MICROECONOMICS

FOURTH EDITION

 S0-AWV-596

David C. Colander

Middlebury College

 McGraw-Hill
Irwin

Boston   Burr Ridge, IL   Dubuque, IA   Madison, WI   New York   San Francisco   St. Louis
Bangkok   Bogotá   Caracas   Lisbon   London   Madrid
Mexico City   Milan   New Delhi   Seoul   Singapore   Sydney   Taipei   Toronto

McGraw-Hill Higher Education

*A Division of The **McGraw-Hill** Companies*

MICROECONOMICS

Published by Irwin/McGraw-Hill, an imprint of The McGraw-Hill Companies, Inc. 1221 Avenue of the Americas, New York, NY, 10020. Copyright ©2001, 1998, 1995, 1993, by The McGraw-Hill Companies, Inc. All rights reserved. No part of this publication may be reproduced or distributed in any form or by any means, or stored in a data base or retrieval system, without the prior written consent of The McGraw-Hill Companies, Inc., including, but not limited to, in any network or other electronic storage or transmission, or broadcast for distance learning. Some ancillaries, including electronic and print components, may not be available to customers outside the United States.

This book is printed on acid-free paper.

1 2 3 4 5 6 7 8 9 0 KPH/KPH 0 9 8 7 6 5 4 3 2 1 0

ISBN 0072317949

Vice president/Editor-in-chief: *Michael W. Junior*
Publisher: *Gary Burke*
Executive editor: *Paul Shensa*
Development editor: *Thomas Thompson*
Marketing manager: *Martin Quinn*
Senior project manager: *Jean Lou Hess*
Production supervisor: *Richard DeVitto*
Coordinator freelance design: *Pam Veros*
Supplement coordinator: *Becky Szura*
Compositor: *GAC/Indianapolis*
Typeface: *Goudy*
Printer: *Quebecor Printing Group/Hawkins*

Library of Congress Cataloging-in-Publication Data
Colander, David C.
  Microeconomics/David C. Colander.—4th ed.
    p. cm.
  A multi-media instructional package with related Website is available to supplement the text.
  Includes index.
  ISBN 0-07-231794-9 (alk. paper)
  1. Microeconomics. I. Title.

HB172.C558 2001
338.5—dc21   00-040690

www.mhhe.com

Dedicated to the memory of Frank Knight and Thorstein Veblen, both of whose economics have significantly influenced the contents of this book.

ABOUT THE AUTHOR

David Colander is the Christian A. Johnson Distinguished Professor of Economics at Middlebury College. He has authored, coauthored, or edited 35 books and over 100 articles on a wide range of economic topics.

He earned his B.A. at Columbia College and his M.Phil and Ph.D. at Columbia University. He also studied at the University of Birmingham in England and at Wilhelmsburg Gymnasium in Germany. Professor Colander has taught at Columbia College, Vassar College, and the University of Miami, as well as having been a consultant to Time-Life Films, a consultant to Congress, a Brookings Policy Fellow, and Visiting Scholar at Nuffield College, Oxford.

He belongs to a variety of professional associations and has served on the board of directors and as vice president and president of both the History of Economic Thought Society and the Eastern Economics Association. He has also served on the editorial boards of the *Journal of Economic Perspectives*, *The Journal of Economic Education*, *The Journal of Economic Methodology*, *The Journal of the History of Economic Thought*, and *The Eastern Economics Journal*.

He is married to a pediatrician, Patrice, who has a private practice in Middlebury, Vermont. In their spare time, the Colanders designed and built their oak post-and-beam house on a ridge overlooking the Green Mountains to the east and the Adirondacks to the west. The house is located on the site of a former drive-in movie theater. (They replaced the speaker poles with fruit trees and used the I-beams from the screen as support for the second story of the carriage house and the garage. Dave's office and library are in the former projection room.)

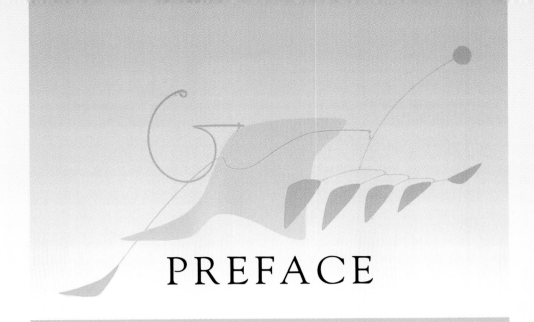

PREFACE

"Imagine . . . a textbook that students enjoy!" An instructor at a large school in the Midwest e-mailed me that comment just as I began to write this preface. It captures what I believe to be the most distinctive feature of my book—students actually enjoy reading it.

The first edition of *Microeconomics* was well received; it was, in large part, a standard book in both tone and structure. Students liked it, but it was seen by some as a bit idiosyncratic; it had some novel metaphors and significantly more history and information about institutions than most books had.

As I have emphasized in my writing about textbooks, there are strong forces pulling all textbooks toward a middle ground, and those forces have affected my book too. In the second and third editions I removed some of the idiosyncrasies while maintaining the voice that appeals to students. This edition continues that process.

NEW TO THE FOURTH EDITION

The fourth edition is the most teachable yet. It is shorter; it reflects many recent changes in the economy and the profession; and many of its more challenging presentations have been simplified. The following sections review the major changes. Please visit the Colander Web site (www.mhhe.com/economics/colander) for a complete list.

● Shorter

There's a fine line between inclusive and encyclopedic; previous editions tried to be inclusive but not encyclopedic. Encyclopedias don't excite students. I've felt this way for a long time but could never decide what material to leave out, which left previous editions bordering on ency-

clopedic. This edition pulls away from that edge. When developing this edition we asked instructors which chapters they assign. The instructors told us that they liked many of the later chapters but didn't have time to teach them. I decided to cut any chapter that was assigned by fewer than 15 percent of our users. The resulting text is five chapters shorter than its predecessor. I used the same criterion to cut numerous appendixes. I also tried to cut out tangents from chapters so that students could more easily focus on core content. This left a shorter, cleaner, more straightforward presentation of the central ideas of economics. For example, Chapter 3, The U.S. Economy in a Global Setting, combines third edition Chapters 5 and 6. The combined chapter is much shorter and surveys the issues while saving the analysis for the micro and macro core chapters.

● Innovation and Globalization

The economy has changed significantly in the last few years, and this edition reflects that change. The revisions emphasize the digital revolution, which affects both technology and innovation, and globalization. Nearly every chapter includes some discussion of one, the other, or both. Chapter 2 gives the example of how the University of Phoenix, which provides online classrooms, competes with traditional "brick-and-mortar" colleges. Besides these chapter-by-chapter changes, specific chapters also focus on these issues. For example, Chapter 14, Globalization, Technology, and Real-World Competition, focuses on these issues.

● Changes in Style and Pedagogy

In response to reviewer feedback, the fourth edition contains fewer nonstandard terms and presentations. For example, the first three editions used metaphors—the invisible handshake and the invisible foot—to describe the social and political forces that influence the economy. I still like those metaphors, but several instructors thought they were distracting, so I eliminated them. I discuss political and social forces; I just don't use the metaphors.

The second and third editions included the "portable tutor," a pedagogical aid that uses the text margins to ask questions that reinforce Learning Objectives and to remind students of important material. The fourth edition continues that practice and expands it by using World Wide Web icons that direct the student to our Web site, which contains content-enriching Internet research exercises.

Terminology is meant to facilitate learning. If it becomes overwhelming, students don't get past the nomenclature to the concepts. In this edition we identified the terms that help students focus on the core material and made sure their definitions are clear and consistent from chapter to chapter. An example of revised terminology appears in Chapter 8, The Logic of Individual Choice: The Foundation of Supply and Demand. Based on reviewer feedback, I replaced the term *utils* with *units of utility*. Not a big change, but one that keeps the terminology standard.

Another major change is, for the most part, invisible. It involves the enormous work done by me; my assistant in writing this book, Jenifer Gamber; my editors at McGraw-Hill; and the reviewers. We went through the book line by line to ensure that the pedagogy was solid. Earlier editions were sometimes described as "big picture" books. The "big picture" remains, but in this fourth edition the details are clearer. This edition presents a brick-by-brick, click-by-click, structure in which the presentation is clear and logical from the ground up. Here are some examples of the changes: Chapter 4, Supply and Demand, now discusses shift factors of demand and supply individually, and Chapter 5 immediately gives students the opportunity to apply those shift factors to the real world, where multiple shift factors may move simultaneously. In Chapter 11, Perfect Competition, I use figures and a graph to demonstrate how a firm's marginal cost curve (above average total costs) is its supply curve.

Learning depends on organization—both mine and the students'. In this edition, we've worked hard to make elements dovetail within chapters. Learning Objectives, which are consistent with the structure of each chapter, serve as quick chapter introductions and can be used by students as self-quizzes. Judiciously chosen key terms are carefully defined in context, and chapter summaries consolidate main points within the Learning Objectives framework. End-of-chapter questions, including many that require Internet research, reinforce Learning Objectives as they test student comprehension.

Pedagogy should reinforce content and help students do well on exams. This requires not only a clearly written book but also a book that gives students an opportunity to try out their new knowledge. In addition to the critical thinking questions that have been a hallmark of previous editions, the fourth edition includes more fundamental questions so students can be sure they know the basics.

Each chapter also ends with a set of Web questions that direct students to a variety of sites from think tanks to government data sites to business-related sites. These new questions fill many roles: They help students see how the concepts in the chapter really do relate to real-world issues; they familiarize students with the mass of information on the Internet; and they give students the chance to apply the concepts they're learning.

In another pedagogical change, we've reorganized the boxed material to fit the theme of "tools, not rules." The boxes in this edition are of three types—Knowing the Tools, Applying the Tools, and Beyond the Tools. Each of the core theory chapters contains a Knowing the Tools box that reviews that chapter's most important concepts, models, and definitions. Applying the Tools boxes provide real-world applications or information related to the chapter. Material that places a concept in a broader or more institutional context appears in Beyond the Tools boxes. These carefully defined boxes help students categorize complementary content as they read through the chapters.

We've also kept the popular colloquial glossary that has been a favorite of ESL students.

● Major Changes

The most significant changes involve a reorganization of the structure—putting more policy earlier, and combining policy discussions, which brings students to interesting policy issues much earlier than before. For example:

- *Early Policy Application.* New Chapter 7, Taxation and Government Intervention, which takes up some of the issues of government intervention first introduced in Chapter 5, gives students the opportunity to apply the concept of consumer and producer surplus learned in Chapter 4 and elasticity learned in Chapter 6. It includes taxation, price floors and ceilings, and quantity restrictions. Efficiency is discussed in relation to all these issues. Politics and rent seeking are introduced as a fight over who gets what portion of total surplus.

- *Increased coverage of technology and globalization.* New Chapter 14, Globalization, Technology, and

Real-World Competition, brings together issues that were dispersed among several third edition chapters. The first half of the chapter continues to discuss how goals of real-world firms are different than assumed by the models and examines the fight between competitive and monopolistic forces. The second half discusses how globalization and technological advances have affected real-world competition. I note how firms have become more specialized, which makes the potential for gain much larger than it used to be. I also examine the ways in which technological advances both affect competition and are affected by it.

- *Revised policy coverage.* New Chapter 15, Government Policy and Market Failures, simplifies the teaching of policy by consolidating the policy discussions that appeared in third edition Chapters 17 and 18. It gives an easily remembered policy framework for students: Anytime there is a market failure, there is a reason for possible government intervention. This chapter considers three market failures (1) externalities, (2) public goods, and (3) incomplete information. Each market failure is introduced and its failure is considered using perfect competition as a benchmark. Alternative methods of dealing with each market failure are also discussed. The chapter ends by questioning whether government can address market failures successfully or whether government intervention makes the situation worse.

- *Revised policy coverage.* The mostly new Chapter 17, Microeconomic Policy, Economic Reasoning, and Beyond, borrows from third edition Chapter 16. Its two parts put economic reasoning into practice. The first part extends the supply/demand model to a broader cost/benefit framework. The second part considers both the costs and the benefits of using economic reasoning. It notes that markets that are working perfectly (no market failures) might still lead to undesirable outcomes. Three failures of market outcomes are considered: (1) failures due to distributional issues, (2) failures due to human irrationality, and (3) failures due to violations of inalienable rights. The chapter also emphasizes that such failures are not necessarily calls for activist policy; policymakers must recognize that government failure exists. Policy is generally a debate about which failure is worse.

● **Standard Updating**
Every chapter has been updated with the latest possible statistics and the most up-to-date policy discussions.

● **Design**
Besides being different, the fourth edition also *looks* different. The design is more open and the typeface more reader-friendly. A lighter color palette makes the graphs and charts easier to read. The Tools boxes are more integrated so that students are less likely to skip over them. Visual elements based on the works of sculptor Alexander Calder provide a subtle, whimsical reminder that the economy, like mobiles, involves intertwined parts that need to be carefully balanced and coordinated.

WHAT WE'VE KEPT

The above discussion may make this seem like a whole new book; it isn't. *Microeconomics* is still written by me with the same essential elements that differentiate it from other books. This includes the focus on teaching economic sensibility and the maintenance of my voice, both in the examples and in the passionate writing style. It also includes an approach that my friend David Littlehale describes as aggressively neutral. He points out that I have this trait of going right into the middle of fights, rather than shying away from them, and picking on both sides. I end up neutral, but not in the standard way.

Finally, while institutions and history receive less coverage, they remain important to me, so you will still find more historical and institutional issues in this book than in almost any other principles book.

ANCILLARIES

All reviewers agreed that the third edition's ancillaries were top rate. If there was a problem it was that there were too many of them. Thus, in this edition we have consolidated and incorporated the best of the previous edition's supplements into an accessible, convenient package.

● **Study Guide**
We combined the best of the *Drill and Review Study Guide* and the *Student Workbook* into a single *Study Guide*. This guide—written by myself, Douglas Copeland of Johnson County Community College, and Jenifer Gamber—reviews the main concepts from each chapter and applies those concepts in a variety of ways: short-answer questions, matching terms with definitions, problems and applications, a brain

teaser, multiple-choice questions, and potential essay questions. Since students learn best not by just knowing the right answer but by understanding how to get there, each answer comes with an explanation. Timed cumulative pretests help students prepare for exams.

● **Instructor's Manual**

In the fourth edition, Tom Adams of Sacramento City College has raised the standard for all instructor's manuals. Eight new features make class preparation easier than ever. "Chapter Overview" and "What's New" provide a quick review of each chapter. "What's New" will be invaluable when modifying lecture notes to fit the new edition. The manual provides you with comprehensive lecture outlines, but it also offers help for inevitable classroom trouble spots. "Discussion Starters" will help engage your students and keep them thinking. "Tips for Teaching Large Sections," written by Gail Hoyt of the University of Kentucky, offers innovative ideas for teaching very large classes. "Student Stumbling Blocks" provides additional explanations or examples that help clarify difficult concepts. "Ties to the Tools" helps bring those text boxes into the classroom; a comprehensive list of relevant URLs brings the Internet in too. Every chapter's 10-question "Pop Quiz" will help students prepare for exams. The "Case Studies" provide contemporary, real-world economic examples. The entire instructor's manual is available in print and electronic forms and on the Colander Web site.

● **Test Banks**

Susan Dadres of Southern Methodist University revised Testbanks A and B (the 5,500-question multiple-choice test banks). Each question is categorized by chapter learning objective; level of difficulty (easy, medium, hard); skill being tested (recall, comprehension, application); and type of question (word problem, calculation, graph). Approximately 30 percent of the questions are new, and many more are revised. Each question was reviewed by Jenifer or myself for accuracy, clarity, and consistency with the textbook. They are available in print form, in the Diploma electronic test generating system.

Expanded Test Bank C, revised by Patrick O'Neill of the University of North Dakota, now consists of over 300 short-answer questions, essay questions, and graphical and mathematical problems. Questions vary in level of difficulty and type of skill being tested. They are available in print and electronic form.

● **DiscoverEcon**

This menu-driven software, which was developed by Gerald Nelson at the University of Illinois, is a complete text-specific student tutorial. Each chapter includes essay questions, Web links and research questions, and a multiple-choice quiz. Interactive graphing problems, animated charts, and live tables help students understand how different data impact the economy. Text references and glossary links help clarify key concepts. Exercises are graded immediately, and results can be submitted to the instructor either on paper or electronically. It is available as a CD version and in an online version.

● **PowerPoint Presentation**

Anthony Zambelli of Cuyameca College has once again prepared an extensive slide program that includes all text exhibits and key concepts. They are available on CD-ROM and on our Web site.

● **Overhead Transparencies**

We offer all key text exhibits in full-color acetate form for use with overhead projectors.

● **Economics Web Newsletter**

This electronic newsletter contains 10 questions related to current economic events that can be used as an in-class quiz and reprints one recent *Wall Street Journal* article along with five in-depth questions (and answers) that are tied to specific text chapters. Seven new exercises will be added each semester.

● **Classic Readings in Economics**

This collection includes selections from the writings of economists, such as Smith, Marx, Hayek, or Veblen, who have raised questions that changed the direction of economic thinking. This material is especially useful for courses that stress the importance of economic ideas.

● **Economics: An Honors Companion**

The Honors Companion presents mathematical techniques that underlie numerous basic economic concepts. It presupposes a solid student background in algebra and geometry and some familiarity with basic calculus, thereby providing a useful ancillary for students with a stronger background such as engineering students.

● **On the Web**

Our new Web site offers a wealth of materials for both students and teachers. The eLearningSessions, prepared by Douglas Copeland of Johnson County Community College, are a set of Internet modules based upon a mastery system of learning, reviewing, and testing. Students are initially presented with an introduction to each chapter and then asked to take a pretest, which is then graded and returned with correct answers and rationales. Students can then address any weaknesses in their understanding by using one of several study modules: Key Terms, a list of the key terms of the chapter with a link to their definitions; Learning Objectives, what students should take away from the chapter; a Tutorial, three to five exercises, with a step-by-step guide to answering each question successfully; and some Practice Exercises, three to five additional problems and answers. The session is completed when students take a multiple-choice posttest.

Students can also broaden their understanding with Web Notes and Current Events, two features prepared by Kit Sims Taylor of Bellevue Community College. Web Notes—Web exercises written for the textbook and identified in the text by margin icons—presents links, articles, short analyses, and follow-up questions focusing on each chapter's key points. Current Events—a set of six current, real-world issues with introductions, links to articles and follow-up questions—will be updated throughout the year as issues facing our economy change. In addition, the student center includes a listing of each chapter's Web Questions, a Bulletin Board, Frequently Asked Questions, Bonus Chapters, a guide to writing economics, a career center, a graphing tool, and the Economics Web Newsletter.

Teachers will also find, among other things, the Instructor's Manual, solutions to end-of-chapter questions, PowerPoints, Sample Syllabi, a bulletin board for instructors, and a link to my own Web site.

I'm very proud of the ancillary package. I think you will find that its high quality, enormous diversity, and exceptional utility make the book a complete learning system.

PEOPLE TO THANK

A book this size is not the work of a single person, despite the fact that only one is listed as author. So many people have contributed so much to this book that it is hard to know where to begin thanking them. But I must begin somewhere, so let me begin by thanking the fourth edition reviewers, whose insightful comments kept me on track.

Tom Adams
Sacramento City College

Peter Alexander
Hartwick College

Rasheed Al-Hmoud
Texas Tech University

Lenard Anyanwu
New Jersey Institute of Technology

Laura Argys
University of Colorado–Denver

Michael Best
Berea College

John Blair
Wright State University

Byron Brown
Michigan State University

Marie Bussing-Burks
University of Southern Indiana

Don Cole
Drew University

Antoinette Criss
Foothill Junior College

Al Culver
California State University, Chico

Susan Dadres
Southern Methodist University

Bridget Daldy
University of Waikato

Tran Huu Dung
Wright State University

Fred Folvary
John F. Kennedy University

Julie Galloway
Southwest Missouri State University

Roger Garrison
Auburn University

William Hall
University of North Carolina–Wilmington

Bassim Harik
Western Michigan University

Tom Head
George Fox University

Paul Heise
Lebanon Valley College

Marc Herold
University of New Hampshire

Vern Hoglund
Hutchinson Community College

Ric Holt
Southern Oregon University

Andy Howard
Rio Hondo College

Gail Hoyt
University of Kentucky

Robert Jerome
James Madison University

Roger Johnson
Messiah College

Nicholas Karatjas
Indiana University of Pennsylvania

Stan Keil
Ball State University

Morris Knapp
Miami-Dade Community College

Andrew Kohen
James Madison University

Mehrene Larudee
University of Kansas

Ann Marie May
University of Nebraska

Richard McIntyre
University of Rhode Island

Barbara Moore
University of Central Florida

Maria Mora
New Mexico State University

Patrick O'Neill
University of North Dakota

Steve Pecsok
Middlebury College

Don Peppard
Connecticut College

Bill Phillips
University of Southern Maine

Irene Powell
Grinnell College

Jaishankar Raman
Valparaiso University

Angela Ritzert
University of New Hampshire

Brian Rungeling
University of Central Florida

Martha Stuffler
Irvine Valley Community College

Kit Taylor
Bellevue Community College

Kay Unger
University of Montana

David Wong
California State University–Fullerton

The following instructors helped guide the fourth edition by responding to an extensive third edition user survey.

Tom Adams
Sacramento City College

Rashid Al-Hmoud
Texas Tech University

Laura Argys
University of Colorado–Denver

John Blair
Wright State University

Kathleen Carroll
University of Maryland, Baltimore Campus

Thomas Cate
Northern Kentucky University

Roger Conover
Azusa Pacifica University

Antoinette Criss
Foothill College

Romesh Diwan
Rensselaer Polytechnical Institute

Thomas Drennen
Hobart & William Smith Colleges

Ishita Edwards
Oxnard College

Rex Edwards
Moorpark College

Charles Fisk, Jr.
Saint Leo's College

Landreth Freeman
Randolph-Macon Woman's College

Roger Garrison
Auburn University

Joe Green
Dixie College

Jay Paul Hamilton
California State University–San Bernadino

Jannett Highfill
Bradley University

Vern Hoglund
Hutchinson Community College

Ric Holt
Southern Oregon University

Kathryn Hulett
Arizona Western College

Matthew Hyle
Winona State University

Andrew Kohen
James Madison University

Mehrene Larudee
University of Kansas

Richard McIntyre
University of Rhode Island

Eric Mitchell
Randolph-Macon Woman's College

Barbara Moore
University of Central Florida

James Murphy
Western Carolina University

Bill O'Connor
Saddleback College

Patrick O'Neill
University of North Dakota

Adenike Osoba
Texas Tech University

Michael Perelman
California State University–Chico

Daniel Powroznik
Chesapeake College

Angela Ritzert
University of New Hampshire

Steve Robinson
University of North Carolina–Wilmington

Denise Robson
University of Wisconsin, Oshkosh

Brian Rungeling
University of Central Florida

Garvin Smith
Daytona Beach Community College

Ugur Soytas
Texas Tech University

Timothy Stanton
Mount Saint Mary's College

Martha Stuffler
Irvine Valley College

Osman Suliman
Millersville University

Neil Terry
West Texas A&M

Robert Wofford
University of the Ozarks

I'd also like to thank the reviewers of the previous three editions. This new book builds on their insights.

First Edition

Jack Adams
University of Arkansas

Stan Antoniotti
Bridgewater State College

Mahmoud P. Arya
Edison Community College

James Q. Aylsworth
Lakeland Community College

George Bohler
University of North Florida

Bijit K. Bora
Carleton College

Gerald E. Breger
Grand Rapids Junior College

Mario Cantu
Northern Virginia Community College

Tom Carroll
Central Oregon Community College

Carol A. M. Clark
Guilford College

Roy Cohn
Illinois State University

Eleanor Craig
University of Delaware

Jerry L. Crawford
Arkansas State University

Ed Dennis
Franklin Pierce College

Phillip Droke
Highline Community College

Fred Englander
Fairleigh Dickinson University

Valerie Englander
St. John's University

Sharon Erenberg
Eastern Michigan University

Rhona C. Free
Eastern Connecticut State University

Joseph Garwood
Valencia Community College

Bernard Gauci
Hollins College

Robert Gentennar
Hope College

Jack B. Goddard
Northeastern State University

Deniek Gondwee
Gettysburg College

Richard Hansen
Southeast Missouri State University

Raymond N. Harvey
Niagara County Community College

Robert Jantzen
Iona College

Walter Johnson
University of Missouri

Diana E. Kraas
Augustana College

Leonard Lardaro
University of Rhode Island

Randall Lutter
State Unviersity of New York–Buffalo

Raymond Mack
Community College of Allegheny County, Boyce Campus

Drew Mattson
Anoka-Ramsey Community College

Bruce McCrea
Lansing Community College

H. Neal McKenzie
Dalton College

Debbie A. Meyer
Brookdale Community College

Craig Milnor
Clarke College

William Morgan
University of Wyoming

Mark Morlock
California State University–Chico

H. Richard Moss
Ricks College

Theodore Muzio
St. Vincent College

Hillar Neumann, Jr.
Northern State University

Maureen O'Brien
University of Minnesota–Duluth

Amar Pari
State University of New York–Fredonia

E. Dale Peterson
Late of Mankato State University

Richard Rosenberg
University of Wisconsin

Linda Schaeffer
California State University–Fresno

Ted Scheinman
Mt. Hood Community College

Timothy Schibik
University of Southern Indiana

Dorothy Siden
Salem State College

R. J. Sidwell
Eastern Illinois University

G. Anthony Spira
University of Tennessee

Mitch Stengel
University of Michigan–Dearborn

Robert Stonebreaker
Indiana University of Pennsylvania

Frank Taylor
McLennan Community College

Wade Thomas
State University of New York College–Oneonta

Joe Turek
Illinois Benedictine College

Alejandro Velez
St. Mary's University

David Weinberg
Xavier University

Kenneth Woodward
Saddleback College

Second Edition

Fatma Antar
Manchester Community College

John Atkins
Pensacola Junior College

Bruce Barnett
Grossmont College

Peter S. Barth
University of Connecticut

William W. Boorman
Palm Beach Community College

Ginny Brannon
Arapahoe Community College

H. L. Brockman
Central Piedmont Community College

Chris Clark
BCIT

Eleanor D. Craig
University of Delaware

Douglas Copeland
Johnson County Community College

Norman V. Cure
Macomb Community College

James W. Eden
Portland Community College

John P. Farrell
Oregon State University

Peter Fortura
Algonquin College

Ann J. Fraedrich
Marquette University

Louis Green
San Diego State University

John B. Hall
Portland State University

Paul A. Heise
Lebanon Valley College

Joseph A. Ilacqua
Bryant College

Susan Kamp
University of Alberta

R. E. Kingery
Hawkeye Community College

Robert Kirk
Indiana University/Purdue University Indianapolis

Evanthis Mavrokordatos
Tarrant County Junior College N.E.

Diana L. McCoy
Truckee Meadows Community College

Shah M. Mehrabi
Montgomery College

Dennis D. Miller
Baldwin Wallace College

James E. Needham
Cuyahoga Community College

Tim Payne
Shoreline Community College

Harmanna Poen
Houston Community College

Edward R. Raupp
Augsburg College

Donald Reddick
Kwantlen College

Mitchell Redlo
Monroe Community College

Balbir S. Sahni
Concordia University

Dennis Shannon
Belleville Area College

Amrick Singh Dua
Mt. San Antonio College

John D. Snead
Bluefield State College

John Somers
Portland Community College

Annie Spears
University of Prince Edward Island

Delores W. Steinhauser
Brookdale Community College

John Stoudenmire
Methodist College

Deborah L. Thorsen
Palm Beach Community College

Marion Walsh
Lansing Community College

James Watson
Jefferson College

Edgar W. Wood
University of Mississippi

Third Edition

Thomas J. Adams
Sacramento City College

Diann Benesh
University of Wisconsin–Eau Claire

David Berrian
Shoreline Community College

David Black
University of Toledo

Geoffrey Black
Marist College

Michael D. Brasselero
Forest Range Community College

Kathleen K. Bromley
Monroe Community College

Sidney L. Carroll
University of Tennessee–Knoxville

Marc C. Chopin
Louisiana Tech University

Curtis Clarke
Mountain View College

John Costley
Iowa Wesleyan College

James Craven
Clark College

Lisa C. DeFelice
University of New Hampshire

James Eden
Portland Community College

James P. Egan
University of Wisconsin–Eau Claire

David N. Feglio
University of Oregon

David W. Findlay
Colby College

Mary Gade
Oklahoma State University

John W. Graham
Rutgers University

Mark E. Haggerty
Clarion University of Pennsylvania

David R. Hakes
University of Northern Iowa

George E. Hoffer
Virginia Commonwealth University

Alexander Holmes
University of Oklahoma

Scott Hunt
Columbus State Community College

Philip A. Klein
The Pennsylvania State University

Morris Knapp
Miami-Dade Community College

Penny Kugler
Central Missouri State University

Randy LaHote
Washtenaw Community College

Jodey Lingg
City University of Renton

Robert T. McLean
Harrisburg Area Community College

Jon R. Miller
University of Idaho

Reynold Nesiba
Augustana College

Norman P. Obst
Michigan State University

Albert Okunade
University of Memphis

Patrick O'Neill
University of North Dakota

Don Powroznik
Chesapeake College

Leila J. Pratt
University of Tennessee–Chattanooga

Renee Prim
Gonzaga University

James J. Rakowski
University of Notre Dame

George D. Santopietro
Radford University

Jacob Sonny
Dowling College

Susan Snyder
Virginia Polytechnic Institute

Ken Woodward
Saddleback College

I have received helpful comments, suggestions, encouragement and assistance from innumerable individuals. Their help made the book better than it otherwise would have been. They include Abby Little, Aditya T. Wresniyandaka, Andrew C. Galbus, Bill Demory, Brendan McCauley, Brian LeTourneau, Cara Tuttle, Chris Bell, Christopher Thompson, Daniel A. Underwood, David Herskowitz, Erich Renner, Evan Donaldson, Frank Gallant, Fred Foldvary, Gail Hoyt, Glen Waddell, James Craven, James DeVault, Jane Paluda, Jennifer Braun, Ji-Hyun Tak, Jill Stoffers, Jim Swaney, Joan McAvoy, John Peters, Karin Sable, Kevin Beck, Larry Ash, Mary King, Matthew Ramsey, Mike Spolum, Nathalie Sweet, Ozkan Ozfidan, Patrick Crowley, Paul Wonnacott, Perry Mehrling, Peter M. Lichtenstein, Phil Shannon, Rasheed Al-Hmoud, Ric Holt, Richard V. Adkisson, Rozi Theohari, S. Scanlon Romer, Sharon Harrison, Stan Smith, Suren Badral, and Trevor Murray. I would also like to thank the many other economists who helped me along the way with a suggestion at a conference or via e-mail.

Special thanks to our supplements authors. Jenifer Gamber guided the ancillary team of Tom Adams, Sacramento City College; Douglas Copeland, Johnson County Community College; Kit Taylor, Bellevue Community College; Gail Hoyt, University of Kentucky; James DeVault, Lafayette College; Susan Dadres, Southern Methodist University; Patrick O'Neill, University of North Dakota; Gerald Nelson, University of Illinois; Anthony Zambelli, Cuyameca College; Harry Landreth, Centre College; Sunder Ramaswamy, Middlebury College; and Kailash Khandke, Furman University. They did a great job.

There is another group of people who helped at various stages. These include Stephen Pecsok and David Horlacher, close friends who read the manuscript and offered many useful suggestions; and Peter Rosenberg, Eli Sugarman, Kaia Laursen, and Kevin Coll, who helped with the proofreading. Helen Reiff also proofread, prepared the glossary, and provided valuable research assistance. A special thank-you goes to Jenifer Gamber, whose role in the book cannot be overestimated. She helped me clarify its vision by providing research, critiquing expositions and often improving them, guiding the ancillaries, and being a good friend. She has an amazing set of skills and I thank her for using them to improve the book.

Next there is the entire McGraw-Hill team: Paul Shensa, the executive editor; Gary Burke, the publisher; Marilea Fried and Tom Thompson, the developmental editors; Jean Lou Hess, the senior project manager; Rich DeVitto, the senior production supervisor; book designers Amy Feldman and Andrew Ogus; Louis Swaim and Becky Szura, the supplements coordinators; Janet Renard, the copyeditor; Roberta Brent, the proofreader; Marty Quinn, the marketing manager; David Littlehale, the national sales manager, and the sales representatives who have been so supportive and helpful. They did a great job and I thank them all.

Finally, I want to thank Pat, my wife, and my sons, Kasey and Zach, for helping me keep my work in perspective, and for providing a loving environment in which to work.

BRIEF CONTENTS

I

INTRODUCTION: THINKING LIKE AN ECONOMIST

II

MICROECONOMICS

I MICROECONOMICS: THE BASICS

II FOUNDATIONS OF SUPPLY AND DEMAND

III MARKET STRUCTURE AND POLICY

IV APPLYING ECONOMIC REASONING TO POLICY

CONTENTS

MICROECONOMICS

I MICROECONOMICS: THE BASICS

V POLICY ISSUES IN DEPTH

INTRODUCTION: THINKING LIKE AN ECONOMIST

I

Part I is an introduction, and an introduction to an introduction seems a little funny. But other sections have introductions, so it seemed a little funny not to have an introduction to Part I; and besides, as you will see, I'm a little funny myself (which, in turn, has two interpretations; I'm sure you will decide which of the two is appropriate). It will, however, be a very brief introduction, consisting of questions you probably have and some answers to those questions.

SOME QUESTIONS AND ANSWERS

Why study economics?
Because it's neat and interesting and helps provide insight into events that are constantly going on around you.

Why is this book so big?
Because there's a lot of important information in it and because the book is designed so your teacher can pick and choose. You'll likely not be required to read all of it, especially if you're on the quarter system. But once you start it, you'll probably read it all anyhow. (Would you believe?)

Why does this book cost so much?
To answer this question you'll have to read the book.

Will this book make me rich?
No.

Will this book make me happy?
It depends.

This book doesn't seem to be written in a normal textbook style. Is this book really written by a professor?
Yes, but he is different. He misspent his youth working on cars; he married his high school sweetheart after they met again at their 20th high school reunion. Twenty-five years after graduating from high school, his wife went back to medical school and got her MD because she was tired of

being treated poorly by doctors. Their five kids make sure he doesn't get carried away in the professorial cloud.

Will the entire book be like this?
No, the introduction is just trying to rope you in. Much of the book will be hard going. Learning happens to be a difficult process: no pain, no gain. But the author isn't a sadist; he tries to make learning as pleasantly painful as possible.

What do the author's students think of him?
Weird, definitely weird—and hard. But fair, interesting, and sincerely interested in getting us to learn. (Answer written by his students.)

So there you have it. Answers to the questions that you might never have thought of if they hadn't been put in front of you. I hope they give you a sense of me and the approach I'll use in the book. There are some neat ideas in it. Let's now briefly consider what's in the first five chapters.

A SURVEY OF THE FIRST FIVE CHAPTERS

This first section is really an introduction to the rest of the book. It gives you the background necessary so that the later chapters make sense. Chapter 1 gives you an overview of the entire field of economics as well as an introduction to my style. Chapter 2 gives you some history of economic systems and shows you how important institutions are. It gives you a sense of how economic forces interact with political and social forces. Chapter 3 introduces you to the institutions of the U.S. economy and discusses how our economy must be viewed in a global setting. Chapters 4 and 5 introduce you to supply and demand, and show you not only the power of those two concepts, but also the limitations.

Now let's get on with the show.

Economics and Economic Reasoning

1

After reading this chapter, you should be able to:

- Define economics and list three coordination problems that an economy must solve.

- Explain how to make decisions by comparing marginal costs and marginal benefits.

- Define opportunity cost and explain its relationship to economic reasoning.

- Explain real-world events in terms of economic forces, social forces, and political forces.

- Differentiate between microeconomics and macroeconomics.

- Distinguish among positive economics, normative economics, and the art of economics.

> *In my vacations, I visited the poorest quarters*
> *of several cities and walked through one street after*
> *another, looking at the faces of the poorest people.*
> *Next I resolved to make as thorough a study*
> *as I could of Political Economy.*
>
> Alfred Marshall

When an artist looks at the world, he sees color. When a musician looks at the world, she hears music. When an economist looks at the world, she sees a symphony of costs and benefits. The economist's world might not be as colorful or as melodic as the others' worlds, but it's more practical. If you want to understand what's going on in the world that's really out there, you need to know economics.

I hardly have to convince you of this fact if you keep up with the news. Unemployment is down; inflation is up; interest rates are up; businesses are going bankrupt. . . . The list is endless. So let's say you grant me that economics is important. That still doesn't mean that it's worth studying. The real question then is: How much will you learn? Most of what you learn depends on you, but part depends on the teacher and another part depends on the textbook. On both these counts, you're in luck; since your teacher chose this book for your course, you must have a super teacher.[1]

WHAT ECONOMICS IS

Economics is *the study of how human beings coordinate their wants and desires, given the decision-making mechanisms, social customs, and political realities of the society.* One of the key words in the definition of the term "economics" is *coordination.* Coordination can mean many things. In the study of economics, coordination refers to how the three central problems facing any economy are solved. These central problems are:

1. What, and how much, to produce.
2. How to produce it.
3. For whom to produce it.

In answering these questions, economies generally find that individuals want more than is available, given how much they're willing to work. That means that in our economy there is a problem of **scarcity**—*the goods available are too few to satisfy individuals' desires.*

Scarcity has two elements—our wants and our means of fulfilling those wants. These can be interrelated since wants are changeable and partially determined by society. The way we fulfill wants can affect those wants. For example, if you work on Wall Street you will probably want upscale and trendy clothes. Up here in Vermont, I am quite happy wearing Levi's and flannel.

The degree of scarcity is constantly changing. The quantity of goods, services, and usable resources depends on technology and human action, which underlie production. Individuals' imagination, innovativeness, and willingness to do what needs to be done can greatly increase available goods and resources. Who knows what technologies are in our future—nannites or micromachines that change atoms into whatever we want could conceivably eliminate scarcity of goods we currently consume. But they would not eliminate scarcity entirely since new wants are constantly developing.

In all known economies, coordination has involved coercion—limiting people's wants and increasing the amount of work individuals are willing to do to fulfill those wants. The reality is that many people would rather play than help solve society's problems. So the basic economic problem involves inspiring people to do things that other people want them to do, and not to do things that other people don't want them to do. Thus, an alternative definition of economics is that it is the study of how to get people to do things they're not wild about doing (such as studying) and not to do things they

Three central coordination problems any economy must solve are what to produce, how to produce it, and for whom to produce it.

The quantity of goods, services, and usable resources depends on technology and human action.

---

[1]This book is written by a person, not a machine. That means that I have my quirks, my odd sense of humor, and my biases. All textbook writers do. Most textbooks have the quirks and eccentricities edited out so that all the books read and sound alike—professional but dull. I choose to sound like me—sometimes professional, sometimes playful, and sometimes stubborn. In my view, that makes the book more human and less dull. So forgive me my quirks—don't always take me too seriously—and I'll try to keep you awake when you're reading this book at 3 A.M. the day of the exam. If you think it's a killer to read a book this long, you ought to try writing one.

are wild about doing (such as eating all the lobster they like), so that the things some people want to do are consistent with the things other people want to do.

To understand an economy you need to learn:

1. *Economic reasoning.*
2. *Economic terminology.*
3. *Economic insights* economists have about issues, and theories that lead to those insights.
4. Information about *economic institutions.*
5. Information about the *economic policy options* facing society today.

Let's consider each in turn.

To understand an economy you need to learn:
<ol>
<li>Economic reasoning.</li>
<li>Economic terminology.</li>
<li>Economic insights.</li>
<li>Economic institutions.</li>
<li>Economic policy options.</li>
</ol>

A GUIDE TO ECONOMIC REASONING

People trained in economics think in a certain way. They analyze everything critically; they compare the costs and the benefits of every issue and make decisions based on those costs and benefits. For example, say you're trying to decide whether protecting baby seals is a good policy or not. Economists are trained to put their emotions aside and ask: What are the costs of protecting baby seals, and what are the benefits? Thus, they are open to the argument that the benefits of allowing baby seals to be killed might exceed the costs. To think like an economist is to address almost all issues using a cost/benefit approach. Economic reasoning—how to think like an economist, making decisions on the basis of costs and benefits—is the most important lesson you'll learn from this book.

Economic reasoning is making decisions on the basis of costs and benefits.

Economic reasoning, once learned, is infectious. If you're susceptible, being exposed to it will change your life. It will influence your analysis of everything, including issues normally considered outside the scope of economics. For example, you will likely use economic reasoning to decide the possibility of getting a date for Saturday night, and who will pay for dinner. You will likely use it to decide whether to read this book, whether to attend class, whom to marry, and what kind of work to go into after you graduate. This is not to say that economic reasoning will provide all the answers. As you will see throughout this book, real-world questions are inevitably complicated, and economic reasoning simply provides a framework within which to approach a question. In the economic way of thinking, every choice has costs and benefits, and decisions are made by comparing them.

Marginal Costs and Marginal Benefits

The relevant costs and relevant benefits to economic reasoning are the expected *incremental* or additional costs incurred and the expected *incremental* benefits that result from a decision. Economists use the term *marginal* when referring to additional or incremental. Marginal costs and marginal benefits are key concepts.

 1.1

A **marginal cost** is *the additional cost to you over and above the costs you have already incurred.* That means eliminating **sunk costs**—*costs that have already been incurred and cannot be recovered*—from the relevant costs when making a decision. Consider, for example, attending class. You've already paid your tuition; it is a sunk cost. So the marginal (or additional) cost of going to class does not include tuition.

Similarly with marginal benefit. A **marginal benefit** is *the additional benefit above what you've already derived.* The marginal benefit of reading this chapter is the *additional* knowledge you get from reading it. If you already knew everything in this chapter before

KNOWING THE TOOLS

Economic Knowledge in One Sentence: TANSTAAFL

Once upon a time, Tanstaafl was made king of all the lands. His first act was to call his economic advisers and tell them to write up all the economic knowledge the society possessed. After years of work, they presented their monumental effort: 25 volumes, each about 400 pages long. But in the interim, King Tanstaafl had become a very busy man, what with running a kingdom of all the lands and everything. Looking at the lengthy volumes, he told his advisers to summarize their findings in one volume.

Despondently, the economists returned to their desks, wondering how they could summarize what they'd been so careful to spell out. After many more years of rewriting, they were finally satisfied with their one-volume effort, and tried to make an appointment to see the king. Unfortunately, affairs of state had become even more pressing than before, and the king couldn't take the time to see them. Instead he sent word to them that he couldn't be bothered with a whole volume, and ordered them,

under threat of death (for he had become a tyrant), to reduce the work to one sentence.

The economists returned to their desks, shivering in their sandals and pondering their impossible task. Thinking about their fate if they were not successful, they decided to send out for one last meal. Unfortunately, when they were collecting money to pay for the meal, they discovered they were broke. The disgusted delivery man took the last meal back to the cook, and the economists started down the path to the beheading station. On the way, the delivery man's parting words echoed in their ears. They looked at each other and suddenly they realized the truth. "We're saved!" they screamed. "That's it! That's economic knowledge in one sentence!" They wrote the sentence down and presented it to the king, who thereafter fully understood all economic problems. (He also gave them a good meal.) The sentence?

There **A**in't **N**o **S**uch **T**hing **A**s **A** **F**ree **L**unch—
TANSTAAFL

---

you picked up the book, the marginal benefit of reading it now is zero. The marginal benefit is not zero if by reading the chapter you learn that you are prepared for class; before, you might only have suspected you were prepared.

Comparing marginal (additional) costs with marginal (additional) benefits will often tell you how you should adjust your activities to be as well off as possible. Just follow the **economic decision rule:**

If the marginal benefits of doing something exceed the marginal costs, do it.

If the marginal costs of doing something exceed the marginal benefits, don't do it.

As an example, let's consider a discussion I might have with a student who tells me that she is too busy to attend my classes. I respond, "Think about the tuition you've spent for this class—it works out to about $30 a lecture." She answers that the book she reads for class is a book that I wrote, and that I wrote it so clearly she fully understands everything. She goes on:

> I've already paid the tuition and whether I go to class or not, I can't get any of the tuition back, so the tuition is a sunk cost and doesn't enter into my decision. The marginal cost to me is what I could be doing with the hour instead of spending it in class. I value my time at $75 an hour [people who understand everything value their time highly], and even though I've heard that your lectures are super, I estimate that the marginal benefit of your class is only $50. The marginal cost, $75, exceeds the marginal benefit, $50, so I don't attend class.

I would congratulate her on her diplomacy and her economic reasoning, but tell her that I give a quiz every week, that students who miss a quiz fail the quiz, that those who fail all the quizzes fail the course, and that those who fail the course do not graduate. In short, she is underestimating the marginal benefits of attending my course. Correctly

If the relevant benefits of doing something exceed the relevant costs, do it. If the relevant costs of doing something exceed the relevant benefits, don't do it.

Q-1 Say you bought stock A for $10 and stock B for $20. The price of each is currently $15. Assuming taxes are not an issue, which would you sell if you need $15?

estimated, the marginal benefits of attending my class exceed the marginal costs. So she should attend my class.

Economics and Passion

Recognizing that everything has a cost is reasonable, but it's a reasonableness that many people don't like. It takes some of the passion out of life. It leads you to consider possibilities like these:

- Saving some people's lives with liver transplants might not be worth the additional cost. The money might be better spent on nutritional programs that would save 20 lives for every 2 lives you might save with transplants.
- Maybe we shouldn't try to eliminate all pollution, because the additional cost of doing so may be too high. To eliminate all pollution might be to forgo too much of some other worthwhile activity.
- Buying a stock that went up 20 percent wasn't necessarily the greatest investment if in doing so you had to forgo some other investment that would have paid you a 30 percent return.
- It might make sense for the automobile industry to save $12 per car by not installing a safety device, even though without the safety device some people will be killed.

You get the idea. This kind of reasonableness is often criticized for being cold-hearted. But, not surprisingly, economists disagree; they argue that their reasoning leads to a better society for the majority of people.

Economists' reasonableness isn't universally appreciated. Businesses love the result; others aren't so sure, as I discovered some years back when my then-girlfriend told me she was leaving me. "Why?" I asked. "Because," she responded, "you're so, so . . . reasonable." It took me many years after she left to learn what she already knew: There are many types of reasonableness, and not everyone thinks an economist's reasonableness is a virtue. I'll discuss such issues later; for now, let me simply warn you that, for better or worse, studying economics will lead you to view questions in a cost/benefit framework.

Opportunity Cost

Putting economists' cost/benefit rules into practice isn't easy. To do so, you have to be able to choose and measure the costs and benefits correctly. Economists have devised the concept of opportunity cost to help you do that. The **opportunity cost** of undertaking an activity is *the benefit forgone by undertaking that activity.* The benefit forgone is the benefit that you might have gained from choosing the next-best alternative. To obtain the benefit of something, you must give up (forgo) something else—namely, the next-best alternative. All activities that have a next-best alternative have an opportunity cost.

Let's consider some examples. The opportunity cost of going out once with Natalia (or Nathaniel), the most beautiful woman (attractive man) in the world, might well be losing your solid steady, Margo (Mike). The opportunity cost of cleaning up the environment might be a reduction in the money available to assist low-income individuals. The opportunity cost of having a child might be two boats, three cars, and a two-week vacation each year for five years.

Examples are endless, but let's consider two that are particularly relevant to you: your choice of courses and your decision about how much to study. Let's say you're a full-time student and at the beginning of the term you had to choose four or five courses to take. Taking one precluded taking some other, and the opportunity cost of taking an

---

Economic reasoning is based on the premise that everything has a cost.

Q-2 Can you think of a reason why a cost/benefit approach to a problem might be inappropriate? Can you give an example?

Opportunity cost is the basis of cost/benefit economic reasoning; it is the benefit forgone, or the cost, of the next-best alternative to the activity you've chosen. In economic reasoning, that cost is less than the benefit of what you've chosen.

economics course may well have been not taking a course on theater. Similarly with studying: you have a limited amount of time to spend studying economics, studying some other subject, sleeping, or partying. The more time you spend on one activity, the less time you have for another. That's opportunity cost.

Notice how neatly the opportunity cost concept takes into account costs and benefits of all other options, and converts these alternative benefits into costs of the decision you're now making.

The relevance of opportunity cost isn't limited to your individual decisions. Opportunity costs are also relevant to government's decisions, which affect everyone in society. A common example is the guns-versus-butter debate. The resources that a society has are limited; therefore, its decision to use those resources to have more guns (more weapons) means that it must have less butter (fewer consumer goods). Thus, when society decides to spent $50 billion more on an improved health care system, the opportunity cost of that decision is $50 billion not spent on helping the homeless, paying off some of the national debt, or providing for national defense.

Opportunity costs have always made choice difficult, as we see in the early-19th-century engraving, "One or the Other." Bleichroeder Print Collection, Baker Library, Harvard Business School.

The opportunity cost concept has endless implications. It can even be turned upon itself. For instance, it takes time to think about alternatives; that means that there's a cost to being reasonable, so it's only reasonable to be somewhat unreasonable. If you followed that argument, you've caught the economic bug. If you didn't, don't worry. Just remember the opportunity cost concept for now; I'll infect you with economic thinking in the rest of the book.

Q.3 John, your study partner, has just said that the opportunity cost of studying this chapter is about 1/35 the price you paid for this book, since the chapter is about 1/35 of the book. Is he right? Why or why not?

Economic and Market Forces

The opportunity cost concept applies to all aspects of life and is fundamental to understanding how society reacts to scarcity. When goods are scarce, those goods must be rationed. That is, a mechanism must be chosen to determine who gets what. Society must deal with the scarcity, thinking about and deciding how to allocate the scarce good.

Let's consider some specific real-world rationing mechanisms. Dormitory rooms are often rationed by lottery, and permission to register in popular classes is often rationed by a first-come, first-registered rule. Food in the United States, however, is generally rationed by price. If price did not ration food, there wouldn't be enough food to go around. All scarce goods or rights must be rationed in some fashion. These rationing mechanisms are examples of **economic forces,** *the necessary reactions to scarcity.*

One of the important choices that a society must make is whether to allow these economic forces to operate freely and openly or to try to rein them in. A **market force** is *an economic force that is given relatively free rein by society to work through the market.* Market forces ration by changing prices. When there's a shortage, the price goes up. When there's a surplus, the price goes down. Much of this book will be devoted to analyzing how the market works like an invisible hand, guiding economic forces to coordinate individual actions and allocate scarce resources. The **invisible hand** is *the price mechanism, the rise and fall of prices that guides our actions in a market.*

Societies can't choose whether or not to allow economic forces to operate—economic forces are always operating. However, societies may choose whether to allow market forces

Q.4 Ali, your study partner, states that rationing health care is immoral—that health care should be freely available to all individuals in society. How would you respond?

When an economic force operates through the market, it becomes a market force.

Economic reality is controlled by three forces:
1. Economic forces (the invisible hand);
2. Social and cultural forces; and
3. Political and legal forces.

Economics in Perspective

All too often, students study economics out of context. They're presented with sterile analysis and boring facts to memorize, and are never shown how economics fits into the larger scheme of things. That's bad; it makes economics seem boring—but economics is not boring. Every so often throughout this book, sometimes in the appendixes and sometimes in boxes, I'll step back and put the analysis in perspective, giving you an idea from whence the analysis sprang and its historical context. In educational jargon, this is called *enrichment*.

I begin here with economics itself.

First, its history: In the 1500s there were few universities. Those that existed taught religion, Latin, Greek, philosophy, history, and mathematics. No economics. Then came the *Enlightenment* (about 1700), in which reasoning replaced God as the explanation of why things were the way they were. Pre-Enlightenment thinkers would answer the question, "Why am I poor?" with "Because God wills it." Enlightenment scholars looked for a different explanation. "Because of the nature of land ownership" is one answer they found.

Such reasoned explanations required more knowledge of the way things were, and the amount of information expanded so rapidly that it had to be divided or categorized for an individual to have hope of knowing a subject. Soon philosophy was subdivided into science and philosophy. In the 1700s, the sciences were split into natural sciences and social sciences. The amount of knowledge kept increasing, and in the late 1800s and early 1900s social science itself split into subdivisions: economics, political science, history, geography, sociology, anthropology, and psychology. Many of the insights about how the economic system worked were codified in Adam Smith's *The Wealth of Nations*, written in 1776. Notice that this is before economics as a subdiscipline developed, and Adam Smith could also be classified as an anthropologist, a sociologist, a political scientist, and a social philosopher.

Throughout the 18th and 19th centuries, economists such as Adam Smith, Thomas Malthus, John Stuart Mill, David Ricardo, and Karl Marx were more than economists; they were social philosophers who covered all aspects of social science. These writers were subsequently called *classical economists*. Alfred Marshall continued in that classical tradition, and his book, *Principles of Economics*, published in the late 1800s, was written with the other social sciences much in evidence. But Marshall also changed the questions economists ask; he focused on those questions that could be asked in a graphical supply/demand framework.

This book falls solidly in the Marshallian tradition. It sees economics as a way of thinking—as an engine of analysis used to understand real-world phenomena.

Marshallian economics is an art, not a science. It is primarily about policy, not theory. It sees institutions as well as political and social dimensions of reality as important, and it shows you how economics ties in to those dimensions.

Social and cultural forces can play a significant role in the economy.

to predominate. Other forces play a major role in deciding whether to let market forces operate. Economic reality is determined by a contest among these forces.

Let's consider an example in which social forces prevent an economic force from becoming a market force: the problem of getting a date for Saturday night. If a school (or a society) has significantly more people of one gender than the other (let's say more men than women), some men may well find themselves without a date—that is, men will be in excess supply—and will have to find something else to do, say study or go to a movie by themselves. An "excess supply" person could solve the problem by paying someone to go out with him or her, but that would probably change the nature of the date in unacceptable ways. It would be revolting to the person who offered payment and to the person who was offered payment. That unacceptability is an example of the complex social and cultural norms that guides and limits our activities. People don't try to buy dates because the social forces prevent them from doing so.

Now let's consider another example in which political and legal influences stop economic forces from becoming market forces. Say you decide that you can make some money delivering mail in your neighborhood. You try to establish a small business, but suddenly you are confronted with the law. The U.S. Postal Service has a legal exclusive

Q.5 Your study partner, Joan, states that market forces are always operative. Is she right? Why or why not?

right to deliver regular mail, so you'll be prohibited from delivering regular mail in competition with the post office. Economic forces—the desire to make money—led you to want to enter the business, but in this case political forces squash the invisible hand.

Often political and social forces work together against the invisible hand. For example, in the United States there aren't enough babies to satisfy all the couples who desire them. Babies born to particular sets of parents are rationed—by luck. Consider a group of parents, all of whom want babies. Those who can, have a baby; those who can't have one, but want one, try to adopt. Adoption agencies ration the available babies. Who gets a baby depends on whom people know at the adoption agency and on the desires of the birth mother, who can often specify the socioeconomic background (and many other characteristics) of the family in which she wants her baby to grow up. That's the economic force in action; it gives more power to the supplier of something that's in short supply.

If our society allowed individuals to buy and sell babies, that economic force would be translated into a market force. The invisible hand would see to it that the quantity of babies supplied would equal the quantity of babies demanded at some price. The market, not the adoption agencies, would do the rationing.[2]

Most people, including me, find the idea of selling babies repugnant. But why? It's the strength of social forces backed up and strengthened by political forces.

What is and isn't allowable differs from one society to another. For example, in Russia, until recently, private businesses were against the law, so not many people started their own businesses. In the United States, until the 1970s, it was against the law to hold gold except in jewelry and for certain limited uses such as dental supplies, so most people refrained from holding gold. Ultimately a country's laws and social norms determine whether the invisible hand will be allowed to work.

Social and political forces are active in all parts of your life. Political forces influence many of your everyday actions. You don't practice medicine without a license; you don't sell body parts or certain addictive drugs. These actions are against the law. But many people do sell alcohol; that's not against the law if you have a permit. Social forces also influence us. You don't make profitable loans to your friends (you don't charge your friends interest); you don't charge your children for their food (parents are supposed to feed their children); many sports and media stars don't sell their autographs (some do, but many consider the practice tacky); you don't lower the wage you'll accept in order to get a job away from someone else (you're no scab). The list is long. You cannot understand economics without understanding the limitations that political and social forces place on economic actions.

In summary, what happens in a society can be seen as the reaction to, and interaction of, these three forces: economic forces, political and legal forces, and social and historical forces. Economics has a role to play in sociology, history, and politics, just as sociology, history, and politics have roles to play in economics.

Economics is about the real world. Throughout this book I'll use the forces just described to talk about real-world events and the interrelationships of economics, history, sociology, and politics.

Economic forces are always operative; society may allow market forces to operate.

 1.2

What happens in society can be seen as a reaction to, and interaction of, economic forces, political forces, social forces, and historical forces.

---

[2]Even though it's against the law, some babies are nonetheless "sold" on a semilegal market, also called a gray market. At the turn of the century, the "market price" for a healthy baby was about $30,000. If it were legal to sell babies (and if people didn't find it morally repugnant to have babies in order to sell them), the price would be much lower, because there would be a larger supply of babies. (It was not against the law to sell human eggs in the late 1990s, and one human egg was sold for $50,000. The average price was much lower; it varied with donor characteristics such as SAT scores and athletic accomplishments.)

ECONOMIC TERMINOLOGY

Economic terminology needs little discussion. It simply needs learning. As terms come up, you'll begin to recognize them. Soon you'll begin to understand them, and finally you'll begin to feel comfortable using them. In this book I'm trying to describe how economics works in the real world, so I introduce you to many of the terms that occur in business and in discussions of the economy. Whenever possible I'll integrate the introduction of new terms into the discussion so that learning them will seem painless. In fact I've already introduced you to a number of economic terms: *opportunity cost, the invisible hand, market forces, economic forces,* just to name a few. By the end of the book I'll have introduced you to hundreds more.

ECONOMIC INSIGHTS

Economists have thought about the economy for a long time, so it's not surprising that they've developed some insights into the way it works.

These insights are often based on generalizations, called theories, about the workings of an abstract economy. Theories tie together economists' terminology and knowledge about economic institutions. Theories are inevitably too abstract to apply in specific cases, and thus a theory is often embodied in an **economic model**—*a framework that places the generalized insights of the theory in a more specific contextual setting*—or in an **economic principle**—*a commonly held economic insight stated as a law or general assumption.* Then these theories, models, and principles are empirically tested (as best one can) to ensure that they correspond to reality. While these models and principles are less general than theories, they are still usually too general to apply in specific cases. Theories, models, and principles must be combined with a knowledge of real-world economic institutions to arrive at specific policy recommendations.

To see the importance of principles, think back to when you learned to add. You didn't memorize the sum of 147 and 138; instead you learned a principle of addition. The principle says that when adding 147 and 138, you first add 7 + 8, which you memorized was 15. You write down the 5 and carry the 1, which you add to 4 + 3 to get 8. Then add 1 + 1 = 2. So the answer is 285. When you know just one principle, you know how to add millions of combinations of numbers.

The Invisible Hand Theory

In the same way, knowing a theory gives you insight into a wide variety of economic phenomena, even though you don't know the particulars of each phenomenon. For example, much of economic theory deals with the *pricing mechanism* and how the market operates to coordinate *individuals' decisions.* Economists have come to the following insights:

When the quantity supplied is greater than the quantity demanded, price has a tendency to fall.

When the quantity demanded is greater than the quantity supplied, price has a tendency to rise.

Using these generalized insights, economists have developed a theory of markets that leads to the further insight that, under certain conditions, markets are efficient. That is, the market will coordinate individuals' decisions, allocating scarce resources to their best possible use. **Efficiency** means *achieving a goal as cheaply as possible.* Economists call this insight the **invisible hand theory**—*a market economy, through the price mechanism, will allocate resources efficiently.*

Theories, models, and principles must be combined with a knowledge of real-world economic institutions to arrive at specific policy recommendations.

Q-6 There has been a superb growing season and the quantity of tomatoes supplied exceeds the quantity demanded. What is likely to happen to the price of tomatoes?

APPLYING THE TOOLS

Winston Churchill and Lady Astor

There are many stories about Nancy Astor, the first woman elected to Britain's Parliament. A vivacious, fearless American woman, she married into the English aristocracy and, during the 1930s and 1940s, became a bright light on the English social and political scenes, which were already quite bright.

One story told about Lady Astor is that she and Winston Churchill, the unorthodox genius who had a long and distinguished political career and who was Britain's prime minister during World War II, were sitting in a pub having a theoretical discussion about morality. Churchill suggested that as a thought experiment Lady Astor ponder the question: If a man were to promise her a huge amount of money—say a million pounds—for the privilege, would she sleep with him? Lady Astor did ponder the question for a while and finally answered, yes, she would, if the money

were guaranteed. Churchill then asked her if she would sleep with him for five pounds. Her response was sharp: "Of course not. What do you think I am—a prostitute?" This time Churchill won the battle of wits by answering, "We have already established that fact; we are now simply negotiating about price."

One moral that economists might draw from this story is that economic incentives, if high enough, can have a powerful influence on behavior. An equally important moral of the story is that noneconomic incentives can also be very strong. Why do most people feel it's wrong to sell sex for money, even if they would be willing to do so if the price were high enough? Keeping this second moral in mind will significantly increase your economic understanding of real-world events.

Theories, and the models used to represent them, are enormously efficient methods of conveying information, but they're also necessarily abstract. They rely on simplifying assumptions, and *if you don't know the assumptions, you don't know the theory*. The result of forgetting assumptions could be similar to what happens if you forget that you're supposed to add numbers in columns. Forgetting that, yet remembering all the steps, can lead to a wildly incorrect answer. For example,

$$147$$
$$+ \ 138$$
$$\overline{}$$
$$1{,}608 \text{ is wrong.}$$

Knowing the assumptions of theories and models allows you to progress beyond gut reaction and better understand the strengths and weaknesses of various economic systems. Let's consider a central economic assumption: the assumption that individuals behave rationally—that what they choose reflects what makes them happiest, given the constraints. If that assumption doesn't hold, the invisible hand theory doesn't hold.

Presenting the invisible hand theory in its full beauty is an important part of any economics course. Presenting the assumptions on which it is based and the limitations of the invisible hand is likewise an important part of the course. I'll do both throughout the book.

Economic Theory and Stories

Economic theory, and the models in which that theory is presented, often developed as a shorthand way of telling a story. These stories are important; they make the theory come alive and convey the insights that give economic theory its power. In this book I present plenty of theories and models, but they're accompanied by stories that provide the context that makes them relevant.

At times, because there are many new terms, discussing models and theories takes up much of the presentation time and becomes a bit oppressive. That's the nature of the

Theory is a shorthand way of telling a story.

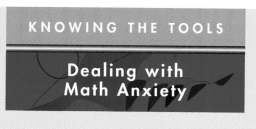

KNOWING THE TOOLS

Dealing with
Math Anxiety

Knowing my own students, I can see the red flags rising, the legs tensing up, the fear flooding over many of you. Here it comes—the math and the graphs.

I wish I could change things by saying to you, "Don't worry—mathematics and graphical analysis are easy." But I can't. That doesn't mean math and graphical analysis aren't wonderful tools that convey ideas neatly and efficiently. They are. But I've had enough teaching experience to know that somewhere back in elementary school some teacher blew it and put about 40 percent of you off mathematics for life. A tool that scares you to death is not useful; it can be a hindrance, not a help, to learning. Nothing your current teacher or I now can say, write, or do is going to completely reassure you, but I'll do my best to relieve your anxiety.

Try to follow the numerical and graphical examples carefully, because they not only cement the knowledge into your minds; they also present in a rigorous manner the ideas I'm discussing. The ideas conveyed in the numerical and graphical examples will be explained in words—and the graphical analysis (the type of mathematical explanation most used in introductory economics) generally will simply be a more precise presentation of the accompanying discussion in words. In most economics courses the exams pose the questions in graphical terms, so there's no getting around the need to understand the ideas graphically. And it is easier than you think. (Appendix A at the end of this chapter discusses the basics of graphical analysis.)

beast. As Albert Einstein said, "Theories should be as simple as possible, but not more so." When a theory or a model becomes oppressive, pause and think about the underlying story that the theory is meant to convey. That story should make sense and be concrete. If you can't translate the theory into a story, you don't understand the theory.

Often economic theories are presented in mathematical—graphical or algebraic—models. In this book I keep models to a minimum, but I cannot avoid them completely. Graphical models are used so much by economists that they must be included. So part of the course will consist of translating the verbal discussions of the economy into graphical models. To prepare you for these graphical models I have written a brief introduction to the basics of graphical presentation in Appendix A of this chapter.

Microeconomics and Macroeconomics

Economic theory is divided into two parts: microeconomic theory and macroeconomic theory. Microeconomic theory considers economic reasoning from the viewpoint of individuals and firms and builds up from there to an analysis of the whole economy. I define **microeconomics** as *the study of individual choice, and how that choice is influenced by economic forces*. Microeconomics studies such things as the pricing policies of firms, households' decisions on what to buy, and how markets allocate resources among alternative ends. Our discussion of opportunity cost was based on microeconomic theory. The invisible hand theory comes from microeconomics.

Microeconomics is the study of how individual choice is influenced by economic forces.

As one builds up from microeconomic analysis to an analysis of the entire economy, everything gets rather complicated. Many economists try to uncomplicate matters by taking a different approach—a macroeconomic approach—first looking at the aggregate, or whole, and then breaking it down into components. I define **macroeconomics** as *the study of the economy as a whole, which includes inflation, unemployment, business cycles, and growth*. Macroeconomics focuses on aggregate relationships such as how household consumption is related to income and how government policies can affect growth. A micro approach would analyze a person by looking first at each individual cell and then building up. A macro approach would start with the person and then go on to his or her components—arms, legs, fingernails, feelings, and so on. Put simply, microeconomics analyzes from the parts to the whole; macroeconomics analyzes from the whole to the parts.

Macroeconomics is the study of inflation, unemployment, business cycles, and growth; it focuses on aggregate relationships.

Microeconomics and macroeconomics are very much interrelated. Clearly, what happens in the economy as a whole is based on individual decisions, but individual decisions are made within an economy and can be understood only within that context. For example, whether a firm decides to expand production capacity will depend on what the owners expect will happen to the demand for their products. Those expectations are determined by macroeconomic conditions. Likewise, decisions by the federal government to change the welfare program in the mid-1990s had to be made based on how those changes would affect the decisions of millions of individuals. Because microeconomics focuses on the individual and macroeconomics focuses on the whole economy, traditionally microeconomics and macroeconomics are taught separately, even though they are interrelated.

> **Q.7** Classify the following topics as macroeconomic or microeconomic:
> 1. The impact of a tax increase on aggregate output.
> 2. The relationship between two competing firms' pricing behavior.
> 3. A farmer's decision to plant soy or wheat.
> 4. The effect of trade on economic growth.

ECONOMIC INSTITUTIONS

To know whether you can apply economic theory to reality, you must know about economic institutions. Corporations, governments, and cultural norms are all economic institutions. Many economic institutions have social, political, and religious dimensions. For example, your job often influences your social standing. In addition, many social institutions, such as the family, have economic functions. If any institution significantly affects economic decisions, I include it as an economic institution because you must understand that institution if you are to understand how the economy functions.

Economic institutions differ significantly among countries. For example, in Germany banks are allowed to own companies; in the United States they cannot. This contributes to a difference in the flow of resources into investment in Germany as compared to the flow in the United States. Or alternatively, in Japan, antitrust laws (laws under which companies can combine or coordinate their activities) are loose; in the United States they are more restrictive. This causes differences in the nature of competition in the two countries.

Economic institutions sometimes seem to operate in ways quite different than economic theory predicts. For example, economic theory says that prices are determined by supply and demand. However, businesses say that prices are set by rules of thumb—often by what are called cost-plus-markup rules. That is, you determine what your costs are, multiply by 1.4 or 1.5, and the result is the price you set. Economic theory says that supply and demand determine who's hired; experience suggests that hiring is often done on the basis of whom you know, not by economic forces.

These apparent contradictions have two complementary explanations. First, economic theory abstracts from many issues. These issues may account for the differences. Second, there's no contradiction; economic principles often affect decisions from behind the scenes. For instance, supply and demand pressures determine what the price markup over cost will be. In all cases, however, to apply economic theory to reality—to gain the full value of economic insights—you've got to have a sense of economic institutions.

> To apply economic theory to reality, you've got to have a sense of economic institutions.

ECONOMIC POLICY OPTIONS

Economic policies are *actions (or inaction) taken by government to influence economic actions.* The final goal of the course is to present the economic policy options facing our society today. For example, should the government restrict mergers between firms? Should it run a budget deficit? Should it do something about the international trade deficit? Should it decrease taxes?

I saved this discussion for last because there's no sense talking about policy options unless you know some economic terminology, some economic theory, and something about economic institutions. Once you know something about them, you're in a position to consider the policy options available for dealing with the economic problems our society faces.

Policies operate within institutions, but policies can also influence the institutions within which they operate. Let's consider an example: welfare policy and the institution of the two-parent family. In the 1960s, the United States developed a variety of policy initiatives designed to eliminate poverty. These initiatives directed income to single parents with children, and assumed that family structure would be unchanged by these policies. But family structure did not remain unchanged; it changed substantially, and, very likely, these policies to eliminate poverty played a role in increasing the number of single-parent families. The result was a failure of the programs to eliminate poverty. Now this is not to say that we should not have programs to eliminate poverty, or that two-parent families are always preferable to one-parent families; it is only to say that we must build into our policies their effect on institutions.

Some policies are designed to change institutions directly. While these policies are much more difficult to implement than policies that don't, they also offer the largest potential for gain. Let's consider an example. In the 1990s, a number of countries decided to replace socialist institutions with market economies. The result: output in those countries fell enormously as the old institutions fell apart. Eventually, these countries hope, once the new market institutions are predominant, output will bounce back and further gains will be made. The temporary hardships these countries are experiencing show the enormous difficulty of implementing policies involving major institutional changes.

Objective Policy Analysis

Good economic policy analysis is objective; that is, it keeps the analyst's value judgments separate from the analysis. Objective analysis does not say, "This is the way things should be," reflecting a goal established by the analyst. That would be subjective analysis because it would reflect the analyst's view of how things should be. Instead, objective analysis says, "This is the way economy works, and if society (or the individual or firm for whom you're doing the analysis) wants to achieve a particular goal, this is how it might go about doing so." Objective analysis keeps, or at least tries to keep, subjective views—value judgments—separate.

To make clear the distinction between objective and subjective analysis, economists have divided economics into three categories: *positive economics, normative economics,* and the *art of economics*. **Positive economics** is *the study of what is, and how the economy works*. It asks such questions as: How does the market for hog bellies work? How do price restrictions affect market forces? These questions fall under the heading of economic theory. **Normative economics** is *the study of what the goals of the economy should be*. Normative economics asks such questions as: What should the distribution of income be? What should tax policy be designed to achieve? In discussing such questions, economists must carefully delineate whose goals they are discussing. One cannot simply assume that one's own goals for society are society's goals.

The **art of economics** is *the application of the knowledge learned in positive economics to the achievement of the goals one has determined in normative economics*. It looks at such questions as: To achieve a certain distribution of income, how would you go about it, given the way the economy works?[3] Most policy discussions fall under the art of economics.

---

[3]This three-part distinction was made back in 1896 by a famous economist, John Neville Keynes, father of John Maynard Keynes, the economist who developed macroeconomics. This distinction was instilled into modern economics by Milton Friedman and Robert Lipsey in the 1950s. They, however, downplayed the art of economics, which J. N. Keynes had seen as central to understanding the economist's role in policy.

To carry out economic policy effectively one must understand how institutions might change as a result of the economic policy.

Q-8 True or false? Economists should focus their policy analysis on institutional changes because such policies offer the largest gains.

Q-9 John, your study partner, is a free market advocate. He argues that the invisible hand theory tells us that the government should not interfere with the economy. Do you agree? Why or why not?

1.3

Positive economics is the study of what is, and how the economy works.

Normative economics is the study of what the goals of the economy should be.

The *art of economics* is the application of the knowledge learned in positive economics to the achievement of the goals determined in normative economics.

In each of these three branches of economics, economists separate their own value judgments from their objective analysis as much as possible. The qualifier "as much as possible" is important, since some value judgments inevitably sneak in. We are products of our environment, and the questions we ask, the framework we use, and the way we interpret empirical evidence all embody value judgments and reflect our backgrounds.

Maintaining objectivity is easiest in positive economics, where one is working with abstract models to understand how the economy works. Maintaining objectivity is harder in normative economics. You must always be objective about whose normative values you are using. It's easy to assume that all of society shares your values, but that assumption is often wrong.

It's hardest to maintain objectivity in the art of economics because it embodies the problems of both positive and normative economics. Because noneconomic forces affect policy, to practice the art of economics we must make judgments about how these noneconomic forces work. These judgments are likely to embody our own value judgments. So we must be exceedingly careful to be as objective as possible in practicing the art of economics.

Policy and Social and Political Forces

When you think about the policy options facing society, you'll quickly discover that the choice of policy options depends on much more than economic theory. You must take into account historical precedent plus social, cultural, and political forces. In an economics course, I don't have time to analyze these forces in as much depth as I'd like. That's one reason there are separate history, political science, sociology, and anthropology courses.

I don't pretend that these forces play an insignificant role in policy decisions, but specialization is necessary. In economics, we focus the analysis on the invisible hand, and much of economic theory is devoted to how the economy would operate if the invisible hand were the only force operating. But as soon as we apply theory to reality and policy, we must take into account political and social forces as well.

An example will make my point more concrete. Most economists agree that holding down or eliminating tariffs (taxes on imports) and quotas (numerical limitations on imports) makes good economic sense. They strongly advise governments to follow a policy of free trade. Do governments follow free trade policies? Almost invariably they do not. Politics leads society in a different direction. If you're advising a policy maker, you need to point out that these other forces must be taken into account, and how other forces should (if they should) and can (if they can) be integrated with your recommendations.

Q.10 State whether the following five statements belong in positive economics, normative economics, or the art of economics.
1. We should support the market because it is efficient.
2. Given certain conditions, the market achieves efficient results.
3. Based on past experience and our understanding of markets, if one wants a reasonably efficient result, markets should probably be relied on.
4. The distribution of income should be left to markets.
5. Markets allocate income according to contributions of factors of production.

CONCLUSION

There's tons more that could be said by way of introducing you to economics, but an introduction must remain an introduction. As it is, this chapter should have:

1. Introduced you to economic reasoning.
2. Surveyed what we're going to cover in this book.
3. Given you an idea of my writing style and approach.

We'll be spending long hours together over the coming term, and before entering into such a commitment it's best to know your partner. While I won't know you, by the end of this book you'll know me. Maybe you won't love me as my mother does, but you'll know me.

This introduction was my opening line. I hope it also conveyed the importance and relevance that belong to economics. If it did, it has served its intended purpose. Economics is tough, but tough can be fun.

Chapter Summary

- The three coordination problems any economy must solve are what to produce, how to produce it, and for whom to produce it. In solving these problems economies have found that there is a problem of scarcity.

- Economic reasoning structures all questions in a cost/benefit frame: If the marginal benefits of doing something exceed the marginal costs, do it. If the marginal costs exceed the marginal benefits, don't do it.

- Sunk costs are not relevant to the economic decision rule.

- The opportunity cost of undertaking an activity is the benefit you might have gained from choosing the next-best alternative.

- "There ain't no such thing as a free lunch" (TANSTAAFL) embodies the opportunity cost concept.

- Economic forces, the forces of scarcity, are always working. Market forces, which ration by changing prices, are not always allowed to work.

- Economic reality is controlled and directed by three types of forces: economic forces, political forces, and social forces.

- Under certain conditions the market, through its price mechanism, will allocate scarce resources efficiently.

- Economics can be divided into microeconomics and macroeconomics. Microeconomics is the study of individual choice and how that choice is influenced by economic forces. Macroeconomics is the study of the economy as a whole, which includes inflation, unemployment, business cycles, and growth.

- Economics can be subdivided into positive economics, normative economics, and the art of economics. Positive economics is the study of what is, normative economics is the study of what should be, and the art of economics relates positive to normative economics.

Key Terms

art of economics *(16)*

economic decision
  rule *(7)*

economic forces *(9)*

economic model *(12)*

economic policies *(15)*

economic principle *(12)*

economics *(5)*

efficiency *(12)*

invisible hand *(9)*

invisible hand theory *(12)*

macroeconomics *(14)*

marginal benefit *(6)*

marginal cost *(6)*

market force *(9)*

microeconomics *(14)*

normative economics *(16)*

opportunity cost *(8)*

positive economics *(16)*

scarcity *(5)*

sunk costs *(6)*

Questions for Thought and Review

1. What is the textbook author's reasoning for focusing the definition of economics on coordination rather than on scarcity?

2. List two recent choices you made and explain why you made those choices in terms of marginal benefits and marginal costs.

3. At times we all regret decisions. Does this necessarily mean we did not use the economic decision rule when making the decision?

4. What is the opportunity cost of buying a $20,000 car?

5. Name three ways a limited number of dormitory rooms could be rationed. How would economic forces determine individual behavior in each? How would social or legal forces determine whether those economic forces become market forces?

6. Give two examples of social forces and explain how they keep economic forces from becoming market forces.

7. Give two examples of political or legal forces and explain how they might interact with the invisible hand.

8. What is an economic model? What besides a model do economists need to make policy recommendations?

9. Does economic theory prove that the free market system is best? Why?

10. List two microeconomic and two macroeconomic problems.

11. Name an economic institution and explain how it either embodies economic principles or affects economic decision making.

12. Is a good economist always objective? Why?

Problems and Exercises

1. You rent a car for $29.95. The first 150 miles are free, but each mile thereafter costs 15 cents. You drive it 200 miles. What is the marginal cost of driving the car?

2. Calculate, using the best estimates you can:
   a. Your opportunity cost of attending college.
   b. Your opportunity cost of taking this course.
   c. Your opportunity cost of attending yesterday's lecture in this course.

3. Individuals have two kidneys but most of us need only one. People who have lost both kidneys through accident or disease must be hooked up to a dialysis machine, which cleanses waste from their bodies. Say a person who has two good kidneys offers to sell one of them to someone whose kidney function has been totally destroyed. The seller asks $30,000 for the kidney, and the person who has lost both kidneys accepts the offer. Who benefits from the deal? Who is hurt? Should a society allow such market transactions? Why?

4. For some years, China has had a one-child-per-family policy. For cultural reasons, there are now many more male than female children born in China. How is this likely to affect who pays the cost of dates in China in 15 or 20 years? Explain your response.

5. State whether the following are microeconomic or macroeconomic policy issues:
   a. Should the U.S. government use a policy of free trade with China to encourage China to advance human rights?
   b. Will the fact that more and more doctors are selling their practices to managed care networks increase the efficiency of medical providers?
   c. Should the current federal income tax structure be eliminated in favor of a flat tax?
   d. Should the federal minimum wage be raised?
   e. Should AT&T and MCI both be allowed to build local phone networks?
   f. Should commercial banks be required to provide loans in all areas of the territory from which they accept deposits?

6. Go to two stores: a supermarket and a convenience store.
   a. Write down the cost of a gallon of milk in each.
   b. The prices are most likely different. Using the terminology used in this chapter, explain why that is the case and why anyone would buy milk in the store with the higher price.
   c. Do the same exercise with shirts or dresses in Wal-Mart (or its equivalent) and Saks (or its equivalent).

7. In the mid-1990s, the German comedian Harald Schmidt attempted to mimic the successful David Letterman show in Germany. The format didn't entertain its German audience. What economic policy lesson can be learned from Harald Schmidt's failure?

8. State whether the following statements belong in positive economics, normative economics, or the art of economics.
   a. In a market, when quantity supplied exceeds quantity demanded, price tends to fall.
   b. When determining tax rates, the government should take into account the income needs of individuals.
   c. What society feels is fair is determined largely by cultural norms.
   d. When deciding which rationing mechanism is best (lottery, price, first-come/first-served), one must take into account the goals of society.
   e. California currently rations water to farmers at subsidized prices. Once California allows the trading of water rights, it will allow economic forces to be a market force.

9. Adam Smith, who wrote *The Wealth of Nations* and is seen as the father of modern economics, also wrote *The Theory of Moral Sentiments*, in which he argued that society would be better off if people weren't so selfish and were more considerate of others. How does this view fit with the discussion of economic reasoning presented in the chapter?

Web Questions

1. Find an employment Web page (an example is www.occ.com) and search for available jobs using "economist" as a keyword. List five jobs that economists have and write a one-sentence description of each.

2. Use an online periodical (an example is www.policy.com) to find two examples of political or legal forces at work. Do those forces keep economic forces from becoming market forces?

3. Using an Internet mapping page (an example is www.mapquest.com), create a map of your neighborhood and answer the following questions:
   a. How is the map like a model?
   b. What are the limitations of the map?
   c. Could you use this map to determine change in elevation in your neighborhood? Distance from one place to another? Traffic speed? What do your answers suggest about what to consider when using a map or a model?

Answers to Margin Questions

The numbers in parentheses refer to the page number of each margin question.

1. Since the price of both stocks is now $15, it doesn't matter which one you sell (assuming no differential capital gains taxation). The price you bought them for doesn't matter; it's a sunk cost. Marginal analysis refers to the future gain, so what you expect to happen to future prices of the stocks—not past prices—should determine which stock you decide to sell. *(7)*

2. A cost/benefit analysis requires that you put a value on a good, and placing a value on a good can be seen as demeaning it. Consider love. Try telling an acquaintance that you'd like to buy his or her spiritual love, and see what response you get. *(8)*

3. John is wrong. The opportunity cost of reading the chapter is primarily the time you spend reading it. Reading the book prevents you from doing other things. Assuming that you already paid for the book, the original price is no longer part of the opportunity cost; it is a sunk cost. Bygones are bygones. *(9)*

4. Whenever there is scarcity, the scarce good must be rationed by some means. Free health care has an opportunity cost in other resources. So if health care is not rationed, to get the resources to supply that care, other goods would have to be more tightly rationed than they currently are. It is likely that the opportunity cost of supplying free health care would be larger than most societies would be willing to pay. *(9)*

5. Joan is wrong. Economic forces are always operative; market forces are not. *(10)*

6. According to the invisible hand theory, the price of tomatoes will likely fall. *(12)*

7. (1) Macroeconomics; (2) Microeconomics; (3) Microeconomics; (4) Macroeconomics. *(15)*

8. False. While such changes have the largest gain, they may also have the largest cost. The policies economists should focus on are those that offer the largest net gain—benefits minus costs—to society. *(16)*

9. He is wrong. The invisible hand theory is a positive theory and does not tell us anything about policy. To do so would be to violate Hume's dictum that a "should" cannot be derived from an "is." This is not to say that government should or should not interfere; whether government should interfere is a very difficult question. *(16)*

10. (1) Normative; (2) Positive; (3) Art; (4) Normative; (5) Positive. *(17)*

APPENDIX A

Graphish: The Language of Graphs

A picture is worth 1,000 words. Economists, being efficient, like to present ideas in **graphs,** *pictures of points in a coordinate system in which points denote relationships between numbers.* But a graph is worth 1,000 words only if the person looking at the graph knows the graphical language: *Graphish,* we'll call it. (It's a bit like English.) Graphish is usually written on graph paper. If the person doesn't know Graphish, the picture isn't worth any words and Graphish can be babble.

I have enormous sympathy for students who don't understand Graphish. A number of my students get thrown for a loop by graphs. They understand the idea, but Graphish confuses them. This appendix is for them, and for those of you like them. It's a primer in Graphish.

TWO WAYS TO USE GRAPHS

In this book I use graphs in two ways:

1. To present an economic model or theory visually; to show how two variables interrelate.

2. To present real-world data visually. To do this, I use primarily bar charts, line charts, and pie charts.

Actually, these two ways of using graphs are related. They are both ways of presenting visually the *relationship* between two things.

Graphs are built around a number line, or axis, like the one in Figure A1-1(a). The numbers are generally placed in order, equal distances from one another. That number

Figure A1-1 (a, b, and c)   Horizontal and Vertical Number Lines and a Coordinate System

(a) **Horizontal number line**   (b) **Vertical number line**   (c) **Coordinate system**

line allows us to represent a number at an appropriate point on the line. For example, point A represents the number 4.

The number line in Figure A1-1(a) is drawn horizontally, but it doesn't have to be; it can also be drawn vertically, as in Figure A1-1(b).

How we divide our axes, or number lines, into intervals, is up to us. In Figure A1-1(a), I called each interval 1; in Figure A1-1(b), I called each interval 10. Point A appears after 4 intervals of 1 (starting at 0 and reading from left to right), so it represents 4. Figure A1-1(b), where each interval represents 10, to represent 5, I place point B halfway in the interval between 0 and 10.

So far, so good. Graphish developed when a vertical and a horizontal number line were combined, as in Figure A1-1(c). When the horizontal and vertical number lines are put together, they're called *axes*. (Each line is an axis. *Axes* is the plural of *axis*.) I now have a **coordinate system**—*a two-dimensional space in which one point represents two numbers*. For example, point A in Figure A1-1(c) represents the numbers (4, 5)—4 on the horizontal number line and 5 on the vertical number line. Point B represents the numbers (1, 20). (By convention, the horizontal numbers are written first.)

Being able to represent two numbers with one point is neat because it allows the relationships between two numbers to be presented visually instead of having to be expressed verbally, which is often cumbersome. For example, say the cost of producing 6 units of something is $4 per unit and the cost of producing 10 units is $3 per unit. By putting both these points on a graph, we can visually see that producing 10 costs less per unit than does producing 6.

Another way to use graphs to present real-world data visually is to use the horizontal line to represent time. Say

that we let each horizontal interval equal a year. and each vertical interval equal $100 in income. By graphing your income each year, you can obtain a visual representation of how your income has changed over time.

Using Graphs in Economic Modeling

I use graphs throughout the book as I present economic models, or simplifications of reality. A few terms are often used in describing these graphs, and we'll now go over them. Consider Figure A1-2(a), which lists the number of pens bought per day (column 2) at various prices (column 1).

We can present the table's information in a graph by combining the pairs of numbers in the two columns of the table and representing, or plotting, them on two axes. I do that in Figure A1-2(b).

By convention, when graphing a relationship between price and quantity, economists place price on the vertical axis and quantity on the horizontal axis.

I can now connect the points, producing a line like the one in Figure A1-2(c). With this line, I interpolate the numbers between the points (which makes for a nice visual presentation). That is, I make the **interpolation assumption**—*the assumption that the relationship between variables is the same between points as it is at the points.* The interpolation assumption allows us to think of a line as a collection of points and therefore to connect the points into a line.

Even though the line in Figure A1-2(c) is straight, economists call any such line drawn on a graph a *curve*. Because it's straight the curve in A1-2(c) is called a **linear curve**—*a curve that is drawn as a straight line.* Notice that this curve starts high on the left-hand side and goes down to the right. Economists say that any curve that looks like that is *downward-sloping*. They also say that a downward-sloping

Figure A1-2 (a, b, c, and d)   A Table and Graphs Showing the Relationships between Price and Quantity

	Price per pen	Quantity of pens bought per day
A	$3.00	4
B	2.50	5
C	2.00	6
D	1.50	7
E	1.00	8

(a) Price quantity table

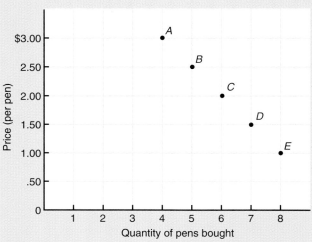

(b) From a table to a graph (1)

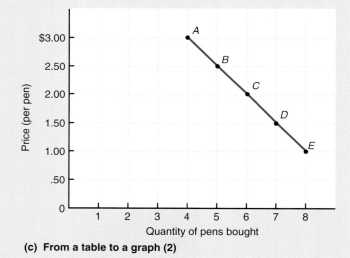

(c) From a table to a graph (2)

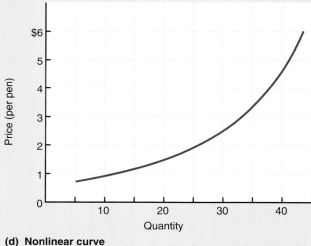

(d) Nonlinear curve

curve represents an **inverse relationship**—*a relationship between two variables in which when one goes up, the other goes down.* In this example, the line demonstrates an inverse relationship between price and quantity—that is, when the price of pens goes up, the quantity bought goes down.

Figure A1-2(d) presents a **nonlinear curve**—*a curve that is drawn as a curved line.* This curve, which really is curved, starts low on the left-hand side and goes up to the right. Economists say any curve that goes up to the right is *upward-sloping.* An upward-sloping curve represents a **direct relationship**—*a relationship in which when one variable goes up, the other goes up too.* The direct relationship I'm

talking about here is the one between the two variables (what's measured on the horizontal and vertical lines). *Downward-sloping* and *upward-sloping* are terms you need to memorize if you want to read, write, and speak Graphish, keeping graphically in your mind the image of the relationships they represent.

Slope

One can, of course, be far more explicit about how much the curve is sloping upward or downward by defining it in terms of **slope**—*the change in the value on the vertical axis*

Figure A1-3 Slopes of Curves

The slope of a curve is determined by rise over run. The slope of curve *a* is shown in the graph. The rest are shown below:

	Rise	÷ Run	= Slope
b	−1	+2	−.5
c	1	1	1
d	4	1	4
e	1	1	1

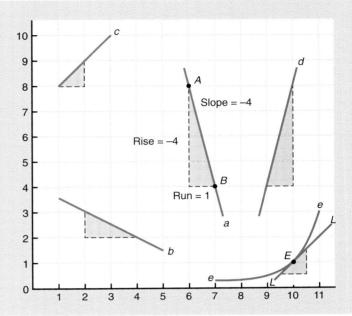

divided by the change in the value on the horizontal axis. Sometimes the slope is presented as "rise over run":

$$\text{Slope} = \frac{\text{Rise}}{\text{Run}} = \frac{\text{Change in value on vertical axis}}{\text{Change in value on horizontal axis}}$$

Slopes of Linear Curves

In Figure A1-3, I present five linear curves and measure their slope. Let's go through an example to show how we can measure slope. To do so, we must pick two points. Let's use points A (6, 8) and B (7, 4) on curve *a*. Looking at these points, we see that as we move from 6 to 7 on the horizontal axis, we move from 8 to 4 on the vertical axis. So when the number on the vertical axis falls by 4, the number on the horizontal axis increases by 1. That means the slope is −4 divided by 1, or −4.

Notice that the inverse relationships represented by the two downward-sloping curves, *a* and *b*, have negative slopes, and that the direct relationships represented by the two upward-sloping curves, *c* and *d*, have positive slopes. Notice also that the flatter the curve, the smaller the numerical value of the slope; and the more vertical, or steeper, the curve, the larger the numerical value of the slope. There are two extreme cases:

1. When the curve is horizontal (flat), the slope is zero.

2. When the curve is vertical (straight up and down), the slope is infinite (larger than large).

Knowing the term *slope* and how it's measured lets us describe verbally the pictures we see visually. For example, if I say a curve has a slope of zero, you should picture in your mind a flat line; if I say "a curve with a slope of minus one," you should picture a falling line that makes a 45° angle with the horizontal and vertical axes. (It's the hypotenuse of an isosceles right triangle with the axes as the other two sides.)

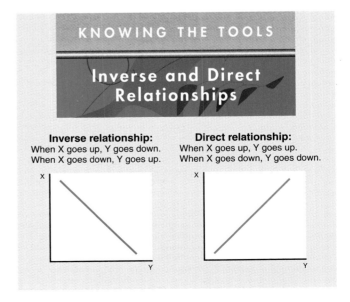

KNOWING THE TOOLS

Inverse and Direct Relationships

Inverse relationship:
When X goes up, Y goes down.
When X goes down, Y goes up.

Direct relationship:
When X goes up, Y goes up.
When X goes down, Y goes down.

Figure A1-4 (a and b)   A Maximum and a Minimum Point

(a) Maximum point

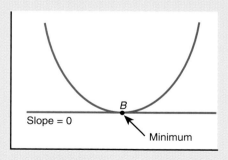

(b) Minimum point

Slopes of Nonlinear Curves

The preceding examples were of *linear (straight) curves.* With *nonlinear curves*—the ones that really do curve—the slope of the curve is constantly changing. As a result, we must talk about the slope of the curve at a particular point, rather than the slope of the whole curve. How can a point have a slope? Well, it can't really, but it can almost, and if that's good enough for mathematicians, it's good enough for us.

Defining the slope of a nonlinear curve is a bit more difficult. The slope at a given point on a nonlinear curve is determined by the slope of a linear (or straight) line that's tangent to that curve. (A line that's tangent to a curve is a line that just touches the curve, and touches it only at one point in the immediate vicinity of the given point.) In Figure A1-3, the line *LL* is tangent to the curve *ee* at point *E*. The slope of that line, and hence the slope of the curve at the one point where the line touches the curve, is +1.

Maximum and Minimum Points

Two points on a nonlinear curve deserve special mention. These points are the ones for which the slope of the curve is zero. I demonstrate those in Figure A1-4(a) and (b). At point A, we're at the top of the curve so it's at a maximum point; at point B, we're at the bottom of the curve so it's at a minimum point. These maximum and minimum points are often referred to by economists, and it's important to realize that the value of the slope of the curve at each of these points is zero.

There are, of course, many other types of curves, and much more can be said about the curves I've talked about.

I won't do so because, for purposes of this course, we won't need to get into those refinements. I've presented as much Graphish as you need to know for this book.

PRESENTING REAL-WORLD DATA IN GRAPHS

The previous discussion treated the Graphish terms that economists use in presenting models which focus on hypothetical relationships. Economists also use graphs in presenting actual economic data. Say, for example, that you want to show how exports have changed over time. Then you would place years on the horizontal axis (by convention) and exports on the vertical axis, as in Figure A1-5(a) and (b). Having done so, you have a couple of choices: you can draw a **line graph**—*a graph where the data are connected by a continuous line;* or you can make a **bar graph**—*a graph where the area under each point is filled in to look like a bar.* Figure A1-5(a) shows a line graph and Figure A1-5(b) shows a bar graph.

Another type of graph is a **pie chart**—*a circle divided into "pie pieces," where the undivided pie represents the total amount and the pie pieces reflect the percentage of the whole pie that the various components make up.* This type of graph is useful in visually presenting how a total amount is divided. Figure A1-5(c) shows a pie chart, which happens to represent the division of grades on a test I gave. Notice that 5 percent of the students got As.

There are other types of graphs, but they're all variations on line and bar graphs and pie charts. Once you understand these three basic types of graphs, you shouldn't have any trouble understanding the other types.

Figure A1-5 (a, b, and c)   Presenting Information Visually

(a) Line graph   (b) Bar graph   (c) Pie chart

INTERPRETING GRAPHS ABOUT THE REAL WORLD

Understanding Graphish is important because, if you don't, you can easily misinterpret the meaning of graphs. For example, consider the two graphs in Figure A1-6 (a) and (b). Which graph demonstrates the larger rise in income? If you said (a), you're wrong. The intervals in the vertical axes differ, and if you look carefully you'll see that the curves in both graphs represent the same combination of points. So when considering graphs, always make sure you understand the markings on the axes. Only then can you interpret the graph.

Let's now review what we've covered.

- A graph is a picture of points on a coordinate system in which the points denote relationships between numbers.
- A downward-sloping line represents an inverse relationship or a negative slope.
- An upward-sloping line represents a direct relationship or a positive slope.
- Slope is measured by rise over run, or a change of y (the number measured on the vertical axis) over a change in x (the number measured on the horizontal axis).

Figure A1-6 (a and b)   The Importance of Scales

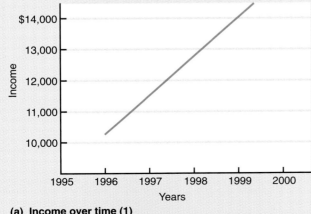

(a) Income over time (1)

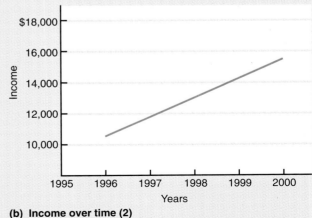

(b) Income over time (2)

- The slope of a point on a nonlinear curve is measured by the rise over run of a line tangent to that point.
- At the maximum and minimum points of a nonlinear curve, the value of the slope is zero.

- In reading graphs, one must be careful to understand what's being measured on the vertical and horizontal axes.

Key Terms

bar graph *(24)*

coordinate system *(21)*

direct relationship *(22)*

graph *(20)*

interpolation assumption *(21)*

inverse relationship *(22)*

line graph *(24)*

linear curve *(21)*

nonlinear curve *(22)*

pie chart *(24)*

slope *(22)*

Questions for Thought and Review

1. Create a coordinate space on graph paper and label the following points:
   a. (0, 5)
   b. (−5, −5)
   c. (2, − 3)
   d. (−1, 1)

2. Graph the following costs per unit, and answer the questions that follow.

Horizontal Axis: Output	Vertical Axis: Cost per Unit
1	$30
2	20
3	12
4	6
5	2
6	6
7	12
8	20
9	30

   a. Is the relationship between cost per unit and output linear or nonlinear? Why?
   b. In what range in output is the relationship inverse? In what range in output is the relationship direct?
   c. In what range in output is the slope negative? In what range in output is the slope positive?
   d. What is the slope between 1 and 2 units?

3. Within a coordinate space, draw a line with:
   a. Zero slope.
   b. Infinite slope.
   c. Positive slope.
   d. Negative slope.

4. Calculate the slope of lines *a* to *e* in the following coordinate system.

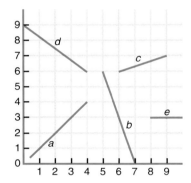

5. Given the following nonlinear curve, answer the following questions:

   a. At what point(s) is the slope negative?
   b. At what point(s) is the slope positive?
   c. At what point(s) is the slope zero?
   d. What point is the maximum? What point is the minimum?

6. State what type of graph or chart you would use to show the following real-world data:
   a. Interest rates from 1929 to 2000.
   b. Median income levels of various ethnic groups in the United States.
   c. Total federal expenditures by selected categories.
   d. Total costs of producing 100–800 shoes.

The Economic Organization of Society

2

After reading this chapter, you should be able to:

- Define capitalism and explain how it relies on markets to coordinate economic activities.

- Define socialism and explain how in practice it solves the three coordination problems.

- Describe how economic systems have evolved from the eighth century to today.

- Demonstrate opportunity cost with a production possibility curve.

- State the principle of increasing marginal opportunity cost.

- Explain why economic reasoning must be considered in context that requires a knowledge of history and institutions.

- Relate the concept of comparative advantage to the production possibility curve.

In capitalism man exploits man;
in socialism it's the other way 'round.

Abba Lerner

Every economy must solve three main coordination problems:

1. What, and how much, to produce.
2. How to produce it.
3. For whom to produce it.

Societies face a universal problem when trying to solve the three problems: Usually what individuals want to do isn't consistent with what "society" wants them to do. Society would often like people to consider what's good for society when making their individual decisions, and to agree that what society wants for them is what they want, too. For example, say society has garbage, and society determines that your neighborhood is the best place to set up a garbage dump. Even if you agree a garbage dump is needed, you probably won't want it in your neighborhood. This attitude of **NIMBY** (*Not In My Back Yard*)—*a mindset of approving a project but not wanting it to be nearby*—is found throughout our society.

Individual goals and social goals also conflict when decisions are being made about how much to produce and consume. Individuals generally like to consume much more than they like to produce. So a society must provide incentives for its members to produce more and consume less to alleviate that scarcity. A sure sign that an economic system isn't working is when people perceive that there are important things that need to be done, but are sitting around doing nothing because the system doesn't provide them with the incentive to do them.

How hard is it to make the three decisions I've listed? Imagine for a moment the problem of living in a family: the fights, arguments, and questions that come up. "Do I have to do the dishes?" "Why can't I have piano lessons?" "Bobby got a new sweater. How come I didn't?" "Mom likes you best." Now multiply the size of the family by millions. The same fights, the same arguments, the same questions—only for society the problems are millions of times more complicated than for one family.

How are these complicated coordination problems solved? The two main economic systems the world has used in the past 50 years—capitalism and socialism—answer this question differently.

> The coordination problems faced by society are immense.

CAPITALISM

Capitalism is *an economic system based on private property and the market in which, in principle, individuals decide how, what, and for whom to produce.* Under capitalism, individuals are encouraged to follow their own self-interest, while market forces of supply and demand are relied on to coordinate those individual pursuits. Distribution of goods is to each individual according to his or her ability, effort, and inherited property.

> Capitalism is an economic system based on private property and the market. It gives private property rights to individuals, and relies on market forces to coordinate economic activity.

Reliance on market forces doesn't mean that political, social, and historical forces play no role in coordinating economic decisions. These other forces do influence how the market works. For example, for a market to exist, government must allocate and defend **private property rights**—*the control a private individual or firm has over an asset or a right.* The concept of private ownership must exist and must be accepted by individuals in society. When you say, "This car is mine," it means that it is unlawful for someone else to take it without your permission. If someone takes it without your permission, he or she is subject to punishment through the legal system.

Reliance on the Market

> **Q.1** John, your study partner, is telling you that the best way to allocate property rights is through the market. How do you respond?

Markets work through a system of rewards and payments. If you do something, you get paid for doing that something; if you take something, you pay for that something. How much you get is determined by how much you give. This relationship seems fair to most people. But there are instances when it doesn't seem fair. Say someone is unable to work. Should that person get nothing? How about Joe down the street, who was given

$10 million by his parents? Is it fair that he gets lots of toys, like Corvettes and skiing trips to Aspen, and doesn't have to work, while the rest of us have to work 40 hours a week and maybe go to school at night?

I'll put those questions about fairness off at this point—they are very difficult questions. For now, all I want to present is the underlying concept of fairness that capitalism embodies: "Them that works, gets; them that don't, starve."[1] In capitalism, individuals are encouraged to follow their own self-interest.

In capitalist economies, individuals are free to do whatever they want as long as it's legal. The market is relied on to see that what people want to get, and want to do, is consistent with what's available. Price is the mechanism through which people's desires are coordinated and goods are rationed. If there's not enough of something to go around, its price goes up; if more of something needs to get done, the price given to individuals willing to do it goes up. If something isn't wanted or doesn't need to be done, its price goes down. Under capitalism, fluctuations in prices play a central role in coordinating individuals' wants.

Under capitalism, fluctuations in prices play a central role in coordinating individuals' wants.

What's Good about the Market?

Is the market a good way to coordinate individuals' activities? Much of this book will be devoted to answering that question. The answer that I, and most U.S. economists, come to is: Yes, it is a reasonable way. True, it has problems; the market can be unfair, mean, and arbitrary, and sometimes it is downright awful. Why then do economists support it? For the same reason that Oliver Wendell Holmes supported democracy—it is a lousy system, but, based on experience with alternatives, it is better than all the others we've thought of.

 2.1

The primary debate among economists is not about using markets; it is about how markets should be structured, and whether they should be modified and adjusted by government regulation. Those are much harder questions, and on these questions, opinions differ enormously.

The primary debate among economists is not about using markets but about how markets are structured.

SOCIALISM

The view that markets are a reasonable way to organize society has not always been shared by all economists. Throughout history strong arguments have been made against markets. These arguments are both philosophical and practical. The philosophical argument against the market is that it brings out the worst in people—it glorifies greed. It encourages people to beat out others rather than to be cooperative. As an alternative some economists have supported **socialism**—which is, in theory, *an economic system based on individuals' goodwill toward others, not on their own self-interest, and in which, in principle, society decides what, how, and for whom to produce.*

---

[1]How come the professor gets to use rotten grammar but screams when he sees rotten grammar in your papers? Well, that's fairness for you. Actually, I should say a bit more about writing style. All writers are expected to know correct grammar; if they don't, they don't deserve to be called writers. Once you know grammar, you can individualize your writing style, breaking the rules of grammar where the meter and flow of the writing require it. In college you're still proving that you know grammar, so in papers handed in to your teacher, you shouldn't break the rules of grammar until you've proved to the teacher that you know them. Me, I've done lots of books, so my editors give me a bit more leeway than your teachers will give you.

Socialism in Theory

Q.2 Are there any activities in a family that you believe should be allocated by a market? What characteristics do those activities have?

You can best understand the idea behind theoretical socialism by thinking about how decisions are made in a family. In most families, benevolent parents decide who gets what, based on the needs of each member of the family. When Sabin gets a new coat and his sister Sally doesn't, it's because Sabin needs a coat while Sally already has two coats that fit her and are in good condition. Victor may be slow as molasses, but from his family he still gets as much as his superefficient brother Jerry gets. In fact, Victor may get more than Jerry because he needs extra help.

Markets have little role in most families. In my family, when food is placed on the table we don't bid on what we want, with the highest bidder getting the food. In my family, every person can eat all he or she wants, although if one child eats more than a fair share, that child gets a lecture from me on the importance of sharing. "Be thoughtful; be considerate. Think of others first," are lessons that many families try to teach.

Socialism is, in theory, an economic system that tries to organize society in the same way as most families are organized—all people contribute what they can, and get what they need.

In theory, socialism is an economic system that tries to organize society in the same way as these families are organized, trying to see that individuals get what they need. Socialism tries to take other people's needs into account and adjust people's own wants in accordance with what's available. In socialist economies, individuals are urged to look out for the other person; if individuals' inherent goodness won't make them consider the general good, government will make them. In contrast, a capitalist economy expects people to be selfish; it relies on markets and competition to direct that selfishness to the general good.[2]

Socialism in Practice

Q.3 Which would be more likely to attempt to foster individualism: socialism or capitalism?

Few economists argue directly in favor of greed. Most accept that it would be great if everyone wanted to be good to others. However, they point out that in practice, economic systems based upon people's goodwill have tended to break down. This is certainly true of the major countries that tried socialism starting in the 1900s. In practice socialist governments had to take a strong role in guiding the economy. Socialism became an economic system based on government ownership of the means of production, with economic activity governed by central planning. What I am describing as "socialism in practice" is often called **Soviet-style socialism**—*an economic system that uses administrative control or central planning to solve the coordination problems: what, how, and for whom*—because it was the system used by the former Soviet Union. In that Soviet-style socialist economic system, government planning boards set society's goals and then directed individuals and firms as to how to achieve those goals.

Soviet-style socialism is an economic system that uses administrative control or central planning to solve the coordination problems: what, how, and for whom.

Q.4 What is the difference between socialism in theory and socialism in practice?

EVOLVING ECONOMIC SYSTEMS[3]

Feudalism is an economic system in which traditions rule.

Capitalism and socialism have not existed forever. Capitalism came into widespread existence in the mid-1700s; socialism came into existence in the early 1900s. Before capitalism and socialism, other forms of economic systems existed, including **feudalism**—*an*

---

[2]As you probably surmised, the above distinction is too sharp. Even capitalist societies want people to be selfless, but not too selfless. Children in capitalist societies are generally taught to be selfless at least in dealing with friends and family. The difficulties parents and societies face is finding a midpoint between the two positions: selfless but not too selfless; selfish but not too selfish.

[3]The appendix to this chapter traces the development of economic systems from feudalism to mercantilism to capitalism to socialism to modern-day forms of welfare capitalism in a bit more detail.

APPLYING THE TOOLS

Tradition and Today's Economy

In a tradition-based society, the social and cultural forces give a society inertia (a tendency to resist change) that predominates over economic and political forces.

"Why did you do it that way?"

"Because that's the way we've always done it."

Tradition-based societies had markets, but they were peripheral, not central, to economic life. In feudal times what was produced, how it was produced, and for whom it was produced were primarily decided by tradition.

In today's U.S. economy, the market plays the central role in economic decisions. But that doesn't mean that tradition is dead. As I said in Chapter 1, tradition still plays a significant role in today's society, and, in many aspects of society, tradition still overwhelms the invisible hand. Consider the following:

1. The persistent view that women should be homemakers rather than factory workers, consumers rather than producers.

2. The raised eyebrows when a man is introduced as a nurse, secretary, homemaker, or member of any other profession conventionally identified as women's work.

3. Society's unwillingness to permit the sale of individuals or body organs.

4. Parents' willingness to care for their children without financial compensation.

Each of these tendencies reflects tradition's influence in Western society. Some are so deep-rooted that we see them as self-evident. Some of tradition's effects we like; others we don't—but we often take them for granted. Economic forces may work against these traditions, but the fact that they're still around indicates the continued strength of tradition in our market economy.

---

economic system in which traditions rule. In feudalism if your parents were serfs (small farmers who lived on a manor), you would be a serf. Feudalism dominated the Western world from about the 8th century to the 15th century.

Throughout the feudalistic period merchants and artisans (small manufacturers who produced goods by hand) grew in importance and wealth and, eventually, their increased importance led to a change in the economic system from feudalism to **mercantilism**—*an economic system in which government determines the what, how, and for whom decisions by doling out the rights to undertake certain economic activities*. Mercantilism remained the dominant economic system until the 1700s, when the **Industrial Revolution**—*a time when technology and machines rapidly modernized industrial production and mass-produced goods replaced handmade goods*—led to a decrease in power of small producers, an increase in power of capitalists, and eventually to a revolution instituting capitalism as the dominant economic system.

Some economists prefer to call the system that evolved from mercantilism a *market economic system* rather than capitalism. Their justification for doing so is that the key element of the new system is not the power of the capitalists but the central reliance on markets to coordinate economic activities. They argue that the market system is not fundamentally changed if the power shifts from a small group of capitalists to corporations, or even to nonprofit organizations, as long as the market remains central. I agree with their argument, but I prefer the term *capitalism* because of its widespread usage, not because I believe that capitalist control is the central element of our modern market economy.

I mention feudalism and mercantilism because aspects of both continue in economies today. For example, governments in Japan and Germany play significant roles in directing their economies. Their economic systems are sometimes referred to as *neomercantilist economies*.

Mercantilism is an economic system in which government doles out the rights to undertake economic activities.

 2.2

Back in the Middle Ages, markets developed spontaneously. "You have something I want; I have something you want. Let's trade" is a basic human attitude we see in all aspects of life. Even children quickly get into trading: chocolate ice cream for vanilla, two Pokémon cards for a ride on a motor scooter. Markets institutionalize such trading by providing a place where people know they can go to trade. New markets are continually being formed. Today there are markets for baseball cards, pork bellies (which become bacon and pork chops), rare coins, and so on. The Internet, with sites like eBay, is expanding markets enormously, allowing ordinary people to trade with people thousands of miles away.

Throughout history, societies have tried to prevent some markets from operating because they feel those markets are ethically wrong or have undesirable side effects. Societies have the power to prevent markets, to make some kinds of markets illegal. In parts of the United States, the addictive drug market, the baby market, and the sex market, to name a few, are illegal. In socialist countries, markets in a much wider range of goods (such as clothes, cars, and soft drinks) and activities (such as private business for individual profit) have been illegal.

BEYOND THE TOOLS

The Rise of Markets in Perspective

But, even if a society prevents the market from operating, society cannot escape the invisible hand. If there's excess supply, there will be downward pressure on prices; if there's excess demand, there will be upward pressure on prices. To maintain an equilibrium in which the quantity supplied does not equal the quantity demanded, a society needs a strong force to prevent the invisible hand from working. In the Middle Ages, that strong force was religion. The Church told people that if they got too far into the market mentality—if they followed their self-interest—they'd go to Hell.

Until recently, in socialist society the state provided the preventive force. The educational system in socialist countries emphasized a more communal set of values. They taught students that a member of socialist society does not try to take advantage of other human beings but, rather, lives by the philosophy "From each according to his ability; to each according to his need."

For whatever reason—whether it be that true socialism wasn't really tried, or that people's self-interest is too strong—the "from each according to his ability; to each according to his need" approach didn't work in socialist countries. They have switched (some say succumbed) to greater reliance on the market.

Q.5 True or false? As economic systems have evolved, there has been less need for planning.

The Need for Coordination in an Economic System

As economic systems evolved from mercantilism to a market economy, many people asked: Who will coordinate economic activities if the government does not? It was in answering this question that modern economics developed. To answer that question, a British moral philosopher named Adam Smith developed, in his famous book *The Wealth of Nations* (1776), the concept of the invisible hand, and used it to explain how markets could coordinate the economy without the active involvement of government. Smith wrote:

Markets coordinate economic activity by using the price mechanism to direct individuals' self-interest into society's interest.

> Man has almost constant occasion for the help of his brethren, and it is in vain for him to expect it from their benevolence only. He will be more likely to prevail, if he can interest their self-love in his favour, and show them that it is for their own advantage to do for him what he requires of them. Whoever offers to another a bargain of any kind proposes to do this. Give me that which I want, and you shall have that which you want, is the meaning of every such offer; and it is in this manner that we obtain from one another the far greater part of those good offices which we stand in need of. It is not from the benevolence of the butcher, the brewer, or the baker, that we expect our dinner, but from their regard to their own interest. We address ourselves, not to their humanity but to their self-love, and never talk to them of our own necessities but of their advantages.

Smith argued that the market's invisible hand would guide suppliers' actions toward the general good. No government coordination was necessary.

Evolutionary Changes within Systems

Revolutionary shifts that give rise to new economic systems are not the only way economic systems change. Systems also evolve. For example, both capitalism and socialism have changed over the years, evolving with changes in social customs, political forces, and the strength of markets. A brief look at their evolution will give us a good sense of the struggles between them that dominate our lives. In the 1930s, during the Great Depression, capitalist countries integrated a number of what might be called socialist institutions into their existing institutions. Distribution of goods was no longer, even in theory, only according to ability; need also played a role. Governments began to play a larger role in the economy, taking control over some of the *how, what,* and *for whom* decisions. For example, most capitalist nations established welfare and social security systems, providing an economic safety net for people whose incomes could not fill their needs. Capitalism became what is sometimes called **welfare capitalism**—*an economic system in which the market is allowed to operate but in which government plays dual roles in determining distribution and making the what, how, and for whom decisions.* In some countries the governments played such an important role that they could reasonably be called market-modified socialist economies. Some countries that allow markets today, such as Sweden, call their economic system a socialist, rather than a capitalist, system.

> Welfare capitalism is an economic system in which the market operates but government regulates markets significantly.

In the 1980s, in socialist countries the reverse process took place: socialism integrated capitalist institutions into its existing institutions. By the 1990s, most of the former socialist countries had given up Soviet-style socialism and had begun to let the market determine the what, how, and for whom decisions. Some government activities in former Socialist economies were privatized—sold to the private sector. Similarly in the 1990s, in capitalist countries governments became even more market oriented and tried to pull back their involvement in the market in favor of private enterprise. For example, governments in Western Europe and the United States tried to eliminate aspects of their welfare systems. In the 1980s and 1990s economic systems moved more toward the capitalist end of the spectrum.

A Blurring of the Distinction between Capitalism and Socialism

The result of these recent changes has been a blending of economic systems and a blurring of the distinctions between capitalism and socialism. China still ostensibly has a socialist system, but a recent trip to China convinced me that it is a very capitalist type of socialism. If the trend toward use of market mechanisms in socialist countries continues, in the 21st century only one general type of economic structure may exist. It won't be pure socialism and it won't be pure capitalism. It will be a blend of the two.

> There has been a blurring of the distinctions between capitalism and socialism.

THE PRODUCTION POSSIBILITY CURVE AND ECONOMIC REASONING

The choices that a society must make are often presented in terms of a production possibility curve. The production possibility curve is related to the concept of opportunity cost that you were introduced to in Chapter 1. It is a tool that shows the trade-offs among choices we make. It can nicely be used to discuss choices societies must make about economic systems. Applying economic reasoning outside of historical and institutional context, however, has difficulties and I'll discuss these difficulties too.

The Production Possibility Table

A production possibility table lists a choice's opportunity costs.

As I discussed in Chapter 1, the concept of opportunity cost—every decision has a cost in forgone opportunities—lies at the center of economic reasoning. Opportunity cost can be seen numerically with a **production possibility table**—*a table that lists a choice's opportunity costs by summarizing what alternative outputs you can achieve with your inputs.* An **output** is simply *a result of an activity,* and an **input** is *what you put into a production process to achieve an output.* For example, your grade in a course is an output and your study time is an input.

Let's present the study-time/grades example numerically. Say you have exactly 20 hours a week to devote to two courses: economics and history. (So, maybe I'm a bit optimistic.) Grades are given numerically and you know that the following relationships exist: if you study 20 hours in economics, you'll get a grade of 100; 18 hours, 94; and so forth.[4]

Let's say that the best you can do in history is a 98 with 20 hours of study a week; 19 hours of study guarantees a 96, and so on. The production possibility table in Figure 2-1(a) shows the highest combination of grades you can get with various allocations of the 20 hours available for studying the two subjects. One possibility is getting 100 in economics and 58 in history. Another is getting 70 in economics and 78 in history.

Notice that the opportunity cost of studying one subject rather than the other is embodied in the production possibility table. The information in the table comes from experience: we are assuming that you've discovered that if you transfer an hour of study from economics to history, you'll lose 3 points on your grade in economics and gain 2 points in history. Thus, the opportunity cost of a 2-point rise in your history grade is a 3-point decrease in your economics grade.

The Production Possibility Curve

The production possibility curve is a curve measuring the maximum combination of outputs that can be obtained from a given number of inputs.

The information in the production possibility table can also be presented graphically in a diagram called a production possibility curve. A **production possibility curve** is *a curve measuring the maximum combination of outputs that can be obtained from a given number of inputs.* It is a graphical presentation of the opportunity cost concept.

A production possibility curve is created from a production possibility table by mapping the table in a two-dimensional graph. I've taken the information from the table in Figure 2-1(a) and mapped it into Figure 2-1(b). The history grade is mapped, or plotted, on the horizontal axis; the economics grade is on the vertical axis.

As you can see from the bottom row of Figure 2-1(a), if you study economics for all 20 hours and study history for 0 hours, you'll get grades of 100 in economics and 58 in history. Point A in Figure 2-1(b) represents that choice. If you study history for all 20 hours and study economics for 0 hours, you'll get a 98 in history and a 40 in economics. Point E represents that choice. Points B, C, and D represent three possible choices between these two extremes.

Notice that the production possibility curve slopes downward from left to right. That means that there is an inverse relationship (a trade-off) between grades in economics and grades in history. The better the grade in economics, the worse the grade in history, and vice versa. That downward slope represents the opportunity cost concept—you get more of one benefit only if you get less of another benefit.

---

[4]Throughout the book I'll be presenting numerical examples to help you understand the concepts. The numbers I choose are often arbitrary. After all, you have to choose something. As an exercise, you might choose different numbers than I did, numbers that apply to your own life, and work out the argument using those numbers.

Figure 2-1 (a and b)   A Production Possibility Table and Curve for Grades in Economics and History
The production possibility table (a) shows the highest combination of grades you can get with only 20 hours available for studying economics and history.
    The information in the production possibility table in (a) can be plotted on a graph, as is done in (b). The grade received in economics is on the vertical axis, and the grade received in history is on the horizontal axis.

Hours of study in history	Grade in history	Hours of study in economics	Grade in economics
20	98	0	40
19	96	1	43
18	94	2	46
17	92	3	49
16	90	4	52
15	88	5	55
14	86	6	58
13	84	7	61
12	82	8	64
11	80	9	67
10	78	10	70
9	76	11	73
8	74	12	76
7	72	13	79
6	70	14	82
5	68	15	85
4	66	16	88
3	64	17	91
2	62	18	94
1	60	19	97
0	58	20	100

(a) Production possibility table

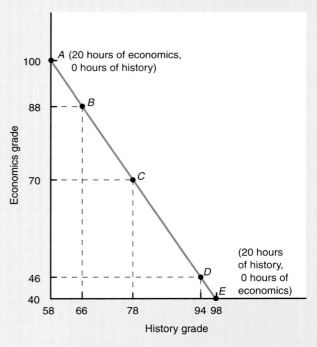

(b) Production possibility curve

The production possibility curve not only represents the opportunity cost concept, it also measures the opportunity cost. For example, in Figure 2-1(b), say you want to raise your grade in history from a 94 to a 98 (move from point *D* to point *E*). The opportunity cost of that 4-point increase would be a 6-point decrease in your economics grade, from 46 to 40.

To summarize, the production possibility curve demonstrates that:

1. There is a limit to what you can achieve, given the existing institutions, resources, and technology.

2. Every choice you make has an opportunity cost. You can get more of something only by giving up something else.

Increasing Marginal Opportunity Cost I chose an unchanging trade-off in the study-time/grade example because it made the initial presentation of the production possibility curve easier. Since, by assumption, you could always trade two points on your history grade for three points on your economics grade, the production possibility curve was a straight line. But is that the way we'd expect reality to be? Probably not. The production possibility curve is generally bowed outward, as in Figure 2-2(b).

Why? Because some resources are better suited for the production of certain kinds of goods than they are for the production of other kinds of goods. To make the answer

The slope of the production possibility curve tells you the opportunity cost of good *X* in terms of good *Y*. You have to give up 2*Y* to get 1*X* when you're around point *A*.

Figure 2-2 (a and b)   A Production Possibility Table and Curve

The table in (a) contains information on the trade-off between the production of guns and butter. This information has been plotted on the graph in (b). Notice in (b) that as we move along the production possibility curve from A to F, trading butter for guns, we get fewer and fewer guns for each pound of butter given up. That is, the opportunity cost of choosing guns over butter increases as we increase the production of guns. This concept is called the principle of increasing marginal opportunity cost. The phenomenon occurs because some resources are better suited for the production of butter than for the production of guns, and we use the better ones first.

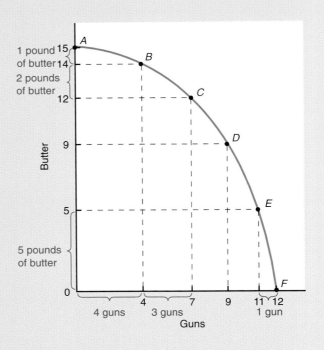

% of resources devoted to production of guns	Number of guns	% of resources devoted to production of butter	Pounds of butter	Row
0	0	100	15	A
20	4	80	14	B
40	7	60	12	C
60	9	40	9	D
80	11	20	5	E
100	12	0	0	F

(a) Production possibility table

(b) Production possibility curve

Q-6   If no resource had a comparative advantage in the production of any good, what would the shape of the production possibility curve be? Why?

more concrete, let's talk specifically about society's choice between defense spending (guns) and spending on domestic needs (butter). The graph in Figure 2-2(b) is derived from the table in Figure 2-2(a).

Let's see what the shape of the curve means in terms of numbers. Let's start with society producing only butter (point A). Giving up a little butter (1 pound) initially gains us a lot of guns (4), moving us to point B. The next 2 pounds of butter we give up gains us slightly fewer guns (point C). If we continue to trade butter for guns, we find that at point D we gain very few guns from giving up a pound of butter. The opportunity cost of choosing guns over butter increases as we increase the production of guns.

The reason the opportunity cost of guns increases as we consume more guns is that some resources are relatively better suited to producing guns, while others are relatively better suited to producing butter. Put in economists' terminology, some resources have a **comparative advantage** over other resources—*the ability to be better suited to the production of one good than to the production of another good.* In this example, some resources have a comparative advantage over other resources in the production of butter, while other resources have a comparative advantage in the production of guns.

When making small amounts of guns and large amounts of butter, in the production of those guns we use the resources whose comparative advantage is in the production of guns. All other resources are devoted to producing butter. Because the resources used in producing guns aren't good at producing butter, we're not giving up much butter to get

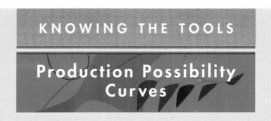

KNOWING THE TOOLS

Production Possibility Curves

Definition	Shape	Shifts	Points In, Out, and On
The production possibility curve is a curve that measures the maximum combination of outputs that can be obtained with a given number of inputs	Most are outward bowed because of increasing marginal opportunity cost; if opportunity cost doesn't change, the production possibility curve is a straight line	Increases in inputs or increases in the productivity of inputs shift the production possibility curve out; decreases have the opposite effect; the production possibility curve shifts along the axis whose input is changing	Points inside the production possibility curve are points of inefficiency; points on the production possibility curve are points of efficiency; points outside the production possibility curve are not obtainable

Remember: when the slope is flat, there's a low opportunity cost of guns (a high opportunity cost of butter). When the slope is steep, there's a high opportunity cost of guns (a low opportunity cost of butter).

those guns. As we produce more and more of a good, we must use resources whose comparative advantage is in the production of the other good—in this case, more suitable for producing butter than for producing guns. As we remove resources from the production of butter to get the same additional amount of guns, we must give up increasing amounts of butter. An alternative way of saying this is that the opportunity cost of producing guns becomes greater as the production of guns increases. As we continue to increase the production of guns, the opportunity cost of more guns becomes very high because we're using resources to produce guns that have a strong comparative advantage for producing butter.

Let's consider two more examples. Say the United States suddenly decides it needs more wheat. To get additional wheat, we must devote additional land to growing it. This land is less fertile than the land we're already using, so our additional output of wheat per acre of land devoted to wheat will be less. Alternatively, consider the use of relief pitchers in a baseball game. If only one relief pitcher is needed, the manager sends in the best; if he must send in a second one, then a third, and even a fourth, the likelihood of winning the game decreases.

For many of the choices society must make, opportunity costs tend to increase as we choose more and more of an item. The reason is that resources are not easily adaptable from the production of one good to the production of another. Such a phenomenon about choice is so common, in fact, that it has acquired a name: the **principle of increasing marginal opportunity cost.** That principle states:

> In order to get more of something, one must give up ever-increasing quantities of something else.

In other words, initially the opportunity costs of an activity are low, but they increase the more we concentrate on that activity. Sometimes this law is called the flowerpot law because, if it didn't hold, all the world's food could be grown in a flowerpot. But it can't be. As we add more seeds to a fixed amount of soil, there won't be enough nutrients or room for the roots, so output per seed decreases.

The principle of increasing marginal opportunity cost states that opportunity costs increase the more you concentrate on the activity. In order to get more of something, one must give up ever-increasing quantities of something else.

Figure 2-3 (a, b, and c)   Efficiency, Inefficiency, and Technological Change

The production possibility curve helps us see what is meant by efficiency. At point A, in (a), all inputs are used to make 4 pounds of butter and 6 guns. This is inefficient since there is a way to obtain more of one without giving up any of the other, that is, to obtain 6 pounds of butter and 6 guns (point C) or 8 guns and 4 pounds of butter (point B). All points inside the production possibility curve are inefficient. With fixed inputs and given technology, we cannot go beyond the production possibility curve. For example, point D is unattainable.

A technological change that improves production techniques will shift the production possibility curve outward, as shown in both (b) and (c). How the curve shifts outward depends on how technology improves. For example, if we become more efficient in the production of both guns and butter, the curve will shift out as in (b). If we become more efficient in producing butter, but not in producing guns, then the curve will shift as in (c).

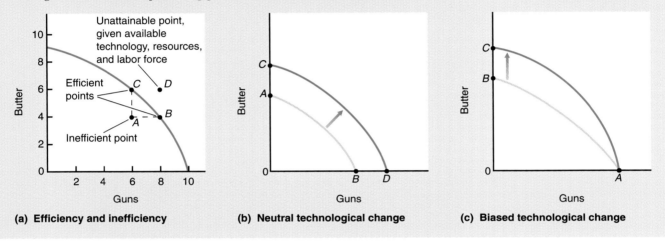

(a) Efficiency and inefficiency   (b) Neutral technological change   (c) Biased technological change

Efficiency We would like, if possible, to get as much output as possible from a given amount of inputs or resources. That's **productive efficiency**—*achieving as much output as possible from a given amount of inputs or resources.* We would like to be efficient. The production possibility curve helps us see what is meant by productive efficiency. Consider point A in Figure 2-3(a), which is inside the production possibility curve. If we are producing at point A, we are using all our resources to produce 6 guns and 4 pounds of butter. Point A represents **inefficiency**—*getting less output from inputs which, if devoted to some other activity, would produce more output.* That's because with the same inputs we could be getting either 8 guns and 4 pounds of butter (point B) or 6 pounds of butter and 6 guns (point C). As long as we prefer more to less, both points B and C represent **efficiency**—*achieving a goal using as few inputs as possible.* We always want to move our production out to a point on the production possibility curve.

Why not move out farther, to point D? If we could, we would, but by definition the production possibility curve represents the most output we can get from a certain combination of inputs. So point D is unattainable, given our resources and technology.

When technology improves, when more resources are discovered, or when the economic institutions get better at fulfilling our wants, we can get more output with the same inputs. What this means is that when technology or an economic institution improves, the entire production possibility curve shifts outward from AB to CD in Figure 2-3(b). How the production possibility curve shifts outward depends on how the technology improves. For example, say we become more efficient in producing butter, but not more efficient in producing guns. Then the production possibility curve shifts outward to AC in Figure 2-3(c).

Efficiency involves achieving a goal as cheaply as possible. Efficiency has meaning only in relation to a specified goal.

Figure 2-4   Examples of Shifts in Production Possibility Curves

Each of these curves reflects a different type of shift. Your assignment is to match these shifts with the situations given in the text on page 40.

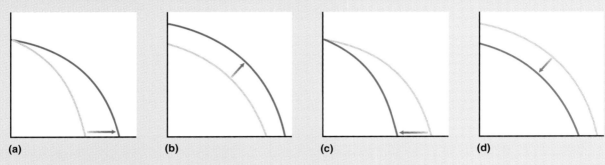

(a)   (b)   (c)   (d)

Policies that costlessly shift the production possibility curve outward are the most desirable policies because they don't require us to decrease our consumption of one good to get more of another. Alas, such policies are the most infrequent. Improving technology and institutions and discovering more resources are not costless; generally there's an opportunity cost of doing so that must be taken into account.

Distribution and Productive Efficiency In discussing the production possibility curve, I avoided questions of distribution: Who gets what? But such questions cannot be ignored in real-world situations. Specifically, if the method of production is tied to a particular income distribution and choosing one method will help some people but hurt others, we can't say that one method of production is efficient and the other inefficient, even if one method produces more total output than the other. As I stated above, the term *efficiency* involves achieving a goal as cheaply as possible. The term has meaning only in regard to a specified goal. Say, for example, that we have a society of ascetics who believe that consumption above some minimum is immoral. For such a society, producing more for less (productive efficiency) would not be efficient since consumption is not its goal. Or say that we have a society that cares that what is produced is fairly distributed. An increase in output that goes to only one person and not to anyone else would not necessarily be efficient.

In our society, however, most people prefer more to less, and many policies have relatively small distributional consequences. On the basis of the assumption that more is better than less, economists use their own kind of shorthand for such policies and talk about efficiency as identical to productive efficiency—increasing total output. But it's important to remember the assumption under which that shorthand is used: that the distributional effects that accompany the policy aren't undesirable and that we, as a society, prefer more output.

Some Examples of Shifts in the Production Possibility Curve

To see whether you understand the production possibility curve, let us now consider some situations that can be shown with the production possibility curve. In Figure 2-4 I demonstrate four situations with production possibility curves. On the following page, I list five situations. To test your understanding of the curve, match each situation to one of the curves in Figure 2-4 (a graph can match more than one situation).

Q-7 Your firm is establishing a trucking business in Saudi Arabia. The firm has noticed that women are generally paid much less than men in Saudi Arabia, and the firm suggests that hiring women would be more efficient than hiring men. What should you respond?

Q.8 When a natural disaster hits the midwestern United States, where most of the U.S. butter is produced, what happens to the U.S. production possibility curve for guns and butter?

1. A new genetic material is found that doubles the speed at which agricultural goods grow.
2. Nanites (micromachines) are perfected that lower the cost of manufactured goods.
3. A meteor hits the world and destroys half the earth's natural resources.
4. A world trade war erupts and trade restrictions grow enormously.
5. Soviet-style socialist countries give up on the socialist system and switch to a market system.

The correct answers are: 1–a; 2–a; 3–d; 4–d; 5–d.

If you got them all right, you are well on your way to understanding the production possibility curve.

The Production Possibility Curve and Economic Systems

Some of you may have rightly wondered about one of the answers in the above examples, specifically, the last one. (If you wondered about the others, a review is in order for you.) The appropriate wondering is the following: According to what I have said previously, the shift by socialist countries toward markets should shift the production possibility curve out, not in; so wouldn't the correct answer be that it shifts the production possibility curve out because it introduces markets that allow trade?

The answer to that question is: Yes, it should *eventually* shift the production possibility curve out. But in the short and medium run (i.e., within 5 to 10 years) the change will shift it in. The explanation of why this is so brings us back to our discussion of economic systems and allows me to tie together that discussion with the discussion of opportunity costs as represented by the production possibility curve.

The production possibility curve presents choices in a timeless fashion and therefore makes opportunity costs clear-cut; there are two choices, one with a higher cost and one with a lower cost. The reality is that most choices are dependent on other choices; they are made sequentially with a time dimension. With sequential choices you cannot simply reverse your decision. Once you have started on a path, to take another path you have to return to the beginning. Thus, following one path often lowers the costs of options along that path, but it raises the costs of options along another path.

Such sequential decisions can best be seen within the framework of a **decision tree**—*a visual description of sequential choices.* A decision tree is shown in Figure 2-5.

Once you make the initial decision to go on path A, the costs of path B options become higher; they include the costs of reversing your path and starting over. The

The production possibility curve presents choices in a timeless fashion, but most choices are dependent upon previous choices.

Q.9 Draw a decision tree that shows the choices you have faced when pursuing your undergraduate degree. Which choices were most costly?

Figure 2-5 A Decision Tree

Decisions are often made sequentially. Decisions made at low levels of the decision tree preclude, or at least significantly increase the costs of, other decisions.

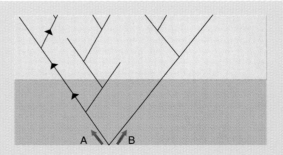

decision trees of life have thousands of branches; each decision you make rules out other paths, or at least increases your costs highly. (Remember that day you decided to blow off your homework? That decision may have changed your future life.)

Another way of putting this same point is that all *decisions are made in context:* What makes sense in one context may not make sense in another. For example, say you're answering the question "Would society be better off if students were taught literature or if they were taught agriculture?" The answer depends on the institutional context. In a developing country whose goal is large increases in material output, teaching agriculture may make sense. In a developed country, where growth in material output is less important, teaching literature may make sense.

Recognizing the contextual nature of decisions is important when interpreting the production possibility curve. Because decisions are contextual, what the production possibility curve for a particular decision looks like depends on the existing institutions, and the analysis can be applied only in institutional and historical context. The production possibility curve is not a purely technical phenomenon. The curve is an engine of analysis to make contextual choices, not a definitive tool to decide what one should do in all cases.

From the above discussion, it should be clear where economic systems fit into this discussion. The choice of economic systems is not the type of decision that the production possibility curve is designed to address. Usually, the curve takes the system as given. The production possibility curve is most useful when analyzing questions that involve policy decisions given existing systems and institutions—slight movements in the production of one good or another.

I sometimes compare the decision the former socialist countries made to my recent decision to give up my beloved Macintosh and to become more Windows-oriented. Mac has a different operating system than Windows, and my wonderful efficiency in Mac does not prevent me being a total klutz in Windows. Why did I change? Because I believe that eventually, as Windows affords me a wider choice of software, the change will make me more efficient. But sometimes I wonder, and in fact this paragraph is being typed on my Mac, which I have stuck with, keeping my Windows machine as a backup. Thus, I have no trouble understanding the difficulties and the switches back and forth that the former socialist countries are making.

Actually, this analogy to a computer operating system is only partially appropriate. With economic systems the problem of changing operating systems or even high-level institutions is even more complex than the analogy is meant to illustrate. Imagine that every software program you used had a mind of its own, and when that program saw that it was going to be made obsolete, it started spewing out viruses and sabotaging the new system. Now, that's the correct analogy. And now you should understand why the former socialist countries may indeed have problems for many years to come.

> Because decisions are contextual, what the production possibility curve for a particular decision looks like depends on the existing institutions, and the analysis can be applied only in an institutional and historical context.

The Production Possibility Curve and Tough Choices

The production possibility curve represents the tough choices society must make. Look at questions such as: Should we save the spotted owl or should we allow logging in the Western forests? Should we expand the government health care system or should we strengthen our national defense system? Should we emphasize policies that allow more consumption now or should we emphasize policies that allow more consumption in the future? Such choices involve difficult trade-offs that can be pictured by the production possibility curve.

Not everyone recognizes these choices. For example, politicians often talk as if the production possibility curve were nonexistent. They promise voters the world, telling

> The production possibility curve represents the tough choices society must make.

Economists continually point out that seemingly free lunches often involve significant hidden costs.

them, "If you elect me, you can have more of everything." When they say that, they obscure the hard choices and increase their probability of getting elected.

Economists do the opposite. They promise little except that life is tough, and they continually point out that seemingly free lunches often involve significant hidden costs. Alas, political candidates who exhibit such reasonableness seldom get elected. Economists' reasonableness has earned economics the nickname *the dismal science*.

COMPARATIVE ADVANTAGE, SPECIALIZATION, AND TRADE

A country has a comparative advantage in a good if it can produce that good at a lower *opportunity* cost than another country can. (Remember, it is a lower opportunity cost, not necessarily a lower absolute cost.)

The same comparative advantage argument I used to explain the shape of the production possibility curve can be used to show how trade (and hence how the markets that facilitate trade) make society better off. Let's start with an international example. Say the United States can produce widgets at a cost of $4 apiece and wadgets at $4 apiece, while Korea can produce widgets at a cost of 300 won (won is the Korean currency) apiece and wadgets at a cost of 100 won apiece. In the United States, the opportunity cost of one widget is one wadget. (Since each costs $4, the United States must reduce its production of wadgets by one to produce another widget.) In Korea, the opportunity cost of a widget is three wadgets since it costs three times as much to produce a widget as it does to produce a wadget. Because the United States' opportunity cost of producing widgets is lower than Korea's, the United States is said to have a comparative advantage in producing widgets. Similarly, Korea is said to have comparative advantage in producing wadgets because its opportunity cost of wadgets is one-third of a widget while the United States' opportunity cost of wadgets is one widget.

If one country has a comparative advantage in one good, the other country must necessarily have a comparative advantage in the other good. Notice how comparative advantage hinges on opportunity cost, not total cost. Even if one country can produce all goods cheaper than another country, trade between them is still possible since the opportunity costs of various goods differ.

The same reasoning can be applied to trade among individuals. To keep the analysis simple, let's consider two individuals. Sunder is a whiz at creative writing; he can turn out four creative writing papers a day or one economics paper a day, or any proportional combination thereof. Ti is an economics whiz; she can turn out four economics papers a day or one creative writing paper a day, or any proportional combination thereof. Figure 2-6(a) shows how many papers each can write in a day.

Sunder and Ti's teacher has given each of them a weekly assignment to do four economics and four creative writing papers. Ti spends four days writing four creative writing papers and one day writing four economics papers. Sunder does the reverse. This will leave no time for partying.

The following week their teacher allows Ti and Sunder to collaborate on their assignment. The team must turn in eight creative writing papers and eight economics papers. Ti and Sunder will receive a collective grade. The question facing Ti and Sunder is how to divide up the work. If they work as they did the week before, it will take each of them all week.

Fortunately Ti is taking an economics course and has just learned about comparative advantage. She points out to Sunder that they can do much better if they avail themselves of their comparative advantages. Since Ti has a comparative advantage in economics and Sunder has a comparative advantage in creative writing, it pays for them to specialize in their respective strengths. Let's say they do that. Their new production possibility table per day is shown in Figure 2-6(b). They both specialize, and in one day the

Q-10 Show, using production possibility curves, that Steve and Sarah would be better off specializing in their baking activities, and then trading, rather than baking only for themselves, given the following production possibility tables.

(a) Steve's Production per Day		(b) Sarah's Production per Day	
Loaves of Bread	Dozens of Cookies	Loaves of Bread	Dozens of Cookies
4	0	4	0
3	2	3	1
2	4	2	2
1	6	1	3
0	8	0	4

Figure 2-6 (a, b, and c)   The Gains from Trade

Trade makes people better off. In this figure I compare individuals' combined production possibilities under two alternative assumptions. The table in (a) shows the number of economics and creative writing papers each student can produce in a day. The table in (b) shows their maximum possibilities when the students collaborate. The graph in (c) plots the production possibility curves associated with the tables in (a) and (b). Notice what trade does to the production possibility frontier. The combined curve is bowed out, reflecting the principle of increasing marginal opportunity costs.

(a) Sunder and Ti's individual possibilities

	Economics papers per day	Creative writing papers per day
Sunder	1	4
Ti	4	1

(b) Sunder and Ti's joint possibilities

	Economics papers per day	Creative writing papers per day
A	5	0
B	4	4
C	0	5

(c) Production possibility curves (numbers of papers per day)

team can turn out four economics papers and four creative writing papers. Now it takes them only two days to do their assignment, leaving them three days to party (or to study for other courses, or to work at a part-time job to pay for their education).

The benefits of collaboration and specialization can also be shown with production possibility curves. Production possibility curves show all the possible combinations of dividing up each student's time and possible combinations when dividing up the work.

Sunder and Ti's respective paper-writing production possibility curves per day are shown in Figure 2-6(c). The blue line represents Sunder's production possibility curve; the red line represents Ti's production possibility curve. The curve connecting points A, B, and C shows the production possibilities if Ti and Sunder collaborate. You should be able to explain the individual production possibility curves. The combined curve is a little more complicated. This curve tells you what they can write when working together. If they both spent the day writing economics papers, they would end up with 5 economics papers and no creative writing papers—point A. If instead, they both wrote creative writing papers, they would have 5 creative writing papers and no economics papers—point C. At these endpoints one person is not taking advantage of his or her comparative advantage. If, instead, they take advantage of their own special skills, Sunder would write 4 creative writing papers and Ti would write 4 economics papers in one day—point B. Connecting points A, B, and C shows all combinations of papers both can write together in one day.

Notice that the combined production possibility curve is shifted out significantly. When individuals collaborate, using their comparative advantages, their production possibilities expand. By collaborating and specializing, each can reach beyond his or her individual production possibility curve. This shifting out of the production possibility curve comes from using comparative advantage and is a geometric representation of the gains to trade.

When individuals trade using their comparative advantages, their combined production possibility curve shifts out.

The Division of Labor

The above examples give a visual sense of the power of markets to make people better off. Markets allow people to trade—to utilize their comparative advantages—and thereby to improve society's combined production possibility curve. Adam Smith, the founder of modern economics, saw this aspect of markets and trade as what differentiated human beings from animals. He wrote:

2.3

> This division of labour, from which so many advantages are derived, is not originally the effect of any human wisdom, which foresees and intends that general opulence to which it gives occasion. It is the necessary, though very slow and gradual consequence of a certain propensity in human nature which has in view no such extensive utility; the propensity to truck, barter, and exchange one thing for another. . . . [This propensity] is common to all men, and to be found in no other race of animals, which seem to know neither this nor any other species of contracts. . . . Nobody ever saw a dog make a fair and deliberate exchange of one bone for another with another dog. Nobody ever saw one animal by its gestures and natural cries signify to another, this is mine, that yours; I am willing to give this for that.

Markets allow specialization and the division of labor. They allow individuals to develop their comparative advantages, thereby increasing the production possibilities of society.

The argument that the division of labor and trade makes individuals better off also holds for countries. Trade shifts out countries' production possibility curves, making them better off. There are, of course, exceptions to this proposition. (Remember all models are dependent on the assumptions of the model.) These exceptions are considered later in microeconomics courses when trade is looked at in more depth. But the general argument that trade and markets make people better off because they allow individuals and economies to assert their comparative advantages carries through and is a primary reason why economists generally support markets.

Markets, Specialization, and Growth

We can see the effect of markets on our well-being empirically by considering the growth of economies. As you can see from Figure 2-7, for 1,700 years the world economy grew very slowly. Then, at the end of the 18th century, the world economy started to grow, and it has grown at an increasing rate since then.

What changed? The introduction of markets and democracy. There's something about markets that leads to economic growth. Markets allow specialization and encourage trade. The bowing out of the production possibilities from trade is part of the story, but a minor part. As individuals compete and specialize they learn by doing, becoming even better at what they do. Markets also foster competition, which pushes individuals

Figure 2-7 Growth in the Past Two Millennia

Source: Angus Maddison, *Monitoring the World Economy*, OECD, 1995; Angus Maddison, "Poor Until 1820," *The Wall Street Journal*, January 11, 1999.

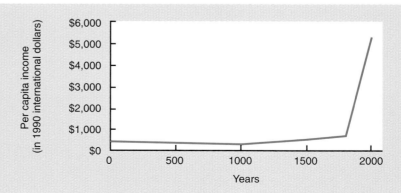

to find better ways of doing things. They devise new technologies that further the growth process.

The new millennium is offering new ways for individuals to specialize and compete. More and more businesses are trading on the Internet. For example, colleges, such as the University of Phoenix, are providing online competition for traditional colleges. Similarly, online bookstores and drugstores are proliferating. As Internet technology becomes built into our economy, we can expect more specialization, more division of labor, and the economic growth that follows.

CONCLUSION

As I will emphasize throughout this book, the tools you will be learning here are powerful but simple, and that simplicity means that much care must be used in their application—to see that the tools fit the situation for which they are used. Businesses tell me that they have much more of a problem with new employees who think they understand things, but actually don't, than they do with new employees who recognize how little they know—who are willing to learn the institutional ropes—and recognize that the time for changing institutions is only when they understand the structural role that the institutions play.

What this means is that economic reasoning is extraordinarily strong, and it really helps you if you apply it in the appropriate time and context. It remains strong when inappropriately applied; but it leads you to the wrong conclusion. The reality is that history and institutions are fundamentally important for making good economic decisions. Economic reasoning alone does not tell anyone, "This is right and this is wrong policy." What economic reasoning does is to provide a framework of analysis that focuses the decision on precisely what are the opportunity costs, and what are the alternative ways of measuring those costs. Fitting that reasoning together with your gut intuitive sense of what is right and wrong is what makes a good economist.

Chapter Summary

- Any economic system must solve three central problems:

    What, and how much, to produce.

    How to produce it.

    For whom to produce it.

- Capitalism is based on private property and the market; socialism is based on individuals' goodwill toward others.

- In capitalism, the what, how, and for whom problems are solved by the market.

- In Soviet-style socialism, the what, how, and for whom problems were solved by government planning boards.

- Political, social, and economic forces are active in both capitalism and socialism.

- Economic systems are in a constant state of evolution.

- Markets use the price mechanism to coordinate economic activity.

- In feudalism, tradition rules; in mercantilism, the government rules; in capitalism, the market rules.

- In welfare capitalism, the market, the government, and tradition each rule components of the economy.

- The production possibility curve measures the maximum combination of outputs that can be obtained from a given number of inputs. It embodies the opportunity cost concept.

- In general, in order to get more and more of something, we must give up ever-increasing quantities of something else. This is the principle of increasing marginal opportunity cost.

- Production possibility curves must be interpreted within the contextual nature of decisions.

- Trade allows people to use their comparative advantage and shift out society's production possibility curve.

- The rise of markets has coincided with significant increases in output. Specialization, trade, and competition have all contributed to the increase.

Key Terms

capitalism *(28)*

comparative
  advantage *(36)*

decision tree *(40)*

efficiency *(38)*

feudalism *(30)*

Industrial Revolution *(31)*

inefficiency *(38)*

input *(34)*

mercantilism *(31)*

NIMBY *(28)*

output *(34)*

principle of increasing
  marginal opportunity
  cost *(37)*

private property
  rights *(28)*

production possibility
  curve *(34)*

production possibility
  table *(34)*

productive efficiency *(38)*

socialism *(29)*

Soviet-style socialism *(30)*

welfare capitalism *(33)*

Questions for Thought and Review

1. What three problems must any economic system solve?

2. How does capitalism solve these three problems?

3. How does Soviet-style socialism solve these three problems?

4. Is capitalism or socialism the better economic system? Why?

5. What arguments can you give for supporting a socialist organization of a family and a capitalist organization of the economy?

6. Design a grade production possibility table and curve that embody the principle of increasing marginal opportunity cost.

7. What would the production possibility curve look like if there were decreasing marginal opportunity costs? Explain. What is an example of decreasing marginal opportunity costs?

8. Show how a production possibility curve would shift if a society became more productive in its output of widgets but less productive in its output of wadgets.

9. How does the theory of comparative advantage relate to production possibility curves?

10. When all people use economic reasoning, inefficiency is impossible, because if the benefit of reducing that inefficiency were greater than the cost, the efficiency would be eliminated. Thus, if people use economic reasoning, it's impossible to be on the interior of a production possibility curve. Is this statement true or false? Why?

11. Why, in the near term, would a switch of socialist countries to a market system cause their production possibility curves to shift in? What institutional and societal characteristics are necessary to carry through that switch successfully?

12. If trade shifts the production possibility curve out, why do some politicians oppose actions to promote trade?

Problems and Exercises

1. Poland, Bulgaria, and Hungary (all former socialist countries) were in the process of changing to a market economy in the early 1990s.
   a. Go to the library and find the latest information about their transitions.
   b. Explain what has happened in the markets, political structures, and social customs of those countries.

2. Economists Edward Lazear and Robert Michael have calculated that the average family spends two and a half times as much on each adult as they do on each child.
   a. Does this mean that children are deprived and that the distribution is unfair?
   b. Do you think these percentages change with family income? If so, how?
   c. Do you think that the allocation would be different in a family in a Soviet-style socialist country than in a capitalist country? Why?

3. One of the specific problems Soviet-style socialist economies had was keeping up with capitalist countries technologically.
   a. Can you think of any reason inherent in a centrally planned economy that would make innovation difficult?
   b. Can you think of any reason inherent in a capitalist country that would foster innovation?
   c. Joseph Schumpeter, a famous Harvard economist of the 1930s, predicted that as firms in capitalist societies grew in size they would innovate less. Can you suggest what his argument might have been?
   d. Schumpeter's prediction did not come true. Modern capitalist economies have had enormous innovations. Can you provide explanations as to why?

4. A country has the following production possibility table:

Resources Devoted to Clothing	Output of Clothing	Resources Devoted to Food	Output of Food
100%	20	0%	0
80	16	20	5
60	12	40	9
40	8	60	12
20	4	80	14
0	0	100	15

a. Draw the country's production possibility curve.
b. What's happening to marginal opportunity costs as output of food increases?
c. Say the country gets better at the production of food. What will happen to the production possibility curve?
d. Say the country gets equally better at producing both food and clothing. What will happen to the production possibility curve?

5. Suppose a country has the following production possibility table:

Resources Devoted to Clothing	Output of Clothing	Resources Devoted to Food	Output of Food
100%	15	0%	0
80	14	20	4
60	12	40	8
40	9	60	12
20	5	80	16
0	0	100	20

a. Draw the country's production possibility curve.

b. What is the combined production possibility curve for this country and the country in question 4 if the countries do not trade and they devote equal proportionate resources to produce each good?
c. What would be the combined production possibility curve of the two countries if they took advantage of their comparative advantages?

6. Assume the United States can produce Toyotas at the cost of $8,000 per car and Chevrolets at $6,000 per car. In Japan, Toyotas can be produced at 1,000,000 yen and Chevrolets at 500,000 yen.
a. In terms of Chevrolets, what is the opportunity cost of producing Toyotas in each country?
b. Who has the comparative advantage in producing Chevrolets?
c. Assume Americans purchase 500,000 Chevrolets and 300,000 Toyotas each year. The Japanese purchase far fewer of each. Using productive efficiency as the guide, who should most likely produce Chevrolets and who should produce Toyotas, assuming Chevrolets are going to be produced in one country and Toyotas in the other?

7. Lawns produce no crops but occupy more land (25 million acres) in the United States than any single crop, such as corn. This means that the United States is operating inefficiently and hence is at a point inside the production possibility curve. Right? If not, what does it mean?

8. Groucho Marx is reported to have said, "The secret of success is honest and fair dealing. If you can fake those, you've got it made." What would likely happen to society's production possibility curve if everyone could fake honesty? Why? (Hint: Remember that society's production possibility curve reflects more than just technical relationships.)

Web Questions

1. The Social Security system is a program that is significant to the evolution of capitalism in the United States. Go to the Social Security Administration's home page (www.ssa.gov) and describe how changes in the Social Security system have moved the U.S. economy toward welfare capitalism. What proposals are being discussed that will change the nature of Social Security? What does this say about the evolution of capitalism today?

2. Using the U.S. International Trade Commission Web site (www.usitc.gov), answer the following:
a. With how many countries does the United States trade?
b. What are its three largest trading partners?
c. How does this trade affect the world production possibility curve?

Answers to Margin Questions

1. He is wrong. Property rights are required for a market to operate. Once property rights are allocated, the market will allocate goods, but the market cannot distribute the property rights that are required for the market to operate. (28)

2. Most families allocate basic needs through control and command. The parents do (or try to do) the controlling and commanding. Generally they are well-intentioned, trying to meet their perception of their children's needs. However, some family activities that are not basic needs

might be allocated through the market. For example, if one child wants a go-cart and is willing to do extra work at home in order to get it, go-carts might be allocated through the market, with the child earning chits that can be used for such nonessentials. *(30)*

3. Capitalism places much more emphasis on fostering individualism. Socialism tries to develop a system in which the individual's needs are placed second to society's needs. *(30)*

4. In theory, socialism is an economic system based upon individuals' goodwill. In practice, socialism follows the Soviet model and involves central planning and government ownership of the primary means of production. *(30)*

5. False. Feudalism, mercantilism, Soviet-style socialism, and capitalism have all involved planning. The difference is in who does the planning. Feudalism relied on tradition for the planning. In mercantilism, the government did most of the planning. In Soviet-style socialism, central planners did the planning. In capitalism, the managers of firms do the planning, with consumers deciding whether those plans are correct. *(32)*

6. If no resource had a comparative advantage, the production possibility curve would be a straight line connecting the points of maximum production of each product as in the graph below.

At all points along this curve, the opportunity cost of producing guns and butter is equal. *(36)*

7. I remind them of the importance of cultural forces. In Saudi Arabia women are not allowed to drive. *(39)*

8. The production possibility curve shifts in along the butter axis as in the graph below. *(40)*

9. A decision tree showing your choices as an undergraduate might look like this: *(40)*

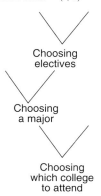

10. If Steve and Sarah do not trade, and divide their time identically, their combined production possibility table is shown in (**a**). If they do collaborate, their production possibility table is shown in (**b**). The corresponding production possibility curves are drawn beneath the tables. The production possibility curve with trade is further to the right than the one without trade. Steve and Sarah can each end up with more bread and cookies if they trade than if they worked on their own. *(42)*

(a) Combined, No Trade		(b) Combined, Trade	
Loaves of Bread	Dozens of Cookies	Loaves of Bread	Dozens of Cookies
8	0	8	0
6	3	6	4
4	6	4	8
2	9	2	10
0	12	0	12

The History of Economic Systems

Remember the distinction between market and economic forces: Economic forces have always existed—they operate in all aspects of our lives; but market forces have not always existed. Markets are social creations societies use to coordinate individuals' actions. Markets developed, sometimes spontaneously, sometimes by design, because they offered a better life for at least some—and usually a large majority of—individuals in a society.

To understand why markets developed, it is helpful to look briefly at the history of the economic systems from which our own system descended.

FEUDAL SOCIETY: RULE OF TRADITION

Let's go back in time to the year 1000 when Europe had no nation-states as we now know them. (Ideally, we would have gone back farther and explained other economic systems, but, given the limited space, I had to draw the line somewhere—an example of trade-off.) The predominant economic system at that time was feudalism. There was no coordinated central government, no unified system of law, no national patriotism, no national defense, although a strong religious institution simply called the Church fulfilled some of these roles. There were few towns; most individuals lived in walled manors or "estates." These manors "belonged to" the "lord of the manor." (Occasionally the "lord" was a lady, but not often.) I say "belonged to" rather than "were owned by" because most of the empires or federations at that time were not formal nation-states that could organize, administer, and regulate ownership. No documents or deeds gave ownership of the land to an individual. Instead, tradition ruled, and in normal times nobody questioned the lord's right to the land. The land "belonged to" the lord because the land "belonged to" him—that's the way it was.

Without a central nation-state, the manor served many functions a nation-state would have served had it existed. The lord provided protection, often within a walled area surrounding the manor house or, if the manor was large enough, a castle. He provided administration and decided disputes. He also decided *what* would be done,

how it would be done, and *who* would get what, but these decisions were limited. In the same way that the land belonged to the lord because that's the way it always had been, what people did and how they did it were determined by what they always had done. Tradition ruled the manor more than the lord did.

Problems of a Tradition-Based Society

Feudalism developed about the 8th and 9th centuries and lasted until about the 15th century, though in isolated countries such as Russia it continued well into the 19th century, and in all European countries its influence lingered for hundreds of years (as late as about 140 years ago in some parts of Germany). Such a long-lived system must have done some things right, and feudalism did: it solved the what, how, and for whom problems in an acceptable way.

But a tradition-based society has problems. In a traditional society, because someone's father was a baker, the son must also be a baker, and because a woman was a homemaker, she wouldn't be allowed to be anything but a homemaker. But what if Joe Blacksmith, Jr., the son of Joe Blacksmith, Sr., is a lousy blacksmith and longs to knead dough, while Joe Baker, Jr., would be a superb blacksmith but hates making pastry? Tough. Tradition dictated who did what. In fact, tradition probably arranged things so that we will never know whether Joe Blacksmith, Jr., would have made a superb baker.

As long as a society doesn't change too much, tradition operates reasonably well, although not especially efficiently, in holding the society together. However, when a society must undergo change, tradition does not work. Change means that the things that were done before no longer need to be done, while new things do need to get done. But if no one has traditionally done these new things, then they don't get done. If the change is important but a society can't figure out some way for the new things to get done, the society falls apart. That's what happened to feudal society. It didn't change when change was required.

The life of individuals living on the land, called *serfs*, was difficult, and feudalism was designed to benefit the lord. Some individuals in feudal society just couldn't take life on the manor, and they set off on their own. Because there was no organized police force, they were unlikely to be caught and forced to return to the manor. Going hungry, being killed, or both, however, were frequent fates of an escaped serf. One place to which serfs could safely escape, though, was a town or city—the remains of what in Roman times had been thriving and active cities. These cities, which had been decimated by plagues, plundering bands, and starvation in the preceding centuries, nevertheless remained an escape hatch for runaway serfs because they relied far less on tradition than did manors. City dwellers had to live by their wits; many became merchants who lived predominantly by trading. They were middlemen; they would buy from one group and sell to another.

Trading in towns was an alternative to the traditional feudal order because trading allowed people to have an income independent of the traditional social structure. Markets broke down tradition. Initially merchants traded using barter (exchange of one kind of good for another): silk and spices from the Orient for wheat, flour, and artisan products in Europe. But soon a generalized purchasing power (money) developed as a medium of exchange. Money greatly expanded the possibilities of trading because its use meant that goods no longer needed to be bartered. They could be sold for money, which could then be spent to buy other goods.

In the beginning, land was not traded, but soon the feudal lord who just had to have a silk robe but had no money was saying, "Why not? I'll sell you a small piece of land so I can buy a shipment of silk." Once land became tradable, the traditional base of the feudal society was undermined. Tradition that can be bought and sold is no longer tradition—it's just another commodity.

FROM FEUDALISM TO MERCANTILISM

Toward the end of the Middle Ages (mid-15th century), markets went from being a sideshow, a fair that spiced up people's lives, to being the main event. Over time, some traders and merchants started to amass fortunes that dwarfed those of the feudal lords. Rich traders settled down; existing towns and cities expanded and new towns were formed. As towns grew and as fortunes shifted from feudal lords to merchants, power in society shifted to the towns. And with that shift came a change in society's political and economic structure.

As these traders became stronger politically and economically, they threw their support behind a king (the strongest lord) in the hope that the king would expand their ability to trade. In doing so, they made the king even

stronger. Eventually, the king became so powerful that his will prevailed over the will of the other lords and even over the will of the Church. As the king consolidated his power, nation-states as we know them today evolved. *The government became an active influence on economic decision making.*

As markets grew, feudalism evolved into mercantilism. The evolution of feudal systems into mercantilism occurred in somewhat this way: As cities and their markets grew in size and power relative to the feudal manors and the traditional economy, a whole new variety of possible economic activities developed. It was only natural that individuals began to look to a king to establish a new tradition that would determine who would do what. Individuals in particular occupations organized into groups called *guilds*, which were similar to strong labor unions today. These guilds, many of which had financed and supported the king, now expected the king and his government to protect their interests.

As new economic activities, such as trading companies, developed, individuals involved in these activities similarly depended on the king for the right to trade and for help in financing and organizing their activities. For example, in 1492, when Christopher Columbus had the wild idea that by sailing west he could get to the East Indies and trade for their riches, he went to Spain's Queen Isabella and King Ferdinand for financial support.

Since many traders had played and continued to play important roles in financing, establishing, and supporting the king, the king was usually happy to protect their interests. The government doled out the rights to undertake a variety of economic activities. By the late 1400s, Western Europe had evolved from a feudal to a mercantilist economy.

The mercantilist period was marked by the increased role of government, which could be classified in two ways: by the way it encouraged growth, and by the way it limited growth. Government legitimized and financed a variety of activities, thus encouraging growth. But government also limited economic activity in order to protect the monopolies of those it favored, thus limiting growth. So mercantilism allowed the market to operate, but it kept the market under its control. The market was not allowed to respond freely to the laws of supply and demand.

FROM MERCANTILISM TO CAPITALISM

Mercantilism provided the source for major growth in Western Europe, but mercantilism also unleashed new tensions within society. Like feudalism, mercantilism limited entry into economic activities. It used a different form of limitation—politics rather than social and cultural tradition—but individuals who were excluded still felt unfairly treated.

The most significant source of tension was the different roles played by craft guilds and owners of new businesses, who were called industrialists or **capitalists**—*businesspeople who have acquired large amounts of money and use it to invest in businesses.* Craft guild members were artists in their own crafts: pottery, shoemaking, and the like. New business owners destroyed the art of production by devising machines to replace hand production. Machines produced goods cheaper and faster than craftsmen.[1] The result was an increase in supply and a downward pressure on the price, which was set by the government. Craftsmen didn't want to be replaced by machines. They argued that machine-manufactured goods didn't have the same quality as hand-crafted goods, and that the new machines would disrupt the economic and social life of the community.

Industrialists were the outsiders with a vested interest in changing the existing system. They wanted the freedom to conduct business as they saw fit. Because of the enormous cost advantage of manufactured goods over crafted goods, a few industrialists overcame government opposition and succeeded within the mercantilist system. They earned their fortunes and became an independent political power.

Once again the economic power base shifted, and two groups competed with each other for power—this time, the guilds and the industrialists. The government had to decide whether the support the industrialists (who wanted government to loosen its power over the country's economic affairs) or the craftsmen and guilds (who argued for strong government limitations and for maintaining traditional values of workmanship). This struggle raged in the 1700s and 1800s. But during this time, governments themselves were changing. This was the Age of Revolutions, and the kings' powers were being limited by democratic reform movements—revolutions supported and financed in large part by the industrialists.

The Need for Coordination in an Economy

Craftsmen argued that coordination of the economy was necessary, and the government had to be involved. If government wasn't going to coordinate economic activity, who would? To answer that question, a British moral philosopher named Adam Smith developed the concept of the invisible hand, in his famous book *The Wealth of Nations* (1776), and used it to explain how markets could coordinate the economy without the active involvement of government.

As stated early in the chapter, Smith argued that the market's invisible hand would guide suppliers' actions toward the general good. No government coordination was necessary.

With the help of economists such as Adam Smith, the industrialists' view won out. Government pulled back from its role in guiding the economy and adopted a **laissez-faire** policy—the *economic policy of leaving coordination of individuals' wants to be controlled by the market.* (*Laissez-faire,* a French term, means "Let events take their course; leave things alone.")

The Industrial Revolution

The invisible hand worked; capitalism thrived. Beginning about 1750 and continuing through the late 1800s, machine production increased enormously, almost totally replacing hand production. This phenomenon has been given a name, the Industrial Revolution. The economy grew faster than ever before. Society was forever transformed. New inventions changed all aspects of life. James Watt's steam engine (1769) made manufacturing and travel easier. Eli Whitney's cotton gin (1793) changed the way cotton was processed. James Kay's flying shuttle (1733),[2] James Hargreaves' spinning jenny (1765), and Richard Arkwright's power loom (1769), combined with the steam engine, changed the way cloth was processed and the clothes people wore.

The need to mine vast amounts of coal to provide power to run the machines changed the economic and physical landscapes. The repeating rifle changed the nature of warfare. Modern economic institutions replaced guilds. Stock markets, insurance companies, and corporations all became important. Trading was no longer financed by government; it was privately financed (although government policies, such as colonial policies giving certain companies monopoly trading rights with a country's colonies, helped in that trading). The Industrial Revolution, democracy, and capitalism all arose in the middle and late 1700s. By the 1800s, they were part of the

---

[1]Throughout this section I use *men* to emphasize that these societies were strongly male-dominated. There were almost no businesswomen. In fact, a woman had to turn over her property to a man upon her marriage, and the marriage contract was written as if she were owned by her husband!

[2]The invention of the flying shuttle frustrated the textile industry because it enabled workers to weave so much cloth that the spinners of thread from which the cloth was woven couldn't keep up. This challenge to the textile industry was met by offering a prize to anyone who could invent something to increase the thread spinners' productivity. The prize was won when the spinning jenny was invented.

institutional landscape of Western society. Capitalism had arrived.

Welfare Capitalism
FROM CAPITALISM TO ~~SOCIALISM~~

Capitalism was marked by significant economic growth in the Western world. But it was also marked by human abuses—18-hour workdays, low wages, children as young as five years old slaving long hours in dirty, dangerous factories and mines—to produce enormous wealth for an elite few. Such conditions and inequalities led to criticism of the capitalist or market economic system.

Marx's Analysis

The best-known critic of this system was Karl Marx, a German philosopher, economist, and sociologist who wrote in the 1800s and who developed an analysis of the dynamics of change in economic systems. Marx argued that economic systems are in a constant state of change, and that capitalism would not last. Workers would revolt, and capitalism would be replaced by a socialist economic system.

Marx saw an economy marked by tensions among economic classes. He saw capitalism as an economic system controlled by the capitalist class (businessmen). His class analysis was that capitalist society is divided into capitalist and worker classes. He said constant tension between these economic classes causes changes in the system. The capitalist class made large profits by exploiting the **proletariat** class—*the working class*—and extracting what he called *surplus value* from workers who, according to Marx's labor theory of value, produced all the value inherent in goods. Surplus value was the additional profit, rent, or interest that, according to Marx's normative views, capitalists added to the price of goods. What economic analysis sees as recognizing a need that society has and fulfilling it, Marx saw as exploitation.

Marx argued that this exploitation would increase as production facilities became larger and larger and as competition among capitalists decreased. At some point, he believed, exploitation would lead to a revolt by the proletariat, who would overthrow their capitalist exploiters.

By the late 1800s, some of what Marx predicted had occurred, although not in the way that he thought it would. Production moved from small to large factories. Corporations developed, and classes became more distinct from one another. Workers were significantly differentiated from owners. Small firms merged and were organized into monopolies and trusts (large combinations of firms).

The trusts developed ways to prevent competition among themselves and ways to limit entry of new competitors into the market. Marx was right in his predictions about these developments, but he was wrong in his prediction about society's response to them.

The Revolution that Did Not Occur

Western society's response to the problems of capitalism was not a revolt by the workers. Instead, governments stepped in to stop the worst abuses of capitalism. The hard edges of capitalism were softened.

Evolution, not revolution, was capitalism's destiny. The democratic state did not act, as Marx argued it would, as a mere representative of the capitalist class. Competing pressure groups developed; workers gained political power that offset the economic power of businesses.

In the late 1930s and the 1940s, workers dominated the political agenda. During this time, capitalist economies developed an economic safety net that included government-funded programs, such as public welfare and unemployment insurance, and established an extensive set of regulations affecting all aspects of the economy. Today, depressions are met with direct government policy. Antitrust laws, regulatory agencies, and social programs of government softened the hard edges of capitalism. Laws were passed prohibiting child labor, mandating a certain minimum wage, and limiting the hours of work. Capitalism became what is sometimes called welfare capitalism.

Due to these developments, government spending now accounts for about a fifth of all spending in the United States, and for more than half in some European countries. Were an economist from the late 1800s to return from the grave, he'd probably say socialism, not capitalism, exists in Western societies. Most modern-day economists wouldn't go that far, but they would agree that our economy today is better described as a welfare capitalist economy than as a capitalist, or even a market, economy. Because of these changes, the U.S. and Western European economies are a far cry from the competitive "capitalist" economy that Karl Marx criticized. Markets operate, but they are constrained by the government.

The concept *capitalism* developed to denote a market system controlled by one group in society, the capitalists. Looking at Western societies today, we see that domination by one group no longer characterizes Western economies. Although in theory capitalists control corporations through their ownership of shares of stock, in practice corporations are controlled in large part by managers. There remains an elite group who control business, but *capitalist* is not a good term to describe them. Managers, not capitalists, exercise primary control over business, and even their control is limited by laws or the fear of laws being passed by governments.

Governments in turn are controlled by a variety of pressure groups. Sometimes one group is in control; at other times, another. Government policies similarly fluctuate. Sometimes they are proworker, sometimes proindustrialist, sometimes progovernment, and sometimes prosociety.

FROM FEUDALISM TO SOCIALISM

You probably noticed that I crossed out *Socialism* in the previous section's heading and replaced it with *Welfare Capitalism*. That's because capitalism did not evolve to socialism as Karl Marx predicted it would. Instead, Marx's socialist ideas took root in feudalist Russia, a society that the Industrial Revolution had in large part bypassed. Arriving at a different place and a different time than Marx predicted it would, you shouldn't be surprised to read that socialism arrived in a different way than Marx predicted. The proletariat did not revolt to establish socialism. Instead, World War I, which the Russians were losing, crippled Russia's feudal economy and government. A small group of socialists overthrew the czar (Russia's king) and took over the government in 1917. They quickly pulled Russia out of the war, and then set out to organize a socialist society and economy.

Russian socialists tried to adhere to Marx's ideas, but they found that Marx had concentrated on how capitalist economies operate, not on how a socialist economy should be run. Thus, Russian socialists faced a huge task with little guidance. Their most immediate problem was how to increase production so that the economy could emerge from feudalism into the modern industrial world. In Marx's analysis, capitalism was a necessary stage in the evolution toward the ideal state for a very practical reason. The capitalists exploit the workers, but in doing so capitalists extract the necessary surplus—an amount of production in excess of what is consumed. That surplus had to be extracted in order to provide the factories and machinery upon which a socialist economic system would be built. But since capitalism did not exist in Russia, a true socialist state could not be established immediately. Instead, the socialists created **state socialism**—*an economic system in which government sees to it that people work for the common good until they can be relied upon to do that on their own.*

Socialists saw state socialism as a transition stage to pure socialism. This transition stage still exploited the workers; when Joseph Stalin took power in Russia in the late 1920s, he took the peasants' and small farmers' land and turned it into collective farms. The government then paid farmers low prices for their produce. When farmers balked at the low prices, millions of them were killed.

Simultaneously, Stalin created central planning agencies that directed individuals what to produce and how to produce it, and determined for whom things would be produced. During this period, *socialism* became synonymous with *central economic planning,* and Soviet-style socialism became the model of socialism in practice.

Also during this time, Russia took control of a number of neighboring states and established the Union of Soviet Socialist Republics (USSR), the formal name of the Soviet Union. The Soviet Union also installed Soviet-dominated governments in a number of Eastern European countries. In 1949 most of China, under the rule of Mao Zedong, adopted Soviet-style socialist principles.

Since the late 1980s, the Soviet socialist economic and political structure has fallen apart. The Soviet Union as a political state broke up, and its former republics became autonomous. Eastern European countries were released from Soviet control. Now they faced a new problem: transition from socialism to a market economy. Why did the Soviet socialist economy fall apart? Because workers lacked incentives to work; production was inefficient; consumer goods were either unavailable or of poor quality; and high Soviet officials were exploiting their positions, keeping the best jobs for themselves and moving themselves up in the waiting lists for consumer goods. In short, the parents of the socialist family (the Communist party) were no longer acting benevolently; they were taking many of the benefits for themselves.

Recent political and economic upheavals in Eastern Europe and the former Soviet Union suggest the kind of socialism these societies tried did not work. However, that failure does not mean that socialist goals are bad; nor does it mean that no type of socialism can ever work. To overthrow socialist-dominated governments it is not necessary to accept capitalism, and many citizens of these countries are looking for an alternative to both systems. Most, however, want to establish market economies.

FROM SOCIALISM TO . . . ?

The upheavals in the former Soviet Union and Eastern Europe have left only China as a major power using a socialist economic system. But even in China there have been changes, and the Chinese economy is socialist in name only. Almost uncontrolled markets exist in numerous sectors of the economy. These changes have led some so-cialists to modify their view that state socialism is the path from capitalism to true socialism, and instead to joke: "So-cialism is the longest path from capitalism to capitalism."

Key Terms

capitalists   *(51)*   laissez-faire   *(51)*   proletariat   *(52)*   state socialism   *(53)*

The U.S. Economy in a Global Setting

3

After reading this chapter, you should be able to:

- Describe how businesses, households, and government interact in a market economy.

- Summarize briefly the advantages and disadvantages of various types of businesses.

- Explain why, even though households have the ultimate power, much of the economic decision making is done by business and government.

- List two general roles of government.

- List the primary areas with which the United States trades.

- State two ways international trade differs from intranational trade.

- List three important global trade organizations.

- List four important international policy organizations.

Letting a hundred flowers blossom and a hundred schools of thought contend is the policy for promoting progress in the arts and sciences and a flourishing socialist culture in our land.

Mao Zedong

The powerful U.S. economic machine generates enormous economic activity and provides a high standard of living (compared to most other countries) for almost all its inhabitants. It also provides economic security for its citizens. Starvation is far from

Ultimately the U.S. economy's strength is its people and its other resources.

most people's minds. Ultimately, what underlies the U.S. economy's strength is its people and its other resources. The United States has vast central plains that are extraordinarily fertile, as are areas in its West and South. It is the world's second-largest producer, and largest exporter, of grains. It has excellent ports and almost 8 million kilometers (5 million miles) of roads.

The positive attributes of the U.S. economy don't mean that the United States has no problems. Critics point out that crime is rampant, drugs are omnipresent, economic resources such as oil and minerals are declining, the environment is deteriorating, the distribution of income is skewed toward the rich, and enormous economic effort goes into economic gamesmanship (real estate deals, stock market deals, deals about deals) that seems simply to reshuffle existing wealth, not to create new wealth.

THE U.S. ECONOMY

Q-1 Into what three groups are market economies generally broken up?

Figure 3-1 diagrams a market economy such as that of the United States. Notice it's divided up into three groups: businesses, households, and government. Households supply labor and other factors of production to businesses and are paid by businesses for doing so. The market where this interaction takes place is called a *factor market*. Businesses produce goods and services and sell them to households and government. The market where this interaction takes place is called the *goods market*.

Notice also the arrows going out to and coming in from both business and households. Those arrows represent the connection of an economy to the world economy. It consists of interrelated flows of goods (exports and imports) and money (capital flows). Finally, consider the arrows connecting government with households and business.

Figure 3-1   Diagrammatic Representation of a Market Economy

This circular flow diagram of the economy is a good way to organize your thinking about the aggregate economy. As you can see, the three sectors—households, government, and business—interact in a variety of ways.

Government taxes business and households. It buys goods and services from business and buys labor services from households. Then, with some of its tax revenue, it provides services (e.g., roads, education) to both business and households and gives some of its tax revenue directly back to individuals. In doing so, it redistributes income. But government also serves a second function. It oversees the interaction of business and households in the goods and factor markets. Government, of course, is not independent. The United States, for instance, is a democracy, so households vote to determine who shall govern.

Now let's look briefly at the individual components.

BUSINESS

President Calvin Coolidge once said, "The business of America is business." That's a bit of an overstatement, but business is responsible for over 80 percent of U.S. production. (Government is responsible for the other 20 percent.) In fact, anytime a household decides to produce something, it becomes a business. **Business** is simply the name given to *private producing units in our society*.

Businesses in the United States decide *what* to produce, *how* much to produce, and *for whom* to produce it. They make these central economic decisions on the basis of their own feelings, which are influenced by market incentives. Anyone who wants to can start a business, provided he or she can come up with the required cash and meet the necessary regulatory requirements. Each year, about 600,000 businesses are started.

Don't think of business as something other than people. Businesses are ultimately made up of a group of people organized together to accomplish some end. Although corporations account for 90 percent of all sales, in terms of numbers of businesses, most are one- or two-person operations. Home-based businesses are easy to start. All you have to do is say you're in business, and you are. However, some businesses require licenses, permits, and approvals from various government agencies. That's one reason why **entrepreneurship** (*the ability to organize and get something done*) is an important part of business.

Businesses in the United States decide *what* to produce, *how* much to produce, and *for whom* to produce it.

Consumer Sovereignty and Business

To say that businesses decide what to produce isn't to say that **consumer sovereignty** (*the consumer's wishes rule what's produced*) doesn't reign in the United States. Businesses decide what to produce based on what they believe will sell. A key question a person in the United States should ask about starting a business is: Can I make a profit from it? **Profit** is *what's left over from total revenues after all the appropriate costs have been subtracted*. Businesses that guess correctly what the consumer wants generally make a profit. Businesses that guess wrong generally operate at a loss.

Although businesses decide what to produce, they are guided by consumer sovereignty.

People are free to start businesses for whatever purposes they want. No one asks them: "What's the social value of your term paper assistance business, your Twinkies business, your pornography business, or your textbook publishing business?" Yet the U.S. economic system is designed to channel individuals' desire to make a profit into the general good of society. That's the invisible hand at work. As long as the business doesn't violate a law and does conform to regulations, people in the United States are free to start whatever business they want, if they can get the money to finance it.

Q.2 In the United States the invisible hand ensures that only socially valuable businesses are started. True or false? Why?

Forms of Business

The three primary forms of business are sole proprietorships, partnerships, and corporations. Of the 23 million businesses in the United States, approximately 73 percent are

Producing physical goods is only one of a society's economic tasks. Another task is to provide services (activities done for others). Services do not involve producing a physical good. When you get your hair cut, you buy a service, not a good. Much of the cost of the physical goods we buy actually is not a cost of producing the good, but is a cost of one of the most important services: distribution (getting the good to where the consumer is). After a good is produced, it has to get to the individuals who are going to consume it at the time they need it. If the distribution system gets botched up, it's as if the good had never been produced.

Let's consider a couple of examples. Take Christmas trees. Say you're sitting on 60,000 cut spruce trees in the Vermont mountains, but an ice storm prevents you from

BEYOND THE TOOLS

Is the United States a Postindustrial Society?

shipping them until December 26. Guess what? You're now stuck with 60,000 spruce trees and the problem of somehow getting rid of them. Or take hot dogs. How many of us have been irked that a hot dog that costs 25¢ to fix at home costs $4 at a football game? But a hot dog at home isn't the same as a hot dog at a game. Distribution of the good is as important as production; you're paying the extra $3.75 for distribution.

The importance of the service economy can be seen in modern technology companies. They provide information and methods of handling information, not physical goods. Operating systems, such as Linux and Windows, can be supplied over the Internet; no physical production is necessary. So, yes, it is fair to say that our economy is a postindustrial economy.

Q.3 Are most businesses in the United States corporations? If not, what are most businesses?

sole proprietorships, 7 percent are partnerships, and 20 percent are corporations, as we see in Figure 3-2 (a). In terms of total receipts, however, we get a quite different picture, with corporations far surpassing all other business forms, as Figure 3-2 (b) shows. In fact, the largest 500 corporations account for almost 90 percent of the total receipts of all U.S. businesses.

Sole proprietorships—*businesses that have only one owner*—are the easiest to start and have the fewest bureaucratic hassles. **Partnerships**—*businesses with two or more owners*—create possibilities for sharing the burden, but they also create unlimited

Figure 3-2 (a and b)   Forms of Business

The charts divide firms by the type of ownership. Approximately 73 percent of businesses in the United States are sole proprietorships (**a**). In terms of annual receipts, however, corporations surpass all other forms (**b**).

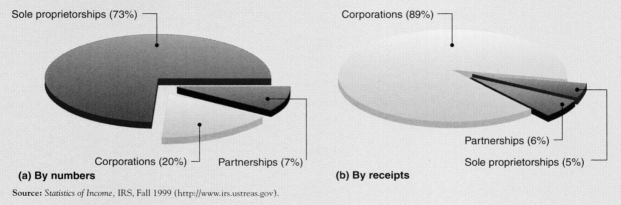

(a) By numbers

Sole proprietorships (73%)
Corporations (20%)
Partnerships (7%)

(b) By receipts

Corporations (89%)
Partnerships (6%)
Sole proprietorships (5%)

Source: *Statistics of Income*, IRS, Fall 1999 (http://www.irs.ustreas.gov).

liability for each of the partners. **Corporations**—*businesses that are treated as a person, and are legally owned by their stockholders who are not liable for the actions of the corporate "person"*—are the largest form of business when measured in terms of receipts.

The advantages and disadvantages of each are summarized in the following table:

Advantages and Disadvantages of Various Forms of For-Profit Businesses

	Sole Proprietor	Partnership	Corporation
Advantages	1. Minimum bureaucratic hassle 2. Direct control by owner	1. Ability to share work and risks 2. Relatively easy to form	1. No personal liability 2. Increasing ability to get funds 3. Ability to shed personal income and gain added expenses
Disadvantages	1. Limited ability to get funds 2. Unlimited personal liability	1. Unlimited personal liability (even for partner's blunder) 2. Limited ability to get funds	1. Legal hassle to organize 2. Possible double taxation of income 3. Monitoring problems

Since corporations are the most complex, let's consider them more carefully. When a corporation is formed, it issues **stock** (*certificates of ownership in a company*), which is sold or given to individuals. Proceeds of the sale of that stock make up what is called the *equity capital* of a company. Ownership of stock entitles you to vote in the election of a corporation's directors.

Corporations were developed as institutions to make it easier for company owners to be separated from company management. A corporation provides the owners with **limited liability**—*the stockholder's liability is limited to the amount that stockholder has invested in the company*. With the other two forms of business, owners can lose everything they possess even if they have only a small amount invested in the company, but in a corporation the owners can lose only what they have invested in that corporation. If you've invested $100, you can lose only $100. In the other kinds of business, even if you've invested only $100, you could lose everything; the business's losses must be covered by the individual owners. Corporations' limited liability makes it easier for them to attract investment capital. Corporations pay taxes, but they also offer their individual owners ways of legally avoiding taxes.

A corporation's stocks can be distributed among as few as three persons or among millions of stockholders. Stocks can be bought and sold either in an independent transaction between two people (an *over-the-counter* trade) or through a broker and a *stock exchange*.

In corporations, ownership is separated from control of the firm. Most stockholders have little input into the decisions a corporation makes. Instead, corporations are often controlled by their managers, who often run them for their own benefit as well as for the owners'. The reason is that owners' control of management is limited.

A large percentage of most corporations' stock is not even controlled by the owners; instead, it is controlled by financial institutions such as mutual funds (financial institutions that invest individuals' money for them) and by pension funds (financial institutions that hold people's money for them until it is to be paid out to them upon their retirement). Thus, ownership of corporations is another step removed from

Most corporations are controlled by managers, with little effective stockholder control.

Stocks are usually traded on a *stock exchange*—a formal market in which stocks are bought and sold. The figure below shows a typical stock exchange listing. Each stock sold on this stock exchange—the Nasdaq—has only one price listed. That's because the exchange has a "specialist" market-maker system, in which a particular broker markets a particular group of stocks. This specialist always stands ready to buy or sell shares of a stock at some price. The specialist sets a price and then varies it according to whether he or she is receiving more buy orders or more sell orders.

In order to buy or sell a stock, you contact a stockbroker (or simply contact the company through the Web—it's cheaper that way) and say you want to buy or sell whatever stock you've decided on— say Ford Motor Company. The commission you're charged for having the broker sell you the stock (or sell it for you) varies. It usually starts at some minimum

KNOWING THE TOOLS

The Stock Market

Source: *The Wall Street Journal*, Jan. 4, 2000. Reprinted by permission of *The Wall Street Journal* © 2000 Dow Jones & Company, Inc. All rights reserved worldwide.

between $10 and $30, and then is so much per share.

There are a number of stock exchanges. The largest and most familiar is the New York Stock Exchange. Somewhere around 50 million individuals own stock they bought on the New York Stock Exchange.

To judge how stocks as a whole are doing, a number of indexes have been developed. These include Standard and Poor's (S&P 500), the Wilshire Index, the Russell 2000, and the Dow Jones Industrial Average. The Dow Jones is the one you're most likely to hear about in the news.

When a share of a corporation's existing stock is sold on the stock exchange, corporations get no money from that sale. The sale is simply a transfer of ownership from one individual (or organization) to another. The only time a corporation gets money from the sale of stock is when it first issues the shares.

Q.4 It is obvious that all for-profit businesses in the United States will maximize profit. True or false? Why?

individuals. Studies have shown that 80 percent of the largest 200 corporations in the United States are essentially controlled by managers and have little effective stockholder control.

Why is the question of who controls a firm important? Because economic theory assumes the goal of business owners is to maximize profits, which would be true of corporations if stockholders made the decisions. Managers don't have the same incentives to maximize profits that owners do. There's pressure on managers to maximize profits, but that pressure can often be weak or ineffective. An example of how firms deal with this problem involves stock options. Many companies give their managers stock options— rights to buy stock at a low price—to encourage them to worry about the price of their company's stock. But these stock options dilute the value of company ownership and decrease profits per share.

Finance and Business

Much of what you hear in the news about business concerns financial assets—assets that acquire value from an obligation of someone else to pay. Stocks are one example of a financial asset; bonds are another. Financial assets are traded in markets such as the New York Stock Exchange. Trading in financial markets can make people rich (or poor) quickly. Stocks and bonds can also provide a means through which corporations can finance expansions and new investments.

Recently there has been much in the news about one part of these financial markets—initial public offerings (IPOs), in which a company first offers some of its stock to the general public, with the owners keeping a large portion for themselves. This is an example of how financial markets work to fund companies, allowing the economy to grow.

 3.2

In the late 1990s many of the stock prices of ".com" (read: dot com) companies, which are firms in some way related to the Internet, exploded. The stocks sold for enormous values—values that many economists felt could not last. (See Appendix A at the end of this chapter for a discussion of how economists value financial assets.) They saw what is called a financial bubble—a situation in which financial assets' valuations are based on what almost everyone believes are insupportable expectations—and were expecting the bubble to burst, or at least to shrink down to a supportable size.

E-Commerce and the Digital Economy

To say that many of the Internet companies are overvalued is not to say that e-commerce—buying and selling over the Internet—will not make an enormous difference to the economy, and to the nature of business. Almost all economists believe it will. E-commerce adds heavy competition to the economy, and will place pressure on existing firms to compete with low prices. If they don't, they will lose their customers. More and more individuals are buying cars, books, prescription drugs, and even groceries on the Web, and the range of what is bought will expand. One reason is that the Internet removes the importance of geography and location for firms. In doing so it reduces the value of firms whose comparative advantage depends on geography, while increasing the value of firms whose comparative advantage does not depend on geography.

Some goods are more conducive to being sold on the Internet than others. For example, there are certain goods customers want to see before they buy them. Until virtual reality is perfected, that is impossible with the Internet. The practice of going to see goods at local stores but then buying them on the Internet will likely lead to some changes in the nature of businesses. Consider cars; because the Internet allows car buyers to compare prices and get a better deal than the local dealer generally gives, more and more people are buying cars over the Internet. Before they do so, however, they generally visit the local car dealership to see and test-drive the car. As Internet car buying expands, such practices are unlikely to continue. The future may well include car showrooms that charge you to test-drive, or even look at, a car (with the charge being rebated by the selling company if you actually buy the car).

E-commerce has grown enormously in the early 2000s, and a terminology developed that is captured in the table below. Initially, B2B (business selling to business) activity grew, but B2C (business selling to consumers) was also growing. Auction sites C2C (consumers selling to consumers) and bidding sites for consumers (C2B) were also beginning to grow.

B2B	B2C
C2B	C2C

HOUSEHOLDS

The second classification we'll consider in this overview of U.S. economic institutions is households. **Households** (*groups of individuals living together and making joint decisions*) are the most powerful economic institution. They ultimately control government and business, the other two economic institutions. Households' votes in the political arena determine government policy; their decisions about supplying labor and capital determine what businesses will have available to work with; and their spending decisions or expenditures (the "votes" they cast with their dollars) determine what business will be able to sell.

In the economy, households vote with their dollars.

The Power of Households

While the ultimate power does in principle lie with the people and households, we, the people, have assigned much of that power to representatives. As I discussed above, corporations are only partially responsive to owners of their stocks, and much of that ownership is once-removed from individuals. Ownership of 1,000 shares in a company with a total of 2 million shares isn't going to get you any influence over the corporation's activities. As a stockholder, you simply accept what the corporation does.

A major decision that corporations make independently of their stockholders concerns what to produce. True, ultimately we, the people, decide whether we will buy what business produces, but business spends a lot of money telling us what services we want, what products make us "with it," what books we want to read, and the like. Most economists believe that consumer sovereignty reigns—that we are not fooled or controlled by advertising. Still, it is an open question in some economists' minds whether we, the people, control business or the business representatives control people.

Because of this assignment of power to other institutions, in many spheres of the economy households are not active producers of output but merely passive recipients of income, primarily in their role as suppliers of labor.

Consumer sovereignty reigns, but it works indirectly by influencing businesses.

Suppliers of Labor

The largest source of household income is wages and salaries (the income households get from labor). Households supply the labor with which businesses produce and government governs. The total U.S. labor force is about 140 million people, about 4.3 percent (5.9 million) of whom were unemployed in 1999. The average U.S. workweek is 42.4 hours for males and 36.2 hours for females. The average pay in the U.S. was $618 per week for males and $473 for females which translates to $15.45 per hour for males and $11.83 for females. Of course, that average has enormous variability and depends on the occupation and region of the country where one is employed. For example, lawyers often earn $100,000 per year; physicians earn about $150,000 per year; and CEOs of large corporations often make $2 million per year or more. A beginning McDonald's employee generally makes about $12,000 per year.

The table below shows predicted growth rates of certain jobs. Notice that many of the fastest-growing jobs are in service industries; many of the fastest-declining are in manufacturing and agriculture. This is not surprising, since the United States has become largely a service economy.

Fastest-Growing Jobs*	Fastest-Declining Jobs*
Computer engineers (107.9%)	Farmers (−13.2%)
Systems analysts (93.6%)	Typists and word processors (−20.4%)
Database administrators (72.2%)	Pressers, hand (−11.4%)
Desktop publishing specialists (72.6%)	Computer operators (−24%)

*Projection for 1998–2008, based on moderate growth assumptions.

Source: *Employment and Earnings*, Bureau of Labor Statistics, and *Occupational Outlook Handbook*, 2000–2001 (http://stats.bls.gov).

GOVERNMENT

The third major U.S. economic institution I'll consider is government. Government plays two general roles in the economy. It's both a referee (setting the rules that determine relations between business and households) and an actor (collecting money in taxes and spending that money on its own projects, such as defense and education). Let's first consider government's role as an actor.

Government as an Actor

The United States has a federal government system, which means we have various levels of government (federal, state, and local), each with its own powers. Together they consume about 20 percent of the country's total output and employ about 21 million individuals. The various levels of government also have a number of programs that redistribute income through taxation or through an array of social welfare and assistance programs designed to help specific groups.

3.3

State and Local Government State and local governments employ over 18 million people and spend over $1 trillion a year. As you can see in Figure 3-3(a), state and local governments get much of their income from taxes: property taxes, sales taxes, and state and local income taxes. They spend their tax revenues on public welfare, administration, education (education through high school is available free in U.S. public schools), and roads, as Figure 3-3(b) shows.

Federal Government Probably the best way to get an initial feel for the federal government and its size is to look at the various categories of its tax revenues and expenditures in Figure 3-4(a). Notice income taxes make up about 48 percent of the federal government's revenue, while social security taxes make up about 33 percent. That's more than 80 percent of the federal government's revenues, most of which shows up as a deduction from your paycheck. In Figure 3-4(b), notice that the federal government's two largest categories of spending are income security and national defense, with expenditures on interest payments close behind.

Q.5 The largest percentage of federal expenditure is in what general category?

Government as a Referee

Even if government spending made up only a small proportion of total expenditures, government would still be central to the study of economics. The reason is that, in a market economy, government sets the rules of interaction between households and businesses, and acts as a referee, changing the rules when it sees fit. Government decides whether economic forces will be allowed to operate freely.

Figure 3-3 (a and b) Income and Expenditures of State and Local Governments

The charts give you a sense of the importance of state and local governments—where they get (a), and where they spend (b), their revenues.

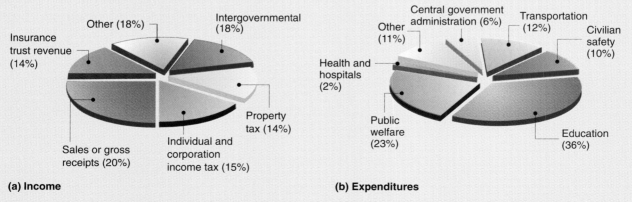

(a) Income

(b) Expenditures

Source: *Survey of Current Business,* 2000, Bureau of Economic Analysis (http://www.bea.doc.gov) and *State and Local Government Finance Estimates,* Bureau of the Census (http://www.census.gov).

Figure 3-4 (a and b)   Income and Expenditures of the Federal Government

The pie charts show the sources and uses of federal government revenue. It is important to note that, when the government runs a deficit, expenditures exceed income and the difference is made up by borrowing, so the size of the income and expenditure pies may not be equal.

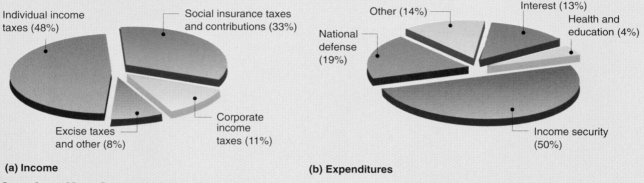

Individual income taxes (48%)

Social insurance taxes and contributions (33%)

Excise taxes and other (8%)

Corporate income taxes (11%)

(a) Income

Other (14%)

National defense (19%)

Interest (13%)

Health and education (4%)

Income security (50%)

(b) Expenditures

Source: *Survey of Current Business,* 1996, Bureau of Economic Analysis (http://www.bea.gov).

Some examples of U.S. laws regulating the interaction between households and businesses today are:

1. Businesses are not free to hire and fire whomever they want. They must comply with equal opportunity and labor laws. Even closing a plant requires 60 days' notice for many kinds of firms.

2. Many working conditions are subject to government regulation: safety rules, wage rules, overtime rules, hours-of-work rules, and the like.

3. Businesses cannot meet with other businesses to agree on prices they will charge.

4. In some businesses workers must join a union to work at certain jobs.

Most of these laws evolved over time. Up until the 1930s, household members, in their roles as workers and consumers, had few rights. Businesses were free to hire and fire at will and, if they chose, to deceive and take advantage of consumers.

Over time, new laws to curb business abuses have been passed, and government agencies have been formed to enforce these laws. Many people think the pendulum has swung too far the other way. They believe businesses are saddled with too many regulatory burdens.

One big question that I'll address throughout this book is: What referee role should the government play in an economy? For example, should government use its taxing powers to redistribute income from the rich to the poor? Should it allow mergers between companies? Should it regulate air traffic? Should it regulate prices? Should it attempt to stabilize fluctuations of aggregate income?

THE GLOBAL SETTING

International issues must now be taken into account in just about any economic decision a country or a firm faces.

There was a time when you could proceed from a discussion of the U.S. economy to a discussion of macroeconomics and microeconomics, the two divisions of economics. No longer. International issues must now also be taken into account in just about every

Figure 3-5   The U.S. Economy in a Global Setting

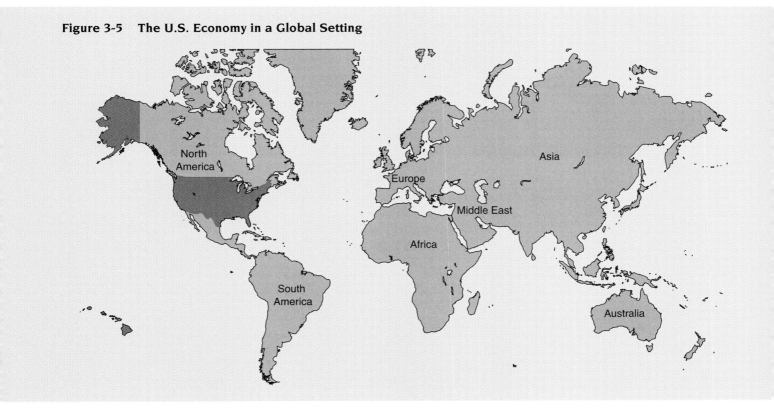

economic decision the United States or a firm in the United States faces. The U.S. economy is now integrated with the world economy, and we cannot reasonably discuss U.S. economic issues without discussing the role that international considerations play in these issues.

Probably the best way to put the U.S. economy into perspective is to look at a map of the world such as the one in Figure 3-5. Notice the physical size of the United States. Compared to the world, it's relatively small. Alternatively, consider population; the U.S. population is 275 million; world population is 6 billion, so the U.S. population is not quite 5 percent of the world population. The importance of the United States increases enormously when we consider that U.S. production accounts for nearly 30 percent of world output, but it is important for Americans to remember that there is a whole world out there, and the United States is simply a part of that world.

Global Corporations

The importance of the world to the U.S. economy can also be seen by considering the clothes on your back. Most likely they were made abroad. Similarly with the cars you drive. It's likely that half of you drive a car that was made abroad. Of course, it's often difficult to tell. Just because a car has a Japanese or German name doesn't mean that it was produced abroad. Some Japanese and German companies now have manufacturing plants in the United States, and some U.S. firms have manufacturing plants abroad. Others, such as Chrysler and Daimler Benz (they make Mercedes) have merged. When goods are produced by **global corporations** (*corporations with substantial operations on both*

Global corporations are corporations with substantial operations on both the production and sales sides in more than one country.

production and sales in more than one country), corporate names don't always tell much about where a good is produced. As global corporations' importance has grown, most manufacturing decisions are made in reference to the international market, not the U.S. domestic market.

Global corporations offer enormous benefits for countries. They create jobs; they bring new ideas and new technologies to a country, and they provide competition for domestic companies, keeping them on their toes. But global corporations also pose a number of problems for governments. One is their implication for domestic and international policy. A domestic corporation exists within a country and can be dealt with using policy measures within that country. A global corporation exists within many countries and there is no global government to regulate or control it. If it doesn't like the policies in one country—say taxes are too high or regulations too tight—it can shift its operations to other countries.

At times it seems that global corporations are governments unto themselves, especially in relation to poorer countries. In terms of sales, a number of global corporations are larger than the economies of middle-size countries. For example, General Motors has a total annual revenue of $177 billion; Ecuador has a total annual income of $60 billion. This comparison is not quite accurate, since sales do not necessarily reflect power; but when a company's decisions can significantly affect what happens in a country's economy, that company has significant economic power.

When global corporations have such power, it is not surprising that they can sometimes dominate a country. The corporation can use its expertise and experience to direct a small country to do its bidding rather than the other way around.

Before you condemn globals, remember: Globals don't have it so easy either. Customs and laws differ among countries. Trying to meet the differing laws and ambiguous limits of acceptable action in various countries is often impossible. For example, in many countries bribery is an acceptable part of doing business. If you want to get permission to sell a good, you must pay the appropriate officials' *baksheesh* (as it's called in Egypt) or *la mordita* (as it's called in Mexico). In the United States, such payments are called bribes and are illegal. Given these differing laws, the only way a U.S. company can do business in some foreign countries is to break U.S. laws.

Moreover, global corporations often work to maintain close ties among countries and to reduce international tension. If part of your company is in an Eastern European country and part in the United States, you want the two countries to be friends. So beware of making judgments about whether global corporations are good or bad. They're both simultaneously.

International Trade

In 1928, total world trade was about $500 billion (in today's dollars). U.S. gross domestic product (GDP) was about $830 billion, so world trade as a percentage of U.S. GDP was almost 60 percent. In 1935, that ratio had fallen to less than 30 percent. In 1950 it was 20 percent. Then it started rising. Today it is about 70 percent, with world trade amounting to nearly $7 trillion. As you can see, international trade has been growing, but with significant fluctuations in that growth. Sometimes international trade has grown rapidly; at other times it has grown slowly or has even fallen.

In part, fluctuations in world trade result from fluctuations in world output. When output rises, international trade rises; when output falls, international trade falls. Fluctuations in world trade are also in part explained by trade restrictions that countries have imposed from time to time. For example, decreases in world income during the Depression caused a large decrease in trade, but that decrease was exacerbated by a worldwide increase in trade restrictions during the 1930s.

Economic geography isn't much covered in most economics courses because it requires learning enormous numbers of facts, and college courses aren't a good place to learn facts. College is designed to teach you how to interpret and relate facts. Unfortunately, if you don't know facts, much of what you learn in college isn't going to do you much good. You'll be relating and interpreting air. The following quiz presents some facts about the world economy. Below I list characteristics of 20 countries or regions in random order. Beneath the characteristics, in alphabetical order, I list 20 countries or regions. Associate the characteristics with the country or region.

If you answer 15 or more correctly, you have a reasonably good sense of economic geography. If you don't, I strongly suggest learning more facts. The study guide has other projects, information, and examples. An encyclopedia has even more, and your library has a wealth of information. You could spend the entire semester following the economic news carefully, paying attention to where various commodities are produced, and picturing in your mind a map whenever you hear about an economic event.

_____ 1. Former British colony, now small independent island country famous for producing rum.

_____ 2. Large sandy country contains world's largest known oil reserves.

_____ 3. Very large country with few people; produces 25 percent of the world's wool.

_____ 4. Temperate country ideal for producing wheat, soybeans, fruits, vegetables, wine, and meat.

_____ 5. Small tropical country produces abundant coffee and bananas.

_____ 6. Has world's largest population and world's largest hydropower potential.

_____ 7. Second-largest country in Europe; famous for wine and romance.

_____ 8. Former Belgian colony with vast copper mines.

_____ 9. European country; exports luxury clothing, footwear, and automobiles.

_____ 10. Country that has depleted many of its natural resources but that has the highest level of GDP of any country in the world.

_____ 11. Long, narrow country of four main islands; most thickly populated country in the world; exports majority of the world's electronics products.

_____ 12. Recently politically reunified country; one important product is steel.

_____ 13. Second-largest country in the world; a good neighbor to the United States; leading paper exporter.

_____ 14. European country for centuries politically repressed; now becoming industrialized; chemicals are one of its leading exports.

_____ 15. 96 percent of its people live on 4 percent of the land; much of the world's finest cotton comes from here.

_____ 16. Politically and radically troubled African nation has world's largest concentration of gold.

_____ 17. Huge, heavily populated country eats most of what it raises but is a major tea exporter.

_____ 18. Country that is a top producer of oil and gold; has recently undergone major political and economic changes.

_____ 19. Has only about 50 people per square mile but lots of trees; timber and fish exporter.

_____ 20. Sliver of a country on Europe's Atlantic coast; by far the world's largest exporter of cork.

A. Argentina
B. Australia
C. Barbados
D. Canada
E. China
F. Costa Rica
G. Egypt
H. France
I. Germany
J. India
K. Italy
L. Japan
M. Portugal
N. Russia
O. Saudi Arabia
P. South Africa
Q. Spain
R. Sweden
S. United States
T. Democratic Republic of the Congo

Answers: 1-C, 2-O, 3-B, 4-A, 5-F, 6-E, 7-H, 8-T, 9-K, 10-S, 11-L, 12-I, 13-D, 14-Q, 15-G, 16-P, 17-J, 18-N, 19-R, 20-M.

Differences in the Importance of Trade The importance of international trade to countries' economies differs widely, as we can see in the table below, which presents the importance of the shares of **exports**—*the value of goods sold abroad*—and **imports**—*the value of goods purchased abroad*—for various countries.

The primary trading partners of the United States are Canada, Mexico, the European Union, and Pacific Rim countries.

	GDP*	Export Ratio	Import Ratio
United States	$9,255	11%	14%
Canada	949	43	40
Netherlands	430	66	59
Germany	2,446	29	27
United Kingdom	1,277	26	27
Italy	1,190	28	22
France	1,619	26	23
Japan	4,003	9	8

*Numbers in billions.
Source: *The World Development Report,* The World Bank, 1999 (http://www.worldbank.org) and individual country Web pages.

Q-6 Among the countries listed in the table, which has the lowest exports and imports as a percentage of GDP?

Among the countries listed, the Netherlands has the highest amount of exports compared to GDP; the United States and Japan have the lowest.

The Netherlands' imports are also the highest as a percentage of GDP. Japan has the lowest. The relationship between a country's imports and its exports is no coincidence. For most countries, imports and exports roughly equal one another, though in any particular year that equality can be rough indeed. For the United States in recent years, imports have generally significantly exceeded exports. But that situation can't continue forever, as I'll discuss.

Total trade figures provide us with only part of the international trade picture. We must also look at what types of goods are traded and with whom that trade is conducted.

What and with Whom the United States Trades The majority of U.S. exports and imports involve significant amounts of manufactured goods. This isn't unusual, since much of international trade is in manufactured goods.

Figure 3-6 shows the regions with which the United States trades. Exports to Canada and Mexico made up the largest percentage of total U.S. exports to individual countries in 1999. The largest regions to whom the U.S. exports are the Pacific Rim and the European Union. Countries from which the United States imports major quantities include Canada and Mexico and the regions of the European Union and the Pacific Rim. Thus, the countries we export to are also the countries we import from.

Notice the **balance of trade**—*the difference between the value of exports and the value of imports* in Figure 3-6. Imports far exceed exports. In economic terms this means that the U.S. economy is running a **trade deficit**—*an excess of imports over exports.* The United States has been running a trade deficit since the 1970s, and in the late 1990s it remained large, at over $300 billion in 1999.

Debtor and Creditor Nations Running a trade deficit isn't necessarily bad. In fact, while you're doing it, it's rather nice. If you were a country, you probably would be running a trade deficit now since, most likely, you're consuming (importing) more than you're producing (exporting). How can you do that? By living off past savings, getting support from your parents or a spouse, or borrowing.

Countries have the same options. They can live off foreign aid, past savings, or loans. For example, the U.S. economy is currently financing its trade deficit by selling

Figure 3-6 (a and b) U.S. Exports and Imports by Region, 1999

Major regions that trade with the United States include Canada, Mexico, the European Union, and the Pacific Rim.

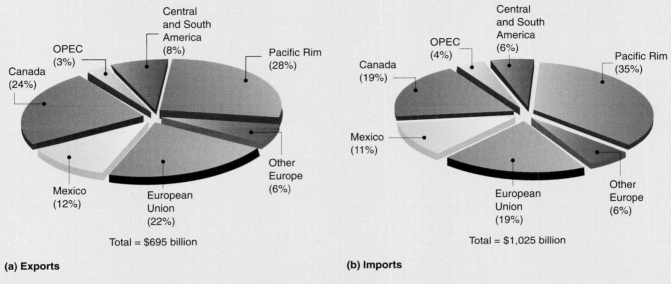

(a) Exports

(b) Imports

Source: FT900 U.S. International Trade in Goods and Services 2000, U.S. Census Bureau (http://www.census.gov).

off assets—financial assets such as stocks and bonds, or real assets such as real estate and corporations. Since the assets of the United States total many trillions of dollars, it can continue to run trade deficits of a similar size for decades to come.

The United States has not always run a trade deficit. Following World War II it ran **trade surpluses**—*an excess of exports over imports*—with other countries, so it was an international lender. Thus, it acquired large amounts of foreign assets. Because of the large trade deficits the United States has run since the 1980s, now the United States is a large debtor nation. The United States has borrowed more from abroad than it has lent abroad.

As the United States has gone from being a large creditor nation to being the world's biggest debtor, international considerations have been forced on the nation. The cushion of being a creditor—of having a flow of interest income—has been replaced by the trials of being a debtor and having to pay out interest every year without getting anything for it.

Q.7 Will a debtor nation necessarily be running a trade deficit?

HOW INTERNATIONAL TRADE DIFFERS FROM DOMESTIC TRADE

*Inter*national trade differs from *intra*national (domestic) trade in two ways. First, international trade involves potential barriers to the flow of imports and exports. Before they can be sold in the United States, international goods must be sent through U.S. Customs; that is, when they enter the United States they are inspected by U.S. officials and usually charged fees, known as *customs*. A company in Texas can produce output to sell in any U.S. state without worrying that its right to sell will be limited; a producer

Two ways in which *inter*national trade differs from *intra*national (domestic) trade are:

1. International trade involves potential barriers to trade; and

2. International trade involves multiple currencies.

Over the past 20 years, international issues have become increasingly important for the U.S. economy. That statement would be correct even if the reference period went back as far as the late 1800s. The late 1800s and the first 40 years of the 1900s was an isolationist period for the United States in which the country turned inward in both economic and foreign policies.

The statement would not be correct if the reference period were earlier than the late 1800s. In the 1600s, 1700s, and most of the 1800s, international trade was vital to the American economy—even more vital than now. The American nation grew from colonial possessions of England, France, and Spain. These "new world" colonial possessions were valued for their gold, agricultural produce, and natural resources. From a European standpoint, international trade was the colonies' reason for being.*

A large portion of the U.S. government's income during much of the 1800s came from tariffs. Our technology was imported from abroad, and international issues played a central role in wars fought here. (Many historians believe that the most important cause of the U.S. Civil War was differences of views about tariffs on manufactured goods. The South opposed them because it wanted cheap manufactured goods, while the North favored them because it wanted to protect its manufacturing industries.) Up until the 1900s, no one would have studied the U.S. economy independently of international issues. Not only was there significant international trade; there was also significant immigration. The United States is a country of immigrants.

Only in the late 1800s did the United States adopt an isolationist philosophy in both politics and trade. So in reference to that isolationist period, the U.S. economy has become more integrated with the world economy. However, in a broader historical perspective, that isolationist period was an anomaly, and today's economy is simply returning international issues to the key role they've usually played.

A second important insight is that international trade has social and cultural dimensions. While much of the chapter deals with specifically economic issues, we must also remember the cultural and social implications of trade.

Let's consider an example from history. In the Middle Ages, Greek ideas and philosophy were lost to Europe

BEYOND THE TOOLS

International Issues in Perspective

when hordes of barbarians swept over the continent. These ideas and that philosophy were only rediscovered in the Renaissance as a by-product of trade between the Italian merchant cities and the Middle East. (The Greek ideas that had spread to the Middle East were protected from European upheavals.) *Renaissance* means rebirth; a rebirth in Europe of Greek learning. Many of our traditions and sensibilities are based on those of the Renaissance, and that Renaissance was caused, or at least significantly influenced, by international trade. Had there been no trade, our entire philosophy of life might have been different.

Fernand Braudel, a French historian, has provided wonderful examples of the broader implications for trade. For instance, he argued that the effects of international trade, specifically Sir Walter Raleigh's introduction of the potato into England from South America in 1588, had more long-run consequences than did the celebrated 1588 battle of the English navy and Spanish Armada.

Another example, which Braudel did not live to see, is the major change in socialist countries in the 1990s. Through the 1960s China, the Soviet Union, and the Eastern European countries were relatively closed societies—behind the Iron Curtain. That changed in the 1970s and 1980s as these socialist countries opened up trade with the West as a way to speed their own economic development. That trade, and the resulting increased contact with the West, gave the people of those countries a better sense of the material goods to be had in the West. That trade also spread Western ideas of the proper organization of government and the economy to these societies. A strong argument can be made that along with trade came the seeds of discontent that changed those societies and their economies forever.

In economics courses we do not focus on these broader cultural issues but instead focus on relatively technical issues such as the reasons for trade and the implications of tariffs. But keep in the back of your mind these broader implications as you go through the various components of international economics. They add a dimension to the story that otherwise might be forgotten.

---

*The American Indian standpoint was, I suspect, somewhat different.

The world economy is often divided into three main areas or trading blocs: The Americas, Europe and Africa, and East Asia. These trading blocs are shown in the map below.

KNOWING THE TOOLS

Our International Competitors

The table below gives you a sense of the similarities and differences in the economies of the United States, Japan, and Europe.

	United States	Japan	Europe
Area (square miles)	3,536,341	145,814	915,330
Population	275 million	125 million	292 million
GDP, 1999	$9.3 trillion	$4.01 trillion	$6.26 trillion
Percentage of world output	26%	16%	28%
GDP per capita	$34,000	$32,000	$22,000
Natural resources	Coal, copper, lead, and others	Very few mineral resources, fish	Coal, iron ore, natural gas, fish, and others
Exports as a percentage of GDP	11%	9%	33%
Imports as a percentage of GDP	14%	8%	28%
Currency value (as of March 1, 2000)	Dollar ($1 = $1)	Yen (¥110 = $1)	Euro (Euro 1.04 = $1)

Source: European Central Bank, Bank of Japan, U.S. Bureau of Economic Analysis.

The three dominant economies in these trading blocs are the Unites States, Germany, and Japan. Each area has a major currency. In the Americas, it is the dollar; in Europe it is the euro, a new currency recently created by the European Union; and in East Asia it is the Japanese yen.

outside the U.S. boundary cannot. At any time, a foreign producer's right to sell in the United States can be limited by government-imposed **quotas** (*limitations on how much of a good can be shipped into a country*), **tariffs** (*taxes on imports*), and **nontariff barriers** (*indirect regulatory restrictions on imports and exports*).

The last category, indirect regulatory restrictions on imports and exports, may be unfamiliar to you, so let's consider an example. U.S. building codes require that plywood have fewer than, say, three flaws per sheet. Canadian building codes require that plywood have fewer than, say, five flaws per sheet. The different building codes are a nontariff barrier, making trade in building materials between the United States and Canada difficult.

The second way international trade differs from domestic or intranational trade is countries' use of different currencies. When people in one country sell something to people in another, they must find a way to exchange currencies as well as goods. **Foreign exchange markets** (*markets where one currency can be exchanged for another*) have developed to provide this service.

How many dollars will an American have to pay to get a given amount of the currency of another country? That depends on the supply of and demand for that currency.

Q-8 What is the difference between a quota and a tariff?

A foreign exchange market is a market in which one currency can be exchanged for another.

To find what you'd have to pay, you look in the newspaper for the **exchange rate**—*the rate at which one currency is traded for another*—such as in the following table:

A Foreign Exchange Rate Table

3.4

From the exchange rate table, you learn how much a dollar is worth in other countries. For example, on this day, Jan. 4, 2000, one dollar would buy 6.36 French francs or 103.29 yen. The table also tells you how many dollars other currencies can buy. For example, one British pound could buy 1.637 dollars.

Tuesday, January 4, 2000

EXCHANGE RATES

The New York foreign exchange mid-range rates below apply to trading among banks in amounts of $1 million and more, as quoted at 4 p.m. Eastern time by Reuters and other sources. Retail transactions provide fewer units of foreign currency per dollar. Rates for the 11 Euro currency countries are derived from the latest dollar-euro rate using the exchange ratios set 1/1/99.

Country	U.S. $ equiv. Tue	U.S. $ equiv. Mon	Currency per U.S. $ Tue	Currency per U.S. $ Mon
Argentina (Peso)	1.0001	1.0002	.9999	.9998
Australia (Dollar)	.6551	.6582	1.5266	1.5192
Austria (Schilling)	.07491	.07462	13.349	13.402
Bahrain (Dinar)	2.6525	2.6525	.3770	.3770
Belgium (Franc)	.0256	.0255	39.1325	39.2885
Brazil (Real)	.5408	.5495	1.8490	1.8200
Britain (Pound)	1.6370	1.6371	.6109	.6108
Canada (Dollar)	.6887	.6913	1.4521	1.4465
Chile (Peso) (d)	.001890	.001894	529.05	527.85
China (Renminbi)	.1208	.1208	8.2799	8.2798
Colombia (Peso)	.0005238	.005306	1909.00	1884.50
Czech. Rep (Koruna)				
Commercial rate	.02839	.02814	35.226	35.541
Denmark (Krone)	.1385	.1379	7.2186	7.2491
Ecuador (Sucre)				
Floating rate	.00004202	.00004598	23800.00	21750.00
Finland (Markka)	.1734	.1727	5.7678	5.7908
France (Franc)	.1572	.1565	6.3633	6.3887
Germany (Mark)	.5273	.5250	1.8966	1.9049
Greece (Drachma)	.003120	.003113	320.52	321.26
Hong Kong (Dollar)	.1286	.1286	7.7773	7.7763
Hungary (Forint)	.004044	.004034	247.30	247.90
India (Rupee)	.02300	.02302	43.480	43.435
Indonesia (Rupiah)	.0001396	.0001417	7165.00	7055.00
Ireland (Punt)	1.3094	1.3040	.7637	.7669
Israel (Shekel)	.2413	.2436	4.1436	4.1053
Italy (Lira)	.0005324	.0005303	1878.33	1885.83
Japan (Yen)	.009681	.009843	103.29	101.60

Country	U.S. $ equiv. Tue	U.S. $ equiv. Mon	Currency per U.S. $ Tue	Currency per U.S. $ Mon
Jordan (Dinar)	1.4085	1.4085	.7100	.7100
Kuwait (Dinar)	3.2927	3.2895	.3037	.3040
Lebanon (Pound)	.0006634	.0006634	1507.50	1507.50
Malaysia (Ringgit)	.2632	.2632	3.8001	3.8000
Malta (Lira)	2.4691	2.4643	.4050	.4058
Mexico (Peso)				
Floating rate	.1045	.1063	9.5700	9.4050
Netherlands (Guilder)	.4678	.4659	2.1378	2.1463
New Zealand (Dollar)	.5209	.5255	1.9198	1.9029
Norway (Krone)	.1260	.1266	7.9388	7.8969
Pakistan (Rupee)	.01929	.01927	51.850	51.890
Peru (new Sol)	.2841	.2840	3.5200	3.5215
Philippines (Peso)	.02509	.02503	39.850	39.950
Poland (Zloty)	.2427	.2418	4.1195	4.1350
Portugal (Escudo)	.005142	.005121	194.49	195.26
Russia (Ruble) (a)	.03632	.03643	27.530	27.450
Saudi Arabia (Riyal)	.2666	.2666	3.7510	3.7508
Singapore (Dollar)	.6039	.6038	1.6560	1.6562
Slovak Rep. (Koruna)	.02434	.02427	41.077	41.202
South Africa (Rand)	.1643	.1632	6.0875	6.1288
South Korea (Won)	.0008909	.0008869	1122.50	1127.50
Spain (Peseta)	.006196	.006171	161.41	162.05
Sweden (Krona)	.1195	.1195	8.3671	8.3668
Switzerland (Franc)	.6429	.6391	1.5555	1.5647
Taiwan (Dollar)	.03276	.03188	30.525	31.365
Thailand (Baht)	.02683	.02702	37.265	37.015
Turkey (Lira)	.00000186	.00000185	536260.00	539255.00
United Arab (Dirham)	.2722	.2723	3.6731	3.6729
Uruguay (New Peso)				
Financial	.08607	.08608	11.619	11.618
Venezuela (Bolivar)	.001538	.001540	650.00	649.25
SDR	1.3820	1.3761	.7236	.7267
Euro	1.0313	1.0268	.9696	.9739

Special Drawing Rights (SDR) are based on exchange rates for the U.S., German, British, French, and Japanese currencies. Source: International Monetary Fund.

a-Russian Central Bank rate. Trading band lowered on 8/17/98. b-Government rate. d-Floating rate; trading band suspended on 9/2/99.

Source: Reprinted by permission of *The Wall Street Journal* © 2000 Dow Jones & Company, Inc. All rights reserved worldwide.

If you want shekels, you'll have to pay about 24¢ apiece. If you want punt, one punt will cost you $1.31. (If you're wondering what shekels and punt are, look at the table above.)

Unless you collect currencies, the reason you want the currency of another country is that you want to buy something that country produces or an existing asset of that country. Say you want to buy a Hyundai car that costs 13,476,000 South Korean won. Looking at the table, you see that the exchange rate is $1 for 1123 won. Dividing 1123 into 13,476,000 won tells you that you need $12,000 to buy the car. So before you can buy the Hyundai, somebody must go to a foreign exchange market with $12,000 and exchange those dollars for 13.476 million won. Only then can the car be bought in the United States. Most final buyers don't do this; the importer does it for them. But whenever a foreign good is bought, someone must trade currencies.

By looking at an exchange rate table, you can determine how much various goods will likely cost in different countries.

Q.9 You are going to Chile and plan to exchange $100. Based on the foreign exchange rate table in the text, how many Chilean pesos will you receive?

INSTITUTIONS SUPPORTING FREE TRADE

As I stated in Chapter 2, economists generally like markets and favor trade being as free as possible. They argue that trade allows specialization and the division of labor. When each country follows its comparative advantage, production is more efficient, and the production possibility curve shifts out. These views mean that most economists, liberal and conservative alike, generally oppose international trade restrictions.

Free Trade Organizations

Despite political pressures to restrict trade, governments have generally tried to follow economists' advice and have entered into a variety of international agreements and organizations. The most important is the **World Trade Organization (WTO),** which is *an organization committed to getting countries to agree not to impose new tariffs or other trade restrictions except under certain limited conditions.* The WTO is the successor to the **General Agreement on Tariffs and Trade (GATT),** *an agreement among many subscribing countries on certain conditions of international trade,* to which you will still occasionally see references, even though the WTO has taken its place. One of the differences between the WTO and GATT is that the WTO includes some enforcement mechanisms.

The push for free trade has a geographic dimension, which includes **free trade associations**—*groups of countries that have reduced or eliminated trade barriers among themselves.* For example, the **European Union** is *a free trade association of 15 western European countries,* 11 of which are also in the process of adopting a single currency called the euro. Other groups have loose trading relationships because of cultural or historical reasons. These loose trading relationships are sometimes called trading zones. For example, many European countries maintain close trading ties with many of their former colonies in Africa where they fit into a number of overlapping trading zones. European companies tend to see that central area as their turf. Similarly, the United States, Canada, and Mexico have created the **North American Free Trade Agreement (NAFTA),** *a U.S.–Canada–Mexico free trade zone that is phasing in reductions in tariffs.* The United States also has close ties in Latin America, making the Western hemisphere another trading zone. Another example of a trading zone is that of Japan and its economic ties with other Far East countries; Japanese companies often see that area as their commercial domain.

These trading zones overlap, sometimes on many levels. For instance, Australia and England, Portugal and Brazil, and the United States and Saudi Arabia are tied together for historical or political reasons, and those ties lead to increased trade between them that seems to deviate from the above trading zones. Similarly, as companies become more and more global, it is harder and harder to associate companies with particular countries. Let me give an example: Do you know who the largest exporters of cars from the United States are? The answer is: Japanese automobile companies!

Thus, there is no hard-and-fast specification of trading zones, and knowing history and politics is important to understanding many of the relationships.

International Economic Policy Organizations

Just as international trade differs from domestic trade, so does international economic policy differ from domestic economic policy. When economists talk about U.S. economic policy, they generally refer to what the U.S. federal government can do to achieve certain goals. In theory, at least, the U.S. federal government has both the power and the legal right of compulsion to make U.S. citizens do what it says. It can tax, it can redistribute income, it can regulate, and it can enforce property rights.

There is no international counterpart to a nation's federal government. Any meeting of a group of countries to discuss trade policies is voluntary. No international body has powers of compulsion. Hence, international problems must be dealt with through negotiation, consensus, bullying, and concessions.

Important international economic organizations include the WTO, GATT, the EU, and NAFTA.

 3.5

To discourage bullying and to encourage negotiation and consensus, governments have developed a variety of international institutions to promote negotiations and coordinate economic relations among countries. These include the United Nations (UN), the World Bank, the World Court, and the International Monetary Fund (IMF). These organizations have a variety of goals. For example, the **World Bank** is *a multinational, international financial institution that works with developing countries to secure low-interest loans*, channeling such loans to them to foster economic growth. The **International Monetary Fund (IMF)** is *a multinational, international financial institution concerned primarily with monetary issues*. It deals with international financial arrangements. When developing countries encountered financial problems in the 1980s and had large international debts that they could not pay, the IMF helped work on repayment plans.

In addition to these formal institutions, there are informal meetings of various countries. These include the **Group of Five,** which *meets to promote negotiations and coordinate economic relations among countries*. The Five are Japan, Germany, Britain, France, and the United States. The **Group of Seven** also *meets to promote negotiations and coordinate economic relations among countries*. The Seven are the five countries just named plus Canada and Italy.

Since governmental membership in international organizations is voluntary, their power is limited. When the United States doesn't like a World Court ruling, it simply states that it isn't going to follow the ruling. When the United States is unhappy with what the United Nations is doing, it withholds some of its dues. Other countries do the same from time to time. Other member countries complain, but can do little to force compliance. It doesn't work that way domestically. If you decide you don't like U.S. policy and refuse to pay your taxes, you'll wind up in jail.

What keeps nations somewhat in line when it comes to international rules is a moral tradition: Countries want to (or at least want to look as if they want to) do what's "right." Countries will sometimes follow international rules to keep international opinion favorable to them. But perceived national self-interest often overrides international scruples.

> Since governmental membership in international organizations is voluntary, their power is limited.

> **Q.10** If the United States chooses not to follow a World Court decision, what are the consequences?

CONCLUSION

This has been a whirlwind tour of the U.S. economy and its global setting. The U.S. economy in the 21st century is a global economy with links through both its trade sector and its financial sector. To understand it, you must understand its components—business, households, and government—and their interrelationship.

The economy is undergoing significant changes because of technological change. E-commerce is growing exponentially and is making markets more global. On the Internet the location of a trade doesn't matter. Countries, however, pose barriers to trade, and there will likely be much conflict as the push for free trade comes up against national boundaries.

Chapter Summary

- A diagram of the U.S. market economy shows the connections among businesses, households, and government. It also shows the U.S. economic connection to other countries.

- In the United States, businesses make the *what, how much,* and *for whom* decisions.
- Although businesses decide what to produce, they succeed or fail depending on their ability to meet consumers' desires. That's consumer sovereignty.

- The three main forms of business are corporations, sole proprietorships, and partnerships. Each has its advantages and disadvantages.
- Government plays two general roles in the economy: (1) as a referee, and (2) as an actor.
- Although households are the most powerful economic institution, they have assigned much of their power to government and business. Economics focuses on households' role as the supplier of labor.
- To understand the U.S. economy, one must understand its role in the world economy.
- Global corporations are corporations with significant operations in more than one country. They are increasing in importance.
- The areas with which the United States trades include Canada, Mexico, the Pacific Rim countries, and the European Union.

- U.S. imports have significantly exceeded exports for so long that the United States has become a debtor nation.
- International trade differs from domestic trade because (1) there are potential barriers to trade and (2) countries use different currencies.
- The rate at which one currency trades for another is that currency's exchange rate.
- Governments of many countries have formed free trade associations that agree to reduce barriers to trade among members. Three well-known free trade organizations are the WTO, NAFTA, and the European Union.
- International policy coordination must be achieved through consensus among nations.

Key Terms

balance of trade (68)

business (57)

consumer sovereignty (57)

corporations (59)

entrepreneurship (57)

European Union (73)

exchange rate (72)

exports (68)

foreign exchange markets (71)

free trade associations (73)

General Agreement on Tariffs and Trade (GATT) (73)

global corporations (65)

Group of Five (74)

Group of Seven (74)

households (61)

imports (68)

International Monetary Fund (IMF) (74)

limited liability (59)

nontariff barriers (71)

North American Free Trade Agreement (NAFTA) (73)

partnerships (58)

profit (57)

quotas (71)

sole proprietorships (58)

stock (59)

tariffs (71)

trade deficit (68)

trade surplus (69)

World Bank (74)

World Trade Organization (WTO) (73)

Questions for Thought and Review

1. Why does an economy's strength ultimately reside in its people?
2. A market system is often said to be based on consumer sovereignty—the consumer determines what's to be produced. Yet business decides what's to be produced. Can these two views be reconciled? How? If not, why?
3. Why is entrepreneurship a central part of any business?
4. You're starting a software company in which you plan to sell software to your fellow students. What form of business organization would you choose? Why?
5. What are the two largest categories of federal government expenditures?
6. A good measure of a country's importance to the world economy is its area and population. True or false? Why?
7. What are the two ways in which international trade differs from domestic trade?

8. If one U.S. dollar will buy .67 Swiss francs, how many U.S. dollars will one Swiss franc buy?
9. The U.S. economy is falling apart because the United States is the biggest debtor nation in the world. Discuss.
10. Why do most economists oppose trade restrictions?
11. What is the relationship between GATT and the WTO?
12. Look up a recent foreign exchange rate table from *The Wall Street Journal* (section C).
    a. How many Portuguese escudos will you receive for $100?
    b. Say you want to buy a Volvo directly from Sweden. The foreign car dealer quotes a price of 235,794 Swedish krona. How many dollars will you have to exchange to purchase the Volvo?

Problems and Exercises

1. Go to a store in your community.
   a. Ask what limitations the owners faced in starting their business.
   b. Were these limitations necessary?
   c. Should there have been more or fewer limitations?
   d. Under what heading of reasons for government intervention would you put each of the limitations?
   e. Ask what kinds of taxes the business pays and what benefits it believes it gets for those taxes.
   f. Is it satisfied with the existing situation? Why? What would it change?

2. You've been appointed to a county counterterrorist squad. Your assignment is to work up a set of plans to stop a group of 10 terrorists the government believes are going to disrupt the economy as much as possible with explosives.
   a. List their five most likely targets in your county, city, or town.
   b. What counterterrorist action would you take?
   c. How would you advise the economy to adjust to a successful attack on each of the targets?

3. Tom Rollins heads a new venture called Teaching Co. He has taped lectures at the top universities, packaged the lectures on audio- and videocassettes, and sells them for $90 and $150 per eight-hour series.
   a. Discuss whether such an idea could be expanded to include college courses that one could take at home.
   b. What are the technical, social, and economic issues involved?
   c. If it is technically possible and cost-effective, will the new venture be a success?

4. This is a library research question.
   a. What are the primary exports of Brazil, Honduras, Italy, Pakistan, and Nigeria?
   b. Which countries produce most of the world's tin, rubber, potatoes, wheat, marble, and refrigerators?

5. This is an entrepreneurial research question. You'd be amazed about the information that's out there if you use a bit of initiative.
   a. Does the largest company in your relevant geographic area (town, city, whatever) have an export division? Why or why not?
   b. If you were an adviser to the company, would you suggest expanding or contracting its export division? Why or why not?
   c. Go to a store and look at 10 products at random. How many were made in the United States? Give a probable explanation why they were produced where they were.

6. Exchange rates can be found in a variety of sources including the Internet.
   a. Using the exchange rate table on page 72, determine the U.S. dollar equivalent of the:
      (1) Lira
      (2) Zloty
      (3) Rand
      (4) Forint
   b. Determine the most recent dollar equivalent of those same currencies. (Use the Web or a recent newspaper.)
   c. Using the information in *a* or *b*, calculate the number of dollars you could get from one unit of each of the above currencies.

Web Questions

1. Go to Levi Strauss' home page (www.levistrauss.com) and answer the following questions:
   a. Is Levi Strauss a sole proprietorship, partnership, or corporation? What reasons do you suspect it has chosen that form of business?
   b. Is Levi Strauss a global corporation? Explain your answer.
   c. Are the shares of Levi Strauss publicly traded?

2. Go to the World Bank's home page (www.worldbank.org) to answer the following questions:
   a. What is the World Bank?
   b. What goals has the World Bank set for the new millennium?
   c. How does the World Bank finance its activities?
   d. Which two regions of the world get the largest loans from the World Bank?

Answers to Margin Questions

1. Market economies are generally broken up into businesses, households, and government.   (56)

2. False. In the United States individuals are free to start any type of business they want, provided it doesn't violate the law. The invisible hand sees to it that only those businesses that customers want earn a profit. The others lose money and eventually go out of business, so in that sense only businesses that customers want stay in business. (57)

3. As can be seen in Figure 3-2, most businesses in the United States are sole proprietorships, not corporations. Corporations, however, generate the most revenue. (58)

4. While profits are important to business, because of internal monitoring problems it is not clear that managers maximize profit. They may waste profit potential in high-priced benefits for themselves and in inefficiency generally. The market, however, provides a limit on inefficiency, and firms that exceed that limit and have losses go out of business. *(60)*

5. The largest percentage of federal expenditure is for income security. *(63)*

6. Japan has the lowest exports and imports as a percentage of GDP, followed closely by the United States. *(68)*

7. A debtor nation will not necessarily be running a trade deficit. *Debt* refers to accumulated past deficits. If a country had accumulated large deficits in the past, it could run a surplus now but still be a debtor nation. *(69)*

8. A quota is a quantitative limitation on trade. A tariff is a type of tax on imports. *(71)*

9. You will receive 52,905 pesos. *(72)*

10. The World Court has no enforcement mechanism. Thus, when a country refuses to follow the Court's decisions, the country cannot be directly punished except through indirect international pressures. *(74)*

APPENDIX A

Valuing Stocks and Bonds

A financial asset's worth comes from the stream of income it will pay in the future. With financial assets like bonds, that stream of income can be calculated rather precisely. With stocks, where the stream of income is a percentage of the firm's profits, which fluctuate significantly, the stream of future income is uncertain and valuations depends significantly on expectations.

Let's start by considering some generally held beliefs among economists and financial experts. The first is that an average share of stock in a company in a mature industry sells for somewhere between 15 and 20 times its normal profits. The second is that bond prices rise as market interest rates fall, and fall as market interest rates rise. The first step in understanding where the beliefs come from is to recognize that $1 today is not equal to $1 next year. Why? Because if I have $1 today I can invest it and earn interest (say 10 percent per year), and next year I will have $1.10, not $1. So if the annual interest rate is 10 percent, $1.10 next year is worth $1 today; alternatively, $1 next year is worth roughly 91 cents today. A dollar two years in the future is worth even less today, and dollars 30 years in the future are worth very little today.

Present value is *a method of translating a flow of future income or savings into its current worth.* For example, say a smooth-talking, high-pressure salesperson is wining and dining you. "Isn't that amazing?" the salesman says. "My company will pay $10 a year not only to you, but also to your great-great-great-grandchildren, and more, for 500 years—thousands of dollars in all. And I will sell this annuity—this promise to pay money at periodic intervals in the future—to you for a payment to me now of only $800, but you must act fast. After tonight the price will rise to $2,000."

Do you buy it? My rhetoric suggests that the answer should be no—but can you explain why? And what price *would* you be willing to pay?

To decide how much an annuity is worth, you need some way of valuing that $10 per year. *You can't simply add up the $10 five hundred times.* Doing so is wrong. Instead you must *discount* all future dollars by the interest rate in the economy. Discounting is required because a dollar in the future is not worth a dollar now.

If you have $1 now, you can take that dollar, put it in the bank, and in a year you will have that dollar plus interest. If the interest rate you can get from the bank is 5 percent, that dollar will grow to $1.05 a year from now. That means also that if the interest rate in the economy is 5 percent, if you have 95 cents now, in a year it will be worth $.9975 (5% × $.95 = $.0475). Reversing the reasoning, $1 one year in the future is worth 95 cents today. So the present value of $1 one year in the future at a 5 percent interest rate is 95 cents.

A dollar *two* years from now is worth even less today. Carry out that same reasoning and you'll find that if the interest rate is 5 percent, $1 two years from now is worth approximately 90 cents today. Why? Because you could take 90 cents now, put it in the bank at 5 percent interest, and in two years have $1.

THE PRESENT VALUE FORMULA

Carrying out such reasoning for every case would be a real pain. But luckily, there's a formula and a table that can be used to determine the present value (PV) of future income. The formula is:

$$PV = A_1/(1 + i) + A_2/(1 + i)^2 + A_3/(1 + i)^3 + \ldots + A_n/(1 + i)^n$$

where

A_n = the amount of money received n periods in the future

i = the interest rate in the economy (assumed constant)

Solving this formula for any time period longer than one or two years is complicated. To deal with it, people either use a business calculator or a present value table like that in Table A3-1.

Table A3-1(a) gives the present value of a single dollar at some time in the future at various interest rates. Notice a couple of things about the chart. First, the further into the future one goes, the lower the present value. Second, the higher the interest rate, the lower the present value. At a 12 percent interest rate, $1 fifty years from now has a present value of essentially zero.

Table A3-1(b) is an annuity table; it tells us how much a constant stream of income for a specific number of years

is worth. Notice that as the interest rate rises, the value of an annuity falls. At an 18 percent interest rate, $1 per year for 50 years has a present value of $5.55. To get the value of amounts other than $1, one simply multiplies the entry in the table by the amount. For example, $10 per year for 50 years at 18 percent interest is 10 × $5.55, or $55.50.

As you can see, the interest rate in the economy is a key to present value. *You must know the interest rate to know the value of money over time.* The higher the current (and assumed constant) interest rate, the more a given amount of money in the present will be worth in the future. Or, alternatively, the higher the current interest rate, the less a given amount of money in the future will be worth in the present.

SOME RULES OF THUMB FOR DETERMINING PRESENT VALUE

Sometimes you don't have a present value table or a business calculator handy. For those times, there are a few rules of thumb and simplified formulas for which you don't need either a present value table or a calculator. Let's consider two of them: the infinite annuity rule and the rule of 72.

The Annuity Rule

To find the present value of an annuity that will pay $1 for an infinite number of years in the future when the interest

Table A3-1 (a and b)   Sample Present Value and Annuity Tables

Year	\multicolumn{7}{c}{Interest Rate}					
	3%	4%	6%	9%	12%	15%	18%
1	$0.97	$0.96	$0.94	$0.92	$0.89	$0.87	$0.85
2	0.94	0.92	0.89	0.84	0.80	0.76	0.72
3	0.92	0.89	0.84	0.77	0.71	0.66	0.61
4	0.89	0.85	0.79	0.71	0.64	0.57	0.52
5	0.86	0.82	0.75	0.65	0.57	0.50	0.44
6	0.84	0.79	0.70	0.60	0.51	0.43	0.37
7	0.81	0.76	0.67	0.55	0.45	0.38	0.31
8	0.79	0.73	0.63	0.50	0.40	0.33	0.27
9	0.77	0.70	0.59	0.46	0.36	0.28	0.23
10	0.74	0.68	0.56	0.42	0.32	0.25	0.19
15	0.64	0.56	0.42	0.27	0.18	0.12	0.08
20	0.55	0.46	0.31	0.18	0.10	0.06	0.04
30	0.41	0.31	0.17	0.08	0.03	0.02	0.01
40	0.31	0.21	0.10	0.03	0.01	0.00	0.00
50	0.23	0.14	0.05	0.01	0.00	0.00	0.00

(a) Present value table (value now of $1 to be received *x* years in the future)
The present value table converts a future amount into a present amount.

Number of years	\multicolumn{7}{c}{Interest Rate}					
	3%	4%	6%	9%	12%	15%	18%
1	$0.97	$0.96	$0.94	$0.92	$0.89	$0.87	$0.85
2	1.91	1.89	1.83	1.76	1.69	1.63	1.57
3	2.83	2.78	2.67	2.53	2.40	2.28	2.17
4	3.72	3.63	3.47	3.24	3.04	2.85	2.69
5	4.58	4.45	4.21	3.89	3.60	3.35	3.13
6	5.42	5.24	4.92	4.49	4.11	3.78	3.50
7	6.23	6.00	5.58	5.03	4.56	4.16	3.81
8	7.02	6.73	6.21	5.53	4.97	4.49	4.08
9	7.79	7.44	6.80	6.00	5.33	4.77	4.30
10	8.53	8.11	7.36	6.42	5.65	5.02	4.49
15	11.94	11.12	9.71	8.06	6.81	5.85	5.09
20	14.88	13.59	11.47	9.13	7.47	6.26	5.35
30	19.60	17.29	13.76	10.27	8.06	6.57	5.52
40	23.11	19.79	15.05	10.76	8.24	6.64	5.55
50	25.73	21.48	15.76	10.96	8.30	6.66	5.55

(b) Annuity table (value now of $1 per year to be received for *x* years)
The annuity table converts a known stream of income into a present amount.

APPLYING THE TOOLS

The Press and Present Value

The failure to understand the concept of present value often shows up in the popular press. Here are three examples.

Headline: **COURT SETTLEMENT IS $40,000,000**

Inside story: The money will be paid out over a 40-year period.

Actual value: $11,925,000 (8 percent interest rate).

Headline: **DISABLED WIDOW WINS $25 MILLION LOTTERY**

Inside story: The money will be paid over 20 years.

Actual value: $13,254,499 (8 percent interest rate).

Headline: **BOND ISSUE TO COST TAXPAYERS $68 MILLION**

Inside story: The $68 million is the total of interest and principal payments. The interest is paid yearly; the principal won't be paid back to the bond purchasers until 30 years from now.

Actual cost: $20,000,000 (8 percent interest rate).

Such stories are common. Be on the lookout for them as you read the newspaper or watch the evening news.

---

rate is 5 percent, we simply divide $1 by 5 percent (.05). Doing so gives us $20. So at 5 percent, $1 a year paid to you forever has a present value of $20. The **annuity rule** is that *the present value of any annuity is the annual income it yields divided by the interest rate.* Our general annuity rule for any annuity is expressed as:

$$PV = X/i$$

That is, the present value of an infinite flow of income, X, is that income divided by the interest rate, i.

Most of the time, people don't offer to sell you annuities for the infinite future. A typical annuity runs for 30, 40, or 50 years. However, the annuity rule is still useful. As you can see from the present value table, in 30 years at a 9 percent interest rate, the present value of $1 isn't much (it's 8 cents), so we can use this infinite flow formula as an approximation of long-lasting, but less than infinite, flows of future income. We simply subtract a little bit from what we get with our formula. The longer the time period, the less we subtract. For example, say you are wondering what $200 a year for 40 years is worth when the interest rate is 8 percent. Dividing $200 by .08 gives $2,500, so we know the annuity must be worth a bit less than $2,500. (It's actually worth $2,411.)

The annuity rule allows us to answer the question posed at the beginning of this section: How much is $10 a year for 500 years worth right now? The answer is that it depends on the interest rate you could earn on a specified amount of money now. If the interest rate is 10 percent, the maximum you should be willing to pay for that 500-year $10 annuity is $100:

$$\$10/.10 = \$100$$

If the interest rate is 5 percent, the most you should pay is $200 ($10/.05 = $200). So now you know why you

should have said no to that supersalesman who offered it to you for $800.

The Rule of 72

A second rule of thumb for determining present values of shorter time periods is the **rule of 72,** which states:

The number of years it takes for a certain amount to double in value is equal to 72 divided by the rate of interest.

Say, for example, that the interest rate is 4 percent. How long will it take for your $100 to become $200? Dividing 72 by 4 gives 18, so the answer is 18 years. Conversely, the present value of $200 at a 4 percent interest rate 18 years in the future is about $100. (Actually it's $102.67.)

Alternatively, say that you will receive $1,000 in 10 years. Is it worth paying $500 for that amount now if the interest rate is 9 percent? Using the rule of 72, we know that at a 9 percent interest rate it will take about eight years for $500 to double:

$$72/9 = 8$$

so the future value of $500 in 10 years is more than $1,000. It's probably about $1,200. (Actually it's $1,184.) So if the interest rate in the economy is 9 percent, it's not worth paying $500 now in order to get that $1,000 in 10 years. By investing that same $500 today at 9 percent, you can have $1,184 in 10 years.

THE IMPORTANCE OF PRESENT VALUE

Many business decisions require such present value calculations. In almost any business, you'll be looking at flows of income in the future and comparing them to present costs or to other flows of money in the future.

Generally, however, when most people calculate present value they don't use any of the formulas. They pull out a handy business calculator, press in the numbers to calculate the present value, and watch while the calculator graphically displays the results.

Let's now use our knowledge of present value to explain the two observations at the beginning of the appendix. Since all financial assets can be broken down into promises to pay certain amounts at certain times in the future, we can determine their value with the present value formula. If the asset is a bond, it consists of a stream of income payments over a number of years and the repayment of the face value of the bond. Each year's interest payment and the eventual repayment of the face value must be calculated separately, and then the results must be added together. If the financial asset is a share of stock, the valuation is a bit less clear since a stock does not guarantee the payment of anything definite—just a share of the profits. No profits, no payment. So, with stocks, expectations of profits are of central importance. Let's consider an example: Say a share of stock is earning $1 per share per year and is expected to continue to earn that long into the future. Using the annuity rule and an interest rate of 6.5 percent, the present value of that future stream of expected earnings is about 1/.065, or a bit more than $15. Assuming profits are expected to grow slightly, that would mean that the stock should sell for somewhere around $20, or 20 times its profit per share, which is the explanation to the first observation in the appendix.

To see the answer to the second, say the interest rate rises to 10 percent. Then the value of the stock or bond that is earning a fixed amount—in this case $1 per share—will go down to $10. Interest rate up, value of stock or bond down. This is the explanation of the second observation.

There is nothing immutable in the above reasoning. For example, if promises to pay aren't trustworthy, you don't put the amount that's promised into your calculation; you put in the amount you actually expect to receive. That's why when a company or a country looks as if it's going to default on loans or stop paying dividends, the value of its bonds and stock will fall considerably. For example, in the late 1980s many people thought Brazil would default on its bonds. That expectation caused the price of Brazilian bonds to fall to about 30 percent on the dollar. Then in the 1990s, when people believed total default was less likely, the value rose.

Of course, the expectations could go in the opposite direction. Say that the interest rate is 10 percent, and that you expect a company's profit, which is now $1 per share, to grow by 10 percent per year. In that case, since expected profit growth is as high as the interest rate, the current value of the stock is infinite. It is such expectations of future profit growth that have fueled the Internet stock craze and have caused the valuation of firms with no current profits (indeed, many are experiencing significant losses) at multiples of sales of 300 or more. Financial valuations based on such optimistic expectations are the reason most economists considered the stock market in Internet stocks to be overvalued in the late 1990s.

ASSET PRICES, INTEREST RATES, AND THE ECONOMY

This appendix isn't meant to cover the intricacies of valuation over time. That's done in a finance course. The point is to help you understand the relationship between interest rates and asset prices. Central to valuing stocks or bonds is the present value formula. From that we know that increases in interest rates (because they make future flows of income coming from an asset worth less now) make financial asset prices fall, and that decreases in interest rates (because they make the future flow of income coming from an asset worth more now) make financial asset prices rise.

Key Terms

annuity rule   (79)   present value   (77)   rule of 72   (79)

Questions for Thought and Review

1. How much is $50 to be received 50 years from now worth if the interest rate is 5 percent? (Use Figure A3-1).

2. How much is $50 to be received 50 years from now worth if the interest rate is 10 percent? (Use Figure A3-1).

3. Your employer offers you a choice of two bonus packages: $1,400 today or $2,000 five years from now. Assuming a 5 percent rate of interest, which is the better value? Assuming an interest rate of 10 percent, which is the better value?

4. Suppose the price of a one-year 10 percent coupon bond with a $100 face value is $98.
   a. Are market interest rates likely to be above or below 10 percent? Explain.
   b. What is the bond's yield or return?
   c. If market interest rates fell, what would happen to the price of the bond?

5. Explain in words why the present value of $100 to be received in 10 years would decline as the interest rate rises.

6. A 6 percent bond will pay you $1,060 one year from now. The interest rate in the economy is 10 percent. How much is that bond worth now?

7. You are to receive $100 a year for the next 40 years. How much is it worth now if the current interest rate in the economy is 6 percent? (Use annuity table.)

8. You are to receive $200 30 years from now. About how much is it worth now? (The interest rate is 3 percent.)

9. A salesperson calls you up and offers you $200 a year for life. If the interest rate is 7 percent, how much should you be willing to pay for that annuity?

10. The same salesperson offers you a lump sum of $20,000 in 10 Years. How much should you be willing to pay? (The interest rate is still 7 percent.)

11. What is the present value of a cash flow of $100 per year forever (a perpetuity), assuming:

    The interest rate is 10 percent.

    The interest rate is 5 percent.

    The interest rate is 20 percent.

    a. Working with those same three interest rates, what are the future values of $100 today in one year? How about in two years?

    b. Working with those same three interest rates, how long will it take you to double your money?

Supply and Demand

After reading this chapter, you should be able to:

- State the law of demand.

- Explain the importance of substitution to the laws of supply and demand.

- Distinguish a shift in demand from a movement along the demand curve.

- Draw a demand curve from a demand table.

- State the law of supply.

- Distinguish a shift in supply from a movement along the supply curve.

- Draw a supply curve from a supply table.

- Explain how the law of demand and the law of supply interact to bring about equilibrium.

- Show how equilibrium maximizes consumer and producer surplus.

Teach a parrot the terms supply *and* demand
and you've got an economist.

Thomas Carlyle

Supply and demand. Supply and demand. Roll the phrase around in your mouth, savor it like a good wine. *Supply* and *demand* are the most-used words in economics. And for good reason. They provide a good off-the-cuff answer for any economic question. Try it.

Why are bacon and oranges so expensive this winter? *Supply and demand.*

Why are interest rates falling? *Supply and demand.*

Why can't I find decent wool socks anymore? *Supply and demand.*

The importance of the interplay of supply and demand makes it only natural that, early in any economics course, you must learn about supply and demand. Let's start with demand.

DEMAND

People want lots of things; they "demand" much less than they want because demand means a willingness and capacity to pay. Unless you are willing and able to pay for it you may *want* it, but you don't *demand* it. For example, I want to own a Maserati. But, I must admit, I'm not willing to do what's necessary to own one. If I really wanted one, I'd mortgage everything I own, increase my income by doubling the number of hours I work, not buy anything else, and get that car. But I don't do any of those things, so at the going price, $240,000, I do not demand a Maserati. Sure, I'd buy one if it cost $10,000, but from my actions it's clear that, at $240,000, I don't demand it. This points to an important aspect of demand: The quantity you demand at a low price differs from the quantity you demand at a high price. Specifically, the quantity you demand varies inversely—in the opposite direction—with price.

Prices are the tool by which the market coordinates individuals' desires and limits how much people are willing to buy—how much they demand. When goods become scarce, the market reduces the quantity of those scarce goods people demand; as their prices go up, people buy fewer goods. As goods become abundant, their prices go down, and people want more of them. The invisible hand—the price mechanism—sees to it that what people demand (do what's necessary to get) matches what's available. In doing so, the invisible hand coordinates individuals' demands.

Prices are the tool by which the market coordinates individual desires.

The Law of Demand

The ideas expressed above are the foundation of the **law of demand:**

> *Quantity demanded rises as price falls, other things constant.*

Or alternatively:

> *Quantity demanded falls as price rises, other things constant.*

This law is fundamental to the invisible hand's ability to coordinate individuals' desires: as prices change, people change how much of a particular good they're willing to buy.

What accounts for the law of demand? Individuals' tendency to substitute other goods for goods whose price has gone up. If the price of CDs rises from $15 to $20 but the price of cassette tapes stays at $9.99, you're more likely to buy that new Christine Aguilera recording on cassette than on CD.

To see that the law of demand makes intuitive sense, just think of something you'd really like but can't afford. If the price is cut in half, you—and other consumers—become more likely to buy it. Quantity demanded goes up as price goes down.

Just to be sure you've got it, let's consider a real-world example: demand for vanity—specifically, vanity license plates. In 1989, the North Carolina state legislature increased the vanity plates' price from $30 to $40. In response, the quantity demanded fell from 60,334 at $30 a year to 31,122 at $40 a year. Assuming other things remained constant, that is the law of demand in action.

The law of demand states that the quantity of a good demanded is inversely related to the good's price. When price goes up, quantity demanded goes down. When price goes down, quantity demanded goes up.

Figure 4-1   A Sample Demand Curve

The law of demand states that the quantity demanded of a good is inversely related to the price of that good, other things constant. As the price of a good goes up, the quantity demanded goes down, so the demand curve is downward sloping.

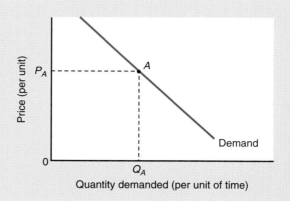

Quantity demanded (per unit of time)

Q-1 Why does the demand curve slope downward?

"Other things constant" places a limitation on the application of the law of demand.

The Demand Curve

A **demand curve** is *the graphic representation of the relationship between price and quantity demanded*. Figure 4-1 shows a demand curve.

As you can see, in graphical terms, the law of demand states that as the price goes up, the quantity demanded goes down, other things constant. An alternative way of saying the same thing is that price and quantity demanded are inversely related, so the demand curve slopes downward to the right.

Notice that in stating the law of demand, I put in the qualification "other things constant." That's three extra words, and unless they were important I wouldn't have put them in. But what does "other things constant" mean? Say that over a period of two years, the price of cars rises as the number of cars purchased likewise rises. That seems to violate the law of demand, since the number of cars purchased should have fallen in response to the rise in price. Looking at the data more closely, however, we see that a third factor has also changed: individuals' income has increased. As income increases, people buy more cars, increasing the demand for cars.

The increase in price works as the law of demand states—it decreases the number of cars bought. But in this case, income doesn't remain constant; it increases. That rise in income increases the demand for cars. That increase in demand outweighs the decrease in quantity demanded that results from a rise in price, so ultimately more cars are sold. If you want to study the effect of price alone—which is what the law of demand refers to—you must make adjustments to hold income constant when you make your study. That's why the qualifying phrase "other things constant" is an important part of the law of demand.

The other things that are held constant include individuals' tastes, prices of other goods, and even the weather. Those other factors must remain constant if you're to make a valid study of the effect of an increase in the price of a good on the quantity demanded. In practice, it's impossible to keep all other things constant, so you have to be careful when you say that when price goes up, quantity demanded goes down. It's likely to go down, but it's always possible that something besides price has changed.

Shifts in Demand versus Movements along a Demand Curve

To distinguish between the effects of price and the effects of other factors on how much of a good is demanded, economists have developed the following precise terminology—

terminology that inevitably shows up on exams. The first distinction to make is between demand and quantity demanded.

- **Demand** refers to *a schedule of quantities of a good that will be bought per unit of time at various prices, other things constant.*
- **Quantity demanded** refers to *a specific amount that will be demanded per unit of time at a specific price, other things constant.*

In graphical terms, the term *demand* refers to the entire demand curve. Demand tells how much of a good will be bought *at various prices. Quantity demanded* refers to a point on a demand curve, such as point A in Figure 4-1. This terminology allows us to distinguish between *changes in quantity demanded* and *shifts in demand.* A change in the quantity demanded refers to the effect of a price change on the quantity demanded. It refers to a **movement along a demand curve**—*the graphical representation of the effect of a change in price on the quantity demanded.* A **shift in demand** refers to *the effect of anything other than price on demand.*

Shift Factors of Demand

Shift factors of demand are factors that cause shifts in the demand curve. A change in anything besides price causes a shift of the entire demand curve.

Important shift factors of demand include:

1. Society's income.
2. The prices of other goods.
3. Tastes.
4. Expectations.

Income From our example above of "the other things constant" qualification, we saw that a rise in income increases the demand for goods. For most goods this is true. As individuals' income rises, they can afford more of the goods they want.

Price of Other Goods Because people make their buying decisions based on the price of related goods, demand will be affected by the prices of other goods. Suppose the price of jeans rose from $25 to $35, but the price of khakis remained at $25. Next time you need pants, you're apt to try khakis instead of jeans. They are substitutes. When the price of a substitute declines, demand for the good whose price has remained the same will fall.

Tastes An old saying goes: "There's no accounting for taste." Of course, many advertisers believe otherwise. Changes in taste can affect the demand for a good without a change in price. As you become older, you may find that your taste for rock concerts has changed to a taste for an evening at the opera or local philharmonic.

Expectations Finally, expectations will also affect demand. Expectations can cover a lot. If you expect your income to rise in the future, you're bound to start spending some of it today. If you expect the price of computers to fall soon, you may put off buying one until later.

These aren't the only shift factors. In fact anything—except the price of the good itself—that affects demand (and many things do) is a shift factor. While economists agree these shift factors are important, they believe that no shift factor influences how much is demanded as consistently as does price of the specific item. That's what makes economists focus first on price as they try to understand the world. That's why economists make the law of demand central to their analysis.

Q-2 In the 1980s and early 1990s, as animal rights activists made wearing fur coats déclassé, the _____ decreased. Should the missing words be "demand for furs" or "quantity of furs demanded"?

Q-3 Explain the effect of each of the following on the demand for new computers:
1. The price of computers falls by 30 percent.
2. Total income in the economy rises.

Figure 4-2   Shift in Demand versus a Change in Quantity Demanded

A rise in a good's price results in a reduction in quantity demanded and is shown by a movement up along a demand curve from point A to point B in (a). A change in any other factor besides price that affects demand leads to a shift in the entire demand curve as shown in (b).

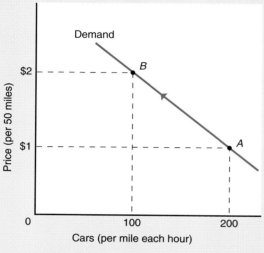

(a) Movement along a demand curve

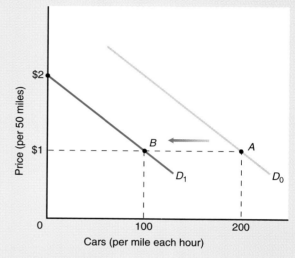

(b) Shift in demand

Change in price causes a movement along a demand curve; a change in a shift factor causes a shift in demand.

To make sure you understand the difference between a movement along a demand curve and a shift in demand, let's consider an example. Singapore has one of the highest number of cars per mile of road. This means that congestion is considerable. Singapore has adopted two policies to reduce road use: It increased the fee charged to use roads, and it provided an expanded public transportation system. Both policies reduced congestion. Figure 4-2(a) shows that increasing the toll charged to use roads from $1 to $2 per 50 miles of road reduces quantity demanded from 200 to 100 cars per mile every hour (a movement along the demand curve). Figure 4-2(b) shows that providing alternative methods of transportation such as buses and subways will shift the demand curve for roads. Demand for road use shifts to the left so that at the $1 fee, demand drops from 200 to 100 cars per mile every hour (a shift in the demand curve).

A Review

Let's test your understanding by having you specify what happens to your demand curve for videocassettes in the following examples: First, let's say you buy a DVD player. Next, let's say that the price of videocassettes falls; and finally, say that you won $1 million in a lottery. What happens to the demand for videocassettes in each case? If you answered: It shifts in; it remains unchanged; and it shifts out—you've got it.

The Demand Table

As I emphasized in Chapter 1, introductory economics depends heavily on graphs and graphical analysis—translating ideas into graphs and back into words. So let's graph the demand curve.

Figure 4-3 (a and b)   From a Demand Table to a Demand Curve

The demand table in (a) is translated into a demand curve in (b). Each combination of price and quantity in the table corresponds to a point on the curve. For example, point A on the graph represents row A in the table: Alice demands 9 videocassette rentals at a price of 50 cents. A demand curve is constructed by plotting all points from the demand table and connecting the points by a line.

	Price per cassette	Cassette rentals demanded per week
A	$0.50	9
B	1.00	8
C	2.00	6
D	3.00	4
E	4.00	2

(a) A demand table

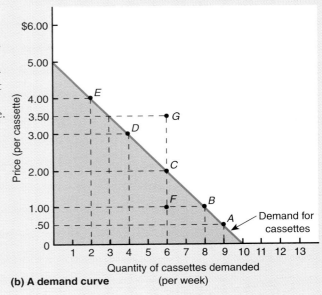

(b) A demand curve

Figure 4-3(a), a demand table, describes Alice's demand for renting videocassettes. For example, at a price of $2, Alice will rent (buy the use of) 6 cassettes per week and at a price of 50 cents she will rent 9.

There are four points about the relationship between the number of videos Alice rents and the price of renting them that are worth mentioning. First, the relationship follows the law of demand: as the rental price rises, quantity demanded decreases. Second, quantity demanded has a specific *time dimension* to it. In this example demand refers to the number of cassette rentals per week. Without the time dimension, the table wouldn't provide us with any useful information. Nine cassette rentals per year is quite a different concept from 9 cassette rentals per week. Third, Alice's cassette rentals are interchangeable—the 9th cassette rental doesn't significantly differ from the 1st, 3rd, or any other cassette rental. The fourth point is already familiar to you: The schedule assumes that everything else is held constant.

From a Demand Table to a Demand Curve

Figure 4-3(b) translates the demand table in Figure 4-3(a) into a graph. Point A (quantity = 9, price = $.50) is graphed first at the (9, $.50) coordinates. Next we plot points B, C, D, and E in the same manner and connect the resulting dots with a solid line. The result is the demand curve, which graphically conveys the same information that's in the demand table. Notice that the demand curve is downward sloping (from left to right), indicating that the law of demand holds in the example.

The demand curve represents the *maximum price* that an individual will pay for various quantities of a good; the individual will happily pay less. For example, say someone offers Alice 6 cassette rentals at a price of $1 each (point F of Figure 4-3(b)). Will she accept? Sure; she'll pay any price within the shaded area to the left of the demand curve. But if someone offers her 6 rentals at $3.50 each (point G), she won't accept. At a rental price of $3.50 apiece, she's willing to buy only 3 cassette rentals.

The demand curve represents the maximum price that an individual will pay.

Individual and Market Demand Curves

Normally, economists talk about market demand curves rather than individual demand curves. A **market demand curve** is *the horizontal sum of all individual demand curves*. Market demand curves are what most firms are interested in. Firms don't care whether individual A or individual B buys their goods; they only care that *someone* buys their goods.

It's a good graphical exercise to add individual demand curves together to create a market demand curve. I do that in Figure 4-4. In it I assume that the market consists of three buyers, Alice, Bruce, and Cathy, whose demand tables are given in Figure 4-4(a). Alice and Bruce have demand tables similar to the demand tables discussed previously. At a price of $3 each, Alice rents 4 cassettes; at a price of $2, she rents 6. Cathy is an all-or-nothing individual. She rents 1 cassette as long as the price is equal to or below $1; otherwise she rents nothing. If you plot Cathy's demand curve, it's a vertical line. However, the law of demand still holds: as price increases, quantity demanded decreases.

The quantity demanded by each consumer is listed in columns 2, 3, and 4 of Figure 4-4(a). Column 5 shows total market demand; each entry is the horizontal sum of the entries in columns 2, 3, and 4. For example, at a price of $3 apiece (row F), Alice demands 4 cassette rentals, Bruce demands 1, and Cathy demands 0, for a total market demand of 5 cassette rentals.

Figure 4-4(b) shows three demand curves: one each for Alice, Bruce, and Cathy. The market, or total, demand curve is the horizontal sum of the individual demand

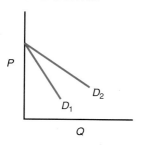

Q.4 Derive a market demand curve from the following two individual demand curves:

Figure 4-4 (a and b)   From Individual Demands to a Market Demand Curve

The table (**a**) shows the demand schedules for Alice, Bruce, and Cathy. Together they make up the market for videocassette rentals. Their total quantity demanded (market demand) for videocassette rentals at each price is given in column 5. As you can see in (**b**), Alice's, Bruce's, and Cathy's demand curves can be added together to get the total market demand curve. For example, at a price of $2, Cathy demands 0, Bruce demands 3, and Alice demands 6, for a market demand of 9 (point D).

	(1)	(2)	(3)	(4)	(5)
	Price (per cassette)	Alice's demand	Bruce's demand	Cathy's demand	Market demand
A	$0.50	9	6	1	16
B	1.00	8	5	1	14
C	1.50	7	4	0	11
D	2.00	6	3	0	9
E	2.50	5	2	0	7
F	3.00	4	1	0	5
G	3.50	3	0	0	3
H	4.00	2	0	0	2

(a) A demand table

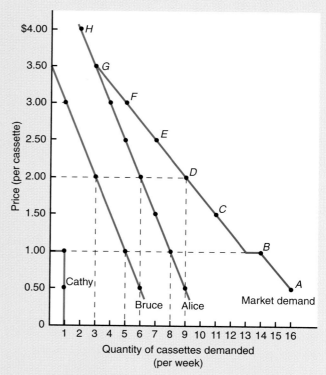

(b) Adding demand curves

KNOWING THE TOOLS

Six Things to Remember When Considering a Demand Curve

- A demand curve had better follow the law of demand: When price rises, quantity demanded falls; and vice versa.
- The horizontal axis—quantity—has a time dimension.
- The quantities are of the same quality.

- The vertical axis—price—assumes all other prices remain the same.
- The curve assumes everything else is held constant.
- Effects of price changes are shown by movements along the demand curve. Effects of anything else on demand (shift factors) are shown by shifts of the entire demand curve.

curves. To see that this is the case, notice that if we take the quantity demanded at $1 by Alice (8), Bruce (5), and Cathy (1), they sum to 14, which is point B (14, $1) on the market demand curve. We can do that for each price. Alternatively, we can simply add the individual quantities demanded, given in the demand tables, prior to graphing (which we do in column 5 of Figure 4-4(a)), and graph that total in relation to price. Not surprisingly, we get the same total market demand curve.

In practice, of course, firms don't measure individual demand curves, so they don't sum them up in this fashion. Instead, they estimate total demand. Still, summing up individual demand curves is a useful exercise because it shows you how the market demand curve is the sum (the horizontal sum, graphically speaking) of the individual demand curves, and it gives you a good sense of where market demand curves come from. It also shows you that, even if individuals don't respond to small changes in price, the market demand curve can still be smooth and downward sloping. That's because, for the market, the law of demand is based on two phenomena:

1. At lower prices, existing demanders buy more.
2. At lower prices, new demanders (some all-or-nothing demanders like Cathy) enter the market.

For the market, the law of demand is based on two phenomena:

1. At lower prices, existing demanders buy more.
2. At lower prices, new demanders enter the market.

SUPPLY

In one sense, supply is the mirror image of demand. Individuals control the factors of production—inputs, or resources, necessary to produce goods. Individuals' supply of these factors to the market mirrors other individuals' demand for those factors. For example, say you decide you want to rest rather than weed your garden. You hire someone to do the weeding; you demand labor. Someone else decides she would prefer more income instead of more rest; she supplies labor to you. You trade money for labor; she trades labor for money. Her supply is the mirror image of your demand.

For a large number of goods and services, however, the supply process is more complicated than demand. For many goods there's an intermediate step in supply: individuals supply factors of production to firms.

Let's consider a simple example. Say you're a taco technician. You supply your labor to the factor market. The taco company demands your labor (hires you). The taco company combines your labor with other inputs like meat, cheese, beans, and tables, and produces many tacos (production), which it supplies to customers in the goods market. For produced goods, supply depends not only on individuals' decisions to supply factors of production but also on firms' ability to produce—to transform those factors of production into usable goods.

Supply of produced goods involves a much more complicated process than demand and is divided into analysis of factors of production and the transformation of those factors into goods.

The supply process of produced goods is generally complicated. Often there are many layers of firms—production firms, wholesale firms, distribution firms, and retailing firms—each of which passes on in-process goods to the next layer of firms. Real-world production and supply of produced goods is a multistage process.

The supply of nonproduced goods is more direct. Individuals supply their labor in the form of services directly to the goods market. For example, an independent contractor may repair your washing machine. That contractor supplies his labor directly to you.

Thus, the analysis of the supply of produced goods has two parts: an analysis of the supply of factors of production to households and to firms, and an analysis of one process by which firms transform those factors of production into usable goods and services.

The Law of Supply

In talking about supply, the same convention exists that we used for demand. Supply refers to the various quantities offered for sale at various prices. Quantity supplied refers to a specific quantity offered for sale at a specific price.

There's a law of supply that corresponds to the law of demand. The **law of supply** states:

Quantity supplied rises as price rises, other things constant.

Or alternatively:

Quantity supplied falls as price falls, other things constant.

Price regulates quantity supplied just as it regulates quantity demanded. Like the law of demand, the law of supply is fundamental to the invisible hand's (the market's) ability to coordinate individuals' actions.

What accounts for the law of supply? When the price of a good rises, individuals and firms can rearrange their activities in order to supply more of that good to the market. The law of supply is based on a firm's ability to substitute production of one good for another, or vice versa. If the price of corn rises and the price of wheat has not changed, farmers will grow less wheat and more corn, other things constant.

With firms, there's a second explanation of the law of supply. Assuming firms' costs are constant, a higher price means higher profits (the difference between a firm's revenues and its costs). The expectation of those higher profits leads it to increase output as price rises, which is what the law of supply states.

The Supply Curve

A **supply curve** is *the graphical representation of the relationship between price and quantity supplied.* A supply curve is shown graphically in Figure 4-5.

Notice how the supply curve slopes upward to the right. That upward slope captures the law of supply. It tells us that the quantity supplied varies *directly*—in the same direction—with the price.

As with the law of demand, the law of supply assumes other things are held constant. Thus, if the price of wheat rises and quantity supplied falls, you'll look for something else that changed—for example, a drought might have caused a drop in supply. Your explanation would go as follows: Had there been no drought, the quantity supplied would have increased in response to the rise in price, but because there was a drought, the supply decreased, which caused prices to rise.

As with the law of demand, the law of supply represents economists' off-the-cuff response to the question "What happens to quantity supplied if price rises?" If the law

Figure 4-5   A Sample Supply Curve

The supply curve demonstrates graphically the law of supply, which states that the quantity supplied of a good is directly related to that good's price, other things constant. As the price of a good goes up, the quantity supplied also goes up, so the supply curve is upward sloping.

seems to be violated, economists search for some other variable that has changed. As was the case with demand, these other variables that might change are called shift factors.

Shifts in Supply versus Movements along a Supply Curve

The same distinctions in terms made for demand apply to supply.

> **Supply** refers to *a schedule of quantities a seller is willing to sell per unit of time at various prices, other things constant.*

> **Quantity supplied** refers to *a specific amount that will be supplied at a specific price.*

In graphical terms, supply refers to the entire supply curve because a supply curve tells us how much will be offered for sale at various prices. "Quantity supplied" refers to a point on a supply curve, such as point A in Figure 4-5.

The second distinction that is important to make is between the effects of a change in price and the effects of shift factors on how much of a good is supplied. Changes in price cause changes in quantity supplied; such changes are represented by a **movement along a supply curve**—*the graphic representation of the effect of a change in price on the quantity supplied.* If the amount supplied is affected by anything other than price, that is, by a shift factor of supply, there will be a **shift in supply**—*the graphic representation of the effect of a change in a factor other than price on supply.*

Shift Factors of Supply

Other factors besides price that affect how much will be supplied include the price of inputs used in production, technology, expectations, and taxes and subsidies. Let's see how.

Price of Inputs Firms produce to earn a profit. Since their profit is tied to costs, it's no surprise that costs will affect how much a firm is willing to supply. If costs rise, profits will decline, and a firm has less incentive to supply. Supply falls when the price of inputs rises. If costs rise substantially, a firm might even shut down.

Technology Advances in technology change the production process, reducing the number of inputs needed to produce a given supply of goods. Thus, a technological advance that reduces the number of workers will reduce costs of production. A reduction in the costs of production increases profits and leads suppliers to increase production. Advances in technology increase supply.

Q.5 In the 1980s and 1990s, as animal activists caused a decrease in the demand for fur coats, the prices of furs fell. This made _____ decline. Should the missing words be "the supply" or "the quantity supplied"?

Expectations Supplier expectations are an important factor in the production decision. If a supplier expects the price of her good to rise at some time in the future, she may store some of today's supply in order to sell it later and reap higher profits, decreasing supply now and increasing it later.

Taxes and Subsidies Taxes on supplies increase the cost of production by requiring a firm to pay the government a portion of the income from products or services sold. Because taxes increases the cost of production, profit declines and suppliers will reduce supply. The opposite is true for subsidies. Subsidies are payments by the government to suppliers to produce goods; thus, they reduce the cost of production. Subsidies increase supply. Taxes on suppliers reduce supply.

These aren't the only shift factors. As was the case with demand, a shift factor of supply is anything that affects supply, other than its price.

Shift in Supply versus a Movement along a Supply Curve

The same "movement along" and "shift of" distinction that we developed for demand exists for supply. To make that distinction clear, let's consider an example: the supply of oil. In 1990 and 1991, world oil prices rose from $15 to $36 a barrel when oil production in the Persian Gulf was disrupted by the Iraqi invasion of Kuwait. U.S. oil producers, seeing that they could sell their oil at a higher price, increased oil production. As the price of oil rose, domestic producers increased the quantity of oil supplied. The change in domestic quantity supplied in response to the rise in world oil prices is illustrated in Figure 4-6(a) as a movement up along the U.S. supply curve from point A to point B. At $15 a barrel, producers supplied 1,500 million barrels of oil a day, and at $36 a barrel they supplied 1,750 million barrels per day.

Q-6 Explain the effect of each of the following on the supply of romance novels:

1. The price of paper rises by 20 percent.
2. Government increases the sales tax on all books by 5 percentage points.

Figure 4-6   Shift in Supply versus Change in Quantity Supplied

A change in quantity supplied results from a change in price and is shown by a movement along a supply curve like the movement from point A to point B in (a). A shift in supply—a shift in the entire supply curve—brought about by a change in a nonprice factor is shown in (b).

(a) Movement along a supply curve

(b) Shift in supply

Earlier, in the 1980s, technological advances in horizontal drilling more than doubled the amount of oil that could be extracted from some oil fields. Technological innovations such as this reduced the cost of supplying oil and shifted the supply of oil to the right as shown in Figure 4-6(b). Before the innovation suppliers were willing to provide 1,250 million barrels of oil per day at $15 a barrel. After the innovation, suppliers were willing to supply 1,500 million barrels of oil per day at $15 a barrel.

A Review

To be sure you understand shifts in supply, explain what is likely to happen to your supply curve for labor in the following cases: (1) You suddenly decide that you absolutely need a new car. (2) You suddenly won a million dollars in the lottery. And finally, (3) the wage you could earn doubled. If you came up with the answers: shift out, shift in, and no change—you've got it down. If not, it's time for a review.

Do we see such shifts in the supply curve often? Yes. A good example is computers. For the past 30 years, technological changes have continually shifted the supply curve for computers out.

The Supply Table

Remember Figure 4-4(a)'s demand table for cassette rentals. In Figure 4-7(a), columns 2 (Ann), 3 (Barry), and 4 (Charlie), we follow the same reasoning to construct a supply table for three hypothetical cassette suppliers. Each supplier follows the law of supply: When price rises, each supplies more, or at least as much as each did at a lower price.

Figure 4-7 (a and b)   From Individual Supplies to a Market Supply

As with market demand, market supply is determined by adding all quantities supplied at a given price. Three suppliers—Ann, Barry, and Charlie—make up the market of videocassette suppliers. The total market supply is the sum of their individual supplies at each price, shown in column 5 of (a).

Each of the individual supply curves and the market supply curve have been plotted in (b). Notice how the market supply curve is the horizontal sum of the individual supply curves.

	(1)	(2)	(3)	(4)	(5)
Quantities supplied	Price (per cassette)	Ann's supply	Barry's supply	Charlie's supply	Market supply
A	$0.00	0	0	0	0
B	0.50	1	0	0	1
C	1.00	2	1	0	3
D	1.50	3	2	0	5
E	2.00	4	3	0	7
F	2.50	5	4	0	9
G	3.00	6	5	0	11
H	3.50	7	5	2	14
I	4.00	8	5	2	15

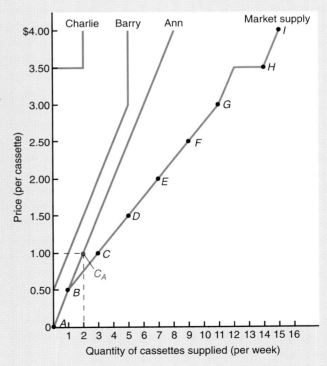

(a) A supply table

(b) Adding supply curves

KNOWING THE TOOLS

Six Things to Remember When Considering a Supply Curve

- A supply curve follows the law of supply. When price rises, quantity supplied increases, and vice versa.
- The horizontal axis—quantity—has a time dimension.
- The quantities are of the same quality.
- The vertical axis—price—assumes all other prices remain constant.
- The curve assumes everything else is constant.
- Effects of price changes are shown by movements along the supply curve. Effects of nonprice determinants of supply are shown by shifts of the entire supply curve.

Q-7 Derive the market supply curve from the following two individual supply curves.

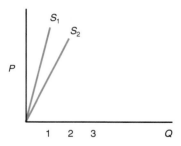

The law of supply is based on two phenomena:

1. At higher prices, existing suppliers supply more.
2. At higher prices, new suppliers enter the market.

From a Supply Table to a Supply Curve

Figure 4-7(b) takes the information in Figure 4-7(a)'s supply table and translates it into a graph of each supplier's supply curve. For instance, point C_A on Ann's supply curve corresponds to the information in columns 1 and 2, row C. Point C_A is at a price of $1 per cassette and a quantity of 2 cassettes per week. Notice that Ann's supply curve is upward sloping, meaning that price is positively related to quantity. Charlie's and Barry's supply curves are similarly derived.

The supply curve represents the set of *minimum* prices an individual seller will accept for various quantities of a good. The market's invisible hand stops suppliers from charging more than the market price. If suppliers could escape the market's invisible hand and charge a higher price, they would gladly do so. Unfortunately for them, and fortunately for consumers, a higher price encourages other suppliers to begin selling cassettes. Competing suppliers' entry into the market sets a limit on the price any supplier can charge.

Individual and Market Supply Curves

The market supply curve is derived from individual supply curves in precisely the same way that the market demand curve was. To emphasize the symmetry, I've made the three suppliers quite similar to the three demanders. Ann (column 2) will supply 2 at $1; if price goes up to $2, she increases her supply to 4. Barry (column 3) begins supplying at $1, and at $3 supplies 5, the most he'll supply regardless of how high price rises. Charlie (column 4) has only two units to supply. At a price of $3.50 he'll supply that quantity, but higher prices won't get him to supply any more.

The **market supply curve** is *the horizontal sum of all individual supply curves.* In Figure 4-7(a) (column 5), we add together Ann's, Barry's, and Charlie's supply to arrive at the market supply curve, which is graphed in Figure 4-7(b). Notice that each point on it corresponds to the information in columns 1 and 5 for each row. For example, point H corresponds to a price of $3.50 and a quantity of 14.

The market supply curve's upward slope is determined by two different sources: by existing suppliers supplying more and by new suppliers entering the market. Sometimes existing suppliers may not be willing to increase their quantity supplied in response to an increase in prices, but a rise in price often brings brand-new suppliers into the market. For example, a rise in teachers' salaries will have little effect on the amount of teaching current teachers do, but it will increase the number of people choosing to be teachers.

THE MARRIAGE OF SUPPLY AND DEMAND

Thomas Carlyle, the English historian who dubbed economics "the dismal science," also wrote this chapter's introductory tidbit. "Teach a parrot the words *supply* and *demand* and you've got an economist." In earlier chapters, I tried to convince you that economics is *not* dismal. In the rest of this chapter, I hope to convince you that, while supply and demand are important to economics, parrots don't make good economists. If students think that when they've learned the terms *supply* and *demand* they've learned economics, they're mistaken. Those terms are just labels for the ideas behind supply and demand, and it's the ideas that are important. What matters about supply and demand isn't the labels but how the concepts interact. For instance, what happens if a freeze kills the blossoms on the orange trees? The quantity of oranges supplied isn't expected to equal the quantity demanded. It's in understanding the interaction of supply and demand that economics becomes interesting and relevant.

Excess Supply

When you have a market in which neither suppliers nor consumers can collude and in which prices are free to adjust, economists have a good answer for the question: What happens if quantity supplied doesn't equal quantity demanded? If there is **excess supply** (a surplus), *quantity supplied is greater than quantity demanded,* and some suppliers won't be able to sell all their goods. Each supplier will think: "Gee, if I offer to sell it for a bit less, I'll be the lucky one who sells my goods; someone else will be stuck with not selling their goods." But because all suppliers with excess goods will be thinking the same thing, the price in the market will fall. As that happens, consumers will increase their quantity demanded. So the movement toward equilibrium caused by excess supply is on both the supply and demand sides.

Excess Demand

The reverse is also true. Say that instead of excess supply, there's **excess demand** (a shortage)—*quantity demanded is greater than quantity supplied.* There are more consumers who want the good than there are suppliers selling the good. Let's consider what's likely to go through demanders' minds. They'll likely call long-lost friends who just happen to be sellers of that good and tell them it's good to talk to them and, by the way, don't they want to sell that . . . ? Suppliers will be rather pleased that so many of their old friends have remembered them, but they'll also likely see the connection between excess demand and their friends' thoughtfulness. To stop their phones from ringing all the time, they'll likely raise their price. The reverse is true for excess supply. It's amazing how friendly suppliers become to potential consumers when there's excess supply.

Q-8 Explain what a sudden popularity of "Economics Professor" brand casual wear would likely do to prices of that brand.

Price Adjusts

This tendency for prices to rise when the quantity demanded exceeds the quantity supplied and for prices to fall when the quantity supplied exceeds the quantity demanded is a central element to understanding supply and demand. So remember:

 4.1

> When quantity demanded is greater than quantity supplied, prices tend to rise.
> When quantity supplied is greater than quantity demanded, prices tend to fall.

Two other things to note about supply and demand are (1) the greater the difference between quantity supplied and quantity demanded, the more pressure there is for prices to rise or fall, and (2) when quantity demanded equals quantity supplied, the market is in equilibrium.

People's tendencies to change prices exist as long as there's some difference between quantity supplied and quantity demanded. But the change in price brings the laws of supply and demand into play. As price falls, quantity supplied decreases as some suppliers leave the business (the law of supply). And as some people who originally weren't really interested in buying the good think, "Well, at this low price, maybe I do want to buy," quantity demanded increases (the law of demand). Similarly, when price rises, quantity supplied will increase (the law of supply) and quantity demanded will decrease (the law of demand).

Whenever quantity supplied and quantity demanded are unequal, price tends to change. If, however, quantity supplied and quantity demanded are equal, price will stay the same because no one will have an incentive to change.

The Graphical Marriage of Supply and Demand

Figure 4-8 shows supply and demand curves for cassette rentals and demonstrates the force of the invisible hand. Let's consider what will happen to the price of cassettes in three cases:

  1. When the price is $3.50 each;

  2. When the price is $1.50 each; and

  3. When the price is $2.50 each.

Q.9 In a flood, it is ironic that usable water supplies tend to decline because the pumps and water lines are damaged. What will a flood likely do to the prices of bottled water?

  1. When price is $3.50, quantity supplied is 7 and quantity demanded is only 3. Excess supply is 4. Individual consumers can get all they want, but most suppliers can't sell all they wish; they'll be stuck with cassettes that they'd like to rent. Suppliers will tend to offer their goods at a lower price and demanders, who see plenty of suppliers out there, will bargain harder for an even lower price. Both these forces will push the price as indicated by the A arrows in Figure 4-8.

Now let's start from the other side.

Figure 4-8   The Marriage of Supply and Demand

Combining Ann's supply from Figure 4-7 and Alice's demand from Figure 4-4, let's see the force of the invisible hand. When there is excess demand there is upward pressure on price. When there is excess supply there is downward pressure on price. Understanding these pressures is essential to understanding how to apply economics to reality.

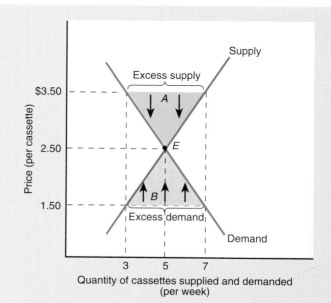

2. Say price is $1.50. The situation is now reversed. Quantity supplied is 3 and quantity demanded is 7. Excess demand is 4. Now it's consumers who can't get what they want and suppliers who are in the strong bargaining position. The pressures will be on price to rise in the direction of the *B* arrows in Figure 4-8.

3. At $2.50, price is at its equilibrium: quantity supplied equals quantity demanded. Suppliers offer to sell 5 and consumers want to buy 5, so there's no pressure on price to rise or fall. Price will tend to remain where it is (point *E* in Figure 4-8). Notice that the equilibrium price is where the supply and demand curves intersect.

EQUILIBRIUM

The concept of equilibrium appears often throughout this text. You need to understand what equilibrium is and what it isn't.

What Equilibrium Is

The concept itself comes from physics—classical mechanics. **Equilibrium** is *a concept in which opposing dynamic forces cancel each other out*. For example, a hot-air balloon is in equilibrium when the upward force exerted by the hot air in the balloon equals the downward pressure exerted on the balloon by gravity. In supply and demand analysis, equilibrium means that the upward pressure on price is exactly offset by the downward pressure on price. **Equilibrium price** is *the price toward which the invisible hand drives the market*. **Equilibrium quantity** is *the amount bought and sold at the equilibrium price*.

4.2

So much for what equilibrium is. Now let's consider what it isn't.

What Equilibrium Isn't

First, equilibrium isn't a state of the world. It's a characteristic of the model—the framework you use to look at the world. The same situation could be seen as an equilibrium in one framework and as a disequilibrium in another. Say you're describing a car that's speeding along at 100 miles an hour. That car is changing position relative to objects on the ground. Its movement could be, and generally is, described as if it were in disequilibrium. However, if you consider this car relative to another car going 100 miles an hour, the cars could be modeled as being in equilibrium because their positions relative to each other aren't changing.

Second, equilibrium isn't inherently good or bad. It's simply a state in which dynamic pressures offset each other. Some equilibria are awful. Say two countries are engaged in a nuclear war against each other and both sides are blown away. An equilibrium will have been reached, but there's nothing good about it.

Equilibrium is not inherently good or bad.

Desirable Characteristics of Supply/Demand Equilibrium

While there is nothing necessarily good about equilibrium, the supply/demand equilibrium has certain desirable characteristics that are very important when applying economic analysis. To see those desirable characteristics, let's consider what the demand curve and supply curve are telling us. Each of these curves tells us how much individuals would be willing to pay (in the case of demand) or accept (in the case of supply) for a good. Thus, in Figure 4-9(a) a consumer at quantity 2 would be willing to pay $8 for a good, and the supplier would be willing to sell it for $2.

Figure 4-9 (a and b)   Consumer and Producer Surplus

Market equilibrium price and quantity maximizes the combination of consumer surplus (shown in blue) and producer surplus (shown in red) as demonstrated in **(a).** When price deviates from its equilibrium as in **(b),** combined consumer and producer surplus falls. The gray shaded region shows the loss of total surplus when price is $1 higher than equilibrium price.

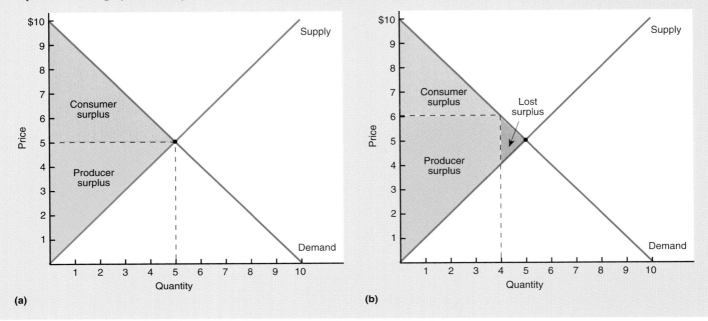

(a)   (b)

Q.10 If price moves from disequilibrium to equilibrium, what happens to the combination of producer and consumer surplus in the market?

If the consumer pays less than what he's willing to pay, he walks away better off. Thus, the distance between the demand curve and the price he pays is a net gain for the consumer. Economists call this net benefit **consumer surplus**—*the value the consumer gets from buying a product less its price.* It is represented by the area underneath the demand curve and above the price that an individual pays. Thus, with the price at equilibrium ($5), consumer surplus is represented by the blue area.

Similarly, if a producer receives more than the price she would be willing to sell it for, she too receives a net benefit. Economists call this gain **producer surplus**—*the price the producer sells a product for less the cost of producing it.* It is represented by the area above the supply curve but below the price the producer receives. Thus, with the price at equilibrium ($5), producer surplus is represented by the red area.

What's good about equilibrium is that it makes the combination of consumer and producer surpluses as large as it can be. To see this, say that for some reason the equilibrium price is held at $6. Consumers will demand only 4 units of the good, and some suppliers are not able to sell all the goods they would like. The combined producer and consumer surplus will decrease, as shown in Figure 4-9(b). The gray triangle represents lost consumer and producer surplus. In general, a deviation of price from equilibrium lowers the combination of producer and consumer surplus. This is one of the reasons economists support markets and why we teach the supply/demand model. It gives us a visual sense of what is good about markets: By allowing trade, markets maximize the combination of consumer and producer surplus.

To fix the ideas of consumer and producer surplus in your mind, let's consider a couple of real-world examples. Think about the water you drink. What does it cost? Almost

APPLYING THE TOOLS

The Supply and Demand for Children

In Chapter 1, I distinguished between an economic force and a market force. Economic forces are operative in all aspects of our lives; market forces are economic forces that are allowed to be expressed through a market. My examples in this chapter are of market forces—of goods sold in a market—but supply and demand can also be used to analyze situations in which economic, but not market, forces operate. An economist who is adept at this is Gary Becker of the University of Chicago. He has applied supply and demand analysis to a wide range of issues, even the supply and demand for children.

Becker doesn't argue that children should be bought and sold. But he does argue that economic considerations play a large role in people's decisions on how many children to have. In farming communities, children can be productive early in life; by age six or seven, they can work on a farm. In an advanced industrial community, children provide pleasure but generally don't contribute productively to family income. Even getting them to help around the house can be difficult.

Becker argues that since the price of having children is lower for a farming society than for an industrial society, farming societies will have more children per family. Quantity of children demanded will be larger. And that's what we find. Developing countries that rely primarily on farming often have three, four, or more children per family. Industrial societies average fewer than two children per family.

nothing. Given that water is readily available, it has a low price. But since you'd die from thirst if you had no water, you are getting an enormous amount of consumer surplus from that water. Next, consider a ballet dancer who loves the ballet so much he'd dance for free. But he finds that people are willing to pay to see him and that he can receive $400 a performance. He is receiving producer surplus.

CONCLUSION

Throughout the book I'll be presenting examples of supply and demand. So I'll end this chapter here because its intended purposes have been served. What were those intended purposes? First, I exposed you to enough economic terminology and economic thinking to allow you to proceed to my more complicated examples. Second, I have set your mind to work putting the events around you into a supply/demand framework. Doing that will give you new insights into the events that shape all our lives. Once you incorporate the supply/demand framework into your way of looking at the world, you will have made an important step toward thinking like an economist.

Chapter Summary

- The law of demand states that quantity demanded rises as price falls, other things constant.
- The law of supply states that quantity supplied rises as price rises, other things constant.
- Factors that affect supply and demand other than price are called shift factors. Shift factors of demand include income, prices of other goods, tastes, and expectations. Shift factors of supply include the price of inputs, technology, expectations, and taxes and subsidies.

- A change in quantity demanded (supplied) is a movement along the demand (supply) curve. A change in demand (supply) is a shift of the entire demand (supply) curve.
- The laws of supply and demand hold true because individuals can substitute.
- A market demand (supply) curve is the horizontal sum of all individual demand (supply) curves.

● When quantity demanded is greater than quantity supplied, prices tend to rise. When quantity supplied is greater than quantity demanded, prices tend to fall.

● When quantity supplied equals quantity demanded, prices have no tendency to change. This is equilibrium.

● Equilibrium maximizes the combination of consumer surplus and producer surplus. Consumer surplus is the net benefit a consumer gets from purchasing a good, while producer surplus is the net benefit a producer gets from selling a good.

Key Terms

consumer surplus (98)
demand (85)
demand curve (84)
equilibrium (97)
equilibrium price (97)
equilibrium quantity (97)

excess demand (95)
excess supply (95)
law of demand (83)
law of supply (90)
market demand
  curve (88)

market supply curve (94)
movement along a demand
  curve (85)
movement along a supply
  curve (91)
quantity demanded (85)
quantity supplied (91)

producer surplus (98)
shift in supply (91)
supply (91)
supply curve (90)

Questions for Thought and Review

1. State the law of demand. Why is price inversely related to quantity demanded?

2. State the law of supply. Why is price directly related to quantity supplied?

3. List four shift factors of demand and explain how each affects demand.

4. Distinguish the effect of a shift factor of demand on the demand curve from the effect of a change in price on the demand curve.

5. Draw a market demand curve from the following demand table.

P	Q
37	20
47	15
57	10
67	5

6. Draw a demand curve from the following demand table.

P	D_1	D_2	D_3
37	20	4	8
47	15	2	7
57	10	0	6
67	5	0	5

7. Mary has just stated that normally, as price rises, supply will increase. Her teacher grimaces. Why?

8. List four shift factors of supply and explain how each affects supply.

9. Draw a market supply curve from the following supply table.

P	S_1	S_2	S_3
37	0	4	14
47	0	8	16
57	10	12	18
67	10	16	20

10. It has just been reported that eating meat is bad for your health. Using supply and demand curves, demonstrate the report's likely effect on the price and quantity of steak sold in the market.

11. Explain why the combination of consumer and producer surplus is not maximized if there is either excess demand or supply.

12. Use economic reasoning to explain why nearly every purchase you make provides you with consumer surplus.

Problems and Exercises

1. You're given the following individual demand tables for comic books.

Price	John	Liz	Alex
$ 2	4	36	24
4	4	32	20
6	0	28	16
8	0	24	12
10	0	20	8
12	0	16	4
14	0	12	0
16	0	8	0

a. Determine the market demand table.
b. Graph the individual and market demand curves.
c. If the current market price is $4, what's total market demand? What happens to total market demand if price rises to $8?
d. Say that an advertising campaign increases demand by 50 percent. Illustrate graphically what will happen to the individual and market demand curves.

2. Draw hypothetical supply and demand curves for tea. Show how the equilibrium price and quantity will be affected by each of the following occurrences:
a. Bad weather wreaks havoc with the tea crop.
b. A medical report implying tea is bad for your health is published.
c. A technological innovation lowers the cost of producing tea.
d. Consumers' income falls.

3. This is a question concerning what economists call the *identification problem*. Say you go out and find figures on the quantity bought of various products. You will find something like the following:

Product	Year	Quantity	Average Price
VCRs	1995	100,000	$210
	1996	110,000	220
	1997	125,000	225
	1998	140,000	215
	1999	135,000	215
	2000	160,000	220

Plot these figures on a graph.
a. Have you plotted a supply curve, a demand curve, or what?

b. If we assume that the market for VCRs is competitive, what information must you know to determine whether these are points on a supply curve or on a demand curve?
c. Say you know that the market is one in which suppliers set the price and allow the quantity to vary. Could you then say anything more about the curves you have plotted?
d. What information about shift factors would you expect to find to make these points reflect the law of demand?

4. You're a commodity trader and you've just heard a report that the winter wheat harvest will be 2.09 billion bushels, a 44 percent jump, rather than an expected 35 percent jump to 1.96 billion bushels.
a. What would you expect would happen to wheat prices?
b. Demonstrate graphically the effect you suggested in *a*.

5. In the United States, gasoline costs consumers about $1.50 per gallon. In Italy it costs consumers about $5 per gallon. What effect does this price differential likely have on:
a. The size of cars in the United States and in Italy?
b. The use of public transportation in the United States and in Italy?
c. The fuel efficiency of cars in the United States and in Italy? What would be the effect of raising the price of gasoline in the United States to $4 per gallon?

6. Use the graph below to answer the following questions:

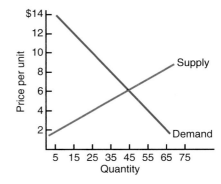

a. What is equilibrium price and quantity?
b. What is producer surplus when the market is in equilibrium?
c. What is consumer surplus when the market is in equilibrium?
d. If price were held at $10 a unit, what is consumer and producer surplus?

Web Questions

1. Go to the U.S. Census Bureau's home page (www.census.gov) and find data about the proportion of the U.S. population in three age groups from 0 to 85+ for this year, for 2025, and for 2050. Report your findings. Other things constant, what do you expect will happen in the next 50 years to the relative demand and supply for each of the following, being careful to distinguish between shifts of and a movement along a curve:
   a. Nursing homes.
   b. Prescription medication.
   c. Baby high chairs.
   d. College education.

2. Go to the Energy Information Administration's home page (www.eia.doe.gov) and look up its most recent "Short-Term Energy Outlook" and answer the following questions:
   a. List the factors that are expected to affect demand and supply for energy in the near term. How will each affect demand? Supply?

   b. What is the EIA's forecast for world oil prices? Show graphically how the factors listed in your answer to (a) are consistent with the EIA's forecast. Label all shifts in demand and supply.
   c. Describe and explain EIA's forecast for the price of gasoline, heating oil and natural gas. Be sure to mention the factors that are affecting the forecast.

3. Go to the Tax Administration home page (www.taxadmin.org) and look up sales tax rates for the 50 U.S. states.
   a. Which states have no sales tax? Which state has the highest sales tax?
   b. Show graphically the effect of sales tax on supply, demand, equilibrium quantity, and equilibrium price.
   c. Name two neighboring states that have significantly different sales tax rates. How does that affect the supply or demand for goods in those states?

Answers to Margin Questions

1. The demand curve slopes downward because price and quantity demanded are inversely related. As the price of a good rises, people switch to purchasing other goods whose prices have not risen by as much. *(84)*

2. *Demand for furs.* The other possibility, *quantity demanded,* is used to refer to movements along (not shifts of) the demand curve. *(85)*

3. (1) The decline in price will increase the quantity of computers demanded (movement down along the demand curve); (2) With more income, demand for computers will rise (shift of the demand curve to the right). *(85)*

4. When adding two demand curves, you sum them horizontally, as in the accompanying diagram. *(88)*

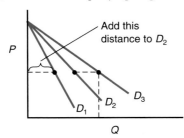

5. "The quantity supplied" declined because there was a movement along the supply curve. The supply curve itself remained unchanged. *(91)*

6. (1) The supply of romance novels declines since paper is an input to production (supply shifts to the left); (2) the supply of romance novels declines since the tax

increases the cost to the producer (supply shifts to the left). *(92)*

7. When adding two supply curves, sum horizontally the two individual supply curves, as in the diagram below. *(94)*

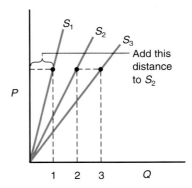

8. Customers will flock to stores demanding that funky "Economics Professor" look, creating excess demand. This excess demand will soon catch the attention of suppliers, and prices will be pushed upward. *(95)*

9. As substitutes—tap water—decrease, demand for bottled water increases enormously, and there will be upward pressure on prices. Social and political forces will, however, likely work in the opposite direction—against "profiteering" in people's misery. *(96)*

10. The combination of consumer and producer surplus will increase since there will be no lost surplus at the equilibrium price. *(98)*

Using Supply and Demand

5

After reading this chapter, you should be able to:

- Show the effect of a shift in demand and supply on equilibrium price and quantity.

- Explain real-world events using supply and demand.

- Demonstrate the effect of a price ceiling and a price floor on a market.

- Explain the effect of taxes, tariffs, and quotas on equilibrium price and quantity.

- State the limitations of demand and supply analysis.

- State six roles of government.

It is by invisible hands that we are bent and tortured worst.

Nietzsche

In the last chapter I introduced you to the concepts of supply and demand. In this chapter I will (1) show you the power of supply and demand, (2) show you how the invisible hand interacts with social and political forces to change the outcome of supply and demand analysis; and (3) discuss how one must adjust supply and demand analysis with other issues kept at the back of one's mind.

THE POWER OF SUPPLY AND DEMAND

To ensure that you understand the supply and demand graphs throughout the book, and can apply them, let's go through an example. Figure 5-1(a) deals with an increase in demand. Figure 5-1(b) deals with a decrease in supply.

Figure 5-1 (a and b)   Shifts in Supply and Demand

When there is an increase in demand (the demand curve shifts outward), there is upward pressure on the price, as shown in (a). If demand increases from D_0 to D_1, the quantity of cassette rentals that was demanded at a price of $2.25, 8, increases to 10, but the quantity supplied remains at 8. This excess demand tends to cause prices to rise. Eventually, a new equilibrium is reached at the price of $2.50, where the quantity supplied and the quantity demanded is 9 (point B).

If supply of cassette rentals decreases, then the entire supply curve shifts inward to the left, as shown in (b), from S_0 to S_1. At the price of $2.25, the quantity supplied has now decreased to 6 cassettes, but the quantity demanded has remained at 8 cassettes. The excess demand tends to force the price upward. Eventually, an equilibrium is reached at the price of $2.50 and quantity 7 (point C).

(a) A shift in demand

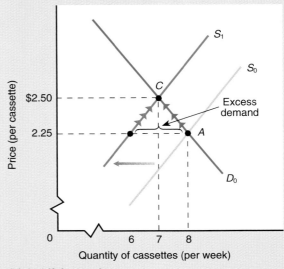

(b) A shift in supply

Q-1 Demonstrate graphically the effect of a heavy frost in Florida on the equilibrium quantity and price of oranges.

Q-2 Say a hormone has been discovered that increases cows' milk production by 20 percent. Demonstrate graphically what effect this discovery would have on the price and quantity of milk sold in a market.

Let's consider again the supply and demand for videocassette rentals from Chapter 4. In Figure 5-1(a), the supply is S_0 and initial demand is D_0. They meet at an equilibrium price of $2.25 per cassette and an equilibrium quantity of 8 cassettes per week (point A). Now say that the demand for cassette rentals increases from D_0 to D_1. At a price of $2.25, the quantity of cassette rentals supplied will be 8 and the quantity demanded will be 10; excess demand of 2 exists.

The excess demand pushes prices upward in the direction of the small arrows, decreasing the quantity demanded and increasing the quantity supplied. As it does so, movement takes place along both the supply curve and the demand curve.

The upward push on price decreases the gap between the quantity supplied and the quantity demanded. As the gap decreases, the upward pressure decreases, but as long as that gap exists at all, price will be pushed upward until the new equilibrium price ($2.50) and new quantity (9) are reached (point B). At point B, quantity supplied equals quantity demanded. So the market is in equilibrium. Notice that the adjustment is twofold: The higher price brings about equilibrium by both increasing the quantity supplied (from 8 to 9) and decreasing the quantity demanded (from 10 to 9).

Figure 5-1(b) begins with the same situation that we started with in Figure 5-1(a); the initial equilibrium quantity and price are 8 cassettes per week and $2.25 per cassette (point A). In this example, however, instead of demand increasing, let's assume supply decreases—say because some suppliers change what they like to do, and decide they will no longer supply cassettes. That means that the entire supply curve shifts inward to the left (from S_0 to S_1). At the initial equilibrium price of $2.25, the quantity demanded is greater than the quantity supplied. Two more cassettes are demanded than are supplied. (Excess demand = 2.)

This excess demand exerts upward pressure on price. Price is pushed in the direction of the small arrows. As the price rises, the upward pressure on price is reduced but will still exist until the new equilibrium price, $2.50, and new quantity, 7, are reached. At $2.50, the quantity supplied equals the quantity demanded. The adjustment has involved a movement along the demand curve and the new supply curve. As price rises, quantity supplied is adjusted upward and quantity demanded is adjusted downward until quantity supplied equals quantity demanded where the new supply curve intersects the demand curve at point C, an equilibrium of 7 and $2.50.

Here is an exercise for you to try. Demonstrate graphically how the price of computers could have fallen dramatically in the past 10 years, even as demand increased. (Hint: Supply has shifted even more, so even at lower prices, far more computers have been supplied than were being supplied 10 years ago.)

Six Real-World Examples

Now that we've been through a generic example of shifts in supply and demand, let's consider some real-world examples. Below are six events. After reading each, try your hand at explaining what happened, using supply and demand curves. To help you in the process Figure 5-2 provides some diagrams. *Before* reading my explanation try to match the shifts to the examples. In each, be careful to explain which curve, or curves, shifted and how those shifts affected equilibrium price and quantity.

1. A 1997 freeze caused more than $300 million in damage to Florida crops. Prices of some vegetables rose by 25 percent just one week after the freeze. Squash, for example, which had cost $1.16 per pound on January 17, cost $1.40 per pound on January 24. Market: Vegetables.

2. In the mid-1990s the 76 million U.S. baby boomers started to put away more and more savings for retirement. This saving was directed toward the purchase of financial assets, driving up the price of stocks. Market: Financial assets.

3. In 1991 Congress imposed a 10 percent tax on the sale of luxury boats. In response, some boat owners held on to their old boats longer. Others bought boats in the Bahamas to escape the tax. Market: Luxury boats. (Because of the uproar from the producers of luxury boats, Congress repealed the tax in 1993.)

4. Rice is crucial to Indonesia's nutritional needs and its rituals. In 1997, drought, pestilence, and a financial crash led to disruptions in the availability of rice. Its price rose so high that in 1998 more than one-fourth of all Indonesians could not buy enough market-priced rice to meet their daily needs. Government programs to deliver subsidized rice were insufficient to bring the price of rice back to affordable levels. Market: Rice in Indonesia.

5. In late summer 1998, U.S. farmers were hard pressed to find enough seasonal farmhands. Why? El Niño's weather patterns compressed the harvest season. Grape, apple, and peach growers who usually harvested at different times were competing for the same workers. In addition, stronger efforts by the Immigration and Naturalization Service (INS) had reduced the flow of illegal workers to the United States. Market: Farm laborers.

6. Every Christmas a new toy becomes the craze. In 1997 it was Tickle Me Elmo and in 1998 it was Furby. Before Christmas Day, these toys were hard to find and sold for as much as 10 times their retail price on what is called the black market. Here we use the Furby as the example. Toymaker Tiger, along with

Q-3   Demonstrate graphically the likely effect of an increase in the price of gas on the equilibrium quantity and price of compact cars.

 5.1

Figure 5-2 (a–f)

In this exhibit, six shifts of supply and demand are shown. Your task is to match them with the events listed in the chapter.

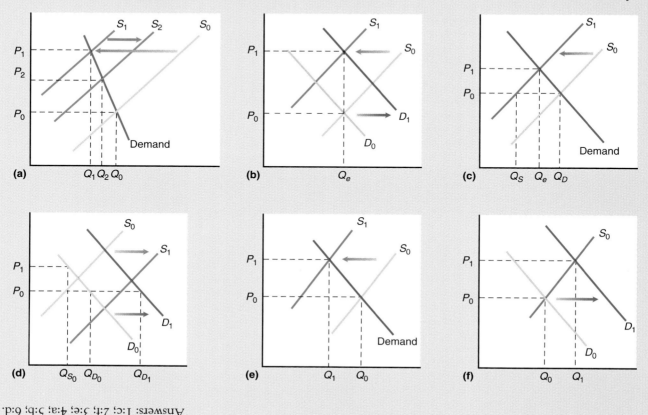

Answers: 1:c; 2:f; 3:e; 4:a; 5:b; 6:d.

retailers, worked up initial interest in Furby just before Thanksgiving, advertising the limited supply. On the day after Thanksgiving, the biggest Christmas shopping day, as early as 2:00 A.M., lines formed at the stores carrying Furbies. Some shoppers (including "toy scouts") who were able to buy Furbies and resold them as soon as that afternoon for as much as $300 apiece in the black market. Even with the shortage, retailers kept the price at its preset advertised price and producers continued to limit distribution. Newspapers carried stories about the lines and black market prices, intensifying demand for Furbies, which became even harder to come by. Days before Christmas the supplier increased shipments of Furbies to meet the increased demand. Customers felt "lucky" when they were able to find Furbies with so few days left before Christmas, and for only $30 instead of $300 on the black market. Market: Furbies in 1998.

Florida Freeze The weather is invariably uncooperative. Nearly every other year, Florida or some other state is hit with a crop-damaging freeze. This is a shift factor of supply because it raises the cost of supplying remaining vegetables. The 1997 freeze shifted the supply curve for Florida vegetables in, as shown in Figure 5-2(c). At the original price, $1.16 per pound (shown by P_0), quantity demanded exceeded quantity supplied and the invisible hand of the market pressured the price to rise until quantity demanded equaled quantity supplied at $1.40 per pound (shown by P_1).

Financial Assets and the Baby Boomers The postwar population swell we call the baby boom resulted in increased demand for all sorts of products as the boomers entered college, then bought houses, and now are demanding more health care and financial assets. In this case, demographic changes have led to a shift out in the demand curve for financial assets, resulting in a rise in stock market prices and an increase in the quantity of stocks and mutual funds supplied. This is depicted in Figure 5-2(f). This figure could also be used to describe the huge rise in housing prices in the 1980s as baby boomers began to purchase houses.

Excise Taxes In Chapter 4's discussion of shift factors, I explained that taxes levied on the supplier will reduce supply. The 10 percent excise tax will shift the supply curve in. That some boat owners hold on to their older boats and others look elsewhere to buy boats is substitution at work, and a movement up along the demand curve. Figure 5-2(e) shows this scenario. After the tax, price rises to P_1 and quantity of boats sold declines to Q_1.

Rice in Indonesia Drought, pestilence, and the financial crash all increased the cost of supplying rice in Indonesia, shifting the supply of rice in from S_0 to S_1 in Figure 5-2(a). Since rice is so important to the well-being of Indonesians, quantity demanded doesn't change much with changes in price. This is shown by the steep demand curve. The price rose to levels unaffordable to many people. In response, the government purchased imported rice and distributed it to the market. This shifted the supply curve out from S_1 to S_2. Since the price was still above its previous level, we know that this second shift in supply is smaller than the first.

Farm Laborers In this case both supply and demand shift, but this time in opposite directions. The previous year's demand is represented in Figure 5-2(b) by D_0 and supply is shown by S_0. Q_e laborers were hired at a wage of P_0. The compressed harvesting season meant that more farmers were looking for laborers, shifting the demand for farm workers out from D_0 to D_1. This put upward pressure on wages and increased quantity of labor supplied. Simultaneously, however, the supply of farm workers shifted in from S_0 to S_1 as the INS increased border patrols. This put further upward pressure on wages and reduced the quantity of labor demanded. Wages are clearly bid up, in this case to P_1. The effect on the number of laborers hired, however, depends on the relative size of the demand and supply shifts. As I have drawn it, the quantity of laborers hired returns to the quantity of the previous year, Q_e. If the supply shift were greater than the shift in demand, the number of laborers would have declined. If it were smaller, the number of laborers would have risen.

Christmas Toys In this example, both supply and demand shift in the same direction. The initial market is shown by D_0 and S_0 in Figure 5-2(d). The price of $30 (shown by P_0) was below the equilibrium price and a shortage of $Q_{D_0} - Q_{S_0}$ existed. The black market price of $300 (shown by P_1) is shown by the amount that consumers are willing to pay for the quantity supplied, Q_{S_0}. As the craze for the toy intensified following the free newspaper publicity of the lines and black market prices, demand shifted out to D_1. Price was kept at $30 and the shortage became even greater, $Q_{D_1} - Q_{S_0}$. When Tiger made more Furbies available, supply shifted to S_1, eliminating most, but not all, of the shortage.

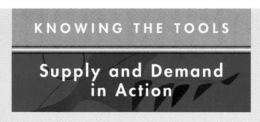

Sorting out the effects of the shifts of supply or demand or both can be confusing. Here are some helpful hints to keep things straight:

- Draw the initial demand and supply curves and label them. The equilibrium price and quantity is where these curves intersect. Label them.

- If only price has changed, no curves will shift and a shortage or surplus will result.

KNOWING THE TOOLS

Supply and Demand in Action

- If a nonprice factor affects demand, determine the direction demand has shifted and add the new demand curve. Do the same for supply.

- Equilibrium price and quantity is where the new demand and supply curves intersect. Label them.

- Compare the initial equilibrium price and quantity to the new equilibrium price and quantity.

See if you can describe what happened in the three graphs below.

A change in price

A shift in demand

A shift in supply

A Review

Anything other than price that affects demand or supply will shift the curves.

As you can see, supply and demand analysis can get quite complicated. That is why you must separate shifts in demand and supply from movements along the supply and demand curves. Remember: Anything that affects demand and supply other than price of the good will shift the curves. Changes in the price of the good result in movements along the curves. Another thing to recognize is that when both curves are shifting you can get a change in price but little change in quantity, or a change in quantity but little change in price.

To test your understanding, I'll now give you six generic results from the interaction of supply and demand. Your job is to decide what shifts produced those results. This exercise is a variation of the first. It goes over the same issues, but this time without the graphs. On the left-hand side of the table below, I list combinations of movements of observed prices and quantities, labeling them 1–6. On the right I give six shifts in supply and demand, labeling them *a–f*.

If you don't confuse your "shifts of" with your "movements along," supply and demand provide good off-the-cuff answers for any economic questions.

Price and Quantity Changes		
1.	P↑	Q↑
2.	P↑	Q↓
3.	P↑	Q?
4.	P↓	Q?
5.	P?	Q↑
6.	P↓	Q↓

Shifts in Supply and Demand

a. Supply shifts in. No change in demand.
b. Demand shifts out. Supply shifts in.
c. Demand shifts in. No change in supply.
d. Demand shifts out. Supply shifts out.
e. Demand shifts out. No change in supply.
f. Demand shifts in. Supply shifts out.

You are to match the shifts with the price and quantity movements that best fit each described shift, using each shift and movement only once. My recommendation to you is to draw the graphs that are described in *a–f*, decide what happens to price and quantity, and then find the match in 1–6.

Now that you've worked them, let me give you the answers I came up with. They are: 1:*e*; 2:*a*; 3:*b*; 4:*f*; 5:*d*; 6:*c*. How did I come up with the answers? I did what I suggested you do—took each of the scenarios on the right and predicted what happens to price and quantity. For case *a*, supply shifts in and there is a movement up along the demand curve. Since the demand curve is downward sloping, the price rises and quantity declines. This matches number *2* on the left. For case *b*, demand shifts out. Along the original supply curve, price and quantity would rise. But supply shifts in, leading to even higher prices, but lower quantity. What happens to quantity is unclear, so the match must be number *3*. For case *c*, demand shifts in. There is movement down along the supply curve with lower price and lower quantity. This matches number 6. For case *d*, demand shifts out and supply shifts out. As demand shifts out, we move along the supply curve to the right and price and quantity rise. But supply shifts out too, and we move out along the new demand curve. Price declines, erasing the previous rise, and the quantity rises even more. This matches number 5.

I'll leave it up to you to confirm my answers to *e* and *f*. Notice that when supply and demand both shift, the change in either price or quantity is uncertain—it depends on the relative size of the shifts. As a summary, I present a diagrammatic of the combinations in Table 5-1.

Q-4 If both demand and supply shift in, what happens to price and quantity?

Table 5-1   Diagram of Effects of Shifts of Demand and Supply on Price and Quantity

This table provides a summary of the effects of shifts in supply and demand on price and quantity. Notice that when both curves shift, the effect on either price or quantity depends on the relative size of the shifts.

	No change in supply.	Supply shifts out.	Supply shifts in.
No change in demand.	No change.	P↓ Q↑ Price declines and quantity rises.	P↑ Q↓ Price rises. Quantity declines.
Demand shifts out.	P↑ Q↑ Price rises. Quantity rises.	P? Q↑ Quantity rises. Price could be higher or lower depending upon relative size of shifts.	P↑ Q? Price rises. Quantity could rise or fall depending upon relative size of shifts.
Demand shifts in.	P↓ Q↓ Price declines. Quantity declines.	P↓ Q? Price declines. Quantity could rise or fall depending upon relative size of shifts.	P? Q↓ Quantity declines. Price rises or falls depending upon relative sizeof shifts.

GOVERNMENT INTERFERENCES: PRICE CEILINGS AND PRICE FLOORS

People don't always like the market-determined price. When prices fall, sellers look to government for ways to hold prices up; when prices rise, buyers look to government for ways to hold prices down. Let's now consider the effect of such actions. Let's start with an example of the price being held down.

Price Ceilings

When government wants to hold prices down, it imposes a **price ceiling**—*a government-imposed limit on how high a price can be charged.* Rent control is an example of a price ceiling. (For the price ceiling to be effective, it must be below the equilibrium price, and throughout this discussion we shall assume that it is.)

5.2

Specifically, let's consider rent control in Paris in 1948. **Rent control** is *a price ceiling on rents set by government.* During World War I, to stabilize housing prices and help out those fighting for France, rents were frozen. Upon the return of veterans, the freeze was held in the interest of society. In 1926, rent control was reviewed but by that time, lifting the controls would have resulted in huge increases in rents. Rents were allowed to rise only slightly. Again, during World War II, rents were frozen. Right after the end of World War II rent was capped at $2.50 a month. Without rent control, rent would have been $17 a month.

This was a good situation for those occupying apartments, but it had drawbacks. For instance, there was an enormous shortage of apartments. The situation is shown in Figure 5-3.

What were the results of the rent control besides the shortage of apartments? More than 80 percent of Parisians had no private bathrooms and 20 percent had no running water. Since rental properties weren't profitable, no new buildings were being constructed and existing buildings weren't kept in repair. From 1914 (before World War I) to 1948, the housing stock increased by only 10 percent. Many couldn't find housing in Paris. Couples lived with their in-laws. Existing apartments had to be rationed in some way. To get into a rent-controlled apartment, individuals paid bribes up to $1,500 per

Figure 5-3   Rent Control In Paris

A price ceiling imposed on housing rent in Paris during World War I created a shortage of housing when World War I ended and veterans returned home. The shortage would have been eliminated if rents had been allowed to rise to $17 per month.

room or watched the obituaries and then simply moved in their furniture before anyone else did. Eventually the situation got so bad that rent controls were lifted.

The system of rent controls is not only of historical interest. Below I list some phenomena that existed in New York City recently.

1. A couple pays $350 a month for a two-bedroom Park Avenue apartment with a solarium and two terraces, while another individual pays $1,200 a month for a studio apartment shared with two roommates.

2. The vacancy rate for apartments in New York City is currently 3.5 percent. Anything under 5 percent is considered a housing emergency.

3. The actress Mia Farrow pays $2,900 a month (a fraction of the market-clearing rent) for 10 rooms on Central Park West. It is an apartment her mother first leased 50 years ago.

4. Would-be tenants make payments, called key money, to current tenants or landlords to get apartments.

Your assignment is to explain how these phenomena might have come about, and to demonstrate, with supply and demand, the situation that likely caused them. (Hint: New York City does have rent control.)

Now that you have done your assignment (you have, haven't you?), let me give you my answers so that you can check them with your answers.

The situation is identical with that presented above in Figure 5-3. Take the first item. The couple lives in a rent-controlled apartment while the individual with roommates does not. If rent control were eliminated, rent on the Park Avenue apartment would rise and rent on the studio would most likely decline. Item 2: The housing emergency is a result of rent control. Below-market rent results in excess demand and little vacancy. Item 3: That Mia Farrow rents a rent-controlled apartment is the result of nonprice rationing. Instead of being rationed by price, other methods of rationing can arise. These other methods of rationing scarce resources are called nonprice rationing. In New York City, strict rules determine the handing down of rent-controlled apartments from family member to family member. Item 4: New residents must search for a long time to find apartments to rent, and many discover that illegal payments to landlords are the only way to obtain a rent-controlled apartment. Key money is a black market payment for a rent-controlled apartment. Because of the limited supply of apartments, individuals are willing to pay far more than the controlled price. Landlords can use other methods of rationing the limited supply of apartments—instituting first-come, first-served policies, and, in practice, selecting tenants based on gender, race, or other personal characteristics, even though such discriminatory selection is illegal.

Price Floors

Sometimes political forces favor suppliers, sometimes consumers. So let us now go briefly through a case when the government is trying to favor suppliers by attempting to prevent the price from falling below a certain level. **Price floors**—*government-imposed limits on how low a price can be charged*—do just this. An example of a price floor is the minimum wage. Both individual states and the federal government impose **minimum wage laws**—*laws specifying the lowest wage a firm can legally pay an employee*. The U.S. federal government first instituted a minimum wage of 25 cents per hour in 1938 as part of the Fair Labor and Standards Act. It has been raised many times since, and in the early 2000s there was a push to raise it to over $6.00 an hour. (With inflation, that's a much smaller increase than it looks.) The minimum wage affects about 10 million U.S.

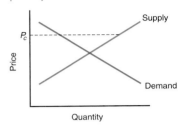

Q-5 What is the effect of the price ceiling, P_c, shown in the graph below on price and quantity?

With price ceilings, existing goods are no longer rationed entirely by price. Other methods of rationing existing goods arise called nonprice rationing.

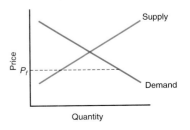

Q-6 What is the effect of the price floor, P_f, shown in the graph below on price and quantity?

Figure 5-4   A Minimum Wage

A minimum wage, W_{min}, above equilibrium wage, W_e, helps those who are able to find work, shown by Q_2, but hurts those who would have been employed at the equilibrium wage but can no longer find employment, shown by $Q_e - Q_2$. A minimum wage also hurts producers who have higher costs of production and consumers who may face higher product prices.

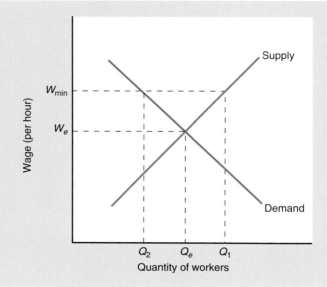

The minimum wage helps some people and hurts others.

workers who are mostly unskilled. The market-determined equilibrium wage for skilled workers is generally above the minimum wage.

The effect of a minimum wage on the unskilled labor market is shown in Figure 5-4. The government-set minimum wage is above equilibrium, as shown by W_{min}. At the market-determined equilibrium wage W_e, the quantity of labor supplied and demanded equals Q_e. At the higher minimum wage, the quantity of labor supplied rises to Q_1 and the quantity of labor demanded declines to Q_2. There is an excess supply of workers (a shortage of jobs) represented by the difference $Q_2 - Q_1$. This represents people who are looking for work but cannot find it.

Who wins and who loses from a minimum wage? The minimum wage improves the wages of the Q_2 workers who are able to find work. Without the minimum wage, they would have earned W_e per hour. The minimum wage hurts those, however, who cannot find work at the minimum wage but who are willing to work, and would have been hired, at the market-determined wage. These workers are represented by the distance $Q_e - Q_2$ in Figure 5-4. The minimum wage also hurts firms who now must pay their workers more, increasing the cost of production. The minimum wage also hurts consumers to the extent that firms are able to pass that increase in production cost on in the form of higher product prices.

All economists agree that the above analysis is logical and correct. But they disagree about whether governments should have minimum wage laws. One reason is that the empirical effects of minimum wage laws are difficult to determine, since "other things" are never remaining constant. A second reason is that some real-world labor markets are not sufficiently competitive to fit the supply/demand model. The third reason is that the minimum wage affects the economy in ways that some economists see as desirable and others see as undesirable. I point this out to remind you that the supply/demand framework is a tool to be used to analyze issues. It does not provide final answers about policy. (In microeconomics, economists explore the policy issues of interferences in markets much more carefully.)

Figure 5-5   The Effect of an Excise Tax

An excise tax on suppliers shifts the entire supply curve up by the amount of the tax. Since at a price equal to the original price plus the tax there is excess supply, the price of the good rises by less than the tax.

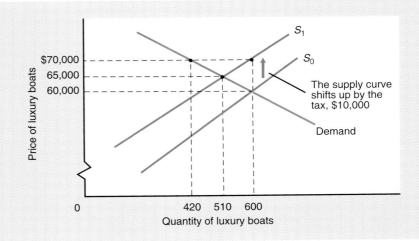

GOVERNMENT INTERFERENCES: TAXES, TARIFFS, AND QUOTAS

Let's now consider an example of the government entering into a market and modifying the results of supply/demand analysis in the form of a tax. An **excise tax** is *a tax that is levied on a specific good.* The luxury tax on expensive cars that the United States imposed in 1991 is an example. A **tariff** is *an excise tax on an imported good.* What effect will excise taxes and tariffs have on the price and quantity in a market?

Excise Taxes and Tariffs

To lend some sense of reality, let's take the example from the early 1990s when the United States put a tax on some luxury goods, in this case expensive boats. This tax was paid by the supplier. Say the price of a boat before the luxury tax was $60,000, and 600 boats were sold at that price. Now the government places a tax of $10,000 on such boats. What will the new price of the boat be, and how many will be sold?

If you were about to answer "The new price will be $70,000," be careful. Ask yourself whether I would have given you that question if the answer were that easy. By looking at supply and demand curves in Figure 5-5 you can see why $70,000 is the wrong answer.

To supply 600 boats, suppliers must be fully compensated for the tax. So the tax of $10,000 on the supplier shifts the supply curve up from S_0 to S_1. However, at $70,000, consumers are not willing to purchase 600 boats. They are willing to purchase only 420 boats. Quantity supplied exceeds quantity demanded at $70,000. Suppliers lower their prices until quantity supplied equals quantity demanded at $65,000, the new equilibrium price. Consumers increase the quantity of boats they are willing to purchase to 510, still less than the original 600 at $60,000. Why? At the higher price of $65,000 some people choose not to buy boats and others find substitute vehicles or purchase their boats outside the United States.

Notice that at the new equilibrium the new price is $65,000, not $70,000. The reason is that at the higher price, the quantity of boats people demand is less. This is a movement up along a demand curve to the left. Excise taxes reduce the quantity of goods demanded. That's why boat manufacturers were up in arms after the tax was

A tax on suppliers shifts the supply curve up by the amount of the tax.

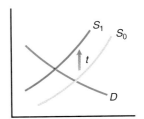

Q-7   Your study partner, Umar, has just stated that a tax on demanders of $2 per unit will raise the equilibrium price from $4 to $6. How do you respond?

Figure 5-6 (a and b)   The Relationship between a Quota and a Tariff

Figure (a) shows the effect of a quota of 5 million cars on the price of Japanese cars sold. Price rises from $9,000 to $17,000. Figure (b) demonstrates that a tax of $11,000 on each Japanese car sold in the United States has the same effect as the quota shown in (a). The difference between a quota and a tariff lies in who gets the revenue. With a quota, the firm selling the good gets the revenue as additional profits. With a tariff, the government gets the revenue shown by the shaded box in (b).

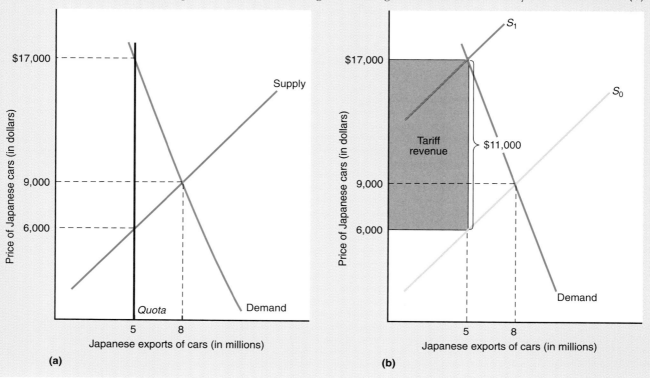

(a)

(b)

imposed and why the revenue generated from the tax was less than expected. Instead of collecting $10,000 × 600 ($6 million), revenue collected was only $10,000 × 510 ($5.1 million). The tax was repealed in 1993.

Quotas

The next example I want to consider is the imposition of a quantity control—a legal restriction on the quantity that can be bought or sold. The most common type of quantity control is the international **quota**—*a quantitative restriction on the amount that one country can export to another.* A recent instance of a quota occurred when the United States wanted to restrict U.S. imports of Japanese cars. I show the effect in Figure 5-6(a).

The market price of a Japanese car is $9,000. At that price, U.S. consumers demand, and Japanese car makers are willing to supply, 8 million cars. But, when the United States places an import quota of, say, 5 million cars into the United States, U.S. consumers are willing to pay $17,000 a car even though Japanese firms are willing to sell them for $6,000 apiece. Of course, sellers will accept what consumers are willing to pay, and the price of Japanese cars rises to $17,000. Notice what the effect of the quota is. It raises the price of Japanese cars in the United States.

The Relationship between a Quota and a Tariff

Above we considered the effect of both quotas and taxes, and I noted that a tariff is a type of excise tax. Both devices increase price and reduce quantity. Let's now compare the effects of the quota above with the results of a tariff that would have achieved the same reduction in output.

I show the effects of such a tariff in Figure 5-6(b). There you can see that a tariff of $11,000 shifts the supply curve in sufficiently to end up with the same sale of 5 million Japanese cars obtained with the quota. Consumers still pay $17,000 for Japanese cars.

Is there a difference between the two cases? The answer is yes. In the quota case, the higher price brings in more revenue to the company. In the tariff case, the revenue goes to the government. So which of the two do you think companies favor? The quota, of course—it means more profits as long as your company is one of those to receive the rights to fill those quotas. In fact, once quotas are instituted Japanese firms compete intensely to get them.

There is such a U.S. tariff on light trucks from Japan, which is why here in the United States you see few light trucks from Japan. You will see Japanese trucks, but these most likely were not produced in Japan. As Japan has internationalized its production facilities, many of its cars and trucks are no longer produced in Japan. They are produced in countries such as Canada and France and, especially, the United States. In fact, as I noted in Chapter 3, Japanese auto companies are the largest exporters of cars from the United States.

A quota of Q_1 has the same effect as a tax t.

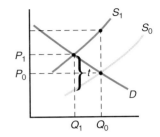

Q.8 Why do firms prefer quotas to tariffs?

THE LIMITATIONS OF SUPPLY AND DEMAND ANALYSIS

I hope the above discussion has convinced you of the power of supply and demand analysis. Now let's discuss some of its limitations. Supply and demand are tools, and, like most tools, they help us enormously when used appropriately. Used inappropriately, however, they can reduce our understanding. Throughout the book I'll introduce you to the limitations of the tools, but let me discuss an important one here.

Other Things Don't Remain Constant

In supply and demand analysis other things are assumed equal. If other things change, then one cannot directly apply supply/demand analysis. Sometimes supply and demand are interconnected, making it impossible to hold other things constant. Let's take an example. Say we are considering the effect of a fall in the wage rate. In supply/demand analysis, you would look at the effect that fall would have on workers' decisions to supply labor, and on business's decision to hire workers. But might there be other effects? For instance, might the fall in the wage lower people's income, and thereby reduce the demand for firms' goods? And might that reduction affect firms' demand for workers? If these effects do occur, and are important enough to affect the result—those effects have to be added to the analysis in order for you to have a complete analysis.

Deciding whether such issues are important enough to affect the result requires a knowledge of the structure of the economy. All actions have a multitude of ripple or feedback effects—they create waves, like those that spread out from a stone thrown into a pool. These waves bounce back, and then hit other waves, which create new waves which . . . . The art of applying supply/demand analysis is determining which of these multitude of ripple effects affect the analysis sufficiently that they must be added back to the analysis.

Q.9 When determining the effect of a shift factor on price and quantity, in which of the following markets could you likely assume that other things will remain constant?

1. Market for eggs.
2. Labor market.
3. World oil market.
4. Market for luxury boats.

There is no single answer to the question of which ripples must be included, and much debate among economists involves which ripple effects to include. But there are some general rules. Supply/demand analysis, used without adjustment, is most appropriate for questions where the goods are a small percentage of the entire economy. That is when the other-things-constant assumption will most likely hold. As soon as one starts analyzing goods that are a large percentage of the entire economy, the other-things-constant assumption is likely not to hold true. The reason is found in the **fallacy of composition**—*the false assumption that what is true for a part will also be true for the whole.*

The Fallacy of Composition

Let's consider the fallacy of composition more carefully. When you are analyzing one individual's actions, small effects of an individual's actions can reasonably be assumed to be too small to change the results of supply/demand analysis. However, when you are analyzing the whole, or a significant portion of the whole, these small effects add up to a big effect. To see this, think of one supplier lowering the price of his or her good. People will substitute that good for other goods, and the quantity of the good demanded will increase. But what if all suppliers lower their prices? Since all prices have gone down, why should consumers switch? The substitution story can't be used in the aggregate. There are many such examples.

An understanding of the fallacy of composition is of central relevance to macroeconomics. In the aggregate, whenever firms produce (whenever they supply), they create income (demand for their goods). So in macro, when supply changes, demand changes. This interdependence is one of the primary reasons we have a separate macroeconomics. In macroeconomics, the other-things-constant assumption central to microeconomic supply/demand analysis cannot hold. In macroeconomics, output creates income and income is spent on output. When the output side increases, so does the income side.

It is to account for these interdependencies that we have a separate macro analysis and micro analysis. In macro we use curves whose underlying foundations are much more complicated than the supply and demand curves we use in micro.

One final comment: The fact that there may be an interdependence between supply and demand does not mean that you can't use supply and demand analysis; it simply means that you must modify its results with the interdependency that, if you've done the analysis correctly, you've kept in the back of your head. Thus using supply and demand analysis is generally a step in any good economic analysis, but you must remember that it may be only a step.

The fallacy of composition gives you some insight into why economists separate micro from macro. One of the important side effects of decisions that must be considered in macro, but not in micro, is the side effect of spending decisions. Your spending decision is someone else's income, and someone else's spending decision creates your income. The circular flow diagram presented in Chapter 3 (Figure 3-1) demonstrated that interconnection.

In our economy people can spend what they want; there is no direct mechanism in the economy that coordinates our spending decisions. Thus, the composite of all spending decisions may be either lots of spending or little spending. As that spending changes, output changes, and the economy experiences a business cycle.

THE ROLES OF GOVERNMENT

It is important to recognize both the strengths and weaknesses of supply and demand analysis because much of this book will involve a consideration of government policy issues within a supply/demand framework. To set the foundation for that discussion I will

---

Margin notes:

The fallacy of composition is the false assumption that what is true for a part will also be true for the whole.

It is to account for interdependency between aggregate supply decisions and aggregate demand decisions that we have a separate micro analysis and a separate macro analysis.

Q-10 Why is the fallacy of composition relevant for macroeconomic issues?

BEYOND THE TOOLS

Laissez-Faire is Not Anarchy

Most reasons for government intervention discussed in this chapter are debatable.

There is, however, one governmental role that even the strongest laissez-faire advocates generally accept. That role is for government to set up an appropriate institutional and legal structure within which markets can operate.

The reason there's little debate about this role is that all economists recognize that markets do not operate when there is anarchy. They require institutional structures that determine the rules of ownership, what types of trade are allowable, how contracts will be enforced, and what productive institutions are most desirable.

Before anyone conducts business, he or she needs to know the rules of the game and must have a reasonable expectation that those rules will not be changed. The operation of the modern economy requires that contractual arrangements be made among individuals. These con-

tractual arrangements must be enforced if the economy is to operate effectively.

Economists differ significantly as to what the rules for such a system should be and whether any rules that already exist should be modified. Even if the rules are currently perceived as unfair, it can be argued that they should be kept in place. Individuals have already made decisions based on those rules, and it's unfair to them to change the rules in the middle of the game.

Stability of rules is a benefit to society. When the rules are perceived as unfair and changing them is also perceived as unfair, the government must find a balance between these two degrees of unfairness. Government often finds itself in that difficult position. Thus, while there's little debate about government's role in providing some institutional framework, there's heated debate about which framework is most appropriate.

---

conclude this chapter by considering the general roles of a government within a market economy. This will establish the framework for consideration of policy in later chapters.

Government's roles in a market economy include (1) providing a stable set of institutions and rules, (2) promoting effective and workable competition, (3) correcting for externalities, (4) ensuring economic stability and growth, (5) providing public goods, and (6) adjusting for undesired market results.

Provide a Stable Set of Institutions and Rules

A basic role of government is to provide a stable institutional framework that includes the set of laws specifying what can and cannot be done as well as a mechanism to enforce those laws. Before people conduct business, they need to know the rules of the game and have a reasonable belief about what those rules will be in the future. These rules can initially develop spontaneously, but as society becomes more complex, the rules must be codified; enforcement mechanisms must be established. The modern market economy requires enforceable complex contractual arrangements among individuals. Where governments don't provide a stable institutional framework, as often happens in developing and transitional countries, economic activity is difficult; usually such economies are stagnant. Russia in the late 1990s is an example. As various groups fought for political control, the Russian economy stagnated.

Promote Effective and Workable Competition

In a market economy the forces of monopoly and competition are always in conflict, and the government must decide what role it is to play in protecting or promoting competition. Historically, U.S. sentiment runs against monopoly power. **Monopoly power** is *the ability of individuals or firms currently in business to prevent other individuals or firms from entering the same kind of business.* Monopoly power gives existing firms and individuals the ability to raise their prices. Similarly, individuals' or firms' ability to enter freely into business activities is generally seen as good. Government's job is to promote competition and prevent excess monopoly power from limiting competition.

Roles of government in a market economy are:

1. providing a stable set of institutions and rules;
2. promoting effective and workable competition;
3. correcting for externalities;
4. ensuring economic stability and growth;
5. providing public goods; and
6. adjusting for undesired market results.

What makes this a difficult function for government is that most individuals and firms believe that competition is far better for the other guy than it is for themselves, that their own monopolies are necessary monopolies, and that competition facing them is unfair competition. For example, most farmers support competition, but these same farmers also support government farm subsidies (payments by government to producers based on production levels) and import restrictions. Likewise, most firms support competition, but these same firms also support tariffs, which protect them from foreign competition. Most professionals, such as architects and engineers, support competition, but they also support professional licensing, which limits the number of competitors who can enter their field. Now, as you will see in reading the newspapers, there are always arguments for limiting entry into fields. The job of the government is to determine whether these arguments are strong enough to overcome the negative effects those limitations have on competition.

Correct for Externalities

When two people freely enter into a trade or agreement, they both believe that they will benefit from the trade. But unless they're required to do so, traders are unlikely to take into account any effect that an action may have on a third party. Economists call *the effect of a decision on a third party not taken into account by the decision maker* an **externality.** An externality can be positive (in which case society as a whole benefits by the trade between the two parties) or negative (in which case society as a whole is harmed by the trade between the two parties).

An example of a positive externality is education. When someone educates herself or himself, all society benefits, since better-educated people usually make better citizens and are better equipped to figure out new approaches to solving problems—approaches that benefit society as a whole. An example of a negative externality is pollution. Air conditioners emit a small amount of chlorofluorocarbons into the earth's atmosphere and contribute to the destruction of the ozone layer. Since the ozone layer protects all living things by filtering some of the sun's harmful ultraviolet light rays, a thinner layer of ozone can contribute to cancer and other harmful or fatal conditions. Neither the firms that produce the air conditioners nor the consumers who buy them take those effects into account. This means that the destruction of the ozone layer is an externality—the result of an effect that is not taken into account by market participants.

When there are externalities, there is a potential role for government to adjust the market result. If one's goal is to benefit society as much as possible, actions with positive externalities should be encouraged and actions with negative externalities should be restricted. Governments can step in and change the rules so that the actors must take into account the effect of their actions on society as a whole. I emphasize that the role is a potential one for two reasons. The first is that government often has difficulty dealing with externalities in such a way that society gains. For example, even if the U.S. government totally banned products that emit chlorofluorocarbons, other countries might not do the same and the ozone layer would continue to be destroyed. The second reason is that government is an institution that reflects, and is often guided by, politics and vested interests. It's not clear that, given the political realities, government intervention to correct externalities would improve the situation. In later chapters I'll have a lot more to say about government's role in correcting for externalities.

Ensure Economic Stability and Growth

In addition to providing general stability, government has the potential role of providing economic stability. If it's possible, most people would agree that government should

When there are externalities, there is a potential role for government.

prevent large fluctuations in the level of economic activity, maintain a relatively constant price level, and provide an economic environment conducive to economic growth. These aims, which became the goals of the U.S. government in 1946 when the Employment Act was passed, are generally considered macroeconomic goals. They're justified as appropriate aims for government to pursue because they involve **macroeconomic externalities** (*externalities that affect the levels of unemployment, inflation, or growth in the economy as a whole*).

Here's how a macro externality could occur. When individuals decide how much to spend, they don't take into account the effects of their decision on others; thus, there may be too much or too little spending. Too little spending often leads to unemployment. But in making their spending decision, people don't take into account the fact that spending less might create unemployment. So their spending decisions can involve a macro externality. Similarly, when people raise their price and don't consider the effect on inflation, they too might be creating a macro externality.

A macroeconomic externality is the effect of an individual decision that affects the levels of unemployment, inflation, or growth in an economy as a whole, but is not taken into account by the individual decision maker.

Provide for Public Goods

A **public good** is *a good that if supplied to one person must be supplied to all and whose consumption by one individual does not prevent its consumption by another individual*. In contrast, a **private good** is *a good that, when consumed by one individual, cannot be consumed by another individual*. An example of a private good is an apple; once I eat that apple, no one else can consume it. National defense is generally considered a public good.

There are very few pure public goods, but many goods have public good aspects to them, and in general economists use the term *public good* to describe goods that are most efficiently provided collectively rather than privately. Parks, playgrounds, roads, and national defense are examples. Let's consider national defense more closely. For technological reasons national defense must protect all individuals in an area; a missile system cannot protect some houses in an area without protecting others nearby.

Everyone agrees that national defense is needed, but not everyone takes part in it. If someone else defends the country, you're defended for free; you can be a **free rider**—*a person who participates in something for free because others have paid for it*. Because self-interested people would like to enjoy the benefits of national defense while letting someone else pay for it, everyone has an incentive to be a free rider. But if everyone tries to be a free rider, there won't be any national defense. In such cases government can step in and require that everyone pay part of the cost of national defense, reducing the free rider problem.

Adjust for Undesired Market Results

A controversial role for government is to adjust the results of the market when those market results are seen as socially undesirable. An example is income distribution. Many people believe the government should see to it that income is "fairly" distributed. Determining what's fair is a difficult philosophical question. Let's consider two of the many manifestations of the fairness problem. Should the government use a **progressive tax** (*a tax whose rates increase as a person's income increases*) to redistribute money from the rich to the poor? (A progressive income tax schedule might tax individuals at a rate of 15 percent for income up to $20,000; at 25 percent for income between $20,000 and $40,000; and at 35 percent for every dollar earned over $40,000.) Or should government impose a **regressive tax** (*a tax whose rates decrease as income rises*) to redistribute money from the poor to the rich? Or should government impose a flat or **proportional tax** (*a tax whose rates are constant at all income levels, no matter what a taxpayer's total annual income is*)? Such a tax might be, say, 25 percent of every dollar of income. The United States has chosen a somewhat progressive income tax, while the social security tax is a proportional tax up to a specified earned income. Economists can tell government the effects of various types of taxes and forms of taxation, but we can't tell government what's fair. That is for the people, through the government, to decide.

Another example of this role involves having government decide what's best for people, independently of their desires. The market allows individuals to decide. But what if people don't know what's best for themselves? Or what if they do know but don't act on that knowledge? For example, people might know that addictive drugs are bad for them, but because of peer pressure, or because they just don't care, they may take drugs anyway. Government action prohibiting such activities through laws or high taxes may then be warranted. *Goods or activities that government believes are bad for people even though they choose to use the goods or engage in the activities* are called **demerit goods or activities.** Illegal drugs are a demerit good and using addictive drugs is a demerit activity.

Alternatively, there are some activities that government believes are good for people, even if people may not choose to engage in them. For example, government may believe that going to the opera or contributing to charity is a good activity. But in the United States only a small percentage of people go to the opera, and not everyone in the United States contributes to charity. Similarly, government may believe that whole-wheat bread is more nutritious than white bread. But many consumers prefer white bread. Goods like whole-wheat bread and activities like contributing to charity are known as **merit goods or activities**—*goods and activities that government believes are good for you even though you may not choose to engage in the activities or consume the goods.* Government sometimes provides support for them through subsidies or tax benefits.

> With merit and demerit goods, individuals are assumed not to be doing what is in their self-interest.

Market Failures and Government Failures

The reasons for government intervention are often summed up in the phrase *market failure*. **Market failures** are *situations in which the market does not lead to a desired result.* In the real world, market failures are pervasive—the market is always failing in one way or another. But the fact that there are market failures does not mean that government intervention will improve the situation. There are also **government failures**—*situations in which the government intervenes and makes things worse.* Government failures are pervasive in the government—the government is always failing in one way or another. So real-world policymakers usually end up choosing which failure—market failure or government failure—will be least problematic.

CONCLUSION

I will conclude the chapter here. We will talk much more about these roles of government in later chapters. For now, I simply want you to understand the general policy framework. When you combine that general policy framework with the supply/demand framework that I presented in Chapter 4 and the first part of this chapter, you have a good foundation for understanding the economic way of thinking about policy issues.

Chapter Summary

- When the demand curve shifts to the right (left), equilibrium price rises (declines) and equilibrium quantity rises (falls).

- When the supply curve shifts to the right (left), equilibrium price declines (rises) and equilibrium quantity rises (falls).

- By minding your *Ps* and *Qs*—the shifts of and movements along curves—you can describe almost all events in terms of supply and demand.

- A price ceiling is a government-imposed limit on how high a price can be charged. Price ceilings below market price create shortages.

● A price floor is a government-imposed limit on how low a price can be charged. Price floors above market price create surpluses.

● Taxes and tariffs paid by suppliers shift the supply curve up by the amount of the tax or tariff. They raise the equilibrium price (inclusive of tax) and decrease the equilibrium quantity.

● Quotas restrict the quantity of goods that one country can export to another. They increase equilibrium price and reduce equilibrium quantity. The effect of a quota on equilibrium price and quantity is the same as a tariff. The difference between the two is who gets the additional revenue.

● In macro, small side effects that can be assumed away in micro are multiplied enormously. Thus, they can significantly change the results and cannot be ignored. To ignore them is to fall into the fallacy of composition.

● Six roles of government are (1) to provide a stable set of institutions and rules, (2) to promote effective and workable competition, (3) to correct for externalities, (4) to ensure economic stability and growth, (5) to provide public goods, and (6) to adjust for undesired market results.

Key Terms

demerit goods or activities *(120)*

excise tax   *(113)*

externality   *(118)*

fallacy of composition   *(116)*

free rider   *(119)*

government failure   *(120)*

macroeconomic externality   *(119)*

market failure   *(120)*

merit goods or activities *(120)*

minimum wage laws   *(111)*

monopoly power   *(117)*

price ceiling   *(110)*

price floor   *(111)*

private good   *(119)*

progressive tax   *(119)*

proportional tax   *(119)*

public good   *(119)*

quota   *(114)*

regressive tax   *(119)*

rent control   *(110)*

tariff   *(113)*

Questions for Thought and Review

1. Say that the price and quantity both fell. What would you say was the most likely cause?

2. Say that price fell and quantity remained constant. What would you say was the most likely cause?

3. Demonstrate graphically the effect of a price ceiling.

4. Demonstrate graphically why rent controls might increase the total payment that new renters pay for an apartment.

5. Demonstrate graphically the effect of a price floor.

6. Graphically show the effects of a minimum wage on the number of unemployed.

7. Oftentimes, to be considered for a job, you have to know someone in the firm. What does this observation tell you about the wage paid for that job?

8. In most developing countries, there are long lines of taxis at airports, and these taxis often wait two or three hours. What does this tell you about the price in that market? Demonstrate with supply and demand analysis.

9. Supply/demand analysis states that equilibrium occurs where quantity supplied equals quantity demanded, but in U.S. agricultural markets quantity supplied almost always exceeds quantity demanded. How can this be?

10. Demonstrate graphically the effect of a tax of $4 per unit on equilibrium price and quantity.

11. Using a graph like the one you drew for question 10 above, show graphically a quota that leads to the same price and quantity.

12. You've set up the rules for a game and started the game, but now realize that the rules are unfair. Should you change the rules?

13. Say the government establishes rights to pollute so that without a pollution permit you aren't allowed to emit pollutants into the air, water, or soil. Firms are allowed to buy and sell these rights. In what way will this correct for an externality?

14. What are six roles of government?

Problems and Exercises

1. Since 1981, the U.S. government has supported the price of sugar produced by U.S. sugar producers by limiting import of sugar into the United States. Restricting imports is effective because the United States consumes more sugar than it produces.

a. Using supply/demand analysis, demonstrate how import restrictions increases the price of domestic sugar.

b. What other import policy could the government implement to have the same effect as the import restriction?

c. Under the Uruguay Round of the General Agreement on Tariffs and Trade in 1997, the United States agreed to permit at least 1.25 million tons of sugar to be imported into the United States. How does this affect the U.S. sugar price support program?

2. "Scalping" is the name given to the buying of tickets at a low price and reselling them at a high price. The following information about a Florida State–Notre Dame game in 1993 comes from a newspaper. At the beginning of the season:

a. Tickets sell for $27 and are sold out in preseason.

b. Halfway through the season, both teams have maintained unbeaten records. Resale price of tickets rises to $200.

c. One week before the game, both teams have remained unbeaten and are ranked 1 and 2. Ticket price rises to $600.

d. Three days before the game, price falls to $400.

Demonstrate, using supply/demand analysis and words, what might have happened to cause these fluctuations in price.

3. In some states and localities "scalping" is against the law, although enforcement of these laws is spotty (difficult).

a. Using supply/demand analysis and words, demonstrate what a weakly enforced antiscalping law would likely do to the price of tickets.

b. Using supply/demand analysis and words, demonstrate what a strongly enforced antiscalping law would likely do to the price of tickets.

4. Apartments in New York City are often hard to find. One of the major reasons is that there is rent control.

a. Demonstrate graphically how rent controls could make apartments hard to find.

b. Often one can get an apartment if one makes a side payment to the current tenant. Can you explain why?

c. What would be the likely effect of eliminating rent controls?

d. What is the political appeal of rent controls?

5. Until recently, angora goat wool (mohair) has been designated as a strategic commodity (it used to be utilized in some military clothing). Because of that, in 1992 for every dollar's worth of mohair sold to manufacturers, ranchers received $3.60.

a. Demonstrate graphically the effect of the elimination of this designation and subsidy.

b. Explain why the program was likely kept in existence for so long.

c. Say that a politician has suggested that the government should pass a law that requires all consumers to pay a price for angora goat wool high enough so that the sellers of that wool would receive $3.60 more than the market price. Demonstrate the effect of the law graphically. Would consumers support it? How about suppliers?

6. The technology is now developing so that road use can be priced by computer. A computer in the surface of the road picks up a signal from your car and automatically charges you for the use of the road.

a. How could this technological change contribute to ending bottlenecks and rush hour congestion?

b. What are some of the problems that might develop with such a system?

c. How would your transportation habits likely change if you had to pay to use roads?

7. In 1938 Congress created a Board of Cosmetology in Washington, D.C., to license beauticians. In 1992 this law was used by the board to close down a hair-braiding salon specializing in cornrows and braids operated by Mr. Uqdah, even though little is taught in cosmetology schools about braiding and cornrows.

a. What possible reason can you give for why this board exists?

b. What options might you propose to change the system?

c. What will be the political difficulties of implementing those options?

Web Questions

1. Go to the Cato Institute's home page (www.cato.org) and search for the article "How Rent Control Drives Out Affordable Housing" by William Tucker. After reading the article, answer the following questions:

a. What is a shadow market, and why does one develop when there is rent control?

b. Why is housing a particularly easy good to hoard? How does this affect newcomers to a city?

c. How do vacancy rates compare among cities with and without rent control? Does this make sense within the supply/demand framework?

2. Go to the Economic Policy Institute's home page (www.epinet.org) and search the catalog for the article "The Next Step" by Jared Bernstein. Using that article, answer the following questions:
   a. What has happened to the minimum wage adjusted for inflation since 1979? Within the standard supply/demand framework, how does this affect unemployment resulting from the minimum wage?
   b. Who is affected by the minimum wage?
   c. What effect does the article say that the minimum wage has on job loss? What evidence does the author cite?

Answers to Margin Questions

1. A heavy frost in Florida will decrease the supply of oranges, increasing the price and decreasing the quantity demanded, as in the accompanying graph. *(104)*

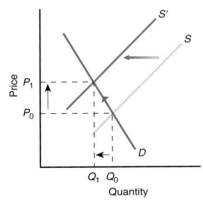

2. A discovery of a hormone that will increase cows' milk production by 20 percent will increase the supply of milk, pushing the price down and increasing the quantity demanded, as in the accompanying graph. *(104)*

3. An increase in the price of gas will likely increase the demand for compact cars, increasing their price and increasing the quantity supplied, as in the accompanying graph. *(105)*

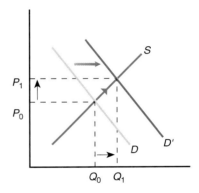

4. Quantity decreases but it is unclear what happens to price. *(109)*

5. Since the price ceiling is above the equilibrium price, it will have no effect on the market-determined equilibrium price and quantity. *(111)*

6. Since the price floor is below the equilibrium price, it will have no effect on the market-determined equilibrium price and quantity. *(111)*

7. I state that the tax will most likely raise the price by less than $2 since the tax will cause the quantity demand to decrease. This will decrease quantity supplied, and hence decrease the price the suppliers receive. In the diagram below, Q falls from Q_0 to Q_1 and the price the supplier receives falls from $4 to $3, making the final price $5, not $6. *(113)*

8. Firms prefer quotas to tariffs because with quotas, they receive additional profit; with tariffs, the government receives tax revenues. *(115)*

9. Other things are most likely to remain constant in the egg and luxury boat markets because each is a small percentage of the whole economy. Factors that affect the world oil market and the labor market will have ripple effects that must be taken into account in any analysis. *(115)*

10. The fallacy of composition is relevant for macroeconomic issues because it reminds us that, in the aggregate, small effects that are immaterial for micro issues can add up and be material. *(116)*

APPENDIX A

Algebraic Representation of Supply, Demand, and Equilibrium

In Chapters 4 and 5, I discussed demand, supply, and the determination of equilibrium price and quantity in words and graphs. These concepts can also be presented in equations. In this appendix I do so, using straight-line supply and demand curves.

THE LAWS OF SUPPLY AND DEMAND IN EQUATIONS

Since the law of supply states that quantity supplied is positively related to price, the slope of an equation specifying a supply curve is positive. (The quantity intercept term is generally less than zero since suppliers are generally unwilling to supply a good at a price less than zero.) An example of a supply equation is:

$$Q_S = -5 + 2P$$

where Q_S is units supplied and P is the price of each unit in dollars per unit. The law of demand states that as price rises, quantity demanded declines. Price and quantity are negatively related, so a demand curve has a negative slope. An example of a demand equation is:

$$Q_D = 10 - P$$

where Q_D is units demanded and P is the price of each unit in dollars per unit.

Determination of Equilibrium

The equilibrium price and quantity can be determined in three steps using these two equations. To find the equilibrium price and quantity for these particular demand and supply curves, you must find the quantity and price that solve both equations simultaneously.

Step 1: Set the quantity demanded equal to quantity supplied:

$$Q_S = Q_D \rightarrow -5 + 2P = 10 - P$$

Step 2: Solve for the price by rearranging terms. Doing so gives:

$$3P = 15$$
$$P = \$5$$

Thus, equilibrium price is $5.

Step 3: To find equilibrium quantity, you can substitute $5 for P in either the demand or supply equation. Let's do it for supply: $Q_S = -5 + (2 \times 5) = 5$ units. I'll leave it to you to confirm that the quantity you obtain by substituting $P = \$5$ in the demand equation is also 5 units.

The answer could also be found graphically. The supply and demand curves specified by these equations are depicted in Figure A5-1. As you can see, demand and supply intersect; quantity demanded equals quantity supplied at a quantity of 5 units and a price of $5.

Movements along a Demand and Supply Curve

The demand and supply curves above represent schedules of quantities demanded and supplied at various prices. Movements along each can be represented by selecting various prices and solving for quantity demanded and supplied. Let's create a supply and demand table using the above equations—supply: $Q_S = -5 + 2P$; demand: $Q_D = 10 - P$.

Figure A5-1   Supply and Demand Equilibrium

The algebra in this appendix leads to the same results as the geometry in the chapter. Equilibrium occurs where quantity supplied equals quantity demanded.

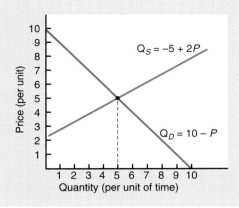

P	$Q_S = -5 + 2P$	$Q_D = 10 - P$
$ 0	−5	10
1	−3	9
2	−1	8
3	1	7
4	3	6
5	5	5
6	7	4
7	9	3
8	11	2
9	13	1
10	15	0

As you move down the rows, you are moving up along the supply schedule, as shown by increasing quantity supplied, and moving down along the demand schedule, as shown by decreasing quantity demanded. Just to confirm your equilibrium quantity and price calculations, notice that at a price of $5, quantity demanded equals quantity supplied.

Shifts of a Demand and Supply Schedule

What would happen if suppliers' expectations changed so that they would be willing to sell more goods at every price? This shift factor of supply would shift the entire supply curve out to the right. Let's say that at every price, quantity supplied increases by three. Mathematically the new equation would be $Q_S = -2 + 2P$. The quantity intercept increases by 3. What would you expect to happen to equilibrium price and quantity? Let's solve the equations mathematically first.

Step 1: To determine equilibrium price, set the new quantity supplied equal to quantity demanded:

$$10 - P = -2 + 2P$$

Step 2: Solve for the equilibrium price:

$$12 = 3P$$
$$P = \$4$$

Step 3: To determine equilibrium quantity, substitute P in either the demand or supply equation:

$$Q_D = 10 - (1 \times 4) = 6 \text{ units}$$
$$Q_S = -2 + (2 \times 4) = 6 \text{ units}$$

Equilibrium price declined to $4 and equilibrium quantity rose to 6, just as you would expect with a rightward shift in a supply curve.

Now let's suppose that demand shifts out to the right. Here we would expect both equilibrium price and equilibrium quantity to rise. We begin with our original supply and demand curves—supply: $Q_S = -5 + 2P$; demand: $Q_D = 10 - P$. Let's say at every price, the quantity demanded rises by 3. The new equation for demand would be $Q_D = 13 - P$. You may want to solve this equation for various prices to confirm that at every price, quantity demanded rises by 3. Let's solve the equations for equilibrium price and quantity.

Step 1: Set the quantities equal to one another:

$$13 - P = -5 + 2P$$

Step 2: Solve for equilibrium price:

$$18 = 3P$$
$$P = \$6$$

Step 3: Substitute P in either the demand or supply equation:

$$Q_D = 13 - (1 \times 6) = 7 \text{ units}$$
$$Q_S = -5 + (2 \times 6) = 7 \text{ units}$$

Equilibrium price rose to $6 and equilibrium quantity rose to 7 units, just as you would expect with a rightward shift in a demand curve.

Just to make sure you've got it, I will do two more examples. First, suppose the demand and supply equations for wheat per year in the United States can be specified as follows (notice that the slope is negative for the demand curve and positive for the supply curve):

$$Q_D = 500 - 2P$$
$$Q_S = -100 + 4P$$

P is the price in dollars per thousand bushels and Q is the quantity of wheat in thousands of bushels. Remember that the units must always be stated. What is the equilibrium price and quantity?

Step 1: Set the quantities equal to one another:

$$500 - 2P = -100 + 4P$$

Step 2: Solve for equilibrium price:

$$600 = 6P$$
$$P = \$100$$

Step 3: Substitute P in either the demand or supply equation:

$$Q_D = 500 - (2 \times 100) = 300$$
$$Q_S = -100 + (4 \times 100) = 300$$

Equilibrium quantity is 300 thousand bushels.

As my final example, take a look at Alice's demand curve depicted in Figure 4-4(b) in Chapter 4. Can you write an equation that represents the demand curve in that figure? It is $Q_D = 10 - 2P$. At a price of zero, the quantity of cassette rentals Alice demands is 10, and for every increase in price of \$1, the quantity she demands falls by 2. Now look at Ann's supply curve shown in Figure 4-7(b) in Chapter 4. Ann's supply curve mathematically is $Q_S = 2P$. At a zero price, the quantity Ann supplies is zero, and for every \$1 increase in price, the quantity she supplies rises by 2. What is the equilibrium price and quantity?

Step 1: Set the quantities equal to one another:

$$10 - 2P = 2P$$

Step 2: Solve for equilibrium price:

$$4P = 10$$
$$P = \$2.5$$

Step 3: Substitute P in either the demand or supply equation:

$$Q_D = 10 - (2 \times 2.5) = 5, \text{ or}$$
$$Q_S = 2 \times 2.5 = 5 \text{ cassettes per week}$$

Ann is willing to supply 5 cassettes per week at \$2.50 per rental and Alice demands 5 cassettes at \$2.50 per cassette rental. Remember that in Figure 4-8 in Chapter 4, I showed you graphically the equilibrium quantity and price of Alice's demand curve and Ann's supply curve. I'll leave it up to you

to check that the graphic solution in Figure 4-8 is the same as the mathematical solution we came up with here.

PRICE CEILINGS AND PRICE FLOORS

Let's now consider a price ceiling and price floor. We start with the supply and demand curves:

$$Q_S = -5 + 2P$$
$$Q_D = 10 - P$$

This gave us the solution:

$$P = 5$$
$$Q = 5$$

Now, say that a price ceiling of \$4 is imposed. Would you expect a shortage or a surplus? If you said "shortage" you're doing well. If not, review the chapter before continuing with this appendix. To find out how much the shortage is we must find out how much will be supplied and how much will be demanded at the price ceiling. Substituting \$4 for price in both lets us see that $Q_S = 3$ units and $Q_D = 6$ units. There will be a shortage of 3 units. Next, let's consider a price floor of \$6. To determine the surplus we follow the same exercise. Substituting \$6 into the two equations gives a quantity supplied of 7 units and a quantity demanded of 4 units, so there is a surplus of 3 units.

TAXES AND SUBSIDIES

Next, let's consider the effect of a tax of \$1 placed on the supplier. That tax would decrease the price received by suppliers by \$1. In other words:

$$Q_S = -5 + 2(P - 1)$$

Multiplying the terms in parentheses by 2 and collecting terms results in

$$Q_S = -7 + 2P$$

This supply equation has the same slope as in the previous case, but a new intercept term—just what you'd expect. To determine the new equilibrium price and quantity, follow steps 1 to 3 discussed earlier. Setting this new equation equal to demand and solving for price gives

$$P = 5\tfrac{2}{3}$$

Substituting this price into the demand and supply equations tells us equilibrium quantity:

$$Q_S = Q_D = 4\tfrac{1}{3} \text{ units}$$

Of that price, the supplier must pay $1 in tax, so the price the supplier receives net of tax is $4⅔.

Next, let's say that the tax were put on the demander rather than on the supplier. In that case, the tax increases the price for demanders by $1 and the demand equation becomes

$$Q_D = 10 - (P + 1), \text{ or}$$
$$Q_D = 9 - P$$

Again solving for equilibrium price and quantity requires setting the demand and supply equations equal to one another and solving for price. I leave the steps to you. The result is:

$$P = 4⅔$$

This is the price the supplier receives. The price demanders pay is $5⅔. The equilibrium quantity will be 4⅓ units.

These are the same results we got in the previous cases showing that, given the assumptions, it doesn't matter who actually pays the tax: The effect on equilibrium price and quantity is identical no matter who pays it.

QUOTAS

Finally, let's consider the effect of a quota of 4⅓ placed on the market. Since a quota limits the quantity supplied, as long as the quota is less than the market equilibrium quantity the supply equation becomes:

$$Q_S = 4⅓$$

where Q_S is the actual amount supplied. The price that the market will arrive at for this quantity is determined by the demand curve. To find that price substitute the quantity 4⅓ into the demand equation ($Q_D = 10 - P$):

$$4⅓ = 10 - P$$

and solve for P:

$$P = 5⅔$$

Since consumers are willing to pay 5⅔, this is what suppliers will receive. The price that suppliers would have been willing to accept for a quantity of 4⅓ is 4⅔. This can be found by substituting the amount of the quota in the supply equation:

$$4⅓ = -5 + 2P$$

and solving for P:

$$2P = 9⅓$$
$$P = 4⅔$$

Notice that this result is very similar to the tax. For demanders it is identical; they pay $5⅔ and receive 4⅓ units. For suppliers, however, the situation is much preferable; instead of receiving a price of $4⅔, the amount they received with the tax, they receive $5⅔. With a quota, suppliers receive the "implicit tax revenue" that results from the higher price.

Questions for Thought and Review

1. Suppose the demand and supply for milk is described by the following equations: $Q_D = 600 - 100P$; $Q_S = -150 + 150P$, where P is price in dollars, Q_D is quantity demanded in millions of gallons per year, and Q_S is quantity supplied in millions of gallons per year.
   a. Create demand and supply tables corresponding to these equations.
   b. Graph supply and demand and determine equilibrium price and quantity.
   c. Confirm your answer to (b) by solving the equations mathematically.

2. Suppose a growth hormone is introduced that allows dairy farmers to offer 125 million more gallons of milk per year at each price.
   a. Construct new demand and supply curves reflecting this change. Describe with words what happened to the supply curve and to the demand curve.
   b. Graph the new curves and determine equilibrium price and quantity.
   c. Determine equilibrium price and quantity by solving the equations mathematically.

   d. Suppose the government set the price of milk at $3 a gallon. Demonstrate the effect of this regulation on the market for milk. What is quantity demanded? What is quantity supplied?

3. Write demand and supply equations that represent demand, D_0, and supply, S_0, in Figure 5-1(a) in the chapter.
   a. Solve for equilibrium price and quantity mathematically.
   b. Rewrite the demand equation to reflect the shift in demand to D_1. What happens to equilibrium price and quantity as shown in Figure 5-1(a) in the chapter? Confirm by solving the equations for equilibrium price and quantity.

4. a. How is a shift in demand reflected in a demand equation?
   b. How is a shift in supply reflected in a supply equation?
   c. How is a movement along a demand (supply) curve reflected in a demand (supply) equation?

5. Suppose the demand and supply for milk is described by the following equations: $Q_D = 600 - 100P$; $Q_S = -150$

+ 150P, where P is the price in dollars; Q_D is quantity demanded in millions of gallons per year; and Q_S is quantity supplied in millions of gallons per year.

a. Solve for equilibrium price and quantity of milk.
b. Would a government-set price of $4 create a surplus or a shortage of milk? How much? Is $4 a price ceiling or a price floor?

6. Suppose the U.S. government imposes a $1 per gallon of milk tax on dairy farmers. Using the demand and supply equations from question 1:

a. What is the effect of the tax on the supply equation? The demand equation?
b. What is the new equilibrium price and quantity?
c. How much do dairy farmers receive per gallon of milk after the tax? How much do demanders pay?

7. Repeat question 6(a) to 6(c) assuming the tax is placed on the buyers of milk. Does it matter who pays the tax?

8. Repeat question 6(a) to 6(c) assuming the government pays a subsidy of $1 per gallon of milk to farmers.

9. Suppose the demand for cassettes is represented by $Q_D = 16 - 4P$, and the supply of cassettes is represented by $Q_S = 4P - 1$. Determine if each of the following is a price floor, price ceiling, or neither. In each case, determine the shortage or surplus.

a. $P = \$3$.
b. $P = \$1.50$.
c. $P = \$2.25$.
d. $P = \$2.50$.

MICROECONOMICS

II

In my vacations, I visited the poorest quarters of several cities and walked through one street after another, looking at the faces of the poorest people. Next I resolved to make as thorough a study as I could of Political Economy.

You may remember having already seen this quotation from Alfred Marshall. It began the first chapter. I chose this beginning for two reasons. First, it gives what I believe to be the best reason to study economics. Second, the quotation is from a hero of mine, one of the economic giants of all times. His *Principles of Economics* was the economists' bible in the late 1800s and early 1900s. How important was Marshall? It was Marshall who first used the supply and demand curves as an engine of analysis.

I repeat this quotation here in the introduction to the microeconomics section because for Marshall economics was microeconomics, and it is his vision of economics that underlies this book's approach to microeconomics. For Marshall, economics was an art that was meant to be applied—used to explain why things were the way they were, and what we could do about them. He had little use for esoteric theory that didn't lead to a direct application to a real-world problem. Reflecting on the state of economics in 1906, Marshall wrote to a friend:

> I had a growing feeling in the later years of my work at the subject that a good mathematical theorem dealing with economic hypotheses was very unlikely to be good economics: and I went more and more on the rules—(1) Use mathematics as a shorthand language, rather than as an engine of inquiry. (2) Keep to them until you have done. (3) Translate into English. (4) Then illustrate by examples that are important in real life. (5) Burn the mathematics. (6) If you can't succeed in (4), burn (3). This last I did often. (From a letter from Marshall to A. L. Bowley, reprinted in A. C. Pigou, *Memorials of Alfred Marshall*, p. 427.)

Marshall didn't feel this way about mathematical economics because he couldn't do mathematics. He was trained as a formal mathematician, and he was a good one. But, for him, mathematics wasn't economics, and the real world was too messy to have applied to it much of the fancy mathematical economic work that some of his fellow economists were doing. Marshall recognized the influence of market, political, and social forces and believed that all three had to be taken into account in applying economic reasoning to reality.

Since 1906, when Marshall wrote this letter, the economics profession has moved away from its Marshallian roots. The profession has found other heroes who have created a mathematical foundation for economics that's both impressive and stultifying. Mathematical economics that has only the slightest connection to the real world has overwhelmed much of the real-world economics that Marshall followed. That's sad.

Not to worry. You won't see such highfalutin mathematical economics in these microeconomic chapters. The chapters follow the Marshallian methodology and present the minimum of formal theory necessary to apply the concepts of economics to the real world, and then they do just that: start talking about real-world issues.

Section I, Microeconomics: The Basics (Chapters 6 and 7), and Section II, Foundations of Supply and Demand (Chapters 8–10), present the background theory necessary to understand the economic way of thinking. These sections introduce you to the foundations of economic reasoning and to some central terms and ideas of microeconomics. But even in these theoretical chapters the focus is on intuition, policy, and on putting the economic approach to problems into perspective, rather than on presenting technique for the sake of technique. Section III, Market Structure and Policy (Chapters 11–14), introduces you to various market structures, providing you with a way of approaching real-world markets.

Section IV, Applying Economic Reasoning to Policy (Chapters 15–17), provides an overview of the implications of microeconomics for policy. Section V, Policy Issues in Depth (Chapters 18 and 19), looks more carefully at two important issues—agriculture policy and trade policy.

Section VI, Factor Markets (Chapters 20–21), looks at a particular set of markets—factor markets. These markets play a central role in determining the distribution of income. These chapters won't tell you how to get rich (you'll have to wait for the sequel for that), but they will give you new insights into how labor markets work.

Describing Supply and Demand: Elasticities

6

After reading this chapter, you should be able to:

- Use the terms *price elasticity of supply* and *price elasticity of demand* to describe the responsiveness of quantity supplied and quantity demanded to changes in price.

- Calculate elasticity graphically and numerically.

- Distinguish five elasticity terms that are used to differentiate varying degrees of responsiveness.

- Explain the importance of substitution in determining elasticity of supply and demand.

- Relate price elasticity of demand to total revenue.

- State how other elasticity concepts are useful in describing the effect of shift factors on demand.

- Explain how the concept of *elasticity* makes supply and demand analysis more useful.

The master economist must understand symbols and speak in words. He must contemplate the particular in terms of the general, and touch abstract and concrete in the same flight of thought.

J. M. Keynes

Chapters 4 and 5 gave you a good sense of supply and demand. In this chapter I introduce you to the concept of elasticity, a term economists use to describe supply and demand. Elasticity refers to responsiveness; for example, elasticity can be used to describe the responsiveness of quantity supplied or quantity demanded to price.

In economics the term elasticity comes up continually For example, policymakers use it to describe by how much quantity demanded will fall in response to an increase in taxes. Firms use elasticity to describe the responsiveness of consumers to an increase in price. In general, the greater the elasticity, the greater the responsiveness.

Information about elasticity is extremely important to firms in making their pricing decisions, and to economists in their study of the economy. Consider the decision by General Mills recently to lower the prices on its brand-name cereals by 10 percent. That decision was based on the prediction that lowering price would increase the quantity of cereal demanded significantly. That is, they were hoping that demand for cereal was highly elastic. Or alternatively, consider some recently reported school boards' decisions to raise teachers' salaries by 10 percent because of a shortage of teachers in their districts. The boards were hoping that the number of individual choosing jobs as teachers would increase significantly with a rise in salaries; that is, they were hoping that the supply of teachers was highly elastic.

PRICE ELASTICITY

The most commonly used elasticity concept is price elasticity of demand and supply. **Price elasticity of demand** is *the percentage change in quantity demanded divided by the percentage change in price:*

$$E_D = \frac{\text{Percentage change in quantity demanded}}{\text{Percentage change in price}}$$

Price elasticity of supply is *the percentage change in quantity supplied divided by the percentage change in price:*

$$E_S = \frac{\text{Percentage change in quantity supplied}}{\text{Percentage change in price}}$$

Let's consider some numerical examples. Say the price of a good rises by 10 percent and, in response, quantity demanded falls by 20 percent. The price elasticity of demand is 2 (-20 percent/10 percent). Notice that I said 2, not -2. Because quantity demanded is inversely related to price, the calculation for the price elasticity of demand comes out negative. Despite this fact, economists talk about price elasticity of demand as a positive number. (Those of you who remember some math can think of elasticity as an *absolute value* of a number, rather than a simple number.) Using this convention makes it easier to remember that a *larger* number for price elasticity of demand means quantity demanded is *more responsive* to price.

To make sure you have the idea down let's consider two more examples. Say that when price falls by 5 percent, quantity supplied falls by 2 percent. In this case, the price elasticity of supply is 0.4 (2 percent/5 percent). And, finally, say the price goes up by 10 percent and in response the quantity supplied rises by 15 percent. Price elasticity of supply is 1.5 (15 percent/10 percent).

Classifying Demand and Supply as Elastic or Inelastic

It is helpful to classify elasticities by relative responsiveness. Economists usually describe supply and demand by the terms *elastic* and *inelastic*. Formally, demand or supply is **elastic** if *the percentage change in quantity is greater than the percentage change in price* ($E > 1$).

Price elasticity of demand is the percentage change in quantity demanded divided by the percentage change in price.

Price elasticity of supply is the percentage change in quantity supplied divided by the percentage change in price.

Q-1 If when price rises by 4 percent, quantity supplied rises by 8 percent, what is the price elasticity of supply?

Q-2 If price elasticity of demand is greater than 1, what would we call demand: elastic or inelastic?

Alternately, demand or supply is **inelastic** if *the percentage change in quantity is less than the percentage change in price* ($E < 1$). In the last two examples, the elasticity of supply was 0.4, so supply was inelastic ($E_S < 1$), and the elasticity of demand was 1.5, so demand was elastic ($E_D > 1$).

The commonsense interpretation of these terms is the following: An *inelastic* supply means that the quantity supplied doesn't change much with a change in price. For example, say the price of land rises. The amount of land supplied won't change much, so the supply of land is inelastic. An *elastic* supply means that quantity supplied changes by a larger percentage than the percentage change in price. For example, say the price of pencils doubles. What do you think will happen to the quantity of pencils supplied? I suspect it will more than double, which means that the supply of pencils is elastic.

The same terminology holds with demand. Consider a good such as a brand A ballpoint pen that has a close substitute, a brand B ballpoint pen. If brand A's price rises, the quantity demanded will fall a lot as people shift to the substitute (a brand B ballpoint pen). So the demand for brand A ballpoint pens would be highly elastic. Alternatively, consider table salt, which has no close substitute at current prices. Demand for table salt is highly inelastic. That is, a rise in the price of table salt does not result in a large decline in quantity demanded.

What Information Price Elasticity Provides

Price elasticity of demand and supply gives us information about the exact quantity response to a change in price. A price elasticity of demand of 3 tells us that a 10 percent rise in price will lead to a 30 percent decline in quantity demanded. If the elasticity of demand were a larger number, say 5, the same 10 percent rise in price will lead to a 50 percent decline in quantity demanded. As elasticity increases, responsiveness of quantity to price increases.

Elasticity Is Independent of Units

Before continuing, notice that elasticity measures the percentage, not the absolute, change in variables. Using percentages allows us to have a measure or responsiveness that is independent of units and thus makes comparisons of responsiveness of different goods easier. Say a $1 increase in the price of a $2,000 computer decreases the quantity demanded by 1, from 10 to 9. Say also that a $1 increase in the price of a pen, from $1 to $2, decreases quantity demanded by 1—from 10,000 to 9,999. Using absolute numbers, the $1 price increase had the same effect on quantities for both pens and computers. But such a comparison of absolute numbers is not very helpful. To see that, ask yourself if you were planning on raising your price, which good you'd rather be selling.

The computer price increased by 1/2,000 of its original price, a relatively small percentage increase, and quantity demanded declined by 1/10 of original sales, a large percentage decline. The percentage decline in quantity demanded exceeded the percentage rise in price, so your total revenue (Price × Quantity) would decrease. The percentage increase in price of pens was relatively large—100 percent—and the percentage decline in quantity demanded was relatively small—1/10 of 1 percent. So if you raise the price of pens, total revenue increases. Clearly, if you're raising your price in these examples, you'd rather be selling pens than computers.

By using percentages, this is made clear: With computers, a 0.05 percent increase in price decreases quantity demanded by 10 percent, so the elasticity is 200. With pens, a 100 percent increase in price decreases quantity demanded by 0.01 percent—an elasticity of 0.0001.

Percentages allow us to have a measure of responsiveness that is independent of units, and thus make comparisons of responsiveness of different goods easier.

CALCULATING ELASTICITIES

To see that you've got the method, calculate price elasticity of demand or supply in the following three real-world examples:

Case 1: In the early 1970s the price of oil rose by 176 percent and the quantity demanded fell by 25 percent.

Case 2: In the 1980s, when gasoline prices rose by 9 percent in Washington, D.C., the quantity of gasoline demanded there fell by 40 percent.

Case 3: In the mid-1990s, when the minimum wage in Vermont rose by 10 percent, the quantity of labor supplied for relevant jobs increased by about 1.8 percent.

In the first case price elasticity of demand is 0.14. The quantity of oil demanded in the United States did not respond much to the increase in oil prices. Elasticity was less than 1, so demand was inelastic. In the second case, price elasticity of demand is 4.4. The quantity of gas demanded in Washington, D.C., responded by a lot to a relatively small change in gas prices. Elasticity was greater than 1, so demand was elastic. The price elasticity of supply in the third case is 0.18. The quantity of labor supplied did not respond much to the change in wage. Elasticity was less than 1, so supply was inelastic.

Elastic: E > 1.
Inelastic: E < 1.

The End-Point Problem

Let's now calculate some elasticities graphically. Let's begin by determining the price elasticity of demand between points A and B in Figure 6-1(a).

Figure 6-1(a, b, and c)   Graphs of Elasticities

In (a) we are calculating the elasticity of the arc between A and B. We essentially calculate the midpoint and use that midpoint in our calculations of percentage changes. This gives us a percentage change in price of 26 percent and a percentage change in quantity of 33 percent, which gives us an elasticity of 1.3. In (b) the percentage change in price is 10.53 percent and the percentage change in quantity is 1.87 percent, giving an elasticity of 0.18. In (c), the calculations are left for you to do.

(a) **Elasticity of demand**

(b) **Elasticity of supply**

(c) **Some examples**

(Answers to (c): $a = 4$; $b = 0.54$; $c = 0.67$)

The demand curve in the figure is a hypothetical demand for WolfPack Simulation Software. You can see that as the price of the software rises from $20 to $26, the quantity demanded falls from 14,000 to 10,000 units a year. To determine the price elasticity of demand, we need to determine the percentage change in quantity and the percentage change in price. In doing so, there is a small problem that is sometimes called the *end-point problem:* The percentage change differs depending on whether you view the change as a rise or a decline. For example, say you calculate the rise in price from $20 to $26, starting from $20. That gives you a percentage increase in price of $[(20 - 26)/20] \times 100 = 30$ percent. If, however, you calculate that same change in price, $6, as a fall in price from $26 to $20, the percentage decrease in price is $[(26 - 20)/26] \times 100 = 23$ percent.

The Arc Convention

To get around this end-point problem in calculating percentages to determine elasticities, economists generally use a convention that I will call the *arc convention.* Using the arc convention, you use the average of the two end points as your starting point when calculating percentage change. In the example, instead of using 20 or 26 as a starting point, you use $(20 + 26)/2$, or 23. So, using the arc convention, the percentage change in price is

$$\frac{P_2 - P_1}{\frac{1}{2}(P_1 + P_2)} = \frac{(26 - 20)}{23} \times 100 = 26 \text{ percent}$$

Using the arc convention for quantity, the percentage change in quantity is

$$\frac{Q_2 - Q_1}{\frac{1}{2}(Q_1 + Q_2)} = \frac{(14 - 10)}{12} \times 100 = 33 \text{ percent}$$

To calculate elasticity (which technically is called *arc elasticity* to emphasize that we are using the arc convention), we divide the percentage change in quantity by the percentage change in price:

$$\text{Elasticity} = \frac{\text{Percentage change in quantity}}{\text{Percentage change in price}} = \frac{33}{26} = 1.27$$

The elasticity of demand between points A and B is approximately 1.3. This means that a 10 percent increase in price will cause a 13 percent fall in quantity demanded. Thus, demand between A and B is elastic.

In Figure 6-1(b) I go through another example, this time using the supply elasticity from case 3 on p. 135. Initially, the Vermont minimum wage was $4.50 an hour; it was then raised to $5 an hour. Using the arc convention, the average of the two end points is $4.75 and so the percentage change in price is $(0.50/4.75) \times 100 = 10.53$ percent. The initial quantity of labor supplied I estimated for my area in Vermont was 476; the rise in the minimum wage increased that number to 485. Using the arc convention, we get a percentage change in quantity of $(9/480.5) \times 100 = 1.87$ percent. To calculate the elasticity of supply, divide the percentage change in quantity by the percentage change in price to get $1.87/10.53 = 0.18$. A 10 percent rise in the minimum wage will bring about a 1.8 percent increase in quantity of labor supplied. The minimum-wage labor supply in Vermont is inelastic.

Learning the mechanics of calculating elasticities takes some practice, so in Figure 6-1(c) I give you three additional examples, leaving the calculations for you.

    a. Move from A to B on the demand curve.

    b. Move from C to D on the demand curve.

    c. Move from E to F on the supply curve.

Now that you've calculated them (you have, haven't you?), I'll let you know that the answers can be found upside down at the bottom of the figure.

Economists use the arc convention to get around the end-point problem.

To calculate elasticity of a range, economists use the arc elasticity method, calculating the percentage change at the midpoint of the range.

Q-3 What is the approximate elasticity between points A and B on the graph below?

The text explained how to calculate elasticity of a range. Let's now turn to a method of calculating the elasticity at a specific point rather than over a range or an arc. The approach we will use is to create a line segment around the point and use the arc elasticity formula to calculate elasticity. Let's go through an example.

Say you want to determine the elasticity at point *A* in Figure (a). First create a line segment, with the point as the segment's midpoint. The segment can be of any length. In Figure (a) I have selected a segment that begins 4 units on the quantity axis before the quantity at *A* and extends 4 units beyond the quantity at *A*. Thus, the quantity arc extends from 20 to 28. Next, determine the price arc relevant for the quantities chosen. In the example, the price corresponding to the lower end on the quantity arc is $3, and the price corresponding to the higher end of the quantity arc is $5.

KNOWING THE TOOLS

Calculating Elasticity at a Point

I've now got my line segment, so I am ready to use the arc elasticity formula to calculate the elasticity at point *A*: Percentage change in quantity = [(28 − 20)/24] × 100 = 33 percent. Percentage change in price = [(5 − 3)/4] × 100 = 50 percent. Elasticity at point *A* is 33/50 = 0.66.

To see that you've got the calculation down, in Figure (b) I present four points—two on the demand curve and two on a supply curve. Your assignment is to determine the elasticity of the four points on your own.

Now that you've done the calculations—you have, right?—you can look at the bottom of Figure (b), where I give you the correct answers. If you got all four right, you're in good shape. If not, it's time for a review. (And if you're taking the easy road and not calculating them on your own, it's time to get yourself in gear and start studying—remember, this stuff doesn't get into your head through osmosis.)

(a) Elasticity of demand

(b) Some examples

(Answers to (b): A = 2.33; B = .11; C = .75; D = .86.)

ELASTICITY AND SUPPLY AND DEMAND CURVES

There are two important points about elasticity and supply and demand curves. The first is that elasticity is related to (but is not the same as) slope and the second is that elasticity changes along straight-line demand and supply curves.

Elasticity Is Not the Same as Slope

Let's begin with the first point. The relationship between elasticity and slope is the following: The steeper the curve becomes at a given point, the less elastic is supply or

Figure 6-2 (a–d) Elasticities and Supply and Demand Curves

In (a) and (b), two special elasticity cases are shown. A perfectly inelastic curve is vertical; a perfectly elastic curve is horizontal. In (c) and (d), I show how elasticity generally varies along both supply and demand curves. Along demand curves it always goes from infinity at the vertical axis intercept to zero at the horizontal axis intercept. How elasticity of supply varies depends on which axis the supply curve intersects. If it intersects the vertical axis, elasticity starts at infinity and declines, and eventually approaches 1. If it intersects the horizontal axis, it starts at zero and increases, and eventually approaches 1. The one exception is when the supply curve intersects the origin. A good exercise is to determine what happens to elasticity in that case. (Hint: See Knowing the Tools box on page 140.)

demand. The limiting examples of this are a vertical curve (most steep), shown in Figure 6-2(a), and a horizontal (least steep) curve, shown in Figure 6-2(b).

The vertical demand curve shown in Figure 6-2(a) demonstrates how a change in price leads to no change in quantity demanded. Economists describe this curve as **perfectly inelastic**—*quantity does not respond at all to changes in price* ($E = 0$). Curves that are vertical are perfectly inelastic. The demand curve shown in Figure 6-2(b), in contrast, is horizontal. A change in price from above or below P_0 results in an infinitely large increase in quantity demanded. This curve is **perfectly elastic** reflecting the fact that *quantity responds enormously to changes in price* ($E = \infty$). Horizontal curves are perfectly elastic. From these extreme cases, you can see that steeper (more vertical) curves at a given point are more *in*elastic and less steep (more horizontal) curves at a given point are more elastic. Elasticity, however, is not the same as slope. The second point illustrates this well.

Elasticity Changes along Straight-Line Curves

On straight-line supply and demand curves, slope does not change, but elasticity does. Figure 6-2(c and d) shows how elasticity changes along demand and supply curves. At the price intercept of the demand curve in Figure 6-2(c), demand is perfectly elastic ($E_D = \infty$); elasticity becomes smaller as price declines until it becomes perfectly inelastic ($E_D = 0$) at the quantity intercept. At one point along the demand curve, between an elasticity of infinity and zero, demand is **unit elastic**—*the percentage change in quantity equals the percentage change in price* ($E = 1$). In Figure 6-2(c) demand is unit elastic at a price of $5. To confirm this, calculate elasticity of demand between $4 and $6. The percentage change in price is $(2/5) \times 100 = 40$ percent, and the percentage change in quantity is $(2/5) \times 100 = 40$ percent. The point at which demand is unit elastic divides the demand curve into two sections—an elastic portion ($E_D > 1$) above the point at which demand is unit elastic and an inelastic portion ($E_D < 1$) below the point at which demand is unit elastic.

The change in elasticity along a supply curve is less dramatic. At the point on a straight-line supply curve that intercepts the price axis, supply is perfectly elastic ($E_S = \infty$). Points become less elastic as you move out along the supply curve. At the point on a straight-line supply curve that intercepts the quantity axis, supply is perfectly inelastic ($E_S = 0$); it becomes more elastic as you move out along the supply curve. These changes are labeled in Figure 6-2(d). I leave it to you to determine what happens to the elasticity of the supply curve if the supply curve intercepts the origin. (Hint: See the Knowing the Tools box "Geometric Tricks for Estimating Price Elasticity.")

As a review, the five terms to describe elasticity along a curve are listed here from most to least elastic:

1. *Perfectly elastic:* Quantity responds enormously to changes in price ($E = \infty$).
2. *Elastic:* The percentage change in quantity exceeds the percentage change in price ($E > 1$).
3. *Unit elastic:* The percentage change in quantity is the same as the percentage change in price ($E = 1$).
4. *Inelastic:* The percentage change in quantity is less than the percentage change in price ($E < 1$).
5. *Perfectly inelastic:* Quantity does not respond at all to changes in price ($E = 0$).

Now that you have seen that elasticity changes along straight-line supply and demand curves, the first point—that elasticity is related to but not the same as slope—should be clear. Whereas elasticity changes along a straight-line curve, slope does not.

SUBSTITUTION AND ELASTICITY

Now that you know how to measure elasticity, let's consider some of the factors that are likely to make supply and demand more or less elastic.

How responsive quantity demanded and quantity supplied will be to changes in price can be summed up in one word: substitution. As a general rule, the more substitutes a good has, the more elastic is its supply or demand.

The reasoning is as follows: If a good has substitutes, a rise in the price of that good will cause the consumer to shift consumption to those substitute goods. Put another way, when

Q-4 Your study partner, Nicole, has just stated that a straight-line demand curve is inelastic. How do you respond?

Five elastic terms are: perfectly elastic ($E = \infty$); elastic ($E > 1$); unit elastic ($E = 1$); inelastic ($E < 1$); and perfectly inelastic ($E = 1$).

Q-5 What is the most important determinant of the price elasticity of demand?

There are a couple of tricks that are useful in determining whether a point on a straight-line supply or demand curve is elastic or inelastic. The trick with demand is the following: (1) Determine where the demand curve intersects the price and quantity axes. (2) At a point midway between the origin and the quantity line intersection draw a vertical line back up to the demand curve. The point where it intersects the demand curve will have an elasticity of 1; it will be unit elastic; all points to the left of that line will be elastic, and all points to the right of that will be inelastic.

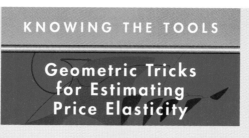

KNOWING THE TOOLS

Geometric Tricks for Estimating Price Elasticity

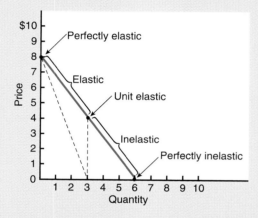

To determine whether a straight-line supply curve is elastic or inelastic you simply extend it to one of the axes, as in the following graph. The point at which this extension intersects the axes indicates the elasticity of the supply curve:

- If the extension intersects the vertical (price) axis, as does S_1, the supply curve has an elasticity greater than 1; the supply curve is elastic.

- If the extension intersects the horizontal (quantity) axis, as does S_2, all points on the supply curve have an elasticity less than 1; the supply curve is inelastic.

- If the extension intersects the two axes at the origin, the supply curve has an elasticity of 1; the supply curve has unit elasticity.

If you combine these tricks with a knowledge that a perfectly elastic supply or demand curve is horizontal and crosses the price axis, and a perfectly inelastic supply or demand curve is vertical and crosses the quantity axis, you can even remember which is which. If a straight-line supply curve crosses the quantity axis, all points on it are inelastic; if it crosses the price axis, all points on it are elastic. Similarly, the top half of the demand curve (the part that crosses the price axis) is elastic; the bottom half (the part that crosses the quantity axis) is inelastic.

a satisfactory substitute is available, a rise in that good's price will have a large effect on the quantity demanded. For example, I think a Whopper is a satisfactory substitute for a Big Mac. If most people agree with me, the demand for Big Macs would be very elastic.

Factors that affect a good's substitutability of demand differ from factors that affect a good's substitutability of supply. So I will consider each separately. I begin with demand.

Substitution and Demand

The number of substitutes a good has is affected by several factors. Four of the most important are:

1. The larger the time interval considered, or the longer the run, the more elastic is the good's demand curve.

2. The less a good is a necessity, the more elastic is its demand curve.

3. As the definition of a good becomes more specific, demand becomes more elastic.

4. Demand for goods that represent a large proportion of one's budget are more elastic than demand for goods that represent a small proportion of one's budget.

These four reasons are derivatives of the substitution factor. Let's consider each to see why.

1. There are more substitutes in the long run than in the short run. That's because the long run provides more alternatives. For example, let's consider the World War II period, when the price of rubber went up considerably. In the short run, there were few substitutes; the demand for rubber was inelastic. In the long run, however, the rise in the price of rubber stimulated research for alternatives. Many alternatives were found. Today automobile tires, which were all made of rubber at the time World War II broke out, are almost entirely made from synthetic materials. In the long run, the demand curve was very elastic.

2. Because by definition one cannot do without necessities, they tend to have fewer substitutes than do luxuries. Insulin for a diabetic is a necessity; the demand is highly inelastic. Chocolate Ecstasy cake, however, is a luxury. A variety of other luxuries can be substituted for it (for example, cheesecake or a ball game).

3. If the good we're talking about is broadly defined (say, transportation), there aren't many substitutes and demand will be inelastic. If you want to get from A to B, you need transportation. If the definition of the good is narrowed—say, to "transportation by bus"—there are more substitutes. Instead of taking a bus you can walk, ride your bicycle, or drive your car. In that case the demand curve is more elastic.

4. Goods that cost very little relative to your total expenditures aren't worth spending a lot of time figuring out whether there's a good substitute. An example is pencils. Their low price means most people would buy just as many even if their price doubled. Their demand is inelastic. It is, however, worth spending lots of time looking for substitutes for goods that take a large portion of one's income. The demand for such goods tends to be more elastic. Many colleges have discovered this as they tried to raise tuition when other colleges did not. The demand curve they faced was inelastic.

> The more substitutes, the more elastic the demand and the more elastic the supply.

> **Q-6** What are four important factors affecting the number of substitutes a good has?

Substitution and Supply

The same general issues involving substitution are relevant when considering determinants of the elasticity of supply. But when it comes to supply, economists focus on time rather than on other factors because time plays such a central role in determining supply elasticity. The general rule is: The longer the time period considered, the more elastic is the supply curve. The reasoning is the same as with demand; in the long run there are more alternatives, so it is easier (less costly) for suppliers to change and produce other goods.

To emphasize the importance of time, economists distinguish three time periods relevant to supply:

1. In the instantaneous period, quantity supplied is fixed, so supply is perfectly inelastic. This supply is sometimes called the momentary supply.

2. In the short run, some substitution is possible, so the short-run supply curve is somewhat elastic.

3. In the long run, significant substitution is possible; the supply curve becomes very elastic.

In determining the elasticity of supply, one must, however, remember an additional factor: Many supplied goods are produced, so we must take into account how easy it is to increase production of those same goods. For example, if the cost per unit of producing a good is constant, its supply is likely highly elastic. Before we can discuss such issues in detail, we need to talk about the production process in detail. And that will take two entire chapters, so I will put off the discussion for now.

> The longer the time period considered, the more elastic the supply.

> **Q-7** Is supply generally more elastic in the short run or in the long run?

How Substitution Factors Affect Specific Decisions

Let's consider how some of the substitution factors affect a specific decision. Let's say you've been hired by two governments (the city of Washington, D.C., and the U.S. government) to advise them about the effect that raising the gas tax by 10 percent will have on tax revenues. You look at the three factors that affect elasticity of demand.

In your report to the two governments, you would point out that in the short run the demand curve is less elastic than in the long run, since people aren't going to trade in their gas-guzzling cars for fuel-efficient cars immediately in response to a 10 percent rise in gas taxes—partly because they can't afford to, partly because they don't want to, and partly because not that many fuel-efficient cars are available to buy at the moment. When the time comes, however, that they would ordinarily purchase a new car, they're likely to switch to cars that are more fuel-efficient than their old cars, and to switch as much as they can to forms of transportation that are more fuel-efficient than cars. In the long run the demand will be far more elastic.

The second point you'd note is that gasoline is generally considered a necessity, although not all driving is necessary. However, since gasoline is only a small part of what it costs to drive a car, demand will probably tend to be inelastic.

As for the third factor (how specifically the good is defined) you have to be careful. It makes your recommendations for the government of the city of Washington, D.C., and the U.S. government quite different from each other. For the U.S. government, which is interested in the demand for gasoline in the entire United States, gasoline has a relatively inelastic demand. The general rule of thumb is that a 1-cent rise in tax will raise tax revenues by $1 billion. That inelasticity can't be carried over to the demand for gasoline in a city such as Washington, D.C. Because of the city's size and location, people in Washington have a choice. A large proportion of the people who buy gas in Washington could as easily buy gas in the adjacent states of Maryland or Virginia. Gasoline in Washington is a narrowly defined good and therefore has a quite elastic demand. A rise in price will mean a large fall in the quantity of gas demanded.

I mention this point because in August 1980 someone forgot about it when the city of Washington, D.C., raised the tax on a gallon of gasoline by 8 cents, a rise at that time of about 9 percent (this was Case 2 in our discussion of calculating elasticities on p. 135). In response, monthly gasoline sales in Washington fell from 16 million gallons to less than 11 million gallons, a 40 percent decrease! The demand for gas in Washington was not inelastic, as it was for the United States as a whole; it was very elastic ($E_D = 4.4$). Washingtonians went elsewhere to buy gas.

The fact that smaller geographic areas have more elastic demands limits how highly state and local governments can tax goods relative to their neighboring localities or states. Where there are tax differences, new stores open all along the border and existing stores expand to entice people to come over that border and save on taxes. For example, the liquor tax is higher in Vermont than in New Hampshire, so it isn't surprising that right across the border from Vermont, New Hampshire has a large number of liquor stores. Here's one final example: If you look at license plates in Janzen Beach, Oregon (right across the Washington state border), you'll see mostly Washington license plates. Why? If you answered that it likely has something to do with differential sales taxes on automobiles in Washington and Oregon, you've got the idea.

In the long run, demand generally becomes more elastic.

Empirical Estimates of Elasticities of Demand and Supply

Table 6-1 presents empirical estimates of elasticity of demand. Notice that, as expected, different estimates are provided for the short- and long-run elasticities of each good.

Table 6-1   Short-Run and Long-Run Elasticities of Demand

| | Price Elasticity | |
Product	Short-Run	Long-Run
Tobacco products	0.46	1.89
Electricity (for household consumption)	0.13	1.89
Health services	0.20	0.92
Toys (nondurable)	0.30	1.02
Movies/motion pictures	0.87	3.67
Foreign travel by U.S. residents	0.14	1.77
Beer	.56	1.39
Wine	.68	.84
University tuition	.52	—
Rail transit	.62	1.59

Sources: Hendrik S. Houthakker and Lester D. Taylor, *Consumer Demand in the United States: Analyses and Projections,* 2nd ed. (Cambridge, Mass.: Harvard University Press, 1970); W. S. Comanor and T. A. Wilson, *Advertising and Market Power* (Cambridge, Mass.: Harvard University Press, 1974); Shermon Folland, Allen C. Goodman, and Miron Stano, *The Economics of Health Care* (New York: Macmillan, 1993); Yu Hsing and Hui S. Change, "Testing Increasing Sensitivity of Enrollment at Private Institutions to Tuition and Other Costs," *The American Economist* 41, no. 1 (Spring 1996); Richard Voith, "The Long-Run Elasticity of Demand for Commuter Rail Transportation," *Journal of Urban Economics* 30 (1991).

Also notice that the estimates are for the entire United States; estimates for a specific region in the United States could be expected to show more elasticity.

Taking an example from Table 6-1, notice that the long-run demand for movies is elastic. If movie theaters raise their prices, it's relatively easy for individuals simply to stay home and watch television. Movies have close substitutes, so we would expect the demand to be relatively elastic.

As a second example, in the short run the demand for electricity is highly inelastic. Either people have electrical appliances or they don't. In the long run, however, it becomes elastic since people can shift to gas for cooking and oil for heating, and can buy more energy-efficient appliances. As an exercise, you might see if you can explain why each of the other goods listed in the table has the elasticity of demand reported.

There are many fewer empirical measurements of supply than there are of demand. The reason concerns the structure of markets of produced goods, and the complicated nature of production. Most retail markets have seller-set or posted prices—you go to the store and pay the listed price of toothpaste. You can buy as much as you want at that price, so in a sense the supply of toothpaste (and most retail goods) is perfectly elastic until the store runs out, whereupon the supply becomes perfectly inelastic. But in another sense there is no supply curve since the selling price is determined by the seller's pricing strategy, not by the market. I will hold off discussion of such issues until after we discuss costs, production, and various market structures.

We do find empirical measurements of supply in factor markets, such as the market for labor services. For example, economist David Blau has estimated that the supply of child care labor is elastic—it may be as high as 1.9—which means that a 10 percent rise in the wages paid to child care workers brings about a 19 percent increase in the quantity of child care workers. More generally, economists have estimated that the labor supply elasticity of heads of households is about 0.1, and for secondary workers is about 1.1. A good test of whether you intuitively understand elasticities is whether you can explain why the latter is more elastic.

Other areas in which elasticities of supply are estimated are agricultural and raw materials markets. Estimating supply elasticities here is possible because these goods are often sold in auction markets where price is directly determined by supply and demand, rather than in posted-price markets. In these markets, economists have generally found that the short-run supplies are highly inelastic, and that the long-run supplies are highly elastic.

ELASTICITY, TOTAL REVENUE, AND DEMAND

For sellers, knowing elasticity of demand is useful because from it they can tell whether the total revenue will go up or down when they raise or lower their prices. The total revenue a supplier receives is the price he or she charges times the quantity he or she sells. (Total revenue equals total quantity sold multiplied by price of good.) Elasticity tells sellers what will happen to total revenue if their price changes. Specifically:

If demand is elastic ($E_D > 1$), a rise in price lowers total revenue. (Price and total revenue move in opposite directions.)

If demand is unit elastic ($E_D = 1$), a rise in price leaves total revenue unchanged.

If demand is inelastic ($E_D < 1$), a rise in price increases total revenue. (Price and total revenue move in the same direction.)

The relationship between elasticity and total revenue is no mystery. There's a very logical reason why they are related, which can be seen most neatly by recognizing that total revenue ($P \times Q$) is represented by the area under the demand curve at that price and quantity. For example, at point E on demand curve D in Figure 6-3(a), the total revenue at price $4 and quantity 6 is the area designated by the A and B rectangles, $24.

If we increase price to $6, quantity demanded decreases to 4, so total revenue is still $24. Total revenue has remained constant, so the demand curve from point E to point F is unit elastic. The new total revenue is represented by the A and C rectangles. The

Q.8 If demand is inelastic and a firm raises price, what happens to total revenue?

Figure 6-3 (a, b, and c)   Elasticity and Total Revenue

Total revenue is measured by the rectangle produced by extending lines from the demand curve to the price and quantity axes. The change in total revenue resulting from a change in price can be estimated by comparing the sizes of the before and after rectangles. If price is being raised, total revenue increases by rectangle C and decreases by rectangle B. As you can see, the effect of a price rise on total revenue differs significantly at different points on a demand curve; (**a**) shows an almost unitary elastic point, (**b**) shows an inelastic point, and (**c**) shows an elastic point.

(a)   **Unit elastic**   (b)   **Inelastic**   (c)   **Elastic** difference between the old total revenue (A and B) and the new total revenue (A and C) is the difference between the rectangles B and C. Comparing these rectangles provides us with a visual method of estimating elasticities.

Figure 6-3(b) shows an inelastic range; Figure 6-3(c) shows a highly elastic range. While in Figure 6-3(b) the slope of the demand curve is the same as in Figure 6-3(a), we begin at a different point on the demand curve (point G). If we raise our price from $1 to $2, quantity demanded falls from 9 to 8. The gained area (rectangle C) is much greater than the lost area (rectangle B). In other words, total revenue increases significantly, so the demand curve at point G is highly inelastic.

In Figure 6-3(c) the demand curve is again the same, but we begin at still another point, J. If we raise our price from $8 to $9, quantity demanded falls from 2 to 1. The gained area (rectangle C) is much smaller than the lost area (rectangle B). In other words, total revenue decreases significantly, so the demand curve at point J is highly elastic.

Total Revenue along a Demand Curve

The way in which elasticity changes along a demand curve and its relationship to total revenue can be seen in Figure 6-4. When output is zero, total revenue is zero; similarly when price is zero, total revenue is zero. That accounts for the two end points of the total revenue curve in Figure 6-4(b). Let's say we start at a price of zero, where demand is

With elastic demands, a rise in price decreases total revenue. With inelastic demands, a rise in price increases total revenue.

Figure 6-4 (a and b)   How Total Revenue Changes

Total revenue is at a maximum when elasticity equals one, as you can see in (a) and (b). When demand is elastic, total revenue decreases with an increase in price. When demand is inelastic, total revenue increases with an increase in price.

perfectly inelastic. As we increase price (decrease quantity demanded), total revenue increases significantly. As we continue to do so, the increases in total revenue become smaller until finally, after output of Q_0, total revenue actually starts decreasing. It continues decreasing at a faster and faster rate until finally, at zero output, total revenue is zero.

6.1

As an example of where such calculations might come in handy, recall the vanity license plates that we used to illustrate the law of demand in Chapter 4. (I am using the arc convention in calculating percentages.) A rise in the price of vanity plates of about 29 percent, from $30 to $40, decreased the quantity demanded about 64 percent, from 60,334 to 31,122, so the price elasticity of demand was about 0.64/0.29 = 2.2. Since demand was elastic, total revenue fell. Specifically, total revenue fell from $1,810,020 ($30 × 60,334) to $1,244,880 ($40 × 31,122).

Elasticity of Individual and Market Demand

In thinking about elasticity of demand, keep in mind the point made in Chapter 4: The market demand curve is the horizontal summation of individual demand curves; some individuals have highly inelastic demands and others have highly elastic demands. A slight rise in the price of a good will cause some people to stop buying the good; the slight increase won't affect other people's quantity demanded for the good at all. Market demand elasticity is influenced both by how many people drop out totally and by how much an existing consumer marginally changes his or her quantity demanded.

If a firm can somehow separate the people with less elastic demand from those with more elastic demand, it can charge more to the individuals with inelastic demands and less to individuals with elastic demands. Economists call this price discrimination. We see firms throughout the economy trying to use price discrimination. Let's consider three examples.

Firms have a strong incentive to separate out people with less elastic demand and charge them a higher price.

1. Airlines' Saturday stay-over specials. If you stay over a Saturday night, usually you can get a much lower airline fare than if you don't. The reason is that businesspeople have inelastic demands and don't like to stay over Saturday nights, while pleasure travelers have more elastic demands. By requiring individuals to stay over Saturday night, airlines can separate out businesspeople and charge them more.

2. The phenomenon of selling new cars. Most new cars don't sell at the listed price. They sell at a discount. Salespeople are trained to separate out comparison shoppers (who have more elastic demands) from impulse buyers (who have inelastic demands). By not listing the selling price of cars so that the discount can be worked out in individual negotiations, salespeople can charge more to customers who have inelastic demands.

3. The almost-continual-sale phenomenon. Some items, such as washing machines, go on sale rather often. Why don't suppliers sell them at a low price all the time? Because some buyers whose washing machines break down have inelastic demand. They can't wait, so they'll pay the "unreduced" price. Others have elastic demands; they can wait for the sale. By running sales (even though they're frequent sales), sellers can separate consumers with inelastic demand curves from consumers with elastic demand curves.

OTHER ELASTICITY CONCEPTS

There are many other elasticity concepts besides the price elasticity of demand and the price elasticity of supply. Since these other elasticities can be useful in specifying the

APPLYING THE TOOLS

Empirically Measuring Elasticities

In the text, the discussion of determining elasticity concentrates on the technical aspects of the calculation. It assumes we know at what point on the supply and demand curve we are. In the real world, economists don't have the luxury of that knowledge. The data points they use involve interactions of supply and demand, and they must use statistical tools to ensure that they are holding "other things constant." Specifically, to determine points on a demand curve we must vary supply (and nothing else); to determine points on a supply curve we must vary demand (and nothing else).

In practice, holding everything else constant is difficult to do, which means real-world estimates of elasticity are often less than perfect. The tables presented in the text are some economists' estimates, but there are often disputes and technical issues that could lead to different estimates.

Where do firms get the information they need to calculate elasticities? Think of the grocery store where you can get a special buyer's card; you show it to the checkout clerk and you get all the discounts. And the card is free! Those grocery stores are not just being nice. When the clerk scans your purchases in, the store gets information that is forwarded to a central processing unit that can see how people react to different prices. This information is valuable; it allows firms to fine-tune their pricing—raising prices on goods for which the demand is inelastic, and lowering prices on goods for which the demand is elastic.

Alternatively, think of the warranty cards that you send in when you buy a new computer or a new TV. The information goes into the firms' information bases and is used by their economists in future price-setting decisions.

effects of shift factors on the demand for a good, I will introduce you to two of them: income elasticity of demand and cross-price elasticity of demand.

The definition of these concepts is straightforward. **Income elasticity of demand** is defined as *the percentage change in demand divided by the percentage change in income*. Put another way,

$$\text{Income elasticity of demand} = \frac{\text{Percentage change in demand}}{\text{Percentage change in income}}$$

It tells us the responsiveness of demand to changes in income. (Notice I used *demand*, not *quantity* demanded, to emphasize that in response to a change in anything but the price of that good, the entire demand curve shifts; there's no movement along the demand curve.) **Cross-price elasticity of demand** is defined as *the percentage change in demand divided by the percentage change in the price of another good*. Put another way,

$$\text{Cross-price elasticity of demand} = \frac{\text{Percentage change in demand}}{\text{Percentage change in price of another good}}$$

These other elasticity concepts tell you how much the demand curve will shift when there is a change in a shift factor. Let's consider each separately.

> Income elasticity of demand shows the responsiveness of demand to changes in income.

> Cross-price elasticity of demand shows the responsiveness of demand to changes in prices of other goods.

Income Elasticity of Demand

The most commonly used of the elasticity terms introduced above is *income elasticity of demand*. Income elasticity of demand tells us how much demand will change with a change in income. An increase in income generally increases one's consumption of almost all goods, although the increase may be greater for some goods than for others. **Normal goods**—*goods whose consumption increases with an increase in income*—have income elasticities greater than zero.

Normal goods are sometimes divided into luxuries and necessities. **Luxuries** are *goods that have an income elasticity greater than 1*—their percentage increase in demand is

> **Q.9** If a good's consumption increases with an increase in income, what type of good would you call it?

Table 6-2   Income Elasticities for Selected Goods

| | Income Elasticity | |
Commodity	Short-Run	Long-Run
Motion pictures	0.81	3.41
Foreign travel	0.24	3.09
Tobacco products	0.21	0.86
Food produced and consumed on farms	−0.61	—
Furniture	2.60	0.53
Jewelry and watches	1.00	1.64
Beer	—	0.84
Hard liquor	—	2.5
Dental services	—	1.6
Private university tuition	—	1.1

Sources: Hendrik S. Houthakker and Lester D. Taylor, *Consumer Demand in the United States: Analyses and Projections,* 2nd ed. (Cambridge, Mass.: Harvard University Press, 1970); E. A. Selvanthan, "Cross-Country Alcohol Consumption: An Application of the Rotterdam Demand System," *Applied Economics* 23 (1991); Shermon Folland, Allen C. Goodman, and Miron Stano, *The Economics of Health Care* (New York: Macmillan, 1993); Yu Hsing and Hui S. Chang, "Testing Increasing Sensitivity of Enrollment at Private Institutions to Tuition and Other Costs," *The American Economist* 41, no. 1 (Spring 1996).

greater than the percentage increase in income. For example, say your incomes goes up 10 percent and your consumption of CDs goes up 20 percent. The income elasticity of CDs is 2; thus, CDs are a luxury good. Alternatively, say your income goes up by 100 percent and your demand for shoes goes up by 50 percent. Your income elasticity for shoes would be 0.5. Shoes are a **necessity**—*a good that has an income elasticity less than 1.* The consumption of a necessity rises by a smaller proportion than the rise in income.

6.2   It is even possible that an increase in income can affect relative preferences so much that an increase in income can cause a *decrease* in the consumption of a particular good. These goods have a negative income elasticity of demand. The term applied to such goods is **inferior goods**—*goods whose consumption decreases when income increases.* In some circumstances, potatoes could be an example of an inferior good. As income goes up, people might so significantly shift their consumption toward meat and away from potatoes that their total consumption of potatoes decreases.

Table 6-2 presents income elasticities measured for some groups of goods. Notice a few things about this table. In the short run, people often save high proportions of their increases in income, so most goods, other than impulse-bought goods, have low income elasticities. To avoid this problem, economists generally focus on long-run income elasticities. Notice which goods are necessities (the ones with long-run income elasticities less than 1). Notice also which goods are luxuries (the ones with elasticities greater than 1).

Finally, notice the one good with a negative income elasticity—food produced and consumed on farms. As mentioned above, such goods are called inferior goods. As income rises, people buy proportionately less of such goods.

Cross-Price Elasticity of Demand

Cross-price elasticity of demand is another frequently used elasticity concept. Let's consider an example. Say the price of Toyotas rises. What is likely to happen to the demand for Fords? It is likely to rise, so the cross-price elasticity between the two is positive. Positive cross-price elasticities of demand mean the goods are **substitutes**—*goods that can*

Income elasticity of demand is defined as *the percentage change in demand divided by the percentage change in income.*

$$\text{Income elasticity of demand} = \frac{\text{Percentage change in demand}}{\text{Percentage change in income}}$$

Cross-price elasticity of demand is defined as *the percentage change in demand divided by the percentage change in the price of a related good.*

$$\text{Cross-price elasticity of demand} = \frac{\text{Percentage change in demand}}{\text{Percentage change in price of a related good}}$$

KNOWING THE TOOLS

A Review of the Alternative Elasticity Terms

Complement: Cross-price elasticity of demand is negative.

Substitute: Cross-price elasticity of demand is positive.

Normal good: Income elasticity of demand is positive.

Luxury: Income elasticity is greater than 1.

Necessity: Income elasticity is less than 1.

Inferior good: Income elasticity of demand is negative.

Table 6-3   Cross-Price Elasticities

Commodities	Cross-Price Elasticity
Beef in response to price changes in pork	0.11
Beef in response to price changes in chicken	0.02
U.S. automobiles in response to price changes in European and Asian automobiles	0.28
European automobiles in response to price changes in U.S. and Asian automobiles	0.61
Beer in response to price changes in wine	0.23
Hard liquor in response to price changes in beer	−0.11

Sources: J. A. Johnson and E. H. Oksanen, "Socioeconomic Determinants of the Consumption of Alcoholic Beverages," *Applied Economics* (1974); Patrick S. McCarthy, "Market Price and Income Elasticities of New Vehicle Demand," *Review of Economics and Statistics* (August 1996); Kuo S. Huang, "Nutrient Elasticities in a Complete Food Demand System," *American Journal of Agricultural Economics* (February 1996).

be used in place of one another. When the price of a good goes up, the demand for the substitute goes up.

Most goods have substitutes, so most cross-price elasticities are positive. But not all. To see that, let's consider another example: Say the price of hot dogs rises; what is likely to happen to the demand for ketchup? If you're like me and use lots of ketchup on your hot dogs, as I cut my consumption of hot dogs I will also cut my consumption of ketchup. Ketchup and hot dogs are not substitutes but rather complements. **Complements** are *goods that are used in conjunction with other goods.* A fall in the price of a good will increase the demand for its complement. The cross-price elasticity of complements is negative.

Some estimate of cross-price elasticities of demand are shown in Table 6-3. You can see that the strongest substitutes are European autos for U.S. and Asian autos. A 10 percent fall in the price of U.S. and Asian autos leads to a 6 percent fall in the quantity of European autos demanded. Hard liquor and beer are complements. If the price of beer falls by 10 percent, the quantity of hard liquor demanded increases by 1.1 percent.

Substitutes have positive cross-price elasticities; complements have negative cross-price elasticities.

Figure 6-5   Calculating Elasticities

Shift factors, such as income or price of another good, shift the entire demand curve. To calculate these elasticities, we see how much demand will shift at a constant price and then calculate the relevant elasticities.

(a) **Calculating income elasticity**   (b) **Calculating cross-price elasticity**

Some Examples

To make sure you've got these concepts down, see Figure 6-5, which demonstrates two examples. In Figure 6-5(a), income has risen by 20 percent, increasing demand at price P_0 from 20 to 26. To determine the income elasticity we must first determine the percentage change in demand. Using our arc convention, we calculate the percentage demand to be $6/[(20 + 26)/2] = (6/23) \times 100 = 26$ percent. The percentage change in income is 20, so the income elasticity is 26/20, or 1.3.

In Figure 6-5(b), a 33 percent fall in the price of pork has caused the demand for beef to fall by 3.8 percent—from 108 to 104 at a price of P_0. The cross-price elasticity of demand is 3.8/33 = 0.12.

THE POWER OF SUPPLY AND DEMAND ANALYSIS

Now that you've got the elasticity terms down, let's consider some examples that demonstrate the power of supply and demand analysis when it is combined with the concept of elasticity. Let's start with some easy cases.

When Should a Supplier Not Raise Price?

First, let's say a firm is trying to increase its profits and hires you to tell it whether it should raise or lower its price. The firm knows that it faces an inelastic demand. Should it raise its price?

I hope your answer was: Definitely yes. How can I be so sure the correct answer is yes? Because I remembered the discussion of the relationship between price elasticity of demand with total revenue. With an inelastic demand the percentage change in quantity is less than the percentage change in price, so total revenue must increase with an increase in price. Total costs will also decrease, so profits—total revenues minus total costs—must also increase.

Along those same lines, consider a university president thinking of raising tuition. Say that raising tuition by 10 percent will decrease the number of students by only

Q-10   A firm faces an elastic demand for its product. It has come to an economist to advise it on whether to lower its price. The answer she gives is: Maybe. Why is this the right answer?

Figure 6-6 (a and b)   Effects of Shifts in Supply on Price and Quantity

In both (**a**) and (**b**) the supply shifts out from S_0 to S_1. Initial price is P_0 and quantity is Q_0. The new equilibrium is P_1 and Q_1. In (**a**), supply intersects demand where demand is inelastic and the quantity effects are relatively small. In (**b**), the demand is more elastic and the quantity effects are much larger. In general the effects of shifts in supply on equilibrium quantity and price are determined by the elasticity of demand. When demand is inelastic, price changes are large and quantity changes are small. A useful exercise is to go through the same two cases for demand shifts, showing how the quantity effect is determined by the elasticity of supply.

(a) Inelastic supply and inelastic demand

(b) Inelastic supply and elastic demand

1 percent. What's the price elasticity? The percentage change in quantity is 1 percent; the percentage change in price is 10. Dividing the percentage change in quantity by the percentage change in price, we have an elasticity of 0.1. That's an inelastic demand ($E_D < 1$), so raising tuition will increase the university's total revenue.

But if a 10 percent rise in tuition will decrease the enrollment by 25 percent, the elasticity will be large (2.5). In response to an increase in tuition, the university's total revenue will significantly decrease. When you have an elastic demand, you should hesitate to increase price. To make sure you're following the argument, explain the likely effect an elastic demand will have on lowering tuition. (Your argument should involve the *possibility* of increasing profit.) If you're not following the argument, go back to the section on elasticity and total revenue, especially Figure 6-3.

Elasticity and Shifting Supply and Demand

Let's now turn to shifts in supply and demand. Knowing the elasticity of the supply and demand curves allows us to be more specific about the effects of shifts in supply and demand. Let's first consider the case of oil. When price rises, quantity falls by only a small amount, so revenue decreases by even more than the rise in price. So obviously oil has an inelastic demand. (If that isn't obvious, review the previous section.)

Figure 6-6 demonstrates the relative effects of supply shifts on equilibrium price and quantity under different assumptions about elasticity. As you can see, the more elastic the demand, the greater the effect of a supply shift on quantity, and the smaller the effect on price. Going through a similar exercise for demand shifts with various supply elasticitites is also a useful exercise. If you do so, you will see that the more elastic the supply, the greater the effect of a demand shift on quantity, and the smaller the effect on price.

To be sure that you have understood elasticity, consider the following three observations about price and quantity and match them with the three descriptions of supply and demand:

Figure 6-6 reviews the effect of shifts in supply with various elasticities.

a. Price rises significantly; quantity hardly changes at all.

b. Price remains almost constant; quantity increases enormously.

c. Price falls significantly; quantity hardly changes at all.

1. Demand highly elastic; supply shifts out.

2. Supply highly inelastic; demand shifts out.

3. Demand is highly inelastic; supply shifts out.

The answers are a–2; b–1; c–3.

CONCLUSION

I'll stop the exercises here. As you can see, the elasticity concept is important. Economists use it all the time when discussing supply and demand.

However, the elasticity concept is not easy to remember, or to calculate, so working with it takes some practice. It becomes a bit less forbidding if you remember that elasticity is what your shorts lose when they've been through the washer and drier too many times. If a relationship is elastic, price (for price elasticity) exerts a strong pull on quantity. If it's inelastic, there's little pull on quantity.

Chapter Summary

- Elasticity is defined as percentage change in quantity over percentage change in some variable that affects demand (or supply) or quantity demanded (or supplied). The most common elasticity concept used is price elasticity.

- Elasticity is a better descriptor than is slope because it is independent of units of measurement.

- To calculate percentage changes in prices and quantities use the arc convention:

$$\text{The percentage change in quantity} = \frac{Q_2 - Q_1}{1/2(Q_1 + Q_2)} \times 100$$

$$\text{The percentage change in price} = \frac{P_2 - P_1}{1/2(P_1 + P_2)} \times 100$$

$$E_D = \frac{\text{Percentage change in quantity demanded}}{\text{Percentage change in price}}$$

$$E_S = \frac{\text{Percentage change in quantity supplied}}{\text{Percentage change in price}}$$

- Five elasticity terms are: *elastic* ($E > 1$); *inelastic* ($E < 1$); *unit elastic* ($E = 1$); *perfectly inelastic* ($E = 0$); and *perfectly elastic* ($E = \infty$).

- The more substitutes a good has, the greater its elasticity.

- Factors affecting the number of substitutes in demand are (1) time interval considered, (2) whether the good is a luxury or a necessity, (3) how specifically the good is defined, and (4) the proportion of one's budget the price of the good is.

- The most important factor affecting the number of substitutes in supply is time. As the time interval lengthens, supply becomes more elastic.

- Elasticity changes along straight-line demand and supply curves. Demand becomes less elastic as we move down along a demand curve.

- When a supplier raises price, if demand is inelastic total revenue increases; if demand is elastic, total revenue decreases; if demand is unit elastic total revenue remains constant.

- Other important elasticity concepts are income elasticity and cross-price elasticity of demand.

- $$\text{Income elasticity of demand} = \frac{\text{Percentage change in demand}}{\text{Percentage change in income}}$$

- $$\text{Cross-price elasticity of demand} = \frac{\text{Percentage change in demand}}{\text{Percentage change in price of a related good}}$$

- Knowing elasticities allows us to be more precise about the qualitative effects that shifts in demand and supply have on prices and quantities.

Key Terms

complements *(149)*

cross-price elasticity of
demand *(147)*

elastic *(133)*

income elasticity of
demand *(147)*

inelastic *(134)*

inferior goods *(148)*

luxuries *(147)*

necessity *(148)*

normal goods *(147)*

perfectly elastic *(138)*

perfectly inelastic *(138)*

price elasticity of
demand *(133)*

price elasticity of
supply *(133)*

substitutes *(148)*

unit elastic *(139)*

Questions for Thought and Review

1. Determine the price elasticity of demand if, in response to an increase in price of 10 percent, quantity demanded decreases by 20 percent. Is demand elastic or inelastic?

2. A firm has just increased its price by 5 percent over last year's price, and it found that quantity sold remained the same. The firm comes to you and wants to know its price elasticity of demand. How would you calculate it? What additional information would you search for before you did your calculation?

3. In 1999 Domino's Pizza, a corporate sponsor of the Washington Redskins (a football team) offered to reduce the price of its medium-size pizza by $1 for every touchdown scored by the Redskins during the previous week. Until that year, the Redskins weren't scoring many touchdowns. Much to the surprise of Domino's, in one week in 1999, the Redskins scored six touchdowns. (Maybe they like pizza.) Domino's pizzas were selling for $2 a pie! The quantity of pizzas demanded soared the following week from 1 pie an hour to 100 pies an hour. What was price elasticity of demand for Domino's pizza?

4. Which of the pairs of goods would you expect to have a greater price elasticity of demand?
   a. Cars, transportation.
   b. Housing, leisure travel.
   c. Rubber during World War II, rubber during the 20th century.

5. Which has greater elasticity: a supply curve that goes through the origin with slope of 1 or a supply curve that goes through the origin with slope of 4?

6. Why would an economist be more hesitant about making an elastic estimate of the effect of an increase in price of 1 percent rather than an increase in price of 50 percent?

7. Demand for "prestige" college education is generally considered to be highly inelastic. What does this suggest about tuition increases at prestige schools in the future? Why don't colleges raise tuition by amounts even greater than they already do?

8. Once a book has been written, would an author facing an inelastic demand curve for the book prefer to raise or lower the book's price? Why?

9. Colleges have increasingly used price sensitivity to formulate financial aid. The more eager the student, the less aid he or she can expect to get. Use elasticity to explain this phenomenon. Is this practice justified?

10. In the discussion of elasticity and raising and lowering prices, the text states that if you have an elastic demand you should hesitate to raise your price, and that lowering price can *possibly* increase profits (total revenue minus total cost). Why is the word *possibly* used?

11. For each of the following goods, state whether it is a normal good, a luxury, a necessity, or an inferior good. Explain your answers.
    a. Vodka.
    b. Table salt.
    c. Furniture.
    d. Perfume.
    e. Beer.
    f. Sugar.

12. For each of the following pairs of goods, state whether the cross-price elasticity is likely positive, negative, or zero.
    a. Lettuce, carrots.
    b. Housing, furniture.
    c. Nike sneakers, LA Gear sneakers.
    d. Jeans, formal suits.

13. If there were only two goods in the world, can you say whether they would be complements or substitutes? Explain your answer.

14. How is elasticity related to the revenue from a sales tax?

Problems and Exercises

1. A major cereal producer decides to lower price from $3.60 to $3 per 15-ounce box.
   a. If quantity demanded increases by 18 percent, what is the price elasticity of demand?
   b. What if, instead of lowering its price, the cereal producer had increased the size of the box from 15 to 17.8 ounces? What would you expect that the response would have been? Why?

2. In the 1960s coffee came in 1-pound cans. Today, most coffee comes in 11-ounce cans.
   a. Can you think of an explanation why?
   b. Can you think of other products besides coffee whose standard size has shrunk? (Often the standard size is supplemented by a "super-size" alternative.)

3. The president of a liberal arts college in Pennsylvania asked economist Paul Heise about the effect of a particular proposal on net income, enrollment, and student GPA. The proposal was the following: "For the incoming class: (1) cut tuition for students in the top 10 percent of their high school class by 50 percent; (2) cut tuition for students in the 10th to 20th percentiles of their high school class by 33 percent; (3) cut tuition for students in the 20th to 30th percentiles of their high school class by 25 percent; (4) leave tuition the same for all others." He believed the demand was highly elastic.
   a. What was Professor Heise's response?
   b. What would his response have been if the demand had been highly inelastic?

4. Economists William Hunter and Mary Rosenbaum wrote an article in which they estimated the demand elasticity for motor fuel to be between 0.4 and 0.85.
   a. If the price rises 10 percent and the initial quantity sold is 10 million gallons, what is the range of estimates of the new quantity demanded?
   b. In carrying out their estimates they came up with different elasticity estimates for rises in price than for falls in price, with an increase in price having a larger elasticity than a decrease in price. What hypothesis might you propose for their findings?

5. In the "Geometric Tricks for Estimating Price Elasticity" box, there are three statements about the elasticities of straight-line supply curves. One of those statements is that supply curves intersecting the quantity axis are inelastic. Can you prove that that is true by algebraic manipulation of the elasticity formula?

6. Calculate the price elasticities of the designated points on the following graph, using the arc elasticity method. (Reread the box "Calculating Elasticity at a Point.")

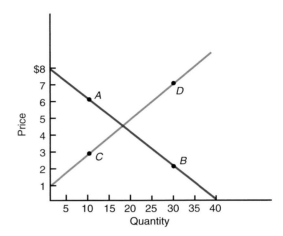

7. Calculate the elasticity of the designated ranges of supply and demand curves on the following graph.

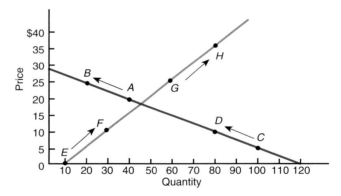

8. Calculate the income elasticities of demand for the following:
   a. Income rises by 20 percent; demand rises by 10 percent.
   b. Income rises from $30,000 to $40,000; demand increases (at a constant price) from 16 to 19.
   c. How would your answer to b differ if you now use the arc convention of calculating percent changes?

9. When the price of ketchup rises by 15 percent, the demand for hot dogs falls by 1 percent.
   a. Calculate the cross-price elasticity of demand.
   b. Are the goods complements or substitutes?
   c. By how much would the demand have to rise for the goods to switch from complements to substitutes, or vice versa?

10. According to *The Wall Street Journal,* in the 1990s the going price for live worms was $1.17 a dozen. Then a drought hit.
    a. Demonstrate graphically what happened to the price and quantity of worms sold.

    b. If the price rose to $1.75 and the quantity sold fell from 90,000 to 60,000, what would your estimate of the elasticity of demand be?

Web Questions

1. Cigarette smoking is widely recognized as the number one cause of cancer in the United States. One method the government can use to reduce cigarette smoking is to tax cigarettes. Read "The Impact of Proposed Cigarette Price Increases" by Frank J. Chaloupka at www.advocacy.org/hsap/tax.htm to answer the following questions about the effect of taxation on cigarette smoking.
    a. Who is likely to be more affected by tax increases on cigarettes—all adults or young adults? Cite specific elasticity of demand estimates from the article to support your answer.
    b. To have the greatest effect on reducing cancer from tobacco use, what other products should government tax?
    c. What is the long-run elasticity of demand for cigarette smoking? What does this mean for the likely impact of taxes on long-run cigarette use?
2. The effect of the minimum wage on employers and employees depends on the elasticity of demand and supply

for labor. Go to the Employment Policies Institute at www.epionlline.org/ to read an article by David A. McPherson, "The Effects of the 1998–1999 Minimum Wage Increase in Oregon," and answer the following questions:
    a. What was the percentage increase in the minimum wage in Oregon from 1998 to 1999?
    b. What is the elasticity of demand for labor used in the study? Is demand elastic or inelastic?
    c. What is the effect of the increase in the minimum wage on labor costs for Oregon firms? Is this consistent with the elasticity of demand for labor? How would the effect on labor costs change if elasticity of demand for labor were greater than 1?
    d. In the long run what will happen to the change in labor costs compared to the change in labor costs in the short run? What accounts for the difference?

Answers to Margin Questions

1. Price elasticity of supply = Percentage change in quantity supplied divided by percentage change in price = 8/4 = 2. *(133)*
2. If price elasticity of demand is greater than 1, by definition demand is elastic. *(133)*
3. Using the arc convention, the percentage change in quantity is 100 (8/8 × 100) and the percentage change in price is 100 (2/2 × 100). Elasticity therefore, is approximately 1 (100/100). *(136)*
4. I tell her that she is partially right (for the bottom part of the curve), but that elasticity on a straight line demand curve changes from perfectly elastic at the vertical axis intersection to perfectly inelastic at the horizontal axis intersection. *(139)*
5. The most important determinant of the price elasticity of demand is the number of substitutes a good has. *(139)*

6. Four factors affecting the number of substitutes in demand are (1) time interval considered, (2) whether the good is a luxury or a necessity, (3) how specifically the good is defined, and (4) the proportion of one's budget the price of the good is. *(141)*
7. Supply is generally more elastic in the long run because there are more alternative goods and services for producers to produce. *(141)*
8. If demand is inelastic, total revenue increases with an increase in price. *(144)*
9. If consumption increases with an increase in income, the good is a normal good. *(147)*
10. With an elastic demand, lowering price will increase total revenue because it will increase sales. But producing more will increase costs, so information about total revenue is not enough to answer the question. *(150)*

Taxation and Government Intervention

7

After reading this chapter, you should be able to:

- Demonstrate the cost of taxation to consumers and producers.

- Distinguish between the benefit principle and the ability-to-pay principle.

- Explain why the person who physically pays the tax is not necessarily the person who bears the burden of the tax.

- Demonstrate how an effective price ceiling is the equivalent of a tax on producers and a subsidy to consumers.

- Define rent seeking and show how it is related to elasticity.

Collecting more taxes than is absolutely necessary is legalized robbery.

Calvin Coolidge

Chapter 6 introduced you to the term elasticity. In this chapter you will apply what you learned. When combined with the concept of elasticity, the supply and demand tools become even more useful. We'll see why by considering two policy issues: taxation and government intervention into markets.

TAXATION AND GOVERNMENT

An old saying goes "The only things in life that are certain are death and taxes." And if you ask individuals what they dislike most about government, many would say taxes.

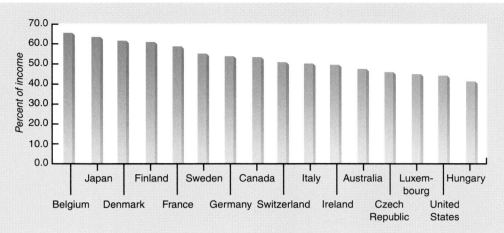

Figure 7-1   Highest Tax Rates on Wage Income (1998)

As you can see from this figure that shows the highest tax rates on wage income for various countries, the United States is one of the lower tax-rate countries.

Source: OECD.

Unfortunately, the government needs taxes to function, and the market likewise needs government. When governments do not have a well-functioning tax system, as is the case in some developing and transitional economies such as Russia's, the government is unable to provide the institutional structure markets need to work effectively. The connection between taxes and the roles of government led American jurist Oliver Wendell Holmes, Jr., to state that taxes are the price we pay for civilization.

Tax rates depend on what goods and services government provides. Having more government-provided goods and services means having higher taxes. The taxes can be low if government plays a minor role in the market—simply providing an institutional framework—or they can be high if government plays a major role such as providing free education and free health care to all citizens. Figure 7-1 gives you a sense of tax rates in various countries. As you can see, the United States is one of the lower tax-rate countries.

Taxes are a pain, but some taxes are necessary.

How Much Should Government Tax?

How should a country decide how much to tax? An economist would answer that question by asking another question: What are the costs and the benefits of taxation? The benefits are the gains to society that result from the goods and services government provides when fulfilling the six roles in a market economy discussed in Chapter 5:

1. Provide a stable set of institutions and rules.
2. Promote effective and workable competition.
3. Correct for externalities.
4. Ensure economic stability and growth.
5. Provide public goods.
6. Adjust for undesired market results.

The Costs of Taxation[1] The costs of taxation to society include the direct cost of the revenue paid to government, the loss of consumer and producer surplus caused by the

---

[1]The analysis presented here is highly simplified. Numerous points can be added to the analysis, some of which will be discussed in later chapters. Despite its limitations, the visual sense of the costs and benefits that the producer and consumer surplus concepts convey is a fundamental building block of the economic way of thinking.

KNOWING THE TOOLS

Consumer and Producer Surplus

In a market most consumers pay less than they would have been willing to pay, and most producers receive more than they would have been willing to accept. As was discussed in Chapter 4 the difference between what consumers would be willing to pay and what they do pay is consumer surplus; the difference between what producers receive and what they would be willing to receive is producer surplus.

Consumer surplus and producer surplus are shown graphically at the right. Consumers would be willing to pay $10 for the second unit, and suppliers would be willing to sell the second unit for $2.

The distance between the demand curve (what the consumer is willing to pay) and the price the consumer actually pays is consumer surplus. When price is at equilibrium ($5), consumer surplus is represented by the blue shaded area. The distance between the supply curve (what the supplier is willing to sell for) and the price the supplier receives is producer surplus. When price is at equilibrium ($5), producer surplus is represented by the red shaded area. At the market equilibrium price, the combination of consumer and producer surpluses is as large as it can be.

A tax paid by the supplier shifts the supply curve up by the amount of the tax.

tax, and the cost of administering the tax codes. Figure 7-2 provides the basic framework for understanding the costs of taxation. For a given good, a per unit tax t paid by the supplier increases the price at which suppliers are willing to sell that good. The increase in price is shown by a shift upward of the supply curve from S_0 to S_1. The equilibrium price of the good rises and the quantity sold declines.

Before the tax, consumer surplus is represented by areas $A + B + C$ and producer surplus is represented by areas $D + E + F$. With the tax t, equilibrium price rises to P_1 and equilibrium quantity falls to Q_1. Tax revenue paid equals the tax t times equilibrium quantity Q_1, or areas B and D.

Figure 7-2   The Costs of Taxation

A per unit tax t paid by the supplier shifts the supply curve up from S_0 to S_1. Equilibrium price rises from P_0 to P_1, and equilibrium quantity falls from Q_0 to Q_1. Consumer surplus is represented by areas A, B, and C before the tax and area A after the tax. Producer surplus is represented by areas D, E, and F before the tax and area F after the tax. Government collects tax shown by areas B and D. The tax imposes a deadweight loss, represented by the welfare loss triangle of areas C and E.

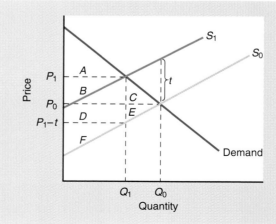

The total cost to consumers and producers is more than tax revenue. Consumers pay area *B* in tax revenue and also lose area *C* in consumer surplus. Producers pay area *D* in tax revenue and lose area *E* in producer surplus. The triangular area *C* + *E* represents a cost of taxation in excess of the revenue paid to government. It is lost consumer and producer surplus that is not gained by government. *The loss of consumer and producer surplus from a tax* is known as **deadweight loss.** Deadweight loss is shown graphically by the **welfare loss triangle**—*a geometric representation of the welfare cost in terms of misallocated resources caused by a deviation from a supply/demand equilibrium.* Keep in mind that with the tax, quantity sold declines. The loss of welfare therefore represents a loss for those consumers and producers who would have traded without the tax but do not trade with the tax.

The costs of taxation don't end there. Resources must be devoted by government to administer the tax code and by individuals to comply with it. Firms and individuals either spend hours filling out income tax forms or pay others to do so. Firms hire accountants and lawyers to take full advantage of any tax-code allowances. Administration costs can be as much as 5 percent of the total tax revenue paid to government. Like the tax itself, these costs increase the price at which producers are willing to sell their goods, reducing quantity sold and further increasing welfare loss.

The Benefits of Taxation The benefits of taxes consist of the goods and services that government provides. Some government-provided goods are part of the basic institutional structure of a market economy and must be supplied if the market is to function effectively. The basic legal system is an example. Other goods are provided by government because they have the qualities of a public good; national defense is an example.

Still other goods are provided by government for reasons of equity or because they create positive externalities. Private markets will provide these goods but perhaps not distribute them equitably or in sufficient quantities. Education up through high school is an example; it is publicly supplied even though it could be privately supplied. A number of governments supply health care publicly. In the United States most health care is supplied privately, although portions of it are paid for by government through Medicare and Medicaid.

The policy debate about the benefits of taxation generally focuses on goods that could be supplied by the market but are, instead, publicly supplied. For example, in the 2000 presidential election one of the candidates, Bill Bradley, suggested that the government provide free health insurance for many individuals without it. Other candidates opposed his plan because it would have required the United States to have higher taxes than it otherwise would have had. The need for taxes increases enormously when the government supplies certain goods to individuals, or pays the private sector to supply those goods.

In the 2000 presidential election some candidates also suggested implementing a voucher system to fund education. In such a system each student is given a certain amount of money, in the form of a voucher, to be used to attend the school of his or her choice. Although a voucher system would likely have decreased the amount of education government supplies, it would not have reduced taxes, since taxes would still have to be collected to fund the vouchers. Private supply of education would have each family paying for their education without any vouchers.

Measuring the benefits of government-supplied goods is difficult, mainly because they are not provided in a market setting. Because of this difficulty, along with the problem of deciding whether certain goods should be provided by government at all, the task of choosing which goods and services to provide and how to finance them is always surrounded by debate.

Q.1 Demonstrate the welfare loss of a tax when the supply is highly elastic and the demand is highly inelastic.

 7.1

Q.2 Would introducing a voucher system to finance education reduce taxes? Why or why not?

Two Principles of Taxation

I'll discuss the problems government faces in choosing what goods to provide in Chapter 15. In this chapter I will focus on the taxes needed to pay for the goods that government does provide. In making decisions about taxes, government follows two general principles: the *benefit principle*, and the *ability-to-pay principle*.

The Benefit Principle The **benefit principle** of taxation follows the same principle as the market: *The individuals who receive the benefit of a good or service should pay the tax necessary to supply that good.* An example of a tax based on the benefit principle is the gasoline tax used to finance road construction in the United States. Since the users of gasoline are using the roads, there is a connection between use and payment; however, unlike a toll, the tax is not direct—people do not pay each time they use the road. Another example is airport use taxes, which provide funding for the building of airports.

The difference between paying for goods through taxes and paying for them in a market is that, with government-supplied goods, consumers aren't directly paying for the goods and consequently do not reveal their preference for the good. The connection between benefit and cost in the decision to buy a publicly provided good is looser than it is with a privately supplied good.

The Ability-to-Pay Principle The **ability-to-pay principle** of taxation does not make any connection between use and payment but simply states: *The individuals who are most able to bear the burden of the tax should pay the tax.* Generally this principle is interpreted as supporting a progressive tax—one whose rate increases with increases in income. With a progressive tax, the tax on the first $10,000 a person earns might be 14 percent and the tax on the next $10,000 might be 20 percent. (A person earning $20,000 would pay an average rate of 17 percent.) During World War II the United States had a highly progressive tax, with the top rate reaching 95 percent; it has declined since then, and the top federal income tax rate is now 39.6 percent. (State income taxes can add another 10 percent.)

The reasoning behind the ability-to-pay principle is that similar tax rates represent a smaller sacrifice for those with higher incomes compared to those with lower incomes. The wealthy should pay more because they can. Since the ability-to-pay principle of taxation makes no attempt to relate the benefit to the tax, the income tax revenue is used to finance a wide variety of government activities such as welfare and defense.

Difficulty of Applying the Principles of Taxation The two principles of taxation discussed above are the ones that economists and policymakers use most often to assess tax structures. Unfortunately, they are not easy to apply and often conflict. For example, benefits of the goods that government supplies are often difficult to assign, making the benefit principle ambiguous. Consider education; it benefits not only the recipient but also the general public. How much does each benefit? (If you asked many high school students whether they would be willing to pay the $7,000 a year it costs to educate them in public school, I suspect many would say no.) Or consider funding health insurance for poor individuals. Under the benefit principle the poor would pay the majority of the costs. Under the ability-to-pay principle the rich would pay.

When taxes are based on the ability-to-pay principle, many high-income individuals ask why they should pay disproportionately more for goods such as income-support programs that are benefiting others, not them. The conflict between these two principles, combined with people's general desire to have "the other person" pay the taxes while they receive the benefits, often leads to significant debates about what to tax.

With government-supplied goods individuals do not reveal their preference for the good.

Q-3 If the tax on the first $20,000 is zero and thereafter the tax is 20 percent, what average tax rate would a person earning $30,000 pay?

The two principles of taxation, the benefit principle and the ability-to-pay principle, are often in conflict with each other.

Thus, we see debates about whether education should be financed by a *property tax*—a tax on houses and land—or by a *sales tax*—a tax on goods and services sold to consumers. Should income be taxed, or should only specific goods, like gasoline, be taxed? Should we use a corporate income tax or the general income tax?

The elasticity concept helps provide insight into the above debates. One of the facts you learned about elasticity is that the more broadly the good is defined, the more inelastic is the demand. Thus, the demand for all goods is much more inelastic than the demand for a particular good, since individuals cannot switch their consumption out of all goods but can switch from one specific good to another. This means that if government, given its targeted revenue, wants to have as little effect on individual actions as possible—or, in the language of consumer and producer surplus, if government wants to minimize the welfare loss—then it should tax goods with inelastic supplies or demands. Broad-based taxes such as income and sales taxes—which represent over 50 percent of state, local, and federal tax revenue—do just that. Most countries use a broad-based income tax, value-added tax, or general sales tax as their primary source of tax revenue.

If the government wants to minimize the welfare loss it should tax goods with inelastic supplies and demands.

Who Bears the Burden of a Tax?

Taxes are like hot potatoes: everyone wants to pass them on to someone else. Nobody wants to pay taxes, and there are usually large political fights about whom government should tax. For example, should the social security tax (mandated by the Federal Insurance Contributions Act, or FICA) be placed on workers or on the company that hires them? Or does it matter? The supply and demand framework gives an unexpected answer to this question.

Burden Depends on Relative Elasticity Let's consider the issue of who bears the burden of a tax by looking at the example involving excise taxes introduced in Chapter 5. There I defined an **excise tax** as *a tax levied on a specific good* and gave the example of a luxury tax on expensive boats that the United States imposed in 1990. An excise tax can be levied on the consumer (who will physically pay the tax) or on the seller.

The person who *physically pays* the tax, however, is not necessarily the person who *bears the burden* of the tax. Who bears the burden of the tax (also known as tax incidence) depends on who is best able to change their behavior in response to the tax, or who has the greater elasticity. Elasticity and supply/demand analysis lets us answer the question "Who will end up bearing the burden of the tax?" (More technically: "What is the incidence of the tax?")

Figure 7-3(a) shows the case I considered in Chapter 5. A $10,000 per unit tax levied on the supplier shifts the supply curve up from S_0 to S_1. That reduces quantity supplied and quantity demanded by 90—from 600 to 510. The equilibrium price rises from $60,000 to $65,000. Suppliers are able to shift $5,000 of the total $10,000 per unit tax onto consumers, leaving the suppliers the burden of the remaining $5,000.

Had we known elasticities at the market equilibrium, we could have stated, without additional calculations, that the tax burden would be shared equally. Specifically, suppliers sold and consumers purchased 90 fewer boats, a 15 percent reduction. The suppliers' price fell by about 8 percent while the consumers' price rose by about 8 percent, meaning the elasticity of both supply and demand was approximately 1.9.[2] With equal elasticities, the tax burden will be divided equally.

[2]There will be slight variations in the measured elasticities depending on how they are calculated. The precise equality holds only for point elasticities, and we are using arc elasticities (see Chapter 6).

Figure 7-3 (a, b, and c)   Who Bears the Burden of a Tax

In the general case the burden of a tax is borne by the relative elasticities of supply and demand. The blue shaded area shows the burden on the consumer; the red shaded area shows the burden on the supplier. This split occurs regardless of who actually pays the tax, as can be seen by noticing that the burden of the tax is equal in (**a**) where the supplier pays the tax and in (**c**) where the consumer pays the tax. In (**b**) you can see how consumers with an inelastic demand bear a greater burden of the tax. The blue shaded area represents the burden paid by consumers; the red area shows the burden on suppliers.

(a)   Supplier pays tax   (b)   Demand is inelastic   (c)   Consumer pays tax

Q.4 Show the tax burden in the case where the demand is elastic and the supply is inelastic.

Tax burden is allocated by relative elasticities.

In reality the tax burden is rarely shared equally because elasticities are rarely equal. The relative burden of the tax follows this general rule: *The more inelastic one's relative supply and demand, the larger the burden of the tax one will bear.* If demand were more inelastic, sellers would have been able to sell the boats at a higher price and could have passed more of the tax along to the buyers.

Figure 7-3(b) shows what the divisions would have been had the demand curve been highly inelastic. In this case the price would rise more, the supplier would pay a lower proportion of the tax (the red area), and the consumer would pay a much larger proportion (the blue area). The general rule about elasticities and the tax burden is this: If demand is more inelastic than supply, consumers will pay a higher percentage of the tax; if supply is more inelastic than demand, suppliers will pay a higher share. This rule makes sense—*elasticity is a measure of how easy it is for the supplier and consumer to change behavior and substitute another good.*

The above rule can lead to some unexpected consequences of taxation. For example, the U.S. luxury tax on boats was initially implemented as a way to tax the wealthy. It turned out, however, that the wealthy found substitutes for American-made boats; their demand was relatively elastic. They either purchased other luxury items or purchased their boats from foreign firms. U.S. boat manufacturers, however, couldn't easily switch to producing other products. Their supply was inelastic. As a result, they tried to pass on the cost increase to consumers, but they saw their sales plummet. They had to lower their price by almost as much as the tax, which meant that they were bearing most of the burden of the tax. As noted in Chapter 5, pressured by boat manufacturers, the government repealed the luxury tax on boats three years after it was instituted.

Who Pays a Tax Is Not Necessarily Who Bears the Burden The allocation of tax burden by relative elasticity means that it doesn't matter who actually pays the tax and

What goods should be taxed depends on the goal of government. If the goal is to fund a program with as little loss as possible in consumer and producer surplus, then the government should tax a good whose supply or demand is inelastic. If the goal is to change behavior, taxes will be most effective if demand or supply is elastic. As a quick review, use the following table:

Goal of Government	Most Effective When
Raise revenue, limit deadweight loss	Demand or supply is inelastic
Change behavior	Demand or supply is elastic

Distributional issues must also be considered when determining what goods are to be taxed. In general, the group with the relatively more inelastic supply or demand will bear a greater portion of the tax. The following table reviews these conclusions:

Elasticity	Who Bears the Burden?
Demand inelastic and supply elastic	Consumers
Supply inelastic and demand elastic	Producers
Both supply and demand elastic	Shared; but the group whose supply or demand is more inelastic

that, as I said earlier, the person who bears the burden can differ from the person who pays. To assure yourself that it doesn't matter who pays the tax, ask yourself how your answer would have differed if the tax of $10,000 had been paid by the consumer. Figure 7-3(c) shows this case. Because the tax is paid by the consumer, the demand curve shifts down by the amount of the tax. As you can see, the results of the tax are identical. The percentage of the tax paid by the supplier and the consumer, after adjusting for the changes in supply and demand price, is independent of who actually makes the physical payment of the tax.

The burden is independent of who physically pays the tax.

Tax Incidence and Current Policy Debates

Now let's consider two policy questions in relation to what we have learned about tax incidence.

Social Security Taxes   The first policy question concerns the social security (or payroll) tax, which accounts for 33 percent of federal government revenue. In 2000, the social security tax rate was 12.4 percent on wages up to an annual maximum wage of $76,200, and another 2.9 percent on all wages, no matter how high, designed to finance Medicare. As a political compromise, half of social security taxes are placed on the employee and half on the employer. But the fact that the law places the tax equally on both does not mean that the burden of the tax is shared equally between employees and employers. On average, labor supply tends to be less elastic than labor demand. This means that the social security tax burden is primarily on the employees, even though employees see only their own statutory portion of the social security tax on their pay stub.

Q.5   If social security taxes were paid only by employees, what would likely happen to workers' pretax pay?

Now, let's say that you are advising a person running for Congress who has come up with the idea to place the entire tax on the employer and eliminate the tax on the employee. What will the effect of that be? Our tax incidence analysis tells us that, ultimately, it will have no effect. Wages paid to employees will fall to compensate employers for the cost of the tax. This example shows that who is assessed the tax can be quite different than who actually bears the burden, or incidence, of the tax. The burden will be borne by those with the most inelastic supply or demand, because they have no way of getting out of paying the tax by substitution.

 7.2

So what do you tell the candidate? Is the idea a good one or not? Although economically it will not make a difference who pays the tax, politically it may be a popular proposal because individuals generally look at statutory assessment, not incidence. The candidate may gain significant support from workers, since they would no longer see a social security tax on their pay stub. The moral, then, is this: Politics often focuses on surface appearance; economics tries to get under the surface, and what is good economics is not always good politics.

Sales Taxes Our second policy question concerns sales taxes paid by retailers on the basis of their sales revenue. In my state the general sales tax is 5 cents on the dollar. Since sales taxes are broadly defined, consumers have little ability to substitute. Demand is inelastic and consumers bear the greater burden of the tax. Although stores could simply incorporate the tax into the price of their goods, most stores add the tax onto the bill after the initial sale is calculated, to make you aware of the tax. Again, it doesn't matter whether the tax is assessed on the store or on you.

Recently, however, the Internet has given consumers a substitute to shopping at actual retail stores. Retail sales over the Internet are over $20 billion annually and are continuing to grow. States have found it very difficult to tax Internet sales because the supplier has no retail address. The point of sale is in cyberspace. Technically in these cases, the buyer is required to pay the tax to the state where he or she lives, but in practice that seldom happens. How to tax Internet sales will be heavily debated over the next few years. The federal government has placed a moratorium on new Internet sales taxes until 2001. As Internet sales grow, states will lose more and more sales tax revenue and retail shops will bear a larger portion of the tax levied on their sales, which together will invite strong pressure to end the moratorium.

GOVERNMENT INTERVENTION

Taxes are not the only way government affects our lives. For example, government establishes laws that dictate what we can do, what prices we can charge for goods, and what working conditions are and are not acceptable. This second part of the chapter continues the discussion of such issues, which began in Chapter 5. I show how the elasticity concept can help us talk about such interventions and how, using the producer and consumer surplus framework, such interventions can be seen as a combination of tax and subsidy that does not show up on government books.

Government Intervention as Implicit Taxation

To see how government intervention in the market can be seen as a combination tax and subsidy, let's first consider the two types of price controls mentioned in Chapter 5: price ceilings and price floors.

Price Ceilings and Floors As I discussed in Chapter 5, a **price ceiling** is *a government-set price below the market equilibrium price*. It is in essence an implicit tax on producers and an implicit subsidy to consumers. Consider the effect of a price ceiling on producer and consumer surplus, shown in Figure 7-4(a).

If the price were at the market equilibrium price, the total surplus would be the combination of the areas A through F. But with an effective price ceiling P_1, the quantity supplied falls from Q_0 to Q_1. The combined producer and consumer surplus is reduced by triangles C and E. The loss of surplus represents those individuals who would like to

What makes sense politically is not always what makes sense economically.

Q-6 Demonstrate the effect of an effective price ceiling on producer and consumer surplus when both supply and demand are highly inelastic.

Figure 7-4 (a and b)   Effect of Price Controls on Consumer and Producer Surplus

Price floors and price ceilings create deadweight loss just as taxes do. In (**a**) we see how a price ceiling, P_1, transfers surplus D from producers to consumers. Price ceilings are equivalent to a tax on producers and a subsidy to consumers. In (**b**) we see how a price floor, P_2, transfers surplus B from consumers to producers. With both a price floor and a price ceiling, areas C and E represent the welfare loss triangle.

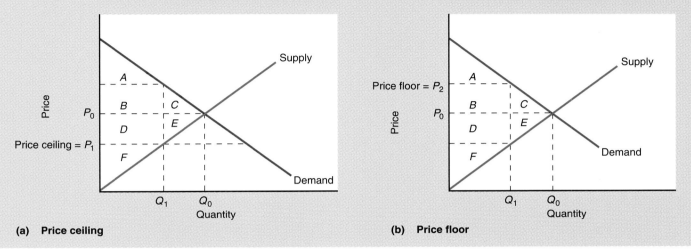

(a)   **Price ceiling**   (b)   **Price floor**

make trades—the individuals represented by the demand and supply curves between Q_1 and Q_0—but cannot do so because of the price ceiling.

This loss of consumer and producer surplus is identical to the welfare loss from taxation.[3] That is not a coincidence. The price ceiling is a combination implicit tax on suppliers, shown by area D, and implicit subsidy to consumers of that same area. It is as if government places a tax on suppliers when they buy the good, and then gives that tax revenue to consumers when they consume the good.

Price floors have the opposite effect on the distribution of consumer and producer surplus. **Price floors**—*government-set prices above equilibrium price*—transfer consumer surplus to producers. They can be seen as a tax on consumers of area B and a subsidy to producers of that same area, as shown in Figure 7-4(b). Price floors also impose a deadweight loss, shown by the welfare loss triangle, areas C and E.

The Difference between Taxes and Price Controls While the effects of taxation and controls are similar, there is an important difference: *Price ceilings create shortages; taxes do not.* The reason is that taxes leave people free to choose how much they want to supply and consume as long as they pay the tax. Thus, taxes create a wedge between the price the consumers pay and the price the suppliers receive. That difference is just enough to equate quantity demanded with quantity supplied.

Since with price ceilings the price consumers pay equals the price suppliers receive, the desired quantity demanded will not be equal to the desired quantity supplied since the price is not the equilibrium price. Some method of rationing—limiting the demand or increasing the supply in the case of price ceilings, and limiting the supply and

A price ceiling is a combination implicit tax on supplies and implicit subsidy on consumers.

Price ceilings create shortages; taxes do not.

 7.3

---

[3]As I will discuss below, for price controls the welfare triangle provides a minimum amount of loss in consumer and producer surplus; the actual loss may be greater.

increasing the demand in the case of price floors—must be found. In the examples of price ceilings so far we have assumed that suppliers can choose to supply how much or how little they want. Thus, there are shortages. Such shortages create black markets—markets in which individuals buy or sell illegally. (Black markets may also be created by taxes if buyers and sellers attempt to evade the tax.)

A Price Ceiling with Forced Supply: The Draft There are other ways of dealing with shortages. For example, there could be "forced supply"—that is, suppliers could be required by law to supply goods at the ceiling price. The military draft is an example. A draft is a law that requires some people to serve a set period in the armed forces at whatever pay the government chooses. It has often been used as a way of meeting the military's need for soldiers. The draft is a price ceiling combined with forced supply. (This case study may become highly relevant because, in recent years, the military has been falling short of the number of recruits it needs and some members of Congress have been suggesting that the United States reinstitute the draft. The legislative authority to do so already exists, and currently all men are legally required to register for the draft when they turn 18.)[4]

The effects of a draft are shown in Figure 7-5. A draft must be imposed when the wage offered by the army is below equilibrium so that the quantity of soldiers demanded is below the quantity supplied. In Figure 7-5 the offered wage W_0 is below the equilibrium wage W_e. The market answer to the shortage would be to increase the wage to W_e. How much the wage would need to be increased to bring about equilibrium depends on the elasticity of supply and demand. If both supply and demand are inelastic, then the pay will need to be increased enormously; if both are elastic, the pay will need to be increased only slightly.

The people who are proposing the draft suspect that both supply and demand are inelastic, in which case the market solution would be very expensive to the government, requiring large increases in taxes. They argue that a draft is much cheaper, and requires lower taxes.

Our supply/demand analysis reveals the fallacy in that reasoning. Government interventions, such as the draft, transfer surplus from one set of individuals to another. Any intervention is the equivalent of a tax on the one from whom the surplus is taken and a subsidy to the one to whom the surplus is given. So the draft imposes a tax, but it is a tax that doesn't show up on the government books. Rather, the tax is on all individuals drafted (young men), and the subsidy is given to those who demand defense services. So, yes, with a draft the government does not have to collect as much revenue as it would if it raised the wage to a market-clearing wage, but the draft places the equivalent of an explicit tax on young men. Instead of being able to do what they want, they must serve in the armed forces.

By paying a lower-than-equilibrium wage, the government is transferring surplus from those drafted to itself. To get around the shortage, the draft requires men to serve whether they want to or not. The effective supply curve becomes the horizontal line W_0. The quantity supplied is forced to meet the quantity demanded at the price ceiling.

In this case of forced supply even more surplus is transferred than in the previous cases we considered. Specifically, in Figure 7-5 the red shaded area is transferred from suppliers to consumers of national defense. The welfare loss triangle is now the triangle

The draft is a price ceiling combined with forced supply.

Q-7   Does a draft allow the government to have lower taxes?

---

[4]Women are not, which raises some questions that will likely be much discussed if the draft is reinstituted.

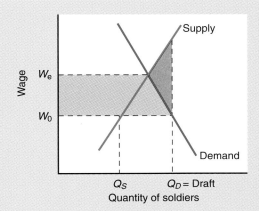

Figure 7-5   Effect of a Draft on Surplus

The military draft is one solution to the shortage that occurs when wages are below the equilibrium wage. The market solution to the shortage of soldiers is for the army to offer soldiers a higher wage. This, however, would require government to raise taxes on the general public. The draft solution would not require an increase in explicit taxes. Instead, it forces young men to supply the quantity demanded by the army. Those who are drafted will accept a lower wage than they could get in the market, which is a transfer of surplus to government. The amount of the transferred surplus is shown by the red shaded region. The gray shaded region shows the deadweight loss associated with the draft.

to the right of the market equilibrium. It is the loss in surplus that the suppliers lose but that the consumers do not receive.

The above analysis of welfare loss due to the price ceiling is the minimum loss that the ceiling will create. The analysis assumes that the individuals drafted will be those whose opportunity cost of being drafted is lowest. In fact, that is not the case. The actual amount of loss depends on how the draft selects individuals. If it selects individuals totally randomly (which in principle is how drafts are structured), it will draft some into the armed forces who would not consider serving even at the equilibrium wage. (For example, Elvis Presley was drafted; when he entered the army he gave up millions of dollars of income, so his opportunity cost was extremely high.) Thus, the welfare loss is larger for interferences in the market such as the draft than it is for an equivalent tax, although it is difficult to specify how much larger it is.

Generally, the welfare loss is larger for controls than for an equivalent tax.

Rent Seeking, Politics, and Elasticities

If price controls reduce total producer and consumer surplus, why do governments institute them? The answer is that *people care more about their own surplus than they do about total surplus*. As we have seen, price ceilings redistribute surplus from producers to consumers, so if the consumers have the political power there will be strong pressures to create price ceilings. Alternatively, if the suppliers have the political power, there will be strong pressures to create price floors.

The possibility of transferring surplus from one set of individuals to another causes people to spend time and resources on doing so. For example, if criminals know that $1 million ransoms are commonly paid for executives, it will be worthwhile for them to figure out ways to kidnap executives—which happens in some developing and transitional economies. (That's why all countries state that they will never pay ransoms; however, not all countries follow their stated policies.)

The possibility of kidnapping, in turn, causes executives to hire bodyguards, which in turn causes kidnappers to think of ingenious ways to kidnap (which in turn …). The result is that, as one group attempts to appropriate surplus from another group, enormous amounts of resources are spent on activities that benefit no one.

Figure 7-6   Inelastic Demand and the Incentive to Restrict Supply

When demand is inelastic, increases in productivity that shift the supply curve to the right result in lower revenue for suppliers. Although suppliers gain area B, they lose the much larger area A. Suppliers have an incentive to restrict supply when demand is inelastic because, by doing so, they will increase their revenues.

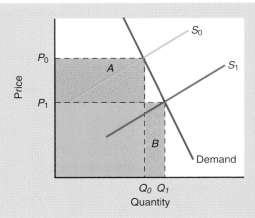

The same reasoning holds for lobbying government. Individuals have an incentive to spend resources to lobby government to institute policies that increase their own surplus. Others have an incentive to spend money to counteract those lobbying efforts. *Activities designed to transfer surplus from one group to another* are called **rent-seeking activities.** Rent-seeking activities require resources, and the net result is unproductive. **Public choice economists**—*economists who integrate an economic analysis of politics with their analysis of the economy*—argue that rent seeking through government is significant, and that much of the transfer of surplus that occurs through government intervention creates an enormous waste of resources. They argue that the taxes and the benefits of government programs affect each other and do not help society significantly, but they do cost resources. These economists point out that much of the redistribution through government is from one group of the middle class to another group of the middle class.

Inelastic Demand and Incentives to Restrict Supply To understand the rent-seeking process a bit better, let's look more carefully at the incentives that consumers and producers have to lobby government to intervene in the market. We'll begin with suppliers. A classic example of the political pressures to limit supply is found in agricultural markets. Within the past century new machinery, new methods of farming, and hybrid seeds have increased the productivity of farmers tremendously. You might think that because farmers can now produce more at a lower cost, they'd be better off. But if you think that, you're ignoring the interaction of supply and demand. As advances in productivity increase supply they do increase the quantity sold, but they also result in lower prices. Farmers sell more but they get less for each unit they sell. Because food is a necessity and has few substitutes, the demand for many agricultural goods is inelastic. Since demand is inelastic the price declines by a greater proportion than the rise in quantity sold, meaning that total revenue declines and the farmers are actually worse off. The situation is shown in Figure 7-6.

Because of the increase in supply, price declines from P_0 to P_1 and quantity sold increases from Q_0 to Q_1. The farmer's revenue rises by area B but also falls by larger area A. To counteract this trend, farmers have an incentive to get government to restrict supply or create a price floor, thereby raising their revenue. In fact, that's what they did in the 1930s. Farmers then were instrumental in getting the government to establish the Farm Board, a federal agency whose job was to manage productivity of agricultural goods. The benefits of limiting competition are greatest for suppliers when demand is inelastic because price will rise proportionately more than quantity will fall.

Q-8 Would a firm's research and development expenditures be classified as rent seeking?

Q-9 How can an increase in productivity harm suppliers?

7.4

When talking about price increases in the text, I mean percentage price increases, which is what the elasticity concept relates to the percentage changes in quantity. A $20 price increase on a $20,000 car is insignificant, because it is such a small percentage of the total price (0.1 percent). So remember, when deciding whether a price increase is significant or not, think of the price increase in percentage, not absolute, terms.

The difference between percentage change and absolute change is a source of constant confusion. Consider the discussions of fluctuations in the Dow Jones Industrial Average. On March 16th, 2000, the Dow Jones Industrial Average rose 499 points—its biggest point gain in a single day and 118 points more than the next-largest single

KNOWING THE TOOLS

Elasticity and Whether a Price Increase Is Significant

day gain. In percentage terms, however, the Dow had risen 4.93%—a less-than-historical gain. It was not even large enough to make the top 35 list of largest single-day percentage gains. The day that holds the record for the largest percentage gain the Dow is October 6, 1931, when it rose by 99.34 points. But, since the day's beginning the Dow was 668, the 99 point rise represented a whopping 14.87% single-day gain.

Another way to look at it is this: A movement of 100 when the Dow was 600 is a 16.7% change in the value of the stocks. A movement of 100 when the Dow is 10,000 is a 1% change. So remember to think percentages when deciding whether a change in price (or in anything) is large or small.

This simple example provides us with an important insight about how markets work and how the politics of government intervention work. Inelastic demand creates an enormous incentive for suppliers either to pressure government to limit the quantity supplied or to get together and look for other ways to limit the quantity supplied. The more inelastic demand is, the more farmers have to gain by restricting supply. By limiting quantity supplied they can raise the price, increasing total revenue.

Sometimes sellers can get government to limit quantity supplied through licensing; other times the existing suppliers can limit supply by force. A well-placed threat ("If you enter this market, I will blow up your store") is often effective. In some transitional economies, such threats are common. What stops existing suppliers from making good on such threats? Government. But the government also creates opportunities for individuals to prevent others from entering the market. Therein lies a central problem of political economy. You need government to see that competition works—to see that existing suppliers don't prevent others from entering the market—but government can also be used to prevent competition and protect existing suppliers. Hence, the point that we will return to throughout this book: Government is part of both the problem and the solution.

The central problem of political economy is that you need government to see that competition works, but government can also be used to prevent competition.

Inelastic Supplies and Incentives to Restrict Prices Firms aren't the only ones who can lobby government to intervene. Consider consumers. When supply is inelastic, consumers can face significant price increases if their demand increases. Thus, when the supply of a good is inelastic and the demand for that good rises, prices will rise significantly and consumers will scream for price controls.

This is what happened in the New York City rent-control example (price ceilings imposed on apartments) in Chapter 5. During World War II an influx of short-term workers into New York City increased demand for apartments. Because supply was inelastic, rents rose tremendously. To keep apartments affordable, the city capped rents.

Such controls are not costless. One of the results of rent control was to create an ongoing shortage of apartments. As we noted earlier, effective price ceilings will cause a shortage unless suppliers are forced to supply a market-clearing quantity. With the knowledge of elasticities you also know whether a large or small shortage will develop with a price ceiling and whether a large or small surplus will develop with a price floor.

Figure 7-7 (a, b, and c)   Price Floors and Elasticity of Demand and Supply

A price floor above equilibrium market price will always create a surplus. The extent of the surplus created depends on the elasticity of the curves. With elastic curves, a large surplus is created by price controls; with inelastic curves, a small surplus is created. Thus, in (a) the intersection of supply and demand occurs where the curves are most elastic and the result is the largest surplus. In (b) demand and supply intersect where the demand curve is less elastic and the surplus declines. In (c) demand and supply intersect where supply and demand are most inelastic and the result is the smallest surplus.

(a) **Price floor with elastic supply and demand**

(b) **Price floor with elastic supply and inelastic demand**

(c) **Price floor with inelastic supply and demand**

To make sure you understand how elasticity can tell you the relative size of a surplus or shortage when there are price controls, look at Figure 7-7, which shows three cases of price floors, each with different elasticities of supply and demand.

As you can see, all three cases create excess supply—surpluses—but the proportional amount of excess supply depends on the elasticity. In Figure 7-7(a), supply and demand intersect at P_E, where they are relatively elastic. There, the price floor, P_F, leads to a relatively large surplus. Figure 7-7(b) represents an intermediate case: the intersection is where supply is elastic and demand is highly inelastic, and a relatively smaller surplus is created by the price floor. In Figure 7-7(c), where the demand and supply curves intersect at relatively inelastic portions, the surplus created by the price floor is relatively small. A good exercise is to go through the same analysis for price ceilings.

> The more elastic supply and demand, the larger the surplus or shortage created by price controls.

The Long-Run/Short-Run Problem of Price Controls Now let's combine our analysis of price controls with another insight from the elasticity chapter—that in the long run, supply and demand tend to be much more elastic than in the short run. This means that price controls will cause only small shortages or surpluses in the short run, but large ones in the long run. Let's consider how this would play out in our rent-control example—see Figure 7-8. In the short run, both supply and demand are inelastic; thus, if the government allows landlords to charge the price they want and demand shifts from D_0 to D_1, they will raise their price significantly, from P_0 to P_1.

In the long run, however, additional apartments will be built and other existing buildings will be converted into apartments. Supply becomes more elastic, rotating from S_0 to S_1. Faced with additional competition, landlords will lower their price to P_2. In the long run price will fall and the number of apartments rented will increase.

Herein lies another political policy problem. In large part, it is the rise in price that brings in new competitors and increases in output. But if the government imposes price controls, the long-run incentives for competitors to enter the market will be eliminated.

> Q-10 Why do price controls tend to create ongoing shortages or surpluses in the long run?

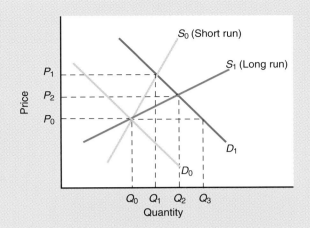

Figure 7-8   Long-Run and Short-Run Effects of Price Controls

This exhibit shows how an increase in demand from D_0 to D_1 raises equilibrium price from P_0 to P_1. As time progresses, the supply curve becomes flatter, which is shown as a rotation of the supply curve from S_0 to S_1. Equilibrium price falls to P_2. If a price ceiling of P_0 had been imposed, the incentive for suppliers to build more apartments would be eliminated. Instead, landlords would convert their apartments to different uses and potential landlords would choose to build fewer apartments, and the shortage resulting from the price control ($Q_3 - Q_0$) would remain.

The political problems arise because politics generally responds to short-run pressures. In the short run demand and supply are generally inelastic, making it look like the price ceiling will not create significant problems. But in the long run, supply is usually elastic. Landlords will convert their rent-controlled apartments to different uses, fewer resources will be spent keeping up existing apartments, and fewer new apartments will be built. In the long run, the shortage becomes even more severe. As we noted in Chapter 5, the rent-control laws in New York City were initially written to be effective whenever the vacancy rate was below 5 percent, which was the vacancy rate at the time. But the rent controls stopped new apartments from being built and old ones from being maintained. Today, the vacancy rate is less than 4 percent and many rent-controlled apartments have deteriorated. The government's imposition of a price ceiling prevents the market from achieving a more desirable long-run equilibrium, at which output has expanded and price has fallen from its initially high level.

CONCLUSION

Government is a part of our life and, therefore, so too are taxes. Economic theory doesn't say government should or shouldn't play any particular role in the economy or what the taxes should be. Those decisions depend on normative judgments and the relevant costs and benefits. What economic theory does is to help point out the costs and benefits. For example, in the case of taxes economists can show that the cost of taxation in terms of lost surplus is independent of who physically pays the tax.

In thinking about taxes and government involvement the public often perceives economic theory and economists as suggesting the best policy is one of laissez-faire, or government noninvolvement in the economy. Many economists do suggest a laissez-faire policy, but that suggestion is based on empirical observations of government's role in the past, not on economic theory.

Still, economists as a group generally favor less government involvement than does the general public. I suspect this is because economists are taught to look below the surface at the long-run effect of government actions. They've discovered that the effects often aren't the intended effects, and that programs frequently have long-run consequences that make the problems worse, not better. Economists, both liberal and

Economists as a group favor less government than does the general public.

conservative, speak in the voice of reason: "Look at all the costs; look at all the bene-fits. Then decide whether government should or should not intervene." The supply/de-mand framework and the elasticity concept are extremely useful tools in making those assessments.

Chapter Summary

- Government taxes firms and individuals in order to carry out its six roles in a market economy. A government will maximize benefits to society only if it chooses to tax when the marginal benefit of the goods and services provided with the revenue of the tax exceeds the cost of the tax.

- Taxes create a loss of consumer and producer surplus known as deadweight loss, which graphically is repre-sented by the welfare loss triangle.

- The cost of taxation to consumers and producers includes the actual tax paid, the deadweight loss, and the costs of administering the tax.

- Government follows both the benefit principle (individu-als who receive the benefit should pay the tax) and the ability-to-pay principle (individuals who are most able to pay should pay the tax) when deciding on whom to levy taxes.

- Who bears the burden of the tax depends on the relative elasticities of demand and supply. The more inelastic one's relative supply and demand, the larger the burden of the tax one will bear.

- Although social security taxes are levied equally on em-ployers and employees, the supply of labor tends to be

more inelastic than the demand for labor, so workers bear the greater burden of these taxes.

- Price ceilings and price floors, like taxes, result in loss of consumer and producer surplus.

- Price ceilings transfer producer surplus to consumers and therefore are equivalent to a tax on producers and a sub-sidy to consumers. Price floors have the opposite effect; they are a tax on consumers and a subsidy to producers.

- Rent-seeking activities are designed to transfer surplus from one group to another. Producers facing inelastic demand for their product will benefit more from rent-seeking activities than producers facing elastic demand. Consumers facing inelastic supply for a product benefit more from rent-seeking activities such as lobbying for price ceilings than consumers facing an elastic supply.

- The more elastic supply and/or demand is, the greater the surplus is with an effective price floor and the greater the shortage is with an effective price ceiling.

- Price controls worsen as the length of time considered rises because elasticity rises as time progresses.

Key Terms

ability-to-pay principle (160)
benefit principle (160)
deadweight loss (159)
excise tax (161)
price ceiling (164)
price floor (165)
public choice economists (168)
rent-seeking activities (168)
welfare loss triangle (159)

Questions for Thought and Review

1. Name one local tax that is based on the ability-to-pay principle and one local tax that is based on the benefit principle. State your reason for categorizing the taxes as you did.

2. How is elasticity related to the revenue from a sales tax?

3. If the federal government wanted to tax a good and sup-pliers were strong lobbyists, but consumers were not, would government prefer supply or demand to be more inelastic? Why?

4. What types of goods would you recommend government tax if it wants the tax to result in no welfare loss? Name a few examples.

5. Suppose demand for cigarettes is inelastic and the sup-ply of cigarettes is elastic. Who would bear the larger burden of a tax placed on cigarettes?

6. If the demand for a good is perfectly elastic and the sup-ply is elastic, who will bear the burden of a tax on the good paid by consumers?

7. Which good would an economist normally recommend taxing if government wanted to minimize welfare loss and maximize revenue: a good with an elastic or inelastic supply? Why?

8. Should tenants who rent apartments worry that increases in property taxes will increase their rent? Does your answer change when considering the long run?

9. Can you explain the tax system that led to this building style, which was common in old Eastern European cities?

10. In which case would the shortage resulting from a price ceiling be greater—when supply is inelastic or elastic? Explain your answer.

11. Define rent seeking. Do firms have a greater incentive to engage in rent-seeking behavior when demand is elastic or when it is inelastic?

Problems and Exercises

1. A political leader comes to you and wonders from whom she will get the most complaints if she institutes a price ceiling when demand is inelastic and supply is elastic.
   a. How do you respond?
   b. Demonstrate why your answer is correct.

2. Suppose the government established a requirement that everyone consume 10 percent more beets than he or she is currently consuming.
   a. Show graphically the welfare loss that would occur.
   b. If someone shows you that the welfare loss is small, say 0.5 percent of the cost of beets, and that eating beets improves people's health, would you support a beet-eating requirement? Why or why not?

3. Demonstrate the welfare loss of:
   a. A restriction on output when supply is perfectly elastic.
   b. A tax *t* placed on suppliers that shifts up a supply curve.
   c. A subsidy *s* given to suppliers that shifts down a supply curve.
   d. A restriction on output when demand is perfectly elastic.

4. Because of the negative incentive effect that taxes have on goods with elastic supply, in the late 1980s Margaret Thatcher (then prime minister of Great Britain) changed the property tax to a poll tax (a tax at a set rate that every individual must pay).
   a. Show why the poll tax is preferable to a property tax in terms of consumer and producer surplus.
   b. What do you think the real-life consequences of the poll tax were?

5. Demonstrate how a price floor is like a tax on consumers and a subsidy to suppliers.
   a. Who gets the revenue in the case of a tax? Label the area that illustrates the tax.
   b. Who gets the revenue in the case of a price floor? Label the transfer of surplus from consumers to suppliers.
   c. Label welfare loss of the tax and the price floor.

6. Suppose government imposed a minimum wage above equilibrium wage.
   a. What do you expect to happen to the resulting shortage of jobs as time progresses? (Assume that inflation and economic growth are both zero.)
   b. What do you expect to happen to the producer surplus transferred to minimum-wage earners as time progresses?

7. New York City has issued 11,797 taxi licenses, called "medallions," and has not changed that number since 1937.
   a. What does that limitation likely do to the price of taxi medallions? Demonstrate graphically.
   b. If the New York City Taxi Commission eliminated a rule that required medallion owners who own only one cab to drive their cabs full time, what would likely happen to the price of the medallion?
   c. If New York City decreased the number of medallions by 1,000 by revoking 1,000 medallions, what would happen to the price of remaining medallions?
   d. What would the political response to such a revocation be?

Web Questions

1. Gasoline taxes are commonly used to fund transportation-related expenditures. Cal-Tax is an advocacy group in California whose mission is to protect taxpayers from unnecessary taxes and to promote efficient, quality government services. Read their analysis of gasoline taxes in California at www.caltax.org/research/gastax.htm to answer the following questions:
   a. How does California rank relative to other states in terms of taxes per gallon?
   b. How does California rank in transportation expenditures relative to other states?
   c. Is the gas tax in California based on the benefit principle, the ability-to-pay principle, or some other principle?
   d. What has happened to revenue from gas taxes on a revenue-per-mile basis over the past few years? What accounts for this change?
   e. Is the gas tax in California a progressive or a regressive tax? (Regressive means that the tax rate falls with income.)

2. Henry George, an American economist living in the 1800s, had very specific views on taxation. Read about these by clicking on *taxation* on the Henry George Institute's home page at www.henrygeorge.org and answer the following questions:
   a. What are the four criteria of a good tax according to Classical economists?
   b. In what way do broad-based taxes fulfill those criteria? In what way do they fail to fulfill those criteria?
   c. What good in our economy, according to Henry George, best fits the four criteria?
   d. Demonstrate the welfare loss associated with the taxation of the good Henry George believes should be taxed. Who will bear the burden of the tax?

Answers to Margin Questions

1. Welfare loss when supply is highly elastic and demand is highly inelastic is shown by the shaded triangle in the graph below. The supply curve shifts up by the amount of the tax. Since equilibrium quantity changes very little, from Q_0 to Q_1, welfare loss is very small.   *(159)*

2. A voucher system to finance education would not reduce taxes because the funding for education would still come from government. Instead of providing the educational services itself, it would be providing the vouchers.   *(159)*

3. The average tax would be total tax divided by total income, or $2,000 (20% of $10,000) divided by $30,000 = 6.7%.   *(160)*

4. The tax burden when demand is elastic and supply is inelastic is shown below. The blue shaded region is the tax burden paid by consumers. The red shaded region is the tax burden paid by producers. Producers pay a larger burden of the tax because they are unable to change their production (supply is inelastic).   *(162)*

5. If the entire amount of the tax were levied on employees, their before-tax income would rise because employers would have to compensate their employees for the increased taxes they would have to physically pay. The burden of the taxation does not depend on who pays the tax. It depends on relative elasticities.   *(163)*

6. The effect of a price ceiling below equilibrium price when demand and supply are inelastic is shown in the following graph. Quantity demanded exceeds quantity supplied, but because demand and supply are both inelastic, the shortage is not big. Likewise, the welfare loss

triangle, shown by the shaded area in the graph, is not large. *(164)*

7. Yes and no. A draft, by reducing the taxes needed to pay wages to soldiers, lowers taxes that show up in government coffers, but does place an implicit tax on young men. Those who are drafted must accept the below-equilibrium wage, and give up the wage they could have made in the marketplace. The difference can be considered a tax paid to government. *(166)*

8. No. Research and development expenditures are an effort to increase technology to either lower production costs or discover a new product that can be marketed. If the firm can get a patent on that new product, the firm will have a monopoly and be able to restrict supply, transferring surplus from consumers to themselves, but this is not rent seeking. Rent-seeking activities are designed to transfer surplus from one group to another given current technology. They are unproductive. *(168)*

9. If suppliers were selling a product for which demand is inelastic, increases in productivity would result in a drop in price that would be proportionately greater than the rise in equilibrium quantity. Total revenue would decline for suppliers. *(168)*

10. Price controls tend to create ongoing shortages and surpluses in the long run because they prevent market forces from working. *(170)*

The Logic of Individual Choice: The Foundation of Supply and Demand

8

After reading this chapter, you should be able to:

- Discuss the principle of diminishing marginal utility.

- Summarize the principle of rational choice.

- Explain why, when $MU_x/P_x = MU_y/P_y$, a consumer is maximizing total utility.

- Explain how the principle of rational choice accounts for the laws of demand and supply.

- Explain why economists can believe there are many explanations of individual choice but nonetheless focus on self-interest.

The theory of economics must begin with a correct theory of consumption.

Stanley Jevons

The analysis of how individuals make choices is central to microeconomics. It is the foundation of economic reasoning and it gives economics much of its power. The first part of this chapter shows you that foundation and leads you through some exercises to make sure you understand the reasoning. The second part of the chapter relates that analysis to the real world, giving you a sense of when the model is useful and when it's not.

As you go through this chapter, think back to Chapter 1, which set out the goals for this book. One goal was to get you to think like an economist. This chapter, which formally develops the reasoning process behind economists' cost/benefit approach to problems, examines the underpinnings of how to think like an economist.

UTILITY THEORY AND INDIVIDUAL CHOICE

Different sciences have various explanations for why people do what they do. For example, Freudian psychology tells us we do what we do because of an internal fight between the id, ego, and superego plus some hangups we have about our bodies. Other psychologists tell us it's a search for approval by our peers; we want to be OK. Economists agree that these are important reasons, but argue that if we want an analysis that's simple enough to apply to problems, these heavy psychological explanations are likely to get us all mixed up. At least to start with, we need an easier underlying psychological foundation. And economists have one—self-interest. People do what they do because it's in their self-interest.

Economists' analysis of individual choice doesn't deny that most of us have our quirks. That's obvious in what we buy. On certain items we're penny-pinchers; on others we're big spenders. For example, how many of you or your parents clip coupons to save 40 cents on cereal but then spend $40 on a haircut? How many save 50 cents a pound by buying a low grade of meat but then spend $20 on a bottle of wine, $75 on dinner at a restaurant, or $60 for a concert ticket?

But through it all comes a certain rationality. Much of what people do reflects their rational self-interest. That's why economists start their analysis of individual choice with a relatively simple, but powerful, underlying psychological foundation.

Using that simple theory, two things determine what people do: the pleasure people get from doing or consuming something, and the price of doing or consuming that something. Price is the tool the market uses to bring the quantity supplied equal to the quantity demanded. Changes in price provide incentives for people to change what they're doing. Through those incentives the invisible hand guides us all. To understand economics you must understand how price affects our choices. That's why we focus on the effect of price on the quantity demanded. We want to understand the way in which a change in price will affect what we do.

In summary, economists' theory of rational choice is a simple, but powerful, theory that shows how these two things—pleasure and price—are related.

> Economists' analysis of individual choice doesn't deny that most of us have our quirks.

Measuring Pleasure

Let's start with an analysis of what we buy. Why do we buy what we buy? Economists' analysis of individual choice starts with the proposition that individuals try to get as much pleasure as possible out of life. To analyze the choice formally we must measure pleasure.

How does one measure pleasure? I don't know the answer to that, but back in the 1800s economists such as Jeremy Bentham thought that eventually they would be able to measure pleasure by measuring brain waves. In the expectation of this discovery they even developed a measure of pleasure they called a *util*. They predicted that someday a machine that could measure utils would be developed. Not surprisingly they called this machine a *utilometer*. This utilometer was to be connected to people's heads and an economist would read it as people went through their daily activities. Eating broccoli might give 10 utils; eating a hot fudge sundae might give 10,000 utils.

Eventually these 19th-century economists gave up hope of developing a utilometer, but economists still use a quaint shorthand term, **utility,** for *the pleasure or satisfaction that one expects to get from consuming a good or service*. (And you thought that economists didn't have a sense of humor.) Utility serves as the basis of economists' analysis of individual choice.

 8.1

> *Utility* refers to the satisfaction one gets from consuming a good or service.

Economists initially used actual numbers to represent utility. But no economist to-day believes that the actual numbers given to utility have meaning. Economists have gone to great lengths to show that all you need is a ranking of goods that people reveal when they choose one good over another. (That means you can say "John is cuter than Bob," but you don't need to say how much cuter.)

It's important to keep in the back of your mind that economists don't need actual numbers to discuss utility, especially if you're going on in economics. In introductory economics there's nothing quite as useful as a unit of utility. It gives us real numbers to work with rather than all kinds of fancy measure theories. So here's the deal: I'll use real numbers in discussing utility and you promise that you'll remember they're not really needed. (If you don't accept this deal, see Appendix A, where I go through the same analysis without using actual numbers.)

Total Utility and Marginal Utility

Q-1 One of the assumptions of economists' theory of choice is that utility must be measured. True or false? Why?

In thinking about utility, it's important to distinguish between *total utility* and *marginal utility*. **Total utility** refers to *the total satisfaction one gets from consuming a product*. **Marginal utility** refers to *the satisfaction one gets from consuming one additional unit of a product above and beyond what one has consumed up to that point*. For example, eating a whole pound of Beluga caviar might give you 4,700 units of utility.[1] Consuming the first 15 ounces may have given you 4,697 units of utility. Consuming the last ounce of caviar might give you an additional 3 units of utility. The 4,700 is total utility; the 3 is the marginal utility of eating that last ounce of caviar.

It is important to distinguish be-tween marginal and total utility.

An example of the relationship between total utility and marginal utility is given in Figure 8-1. Let's say that the marginal utility of the 1st slice of pizza is 14, and since you've eaten only 1 slice, the total utility is also 14. Let's also say that the marginal utility of the 2nd slice of pizza is 12, which means that the total utility of 2 slices of pizza is 26 (14 + 12). Similarly for the 3rd, 4th, and 5th slices of pizza, whose marginal utilities are 10, 8, and 6, respectively. The total utility of your eating those 5 pieces of pizza is the sum of the marginal utilities you get from eating each of the 5 slices. The fifth row of column 2 of Figure 8-1(a) shows that sum.

Notice that marginal utility shows up between the lines. It is the utility of changing consumption levels. For example, the marginal utility of changing from 1 to 2 slices of pizza is 12. The relationship between total and marginal utility can also be seen graphically. In Figure 8-1(b) we graph total utility (column 2 of the utility table) on the vertical axis, and the number of slices of pizza (column 1 of the utility table) on the horizontal axis. As you can see, total utility increases up to 7 slices of pizza; after 8 slices it starts decreasing—after 8 pieces of pizza you're so stuffed that you can't stand to look at another slice.

Q-2 If the total utility curve is a straight line—that is, does not exhibit diminishing marginal utility—what will the marginal utility curve look like?

In Figure 8-1(c) we graph marginal utility (column 3 of the utility table) on the vertical axis and slices of pizza (column 1) on the horizontal axis. Notice how marginal utility decreases while total utility increases. When total utility stops increasing (between 7 and 8 slices), marginal utility is zero. Beyond this point total utility decreases and marginal utility is negative. An additional slice of pizza will actually make you worse off.

---

[1] I choose specific numbers to make the examples more understandable and to make the points I want to make. A useful exercise is for you to choose different numbers and reason your way through the same analysis.

Figure 8-1 (a, b, and c)   Marginal and Total Utility

Marginal utility tends to decrease as consumption of a good increases. Notice how the information in the table (a) can be presented graphically in two different ways. The two different ways are, however, related. The downward slope of the marginal utility curve (c) is reflected in the total utility curve bowed downwards in (b). Notice that marginal utility relates to changes in quantity so the marginal utility line is graphed at the halfway point. For example, in (c), between 7 and 8, marginal utility becomes zero.

Number of pizza slices	Total utility	Marginal utility
1	14	14
2	26	12
3	36	10
4	44	8
5	50	6
6	54	4
7	56	2
8	56	0
9	54	-2

(a) Utility table   (b) Total utility   (c) Marginal utility

Diminishing Marginal Utility

Now let's consider the shapes of these curves a bit more carefully: What are they telling us about people's choices? As we've drawn the curves, the marginal utility that a person gets from each additional slice of pizza decreases with each slice of pizza eaten. Economists believe that the shapes of these curves accurately describe the pattern of people's enjoyment. They call that pattern the **principle of diminishing marginal utility:**

> *As you consume more of a good, after some point the marginal utility received from each additional unit of a good decreases with each additional unit consumed.*

As individuals increase their consumption of a good, at some point consuming another unit of the product will simply not yield as much additional pleasure as did consuming the preceding unit.

Consider, for example, that late-night craving for a double-cheese-and-pepperoni pizza. You order one and bite into it. Ah, pleasure! But if you've ordered a large pizza and you're eating it all by yourself, eventually you'll get less additional enjoyment from eating additional slices. In other words, the marginal utility you get is going to decrease with each additional slice of pizza you consume. That's the principle of diminishing marginal utility.

Notice that the principle of diminishing marginal utility does not say that you don't enjoy consuming more of a good; it simply states that as you consume more of the good, you enjoy the additional units less than you did the initial units. A fourth slice of pizza still tastes good, but it doesn't match the taste of the third slice. At some point, however, marginal utility can become negative. Say you had two large pizzas and only two hours in which to eat them. Eating the last slice could be pure torture. But in most situations you have the option *not* to consume any more of a good. When consuming a good becomes torture (meaning its utility is negative), you simply don't consume any

The principle of diminishing marginal utility states that, after some point, the marginal utility received from each additional unit of a good decreases with each additional unit consumed.

Q-3   Consuming more of a good generally increases its marginal utility. True or false? Why?

more of it. If you eat a slice of pizza (or consume an additional unit of a good), that's a good indication that its marginal utility is still positive.

RATIONAL CHOICE AND MARGINAL UTILITY

The analysis of rational choice is the analysis of how individuals choose goods in order to maximize total utility, and how maximizing total utility can be accomplished by considering marginal utility. That analysis begins with the premise that rational individuals want as much satisfaction as they can get from their available income. The term *rational* in economics means, specifically, that people prefer more to less and will make choices that give them as much satisfaction as possible. The problem is that people face an income constraint. They must choose among the alternatives. How do they do that?

Because people face an income constraint, they must choose among alternatives.

Some Choices

8.2

Let's start by considering three choices. (Answer each choice as you read it.)

Choice 1: Between spending another dollar on a slice of pizza that gives you an additional 41 units of utility or spending another dollar on a hero sandwich that gives you an additional 30 units of utility.

Choice 2: Between reading an additional chapter in this book that gives you an additional 200 units of utility at a cost of one hour of your time, or reading an additional chapter in psychology that gives you an additional 100 units of utility at a cost of 40 minutes of your time.

Choice 3: Between having your next date with that awesome guy Jerry, which gives you an additional 2,000 units of utility and costs you $70, or taking out plain Jeff on your next date, which gives you an additional 200 units of utility and costs you $10.

The correct choices, in terms of marginal utility, are (1) the pizza, (2) a chapter of this book, and (3) Jerry.

If you answered all three correctly, either you're lucky or you have a good intuitive understanding of the principle of rational choice. Now let's explore the principle of rational choice more thoroughly by considering each of the three examples.

Choice 1 Since the slice of pizza and the hero sandwich both cost $1, and the pizza gives you more units of utility than the hero, the pizza is the rational choice. If you spend $1 on the hero rather than the pizza, you're losing 11 units of utility and not making yourself as happy as you could be. You're being irrational. Any choice (for the same amount of money) that doesn't give you as much utility as possible is an irrational choice.

But now let's say that the price of heroes falls to 50 cents so that you can buy two heroes for the same price you previously had to pay for only one. Let's also say that two heroes would give you 56 units of utility (not $2 \times 30 = 60$—remember the principle of diminishing marginal utility). Which would now be the more rational choice? The two heroes, because their 56 units of utility are 15 more than you would get from that dollar spent on one slice of pizza.

Another way of thinking about your choice is to recognize that essentially what you're doing is buying units of utility. Obviously you want to get the most for your money, so you choose goods that have the highest units of utility per unit of cost. Let's see how this way of thinking about it works by considering our second choice.

Choice 2 Here the two alternatives have a cost in time, not money. The analysis, however, is the same. You calculate the marginal utility (additional units of utility) of the

Q-4 Which is the rational choice—watching one hour of MTV that gives you 20 units of utility or watching a two-hour movie that gives you 30 units of utility?

choice facing you, and divide that by the costs of the activity; that gives you the marginal utility per unit of cost. Then choose the activity that has the highest marginal utility per unit of cost or lowest cost per unit of utility. When you do that, you see that this chapter gives you 3⅓ units of utility per minute (200/60 = 3⅓), while the psychology chapter gives you 2½ units of utility per minute. So you choose to read another chapter in this book.[2]

Choice 3 Taking out Jerry gives you 28½ units of utility per dollar (2,000/$70), while taking out Jeff gives you 20 units of utility per dollar (200/$10). So you choose to take out Jerry.[3]

The Principle of Rational Choice

The **principle of rational choice** is as follows: *Spend your money on those goods that give you the most marginal utility (MU) per dollar.* The principle of rational choice is important enough for us to emphasize.

If $\frac{MU_x}{P_x} > \frac{MU_y}{P_y}$, choose to consume an additional unit of good x.

If $\frac{MU_x}{P_x} < \frac{MU_y}{P_y}$, choose to consume an additional unit of good y.

By substituting the marginal utilities and prices of goods into these formulas, you can always decide which good it makes more sense to consume. Consume the one with the highest marginal utility per dollar.

Simultaneous Decisions

So far in discussing our examples, we've considered the choices separately. But in real life, choices aren't so neatly separated. Say you were presented with all three choices simultaneously. If you make all three of the decisions given in the examples, are you being rational? The answer is no. Why? The pizza gives you 41 units of utility per dollar; taking out Jerry gives you 28½ units of utility per dollar. You aren't being rational; you aren't maximizing your utility. It would clearly make sense to eat more pizza, paying for it by cutting the date with Jerry short. (Skip the coffee at the end of the meal.)

But what about the other choice: studying psychology or economics? We can't compare the costs of studying to the costs of the other goods because, as I noted earlier, the costs of both studying alternatives are expressed in terms of time, not money. If we can assign a money value to the time, however, we can make the comparison. Let's say you can earn $6 per hour, so the value of your time is 10 cents per minute. This allows us to think about both alternatives in terms of dollars and cents. Since a chapter in economics takes an hour to read, the cost in money of reading a chapter is 60 minutes × 10 cents = $6. Similarly, the cost of the 40 minutes you'd take to read the psychology chapter is $4.

With these values we can compare our studying decisions with our other decisions. The value in units of utility per dollar of reading a chapter of this book is:

$$\frac{200}{\$6} = 33⅓ \text{ units of utility per dollar}$$

The principle of rational choice tells us to spend our money on those goods that give us the most marginal utility per dollar.

Q-5 True or False? You are maximizing total utility only when the marginal utility of all goods is zero. Explain your answer.

[2] As I've pointed out before, I choose the numbers to make the points I want to make. A good exercise for you is to choose different numbers that reflect your estimate of the marginal utility you get from choice, and see what your rational choices are. And remember our deal.

[3] In these examples I am implicitly assuming that the "goods" are divisible. Technically, this assumption is needed for marginal utilities to be fully specified.

So forget about dating Jerry with its 28½ units of utility per dollar. Your rational choice is to study this chapter while stuffing yourself with pizza.

But wait. Remember that, according to the principle of diminishing marginal utility, as you consume more of something, the marginal utility you get from it falls. So as you consume more pizza and spend more time reading this book, the marginal utilities of these activities will fall. Thus, as you vary your consumption, the marginal utilities you get from the goods are changing.

MAXIMIZING UTILITY AND EQUILIBRIUM

When do you stop changing your consumption? The principle of rational choice tells you to keep adjusting your spending if the marginal utility per dollar (MU/P) of two goods differs. The only time you don't adjust your spending is when there is no clear winner. *When the ratios of the marginal utility to price of the two goods are equal*, you're maximizing utility; this is the **utility-maximizing rule:**

The utility maximizing rule:

$$\frac{MU_x}{P_x} = \frac{MU_y}{P_y}$$

$$If \frac{MU_x}{P_x} = \frac{MU_y}{P_y}, \text{ you're maximizing utility.}$$

When you're maximizing utility, you're in equilibrium. To understand how, by adjusting your spending, you can achieve equilibrium, it's important to remember the principle of diminishing marginal utility. As we consume more of an item, the marginal utility we get from the last unit consumed decreases. Conversely, as we consume *less* of an item, the marginal utility we get from the last unit consumed *increases*. (The principle of diminishing marginal utility operates in reverse.)

Achieving equilibrium by maximizing utility (juggling your choices, adding a bit more of one and choosing a bit less of another) requires more information than I've so far presented. We need to know the marginal utility of alternative amounts of consumption for each choice and how much income we have to spend on all those items. With that information we can choose among alternatives, given our available resources.

An Example of Maximizing Utility

Table 8-1 offers an example in which we have the necessary information to make simultaneous decisions and maximize utility. In this example, we have $7 to spend on ice cream cones and Big Macs. The choice is between ice cream at $1 a cone and Big Macs at $2 apiece. In the table you can see the principle of diminishing marginal utility in action. The marginal utility (MU) we get from either good decreases as we consume more of it. Marginal utility (MU) becomes negative after 5 Big Macs or 6 ice cream cones.

The key columns for your decision are the *MU/P* columns. They tell you the *MU* per dollar spent on each of the items. By following the rule that we choose the good with the higher marginal utility per dollar, we can quickly determine the optimal choice.

Let's start by considering what we'd do with our first $2. Clearly we'd only eat ice cream. Doing so would give us 29 + 17 = 46 units of utility, compared to 20 units of utility if we spent the $2 on a Big Mac. How about our next $2? Again the choice is clear; the 10 units of utility per dollar from the Big Mac are plainly better than the 7 units of utility per dollar we can get from ice cream cones. So we buy 1 Big Mac and 2 ice cream cones with our first $4.

Now let's consider our fifth and sixth dollars. The *MU/P* for a second Big Mac is 7. The *MU/P* for a third ice cream cone is also 7, so we could spend the fifth dollar on either—if McDonald's will sell us half a Big Mac. We ask them if they will, and they tell us no, so we must make a choice between either two additional ice cream cones or

Table 8-1   Maximizing Utility

This table provides the information needed to make simultaneous decisions. Notice that the marginal utility we get from another good declines as we consume more of it. To maximize utility, adjust your choices until the marginal utility of all goods is equal.

Big Macs (P = $2)				Ice Cream (P = $1)			
Q	TU	MU	MU/P	Q	TU	MU	MU/P
0	0			0	0		
		20	10			29	29
1	20			1	29		
		14	7			17	17
2	34			2	46		
		10	5			7	7
3	44			3	53		
		3	1.5			2	2
4	47			4	55		
		0	0			1	1
5	47			5	56		
		−5	−2.5			0	0
6	42			6	56		
		−10	−5			−4	−4
7	32			7	52		

another Big Mac for our fifth and sixth dollars. Since the marginal utility per dollar of the fourth ice cream cone is only 2, it makes sense to spend our fifth and sixth dollars on another Big Mac. So now we're up to 2 Big Macs and 2 ice cream cones and we have one more dollar to spend.

Now how about our last dollar? If we spend it on a third ice cream cone we get 7 additional units of utility. If McDonald's maintains its position and only sells whole Big Macs, this is our sole choice since we only have a dollar and Big Macs sell for $2. But let's say that McDonald's wants the sale and this time offers to sell us half a Big Mac for $1. Would we take it? The answer is no. One-half of the next Big Mac gives us only 5 units of utility per dollar whereas the third ice cream cone gives us 7 units of utility per dollar. So we spend the seventh dollar on a third ice cream cone.

With these choices we've arrived at equilibrium—the marginal utilities per dollar are the same for both goods and we're maximizing total utility. Our total utility is 34 from 2 Big Macs and 53 units of utility from the 3 ice cream cones, making a total utility of 87.

Why do these two choices make sense? Because they give us the most total utility for the $7 we have to spend. We've followed the utility-maximizing rule: Maximize utility by adjusting your choices until the marginal utilities per dollar are the same. These choices make the marginal utility per dollar between the last Big Mac and the last ice cream cone equal. The marginal utility per dollar we get from our last Big Mac is:

$$\frac{MU}{P} = \frac{14}{\$2} = 7$$

The marginal utility per dollar we get from our last ice cream cone is:

$$\frac{MU}{P} = \frac{7}{\$1} = 7$$

The marginal utility per dollar of each choice is equal, so we know we can't do any better. For any other choice we would get less total utility, so we could increase our total utility by switching to one of these two choices.

Extending the Principle of Rational Choice

Our example involved only two goods, but the reasoning can be extended to the choice among many goods. Our analysis has shown us that the principle of rational choice among many goods is simply an extension of the principle of rational choice applied to two goods. That general principle of rational choice is to consume more of the good that provides a higher marginal utility per dollar.

When $\dfrac{MU_x}{P_x} > \dfrac{MU_z}{P_z}$, consume more of good x.

When $\dfrac{MU_y}{P_y} > \dfrac{MU_z}{P_z}$, consume more of good y.

Stop adjusting your consumption when the marginal utilities per dollar are equal.

So the general utility-maximizing rule is that you are maximizing utility when the marginal utilities per dollar of the goods consumed are equal.

When $\dfrac{MU_x}{P_x} = \dfrac{MU_y}{P_y} = \dfrac{MU_z}{P_z}$ you are maximizing utility.

When this rule is met, the consumer is in equilibrium; the cost per additional unit of utility is equal for all goods and the consumer is as well off as it is possible to be.

Notice that the rule does not say that the rational consumer should consume a good until its marginal utility reaches zero. The reason is that the consumer doesn't have enough money to buy all she wants. She faces an income constraint and does the best she can under that constraint—that is, she maximizes utility. To buy more goods she has to work more, so she should work until the marginal utility of another dollar earned just equals the marginal utility of goods purchased with another dollar. According to economists' analysis of rational choice, a person's choice of how much to work is made simultaneously with the person's decision of how much to consume So when you say you want a Porsche but can't afford one, economists ask whether you're working two jobs and saving all your money to buy a Porsche. If you aren't, you're demonstrating that you don't really want a Porsche, given what you would have to do to get it.

Q-6 If you are initially in equilibrium and the price of one good rises, how would you adjust your consumption to return to equilibrium?

RATIONAL CHOICE AND THE LAWS OF DEMAND AND SUPPLY

Now that you know the rule for maximizing utility, let's see how it relates to the laws of demand and supply. We begin with demand. The law of demand says that the quantity demanded of a good is inversely related to its price. That is, when the price of a good goes up, the quantity we consume of it goes down.

Now let's consider the law of demand in relation to our principle of rational choice. When the price of a good goes up, the marginal utility *per dollar* we get from that good goes down. So when the price of a good goes up, if we were initially in equilibrium, we no longer are. Therefore, we choose to consume less of that good. The principle of rational choice shows us formally that following the law of demand is the rational thing to do.

In the discussion of the law of demand I didn't say precisely how much the quantity demanded would decrease with an increase in the price of an ice cream cone from $1 to $2. I didn't because of a certain ambiguity that arises when one talks about changes in nominal prices. To understand the cause of this ambiguity, notice that if the price of an ice cream cone has risen to $2, with $7 we can no longer consume 2 Big Macs and 3 ice cream cones. We've got to cut back for two reasons: First, we're poorer due to the rise in price. The reduction in quantity demanded because we're poorer is called the *income effect*. Second, the *relative* prices have changed. The price of ice cream has risen relative to the price of Big Macs. The reduction in quantity demanded because relative price has risen is called a *substitution effect*. Technically the law of demand is based only on the substitution effect.

To separate the two effects, let's assume that somebody compensates us for the rise in price of ice cream cones. Since it would cost $10 [(2 × $2 = $4) + (3 × $2 = $6)] to buy what $7 bought previously, we'll assume that someone gives us an extra $3 to compensate us for the rise in price. Since we are not any poorer because of the price change, this eliminates the income ef-

KNOWING THE TOOLS

Income and Substitution Effects

Big Macs ($P = \$2$)				Ice Cream ($P = \$2$)			
Q	TU	MU	MU/P	Q	TU	MU	MU/P
0	0			0	0		
		20	10			29	14.5
1	20			1	29		
		14	7			17	8.5
2	34			2	46		
		10	5			7	3.5
3	44			3	53		

fect. We now have $10, so we can buy 2 Big Macs and the 3 ice cream cones as we did before. If we do so, our total utility is once again 87 (34 units of utility from 2 Big Macs and 53 units of utility from 3 ice cream cones). But will we do so? We can answer that with the table.

We see that Big Macs give us more *MU* per dollar. What happens if we exchange an ice cream cone for an additional Big Mac, so instead of buying 3 ice cream cones and 2 Big Macs, we buy 3 Big Macs and 2 ice cream cones? The *MU* per dollar of Big Macs falls from 7 to 5 and the *MU* per dollar of the ice cream cone (whose price is now $2) rises from 3.5 to 8.5. Our total utility rises to 44 from 3 Big Macs and 46 from 2 ice cream cones, for a total of 90 units of utility rather than the previous 87. We've increased our total utility by shifting our consumption out of ice cream, the good whose price has risen. The price of ice cream went up and, even though we were given more money so we could buy the same amount as before, we did not; we bought fewer ice cream cones. That's the substitution effect in action: It tells us that when the relative price of a good goes up, the quantity purchased of that good decreases, *even if you're given money to compensate you for the rise.*

Let's see how. If:

$$\frac{MU_x}{P_x} = \frac{MU_y}{P_y}$$

and the price of good y goes up, then:

$$\frac{MU_x}{P_x} > \frac{MU_y}{P_y}$$

Our utility-maximizing rule is no longer satisfied. Consider the preceding example, in which we were in equilibrium with 87 units of utility (34 from 2 Big Macs and 53 from 3 ice cream cones) with the utility-maximizing rule fulfilled:

Big Mac   Ice cream

$$\frac{14 \text{ units of utility}}{\$2} = \frac{7 \text{ units of utility}}{\$1} = 7$$

According to the principle of rational choice, if there is diminishing marginal utility and the price of a good goes up, we consume less of that good. Hence, the principle of rational choice leads to the law of demand.

If the price of an ice cream cone rises from $1 to $2, the marginal utility per dollar for Big Macs (whose price hasn't changed) exceeds the marginal utility per dollar of ice cream cones:

Big Mac   Ice cream

$$\frac{14}{\$2} > \frac{7}{\$2}$$

To satisfy our utility-maximizing rule so that our choice will be rational, we must somehow raise the marginal utility we get from the good whose price has risen. Following the principle of diminishing marginal utility, we can increase marginal utility only by *decreasing* our consumption of the good whose price has risen. As we consume fewer ice cream cones and more Big Macs, the marginal utility of ice cream rises and the marginal utility of a Big Mac falls.

This example can be extended to a general rule: If the price of a good rises, you'll increase your total utility by consuming less of it. When the price of a good goes up, consumption of that good will go down. Our principle of rational choice underlies the law of demand:

Quantity demanded rises as price falls, other things constant.

Or alternatively:

Quantity demanded falls as price rises, other things constant.

This discussion of marginal utility and rational choice shows the relationship between marginal utility and the price we're willing to pay. When marginal utility is high, as it is with diamonds, the price we're willing to pay is high. When marginal utility is low, as it is with tap water, the price we're willing to pay is low. Since our demand for a good is an expression of our willingness to pay for it, quantity demanded is related to marginal utility.

The Law of Supply

According to the principle of rational choice, if there is diminishing marginal utility and the price of supplying a good goes up, you supply more of that good.

The above discussion focused on demand and goods we consume, but this analysis of choice holds for the law of supply of factors of production, such as labor, that individuals supply to the market, as well as for demand. In supply decisions you are giving up something—your time, land, or some other factor of production—and getting money in return. To show you how this works, let's consider one final example—how much labor you should supply to the market.

Say that working another hour at your part-time job pays you another $5 and that you currently work 20 hours per week. That additional income from the final hour of work gives you an additional 24 units of utility. Also assume that your best alternative use of that hour—studying economics—gives you another 24 units of utility. (You didn't know economics gave you so much pleasure, did you?) So what should you do when your boss asks you to work an extra hour? Tell her no, you are already satisfying the utility-maximum rule $MU_w/W = MU_s/W$.

Studying   Working

$$\frac{24 \text{ units of utility}}{\$5} = \frac{24 \text{ units of utility}}{\$5}$$

The price of studying an additional hour is also your wage per hour because that wage is the opportunity cost of studying.

But now say that your boss offers to raise your wage to $5.50 per hour for work you do over 20 hours. That means that both your wage at work and the price of studying

Figure 8-2   Deriving Labor Supply from Marginal Utility

Factor supply curves can be derived from a comparison of marginal utilities for various activities in relation to work. In this example the higher the wage, the higher the marginal utility of the goods you can get for the wage relative to the next-best alternative, giving you an upward-sloping labor supply curve.

have increased. But now you can get more goods for working that additional hour. Let's say that those additional goods raise the marginal utility you get from an additional hour of work to 32 additional units of utility. Now, the marginal utility of working an additional hour exceeds the marginal utility of studying an additional hour:

$$\underset{\$5.50}{\underbrace{\text{Studying}}} \qquad\qquad \underset{\$5.50}{\underbrace{\text{Working}}}$$

$$\frac{24 \text{ units of utility}}{\$5.50} < \frac{32 \text{ units of utility}}{\$5.50}$$

So you work the extra hour.

Now say your boss comes to you and asks what it would take to get you to work five hours more per week. After running the numbers through your computer-mind you solve the utility-maximizing rule, and tell her, "$8.00 an hour for overtime work and you've got your worker." Combining these hours and wages gives you the supply curve shown in Figure 8-2, which demonstrates the law of supply.

To see that you have the reasoning down, say that an exam is coming, and you haven't studied. This will likely raise the marginal utility of studying sufficiently, so you will choose to work less, if you have a choice. What will that change do to the supply curve?

If you answered that it will shift it to the left, you're in good shape.

Opportunity Cost

Before we leave the principle of rational choice let's consider how it relates to the opportunity cost concept that I presented in earlier chapters. *Opportunity cost* was the benefit forgone of the next-best alternative. Now that you've been through the principle of rational choice, you have a better sense of what is meant by opportunity cost of a forgone opportunity—it is essentially the marginal utility per dollar you forgo from the consumption of the next-best alternative.

To say

$$\frac{MU_x}{P_x} > \frac{MU_y}{P_y}$$

is to say that the opportunity cost of not consuming good *x* is greater than the opportunity cost of not consuming good *y*. So you consume *x*.

When the marginal utilities per dollar spent are equal, the opportunity cost of the alternatives are equal. In reality people don't use the utility terminology, and, indeed, a specific measure of utility doesn't exist. But the choice based on the price of goods relative to the benefit they provide is used all the time. Instead of utility terminology,

Q-7 Use the principle of rational choice to explain how you would change your supply of work if your employer raised your wage by $1 per hour.

The principle of rational choice states that, to maximize utility, choose goods until the opportunity costs of all alternatives are equal.

Q.8 If the opportunity cost of consuming good *x* is greater than the opportunity cost of consuming good *y*, which good has the higher marginal utility per dollar?

people use the "really need" terminology. They say they will work the extra hour rather than study because they *really need* the money. To say you are working because you "really need" the money is the equivalent of saying the marginal utility of working is higher than the opportunity cost of other choices. So the general rule fits decisions about supply, even if most people don't use the word *utility*. The more you "really, really need" something, the higher its marginal utility.

APPLYING ECONOMISTS' THEORY OF CHOICE TO THE REAL WORLD

Understanding a theory involves more than understanding how a theory works; it also involves understanding the limits the assumptions underlying the theory place on the use of the theory. So let's consider some of the assumptions on which economists' analysis of choice is based. The first assumption we'll consider is the implicit assumption that decisions can be made costlessly.

The Cost of Decision Making

Q.9 Bounded rationality violates the principle of rational choice. True or false?

The principle of rational choice makes reasonably good intuitive sense when we limit our examples to two or three choices, as I did in this chapter. But in reality, we make hundreds of thousands of choices simultaneously. It simply doesn't make intuitive sense that we're going to apply rational choice to all those choices at once—that would exceed our decision-making abilities. This cost of decision making means that it is only rational to be somewhat irrational—to do things without applying the principle of rational choice. Thinking about decisions is one of the things we all economize on.

How real-world people make decisions in real-world situations is an open question that modern economists are spending a lot of time researching. Following the work of Nobel Prize winner Herbert Simon, a number of economists have come to believe that, to make real-world decisions, most people use *bounded rationality*—rationality based on rules of thumb—rather than using the principle of rational choice. They argue that many of our decisions are made with our minds on automatic pilot. This view of rationality has significant implications for interpreting and predicting economic events. For example, one rule of thumb is "You get what you pay for," which means that something with a high price is better than something with a low price. Put technically, we rely on price to convey information about quality. This reliance on price for information changes the inferences one can draw from the analysis, and can lead to upward-sloping demand curves.

A second rule of thumb that people sometimes use is "Follow the leader." If you don't know what to do, do what you think smart people are doing. Consider the clothes you're wearing. I suspect many of your choices of what to wear reflect this and the previous rules of thumb. Suppliers of clothing certainly think so and spend enormous amounts of money to exploit these rules of thumb. They try to steer your automatic pilot toward their goods. The suppliers emphasize these two rules ("You get what you pay for" and "Follow the leader") to convince people their product is the "in" thing to buy. If they succeed, they've got a gold mine; if they fail, they've got a flop. Advertising is designed to mine these rules of thumb.

Advertising is designed to mine rules of thumb.

In technical terms, the "Follow the leader" rule leads to *focal point equilibria*, in which a set of goods is consumed, not because the goods are objectively preferred to all other goods, but simply because through luck, or advertising, they have become focal points to which people have gravitated. Once some people started consuming a good, others followed.

Given Tastes

A second assumption implicit in economists' theory of rational choice is that our preferences are given, and are not shaped by society. In reality our preferences are determined not only by nature but also by our experiences—by nurture. Let's consider an example: Forty percent of major league baseball players chew tobacco, but close to zero percent of college professors chew tobacco. Why? Are major league baseball players somehow born with a tobacco-chewing gene while college professors are not? I doubt it. Tastes often are significantly influenced by society.

Tastes and Individual Choice

One way in which economists integrate the above insights into economics is by emphasizing that the analysis is conducted on the assumption of "given tastes." As discussed above, in reality, economists agree that often forces besides price and marginal utility play a role in determining what people demand. They fully recognize that a whole other analysis is necessary to supplement theirs—an analysis of what determines taste.

 8.3

Ask yourself what you ate today. Was it health food? Pizza? Candy? Whatever it was, it was probably not the most efficient way to satisfy your nutritional needs. The most efficient way to do that would be to eat only soybean mush and vitamin supplements at a cost of about $300 per year. That's less than one-tenth of what the average individual today spends on food per year. Most of us turn up our noses at soybean mush. Why? Because tastes are important.

I emphasize this point because some economists have been guilty of forgetting their simplifying assumption. Some economists in the 1800s thought that society's economic needs eventually would be fully met and that we would enter a golden age of affluence where all our material wants would be satisfied. They thought there would be surpluses of everything. Clearly that hasn't happened. Somehow it seems that whenever a need is met, it's replaced by a want, which soon becomes another need.

There are, of course, examples of wants being temporarily satisfied, as a U.S. company on a small island in the Caribbean is reported to have discovered. Employees weren't showing up for work. The company sent in a team of efficiency experts who discovered the cause of their problem: The firm had recently raised wages, and workers had decided they could get all they wanted (warm weather, a gorgeous beach, plenty of food, and a little bit of spending money) by showing up for work once, maybe twice, a week. Such a situation was clearly not good for business, but the firm found a solution. It sent in thousands of Sears catalogs (back when Sears sent catalogs), and suddenly the workers were no longer satisfied with what they already had. They wanted more and went back to work to get it. When they were presented with new possibilities, their wants increased. Companies know that tastes aren't constant, and they spend significant amounts of money on advertising to make consumers have a taste for their goods. It works, too.

Tastes are also important in explaining differences in consumption between countries. For example, a Japanese person wouldn't consider having a meal without rice. Rice has a ceremonial, almost mystical value in Japan. In many parts of the United States supper means meat and potatoes. In Germany, carp (a large goldfish) is a delicacy; in the United States many people consider carp inedible. In the United States corn is a desirable vegetable; in parts of Europe, until recently, it was considered pig food.

Somehow, whenever a need is met, it's replaced by a want, which soon becomes another need.

Q.10 Using the principle of rational choice, explain why a change in tastes will shift a demand curve.

It is hard to make good decisions. You need lots of training—in math, in economics, in logic. Think of kids—do five-year-olds make rational decisions? Some dyed-in-the-wool utilitarians might argue that whatever decision one makes must, by definition, be rational, but such usage makes the concept tautological—true by definition.

When applying the theory of rational choice, most economists agree that some decisions people make can be irrational. For example, they will concede that five-year-olds make a lot of what most parents would call stupid (or irrational) decisions. By a stupid decision they mean a decision with expected consequences that, if the child had logically thought about them, would have caused the child not to make that particular decision. But five-year-olds often haven't learned how to think logically about expected consequences, so economists don't assume decisions made by five-year-olds reflect the rational choice model.

In the real world, parents and teachers spend enormous effort to teach children what is rational, reasonable, and

APPLYING THE TOOLS

Making Stupid Decisions

"appropriate." Children's decision-making process reflects that teaching. But parents and teachers teach more than a decision-making process; they also teach children a moral code that often includes the value of honor and the value of selflessness. These teachings shape their children's decision-making process (although not always in the way that parents or teachers think or hope) and modify their preferences. So our decision-making process and our preferences are, to some degree, taught to us.

Recognizing that preferences and decision-making processes are, to some degree, taught, not inherent, eliminates the fixed point by which to judge people's decisions: Are they making decisions that reflect their true needs, or are they simply reflecting what they have been taught? Eliminating that fixed point makes it difficult to draw unambiguous policy implications from economists' model of rational choice.

Economists take into account changes in tastes as shift factors of demand.

To say we don't analyze tastes in the core of economic theory doesn't mean that we don't take them into account. Think back to Chapter 4, when we distinguished shifts in demand (the entire demand schedule shifts) from movements along the demand curve. Those movements along the demand curve were the effect of price. Tastes were one of the shift factors of demand. So economists do include tastes in their analysis; a change in tastes makes the demand curve shift.

CONCLUSION

We began this chapter with a discussion of the simplifying nature of the economists' analysis of rational choice. Now that you've been through it, you may be wondering if it's all that simple. In any case, I'm sure most of you would agree that it's complicated enough. When we're talking about formal analysis, I'm in total agreement.

But if you're talking about informal analysis and applying the analysis to the real world, most economists would also agree that this theory of choice is in no way acceptable. Economists believe that there's more to life than maximizing utility. We believe in love, anger, and doing crazy things just for the sake of doing crazy things. We're real people.

Economists use their simple self-interest theory of choice because it cuts through many obfuscations, and in doing so, often captures a part of reality that others miss.

But, we argue, simplicity has its virtue, and often people hide their selfish motivations. Few people like to go around and say, "I did this because I'm a self-interested, calculating person who cares primarily about myself." Instead they usually emphasize other motives. "Society conditioned me to do it"; "I'm doing this to achieve fairness"; "It's my upbringing." And they're probably partially right, but often they hide and obscure their self-interested motives in their psychological explanations. The beauty of economists' simple psychological assumption is that it cuts through many obfuscations (that's an obfuscating word meaning smokescreens) and, in doing so, often captures a part of reality that others miss. Let's consider a couple of examples.

Why does government have restrictions on who's allowed to practice law? The typical layperson's answer is that these restrictions exist to protect the public. The economists' answer is that many of the restrictions do little to protect the public. Instead their primary function is to restrict the number of lawyers and thereby increase the marginal utility of existing lawyers and the price they can charge.

Why do museum directors almost always want to increase the size of their collections? The layperson's (and museum directors') answer is that they're out to preserve our artistic heritage. The economists' answer is that it often has more to do with maximizing the utility of the museum staff. (Economist William Grampp made this argument in a book about the economics of art. He supported his argument by pointing out that more than half of museums' art is in storage and not accessible to the public. Acquiring more art will simply lead to more art going into storage.)

Now in no way am I claiming that the economic answer based on pure self-interest is always the correct one. But I am arguing that approaching problems by asking the question "What's in it for the people making the decisions?" is a useful approach that will give you more insight into what's going on than many other approaches. It gets people to ask tough, rather than easy, questions. After you've asked the tough questions, then you can see how to modify the conclusions by looking deeply into the real-world institutions.

Approaching problems by asking the question "What's in it for the people making the decision?" is a useful approach that will give you more insight than many other approaches.

All too often students think of economics and economic reasoning as establishment reasoning. That's not true. Economic reasoning can be extremely subversive to existing establishments. But whatever it is, it is not subversive in order to be subversive, or proestablishment to be proestablishment. It's simply a logical application of a simple idea—individual choice theory—to a variety of problems.

Chapter Summary

- Total utility is the satisfaction obtained from consuming a product; marginal utility is the satisfaction obtained from consuming one additional unit of a product.

- The principle of diminishing marginal utility states that after some point, the marginal utility of consuming more of the good will fall.

- The principle of rational choice is:

  If $\dfrac{MU_x}{P_x} > \dfrac{MU_y}{P_y}$, choose to consume more of good x.

  If $\dfrac{MU_x}{P_x} < \dfrac{MU_y}{P_y}$, choose to consume more of good y.

- The utility-maximizing rule says:

  If $\dfrac{MU_x}{P_x} = \dfrac{MU_y}{P_y}$, you're maximizing utility; you're indifferent between good x and good y.

- Unless $MU_x/P_x = MU_y/P_y$, an individual can rearrange his or her consumption to increase total utility.

- Opportunity cost is essentially the marginal utility per dollar one forgoes from the consumption of the next-best alternative.

- The law of demand can be derived from the principle of rational choice.

- If you're in equilibrium and the price of a good rises, you'll reduce your consumption of that good to reestablish equilibrium.

- The law of supply can be derived from the principle of rational choice.

- If your wage rises, the marginal utility of the goods you can buy with that wage will rise and you will work more to satisfy the utility-maximizing rule.

- To apply economists' analysis of choice to the real world, we must carefully consider, and adjust for, the underlying assumptions, such as costlessness of decision making and given tastes.

Key Terms

marginal utility   *(178)*

principle of diminishing marginal
  utility   *(179)*

principle of rational choice   *(181)*

total utility   *(178)*

utility   *(177)*

utility-maximizing rule   *(182)*

Questions for Thought and Review

1. Explain how marginal utility differs from total utility.
2. According to the principle of diminishing marginal utility, how does marginal utility change as more of a good is consumed? As less of a good is consumed?
3. How would the world be different than it is if the principle of diminishing marginal utility seldom held true?
4. It is sometimes said that an economist is a person who knows the price of everything but the value of nothing. Is this statement true or false? Why?
5. Assign a measure of utility to your studying for various courses. Do your study habits follow the principle of rational choice?
6. What key psychological assumptions do economists make in their theory of individual choice?
7. Explain your motivation for four personal decisions you have made in the past year, using economists' model of individual choice.
8. State the law of demand and explain how it relates to the principle of rational choice.
9. State the law of supply and explain how it relates to opportunity cost.
10. If the supply curve is perfectly inelastic, what is the opportunity cost of the supplier?
11. There is a small but growing movement known as "voluntary simplicity," which is founded on the belief in a simple life of working less and spending less. Do Americans who belong to this movement follow the principle of rational choice?
12. Although the share of Americans who say they are "very happy" hasn't changed much in the last five decades, the number of products produced and consumed per person has risen tremendously. How can this be?
13. Early Classical economists found the following "diamond/water" paradox perplexing: "Why is water, which is so useful and necessary, so cheap, when diamonds, which are so useless and unnecessary, so expensive?" Using the utility concept, explain why it is not really a paradox.
14. Give an example of a recent purchase for which you used a rule of thumb in your decision-making process. Did your decision follow the principle of rational choice? Explain.

Problems and Exercises

1. Complete the following table of Scout's utility from drinking cans of soda and answer the questions below.

Cans of Soda	Total Utility	Marginal Utility
0	———	
		10
1	———	
		12
2	22	
3	32	
		8
4	———	
		4
5	———	
6	44	———
7	42	———

a. At what point does marginal utility begin to fall?
b. Will Scout consume the 7th can of soda? Explain your answer.
c. True or false? Scout will be following the utility-maximizing rule by consuming 2 cans of soda. Explain your answer.

2. The following table gives the price and total units of three goods: A, B, and C.

			Total Utility						
Good	Price	1	2	3	4	5	6	7	8
A	$10	200	380	530	630	680	700	630	430
B	2	20	34	46	56	64	72	78	82
C	6	50	60	70	80	90	100	90	80

As closely as possible, determine how much of the three goods you would buy with $20. Explain why you chose what you did.

3. The following table gives the marginal utility of John's consumption of three goods: A, B, and C.

Units of Consumption	MU of A	MU of B	MU of C
1		25	45
	20		
2		20	30
	18		
3		15	24
	16		
4		10	18
	14		
5		8	15
	12		
6		6	12
	10		

a. Good A costs $2 per unit, good B costs $1, and good C costs $3. How many units of each should a consumer with $12 buy to maximize his or her utility?

b. How will the answer change if the price of B rises to $2?

c. How about if the price of C is 50 cents but the other prices are as in *a*?

4. The total utility of your consumption of widgets is 40; it changes by 2 with each change in widgets consumed. The total utility of your consumption of wadgets is also 40 but changes by 3 with each change in wadgets consumed. The price of widgets is $2 and the price of wadgets is $3. How many widgets and wadgets should you consume?

5. Nobel Prize–winning economist George Stigler explains how the famous British economist Phillip Wicksteed decided where to live. His two loves were fresh farm eggs, which were more easily obtained the farther from London he was, and visits from friends, which decreased the farther he moved away from London. Given these two loves, describe the decision rule that you would have expected Wicksteed to follow.

6. You are buying your spouse, significant other, or close friend a ring. You decide to show your reasonableness, and buy a cubic zirconium ring that sells at ⅕₀ the cost of a mined diamond and that any normal person could not tell from a mined diamond just by looking at it. In fact,

the zirconium will have more brilliance and fewer occlusions (imperfections) than a mined diamond.

a. How will your spouse (significant other, close friend) likely react?

b. Why?

c. Is this reaction justified?

7. Suppose Charlie Parker CDs cost $10 apiece and Lester Young CDs cost $5 apiece. You have $40 to spend on CDs. The marginal utility that you derive from additional CDs is as follows:

Number of CDs	Charlie Parker	Lester Young
0		
1	60	30
2	40	28
3	30	24
4	20	20
5	10	10

How many of each CD would you buy? Suppose the price of a Lester Young CD rises to $10. How many of each CDs would you buy? Use this to show how the principle of rational choice leads to the law of demand.

Web Questions

1. Go to http://www.travelocity.com.
   a. Find a selection of prices of airline fares between two cities for a period of one month ahead of time and staying over a Saturday night. If there are differences in the prices explain why they likely differ.
   b. Now shorten your stay, and do not include a Saturday night stay. What happens to the prices? Explain why.
   c. Now find the price of the same flight you had in *a* only this time booking only three days ahead. What happens to prices? Explain why.

2. Go to http://www.iwon.com.
   a. What does this site do?
   b. Why do they give out a $10,000 daily prize and a $10 million yearly prize for using the site?
   c. What advertisements were shown there?
   d. What does the existence of these advertisements suggest about economists' assumption that tastes are fixed?

Answers to Margin Questions

1. False. Economists' theory of choice does not require them to measure utility. It only requires that the marginal utility of one good be compared to the marginal utility of another. *(178)*

2. If the total utility curve is a straight line, the marginal utility curve will be flat with a slope of zero since marginal utility would not change with additional units. *(178)*

3. False. The principle of diminishing marginal utility is that as one increases consumption of a good, the good's marginal utility decreases. *(179)*

4. Given a choice between the two, the rational choice is to watch MTV for one hour since it provides the highest marginal utility per hour. *(180)*

5. False. You are maximizing total utility when the marginal utilities per dollar are the same for all goods. This does not have to be where marginal utility is zero. *(181)*

6. If I am currently in equilibrium, then $MU_x/P_x = MU_y/P_y = MU_z/P_z$ for all goods I consume. If the price of one good goes up, I will decrease my consumption of that good and increase the consumption of other goods until the equilibrium is met again where $MU_x/P_x = MU_y/P_y = MU_z/P_z$. *(184)*

7. If offered one more dollar per hour, I would choose to substitute labor for leisure since the price of leisure (pay per hour of work) has increased. Following the principle of rational choice, I would work more to lower the marginal utility of work so that $MU_w/P_w = MU_l/P_l$. *(187)*

8. Good y has the higher marginal utility per dollar since the opportunity cost of consuming good x is the marginal utility per dollar of consuming good y. *(188)*

9. This could be true or false. It depends on how you interpret bounded rationality. If it is interpreted within a costless decision-making environment, it does violate the principle of rational choice since there is no reason to be less than rational. If, however, it is interpreted within a costly decision-making environment, then you can be making decisions within a range because the marginal cost of increasing the range of choices exceeds the marginal benefit of doing so, and in that case bounded rationality is consistent with the principle of rational choice. Information is not costless. *(188)*

10. If a person is in equilibrium and a change in tastes leads to an increase in the marginal utility for one good, he will increase consumption of that good to reestablish equilibrium. A change in tastes will shift a demand curve because it will cause a change in quantity consumed without a change in the good's price. *(189)*

Indifference Curve Analysis

As I stated in the chapter, analyzing individual choice using actual numbers is unnecessary. In the chapter, I asked you to make a deal with me: You'd remember that actual numbers are unnecessary and I'd use them anyway. This appendix is for those who didn't accept my deal (and for those whose professors want them to get some practice in Graphish). It presents an example of a more formal analysis of individual choice.

SOPHIE'S CHOICE

Sophie is a junk food devotee. She lives on two goods: chocolate bars, which cost $1 each, and cans of soda, which sell for 50 cents apiece. Sophie is trying to get as much pleasure as possible, given her income. Alternatively expressed, Sophie is trying to maximize her utility, given an income constraint.

By translating this statement of Sophie's choice into graphs, I can demonstrate the principle of rational choice without ever mentioning any specific amount of utility.

The graph we'll use will have chocolate bars on the vertical axis and cans of soda on the horizontal axis, as in Figure A8-1.

GRAPHING THE INCOME CONSTRAINT

Let's begin by asking: How can we translate her income constraint (the $10 maximum she has to spend) into Graphish? The easiest way to do that is to ask what would happen if she spends her $10 all on chocolate bars or all on cans of soda. Since a chocolate bar costs $1, if she spends it all on chocolate bars she can get 10 bars (point A

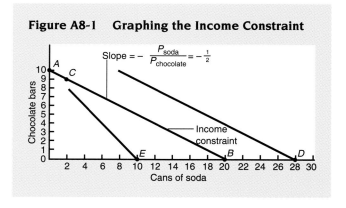

Figure A8-1   Graphing the Income Constraint

in Figure A8-1). If she spends it all on cans of soda, she can get 20 cans of soda (point B). This gives us two points.

But what if she wants some combination of soda and chocolate bars? If we draw a line between points A and B, we'll have a graphical picture of her income constraint and can answer that question because an **income constraint** is *a curve that shows us the various combinations of goods an individual can buy with a given income*. The line is her income constraint in Graphish.

To see that it is, say Sophie is spending all her money on chocolate bars. She then decides to buy one fewer chocolate bar. That gives her $1 to spend on soda, which, since those cans cost 50 cents each, allows her to buy 2 cans. Point C (9 chocolate bars and 2 cans of soda) represents that decision. Notice how point C is on the income constraint. Repeat this exercise from various starting points until you're comfortable with the fact that the line does indeed represent the various combinations of soda and chocolate bars Sophie can buy with the $10. It's a line with a slope of −½ and intersects the chocolate bar axis at 10 and the cans-of-soda axis at 20.

To be sure that you've got it, ask yourself what would happen to the income constraint if Sophie got another $4 to spend on the two goods. Going through the same reasoning should lead you to the conclusion that the income constraint will shift to the right so that it will intersect the cans-of-soda axis at 28 (point D), but its slope won't change. (I started the new line for you.) Make sure you can explain why.

Now what if the price of a can of soda goes up to $1? What happens to the income line? (This is a question many people miss.) If you said the income line becomes steeper, shifting in along the cans-of-soda axis to point E while remaining anchored along the chocolate bar axis until the slope equals −1, you've got it. If you didn't say that, go through the same reasoning we went through at first (if Sophie buys only cans of soda . . .) and then draw the new line. You'll see it becomes steeper. Put another way, the absolute value of the slope of the curve is the ratio of the price of cans of soda to the price of chocolate bars; the absolute value of the slope becomes greater with a rise in the price of cans of soda.

GRAPHING THE INDIFFERENCE CURVE

Now let's consider the second part of Sophie's choice: the pleasure part. Sophie is trying to get as much pleasure as she can from her $10. How do we deal with this in Graphish?

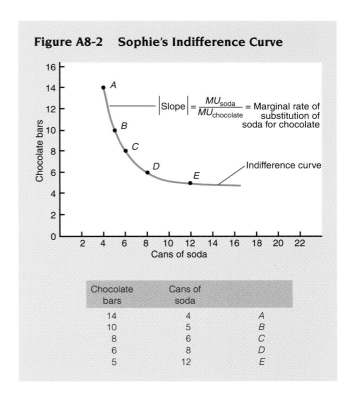

Figure A8-2   Sophie's Indifference Curve

$$\left|\text{Slope}\right| = \frac{MU_{soda}}{MU_{chocolate}} = \text{Marginal rate of substitution of soda for chocolate}$$

Chocolate bars	Cans of soda	
14	4	A
10	5	B
8	6	C
6	8	D
5	12	E

To see, let's go through a thought experiment. Say Sophie had 14 chocolate bars and 4 cans of soda (point A in Figure A8-2). Let's ask her, "Say you didn't know the price of either good and we took away 4 of those chocolate bars (so you had 10). How many cans of soda would we have to give you so that you would be just as happy as before we took away the 4 chocolate bars?"

Since she's got lots of chocolate bars and few cans of soda, her answer is probably "Not too many; say, 1 can of soda." This means that she would be just as happy to have 10 chocolate bars and 5 cans of soda (point B) as she would to have 14 chocolate bars and 4 cans of soda (point A). Connect those points and you have the beginning of a "just-as-happy" curve. But that doesn't sound impressive enough, so, following economists' terminology, we'll call it an **indifference curve**—*a curve that shows combinations of goods among which an individual is indifferent*. She's indifferent between points A and B.

If you continue our thought experiment, you'll get a set of combinations of chocolate bars and cans of soda like that shown in the table in Figure A8-2.

If you plot each of these combinations of points on the graph in Figure A8-2 and connect all these points, you have one of Sophie's indifference curves: a curve representing combinations of cans of soda and chocolate bars among which Sophie is indifferent.

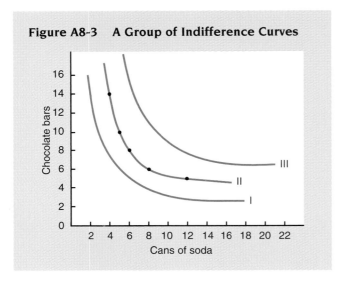

Figure A8-3   A Group of Indifference Curves

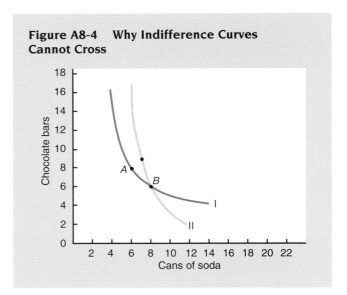

Figure A8-4   Why Indifference Curves Cannot Cross

Let's consider the shape of this curve. First, it's downward sloping. That's reasonable; it simply says that if you take something away from Sophie, you've got to give her something in return if you want to keep her indifferent between what she had before and what she has now. The absolute value of the slope of an indifference curve is the **marginal rate of substitution**—*the rate at which one good must be added when the other is taken away in order to keep the individual indifferent between the two combinations.*

Second, it's bowed inward. That's because as Sophie gets more and more of one good, it takes fewer and fewer of another good to compensate for the loss of the good she incurred in order to get more of the other good. The underlying reasoning is similar to that in our discussion of the law of diminishing marginal utility, but notice we haven't even mentioned utility. Technically the reasoning for the indifference curve being bowed inward is called the **law of diminishing marginal rate of substitution**—which tells us that *as you get more and more of a good, if some of that good is taken away, then the marginal addition of another good you need to keep you on your indifference curve gets less and less.*

Even more technically we can say that the absolute value of the slope of the indifference curve equals the ratio of the marginal utility of cans of soda to the marginal utility of chocolate bars:

$$\left|\text{Slope}\right| = \frac{MU_{\text{soda}}}{MU_{\text{chocolate}}} = \begin{array}{l}\text{Marginal rate}\\ \text{of substitution}\end{array}$$

That ratio equals the marginal rate of substitution of cans of soda for chocolate bars. Let's consider an example. Say

that in Figure A8-2 Sophie is at point A and that the marginal utility she gets from an increase from 4 to 5 cans of soda is 10. Since we know that she was willing to give up 4 chocolate bars to get that 1 can of soda (and thereby move from point A to point B), that 10 must equal the loss of utility she gets from the loss of 4 chocolate bars out of the 14 she originally had. So the marginal rate of substitution of cans of soda for chocolate bars between points A and B must be 4. That's the absolute value of the slope of that curve. Therefore, her *MU* of a chocolate bar must be about 2.5 (10 for 4 chocolate bars).

You can continue this same reasoning, starting with various combinations of goods. If you do so, you can get a whole group of indifference curves like that in Figure A8-3. Each curve represents a different level of happiness. Assuming she prefers more to less, Sophie is better off if she's on Curve II than if she's on Curve I, and even better off if she's on Curve III. Her goal in life is to get out to the furthest indifference curve she can.

To see whether you've followed the reasoning, ask yourself the following question: "Assuming Sophie prefers more of a good to less (which seems reasonable), can any two of Sophie's indifference curves cross each other as the ones in Figure A8-4 do?"

The answer is no, no, no! Why? Because they're indifference curves. If the curves were to cross, the "prefer-more-to-less" principle would be violated. Say we start at point A: Sophie has 8 chocolate bars and 6 cans of soda. We know that since A (8 chocolate bars and 6 sodas) and B (6 chocolate bars and 8 cans of soda) are on the same indifference curve, Sophie is indifferent between A and B.

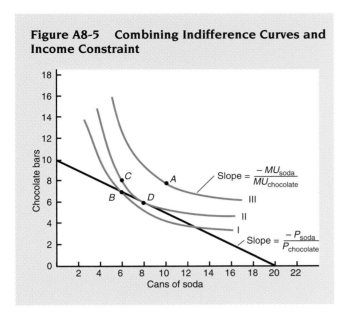

Figure A8-5   Combining Indifference Curves and Income Constraint

Similarly with points B and C: Sophie would just as soon have 9 chocolate bars and 7 cans of soda as she would 6 chocolate bars and 8 cans of soda.

It follows by logical deduction that point A must be indifferent to C. But consider points A and C carefully. At point C, Sophie has 7 cans of soda and 9 chocolate bars. At point A she has 6 cans of soda and 8 chocolate bars. At point C she has more of both goods than she has at point A, so to say she's indifferent between these two points violates the "prefer-more-to-less" criterion. Ergo (that's Latin, meaning "therefore"), two indifference curves cannot intersect. That's why we drew the group of indifference curves in Figure A8-3 so that they do not intersect.

COMBINING INDIFFERENCE CURVES AND INCOME CONSTRAINTS

Now let's put the income constraint and the indifference curves together and ask how many chocolate bars and cans of soda Sophie will buy if she has $10, given the psychological makeup described by the indifference curves in Figure A8-3.

To answer that question, we must put the income line of Figure A8-1 and the indifference curves of Figure A8-3 together, as we do in Figure A8-5.

As we discussed, Sophie's problem is to get to as high an indifference curve as possible, given her income con-

straint. Let's first ask if she should move to point A (8 chocolate bars and 10 cans of soda). That looks like a good point. But you should quickly recognize that she can't get to point A; her income line won't let her. (She doesn't have enough money.) Well then, how about point B (7 chocolate bars and 6 cans of soda)? She can afford that combination; it's on her income constraint. The problem with point B is the following: She'd rather be at point C since point C has more chocolate bars and the same amount of soda (8 chocolate bars and 6 cans of soda). But, you say, she can't reach point C. Yes, that's true, but she can reach point D. And, by the definition of indifference curve, she's indifferent between point C and point D, so point D (6 chocolate bars and 8 cans of soda), which she can reach given her income constraint, is preferred to point B.

The same reasoning holds for all other points. The reason is that the combination of chocolate bars and cans of soda represented by point D is the best she can do. It is the point where the indifference curve and the income line are tangent—the point at which the slope of the income line ($-P_s/P_c$) equals the slope of the indifference curve ($-MU_s/MU_c$). Equating those slopes gives $P_s/P_c = (MU_s/MU_c)$, or:

$$MU_c/P_c = MU_s/P_s$$

This equation, you may remember from the chapter, is the equilibrium condition of our principle of rational choice. So by our Graphish analysis we arrived at the same conclusion we arrived at in the chapter, only this time we did it without using actual numbers. This means that even without a utilometer, economists' principle of rational choice is internally logical.

DERIVING A DEMAND CURVE FROM THE INDIFFERENCE CURVE

Not only can we derive the principle of rational choice with indifference curve/income line analysis, we can also derive a demand curve. To do so, ask yourself what a demand curve is. It's the quantity of a good that a person will buy at various prices. Since the income line gives us the relative price of a good, and the point of tangency of the indifference curve gives us the quantity that a person would buy at that price, we can derive a demand curve from the indifference curves and income lines. To derive a demand curve we go through a set of thought experiments asking how many cans of soda Sophie would buy at various prices. We'll go through one of those experiments.

Figure A8-6 (a and b)   From Indifference Curves to Demand Curves

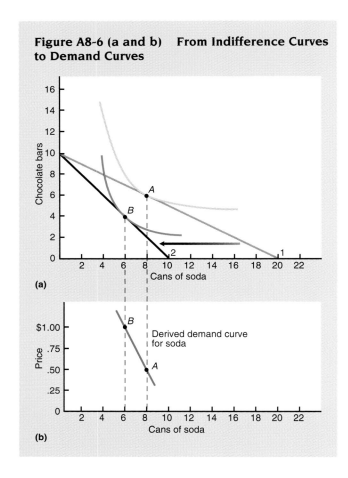

(a)

(b)

We start with the analysis we used before when Sophie started with $10 and chose to buy 8 cans of soda when the price of a can of soda was 50 cents (point A in Figure A8-6(a)). That analysis provides us with one point on the demand curve. I represent that by point A in Figure A8-6(b). At a price of 50 cents, Sophie buys 8 cans of soda.

Now say the price of a can of soda rises to $1. That rotates the income line in, from income line 1 to income line 2 as in Figure A8-6(a). She can't buy as much as she could before. But we can determine how much she'll buy by the same reasoning we used previously. She'll choose a point at which her lower indifference curve is tangent to her new income line. As you can see, she'll choose point B, which means that she buys 6 cans of soda when the price of a can of soda is $1. Graphing that point (6 cans of soda at $1 each) on our price/quantity axis in Figure A8-6(b), we have another point on our demand curve, point B. Connect these two together and you can see we're getting a downward-sloping demand curve, just as the law of demand said we would. To make sure you understand, continue the analysis for a couple of additional price changes. You'll see that the demand curve you derive will be downward sloping.

There's much more we can do with indifference curves. We can distinguish income effects and substitution effects. (Remember, when the price of a can of soda rose, Sophie was worse off. So to be as well off as before, as is required by the substitution effect, she'd have to be compensated for that rise in price by an offsetting fall in the price of chocolate bars.) But let's make a deal. You tentatively believe me when I say that all kinds of stuff can be done with indifference curves and income constraints, and I'll leave the further demonstration and the proofs for you to experience in the intermediate microeconomics courses.

Key Terms

income constraint   (195)

indifference curve   (195)

law of diminishing marginal rate of
     substitution   (196)

marginal rate of substitution   (196)

Questions for Thought and Review

1. Zachary has $5 to spend on two goods: video games and hot dogs. Hot dogs cost $1 apiece while video games cost 50 cents apiece.
    a. Draw a graph of Zachary's income constraint, placing videos on the Y axis.

    b. Suppose the price of hot dogs falls to 50 cents apiece. Draw the new income constraint.
    c. Suppose Zachary now has $8 to spend. Draw the new income constraint using the prices from b.

2. Zachary's indifference curves are shown in the following graph. Determine on which indifference curve Zachary will be, given the income constraints in *a*, *b*, and *c* from problem 1.

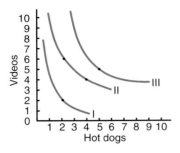

a. Given a choice, which income constraint would Zachary prefer most? Least?

b. What is the marginal rate of substitution of hot dogs for videos at each of the combinations chosen with income constraints *a*, *b*, and *c* in problem 1?

3. What would an indifference curve look like if the marginal rate of substitution were zero? If it were constant?

4. What might an indifference curve look like if the law of diminishing marginal utility did not hold?

Production and Cost Analysis I

9

After reading this chapter, you should be able to:

- Differentiate economic profit from accounting profit.

- Distinguish between long-run and short-run production.

- State the law of diminishing marginal productivity.

- Calculate fixed costs, variable costs, marginal costs, total costs, average fixed costs, average variable costs, and average total costs, given the appropriate information.

- Distinguish the various kinds of cost curves and describe the relationships among them.

- Explain why the marginal and average cost curves are U-shaped.

- Explain why the marginal cost curve always goes through the minimum point of an average cost curve.

Production is not the application of tools
to materials, but logic to work.

Peter Drucker

The ability of market economies to supply material goods and services to members of their societies make them the envy of many other societies and is one of the strongest arguments for using the market as a means of organizing society. Somehow markets are able to channel individuals' imagination, creativity, and drive into the production of material goods and services that other people want. They do this by giving people incentives to supply goods and services to the market.

Ultimately all supply comes from individuals. Individuals control the factors of production such as land, labor, and capital. Why do individuals supply these factors to the market? Because they want something in return. This means that industry's ability to supply goods is dependent on individuals' willingness to supply the factors of production they control. This connection became obvious in the formerly socialist countries in the late 1980s and early 1990s when consumer goods were unavailable. People in those countries stopped working (supplying their labor). They reasoned: Why supply our labor if there's nothing to get in return?

The analysis of supply is more complicated than the analysis of demand. In the supply process, people first offer their factors of production to the market. Then the factors are transformed by firms, such as GM or IBM, into goods that consumers want. **Production** is the name given to that *transformation of factors into goods and services.*

To make it simple for you, I separate out the analysis of the supply of factors of production (considered in detail in later chapters) from the supply of produced goods. This allows us to assume that the prices of factors of production are constant, which simplifies the analysis of the supply of produced goods enormously. There's no problem with doing this as long as you remember that behind any produced good are individuals' factor supplies. Ultimately people, not firms, are responsible for supply.

Even with the analysis so simplified, there's still a lot to cover—so much, in fact, that we devote two chapters (this chapter and the next) to considering production, costs, and supply. In this chapter I introduce you to the production process and short-run cost analysis. Then, in the next chapter, I focus on long-run costs and how cost analysis is used in the real world.

THE ROLE OF THE FIRM

With goods that already exist, like housing and labor, the law of supply is rather intuitive. Their supply to the market depends on people's opportunity costs of keeping them for themselves and of supplying them to the market. But many of the things we buy (such as VCRs, cars, and jackets) don't automatically exist; they must be produced. The supply of such goods depends on production.

 9.1

A key concept in production is the firm. A **firm** is *an economic institution that transforms factors of production into goods and services.* A firm (1) organizes factors of production, and/or (2) produces goods, and/or (3) sells produced goods to individuals, businesses, or government.

Which combination of activities a firm will undertake depends on the cost of undertaking each activity relative to the cost of subcontracting the work out to another firm. When the firm only organizes production, it is called a *virtual firm.* Virtual firms organize the factors of production and subcontract out all production. Let's consider an example—a "psychic superline" that provides super psychic advice to individuals. If it is a virtual firm, it hires individuals to act as psychics, hires an advertising company to convince gullible people to call in, hires a phone routing company to route incoming calls, and hires a billing company to bill callers (the telephone company does this for them). The firm's sole role is organization. While most firms are not totally virtual, more and more of the organizational structure of businesses is being separated from the production process. As cost structures change because of technological advances such as the Internet, an increasing number of well-known firms will likely concentrate on organizational instead of production activities.

Firms:

1. Organize factors of production,
2. produce goods and services, and/or
3. sell produced goods and services.

More and more of the organization structure of business is being separated from the production process.

The Firm and the Market

The firm operates within a market, but, simultaneously, it is a negation of the market in the sense that it replaces the market with command and control. How an economy

This book (like all economics text-books) treats production as if it were a one-stage process—as if a single firm transformed a factor of production into a consumer good. Economists write like that to keep the analysis manageable. (Believe me, it's complicated enough.) But you should keep in mind that reality is more complicated. Most goods go through a variety of stages of production.

For example, consider the production of desks. One firm transforms raw materials into usable raw materials (iron ore into steel); another firm transforms usable raw materials into more usable inputs (steel into steel rods, bolts, and nuts); another firm transforms those inputs into desks, which it sells wholesale to a general distributor, which then sells them to a retailer, which sells them to consumers. Many goods go through five or six stages of production and distribution. As a result, if you added up all the sales of all the firms you would overstate how much total production was taking place.

To figure out how much total production is actually taking place, economists use the concept *value added*. Value added is the contribution that each stage of production makes to the final value of a good. A firm's value added is determined by subtracting from the firm's total output

APPLYING THE TOOLS

Value Added and the Calculation of Total Production

the cost of the inputs bought from other firms. For example, if a desk assembly firm spends $4,000 of its revenue on component parts and sells its output for $6,000, its value added is $2,000, or 33⅓ percent of its revenue.

When you add up all the stages of production, the value added of all the firms involved must equal 100 percent, and no more, of the total output. When I discuss "a firm's" production of a good in this book, to relate that discussion to reality, you should think of that firm as a composite firm consisting of all the firms contributing to the production and distribution of that product.

Why is it important to remember that there are various stages of production? Because it brings home to you how complicated producing a good is. If any one stage gets messed up, the good doesn't get to the consumer. Producing a better mousetrap isn't enough. The firm must also be able to get it out to consumers and let them know that it's a better mousetrap. The standard economic model doesn't bring home this point. But if you're ever planning to go into business for yourself, you'd better remember it. Many people's dreams of supplying a better product to the market have been squashed by this reality.

Firms replace the market with command and control.

operates—which activities are organized through markets, and which activities are organized through firms—depends on *transactions costs* (costs of undertaking trades through the market) and the rent or command over resources that organizers can appropriate to themselves by organizing production in a certain way. Ronald Coase won a Nobel Prize in 1991 for pathbreaking work on the nature of the firm and transactions costs.

In Chapter 3 we discussed the types of firms that exist in real life. They include sole proprietorships, partnerships, corporations, for-profit firms, nonprofit firms, and cooperatives. These various firms are the production organizations that translate factors of production into consumer goods.

Firms Maximize Profit

The firm plays the same role in the theory of supply that the individual does in the theory of demand. The difference is that whereas individuals maximize utility, firms maximize profit. Profit is defined as follows:

Profit = *Total revenue* − *Total cost*

In accounting, total revenue equals total sales times price; if a firm sells 1,000 pairs of earrings at $5 each, its total revenue is $5,000. For an accountant, total costs are the wages paid to labor, rent paid to owners of capital, interest paid to lenders, and actual payments to other factors of production. If the firm paid $2,000 to employees to make the earrings and $1,000 for the materials, total cost is $3,000.

In determining what to include in total revenue and total costs, accountants focus on explicit revenues and explicit costs. That's because they must have explicit measures that go into a firm's income statement. For this reason, you can think of *accounting profit* as explicit revenue less explicit cost. The accounting profit for the earring firm is $2,000.

Economists have different measures of revenues and costs and hence have a different measure of profit. Economists include in revenue and costs both explicit and implicit costs and revenues. Their measure of profit is both explicit and implicit revenue less both explicit and implicit costs.

What are implicit costs and implicit revenue? Implicit costs include the opportunity costs of the factors of production provided by the owners of the business. Say that the owner of our earring firm could have earned $1,500 working elsewhere if he did not own the earring firm. The opportunity cost of working in his own business is $1,500. It is an implicit cost of doing business and would be included as a cost. For economists, **total cost** is *explicit payments to the factors of production plus the opportunity cost of the factors provided by the owners of the firm*. Total cost of the earring firm is $3,000 in explicit cost and $1,500 in implicit cost, or $4,500. Generally implicit costs must be estimated and are not directly measurable, which is why accountants do not include them.

Implicit revenues include the increase in the value of assets. Say the earring firm owns a kiosk whose market value rises from $10,000 to $11,000. The economic concept of revenue would include the $1,000 increase in the value of the kiosk as part of total revenue. For economists, **total revenue** is *the amount a firm receives for selling its product or service plus any increase in the value of the assets owned by the firm*. Total revenue of the earring firm is $5,000 in explicit revenue plus $1,000 in implicit revenue, or $6,000. For economists,

Economic profit = (*Explicit and implicit revenue*) − (*Explicit and implicit cost*)

So in this case, economic profit is ($5,000 + $1,000) − ($3,000 + $1,500) = $1,500. The difference really has to do with measurability. Implicit costs must be estimated, and the estimations can sometimes be inexact. General accounting rules do not permit such inexactness because it might allow firms to misstate their profit, something accounting rules are designed to avoid.

> In accounting, explicit costs and revenues are focused on; in economics, both explicit and implicit costs and revenues are focused on.

THE PRODUCTION PROCESS

As I stated at the beginning of the chapter, supply is the key to the market's ability to provide the goods people want. Underlying supply is production; firms are important because they control the production process.

The Long Run and the Short Run

The production process is generally divided into a *long-run* planning decision, in which a firm chooses the least expensive method of producing from among all possible methods, and a *short-run* adjustment decision, in which a firm adjusts its long-run planning decision to reflect new information.

In a **long-run decision** *a firm chooses among all possible production techniques*. This means that it can choose the size of the plant it wants, the type of machines it wants, and the location it wants. The firm has fewer options in a **short-run decision,** in which *the firm is constrained in regard to what production decisions it can make.*

The terms *long run* and *short run* do not necessarily refer to specific periods of time independent of the nature of the production process. They refer to the degree of flexibility the firm has in changing the level of output. In the long run, by definition, the firm can vary the inputs as much as it wants. In the short run some of the flexibility that

> A long-run decision is a decision in which the firm can choose among all possible production techniques. A short-run decision is a decision in which the firm is constrained in regard to what production decisions it can make.

existed in the long run no longer exists. In the short run some inputs are so costly to adjust that they are treated as fixed. *So in the long run all inputs are variable; in the short run some inputs are fixed.*

Production Tables and Production Functions

How a firm combines factors of production to produce goods and services can be presented in a **production table** *(a table showing the output resulting from various combinations of factors of production or inputs).*

Real-world production tables are complicated. They often involve hundreds of inputs, hundreds of outputs, and millions of possible combinations of inputs and outputs. Studying these various combinations and determining which is best requires expertise and experience. Business schools devote entire courses to it (operations research and production analysis); engineering schools devote entire specialties to it (industrial engineering).

Studying the problems and answering the questions that surround production make up much of what a firm does: What combination of outputs should it produce? What combination of inputs should it use? What combination of techniques should it use? What new techniques should it explore? To answer these questions, the managers of a firm look at a production table.

Production tables are so complicated that in introductory economics we concentrate on short-run production analysis in which one of the factors is fixed. Doing so allows us to capture some important technical relationships of production without getting too tied up in numbers. The relevant part of a production table of earrings appears in Figure 9-1(c). In it the number of the assumed fixed inputs (machines) has already been determined. Columns 1 and 2 of the table tell us how output of earrings varies as the variable input (the number of workers) changes. For example, you can see that with 3 workers the firm can produce 17 pairs of earrings. Column 3 tells us workers' **marginal product** *(the additional output that will be forthcoming from an additional worker, other inputs constant).* Column 4 tells us workers' **average product** *(output per worker).*

It is important to distinguish marginal product from average product. Workers' average product is the total output divided by the number of workers. For example, let's consider the case of 5 workers. Total output is 28, so average product is 5.6 (28 divided by 5). To find the marginal product we must ask how much additional output will be forthcoming if we change the number of workers. For example, if we change from 4 to 5 workers, the additional worker's marginal product will be 5; if we change from 5 to 6, the additional worker's marginal product will be 3. That's why the marginal products are written between each level of output.

The information in a production table is often summarized in a production function. A **production function** is *the relationship between the inputs (factors of production) and outputs.* Specifically, the production function tells the maximum amount of output that can be derived from a given number of inputs. Figure 9-1(a) is the production function that displays the information in the production table in Figure 9-1(c). The number of workers is on the horizontal axis and the output of earrings is on the vertical axis.

The Law of Diminishing Marginal Productivity

Figure 9-1(b) graphs the workers' average and marginal productivities from the production function in Figure 9-1(a). (Alternatively you can determine those graphs by plotting columns 3 and 4 from the table in Figure 9-1(c).) Notice that both marginal and average productivities are initially increasing, but that eventually they both decrease. Between 7 and 8 workers, the marginal productivity of workers actually becomes negative.

The marginal product is the additional output forthcoming from an additional input, other inputs constant; the average product is the total output divided by the quantity of the input.

Figure 9-1 (a, b, and c) A Production Table and Production Function

The production function in (a) is a graph of the production table in (c). Its shape reflects the underlying production technology. The graph in (b) shows the marginal and average product. Notice that when marginal product is increasing, the production function is bowed upward; when marginal product is decreasing, the production function is bowed downward, and when marginal product is zero, the production function is at its highest point. Firms are interested in producing where both average product and marginal product are positive and falling, which starts at 4 workers and ends at 7.5 workers.

Number of workers	Total output	Marginal product (change in total output)	Average product (total product/number of workers)	
1	4	4	4	Increasing marginal productivity
2	10	6	5	
3	17	7	5.7	
4	23	6	5.8	Diminishing marginal productivity
5	28	5	5.6	
6	31	3	5.2	
7	32	1	4.6	
8	32	0	4.0	Diminishing absolute productivity
9	30	−2	3.3	
10	25	−5	2.5	

(c)

This means that initially this production function exhibits increasing marginal productivity and then it exhibits *diminishing marginal productivity*. Eventually it exhibits negative marginal productivity.

The same information can be gathered from Figure 9-1(a), but it's a bit harder to interpret.[1] Notice that initially the production function is bowed upward. Where it's bowed upward there is increasing marginal productivity, as you can see if you extend a line down to Figure 9-1(b). Then, between 2.5 and 7.5 workers, the production function is bowed downward but is still rising. In this range there's diminishing marginal productivity, as you can see by extending a line down to Figure 9-1(b). Finally marginal productivity is negative.

The most important area of these relationships is the area of diminishing marginal productivity and falling average product (between 4 and 7.5 workers). Why? Because that's the most likely area for a firm to operate in. For example, if it's in the first range and

Q-1 What are the normal shapes of marginal productivity and average productivity curves?

[1]Technically the marginal productivity curve is a graph of the slope of the total product curve.

Q-2 Firms are likely to operate on what portion of the marginal productivity curve?

The law of diminishing marginal productivity states that as more and more of a variable input is added to an existing fixed input, after some point the additional output one gets from the additional input will fall.

marginal productivity is increasing, a firm can increase its existing workers' output by hiring more workers; it will have a strong incentive to do so and get out of that range. Similarly, if hiring an additional worker actually cuts total output (as it does when marginal productivity is negative), the firm would be crazy to hire that worker. So it stays out of that range.

This range of the relationship between fixed and variable inputs is so important that economists have formulated a law that describes what happens in production processes when firms reach this range—when more and more of one input is added to a fixed amount of another input. The **law of diminishing marginal productivity** states that *as more and more of a variable input is added to an existing fixed input, eventually the additional output one gets from that additional input is going to fall.*

As I stated in Chapter 2, the law of diminishing marginal productivity is sometimes called the *flowerpot law* because if it didn't hold true, the world's entire food supply could be grown in one flowerpot. In the absence of diminishing marginal productivity, we could take a flowerpot and keep adding seeds to it, getting more and more food per seed until we had enough to feed the world. In reality, however, a given flowerpot is capable of producing only so much food no matter how many seeds we add to it. At some point, as we add more and more seeds, each additional seed will produce less food than did the seed before it. Eventually the pot reaches a stage of diminishing absolute productivity, in which the total output, not simply the output per unit of input, decreases as inputs are increased.

THE COSTS OF PRODUCTION

In any given firm, owners and managers probably discuss costs far more than anything else. Invariably costs are too high and the firm is trying to figure out ways to lower them. But the concept *costs* is ambiguous; there are many different types of costs and it's important to know what they are. Let's consider some of the most important categories of costs in reference to Table 9-1, which shows costs associated with making between 3 and 32 pairs of earrings.

Fixed Costs, Variable Costs, and Total Costs

9.2

Fixed costs are *costs that are spent and cannot be changed in the period of time under consideration.* There are no fixed costs in the long run since all inputs are variable and hence their costs are variable. In the short run, however, a number of costs will be fixed. For example, say you make earrings. You buy a machine for working with silver, but suddenly there's no demand for silver earrings. Assuming that machine can't be modified and used for other purposes, the money you spent on it is a fixed cost.

Fixed costs are shown in column 2 of Table 9-1. Notice that fixed costs remain the same ($50) regardless of the level of production. As you can see, it doesn't matter whether output is 15 or 20; fixed costs are always $50.

Besides buying the machine, the silversmith must also hire workers. These workers are the earring firm's **variable costs**—*costs that change as output changes.* The earring firm's variable costs are shown in column 3. Notice that as output increases, variable costs increase. For example, when the firm produces 10 pairs of earrings, variable costs are $108; when it produces 16, variable costs rise to $150.

All costs are either fixed or variable in the standard model, so the *total cost* is the sum of the fixed and variable costs:

$$TC = FC + VC$$

$TC = FC + VC$

The earring firm's total costs are presented in column 4. Each entry in column 4 is the sum of the entries in columns 2 and 3 in the same row. For example, to produce 16 pairs of earrings, fixed costs are $50 and variable costs are $150, so total cost is $200.

Table 9-1 The Cost of Producing Earrings

1	2	3	4	5	6	7	8
Output	Fixed Costs (FC)	Variable Costs (VC)	Total Costs (TC) (FC + VC)	Marginal Costs (MC) (Change in total costs/ Change in output)	Average Fixed Costs (AFC) (FC/Output)	Average Variable Costs (AVC) (VC/Output)	Average Total Costs (ATC) (AFC + AVC)
3	$50	$ 38	$ 88	$12	$16.67	$12.66	$29.33
4	50	50	100		12.50	12.50	25.00
9	50	100	150	8	5.56	11.11	16.67
10	50	108	158		5.00	10.80	15.80
16	50	150	200	7	3.13	9.38	12.50
17	50	157	207		2.94	9.24	12.18
22	50	200	250	10	2.27	9.09	11.36
23	50	210	260		2.17	9.13	11.30
27	50	255	305	15	1.85	9.44	11.30
28	50	270	320		1.79	9.64	11.43
32	50	350	400		1.56	10.94	12.50

Average Total Cost, Average Fixed Cost, and Average Variable Cost

Total cost, fixed cost, and variable cost are important, but much of a firm's discussion is of average cost. So the next distinction we want to make is between total cost and average cost. To arrive at the earring firm's average cost, we simply divide the total amount of whatever cost we're talking about by the quantity produced. Each of the three costs we've discussed has a corresponding average cost.

For example, **average total cost** (often called average cost) equals *total cost divided by the quantity produced*. Thus:

$$ATC = TC/Q$$

Average fixed cost equals *fixed cost divided by quantity produced:*

$$AFC = FC/Q$$

Average variable cost equals *variable cost divided by quantity produced:*

$$AVC = VC/Q$$

Average fixed cost and average variable cost are shown in columns 6 and 7 of Table 9-1. The most important average cost concept, average total cost, is shown in column 8. Average total cost can also be thought of as the sum of average fixed cost and average variable cost:

$$ATC = AFC + AVC$$

As you can see, the average total cost of producing 16 pairs of earrings is $12.50. It can be calculated by dividing total cost ($200) by output (16).

Average cost equals total cost divided by quantity.

Marginal Cost

All these costs are important to our earring firm but they are not the most important cost it considers when deciding how many pairs of earrings to produce. That distinction goes to marginal cost, which appears in column 5.[2] **Marginal cost** is *the increase*

Q-3 If total costs are 400, fixed costs are 0, and output is 10, what are average variable costs?

---

[2]Since only selected output levels are shown, not all entries have marginal costs. For a marginal cost to exist, there must be a marginal change, a change by only one unit.

(decrease) in total cost from increasing (or decreasing) the level of output by one unit. Let's find marginal cost by considering what happens if our earring firm increases production by one unit—from 9 to 10. Looking again at Table 9-1, we see that the total cost rises from $150 to $158. In this case the marginal cost of producing the 10th unit is $8.

GRAPHING COST CURVES

Let's say that the owner of the earring firm is a visually-oriented person who asks you (an economics consultant) to show her what all those numbers in Table 9-1 mean. To do so, you first draw a graph, putting quantity on the horizontal axis and a dollar measure of various costs on the vertical axis.

Total Cost Curves

Figure 9-2(a) graphs the total cost, total fixed cost, and total variable costs of all the levels of output given in Table 9-1.[3] The total cost curve is determined by plotting the entries in column 1 and the corresponding entries in column 4. For example, point *L* corresponds to a quantity of 10 and a total cost of $158. Notice that the curve is upward sloping: Increasing output increases total cost.

The total fixed cost curve is determined by plotting column 1 and column 2 on the graph. The total variable cost curve is determined by plotting column 1 and column 3.

As you can see, the total variable cost curve has the same shape as the total cost curve: Increasing output increases variable cost. This isn't surprising, since the total cost curve is the vertical summation of total fixed cost and total variable cost. For example, at output 10, total fixed cost equals $50 (point M); total variable cost equals $108 (point O); and total cost equals $158 (point *L*).

Average and Marginal Cost Curves

Figure 9-2(b) presents the average fixed cost curve, average total cost curve (or average cost curve, as it's generally called), average variable cost curve, and marginal cost curve associated with the cost figures in Table 9-1. Each point on the four curves represents a combination of two corresponding entries in Table 9-1. Points on the average variable cost curve are determined by plotting the entries in column 1 and the corresponding entries in column 7. Points on the average fixed cost curve are determined by entries in column 1 and the corresponding entries in column 6. Points on the average total cost curve are determined by entries in column 1 and the corresponding entries in column 8. Finally, the marginal cost curve is determined by plotting the entries in column 1 and the corresponding entries in column 5. As was the case with the total cost curves, all the firm's owner need do is look at this graph to find the various costs associated with different levels of output.

One reason the graphical visualization of cost curves is important is that the graphs of the curves give us a good sense of what happens to costs as we change output.

Downward-Sloping Shape of the Average Fixed Cost Curve

Let's start our consideration with average fixed cost. Average fixed cost is decreasing throughout. The average fixed cost curve looks like a child's slide: It starts out with a steep decline; then it becomes flatter and flatter. What this tells us about production is

The marginal cost curve goes through the minimum point of the average total cost curve and average variable cost curve; each of these curves is U-shaped. The average fixed cost curve slopes down continuously.

Q-4 Draw a graph of both the marginal cost curve and the average cost curve.

Q-5 What determines the distance between the average total cost and the average variable cost?

---

[3]To keep the presentation simple, we focus only on the most important part of the total cost curve, that part that follows the simplest rules. Other areas of the total cost curve can be bowed downward rather than bowed upward.

Figure 9-2 (a and b)   Total and Per Unit Output Cost Curves

Total fixed costs, shown in (**a**), are always constant; they don't change with output. All other total costs increase with output. As output gets high, the rate of increase has a tendency to increase. The average fixed cost curve shown in (**b**), is downward sloping; the average variable cost curve and average total cost curve are U-shaped. The U-shaped MC curve goes through the minimum points of the AVC and ATC curves. (The AFC curve is often not drawn since AFC is also represented by the distance between the AVC and ATC.)

(a) Total cost curves

(b) Per unit output cost curves

straightforward: As output increases, the same fixed cost can be spread over a wider range of output, so average fixed cost falls. Average fixed cost initially falls quickly but then falls more and more slowly. As the denominator gets bigger while the numerator stays the same, the increase has a smaller and smaller effect.

The U Shape of the Average and Marginal Cost Curves

Let's now move on to the average and marginal cost curves. Why do they have the shapes they do? Or expressed another way, how does our analysis of production relate to our analysis of costs? You may have already gotten an idea of how production and costs relate if you remembered Figure 9-1 and recognized the output numbers that we presented there were similar output numbers to those that we used in the cost analysis. Cost analysis is simply another way of considering production analysis. The laws governing costs are the same laws governing productivity that we just saw in our consideration of production.

In the short run, output can only be raised by increasing the variable input. But as more and more of a variable input is added to a fixed input, the law of diminishing marginal productivity enters in. Marginal and average productivities fall. The key insight here is that when marginal productivity falls, marginal cost must rise, and when average productivity of the variable input falls, average variable cost must rise. So to say that productivity falls is equivalent to saying that cost rises.

It follows that if eventually the law of diminishing marginal productivity holds true, then eventually both the marginal cost curve and the average cost curve must be upward sloping. And, indeed, in our examples they are. It's also generally held that at low levels of production, marginal and average productivities are increasing. This means that marginal cost and average variable cost are initially falling. If they're falling initially and

As more and more of a variable input is added to a fixed input, the law of diminishing marginal productivity causes marginal and average productivities to fall. As these fall, marginal and average costs rise.

Q-6 If you increase output enormously, what two cost curves would almost meet?

rising eventually, at some point they must be neither rising nor falling. This means that both the marginal cost curve and the average variable cost curve are U-shaped.

As you can see in Figure 9-2(b), the average total cost curve has the same general U shape as the average variable cost curve. It has the same U shape because it is the vertical summation of the average fixed cost curve and the average variable cost curve. Its minimum, however, is to the right of the minimum of the average variable cost curve. We'll discuss why after we cover the shape of the average variable cost curve.

Average total cost initially falls faster and then rises more slowly than average variable cost. If we increased output enormously, the average variable cost curve and the average total cost curve would almost meet. Average total cost is of key importance to the firm's owner. She wants to keep it low.

The Relationship between the Marginal Productivity and Marginal Cost Curves

Let's now consider the relationship between marginal product and marginal cost. In Figure 9-3(a), I draw a marginal cost curve and average variable cost curve. Notice their U shape. Initially costs are falling. Then there's some minimum point. After that, costs are rising.

Figure 9-3 (a and b)   The Relationship between Productivity and Costs

The shapes of the cost curves are mirror-image reflections of the shapes of the corresponding productivity curves. (The corresponding productivity curve is an implicit function in which marginal productivity is related to output rather than inputs. At each output there is an implicit number of workers who would supply that output.) When one is increasing, the other is decreasing; when one is at a minimum, the other is at a maximum.

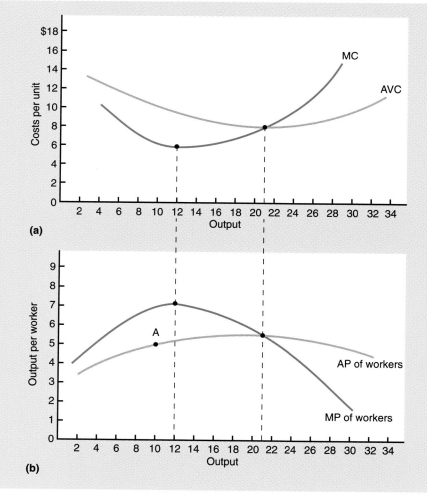

In Figure 9-3(b), I graph the average and marginal productivity curves similar to those that I presented in Figure 9-1(b), although this time I relate average and marginal productivities to output, rather than to the number of workers. Thus, we know that the average product of 2 workers is 5, and that 2 workers can produce an output of 10, so when output is 10, the workers' average productivity is 5. Point A corresponds to an output of 10 and average productivity of 5.

Now let's compare the graphs in Figure 9-3 (a and b). If you look at the two graphs carefully, you'll see that one is simply the mirror image of the other. The minimum point of the average variable cost curve (output = 21) is the same level of output as the maximum point of the average productivity curve; the minimum point of the marginal cost curve (output = 12) is at the same level of output as the maximum point on the marginal productivity curve. When the productivity curves are falling, the corresponding cost curves are rising. Why is that the case? Because as productivity falls, costs per unit increase; and as productivity increases, costs per unit decrease.

The Relationship between the Marginal Cost and Average Cost Curves

Now that we've considered the shapes of each cost curve, let's consider some of the important relationships among them—specifically the relationships between the marginal cost curve on the one hand and the average variable cost and average total cost curves on the other. These relationships are shown graphically for a different production process in Figure 9-4.

If $MP > AP$, then AP is rising.
If $MP < AP$, then AP is falling.

Q.7 When the marginal cost equals the minimum point of the average variable cost, what is true about the average productivity and marginal productivity of workers?

When the productivity curves are falling, the corresponding cost curves are rising.

 9.3

Figure 9-4   The Relationship of Marginal Cost Curve to Average Variable Cost and Average Total Cost Curves

The marginal cost curve goes through the minimum point of both the average variable cost curve and the average total cost curve. Thus, there is a small range where average total costs are falling and average variable costs are rising.

If $MC > ATC$, then ATC is rising.
If $MC = ATC$, then ATC is at its low point.
If $MC < ATC$, then ATC is falling.

If $MC > AVC$, then AVC is rising.
If $MC = AVC$, then AVC is at its low point.
If $MC < AVC$, then AVC is falling.

We've covered a lot of costs and cost curves quickly so a review is in order. First, let's list the cost concepts and their definitions.

KNOWING THE TOOLS

Review of Costs

1. Marginal cost: the additional cost resulting from a one-unit increase in output.
2. Total cost: the sum of all costs.
3. Average total cost: total cost divided by total output (*TC/Q*).
4. Fixed cost: cost that is already spent and cannot be recovered. (It exists only in the short run.)
5. Average fixed cost: fixed cost divided by total output (*FC/Q*).
6. Variable cost: cost of variable inputs. Variable cost does not include fixed cost.
7. Average variable cost: variable cost divided by total output (*VC/Q*).

Each of these costs can be represented by a curve. A number of these curves have specific relationships to the other cost curves.

1. *MC:* MC intersects AVC and ATC at their minimum points.
2. If *MC > AVC*, then *AVC* is rising. If *MC < AVC*, then *AVC* is falling.
3. If *MC > ATC*, then *ATC* is rising. If *MC < ATC*, then *ATC* is falling.
4. *ATC:* a U-shaped curve higher than the *AVC*.
5. *AVC:* a U-shaped curve lower than the *ATC*, with the minimum point slightly to the left.
6. *AFC:* a downward-sloping curve that starts high, initially decreases rapidly, and then decreases slowly.

When marginal cost exceeds average cost, average cost must be rising. When marginal cost is less than average cost, average cost must be falling. This relationship explains why marginal cost curves always intersect the average cost curve at the minimum of the average cost curve.

Marginal cost is relevant for production decisions; average cost is relevant for profit calculations.

Q.8 If marginal costs are increasing, what is happening to average total costs?

Q.9 If marginal costs are decreasing, what must be happening to average variable costs?

Let's first look at the relationship between marginal cost and average total cost. In areas A and B at output below 5, even though marginal cost is rising, average total cost is falling. Why? Because in areas A and B the marginal cost curve is below the average total cost curve. At point B, where average total cost is at its lowest, the marginal cost curve intersects the average total cost curve. In area C, above output 5, where average total cost is rising, the marginal cost curve is above the ATC curve.

The positioning of the marginal cost curve is not happenstance. The position of marginal cost relative to average total cost tells us whether average total cost is rising or falling.

If $MC > ATC$, then ATC is rising.

If $MC = ATC$, then ATC is at its low point.

If $MC < ATC$, then ATC is falling.

To understand why this is, think of it in terms of your grade point average. If you have a B average and you get a C on the next test (that is, your marginal grade is a C), your grade point average will fall below a B. Your marginal grade is below your average grade, so your average grade is falling. If you get a C+ on the next exam (that is, your marginal grade is a C+), *even though your marginal grade has risen from a C to a C+,* your grade point average will fall. Why? Because your marginal grade is still below your average grade. To make sure you understand the concept, explain the next two cases:

1. If your marginal grade is above your average grade, your average grade will rise.
2. If your marginal grade and average grade are equal, the average grade will remain unchanged.

Marginal and average reflect a general relationship that also holds for marginal cost and average variable cost.

If $MC > AVC$, then AVC is rising.

If $MC = AVC$, then AVC is at its low point.

If $MC < AVC$, then AVC is falling.

This relationship is best seen in area B of Figure 9-4, when output is between Q_0 and Q_1. In this area the marginal cost curve is above the average variable cost curve, so average variable cost is rising; but the MC curve is below the average total cost curve, so average total cost is falling.

The intuitive explanation for what is represented in this area is that average total cost includes average variable cost, but it also includes average fixed cost, which is falling. As long as short-run marginal cost is only slightly above average variable cost, the average total cost will continue to fall. Put another way: Once marginal cost is above average variable cost, as long as average variable cost doesn't rise by more than average fixed cost falls, average total cost will still fall.

Q.10 Why does the marginal cost curve intersect the average total cost curve at the minimum point?

INTERMISSION

At this point I'm going to cut off the chapter, not because we're finished with the subject, but because there's only so much that anyone can absorb in one chapter. It's time for a break.

Those of you with significant others, go out and do something significant. Those of you with parents bearing the cost of this education, give them a call and tell them that you appreciate their expenditure on your education. Think of the opportunity cost of that education to them; it's not peanuts. Those of you who are married should go out and give your spouse a big kiss; tell him or her that the opportunity cost of being away for another minute was so high that you couldn't control yourself. Those of you with kids, go out and read them a Dr. Seuss book. (My favorite is about Horton.) Let's face it—Seuss is a better writer than I, and if you've been conscientious about this course, you may not have paid your kids enough attention. We'll return to the grind in the next chapter.

Dr. Seuss books are often more interesting than economics books.

Chapter Summary

- Accounting profit is explicit revenue less explicit cost. Economists include implicit revenue and cost in their determination of profit.

- Implicit revenue includes the increases in the value of assets owned by the firm. Implicit costs include opportunity cost of time and capital provided by the owners of the firm.

- In the long run a firm can choose among all possible production techniques; in the short run it is constrained in its choices.

- The law of diminishing marginal productivity states that as more and more of a variable input is added to a fixed input, the additional output the firm gets will eventually be decreasing.

- Costs are generally divided into fixed costs, variable costs, and total costs.

- $TC = FC + VC$; MC = change in TC; $AFC = FC/Q$; $AVC = VC/Q$; $ATC = AFC + AVC$.

- The average variable cost curve and marginal cost curve are mirror images of the average product curve and the marginal product curve, respectively.

- The law of diminishing marginal productivity causes marginal and average costs to rise.

- If $MC > ATC$, then ATC is rising.
  If $MC = ATC$, then ATC is constant.
  If $MC < ATC$, then ATC is falling.

- The marginal cost curve goes through the minimum points of the average variable cost curve and average total cost curve.

Key Terms

Questions for Thought and Review

1. What costs and revenues do economists include when calculating profit that accountants don't include? Give an example of each.

2. "There is no long run; there are only short and shorter runs." Evaluate that statement.

3. What is the difference between marginal product and average product?

4. If average product is falling, what is happening to short-run average variable cost?

5. If marginal cost is increasing, what do we know about average cost?

6. If average productivity falls, will marginal cost necessarily rise? How about average cost?

7. Say that neither labor nor machines are fixed but that there is a 50 percent quick-order premium paid to both workers and machines for delivery of them in the short run. Once you buy them, they cannot be returned, however. What do your short-run marginal cost and short-run average total cost curves look like?

8. If machines are variable and labor fixed, how will the general shapes of the short-run average cost curve and marginal cost curve change?

9. If you increase production to an infinitely large level, the average variable cost and the average total cost will merge. Why?

10. Explain whether the following statements are true or false: Supplying labor depends on opportunity costs because labor already exists. Supplying goods that need to be produced does not depend on opportunity costs since they do not already exist.

11. Explain how studying for an exam is subject to the law of diminishing marginal productivity.

12. Labor costs are 17.5 percent of revenue per vehicle for General Motors. In union negotiations in the late 1990s, GM attempted to cut its workforce to increase productivity. Together with the reductions they expected in jobs, GM officials hoped to make its North American operations fully competitive with its U.S. and Japanese rivals on total costs. Why are productivity gains so important to GM?

Problems and Exercises

1. Peggy-Sue's cookies are the best in the world, or so I hear. She has been offered a job by Cookie Monster, Inc., to come to work for them at $125,000 per year. Currently, she is producing her own cookies, and she has revenues of $260,000 per year. Her costs are $40,000 for labor, $10,000 for rent, $35,000 for ingredients, and $5,000 for utilities. She has $100,000 of her own money invested in the operation, which, if she leaves, can be sold for $40,000 that she can invest at 10 percent per year.
   a. Calculate her accounting and economic profits.
   b. Advise her as to what she should do.

2. Economan has been infected by the free enterprise bug. He sets up a firm on extraterrestrial affairs. The rent of the building is $4,000, the cost of the two secretaries is $40,000, and the cost of electricity and gas comes to $5,000. There's a great demand for his information, and his total revenue amounts to $100,000. By working in the firm, though, Economan forfeits the $50,000 he could earn by working for the Friendly Space Agency and the $4,000 he could have earned as interest had he saved his funds instead of putting them in this business. Is he making a profit or loss by an accountant's definitions of profit and loss? How about by an economist's definition?

3. Find and graph the TC, AFC, AVC, AC, and MC from the following table.

Units	FC	VC
0	$100	$ 0
1	100	40
2	100	60
3	100	70
4	100	85
5	100	130

4. An economic consultant is presented with the following total product table and asked to derive a table for average variable costs. The price of labor is $15 per hour.

Labor	TP
1	5
2	15
3	30
4	36
5	40

a. Help him do so.
b. Show that the graph of the average productivity curve and average variable cost curve are mirror images of each other.
c. Show the marginal productivity curve for labor inputs between 1 and 5.
d. Show that the marginal productivity curve and marginal cost curve are mirror images of each other.

5. A firm has fixed costs of $100 and variable costs of the following:

Output	1	2	3	4	5	6	7	8	9
Variable costs	$35	75	110	140	175	215	260	315	390

a. Graph the AFC, ATC, AVC, and MC curves.
b. Explain the relationship between the MC curve and the two average cost curves.
c. Say fixed costs dropped to $50. Graph the new AFC, ATC, AVC, and MC curves.
d. Which curves shifted in c? Why?

6. Say that a firm has fixed costs of $200 and constant average variable costs of $25.

a. Graph the AFC, ATC, AVC, and MC curves.
b. Explain why the curves have the shapes they do.
c. What law is not operative for this firm?
d. Say that instead of remaining a constant $25, average variable costs increase by $5 for each unit, so that the cost of 1 is $25, the cost of 2 is $30, the cost of 3 is $35, and so on. Graph the AFC, ATC, AVC, and MC curves associated with these costs.
e. Explain how costs would have to increase in d in order for the curves to have the "normal" shapes of the curves presented in the text.

7. Explain how each of the following will affect the average fixed cost, average variable cost, average total cost, and marginal cost curves faced by a steel manufacturer:
a. New union agreement increases hourly pay.
b. Local government imposes an annual lump-sum tax per plant.
c. Federal government imposes a "stack tax" on emission of air pollutants by steel mills.
d. New steel-making technology increases productivity of every worker.

Web Questions

1. Go to the Avis Rent A Car, Inc., home page at www.avis.com and find out how much it costs to rent a car for a week, driving from your city to a city in another state.
a. Fill in the following cost table:

Miles	Total Cost	Marginal Cost	Average Fixed Cost	Average Variable Cost
0	____	____	____	____
500	____	____	____	____
1,000	____	____	____	____
1,500	____	____	____	____
2,500	____	____	____	____

b. How does average fixed cost change as total number of miles driven increases?
c. How does marginal cost change as total number of miles driven increases?

2. Go to http://www.econ.ag.gov. Using the on-site search engine, answer the following questions:
a. Determine the cost of production of an acre of corn.
b. State two major components of the variable (operating) costs of corn production.
c. State two major components of fixed (allocated overhead) costs of corn production.
d. What price of corn was needed to cover operating costs?
e. What price of corn was needed to cover corn's total operating costs?

Answers to Margin Questions

1. Normally the marginal productivity curve and average productivity curve are both inverted U shapes. (205)
2. Firms are likely to operate on the downward-sloping portion of the marginal productivity curve because on the upward-sloping portion, firms could increase workers' output by hiring more workers. It will continue to hire more workers at least to the point where diminishing marginal productivity sets in. (205)
3. Average variable costs would be 40. (207)
4. As you can see in the graph, both these curves are U-shaped and the marginal cost curve goes through the average cost curve at the minimum point of the average cost curve. (208)

Quantity

5. The distance between the average total cost and the average variable cost is determined by the average fixed cost at that quantity. If quantity increases, the average fixed cost decreases, so the two curves get closer and closer together. *(208)*

6. As output increases, the average total costs and average variable costs come closer and closer together. *(210)*

7. Since the average productivity and marginal productivity of workers are the mirror images of average costs and marginal costs, and when the marginal costs and average costs intersect the two are equal, it follows that the average productivity and marginal productivity of workers must be equal at that point. *(211)*

8. It is impossible to say what is happening to average total costs on the basis of what is happening to marginal costs. It is the position of marginal costs relative to average total costs that is important. *(212)*

9. It is impossible to say because it is the position of marginal cost relative to average variable cost that determines what is happening to average variable cost. *(212)*

10. The marginal cost curve intersects the average total cost curve at the minimum point because once the marginal cost exceeds average total costs, the average total costs must necessarily begin to rise, and vice versa. *(213)*

Production and Cost Analysis II

10

After reading this chapter, you should be able to:

- Distinguish technical efficiency from economic efficiency.

- Explain how economies and diseconomies of scale influence the shape of long-run cost curves.

- State the envelope relationship between short-run cost curves and long-run cost curves.

- Explain the role of the entrepreneur in translating cost of production to supply.

- Discuss some of the problems of using cost analysis in the real world.

Economic efficiency consists of making things that are worth more than they cost.

J. M. Clark

Welcome back. I hope you've reestablished your relationship with the real world and are ready to return, with renewed vigor, to the world of economics. When we took our intermission last chapter we had worked our way through the various short-run costs. That short run is a time period in which some inputs are fixed. In the first part of this chapter we consider firms' long-run decisions and the determinants of the long-run cost curves. Then in the second part we'll talk about applying cost analysis to the real world.

MAKING LONG-RUN PRODUCTION DECISIONS

Firms have many more options in the long run than they do in the short run. They can change any input they want. Plant size is not given; neither is the technology available given.

To make their long-run decisions, firms look at the costs of the various inputs and the technologies available for combining those inputs, and then decide which combination offers the lowest cost.

Say you're opening a hamburger stand. One decision you'll have to make is what type of stove to buy. You'll quickly discover that many different types are available. Some use more gas than others but cost less to buy; some are electric; some are self-cleaning and hence use less labor; some are big; some are little; some use microwaves; some use convection. Some have long-term guarantees; some have no guarantees. Each has a colorful brochure telling you how wonderful it is. After studying the various detailed specifications and aspects of the production technology, you choose the stove that has the combination of characteristics that you believe best fits your needs.

Next you decide on workers. Do you want bilingual workers, college-educated workers, part-time workers, experienced workers . . . ? You get the idea: Even simple production decisions involve complicated questions. These decisions are made on the basis of the expected costs, and expected usefulness, of inputs.

TECHNICAL EFFICIENCY AND ECONOMIC EFFICIENCY

When choosing among existing technologies in the long run, firms are interested in the lowest cost, or most economically efficient, methods of production. They consider all technically efficient methods and compare their costs. The terms *economically efficient* and *technically efficient* differ in meaning. Here's how: **Technical efficiency** in production means that *as few inputs as possible are used to produce a given output.*

Many different production processes can be technically efficient. For example, say you know that to produce 100 tons of wheat you can use 10 workers and 1 acre or use 1 worker and 100 acres. Which of these two production techniques is more efficient? Both can be technically efficient since neither involves the use of more of both inputs than the other technique. But that doesn't mean that both are equally economically efficient. That question can't be answered unless you know the relative costs of the two inputs. If an acre of land rents for $1 million and each worker costs $10 a day, our answer likely will be different than if land rents for $40 an acre and each worker costs $100 a day. The **economically efficient** method of production is *the method that produces a given level of output at the lowest possible cost.*

In long-run production decisions, firms will look at all available production technologies and choose the technology that, given the available inputs and their prices, is the economically efficient way to produce. These choices will reflect the prices of the various factors of production. Those prices, in turn, will reflect the factors' relative scarcities.

Consider the use of land by firms in the United States and in Japan. The United States has large amounts of land (9 acres) per person, so the price of land is lower than in Japan, which has only 0.71 acre per person. An acre of rural land in the United States might cost about $700; in Japan it costs about $15,000. Because of this difference in the price of inputs, production techniques use land much more intensively in Japan than in the United States. Similarly with China: Labor is more abundant and capital is scarcer, so production techniques in China use capital much more intensively than it is used in the United States. Whereas China would use hundreds of workers, and very little machinery, to build a road, the United States would use three or four people along with three machines. Both countries are being economically efficient, but because costs of inputs differ, the economically efficient method of production differs. Thus, the

Q-1 True or false? If a process is economically efficient it is also technically efficient. Explain your answer.

10.1

Q-2 Why does China use more labor-intensive techniques than does the United States?

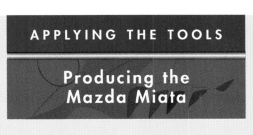

APPLYING THE TOOLS

Producing the Mazda Miata

In the late 1980s the normal production run of a U.S. automobile was 200,000 units per year. Why was it so high? Because of indivisible setup costs of the then-current production technology. In order to reduce those indivisible setup costs to an acceptable level, the production level per year had to equal at least 200,000 or the car was considered an economic failure. The Pontiac Fiero, a sporty two-seater, was dropped in 1988 because it didn't sell well enough to sustain that production level.

But what is an indivisible setup cost depends on the structure of production. Japanese companies structured production differently from U.S. companies and had a much lower level of indivisible setup costs. For example, at just about the same time as Pontiac dropped the Fiero,

a Japanese company, Mazda, entered the market with the Miata, another sporty two-seater. Because Mazda's assembly line was designed to handle different sizes and shapes of vehicles (which permits economies of scope, discussed later in the chapter), its minimum profitable production level for the Miata was about 30,000, not 200,000. This alternative structure of production made it possible for the Miata to do well in a market that buys a total of about 40,000 two-seater sports coupes annually. In response to this competition, U.S. companies followed suit; they changed production methods and, now, indivisible setup costs make up a smaller portion of the total costs, thereby lowering their minimum efficient level of production.

economically efficient method of production is the technically efficient method of production that has the lowest cost. (For a further, graphical analysis of economic efficiency, see Appendix A.)

DETERMINANTS OF THE SHAPE OF THE LONG-RUN COST CURVE

In Chapter 9 we saw that the law of diminishing marginal productivity accounted for the shape of the short-run average cost curve. The firm was adding more of a variable input to a fixed input. The law of diminishing marginal productivity doesn't apply to the long run since in the long run all inputs are variable. The most important determinants of what is economically efficient in the long run are economies and diseconomies of scale. Let's consider each of these in turn and see what effect they will have on the shape of the long-run average cost curve.

> The shape of the long-run cost curve is due to the existence of economies and diseconomies of scale.

Economies of Scale

We say that there are **economies of scale** in production *when long-run average total costs decrease as output increases.* For example, if producing 40,000 VCRs costs the firm $16 million ($400 each), but producing 200,000 VCRs costs the firm $40 million ($200 each), there are significant economies of scale associated with choosing to produce 200,000 rather than 40,000 VCRs.

In real-world production processes, at low levels of production economies of scale are extremely important because many production techniques require a certain minimum level of output to be useful. For example, say you want to produce a pound of steel. You can't just build a mini blast furnace, stick in some coke and iron ore, and come out with a single pound of steel. The smallest technically efficient blast furnaces have a production capacity measured in tons per hour, not pounds per year. The cost of the blast furnace is said to be an **indivisible setup cost** (*the cost of an indivisible input for which a certain minimum amount of production must be undertaken before the input becomes economically feasible to use*).

> In the production of steel, the cost of a blast furnace is an indivisible setup cost that requires a minimum level of production to be economically feasible.

Q₃ Why are larger production runs often cheaper per unit than smaller production runs?

In the longer run all inputs are variable, so only economies of scale can influence the shape of the long-run cost curve.

Indivisible setup costs are important because they create many real-world economies of scale: As output increases, the costs per unit of output decrease. As an example, consider this book. Setting the type for it is an indivisible setup cost; it is a cost that must be incurred if any production is to take place, but it is not a cost that increases with the number of books produced. That means that the more copies of the book that are produced, the lower the typesetting cost per book. That's why it costs more per book to produce a textbook for an upper-level, low-enrollment course than it does for a lower-level, high-enrollment course. The same amount of work goes into both (both need to be written, edited, and set into type), and the printing costs differ only slightly. The actual print-run costs of printing a book are only about $1 to $8 per book. The other costs are indivisible setup costs. Prices of produced goods, including books, reflect their costs of production. As you move to upper-level academic courses, where print runs are smaller, you'll likely discover that the books are smaller and less colorful but are priced the same as, or more than, this introductory text.

In the long-run planning decisions about the cost of producing this book, the expected number of copies to be sold was an important element. That figure influenced the number of books produced, which in turn affected the expected cost per unit. This will be the case anytime there are economies of scale. With economies of scale, cost per unit of a small production run is higher than cost per unit of a large production run.

Figure 10-1(a) demonstrates a normal long-run production table; Figure 10-1(b) shows the related typical shape of a long-run average cost curve. (Notice that there are no fixed costs. Because we're in the long run, all costs are variable.) Economies of scale account for the downward-sloping part. Cost per unit of output is decreasing.

Because of the importance of economies of scale, businesspeople often talk of a minimum efficient level of production. What they mean by minimum efficient level of production is that, given the price at which they expect to be able to sell a good, the indivisible setup costs are so high that production runs of less than a certain size don't

---

Figure 10-1 (a and b)   A Typical Long-Run Average Total Cost Table and Curve

In the long run, average costs initially fall because of economies of scale; then they are constant for a while, and finally they tend to rise due to diseconomies of scale.

Quantity	Total Costs of Labor	Total Costs of Machines	Total Costs = $TC_L + TC_M$	Average Total Costs = TC/Q
11	$381	$254	$635	$58
12	390	260	650	54
13	402	268	670	52
14	420	280	700	50
15	450	300	750	50
16	480	320	800	50
17	510	340	850	50
18	549	366	915	51
19	600	400	1,000	53
20	666	444	1,110	56

(a) Long-run production table

(b) Long-run average cost curve

make economic sense. Thus, the **minimum efficient level of production** is *the amount of production that spreads setup costs out sufficiently for a firm to undertake production profitably.* At this point, the market has expanded to a size large enough for firms to take advantage of all economies of scale. The minimum efficient level of production is where the average total costs are at a minimum.

Diseconomies of Scale

Notice that on the right side of Figure 10-1(b) the long-run average cost curve is upward sloping. Average cost is increasing. We say that there are **diseconomies of scale** in production *when long-run average total cost increases as output increases.* For example, if producing 200,000 VCRs costs the firm $40 million ($200 each) and producing 400,000 VCRs costs the firm $100 million ($250 each), there are diseconomies of scale associated with choosing to produce 400,000 rather than 200,000. Diseconomies of scale usually, but not always, start occurring as firms get large.

Diseconomies of scale could not occur if production relationships were only technical relationships. If that were the case, the same technical process could be used over and over again at the same cost. In reality, however, production relationships have social dimensions, which introduce the potential for important diseconomies of scale into the production process in two ways:

1. As the size of the firm increases, monitoring costs generally increase.
2. As the size of the firm increases, team spirit or morale generally decreases.

Monitoring costs are *the costs incurred by the organizer of production in seeing to it that the employees do what they're supposed to do.* If you're producing something yourself, the job gets done the way you want it done; monitoring costs are zero. However, as the scale of production increases, you have to hire people to help you produce. This means that if the job is to be done the way you want it done, you have to monitor (supervise) your employees' performance. The cost of monitoring can increase significantly as output increases; it's a major contributor to diseconomies of scale. Most big firms have several layers of bureaucracy devoted simply to monitoring employees. The job of middle managers is, to a large extent, monitoring.

The other social dimension that can contribute to diseconomies of scale is the loss of **team spirit** (*the feelings of friendship and being part of a team that bring out people's best efforts*). Most types of production are highly dependent on team spirit. When the team spirit or morale is lost, production slows considerably. The larger the firm is, the more difficult it is to maintain team spirit.

An important reason diseconomies of scale can come about is that the bigger things get, the more checks and balances are needed to ensure that the right hand and the left hand are coordinated. The larger the organization, the more checks and balances and the more paperwork.

Some large firms manage to solve these problems and thus avoid diseconomies of scale. But problems of monitoring and loss of team spirit often limit the size of firms. They underlie diseconomies of scale in which relatively less output is produced for a given increase in inputs, so that per-unit costs of output increase.

Constant Returns to Scale

Sometimes in a range of output a firm does not experience either economies of scale or diseconomies of scale. In this range there are **constant returns to scale** where *long-run average total costs do not change with an increase in output.* Constant returns to scale are shown by the flat portion of the average total cost curve in Figure 10-1(b). Constant

Diminishing marginal productivity refers to the decline in productivity caused by increasing units of a variable input being added to a fixed input. Diseconomies of scale refer to the decreases in productivity which occur when there are equal increases of all inputs (no input is fixed).

Q-4 If production involved only technical relationships and had no social dimension, what would the long-run average total cost curve look like?

As firms become larger, monitoring costs increase and achieving team spirit is more difficult.

As pointed out in the text, the shapes of the short-run average cost curve and the long-run average cost curve are similar. But the reasons underlying those shapes are quite different. It is important to reemphasize that difference. In the short run, some inputs are fixed; in the long run, all inputs vary.

Let's first review why the short-run average cost curve is U-shaped. What accounts for its shape is what's happening to marginal productivity of each additional unit of input *keeping all other inputs fixed*. Since costs are based on inputs, how much an input contributes to output directly affects the costs of production. Average total costs in the short run fall initially because of the assumption of increasing marginal productivity: additional inputs are able to produce increasing increments of output. An example of increasing marginal productivity is a 5 percent increase in the quantity of labor, holding capital constant, leading to a 5 percent increase in output, and the next 5 percent increase leading to a 10 percent increase in output.

Eventually, marginal productivity falls and the short-run average cost curve slopes upward. Adding more of *one* factor of production, holding the others constant, contributes less and less to output, causing marginal costs, and eventually average costs, to rise. An example of diminishing marginal productivity is a 5 percent increase in the quantity of labor, holding capital constant, leading to a 2 percent increase in output and the next 5 percent increase, holding capital constant, leading to a 1 percent increase in output. The assumption of initially increasing

KNOWING THE TOOLS

Distinguishing Diseconomies of Scale from Diminishing Marginal Productivity

marginal productivity and eventually diminishing marginal productivity leads to the U shape of the short-run average cost curve.

Now consider the long-run average cost curve. Its shape is determined by what's happening to returns to scale. Returns to scale are not about how changes in one input affect output. Instead, they involve changing *all inputs equally*. If there are economies of scale, increasing all factors of production equally, say by 5 percent, leads to a greater increase in output, say by 8 percent.

The assumption economists make in the long run is that initially economies of scale cause the long-run average total cost curve to slope downward. Eventually, however, there are diseconomies of scale. That is, increasing all inputs equally, say by 5 percent, leads to a smaller increase in output, say by 3 percent. Diseconomies of scale cause average total costs to rise and the long-run average total cost curve to slope upward. If there are neither economies of scale nor diseconomies of scale, the average total cost curve is flat because inputs and output both are changing by equal proportions. An example of constant returns to scale is a 5 percent increase in all inputs leading to a 5 percent increase in output. With constant returns to scale, average costs do not change.

The assumption we make about production in the long run is that there are first increasing, then constant, and finally decreasing returns to scale. That assumption about returns to scale accounts for the U shape of the long-run average cost curve.

returns to scale occur when production techniques can be replicated again and again to increase output. This occurs before monitoring costs rise and team spirit is lost.

The Importance of Economies and Diseconomies of Scale

Economies and diseconomies of scale play important roles in real-world long-run production decisions.

Economies and diseconomies of scale play important roles in real-world long-run production decisions. Economies of scale underlie firms' attempts to expand their markets either at home or abroad. If they can make and sell more at lower per-unit costs, they will make more profits. Diseconomies of scale prevent a firm from expanding and can lead corporate raiders to buy the firm and break it up in the hope that the smaller production units will be more efficient, thus eliminating some of the diseconomies of scale.

The long-run and the short-run average cost curves have the same U shape. But it's important to remember that the reasons why they have this U shape are quite different. The assumption of initially increasing and then eventually diminishing marginal productivity (as a variable input is added to a fixed input) accounts for the shape of the short-run average cost curve. Economies and diseconomies of scale account for the shape of the long-run average total cost curve. (See the Knowing the Tools box for a review of why.)

Q.5 Why is the short-run average cost curve a U-shaped curve?

Q.6 Why is the long-run average total cost curve generally considered to be a U-shaped curve?

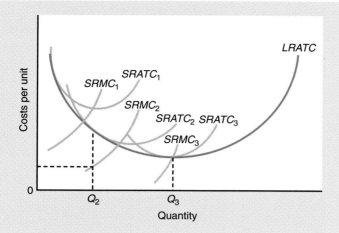

Figure 10-2   Envelope of Short-Run Average Total Cost Curves

The long-run average total cost curve is an envelope of the short-run average total cost curves. Each short-run average total cost curve touches the long-run average total cost curve at only one point. (*SR* stands for short run; *LR* stands for long run.)

ENVELOPE RELATIONSHIP

Since in the long run all inputs are flexible, while in the short run some inputs are not flexible, long-run cost will always be less than or equal to short-run cost at the same level of output. To see this, let's consider a firm that had planned to produce 100 but now adjusts its plan to produce more than 100. We know that in the long run the firm chooses the lowest-cost method of production. In the short run it faces an additional constraint: All expansion must be done by increasing only the variable input. That constraint must increase average cost (or at least not decrease it) compared to what average cost would have been had the firm planned to produce that level to begin with. If it didn't, the firm would have chosen that new combination of inputs in the long run. Additional constraints increase cost. The *envelope relationship* is the relationship between long-run and short-run average total costs. It is shown in Figure 10-2.

The envelope relationship is the relationship explaining that, at the planned output level, short-run average total cost equals long-run average total cost, but at all other levels of output, short-run average total cost is higher than long-run average total cost.

Why it's called an envelope relationship should be clear from the figure. Each short-run average total cost curve touches (is tangent to) the long-run average total cost curve at one, and only one, output level; at all other output levels, short-run average cost exceeds long-run average cost. The long-run average total cost curve is an envelope of short-run average total cost curves.

The intuitive reason why the short-run average total cost curves always lie above the long-run average cost curve is simple. In the short run, you have chosen a plant; that plant is fixed, and its costs for that period are part of your average fixed costs. Changes must be made within the confines of that plant. In the long run you can change everything, choosing the combination of inputs in the most efficient manner. The more options you have to choose from, the lower the costs of production. Put another way: constraints always raise costs. So in the long run, costs must be lower.

Another insight to note about this envelope relationship is the following: When there are economies of scale and you have chosen a plant size that is efficient, given output, your short-run average costs will fall as you increase production. Technically, this must be the case because the short-run marginal cost (*SRMC*) curve goes through the minimum point of the short-run average total cost (*SRATC*) curve, and the minimum point of the *SRATC* curve is to the right of the efficient level of production in the long run. That means that at output Q_2, $SRMC_2$ has to be below $SRATC_2$ and short-run average total cost is falling. Intuitively, what's happening is that at output Q_2, your fixed

APPLYING THE TOOLS

Why Are Textbooks So Long?

Understanding costs and their structure will help you understand why intro economics textbooks are so long—and why their length is to your advantage.

The majority of the costs of a book are fixed costs in relation to the length of the book. The initial costs in terms of length are about 20 percent of the total price of the book. So increasing the length of the book increases costs slightly. But the longer length allows the writer to include more issues that some professors want, and many professors will not consider using the book unless it does include these issues. That means that greater length can allow publishers to sell more books, allowing the fixed costs to be divided over more output. This decrease in fixed cost per unit can lower average total cost more than

increasing the length of the book increases average total costs per unit. So if the added length increases the number of users, the additional length can lower the average cost of the book.

It does lower the costs of the book—up to a point. Textbook publishers are continually looking for that point. They direct authors to shorten their books but also to include almost all issues that various groups want. The latter direction—in favor of inclusion—often takes precedence, which is why textbooks are so long. This doesn't mean that textbooks will always be longer. Recently, economics textbooks have become smaller because students began to complain that the texts were getting too heavy to carry.

costs are high. Now demand increases and you increase production. Your average fixed costs are high; your marginal costs are low; and initially the fall in average fixed costs more than offsets the increased marginal cost. Once marginal cost exceeds *SRATC*, that no longer is the case.[1]

Only when the firm is at the minimum point of the long-run average total cost (*LRATC*) curve (at output Q_3) is the $SRATC_3$ curve tangent to the *LRATC* curve at a point where the *SRMC* curve intersects both the curves. For large markets, this point is the optimal production level of a firm.

ENTREPRENEURIAL ACTIVITY AND THE SUPPLY DECISION

In this chapter and the preceding one we have discussed the technical nature of costs and production. In the next chapter we will formally relate costs of production to the supply of goods. As a bridge between the two chapters, let's conclude this chapter with a consideration of the entrepreneur, who establishes the relationship between costs and the supply decision, and of some of the problems of using cost analysis in the real world.

In thinking about the connection between cost and supply, one fundamental insight is that the revenue received for a good must be greater than the planned cost of producing it. Otherwise why would anyone supply it? The difference between the expected price of a good and the expected average total cost of producing it is the supplier's

The difference between the expected price of a good and the expected average total cost of producing it is the supplier's expected economic profit per unit. The expected profit per unit must exceed the opportunity cost of supplying the good for a good to be supplied.

---

[1]The above reasoning is dependent on the curves being smooth—i.e., having no kinks. This smoothness is a standard assumption of the model. If we give up the smoothness assumption, the *SRATC* curve could be kinked and the *SRMC* curve could be discontinuous. In that case, the *SRATC* curve might be tangent to the *LRATC* curve from the left, but not from the right, and it might not decrease. This would make movement from the long to the short run a discrete jump, whereas the existing model and smoothness assumption make it a smooth continuous movement. So if your intuition doesn't lead you to understand the model, you are probably thinking of a model with different assumptions. You'll be in good company, too. When an economist by the name of Jacob Viner first created this model, his intuition led him to a different result because his intuition was basing the analysis on different assumptions than he was using in his formal model.

expected economic profit per unit. It's profit that underlies the dynamics of production in a market economy.

Cost curves do not become supply curves through some magic process. To move from cost to supply, entrepreneurial initiative is needed. An **entrepreneur** is *an individual who sees an opportunity to sell an item at a price higher than the average cost of producing it.* The entrepreneur is the organizer of production and the one who visualizes the demand and convinces the individuals who own the factors of production that they want to produce that good. Businesses work hard at maintaining the entrepreneurial spirit in their employees. The greater the difference between price and average total cost, the greater the entrepreneur's incentive to tackle the organizational problems and supply the good.

Q-7 Why is the role of the entrepreneur central to the production process in the economy?

USING COST ANALYSIS IN THE REAL WORLD

All too often students walk away from an introductory economics course thinking that cost analysis is a relatively easy topic. Memorize the names, shapes, and relationships of the curves, and you're home free. In the textbook model, that's right. In real life, it's not, because actual production processes are marked by economies of scope, learning by doing and technological change, many dimensions, unmeasured costs, joint costs, indivisible costs, uncertainty, asymmetries, and multiple planning and adjustment periods with many different short runs. And this is a short list!

Economies of Scope

The cost of production of one product often depends on what other products a firm is producing. Economists say that in the production of two goods there are **economies of scope** *when the costs of producing products are interdependent so that it's less costly for a firm to produce one good when it's already producing another.* For example, once a firm has set up a large marketing department to sell cereal, the department might be able to use its expertise in marketing a different product—say, dog food. A firm that sells gasoline can simultaneously use its gas station attendants to sell soda, milk, and incidentals. The minimarts so common along our highways and neighborhood streets developed because gasoline companies became aware of economies of scope.

 10.2

Economies of scope play an important role in firms' decisions of what combination of goods to produce. They look for both economies of scope and economies of scale. When you read about firms' mergers, think about whether the combination of their products will generate economies of scope. Many otherwise unexplainable mergers between seemingly incompatible firms can be explained by economies of scope.

Q-8 What is the difference between an economy of scope and an economy of scale?

By allowing firms to segment the production process, globalization has made economies of scope even more important to firms in their production decisions. Low-cost labor in other countries has led U.S. firms to locate their manufacturing processes in those countries and to concentrate domestic activities on other aspects of production. As I have stressed throughout this book, production is more than simply manufacturing; the costs of marketing, advertising, and distribution are often larger components of the cost of a good than are manufacturing costs. Each of these involves special knowledge and expertise, and the U.S. companies are specializing in the marketing, advertising, and distribution aspects of the production process. By concentrating on those aspects, and by making themselves highly competitive by taking advantage of low-cost manufacturing elsewhere, U.S. firms become more competitive and expand, increasing demand for U.S. labor. Often they expand into new areas, taking advantage of economies of scope in distribution and marketing.

Consider Nike—it produces shoes, right? Wrong. It is a U.S. marketing and distribution company; it outsources all its production to affiliate companies. Nike is expanding, but not in the production of shoes. It is expanding into leisure clothing, where it hopes economies of scope in its marketing and distribution specialties will bring it success.

Nike is only one of many examples. The large wage differentials in the global economy are causing firms to continually reinvent themselves—to shed aspects of their business where they do not have a comparative advantage, and to add new businesses where their abilities can achieve synergies and economies of scope.

Learning by Doing and Technological Change

The production terminology that we've been discussing is central to the standard economic models. In the real world, however, other terms and concepts are also important. The production techniques available to real-world firms are constantly changing because of *learning by doing* and *technological change*. These changes occur over time and cannot be accurately predicted.

Unlike events in the standard economic model, all events in the real world are influenced by the past. That's why learning by doing is important in the real world, but isn't a part of the standard economic model. **Learning by doing** simply means that *as we do something, we learn what works and what doesn't, and over time we become more proficient at it*. Practice may not make perfect, but it certainly makes better and more efficient. Many firms estimate that output per unit input will increase by 1 or 2 percent a year, even if no changes in inputs or technologies occur, as employees learn by doing.

The concept of learning by doing emphasizes the importance of the past in trying to predict performance. Let's say a firm is deciding between two applicants for the job of managing its restaurant. One was a highly successful student but has never run a

Q.9 Does learning by doing cause the cost curve to be downward sloping?

Many firms estimate worker productivity to grow 1 to 2 percent a year because of learning by doing.

Production then: The nature of production has changed considerably in the last 60 years. This picture shows a 1933 production line in which people did the work as the goods moved along the line.   Bettmann/CORBIS.

restaurant; the other was an OK student who has run a restaurant that failed. Which one does the firm hire? The answer is unclear. The first applicant may be brighter, but the lack of experience will likely mean that the person won't be hired. Businesses give enormous weight to experience. So this firm may reason that in failing, the second applicant will have learned lessons that make her the better candidate. U.S. firms faced such a choice when they were invited to expand into the new market economies of Eastern Europe in the early 1990s. Should they hire the former communist managers who had failed to produce efficiently, or should they hire the reformers? (Generally they decided on the former communist managers, hoping they had learned by failing.)

Technological change is *an increase in the range of production techniques that provides new ways of producing goods.* That is, technological change offers an increase in the known range of production. For example, at one point automobile tires were made from rubber, clothing was made from cotton and wool, and buildings were made of wood. As a result of technological change, many tires are now made from petroleum distillates, much clothing is made from synthetic fibers (which in turn are made from petroleum distillates), and many buildings are constructed from steel.

The standard long-run model takes technology as a given. From our experience, we know that technological change affects firms' decisions and production. Technological change can fundamentally alter the nature of production costs.

In some industries technological change is occurring so fast that it overwhelms all other cost issues. The computer industry is a good example. The expectation of technological change has been built into the plans of firms in that industry. The industry has followed Moore's law, which states that the cost of computing will fall by half every 18 months. Indeed, that has happened since the 1980s. With costs falling that fast

Technological change can fundamentally alter the nature of production costs.

Production now: The nature of production has changed considerably in the last 60 years. This picture shows a modern production line. Robots do much of the work. © Keystone/ The Image Works.

because of learning by doing and technological change, all other cost components are overwhelmed, and, instead of costs increasing as output rises significantly, as might be predicted because of diseconomies of scale, costs keep going down.

The fall in the cost of computer chips has affected other industries as well. All types of household goods that use computer technology—including telephones, refrigerators, automobiles, TVs and VCRs, and compact disc players—are undergoing enormous change. For instance, in Asia, VCRs are now almost extinct; they have been replaced by digital video disc (DVD) players—where all images are transmitted digitally. The same will happen in the United States. Another change is that mass-stamped CDs will soon be replaced by individual CDs created by downloading files from the Internet using MP3 technology. In a few years, CDs may not be used at all—music will be stored in music memory banks that will be modified computer hard drives. Computer technology has also revolutionized automobiles, making them more reliable and cheaper. In the 1960s, I could work on my own car, changing the points or modifying the carburetor. Modern cars have no such parts; they have been replaced by electronic parts. When a car isn't running right its owner must now take it to a garage. My point, however, is that automobiles have fundamentally changed; they are much more efficient and reliable and their price has fallen because of the introduction of computer technology. Technological change drives costs down, and can overwhelm diseconomies of scale, causing prices to fall more and more.

Technological change occurs in all industries, not only "high-tech" industries.

Don't think of technological change as occurring only in high-tech industries. Consider chicken production. The price of chickens has fallen enormously over the past 50 years. Why? Because of technological change. At one time chickens were raised in farmyards. They walked around, ate scraps and feed, and generally led a chicken's life. Walking around had definite drawbacks—it took space (which cost money); it made standardization (a requirement of taking advantage of economies of scale) difficult, which prevented lowering costs; it used energy, which meant more feed per pound of chicken; and sometimes it led to disease, since chickens walked in their own manure.

The technological change was to put the chickens in wire cages, so the manure falls through to a conveyor belt and is transferred outside. Another conveyor belt feeds the chickens food laced with antibiotics to prevent disease. Soft music is played to keep them calm (they burn fewer calories). Once they reach the proper weight, they are slaughtered in a similar automated process. Perdue Farms Inc., which led the way in developing this new technology, does not grow any chickens itself. It outsources this approach to chicken farms. Farmers bid for the right to grow the chickens for Perdue. Perdue then puts its label on the chickens, ships them to the supermarkets, and advertises the plump chickens with its name on them. How the chickens feel about this technological change is not clear. (When I asked them all they had to say was cluck.)

This method of raising chickens will likely be replaced in the next couple of decades by another technological change—genetic engineering that will allow chicken parts to be produced directly from single cells. Only the breasts and drumsticks will be produced (and wings if you live in Buffalo). All low-efficiency, low-profit-margin parts such as necks, feet, and heads will be eliminated.

In many businesses the effect of learning by doing and technological change on prices is built into the firm's pricing structure. If they expect their costs to fall with more experience, or if they expect technological advances to lower costs in the future, they might bid low for a big order to give themselves the chance to lower their costs through learning by doing or technological change.

Technological change and learning by doing are intricately related.

Technological change and learning by doing are intricately related. The efficient chicken production we now have did not come about overnight. It occurred over a 20-year period as firms learned how to do it better. Chickens respond to Mozart better than to hip-hop. That had to be learned. Similarly, genetic reproduction of chicken parts will evolve as scientists and firms learn more about cloning and DNA.

Many Dimensions

The only dimension of output in the standard model is how much to produce. Many, if not most, decisions that firms make are not the one-dimensional decisions of the standard model, such as "Should we produce more or less?" They're multidimensional questions like "Should we change the quality? Should we change the wrapper? Should we improve our shipping speed? Should we increase our inventory?" Each of these questions relates to a different dimension of the production decision and each has its own marginal costs. Thus, there isn't just one marginal cost; there are 10 or 20 of them. Good economic decisions take all relevant margins into account.

Good economic decisions take all relevant margins into account.

The reason that the standard model is important is that each of these questions can be analyzed using the same reasoning used in the standard model. But you must remember, *in applying the analysis, it's the reasoning, not the specific model, that's important.*

Unmeasured Costs

If asked, "In what area of decision making do businesses most often fail to use economic insights?" most economists would say costs. The relevant costs are generally not the costs you'll find in a firm's accounts.

Why the difference? Economists operate conceptually; they include in costs exactly what their theory says they should. They include all opportunity costs. Accountants who have to measure firms' costs in practice and provide the actual dollar figures take a much more pragmatic approach; their concepts of costs must reflect only explicit costs—those costs that are reasonably precisely measurable.

Here I review the difference between explicit and implicit costs (discussed in Chapter 9) and introduce another difference—how economists and accountants measure depreciation of capital.

Economists Include Opportunity Cost First, say that a business produces 1,000 widgets[2] that sell at $3 each for a total revenue of $3,000. To produce these widgets the business had to buy $1,000 worth of widgetgoo, which the owner has hand-shaped into widgets. An accountant would say that the total cost of producing 1,000 widgets was $1,000 and that the firm's profit was $2,000. That's because an accountant uses explicit costs that can be measured.

Economic profit is different. An economist, looking at that same example, would point out that the accountant's calculation doesn't take into account the time and effort that the owner put into making the widgets. While a person's time involves no explicit cost in money, it does involve an opportunity cost, the forgone income that the owner could have made by spending that time working in another job. If the business takes 400 hours of the person's time and the person could have earned $6 an hour working for someone else, then the person is forgoing $2,400 in income. Economists include that implicit cost in their concept of cost. When that implicit cost is included, what looks like a $2,000 profit becomes a $400 economic loss.

Q-10 As the owner of the firm, Jim pays himself $1,000. All other expenses of the firm add up to $2,000. What would an economist say are the total costs for Jim's firm?

Economic Depreciation versus Accounting Depreciation Now let's take depreciation. Say a firm buys a machine for $10,000 that's meant to last 10 years. After 1 year,

---

[2]What's a widget? It's a wonderful little gadget that's the opposite of a wadget. (No one knows what they look like or what they are used for.) Why discuss widgets? For the same reason that scientists discuss fruit flies—their production process is simple, unlike most real-world production processes.

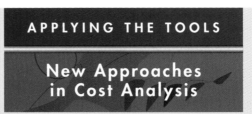

"Factories run by numbers. Numbers to calculate profit and losses; to analyze the costs of new products; and to chart corporate strategy. But a lot of managers are relying on the wrong numbers.

As they adopt new manufacturing techniques like computer-aided design, just-in-time stock management, and total quality control, many firms are discovering that their existing account systems also need dragging into the 1990s. Unless the bean-counters join the manufacturing revolution, traditional cost accounting will have little place in the factory of the future."

The above quote introduced an article in *The Economist* (March 3, 1990, p. 61) describing a conference on strategic manufacturing. This conference focused on managerial or cost accounting (the application of cost analysis to managerial decisions). Unlike *financial accounting* (which involves keeping track of income, assets, and liabilities), managerial accounting is used to help managers determine the cost of producing products and plan future investment. It's the direct application of microeconomics to production.

In the 1980s and 1990s cost accounting changed enormously. The leaders of this change—such as Robert Kaplan of the Harvard Business School—argue that cost accounting systems based on traditional concepts of fixed and variable costs lead firms consistently to make the wrong decisions. They argue that in today's manufacturing, direct labor costs have fallen substantially—in many industries to only 2 or 3 percent of the total cost—and overhead costs have risen substantially. This change in costs facing firms requires a much more careful division among types of overhead costs, and a recognition that what should and should not be assigned as a cost to a particular product differs with each decision.

These developments in managerial accounting require an even deeper understanding of costs than accountants have previously needed. As one firm's director of manufacturing was quoted in *The Economist* article, "Unless management accountants move fast [to incorporate these new concepts], they will be almost without use to the manufacturing manager."

machines like that become in short supply, so instead of falling, its value rises to $12,000. An accountant, looking at the firm's costs that year, would use historical cost (what the machine cost in terms of money actually spent) depreciated at, say, 10 percent per year, so the machine's cost for each of its 10 years of existence would be $1,000. An economist would say that since the value of the machine is rising, the machine has no cost; in fact, it provides a revenue of $2,000 to the firm. The standard model avoids such messy, real-world issues of measuring costs and instead assumes that all costs are measurable in a single time period.

The Standard Model as a Framework

Despite its limitations the standard model provides a good framework for cost analysis.

The standard model can be expanded to include these real-world complications. I don't do so because I suspect that even with its simplifications, the standard model has been more than enough to learn in an introductory course. Learning the standard model, however, only provides you with the rudiments of cost analysis, in the same way that learning the rules of mechanics only provides you with the basics of mechanical engineering. In addition to a knowledge of the laws of mechanics, building a machine requires years of experience. Similarly for economics and cost analysis. Introductory economics provides you with a superb framework for starting to think about real-world cost measurement, but it can't make you an expert cost analyst.

CONCLUSION AND A LOOK AHEAD

We've come to the end of our discussion of production, cost, and supply. The two chapters we spent on them weren't easy; there's tons of material here, and, quite frankly, it will likely require at least two or three reads and careful attention to your professor's lecture before your mind can absorb it. So if you're planning to sleep through a lecture, the ones on these chapters aren't the ones for that.

These chapters, in combination with our discussion of individual choice, will provide the framework for most of the later chapters, which really do get into interesting real-world issues. But you've got to know the basics to truly understand those issues. So, now that you've come to the end of these two chapters, unless you really feel comfortable with the analysis, it's probably time to review them from the beginning. (Sorry, but remember, there ain't no such thing as a free lunch.)

Chapter Summary

- An economically efficient production process must be technically efficient, but a technically efficient process need not be economically efficient.

- The long-run average total cost curve is U-shaped. Economies of scale initially cause average total cost to decrease; diseconomies eventually cause average total cost to increase.

- Production is a social, as well as a technical, phenomenon; that's why concepts like team spirit are important—and that's why diseconomies of scale occur.

- The marginal cost and short-run average cost curves slope upward because of diminishing marginal productivity. The long-run average cost curve slopes upward because of diseconomies of scale.

- There is an envelope relationship between short-run average cost curves and long-run average cost curves. The short-run average cost curves are always above the long-run average cost curve.

- An entrepreneur is an individual who sees an opportunity to sell an item at a price higher than the average cost of producing it.

- Once we start applying cost analysis to the real world, we must include a variety of other dimensions of costs that the standard model does not cover.

- Costs in the real world are affected by economies of scope, learning by doing and technological change, the many dimensions to output and unmeasured costs such as opportunity costs.

Key Terms

constant returns to
scale *(221)*

diseconomies of
scale *(221)*

economically
efficient *(218)*

economies of scale *(219)*

economies of scope *(225)*

entrepreneur *(225)*

indivisible setup
cost *(219)*

learning by doing *(226)*

minimum efficient level of
production *(221)*

monitoring costs *(221)*

team spirit *(221)*

technical efficiency *(218)*

technological change
(227)

Questions for Thought and Review

1. Distinguish technical efficiency from economic efficiency.

2. A student has just written on an exam that in the long run fixed cost will make the average total cost curve slope downward. Why will the professor mark it incorrect?

3. What inputs do you use in studying this book? What would the long-run average total cost and marginal cost curves for studying look like? Why?

4. Why could diseconomies of scale never occur if production relationships were only technical relationships?

5. When economist Jacob Viner first developed the envelope relationship, he told his draftsman to make sure that all the marginal cost curves went through both (1) the minimum point of the short-run average cost curve and (2) the point where the short-run average total cost curve was tangent to the long-run average total cost curve. The draftsman told him it couldn't be done. Viner told him to do it anyhow. Why was the draftsman right?

6. What is the role of the entrepreneur in translating cost of production into supply?

7. Your average total cost is $40; the price you receive for the good is $12. Should you keep on producing the good? Why?

8. A student has just written on an exam that technological change will mean that the cost curve is downward sloping. Why did the teacher mark it wrong?

9. If you were describing the marginal cost of an additional car driving on a road, what costs would you look at? What is the likely shape of the marginal cost curve?

10. The cost of setting up a steel mill is enormous. For example, a Gary, Indiana, hot-strip mill would cost an estimated $1.5 billion to build. Using this information and the cost concepts from the chapter, explain the following quotation: "To make operations even marginally profitable, big steel makers must run full-out. It's like a car that is more efficient at 55 miles an hour than in stop-and-go traffic at 25."

Problems and Exercises

1. Visit a nearby company and ask it what would happen to its per-unit costs if sales increased by 10 percent. Try to figure out how its answer relates to the concepts in this and the preceding chapter, remembering especially the discussion about using cost analysis in the real world.

2. Find out the total budget of your college or university. (It often takes a bit of sleuthing, but almost all college and university budgets are in the public record.) Find out the number of students. What is the total cost per student? What is the relevant marginal cost of an additional student?

    Now say you're on a planning committee charged with eliminating an expected 2 percent budget deficit next year. Using the budget figures, make some suggestions. Have a college administrator (preferably the treasurer or comptroller) visit your class and react to those suggestions. Explain why presidents of universities and colleges don't last long.

3. A pair of shoes that wholesale for $28.79 has approximately the following costs:

Manufacturing labor	$2.25
Materials	4.95
Factory overhead, operating expenses, and profit	8.50
Sales costs	4.50
Advertising	2.93
Research and development	2.00
Interest	.33
Net income	3.33
Total	$28.79

    a. Which of these costs would likely be a variable cost?
    b. Which would likely be a fixed cost?
    c. If output were to rise, what would likely happen to average total costs? Why?

4. Draw a long-run cost curve.
    a. Why does it slope downward initially?
    b. Why does it eventually slope upward?
    c. How would your answer to a and b differ if you had drawn a short-run cost curve?
    d. How large is the fixed cost component of the long-run cost curve?
    e. If there were constant returns to scale everywhere, what would the long-run cost curve look like?

5. A major issue of contention at many colleges concerns the cost of meals that is rebated when a student does not sign up for the meal plan. The administration usually says that it should rebate only the marginal cost of the food alone, which it calculates at, say, $1.25 per meal. Students say that the marginal cost should include more costs, such as the saved space from fewer students using the facilities and the reduced labor expenses on food preparation. This can raise the marginal cost to $6.00.
    a. Who is correct, the administration or the students?
    b. How might your answer differ if this argument were being conducted in the planning stage, before the dining hall is built?
    c. If you accept the $1.25 figure of a person not eating, how could you justify using a higher figure of about $6.00 for the cost of feeding a guest at the dining hall, as many schools do?

Web Questions

1. Go to the Internet site About.com (www.about.com) and answer the following questions:
    a. What services does About.com provide? What does it charge for those services?
    b. What are the fixed costs associated with running About.com? What is the marginal cost of providing About.com to one additional person?
    c. List the advertising you saw while visiting About.com.
    d. Under what circumstances will an entrepreneur supply a good to the market? What incentives do the owners of About.com have to supply this product on the Internet? (Hint: Look at your answer to c).

2. Go to www.about.com and search for an article entitled "Telecom Mergers and Regulation." Read the article to answer the following questions:
   a. Why are Bell Atlantic and GTE merging?
   b. Along what portion of the long-run average total cost curve are Bell Atlantic and GTE operating separately?

   Along what portion do they expect to be operating as a merged company?
   c. Why does the telecom industry experience economies of scale?

Answers to Margin Questions

1. True. Since an economically efficient method of production is that method that produces a given level of output at the lowest possible cost, it must also use as few inputs as possible. It is also technically efficient. *(218)*

2. China uses more labor-intensive techniques than does the United States because the price of labor is much lower in China relative to the United States. Both countries are producing economically efficiently. *(218)*

3. Larger production runs are generally cheaper per unit than smaller production runs because of indivisible setup costs, which do not vary with the size of the run. *(220)*

4. Because the same technical process could be used over and over again at the same cost, the long-run average cost curve would never become upward sloping. *(221)*

5. The short-run average total cost curve initially slopes downward because of large average fixed costs, then begins sloping upward because of diminishing marginal productivity, giving it a U shape. *(222)*

6. The long-run average total cost curve is generally considered to be U-shaped because initially there are economies of scale and, for large amounts of production, there are diseconomies of scale. *(222)*

7. Economic activity does not just happen. Some dynamic, driven individual must instigate production. That dynamic individual is called an entrepreneur. *(225)*

8. Economies of scale are economies that occur because of increases in the amount of a good one is producing. Economies of scope occur when producing different types of goods lowers the cost of each of those goods. *(225)*

9. Learning by doing causes a shift in the cost curve because it is a change in the technical characteristics of production. It does not cause the cost curve to be downward sloping—it causes it to shift downward. *(226)*

10. An economist would say that he doesn't know what total cost is without knowing what Jim could have earned if he had undertaken another activity besides running his business. Just because he paid himself $1,000 doesn't mean that $1,000 is his opportunity cost. *(229)*

Isocost/Isoquant Analysis

In the long run, a firm can vary more than one factor of production. One of the decisions firms face in this long run is which combination of factors of production to use. Economic efficiency involves choosing those factors so that the cost of production is at a minimum.

In analyzing this choice of which combination of factors to use, economists have developed a graphical technique called *isocost/isoquant analysis*. In this technique the analyst creates a graph placing one factor of production, say labor, on one axis and another factor, say machines, on the other axis, as I have done in Figure A10-1. Any point on that graph represents a combination of machines and labor that can produce a certain amount of output, say

pairs of earrings. For example, point A represents 3 machines and 4 units of labor being used to produce 8 pairs of earrings. Any point in the blue shaded area represents more of one or both factors and any point in the red shaded area represents less of one or both factors.

THE ISOQUANT CURVE

The firm's problem is to figure out how to produce its output—let's say it has chosen an output of 60 pairs of earrings—at as low a cost as possible. That means somehow we must show graphically the combinations of machines

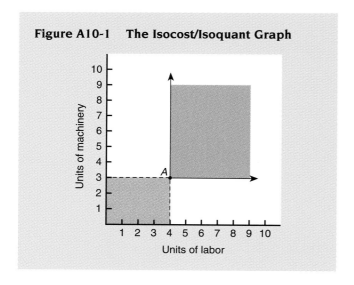

Figure A10-1   The Isocost/Isoquant Graph

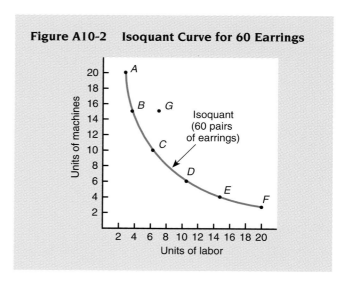

Figure A10-2   Isoquant Curve for 60 Earrings

and labor that can produce 60 pairs of earrings as cheaply as possible. We do so with what is called an isoquant curve. An **isoquant curve** is *a curve that represents combinations of factors of production that result in equal amounts of output.* (*Isoquant* is a big name for an "equal quantity.") At all points on an isoquant curve the firm can produce the same amount of output. So, given a level of output, a firm can find out what combinations of the factors of production will produce that output. Suppose a firm can produce 60 pairs of earrings with the following combination of labor and machines:

	Labor	Machines	Pairs of Earrings
A	3	20	60
B	4	15	60
C	6	10	60
D	10	6	60
E	15	4	60
F	20	3	60

This table shows the technical limits of production. It shows that the firm can use, for example, 3 units of labor and 20 machines or 20 units of labor and 3 machines to produce 60 pairs of earrings. The isoquant curve is a graphical representation of the table. I show the isoquant curve for producing 60 pairs in Figure A10-2. Points A to F represent rows A to F in the table.

To be sure you understand it, let's consider some points on the curve. Let's start at point A. At point A the firm is producing 60 pairs of earrings using 20 machines and 3 workers. If the firm wants to reduce the number of machines by 5, it must increase the number of units of labor by 1 to keep output constant. Doing so moves the firm to point B. At point B the firm is also producing 60 pairs of earrings, but is doing it with 15 machines and 4 workers. Alternatively, if the firm were at point D, and it wants to reduce the number of machines from 6 to 4, it must increase the number of units of labor from 10 to 15 to keep output constant at 60. At any point on this isoquant curve the firm is being technically efficient—it is using as few resources as possible to produce 60 pairs of earrings. Thus, it would never want to produce 60 at a point like G, because that point uses more inputs. It is a technically inefficient method of production.

The numbers in the production table and the shape of the curve were not chosen randomly. They were chosen to be consistent with the law of diminishing marginal productivity which means the curve is bowed inward. That is because as the firm increases the use of one factor more and more, it must use fewer and fewer units of the other factor to keep output constant. This reflects the technical considerations embodied in the law of diminishing marginal productivity. Thus, the chosen numbers tell us that if a firm wants to keep output constant, as it adds more and more of one factor (and less of the other factor), it has to use relatively more of that factor. For example, initially it might add 1 machine to replace 1 worker, holding output constant. If it continues it will have to use 1.5 machines, then 2 machines, and so on.

The rate at which one factor must be added to compensate for the loss of another factor, to keep output constant, is called

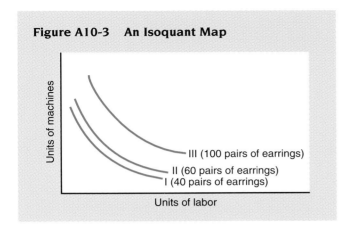

Figure A10-3   An Isoquant Map

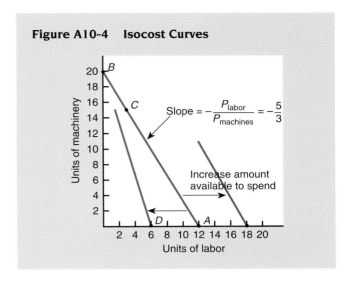

Figure A10-4   Isocost Curves

the **marginal rate of substitution.** To say that there is diminishing marginal productivity is to say that there is a diminishing marginal rate of substitution. It is because the table assumes a diminishing marginal rate of substitution that the isoquant curve is bowed inward.

Graphically, the slope of the isoquant curve is the marginal rate of substitution. To be exact, the absolute value of the slope at a point on the isoquant curve equals the ratio of the marginal productivity of labor to the marginal productivity of machines:

$$|\text{Slope}| = MP_{\text{labor}}/MP_{\text{machines}}$$
$$= \text{Marginal rate of substitution}$$

With this equation, you can really see why the isoquant is downward sloping. As the firm moves from point *A* to point *F* it is using more labor and fewer machines. Because of the law of diminishing marginal productivity, as the firm moves from *A* to *F*, the marginal productivity of labor decreases and the marginal productivity of machines increases. The slope of the isoquant falls since the marginal rate of substitution is decreasing.

Let's consider a specific example. Say in Figure A10-2 the firm is producing at point *B*. If it cuts its input by 5 machines but also wants to keep output constant, it must increase labor by 2 (move from point *B* to point *C*). So the marginal rate of substitution of labor for machines between points *B* and *C* must be 5/2 or 2.5.

The firm can complete this exercise for many different levels of output. Doing so will result in an **isoquant map,** *a set of isoquant curves that show technically efficient combinations of inputs that can produce different levels of output.* Such a map for output levels of 40, 60, and 100 is shown in Figure A10-3.

Each curve represents a different level of output. Isoquant I is the lower level of output, 40, and the isoquant

III is the highest level of output. When a firm chooses an output level it is choosing one of those isoquants. The chosen isoquant represents the technically efficient combinations of resources that can produce the desired output.

THE ISOCOST LINE

So far I have only talked about technical efficiency. To move to economic efficiency, we have to bring in the costs of production. We do so with the **isocost line**—*a line that represents alternative combinations of factors of production that have the same costs.* (Isocost is a fancy name for "equal cost.") Each point on the isocost line represents a combination of factors of production which, in total, cost the firm an equal amount.

To draw the isocost line you must know the cost per unit of each input as well as the amount the firm has chosen to spend on production. Say labor costs $5 a unit and machinery costs $3 a unit and that the firm has chosen to spend $60. What is the greatest number of earrings it can produce with that $60? To answer that question, we need to create a curve representing the various amounts of inputs a firm can get with that $60. We do so in the following manner. Say the firm decides to spend the entire $60 on labor. Since labor costs $5 a unit, if the firm spends all of the $60 on labor it can buy 12 units of labor. This alternative is represented by point *A* in Figure A10-4.

Alternatively, since machines cost $3 a unit, if the firm chooses to spend all of the $60 on machines it can buy 20 machines (point *B* in Figure A10-4). This gives us two points on the isocost curve. Of course, the assumption of diminishing marginal rates of substitutions makes it highly unlikely that firm would want to produce at either of these points. Instead, it would likely use some combination of inputs. But these extreme points are useful nonetheless, because by connecting them (the line that goes from *A* to *B* in Figure A10-4), we can see the various combinations of inputs that also cost $60.

To see that this is indeed the case, say the firm starts with 20 machines and no labor. If the firm wants to use some combination of labor and machinery, it can give up some machines and use the money it saves by using fewer machines to purchase units of labor. Let's say it gives up 5 machines, leaving it with 15. That means it has $15 to spend on labor, for which it can buy 3 units of labor. That means 15 machines and 3 units of labor is another combination of labor and machines that cost the firm $60. This means that point *C* is also a point on the isocost line. You can continue with this exercise to prove to yourself that the line connecting points *A* and *B* does represent various combinations of labor and machinery the firm can buy with $60. Thus, the line connecting *A* and *B* is the $60 isocost line.

To see that you understand the isocost line, it is useful to go through a couple of examples that would make it shift. For example, what would happen to the isocost line if the firm chooses to increase its spending on production to $90? To see the effect we go through the same exercise as before: If it spent it all on labor, it could buy 18 units of labor. If it spent it all on machines, it could buy 30 units of machinery. Connecting these points will give us a curve to the right of and parallel to the original curve. It has the same slope because the relative prices of the factors of production, which determines the slope, have not changed.

Now ask yourself, What happens to the isocost line if the price of labor rises to $10 a unit? If you said the isocost curve becomes steeper, shifting along the labor axis to point *D* while remaining anchored along the machinery axis until the slope is −10/3, you've got it. In general, the absolute value of the slope of the isocost curve is the ratio of the price of the factor of production on the *x*-axis to the price of the factor of production on the *y*-axis. That means that as the price of a factor rises, the end point of the isocost curve shifts in on the axis on which that factor is measured.

CHOOSING THE ECONOMICALLY EFFICIENT POINT OF PRODUCTION

Now let's move on to a consideration of the economically efficient combination of resources to produce 60 pairs of

Figure A10-5   Combining Isoquant and Isocost Curves

earrings with $60. To do that we must put the isoquant cost curve from Figure A10-2 and the isocost curve from Figure A10-4 together. We do so in Figure A10-5.

The problem for the firm is to produce as many pairs of earrings as possible with the $60 it has to spend. Or, put another way, given a level of production it has chosen, it wants to produce at the least-cost combination of the factors of production.

Let's now find the least-cost combination of inputs to produce 60 pairs of earrings. Let's say that, initially, the firm chooses point *A* on its isoquant curve—that's at 15 machines and 4 workers. That produces 60 pairs of earrings, but has a cost of $45 + $20 = $65. The firm can't produce 60 pairs of earrings unless it is willing to spend more than $60. If it fires a worker to bring its cost in line, moving it to point *B*, it moves down to a lower isoquant— it is producing only 40 pairs.

If the firm has a less-than-competent manager, that manager will conclude that you can't produce 60 for $60. But say the firm has an efficient manager—one who has taken introductory economics. As opposed to *reducing* the number of workers as the other manager did, she *increases* the number of workers to 6 and reduces the number of machines to 10. Doing so still produces 60 pairs of earrings, since *C* is a point on the isoquant curve, but the strategy reduces the cost from $65 at point *A* to $60 (10 machines at $3 = $30, and 6 workers at $5 = $30). So she is producing 60 pairs of earrings at a cost of $60. She is operating at the economic efficient point—point *C*.

Let's talk about the characteristics of Point *C*. Point *C* is the point where the isoquant curve is tangent to the isocost curve—the point at which the slope of the isoquant curve $(-MP_L/MP_M)$ equals the slope of the isocost curve $(-P_L/P_M)$. That is, $-MP_L/MP_M = -P_L/P_M$. This can be rewritten as:

$$MP_L/P_L = MP_M/P_M$$

What this equation says is that when the additional output per dollar spent on labor equals the additional output per dollar spent on machines, the firm is operating efficiently. It makes sense. If the additional output per dollar spent on labor exceeded the additional output per dollar spent on machines, the firm would do better by increasing its use of labor and decreasing its use of machines.

Point C represents the combination of labor and machines that will result in the highest output given the isocost curve facing the firm. To put it in technical terms, the firm is operating at an economically efficient point where marginal rate of substitution equals the ratio of the factor prices. Any point other than C on the isocost curve will cost $60 but produce fewer than 60 pairs of earrings. Any other point than C on the isoquant curve will produce 60 pairs of earrings but cost more than $60. Only C is the economically efficient point given the factor costs.

To see that you understand the analysis, say that the price of labor falls to $3 and you still want to produce 60. What will happen to the amount of labor and machines you hire? Alternatively, say that the price of machines rises to $5 and you want to spend only $60. What will happen to the amount of labor and machines you hire?

If your answers are (1) you hire more workers and fewer machines, and (2) you reduce production using fewer machines and, maybe, less labor, you've got the analyses down. If you didn't give those answers, I suggest rereading this appendix, if it is to be on the exam, and working through the questions for thought and review.

Key Terms

isocost line   *(235)*

isoquant curve   *(234)*

isoquant map   *(235)*

marginal rate of substitution   *(235)*

Questions for Thought and Review

1. What happens to the marginal rate of substitution as a firm increases the use of one input, keeping output constant? What accounts for this?

2. Draw an isocost curve for a firm that has $100 to spend on producing jeans. Input includes labor and materials. Labor costs $8 and materials cost $4 a unit. How does each of the following affect the isocost curve? Show your answer graphically.
   a. Production budget doubles.
   b. Cost of materials rises to $10 a unit.
   c. Costs of labor and materials each rise by 25 percent.

3. Show, using isocost/isoquant analysis, how firms in the United States use relatively less labor and relatively more land than Japan for the production of similar goods, yet both are behaving economically efficiently.

4. Demonstrate the difference between economic efficiency and technical efficiency, using the isocost/isoquant analysis.

5. Draw a hypothetical isocost curve and an isoquant curve tangent to the isocost curve. Label the combination of inputs that represents an efficient use of resources.
   a. How does a technological innovation affect your analysis?
   b. How does the increase in the price of the input on the x-axis affect your analysis?

6. Show graphically the analysis of the example in Figure A10-5 if the price of labor falls to $3. Demonstrate that the firm can increase production given the same budget.

7. Show graphically the analysis of the example in Figure A10-5 if the price of machines rises to $5. Demonstrate that the firm must reduce production if it keeps the same budget.

Perfect Competition

11

After reading this chapter, you should be able to:

- List the six conditions for a perfectly competitive market.

- Explain why producing an output at which marginal cost equals price maximizes total profit for a perfect competitor.

- Demonstrate why the marginal cost curve is the supply curve for a perfectly competitive firm.

- Determine the output and profit of a perfect competitor graphically and numerically.

- Construct a market supply curve by adding together individual firms' marginal cost curves.

- Explain why perfectly competitive firms make zero economic profit in the long run.

- Explain the adjustment process from short-run equilibrium to long-run equilibrium.

> *There's no resting place for an enterprise*
> *in a competitive economy.*
>
> Alfred P. Sloan

The concept *competition* is used in two ways in economics. One way is as a process. *Competition as a process* is a rivalry among firms and is prevalent throughout our economy. It involves one firm trying to figure out how to take away market share from another firm. An example is my publishing firm giving me a contract to write a great book like this in order for the firm to take market share away from other publishing firms that are also selling economics textbooks. The other use of *competition* is as a *perfectly competitive market structure*. It is this use that is the subject of this chapter. Although perfect competition has highly restrictive assumptions, it provides us with a reference point we can use to think about various market structures and competitive processes. Why is such a reference point important? Think of the following analogy.

In physics when you study the laws of gravity, you initially study what would happen in a vacuum. Perfect vacuums don't exist, but talking about what would happen if you dropped an object in a perfect vacuum makes the analysis easier. So too with economics. Our equivalent of a perfect vacuum is perfect competition. In perfect competition the invisible hand of the market operates unimpeded. In this chapter we'll consider how perfectly competitive markets work and see how to apply the cost analysis developed in Chapters 9 and 10.

> The process of competition involves a rivalry among firms and is prevalent throughout our economy. The state of competition is the end result of the competitive process under certain conditions.

A PERFECTLY COMPETITIVE MARKET

A **perfectly competitive** market is *a market in which economic forces operate unimpeded*. For a market to be called *perfectly competitive*, it must meet some stringent conditions:

> A perfectly competitive market is one in which economic forces operate unimpeded.

1. Both buyers and sellers are price takers.
2. The number of firms is large.
3. There are no barriers to entry.
4. Firms' products are identical.
5. There is complete information.
6. Selling firms are profit-maximizing entrepreneurial firms.

These conditions are needed to ensure that economic forces operate instantaneously and are unimpeded by political and social forces. For example, if there weren't a large number of firms, the few firms in the industry would have an incentive to get together and limit output so they could get a higher price. They would stop the invisible hand from working. Similarly for the other conditions, although the reasoning why they're necessary can get rather complicated.

The Necessary Conditions for Perfect Competition

To give you a sense of these conditions, let's consider each a bit more carefully.

> Six conditions for a market to be perfectly competitive are:
> 1. Both buyers and sellers are price takers.
> 2. Large number of firms.
> 3. No barriers to entry.
> 4. Identical product.
> 5. Complete information.
> 6. Profit-maximizing entrepreneurial firms.

1. *Both buyers and sellers are price takers.* A **price taker** is *a firm or individual who takes the price determined by market supply and demand as given*. When you buy, say, toothpaste, you go to the store and find that the price of toothpaste is, say, $1.38 for the medium-size tube; you're a price taker. The firm, however, is a price maker since it set the price at $1.38. So even though the toothpaste industry is highly competitive, it's not a perfectly competitive market. In a perfectly competitive market, market supply and demand determine the price; both firms and consumers take the market price as given.

2. *The number of firms is large.* This is almost self-explanatory. *Large* means sufficiently large so that any one firm's output compared to the market output is imperceptible, and what one firm does has no influence on what other firms do.

3. *There are no barriers to entry.* **Barriers to entry** are *social, political, or economic impediments that prevent other firms from entering a market*. They might be legal barriers such as exist when firms acquire a patent to produce a certain product.

Q-1 Why is the assumption
of no barriers to entry necessary
for the existence of perfect
competition?

Barriers might be technological, such as when the minimum efficient scale of production allows only one firm to produce at the lowest average total cost. Or barriers might be created by social forces, such as when bankers will lend only to individuals with specific racial characteristics. Perfect competition can have no barriers to entry.

4. *Firms' products are identical.* This requirement means that each firm's output is indistinguishable from any other firm's output. Corn bought by the bushel is relatively homogeneous. One kernel is indistinguishable from any other kernel. In contrast, you can buy 30 different brands of many goods—soft drinks, for instance: Pepsi, Coke, 7UP, and so on. They are all slightly different from one another and thus not identical.

5. *There is complete information.* In a perfectly competitive market, firms and consumers know all there is to know about the market—prices, products, and available technology, to name a few aspects. If any firm experiences a technological breakthrough, all firms know about it and are able to use the same technology instantaneously. No firm or consumer has a competitive edge over another.

6. *Selling firms are profit-maximizing entrepreneurial firms.* Firms can have many goals and be organized in a variety of ways. For perfect competition to exist, firms must seek maximum profit and only profit, and the people who make the decisions must receive only profits and no other form of income from the firms.

The Definition of Supply and Perfect Competition

These are enormously strong conditions and are seldom met simultaneously. But they are necessary for a perfectly competitive market to exist. Combined, they create an environment in which each firm, following its own self-interest, will offer goods to the market in a predictable way. If these conditions hold, we can talk formally about the supply of a produced good and how it relates to costs. This follows from the definition of supply we gave in Chapter 4:

> Supply is a schedule of quantities of goods that will be offered to the market at various prices.

This definition requires the supplier to be a price taker (our first condition). In almost all other market structures (frameworks within which firms interact economically), firms are not price takers; they are price makers. They don't ask, "How much should I supply, given the market price?" Instead they ask, "Given a demand curve, how much should I produce and what price should I charge?" In other market structures, the supplier sets the quantity and price, based on costs, at whatever level is best for it.[1]

The second condition—that the number of firms is large—is necessary so that firms have no ability to *collude* (to operate in concert so that they can get more for themselves). Conditions 3 through 5 are closely related to the first two; they make it impossible for any firm to forget about the hundreds of other firms out there just waiting to replace their supply. Condition 6 tells us a firm's goals. If we didn't know the goals, we wouldn't know how firms would react when faced with the given price.

---

[1]A firm's ability to set price doesn't mean that it can choose just any price it pleases. Other market structures can be highly competitive, so the range of prices a firm can charge and still stay in business is often limited. Such highly competitive firms are not perfectly competitive—they still set price rather than supply a certain quantity and accept whatever price they get.

APPLYING THE TOOLS

The Internet and the Perfectly Competitive Model

Recent technological developments are making the perfectly competitive model more directly relevant to our economy. Specifically, the Internet has eliminated the spatial dimension of competition (except for shipping), allowing individuals to compete globally rather than locally. When you see a bid on the Internet, you don't care where the supplier is (as long as you do not have to pay shipping fees). Because it allows access to so many buyers and sellers, the Internet reduces the number of seller-set posted price markets (such as found in retail stores), and replaces them with auction markets.

The Internet has had its biggest impact in firms' buying practices. When firms want to buy standardized products in the 2000s, they will often post their technical requirements for desired components on the net and allow suppliers from all over the world to bid to fill their orders. Firms have found that buying in this fashion over the In-ternet has on average lowered the prices they pay by over 10%.

Similar changes are occurring in consumer markets. With sites like Priceline.com, individuals can set the price they are willing to pay for goods and services (such as hotel rooms and airline tickets) and see if anyone wants to supply them. (Recently, I successfully bid $120 for a $460 retail price hotel room in New York City.) With sites such as eBay you can buy and sell almost anything. The Internet is even developing its own currency, beenz (www.beenz.com).

In short, with the Internet, entry and exit are much easier than in traditional "brick and mortar" business, and that makes the market more like a perfectly competitive market. As Internet search engines become better designed for commerce, and as more people become Internet savvy, the economy will more and more closely resemble the perfectly competitive model.

What's nice about these conditions is that they allow us to formally relate supply to the cost concept we developed in Chapters 9 and 10: marginal cost. If the conditions hold, a firm's supply curve will be that portion of the firm's short-run marginal cost curve above the average variable cost curve, as we'll see shortly.

If the conditions for perfect competition aren't met, then we can't use our formal concept of supply and how it relates to cost; we can still talk *informally* about the supply of produced goods and cost conditions. We generally talk informally about perfect competition, keeping in the back of our minds which conditions aren't met and modifying the analysis accordingly. Even if the conditions for perfect competition don't fully exist, supply forces are still strong and many of the insights of the competitive model can be applied to firm behavior in other market structures.

11.1

Even if we can't technically specify a supply curve, supply forces are still strong and many of the insights of the competitive model carry over.

Demand Curves for the Firm and the Industry

Now that we've considered the competitive supply curve for the firm, let's turn our attention to the competitive demand curve for the firm. Here we must recognize that the demand curve for the industry is downward sloping as in Figure 11-1(a), but the perceived demand curve for the firm is horizontal (perfectly elastic), as in Figure 11-1(b).

Why the difference? It's a difference in perception. Each firm in a competitive industry is so small that it perceives that its actions will not affect the price it can get for its product. Price is the same no matter how much it produces. Think of an individual firm's actions as removing one piece of sand from a beach. Does that lower the level of the beach? For all practical, and even most impractical, purposes, we can assume it doesn't. Similarly for a perfectly competitive firm. That is why we consider the demand curve facing the firm to be horizontal.

The price the firm can get is determined by the market supply and demand curves shown in Figure 11-1(a). Market price is $7, and the firm represented in Figure 11-1(b) will get $7 for each unit of its product whether it produces 10 units (point A), 20 units

Q-2 How can the demand curve for the market be downward sloping but the demand curve for a competitive firm be perfectly elastic?

Figure 11-1 (a and b)   Market Demand Curve versus Individual Firm Demand Curve

Even though the demand curve for the market is downward sloping, the perceived demand curve of an individual firm is perfectly elastic because each firm is so small relative to the market.

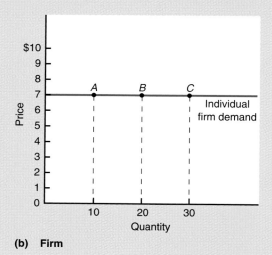

(a) **Market**   (b) **Firm**

(point B), or 30 units (point C). Its demand curve is perfectly elastic even though the demand curve for the market is downward sloping.

> A perfectly competitive firm's demand schedule is perfectly elastic even though the demand curve for the market is downward sloping.

This difference in perception is extremely important. It means that firms will increase their output in response to an increase in market demand even though that increase in output will cause price to fall and can make all firms collectively worse off. But since, by the assumptions of perfect competition, they don't act collectively, each firm follows its self-interest. Let's now consider that self-interest in more detail.

THE PROFIT-MAXIMIZING LEVEL OF OUTPUT

The goal of a firm is to maximize profits—to get as much for itself as possible. So when it decides what quantity to produce, it will continually ask the question "What will changes in quantity do to profit?" Since profit is the difference between total revenue and total cost, what happens to profit in response to a change in output is determined by **marginal revenue (MR),** *the change in total revenue associated with a change in quantity,* and **marginal cost (MC),** *the change in total cost associated with a change in quantity.* That's why marginal revenue and marginal cost are key concepts in determining the profit-maximizing or loss-minimizing level of output of any firm.

> To determine the profit-maximizing output, all you need to know is MC and MR.

To emphasize the importance of MR and MC, those are the only cost and revenue figures shown in Figure 11-2. Notice that we don't illustrate profit at all. We'll calculate profit later. All we want to determine now is the profit-maximizing level of output. To do this you need only know MC and MR. Specifically, a firm maximizes profit when MC = MR. To see why, let's first look at MC and MR more closely.

Marginal Revenue

Let's first consider marginal revenue. Since a perfect competitor accepts the market price as given, marginal revenue is simply the market price. For example, if the firm

Figure 11-2 (a and b)   Marginal Cost, Marginal Revenue, and Price

The profit-maximizing output for a firm occurs where marginal cost equals marginal revenue. Since for a competitive firm $P = MR$, its profit-maximizing output is where $MC = P$. At any other output it is forgoing profit.

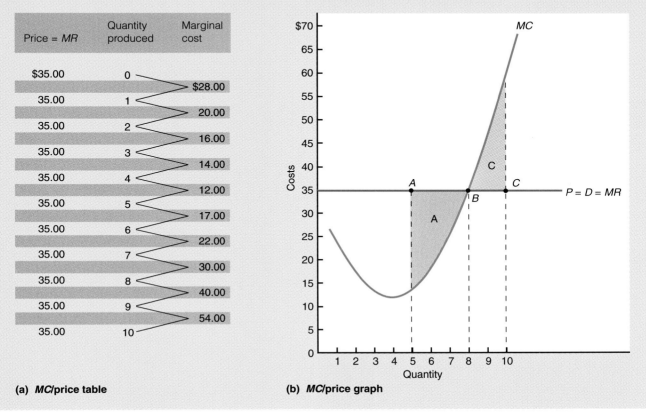

Price = MR	Quantity produced	Marginal cost
$35.00	0	
		$28.00
35.00	1	
		20.00
35.00	2	
		16.00
35.00	3	
		14.00
35.00	4	
		12.00
35.00	5	
		17.00
35.00	6	
		22.00
35.00	7	
		30.00
35.00	8	
		40.00
35.00	9	
		54.00
35.00	10	

(a) *MC*/price table

(b) *MC*/price graph

increases output from 2 to 3, its revenue rises by $35 (from $70 to $105). So its marginal revenue is $35, the price of the good. Since at a price of $35 it can sell as much as it wants, for a competitive firm, $MR = P$.

For a competitive firm, $MR = P$.

Marginal revenue is given in column 1 of Figure 11-2(a). As you can see, MR equals $35 for all levels of output. But that's what we saw in Figure 11-1, which showed that the demand curve for a perfect competitor is perfectly elastic at the market price. For a perfect competitor, the marginal revenue curve and demand curve it faces are the same.

Marginal Cost

Now let's move on to marginal cost. I'll be brief since I discussed marginal cost in detail in Chapter 9. Marginal cost is that change in total cost that accompanies a change in output. Figure 11-2(a) shows marginal cost in column 3. Notice that initially in this example, marginal cost is falling, but by the fifth unit of output, it's increasing. This is consistent with our discussion in earlier chapters.

Notice also that the marginal cost figures are given for movements from one quantity to another. That's because marginal concepts tell us what happens when there's a change in something, so marginal concepts are best defined between numbers. The numbers in the shaded rows are the marginal costs. So the marginal cost of increasing output from 1 to 2 is $20, and the marginal cost of increasing output from 2 to 3 is $16. The marginal cost right at 2 (which the marginal cost graph shows) would be between $20 and $16 at approximately $18.

Profit Maximization: MC = MR

As I noted above, to maximize profit, a firm should produce where marginal cost equals marginal revenue. Looking at Figure 11-2(b), we see that a firm following that rule should produce at an output of 8 where MC = MR = $35. Now let me try to convince you that 8 is indeed the profit-maximizing output. To do so, let's consider three different possible quantities the firm might look at.

Let's say that initially the firm decides to produce 5, placing it at point A in Figure 11-2(b). At output A, the firm gets $35 for each widget but its marginal cost of increasing output is $17. We don't yet know the firm's total profit, but we do know how changing output will affect profit. For example, say the firm increases production from 5 to 6. Its revenue will rise by $35. (In other words, its marginal revenue is $35.) Its marginal cost of increasing output is $17. Since profit increases by $18 (the difference between MR, $35, and MC, $17), it makes sense (meaning the firm can increase its profit) to increase output from 5 to 6 units. It makes sense to increase output as long as the marginal cost is below the marginal revenue. The blue shaded area (A) represents the entire increase in profit the firm can get by increasing output.

Now let's say that the firm decides to produce 10 widgets, placing it at point C. Here the firm gets $35 for each widget. The marginal cost of producing that 10th unit is $54. So, MC > MR. If the firm decreases production by one unit, its cost decreases by $54 and its revenue decreases by $35. Profit increases by $19 ($54 − $35 = $19), so at point C, it makes sense to decrease output. This reasoning holds true as long as the marginal cost is above the marginal revenue. The red shaded area (C) represents the increase in profits the firm can get by decreasing output.

At point B (output = 8) the firm gets $35 for each widget, and its marginal cost is $35, as you can see in Figure 11-2(b). The marginal cost of increasing output by one unit is $40 and the marginal revenue of selling one more unit is $35, so its profit falls by $5. If the firm decreases output by one unit, its MC is $30 and its MR is $35, so its profit falls by $5. Either increasing or decreasing production will decrease profit, so at point B, an output of 8, the firm is maximizing profit.

Since MR is just market price, we can state the **profit-maximizing condition** of a competitive firm as MC = MR = P.

You should commit this profit-maximizing condition to memory. You should also be sure that you understand the intuition behind it. If marginal revenue isn't equal to marginal cost, a firm obviously can increase profit by changing output. If that isn't obvious, the marginal benefit of an additional hour of thinking about this condition will exceed the marginal cost (whatever it is), meaning that you should . . . right, you guessed it . . . study some more.

The Marginal Cost Curve Is the Supply Curve

Now let's consider again the definition of the supply curve as a schedule of quantities of goods that will be offered to the market at various prices. Notice that the marginal cost curve fits that definition. It tells how much the firm will supply at a given price. Figure 11-3 shows the various quantities the firm will supply at different market prices. If the price is $35, we showed that the firm would supply 8 (point A). If the price had been $19.50, the firm would have supplied 6 (point B); if the price had been $61, the firm

Q.3 What are the two things you must know to determine the profit-maximizing output?

Profit-maximizing condition for a competitive firm: MR = P = MC.

If marginal revenue does not equal marginal cost, a firm can increase profit by changing output. Therefore, profit is maximized when MC = MR = P.

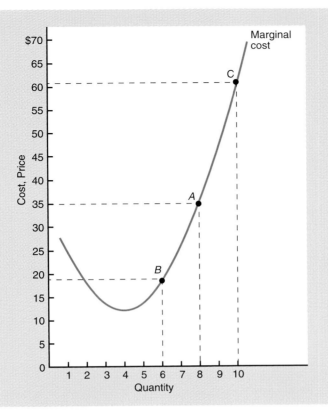

Figure 11-3   The Marginal Cost Curve Is a Firm's Supply Curve

A perfectly competitive firm maximizes profit by producing the quantity at which marginal revenue equals marginal cost equals price. A perfectly competitive firm produces the quantity at which market price intersects the marginal cost curve. Since the marginal cost curve tells the firm how much to produce, the marginal cost curve is the perfectly competitive firm's supply curve. This exhibit shows three points on a firm's supply curve; as you can see the quantity the firm chooses to supply depends on the price. For example, if market price is $19.50 the firm produces 6 units.

would have supplied 10 (point C). Because the marginal cost curve tells us how much of a produced good a firm will supply at a given price, *the marginal cost curve is the firm's supply curve*. The MC curve tells the competitive firm how much it should produce at a given price. (As you'll see later, there's an addendum to this statement. Specifically, the marginal cost curve is the firm's supply curve only if price exceeds average variable cost.)

Because the marginal cost curve tells us how much of a produced good a firm will supply at a given price, the marginal cost curve is the firm's supply curve.

Firms Maximize Total Profit

Notice that when you talk about maximizing profit, you're talking about maximizing *total profit*, not profit per unit. Profit per unit would be maximized at a much lower output level than is total profit. Firms don't care about profit per unit; as long as an increase in output will increase total profits, a profit-maximizing firm should increase output. That's difficult to grasp, so let's consider a concrete example.

Q.4 Why do firms maximize total profit rather than profit per unit?

Say two people are selling T-shirts that cost $4 each. One sells 2 T-shirts at a price of $6 each and makes a profit per shirt of $2. His total profit is $4. The second person sells 8 T-shirts at $5 each, making a profit per unit of only $1 but selling 8. Her total profit is $8, twice as much as the fellow who had the $2 profit per unit. In this case, $5 (the price with the lower profit per unit), not $6, yields more total profit.

Profit Maximization Using Total Revenue and Total Cost

An alternative method of determining the profit-maximizing level of output is to look at the total revenue and total cost curves directly. Figure 11-4 shows total cost and total

This marginal revenue = marginal cost equilibrium condition is simple, but it's enormously powerful. As we'll see, it carries over to other market structures. If you replace revenue with benefits, it also forms the basis of economic reasoning. With whom should you go out? What's the marginal benefit? What's the marginal cost? Should you marry Pat? What's the marginal benefit?

APPLYING THE TOOLS

The Broader Importance of the MR = MC Equilibrium Condition

What's the marginal cost? As we discussed in Chapter 1, thinking like an economist requires thinking in these marginal terms and applying this marginal reasoning to a wide variety of activities. Understanding this condition is to economics what understanding gravity is to physics. It gives you a sense of if, how, and why prices and quantities will move.

revenue for the firm we're considering so far. The table in Figure 11-4(a) shows total revenue in column 2, which is just the number of units sold times market price. Total cost is in column 3. Total cost is the cumulative sum of the marginal costs from Figure 11-2(a) plus a fixed cost of $40. Total profit (column 4) is the difference between total revenue and total cost. The firm is interested in maximizing total profit. Looking down column 4 of Figure 11-4(a), you can quickly see that the profit-maximizing level of output is 8, as it was using the $MR = MC$ rule, since total profit is highest at an output of 8.

Figure 11-4 (a and b)   Determination of Profits by Total Cost and Total Revenue Curves

The profit-maximizing output level can also be seen by considering the total cost curve and the total revenue curve. Profit is maximized at the output where total revenue exceeds total cost by the largest amount. This occurs at an output of 8.

Quantity	Total revenue	Total cost	Total profit
0	$ 0	$ 40	$−40
1	35	68	−33
2	70	88	−18
3	105	104	1
4	140	118	22
5	175	130	45
6	210	147	63
7	245	169	76
8	280	199	81
9	315	239	76
10	350	293	57

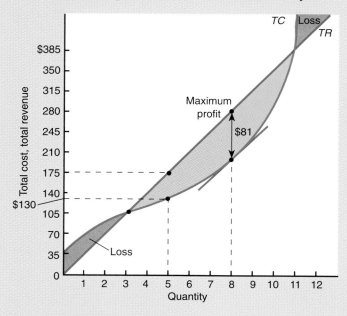

(a) Total revenue and total cost table

(b) Total revenue and total cost curves

In Figure 11-4(b) we plot the firm's total revenue and total cost curves from the table in Figure 11-4(a). The total revenue curve is a straight line; each additional unit sold increases revenue by the same amount, $35. The total cost curve is bowed upward at most quantities, reflecting the increasing marginal cost at different levels of output. The firm's profit is represented by the distance between the total revenue curve and the total cost curve. For example, at output 5, the firm makes $45 in profit.

Total profit is maximized where the vertical distance between total revenue and total cost is greatest. In this example total profit is maximized at output 8, just as in the alternative approach. At that output, marginal revenue (the slope of the total revenue curve) and marginal cost (the slope of the total cost curve) are equal.

TOTAL PROFIT AT THE PROFIT-MAXIMIZING LEVEL OF OUTPUT

In the initial discussion of the firm's choice of output, given price, I carefully presented only marginal cost and price. We talked about maximizing profit, but nowhere did I mention what profit, average total cost, average variable cost, or average fixed cost is. I mentioned only marginal cost and price to emphasize that marginal cost is all that's needed to determine a competitive firm's supply curve (and a competitive firm is the only firm that has a supply curve) and the output that will maximize profit. Now that you know that, let's turn our attention more closely to profit.

Marginal cost is all that is needed to determine a competitive firm's supply curve.

Determining Profit from a Table of Costs and Revenue

The $P = MR = MC$ condition tells us how much output a competitive firm should produce to maximize profit. It does not tell us the profit the firm makes. Profit is determined by total revenue minus total cost. Table 11-1 expands Figure 11-2(a) and presents a table of all the costs relevant to the firm. Going through the columns and reminding yourself of the definition of each is a good review of Chapters 9 and 10. If the definitions don't come to mind immediately, you need a review. If you don't know the definitions of MC, AVC, ATC, FC, and AFC, go back and reread Chapters 9 and 10.

The firm is interested in maximizing profit. Looking at Table 11-1 you can quickly see that the profit-maximizing position is 8, as it was before, since at an output of 8, total profit is highest.

Using the $MC = MR = P$ rule, you can also see that the profit-maximizing level of output is 8. Increasing output from 7 to 8 has a marginal cost of $30, which is less than $35, so it makes sense to do so. Increasing output from 8 to 9 has a marginal cost of $40, which is more than $35, so it does not make sense to do so. The output 8 is the profit-maximizing output. At that profit-maximizing level of output, the profit the firm earns is $81, which is calculated by subtracting total cost of $199 from total revenue of $280. Notice also that average total cost is lowest at an output of about 7, and the average variable cost is lowest at an output of about 6.[2] Thus, the profit-maximizing position (which is 8) is *not* necessarily a position that minimizes either average variable cost or average total cost. It is only the position that maximizes total profit.

---

[2] I say "about 6" and "about 7" because the table gives only whole numbers. The actual minimum point occurs at 5.55 for average variable cost and 6.55 for average total cost. The nearest whole numbers to these are 6 and 7.

Table 11-1   Costs Relevant to a Firm

	1	2	3	4	5	6	7	8	9	10
Price = Marginal Revenue	Quantity Produced	Total Fixed Cost	Average Fixed Cost	Total Variable Cost	Average Variable Cost	Total Cost	Marginal Cost	Average Total Cost	Total Revenue	Total Profit
$35.00	0	$40.00	—	0	—	$ 40.00		—	0	$−40.00
							$28.00			
35.00	1	40.00	$40.00	$ 28.00	$28.00	68.00		$68.00	$ 35.00	−33.00
							20.00			
35.00	2	40.00	20.00	48.00	24.00	88.00		44.00	70.00	−18.00
							16.00			
35.00	3	40.00	13.33	64.00	21.33	104.00		34.67	105.00	1.00
							14.00			
35.00	4	40.00	10.00	78.00	19.50	118.00		29.50	140.00	22.00
							12.00			
35.00	5	40.00	8.00	90.00	18.00	130.00		26.00	175.00	45.00
							17.00			
35.00	6	40.00	6.67	107.00	17.83	147.00		24.50	210.00	63.00
							22.00			
35.00	7	40.00	5.71	129.00	18.43	169.00		24.14	245.00	76.00
							30.00			
35.00	8	40.00	5.00	159.00	19.88	199.00		24.88	280.00	81.00
							40.00			
35.00	9	40.00	4.44	199.00	22.11	239.00		26.56	315.00	76.00
							54.00			
35.00	10	40.00	4.00	253.00	25.30	293.00		29.30	350.00	57.00

Determining Profit from a Graph

The profit-maximizing output can be determined in a table (as in Table 11-1) or in a graph (as in Figure 11-5).

These relationships can be seen in a graph. In Figure 11-5(a) I add the average total cost and average variable cost curves to the graph of marginal cost and price first presented in Figure 11-2. Notice that the marginal cost curve goes through the lowest points of both average cost curves. (If you don't know why, it would be a good idea to go back and review Chapter 9.)

Q.5 If the firm described in Figure 11-5 is producing 4 units, what would you advise it to do, and why?

Find Output Where MC = MR The way you find profit graphically is first to find the point where MC = MR (point A). That intersection determines the quantity the firm will produce if it wants to maximize profit. Why? Because the vertical distance between a point on the marginal cost curve and a point on the marginal revenue curve represents the additional profit the firm can make by changing output. For example, if it increases production from 6 to 7, its marginal cost is $22 and its marginal revenue is $35. By increasing output it can increase profit by $13 (from $63 to $76). The same reasoning holds true for any output less than 8. For outputs higher than 8, the opposite reasoning holds true. Marginal cost exceeds marginal revenue, so it pays to decrease output. So to maximize profit, the firm must see that there is no distance between the two curves—it must see where they intersect.

When the ATC curve is below the marginal revenue curve, the firm makes a profit. When the ATC curve is above the marginal revenue curve, the firm incurs a loss.

Find Profit Per Unit Where MC = MR After having determined the profit-maximizing quantity, drop a vertical line down to the horizontal axis and see what average total cost is at that output level (point B). Doing so determines the profit per unit at the profit-maximizing output because it's the difference between the price the firm receives (its

Figure 11-5 (a, b, and c)   Determining Profits Graphically

The profit-maximizing output depends *only* on where the MC and MR curves intersect. The total amount of profit or loss that a firm makes depends on the price it receives and its average total cost of producing the profit-maximizing output. This exhibit shows the case of (**a**) a profit, (**b**) zero profit, and (**c**) a loss.

(a) Profit case   (b) Zero profit case   (c) Loss case

average revenue) and its average cost. Since the firm will earn that profit on each unit sold, you next extend a line back to the vertical axis (point C). That tells us that the average total costs per unit are $25. Next go up the price axis to the price that the firm receives (point D). For a competitive firm, that price is the marginal revenue. Connecting these points gives us the shaded rectangle, *ABCD*, which is the total profit earned by the firm (the total quantity times the profit per unit).

Notice that at the profit-maximizing position, the profit per unit isn't at its highest because average total cost is *not* at its minimum point. Profit per unit of output would be highest at point E. A common mistake that students make is to draw a line up from point E when they are finding profits. That is wrong. It is important to remember: *To determine maximum profit you must first determine what output the firm will choose to produce by seeing where* MC *equals* MR *and then determine the average total cost at that quantity by dropping a line down to the* ATC *curve.* Only then can you determine what maximum profit will be.

To determine maximum profit, you must first determine what output the firm will choose to produce by seeing where *MC* equals *MR*, and then dropping a line down to the *ATC* curve.

Zero Profit or Loss Where MC = MR Notice also that as the curves in Figure 11-5(a) are drawn, *ATC* at the profit-maximizing position is below the price, and the firm makes a profit per unit of a little over $10. The choice of short-run average total cost curves was arbitrary and doesn't affect the firm's profit-maximizing condition: MC = MR. It could have been assumed that fixed cost was higher, which would have shifted the *ATC* curve up. In Figure 11-5(b) it's assumed that fixed cost is $81 higher than in Figure 11-5(a). Instead of $40, it's $121. The appropriate average total cost curve for a fixed cost of $121 is drawn in Figure 11-5(b). Notice that in this case economic profit is zero and the marginal cost curve intersects the minimum point of the average total

APPLYING THE TOOLS

Profit Maximization and Real-World Firms

Most real-world firms do not have profit as their only goal. The reason is that, in the real world, the decision-maker's income is part of the cost of production. For example, a paid manager has an incentive to hold down costs, but has little incentive to hold down his income which, for the firm, is a cost. Alternatively, say that a firm is a worker-managed firm. If workers receive a share of the profits, they'll push for higher profits, but they'll also see to it that in the process of maximizing profits they don't hurt their own interest—maximizing their wages.

A manager-managed firm will push for high profits but will see to it that it doesn't achieve those profits by hurting the manager's interests. Managers' pay will be high. In short, real-world firms will hold down the costs of factors of production *except* the cost of the decision maker.

In real life, this problem of the lack of incentives to hold down costs is important. For example, firms' managerial expenses often balloon even as firms are cutting "costs."

Similarly, CEOs and other high-ranking officers of the firm often have enormously high salaries. How and why the lack of incentives to hold down costs affects the economy is best seen by first considering the nature of an economy with incentives to hold down all costs. That's why we use as our standard model the profit-maximizing firm. (*Standard model* means the model that economists use as our basis of reasoning; from it, we branch out.)

Q.6 What is wrong with the following diagram?

Q.7 In the 1990s, many airlines were making losses, yet they continued to operate. Why?

The shutdown point is the point at which the firm will be better off if it shuts down than it will if it stays in business.

cost curve at an output of 8 and a price of $35. In this case, the firm is making zero economic profit. (Remember from Chapter 10 that even though economic profit is zero, all resources, including entrepreneurs, are being paid their opportunity cost.)

In Figure 11-5(c), fixed cost is much higher—$169. Profit-maximizing output is still 8, but now at an output of 8, the firm is making an economic loss of $6 on each unit sold, since its average total cost is $41. The loss is given by the shaded rectangle. In this case, the profit-maximizing condition is actually a loss-minimizing condition. So MC = MR = P is both a *profit-maximizing condition* and a *loss-minimization condition*.

I draw these three cases to emphasize to you that determining the profit-maximizing output level doesn't depend on fixed cost or average total cost. It depends only on where marginal cost equals price.

The Shutdown Point

Earlier I stated the supply curve of a competitive firm is its marginal cost curve. More specifically, the supply curve is the part of the marginal cost curve that is above the average variable cost curve. Considering why this is the case should help the analysis stick in your mind.

Let's consider Figure 11-6(a)—a reproduction of Figure 11-5(c)—and the firm's decision at various prices. At a price of $35, it's incurring a loss of $6 per unit. If it's making a loss, why doesn't it shut down? The answer lies in the fixed costs. There's no use crying over spilt milk. In the short run a firm knows it must pay these fixed costs regardless of whether or not it produces. The firm only considers the costs it can save by stopping production, and those costs are its variable costs. As long as a firm is covering its variable costs, it pays to keep on producing. By producing, its loss is $48; if it stopped producing, its loss would be all the fixed costs ($169). So it makes a smaller loss by producing.

However, once the price falls below average variable costs (below $17.80), it will pay to shut down (point A in Figure 11-6(a)). In that case the firm's loss from producing would be more than $169, and it would do better to simply stop producing temporarily and avoid paying the variable cost. Thus, the point at which price equals AVC is the **shutdown point** (*that point at which the firm will be better off if it temporarily shuts down than it will if it stays in business*). When price falls below the shutdown point, the average

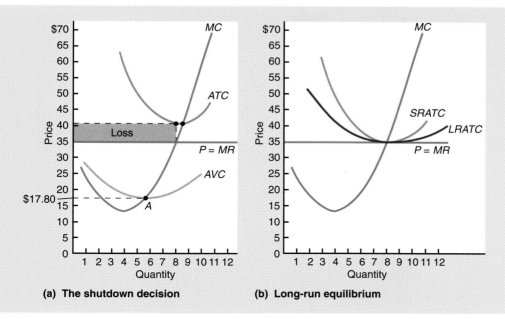

Figure 11-6   The Shutdown Decision and Long-Run Equilibrium

A firm should continue to produce as long as price exceeds average variable cost. Once price falls below that, it will do better by temporarily shutting down and saving the variable costs. This occurs at point A in (a). In (b), the long-run equilibrium position for a marginal firm in an industry is shown. In that long-run equilibrium, only normal profits are made.

variable costs the firm can avoid paying by shutting down exceed the price it would get for selling the good. When price is above average variable cost, in the short run a firm should keep on producing even though it's making a loss. As long as a firm's total revenue is covering its total variable cost, temporarily producing at a loss is the firm's best strategy because it's making a smaller loss than it would make if it were to shut down.

If $P >$ minimum of AVC, the firm will continue to produce in the short run. If $P \leq$ minimum of AVC, the firm will shut down.

SHORT-RUN MARKET SUPPLY AND DEMAND

Most of the preceding discussion has focused on supply and demand analysis of a firm. Now let's consider supply and demand in an industry. We've already discussed industry demand. Even though the demand curve faced by the firm is perfectly elastic, the industry demand curve is downward sloping.

How about the industry supply curve? We previously demonstrated that the supply curve for a competitive firm is that firm's marginal cost curve (above the average variable cost curve). To discuss the industry supply curve, we must use a market supply curve. In the short run when the number of firms in the market is fixed, the **market supply curve** is just the *horizontal sum of all the firms' marginal cost curves, taking account of any changes in input prices that might occur*. To move from individual firms' marginal cost curves or supply curves to the market supply curve we add the quantities all firms will supply at each possible price. Since all firms have identical marginal cost curves, a quick way of summing the quantities is to multiply the quantities from the marginal cost curve of a representative firm at each price by the number of firms in the market. As the short run evolves into the long run, the number of firms in the market can change. As more firms enter the market, the market supply curve shifts to the right because more firms are supplying the quantity indicated by the representative marginal cost curve. Likewise, as the number of firms in the market declines, the market supply curve shifts to the left. Knowing how the number of firms in the market affects the market supply curve is important to understanding long-run equilibrium in perfectly competitive markets.

The market supply curve is the horizontal sum of all the firms' marginal cost curves, taking account of any changes in input prices that might occur.

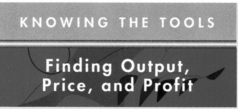

To find a competitive firm's price, level of output, and profit given a firm's marginal cost curve and average total cost curve, use the following three steps:

1. Determine the market price at which market supply and demand curves intersect. This is the price the competitive firm accepts for its products. Draw the horizontal marginal revenue (*MR*) curve at the market price.

2. Determine the profit-maximizing level of output by finding the level of output where the *MR* and *MC* curves intersect.

KNOWING THE TOOLS

Finding Output, Price, and Profit

3. Determine profit by subtracting average total costs at the profit-maximizing level of output from the price and multiplying by the firm's output.

If you are demonstrating profit graphically, find the point at which $MC = MR$. Extend a line down to the *ATC* curve. Extend a line from this point to the vertical axis. To complete the box indicating profit, go up the vertical axis to the market price.

LONG-RUN COMPETITIVE EQUILIBRIUM

The analysis of the competitive firm consists of two parts: the short-run analysis just presented and the long-run analysis. In the short run the number of firms is fixed and the firm can either earn economic profit or incur economic loss. In the long run, firms enter and exit the market and neither economic profits nor economic losses are possible. In the long run, firms make zero economic profit. Thus, in the long run, only the zero profit equilibrium shown in Figure 11-6(b) is possible. As you can see, at that long-run equilibrium, the firm is at the minimum of both the short-run and the long-run average total cost curves.

Why can't firms earn economic profit or make economic losses in the long run? Because of the entry and exit of firms: If there are economic profits, firms would enter the market, shifting the market supply curve to the right. As market supply increased, the market price would decline and reduce profits for each firm. Firms would continue to enter the market and the market price would continue to decline until the incentive of economic profits was eliminated. At that price, all firms are earning zero profit. Similarly, if the price was lower than the price necessary to earn a profit, firms incurring losses would leave the market and the market supply curve would shift to the left. As market supply shifts to the left, market price will rise. Firms will continue to exit the market and market price will continue to rise until all remaining firms are no longer incurring losses and are earning zero profit. Only at zero profit do entry and exit stop.

Zero profit does not mean that entrepreneurs don't get anything for their efforts. The entrepreneur is an input to production just like any other factor of production. In order to stay in the business the entrepreneur must receive the opportunity cost, or **normal profit** (*the amount the owners of business would have received in the next-best alternative*). That normal profit is built into the costs of the firm; economic profits are profits above normal profits.

Another aspect of the zero profit position deserves mentioning. What if one firm has superefficient workers or machinery? Won't the firm make a profit in the long run? The answer is, again, no. In a long-run competitive market, other firms will see the value of those workers and machines and will compete to get them for themselves. As firms compete for the superefficient factors of production, the price of those specialized inputs

Since profits create incentives for new firms to enter, output will increase, and the price will fall until zero profits are being made.

11.2

Q-8 If a competitive firm makes zero profit, why does it stay in business?

APPLYING THE TOOLS

The Shutdown Decision and the Relevant Costs

Chapters 9 and 10 emphasized that it is vital to choose the relevant costs to the decision at hand. Discussing the shutdown decision gives us a chance to demonstrate the importance of those choices. Say the firm leases a large computer it needs to operate. The rental cost of that computer is a fixed cost for most decisions, if, as long as the firm keeps the computer, the rent must be paid whether or not the computer is used. However, if the firm can end the rental contract at any time, and thereby save the rental cost, the computer is not a fixed cost. But nei-ther is it your normal variable cost. Since the firm can end the rental contract and save the cost only if it shuts down, that rental cost of the computer is an *indivisible setup cost*. For the shutdown decision, the computer cost is a variable cost. For other decisions about changing quantity, it's a fixed cost.

The moral: The relevant cost can change with the decision at hand, so when you apply the analysis to real-world situations, be sure to think carefully about what the *relevant cost* is.

will rise until all profits are eliminated. Those factors will receive what are called *rents* to their specialized ability. For example, say the average worker receives $400 per week, but Sarah, because she's such a good worker, receives $600. So $200 of the $600 she receives is a rent to her specialized ability. Either her existing firm matches that $600 wage or she will change employment.

The zero profit condition is enormously powerful; it makes the analysis of competitive markets far more applicable to the real world than can a strict application of the assumption of perfect competition. If economic profit is being made, firms will enter and compete that profit away. Price will be pushed down to the average total cost of production as long as there are no barriers to entry. As we'll see in later chapters, in their analysis of whether markets are competitive, many economists focus primarily on whether barriers to entry exist.

> The zero profit condition is enormously powerful; it makes the analysis of competitive markets far more applicable to the real world than would otherwise be the case.

ADJUSTMENT FROM THE SHORT RUN TO THE LONG RUN

Now that we've been through the basics of the perfectly competitive supply and demand curves, we're ready to consider the two together and to see how the adjustment to long-run equilibrium will likely take place in the firm and in the market.

An Increase in Demand

First, in Figure 11-7(a and b), let's consider a market that's in equilibrium but that suddenly experiences an increase in demand. Figure 11-7(a) shows the market reaction. Figure 11-7(b) shows a representative firm's reaction. Originally market equilibrium occurs at a price of $7 and market quantity supplied of 700 thousand units (point A in (a)), with each of 70 firms producing 10 thousand units (point a in (b)). Firms are making zero profit because they're in long-run equilibrium. If demand increases from D_0 to D_1, the firms will see the market price increasing and will increase their output until they're once again at a position where $MC = P$. This occurs at point B at a market output of 840 thousand units in (a) and at point b at a firm output of 12 in (b). In the short run the 70 existing firms each make an economic profit (the shaded area in Figure 11-7(b)). Price has risen to $9, but average cost is only $7.10, so if the price remains $9 each firm is making a profit of $1.90 per unit. But price cannot remain at $9 since each firm will have an incentive to expand output and new firms will have an incentive to enter the market.

> **Q.9** If berets suddenly became the "in" thing to wear, what would you expect to happen to the price in the short run? In the long run?

Figure 11-7 (a and b)   Market Response to an Increase in Demand

Faced with an increase in demand which it sees as an increase in price and hence profits, a competitive firm will respond by increasing output (from A to B) in order to maximize profit. The market response is shown in (a); the firm's response is shown in (b). As all firms increase output and as new firms enter, price will fall until all profit is competed away. Thus the long-run market supply curve will be perfectly elastic, as is S_{LR} in (a). The final equilibrium will be the original price but a higher output. The original firms return to their original output (A), but since there are more firms in the market, the market output increases to C.

(a) Market

(b) Firm

As existing firms expand and new firms enter, if input prices remain constant, the short-run market supply curve shifts from S_0 to S_1 and the market price returns to $7. The entry of 50 new firms provides the additional output in this example, bringing market output to 1.2 million units sold for $7 apiece. The final equilibrium will be at a higher market output but the same price.

Long-Run Market Supply

In the long run firms earn zero profits.

The long-run market supply curve is a schedule of quantities supplied when firms are no longer entering or exiting the market. This occurs when firms are earning zero profit. In this case, the long-run supply curve is created by extending to the right the line connecting points A and C. Since equilibrium price remains at $7, the long-run supply curve is perfectly elastic. The long-run supply curve is horizontal because factor prices are constant. That is, factor prices do not increase as industry output increases. Economists call this market a *constant-cost industry*. Two other possibilities exist: an *increasing-cost industry* (in which factor prices rise as more firms enter the market and existing firms expand production) and a *decreasing-cost industry* (in which factor prices fall as industry output expands).

Factor prices are likely to rise when industry output increases if the factors of production are specialized. An increase in the demand for the factors of production that accompanies an increase in output, in this case, will bid up factor prices. The effect on long-run supply is the following: The rise in factor prices forces costs up for each individual firm and increases the price at which firms earn zero profit. Firms will stop

KNOWING THE TOOLS

A Summary of a
Perfectly Competitive
Industry

Four things to remember when considering a perfectly competitive industry are

1. The profit-maximizing condition for perfectly competitive firms is $MC = MR = P$.

2. To determine profit or loss at the profit-maximizing level of output, subtract the average total cost at that level of output from the price and multiply the result by the output level.

3. Firms will shut down production if price is equal to or falls below the minimum of their average variable costs.

4. A perfectly competitive firm is in long-run equilibrium only when it is earning zero economic profit, or when price equals the minimum of long-run average total costs.

entering the market and expanding production at a higher equilibrium price since the price at which zero profit is made has risen. Therefore, in increasing cost industries, the long-run supply curve is upward sloping. In the extreme case, in which all firms in an industry are competitively supplying a perfectly inelastic resource or factor input, the long-run market supply curve is perfectly inelastic (vertical). Any increase in demand would increase the price of that factor. Costs would rise in response to the increase in demand; output would not. Input costs would also rise if there are diseconomies of scale. In both cases, the long-run equilibrium price would have been higher and output would have been lower than if input prices remained constant.[3]

The other possibility is a decreasing-cost industry. If factor prices decline when industry output expands, individual firms' cost curves shift down. As they do, the price at which the zero profit condition falls and the price at which firms cease to enter the market also falls. In this case, the long-run market supply curve is downward sloping. Factor prices may decline as output rises when new entrants make it more cost-effective for other firms to provide services to all firms in the area. The supply of factors of production expands and reduces the price of inputs to production.

Notice that in the long-run equilibrium, once again zero profit is being made. Long-run equilibrium is defined by zero economic profit. Notice also that the long-run supply curve is more elastic than the short-run supply curve. That's because output changes are much less costly in the long run than in the short run. *In the short run, the price does more of the adjusting. In the long run, more of the adjustment is done by quantity.*

In the short run, the price does more of the adjusting. In the long run, more of the adjustment is done by quantity.

An Example in the Real World

The perfectly competitive model and the reasoning underlying it are extremely powerful. With them you have a simple model to use as a first approach to predict the effect of an event, or to explain why an event occurred. For example, consider the decision of the owners of the Ames chain of department stores to close over 100 stores after experiencing two years of losses.

Figure 11-8 shows what happened. Initially, Ames saw the losses it was suffering as temporary. In the two years prior to the shutdown decision, Ames' cost curves looked

---

[3]To check your understanding, ask yourself the following question: What if there had been economies of scale? If you answered, "There couldn't have been," you're really into economic thinking. (For those of you who aren't all that heavily into economic thinking, the reason is that if there had been economies of scale, the market structure would not have been perfectly competitive. One firm would have kept expanding and expanding and, as it did, its costs would have kept falling.

Figure 11-8   A Real-World Example: A Shutdown Decision

Supply-demand analysis can be applied to a wide variety of real-world examples. This exhibit shows one, but there are many more. As you experience life today, a good exercise is to put on your supply-demand glasses and interpret everything you see in a supply/demand framework.

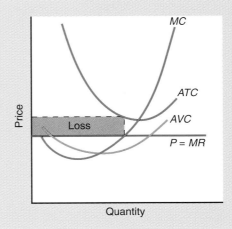

Supply and demand curves can be used to describe most real-world events.

Q-10 In the early 1990s, demand for hotel rooms in Hawaii decreased substantially because the value of the Japanese yen fell. In the short run, what would you expect to happen to the prices of these hotel rooms? How about in the long run?

like those in Figure 11-8. Since price exceeded average variable cost, Ames continued to produce even though it was making a loss.

But after two years of losses Ames' perspective changed. The company moved from the short run to the long run. Ames began to believe that the demand wasn't temporarily low but rather permanently low. It began to ask: What costs are truly fixed and what costs are simply indivisible costs that we can save if we close down completely, selling our buildings and reducing our overhead? Since in the long run all costs are variable, the ATC became its relevant AVC. Ames recognized that demand had fallen below these long-run average costs. At that point, it shut down those stores for which $P < AVC$.

There are hundreds of other real-world examples to which the perfectly competitive model adds insight. That's one reason why it's important to keep it in the back of your mind.

CONCLUSION

We've come to the end of the presentation of perfect competition. It was tough going, but if you went through it carefully, it will serve you well, both as a basis for later chapters and as a reference point for how real-world economies work. But like many good things, a complete understanding of the chapter doesn't come easy.

Chapter Summary

- The necessary conditions for perfect competition are that buyers and sellers be price takers, the number of firms be large, there be no barriers to entry, firms' products be homogeneous (identical), there be complete information, and sellers be profit-maximizing entrepreneurial firms.

- The profit-maximizing position of a competitive firm is where marginal revenue equals marginal cost.

- The supply curve of a competitive firm is its marginal cost curve. Only competitive firms have supply curves.

- To find the profit-maximizing level of output for a perfect competitor, find that level of output where $MC = MR$. Profit is price less average total cost times output at the profit-maximizing level of output.

- In the short run, competitive firms can make a profit or loss. In the long run, they make zero profits.

- The shutdown price for a perfectly competitive firm is a price below the minimum point of the average variable cost curve.

- The short-run market supply curve is the horizontal summation of the marginal cost curves for all firms in the market. An increase in the number of firms in the market shifts the market supply curve to the right, while a decrease shifts it to the left.

- Perfectly competitive firms make zero profit in the long run because if profit were being made, new firms would enter and the market price would decline, eliminating the profit. If losses were being made, firms would exit and the market price would rise, eliminating the loss.

- The long-run supply curve is a schedule of quantities supplied where firms are making zero profit. The slope of the long-run supply curve depends on what happens to factor prices when output increases. Constant-cost industries have horizontal long-run supply curves. Increasing-cost industries have upward-sloping long-run supply curves, and decreasing-cost industries have downward-sloping long-run supply curves.

Key Terms

barriers to entry *(239)*

marginal cost *(242)*

marginal revenue *(242)*

market supply curve *(251)*

normal profit *(252)*

perfectly competitive *(239)*

price taker *(239)*

profit-maximizing condition *(244)*

shutdown point *(250)*

Questions for Thought and Review

1. Why must buyers and sellers be price takers for a market to be perfectly competitive?

2. Draw marginal cost, marginal revenue, and average total cost curves for a typical perfectly competitive firm and indicate the profit-maximizing level of output and total profit for that firm. Is the firm in long-run equilibrium? Why or why not?

3. Draw marginal cost, marginal revenue, and average total cost curves for a typical perfectly competitive firm in long-run equilibrium and indicate the profit-maximizing level of output and total profit for that firm.

4. What portion of the marginal cost curve is the firm's supply curve? How is a firm's marginal cost curve related to the market supply curve?

5. Draw the ATC, AVC, and MC curves for a typical firm. Label the price at which the firm would shut down temporarily and the price at which the firm would exit the market in the long run.

6. Under what cost condition is the shutdown point the same as the point at which a firm exits the market?

7. Why is long-run market supply curve upward sloping in an increasing-cost industry, downward sloping in a decreasing-cost industry, and horizontal in a constant-cost industry?

8. What will be the effect of a technological development that reduces marginal costs in a competitive market on short-run price, quantity, and profit?

9. If a firm is owned by its workers but otherwise meets all the qualifications for a perfectly competitive firm, will its price and output decisions differ from the price and output decisions of a perfectly competitive firm? Why?

10. You're thinking of buying one of two firms. One has a profit margin of $8 per unit; the other has a profit margin of $4 per unit. Which should you buy? Why?

11. If marginal cost is four times the quantity produced and the price is $20, how much should the firm produce? Why?

12. Find three events in the newspaper that can be explained or interpreted with supply/demand analysis.

13. State what is wrong with each of the graphs.

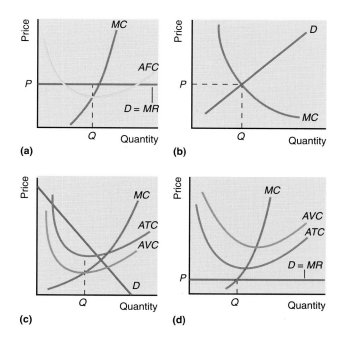

14. In the late 1990s, hundreds of music stores closed in the face of stagnant demand for CDs and new competitors—online music vendors and discount retailers. Explain how price competition from these new sources would cause a retail store to close. In the long run, what effect will new entrants have on the price of CDs?

Problems and Exercises

1. a. Based on the following table, what is the profit-maximizing output?

Output	Price	Total Costs
0	$10	$ 30
1	10	40
2	10	45
3	10	48
4	10	55
5	10	65
6	10	80
7	10	100
8	10	140
9	10	220
10	10	340

b. How would your answer change if, in response to an increase in demand, the price of the good increased to $15?

2. A profit-maximizing firm has an average total cost of $4, but it gets a price of $3 for each good it sells.
   a. What would you advise the firm to do?
   b. What would you advise the firm to do if you knew average variable costs were $3.50?

3. Say that half of the cost of producing wheat is the rental cost of land (a fixed cost) and half is the cost of labor and machines (a variable cost). If the average total cost of producing wheat is $8 and the price of wheat is $6, what would you advise the farmer to do? ("Grow something else" is not allowed.)

4. Use the accompanying graph, which shows the marginal cost and average total cost curves for the shoe store, Zapateria, a perfectly competitive firm.

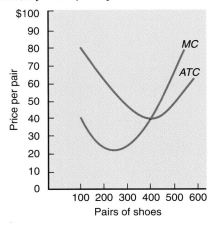

a. How many pairs of shoes will Zapateria produce if the market price of shoes is $70 a pair?
b. What is the total profit Zapateria will earn if the market price of shoes is $70 a pair?
c. Should Zapateria expect more shoe stores to enter this market? Why or why not?
d. What is the long-run equilibrium price in the shoe market assuming it is a constant-cost industry?

5. Each of 10 firms in a given industry has the costs given in the left-hand table. The market demand schedule is given in the right-hand table.

Quantity	Total Cost	Price	Quantity Demanded
0	12	2	110
1	24	4	100
2	27	6	90
3	31	8	80
4	39	10	70
5	53	12	60
6	73	14	50
7	99	16	40

a. What is the market equilibrium price and the price each firm gets for its product?
b. What is the equilibrium market quantity and the quantity each firm produces?
c. What profit is each firm making?
d. Below what price will firms begin to exit the market?

6. Suppose an increasing-cost industry is in both long-run and short-run equilibrium. Explain what will happen to the following in the long run if the demand for that product declines:
   a. Price.
   b. Quantity.
   c. Number of firms in the market.
   d. Profit.

7. Graphically demonstrate the quantity and price of a perfectly competitive firm.
   a. Explain why a slightly larger quantity would not be preferred.
   b. Explain why a slightly lower quantity would not be preferred.
   c. Label the shutdown point in your diagram.
   d. You have just discovered that shutting down means that you would lose your land zoning permit which is required to start operating again. How does that change your answer to c?

8. A California biotechnology firm submitted a tomato to the U.S. Food and Drug Administration that will not rot for weeks. It designed such a fruit by changing the genetic structure of the tomato. What effect will this technological change have:
   a. On the price of tomatoes?
   b. On farmers who grow tomatoes?
   c. On the geographic areas where tomatoes are grown?
   d. On where tomatoes are generally placed on salad bars in winter?

9. Currently central banks (banks of governments) hold 35,000 tons of gold—one-third of the world's supply. This is the equivalent of 17 years' production. In the 1990s there was discussion about the central banks selling off their gold, since it is no longer tied to money supplies. Assuming they did sell it:
   a. Demonstrate, using supply and demand analysis, the effect on the price of gold in the long run and the short run.
   b. If you were an economist advising the central banks and you believed that selling off the gold made sense, would you advise them to do it quickly or slowly? Why?

10. The milk industry has a number of interesting aspects. Provide economic explanations for the following:
   a. Fluid milk is 87 percent water. It can be dried and reconstituted so that it is almost indistinguishable from fresh milk. What is a likely reason that such reconstituted milk is not produced?
   b. The United States has regional milk-marketing regulations whose goals are to make each of the regions self-sufficient in milk. What is a likely reason for this?

c. A U.S. senator from a milk-producing state has been quoted as saying, "I am absolutely convinced . . . that simply bringing down dairy price supports is not a way to cut production." Is it likely that he is correct? What is a probable reason for his statement?

11. Subtle changes in the tax laws often mean enormous amounts of money to individuals and groups. Consider the case of whiskey, as did economists Jack High and Clayton Coppin. Whiskey is distilled grain. The distilling process produces poisonous impurities, called fusel oil, that must be removed before the whiskey is drinkable. One way to remove these impurities is by aging the whiskey in wooden barrels. Whiskey produced in this manner is "straight whiskey." The second method is distillation—removing the fusel oil through additional distilling. The latter method removes more impurities and is cheaper, but it results in a whiskey with little taste. However, taste can be added back through flavorings or blending with aged whiskey. Up until 1868 distilled or blended whiskey predominated, but in that year a law was passed that allowed straight-whiskey producers who stored their whiskey in government warehouses to defer their taxes on it until it was fully aged.
   a. What advantage would this law have for straight-whiskey producers?
   b. After the tax was paid the whiskey received a tax stamp, certifying that its producers had paid the tax and that their straight whiskey had been stored in a "bonded government warehouse." If you were a straight-whiskey producer, how might you try to use that tax stamp to your advantage in advertising?
   c. How might competing producers of distilled whiskey certify the quality of their product?

Web Questions

1. A number of markets are developing on the Internet. One of those markets is eBay. Check out eBay at www.ebay.com and explain whether you believe that the eBay Internet auction market is perfectly competitive. Be sure to explain which of the six conditions are met and how.

2. Find 60-month new auto loans in five different states using a loan information center on the Internet such as www.rates.net and answer the following questions:

   a. By how much did the interest rates differ among those institutions you sampled?
   b. Which of the six conditions for perfect competition does the auto loan market meet?
   c. Is your answer to b consistent with your answer to a? Why or why not?

Answers to Margin Questions

1. Without the assumption of no barriers to entry, firms could make a profit by raising price; hence, their demand curve would not be perfectly elastic and, hence, perfect competition would not exist. (240)

2. The competitive firm is such a small portion of the total market that it can have no effect on price. Consequently

it takes the price as given, and hence its perceived demand curve is perfectly elastic. (241)

3. To determine the profit-maximizing output of a competitive firm, you must know price and marginal cost. (244)

4. Firms are interested in getting as much for themselves as they possibly can. Maximizing total profit does this.

Maximizing profit per unit might yield very small total profits. *(245)*

5. If the firm in Figure 11-5 were producing 4 units, I would explain to it that the marginal cost of increasing output is only $12 and the marginal revenue is $35, so they should significantly expand output until 8, where the marginal cost equals the marginal revenue, or price. *(248)*

6. The diagram is drawn with the wrong profit-maximizing output and hence the wrong profit. Output is determined where marginal cost equals price and profit is the difference between the average total cost and price at that output, not at the output where marginal cost equals average total cost. The correct diagram is shown here. *(250)*

7. The marginal cost for airlines is significantly below average total cost. Since they're recovering their average variable cost, they continue to operate. In the long run, if this continues, some airlines will be forced out of business. *(250)*

8. The costs for a firm include the normal costs, which in turn include a return for all factors. Thus it is worthwhile for a competitive firm to stay in business, since it is doing better, or at least as well, as it could in any other activity. *(252)*

9. Suddenly becoming the "in" thing to wear would cause the demand for berets to shift up, pushing the price up in the short run. In the long run it would probably push the price down, as there probably are considerable economies of scale in the production of berets. *(253)*

10. A decline in demand should push the short-run price of these hotel rooms down. In the long run, however, once a number of hotels go out of business, the price of hotel rooms should eventually move back to approximately where it was before the decline, assuming constant returns to scale. *(256)*

Monopoly

12

After reading this chapter, you should be able to:

- Summarize how and why the decisions facing a monopolist differ from the collective decisions of competing firms.

- Explain why $MC = MR$ maximizes total profit for a monopolist.

- Determine a monopolist's price, output, and profit graphically and numerically.

- Explain why a price-discriminating monopolist will earn more profit than a normal monopolist.

- Show graphically the welfare loss from monopoly.

- Explain why there would be no monopoly without barriers to entry.

- List three normative arguments against monopoly.

Monopoly is business at the end of its journey.

Henry Demarest Lloyd

In Chapter 11 we considered perfect competition. We now move to the other end of the spectrum: monopoly. **Monopoly** is *a market structure in which one firm makes up the entire market.* It is the polar opposite to competition. It is a market structure in which the firm faces no competitive pressure from other firms.

Monopolies exist because of barriers to entry into a market that prevent competition. These can be legal barriers (as in the case where a firm has a patent that prevents other firms from entering), sociological barriers where entry is prevented by custom or tradition, natural barriers where the firm has a unique ability to produce what other firms can't duplicate, or technological barriers where the size of the market can support only one firm.

THE KEY DIFFERENCE BETWEEN A MONOPOLIST AND A PERFECT COMPETITOR

For a competitive firm, marginal revenue equals price. For a monopolist, it does not. The monopolist takes into account the fact that its decision can affect price.

A key question we want to answer in this chapter is: How does a monopolist's decision differ from the collective decision of competing firms (i.e., from the competitive solution)? Answering that question brings out a key difference between a competitive firm and a monopoly. Since a competitive firm is too small to affect the price, it does not take into account the effect of its output decision on the price it receives. A competitive firm's marginal revenue (the additional revenue it receives from selling an additional unit of output) is the given market price. A monopolistic firm takes into account that its output decision can affect price; its marginal revenue is not its price. A monopolistic firm will reason: "If I increase production, the price I can get for each unit sold will fall, so I had better be careful about how much I increase production."

Let's consider an example. Say your drawings in the margins of this book are seen by a traveling art critic who decides you're the greatest thing since Rembrandt, or at least since Andy Warhol. Carefully he tears each page out of the book, mounts them on special paper, and numbers them: Doodle Number 1 (Doodle While Contemplating Demand), Doodle Number 2 (Doodle While Contemplating Production), and so on.

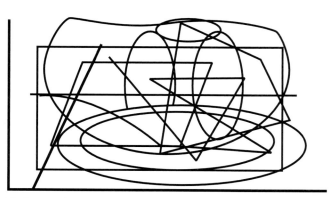

Doodle Number 27: Contemplating Costs

All told, he has 100. He figures, with the right advertising and if you're a hit on the art circuit, he'll have a monopoly in your doodles. He plans to sell them for $20,000 each: He gets 50 percent, you get 50 percent. That's $1 million for you. You tell him, "Hey, man! I can doodle my way through the entire book. I'll get you 500 doodles. Then I get $5 million and you get $5 million."

Q₁ Why should you study rather than doodle?

The art critic has a pained look on his face. He says, "You've been doodling when you should have been studying. Your doodles are worth $20,000 each only if they're rare. If there are 500, they're worth $1,000 each. And if it becomes known that you can turn them out that fast, they'll be worth nothing. I won't be able to limit quantity at all, and my monopoly will be lost. So obviously we must figure out some way that you won't doodle anymore—and study instead. Oh, by the way, did you know that the price of an artist's work goes up significantly when he or she dies? Hmm?" At that point you decide to forget doodling and to start studying, and to remember always that increasing production doesn't necessarily make suppliers better off.

Table 12-1   Monopolistic Profit Maximization

1	2	3	4	5	6	7	8
Quantity	Price	Total Revenue	Marginal Revenue	Total Cost	Marginal Cost	Average Total Cost	Profit
0	$36	$ 0		$ 47			$−47
			$33		$ 1		
1	33	33		48		$48.00	−15
			27		2		
2	30	60		50		25.00	10
			21		4		
3	27	81		54		18.00	27
			15		8		
4	24	96		62		15.50	34
			9		16		
5	21	105		78		15.60	27
			3		24		
6	18	108		102		17.00	6
			−3		40		
7	15	105		142		20.29	−37
			−9		56		
8	12	96		198		24.75	−102
			−15		80		
9	9	81		278		30.89	−197

As we saw in Chapter 11, competitive firms do not take advantage of that insight. Each individual competitive firm, responding to its self-interest, is not doing what is in the interest of the firms collectively. In competitive markets, as one supplier is pitted against another, consumers benefit. In monopolistic markets, the firm faces no competitors and does what is in its best interest. Monopolists can see to it that the monopolists, not the consumers, benefit; perfectly competitive firms cannot.

> Monopolists see to it that monopolists, not consumers, benefit.

A MODEL OF MONOPOLY

How much should the monopolistic firm choose to produce if it wants to maximize profit? To answer that we have to consider more carefully the effect that changing output has on the total profit of the monopolist. That's what we do in this section. First, we consider a numerical example; then we consider that same example graphically. The relevant information for our example is presented in Table 12-1.

Determining the Monopolist's Price and Output Numerically

Table 12-1 shows the price, total revenue, marginal revenue, total cost, marginal cost, average total cost, and profit at various levels of production. It's similar to the table in the last chapter where we determined a competitive firm's output. The big difference is that marginal revenue changes as output changes and is not equal to the price. Why?

First, let's remember the definition of marginal revenue: Marginal revenue is the change in total revenue associated with a change in quantity. In this example, if a monopolist increases output from 4 to 5, the price it can charge falls from $24 to $21 and its revenue increases from $96 to $105, so marginal revenue is $9. Marginal revenue of

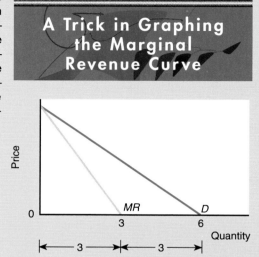

KNOWING THE TOOLS

A Trick in Graphing the Marginal Revenue Curve

Here's a trick to help you graph the marginal revenue curve. The *MR* line starts at the same point on the price axis as does a linear demand curve, but it intersects the quantity axis at a point half the distance from where the demand curve intersects the quantity axis. (If the demand curve isn't linear, you can use the same trick if you use lines tan-

gent to the curved demand curve.) So you can extend the demand curve to the two axes and measure halfway on the quantity axis (3 in the graph below). Then draw a line from where the demand curve intersects the price axis to that halfway mark. That line is the marginal revenue curve.

increasing output from 4 to 5 for the monopolist reflects two changes: a $21 gain in revenue from selling the 5th unit and a $12 decline in revenue because the monopolist must lower the price on the previous 4 units it produces by $3 a unit, from $24 to $21. This highlights the key characteristic of a monopolist—its output decision affects its price. Because an increase in output lowers the price on all previous units, a monopolist's marginal revenue is always below its price. Comparing columns 2 and 4, you can confirm that this is true.

Now let's see if the monopolist will increase production from 4 to 5 units. The marginal revenue of increasing output from 4 to 5 is $9, and the marginal cost of doing so is $13. Since marginal cost exceeds marginal revenue, increasing production from 4 to 5 will reduce total profit and the monopolist will not increase production. If it decreases output from 4 to 3, where $MC < MR$, the revenue it loses ($15) exceeds the reduction in costs ($8). It will not reduce output from 4 to 3. Since it cannot increase total profit by increasing output to 5 or decreasing output to 3, it is maximizing output at 4 units.

As you can tell from the table, profits are highest ($34) at 4 units of output and a price of $24. At 3 units of output and a price of $27, the firm has total revenue of $81 and total cost of $54, yielding a profit of $27. At 5 units of output and a price of $21, the firm has a total revenue of $105 and a total cost of $78, also for a profit of $27. The highest profit it can make is $34, which the firm earns when it produces 4 units. This is its profit-maximizing level.

Q-2 In Table 12-1, explain why 4 is the profit-maximizing output.

Determining the Monopolist's Price and Output Graphically

The monopolist's output decision can also be seen graphically. Figure 12-1 graphs the table's information into a demand curve, a marginal revenue curve, and a marginal cost curve. The marginal cost curve is a graph of the change in the firm's total cost as it changes output. It's the same curve as we saw in our discussion of perfect competition.

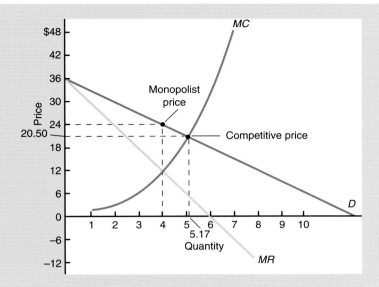

Figure 12-1   Determining the Monopolist's Price and Output Graphically

The profit-maximizing output is determined where the MC curve intersects the *MR* curve. To determine the price (at which MC = MR) that would be charged if this industry were a monopolist with the same cost structure, we first find that output and then extend a line to the demand curve, in this case finding a price of $24. This price is higher than the competitive price, $20.50, and the quantity, 4, is lower than the competitor's quantity, 5.17.

The marginal revenue curve tells us the change in total revenue when quantity changes. It is graphed by plotting and connecting the points given by quantity and marginal revenue in Table 12-1.

The marginal revenue curve for a monopolist is new, so let's consider it a bit more carefully. It tells us the additional revenue the firm will get by expanding output. It is a downward-sloping curve that begins at the same point as the demand curve but has a steeper slope. In this example, marginal revenue is positive up until the firm produces 6 units. Then marginal revenue is negative; after 6 units the firm's total revenue decreases when it increases output.

Notice specifically the relationship between the demand curve (which is the average revenue curve) and the marginal revenue curve. Since the demand curve is downward sloping, the marginal revenue curve is below the average revenue curve. (Remember, if the average curve is falling, the marginal curve must be below it.)

Having plotted these curves, let's ask the same questions as we did before: What output should the monopolist produce, and what price can it charge? To answer those questions, the key curves to look at are the marginal cost curve and the marginal revenue curve.

MR = MC Determines the Profit-Maximizing Output The monopolist uses the general rule that any firm must follow to maximize profit: Produce the quantity at which MC = MR. If you think about it, it makes sense that the point where marginal revenue equals marginal cost determines the profit-maximizing output. If the marginal revenue is below the marginal cost, it makes sense to reduce production. Doing so decreases marginal cost and increases marginal revenue. When MR < MC, reducing output increases total profit. If marginal cost is below marginal revenue, you should increase production because total profit will rise. If the marginal revenue is equal to marginal cost, it does not make sense to increase or reduce production. So the monopolist should produce at the output level where MC = MR. As you can see, the output the monopolist chooses

Q.3 In the graph below, indicate the monopolist's profit-maximizing level of output and the price it would charge.

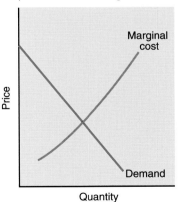

The general rule that any firm must follow to maximize profit is: Produce at an output level at which $MC = MR$.

is 4 units, the same output that we determined numerically.[1] This leads to the following insights:

If $MR > MC$, the monopolist gains profit by increasing output.

If $MR < MC$, the monopolist gains profit by decreasing output.

If $MC = MR$, the monopolist is maximizing profit.

Thus, $MR = MC$ is the profit-maximizing rule for a monopolist.

The Price a Monopolist Will Charge The $MR = MC$ condition determines the quantity a monopolist produces; in turn, that quantity determines the price the firm will charge. A monopolist will charge the maximum price consumers are willing to pay for that quantity. Since the demand curve tells us what consumers will pay for a given quantity, to find the price a monopolist will charge you must extend the quantity line up to the demand curve. We do so in Figure 12-1 and see that the profit-maximizing output level of 4 allows a monopolist to charge a price of $24.

Q-4 Why does a monopolist produce less output than would perfectly competitive firms in the same industry?

Comparing Monopoly and Perfect Competition

For a competitive industry, the horizontal summation of firms' marginal cost curves is the supply curve.[2] Output for a perfectly competitive industry would be 5.17, and price would be $20.50, as Figure 12-1 shows. The monopolist's output was 4 and its price was $24. So, if a competitive market is made into a monopoly, you can see that output would be lower and price would be higher. The reason is that the monopolist takes into account the effect that restricting output has on price.

Equilibrium output for the monopolist, like equilibrium output for the competitor, is determined by the $MC = MR$ condition, but because the monopolist's marginal revenue is below its price, its equilibrium output is different from a competitive market.

An Example of Finding Output and Price

We've covered a lot of material quickly, so it's probably helpful to go through an example slowly and carefully review the reasoning process. Here's the problem:

Say that a monopolist with marginal cost curve MC faces a demand curve D in Figure 12-2(a). Determine the price and output the monopolist would choose.

The first step is to draw the marginal revenue curve, since we know that a monopolist's profit-maximizing output level is determined where $MC = MR$. We do that in Figure 12-2(b), remembering the trick in the box on page 264 of extending our demand curve back to the vertical and horizontal axes and then bisecting the horizontal axis.

The second step is to determine where $MC = MR$. Having found that point, we extend a line up to the demand curve and down to the quantity axis to determine the output the monopolist chooses, Q_M. We do this in Figure 12-2(c).

Finally we see where the quantity line intersects the demand curve. Then we extend a horizontal line from that point to the price axis, as in Figure 12-2(d). This determines the price the monopolist will charge, P_M.

---

[1]This could not be seen precisely in Table 12-1 since the table is for discrete jumps and does not tell us the marginal cost and marginal revenue exactly at 4; it only tells us the marginal cost and marginal revenue ($8 and $15, respectively) of moving from 3 to 4 and the marginal cost and marginal revenue ($16 and $9, respectively) of moving from 4 to 5. If small adjustments (1/100 of a unit or so) were possible, the marginal cost and marginal revenue precisely at 4 would be $12. Because drawing the curve implicitly assumes we can make very small changes, the graphs of the marginal revenue curve and marginal cost curve will intersect at an output of 4 and a marginal cost and marginal revenue of $12.

[2]The above statement has some qualifications best left to intermediate classes.

Figure 12-2 (a, b, c, and d)   Finding the Monopolist's Price and Output
Determining a monopolist's price and output can be tricky. The text discusses the steps shown in this exhibit. To make sure you understand, try to go through the steps on your own, and then check your work with the text.

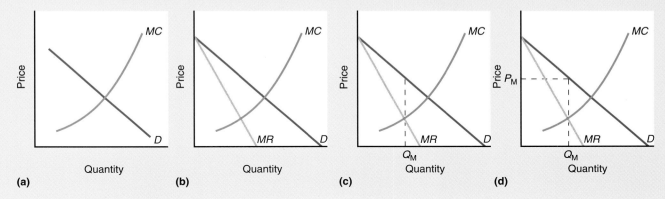

(a)   (b)   (c)   (d)

PROFITS AND MONOPOLY

The monopolist's profit can be determined only by comparing average total cost to price. So before we can determine profit, we need to add another curve: the average total cost curve. As we saw with a perfect competitor, it's important to follow the correct sequence when finding profit:

- First, draw the firm's marginal revenue curve.
- Second, determine the output the monopolist will produce by the intersection of the marginal cost and marginal revenue curves.
- Third, determine the price the monopolist will charge for that output. (Remember, the price it will charge depends on the demand curve.)
- Fourth, determine the monopolist's profit (loss) by subtracting average total cost from average revenue (P) at that level of output and multiplying by the chosen output.

If price exceeds average total cost at the output it chooses, the monopolist will make a profit. If price equals average total cost, the monopolist will make no profit (but it will make a normal return). If price is less than average cost, the monopolist will incur a loss: Total cost exceeds total revenue.

A Monopolist Making a Profit

I consider the case of a profit in Figure 12-3, going through the steps slowly. The monopolist's demand, marginal cost, and average total cost curves are presented in Figure 12-3(a). Our first step is to draw the marginal revenue curve, which has been added in Figure 12-3(b). The second step is to find the output level at which marginal cost equals marginal revenue. From that point draw a vertical line to the horizontal (quantity) axis. That intersection tells us the monopolist's output, Q_M in Figure 12-3(b). The third step is to find what price the monopolist will charge at that output. We do so by extending the vertical line to the demand curve (point A) and then extending a horizontal line over to the price axis. Doing so gives price, P_M. Our fourth step is to determine the average total cost at that quantity. We do so by seeing where our vertical line at the chosen

Q-5 Indicate the profit that the monopolist shown in the graph below earns.

Figure 12-3 (a, b, and c)   The Monopolist Makes a Profit

(a)   (b)   (c)

output intersects the average total cost curve (point B). That tells us the monopolist's average cost at its chosen output.

To determine profit, we extend lines from where the quantity line intersects the demand curve (point A) and the average total cost curve (point B) to the price axis in Figure 12-3(c). The resulting shaded rectangle in Figure 12-3(c) represents the monopolist's profit.

A Monopolist Breaking Even and Making a Loss

In Figure 12-4(a) and (b) we consider two other average total cost curves to show you that a monopolist may make a loss or no profit as well as an economic profit. In Figure 12-4(a) the monopolist is making zero profit; in Figure 12-4(b) it's making a loss. Whether a firm is making a profit, zero profit, or a loss depends on average total costs

**Figure 12-4 (a and b)
Other Monopoly Cases**

Depending on where the ATC curve falls, a monopolist can make a profit, break even (as in (a)), or make a loss (as in (b)) in the short run. In the long run, a monopolist who is making a loss will get out of business.

(a)   **Zero profit**   (b)   **Loss**

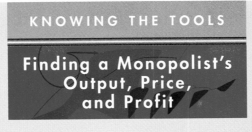

KNOWING THE TOOLS

Finding a Monopolist's Output, Price, and Profit

To find a monopolist's level of output, price, and profit, follow these four steps:

1. Draw the marginal revenue curve.
2. Determine the output the monopolist will produce: The profit-maximizing level of output is where *MR* and *MC* curves intersect.
3. Determine the price the monopolist will charge: Extend a line from where *MR* = *MC* up to the demand

curve. Where this line intersects the demand curve is the monopolist's price.

4. Determine the profit the monopolist will earn: Subtract the *ATC* from price at the profit-maximizing level of output to get profit per unit. Multiply profit per unit by quantity of output to get total profit.

relative to price. So clearly in the short run a monopolist can be making either a profit or a loss, or it can be breaking even.

THE PRICE-DISCRIMINATING MONOPOLIST

So far we've considered monopolists that charge the same price to all consumers. Let's consider what would happen if our monopolist suddenly gained the ability to **price discriminate**—*to charge different prices to different individuals or groups of individuals* (for example, students as compared to businesspeople). If a monopolist can identify groups of customers who have different elasticities of demand, separate them in some way, and limit their ability to resell its product between groups, it can charge each group a different price. Specifically, it could charge consumers with less elastic demands a higher price and individuals with more elastic demands a lower price. By doing so, it will increase total profit. Suppose, for instance, Megamovie knew that at $6 it would sell 1,000 movie tickets and at $3 a ticket it would sell 1,500 tickets. Assuming Megamovie could show the film without cost, it would maximize profits by charging $6 to 1,000 moviegoers, earning a total profit of $6,000. If, however, it could somehow attract the additional 500 viewers at $3 a ticket without reducing the price to the first 1,000 moviegoers, it could raise its profit by $1,500, to $7,500. As you can see, a price-discriminating monopolist increases its profit.

We see many examples of price discrimination in the real world.

1. *Movie theaters give discounts to senior citizens and children.* Movie theaters charge senior citizens and children a lower price because they have a more elastic demand for movies.
2. *All Airline Super Saver fares include Saturday-night stayovers.* This is a method of price discrimination. Businesspeople who have highly inelastic demands generally aren't willing to stay over a Saturday night, so they're charged a high price while tourists and leisure travelers who have a far more elastic demands and who are willing to stay over a Saturday night are charged a lower price.
3. *Automobiles are seldom sold at list price.* Once again we have an example of price discrimination. Salespeople can size up the customer and determine the customer's elasticity. People who haven't done the research and don't know that selling at 10 percent off list is normal (i.e., people with inelastic demands) pay higher prices than people who search out all the alternatives (people with elastic demand).

When a monopolist price discriminates, it charges individuals high up on the demand curve higher prices and those low on the demand curve lower prices.

12.1

BEYOND THE TOOLS

Monopsony

Monopoly occurs when there is a single seller; there are also markets in which there is a single buyer. Such markets are called monopsonies. An example of a monopsony is a "company town" in which a single firm is the only employer. Whereas a monopolist takes into account the fact that if it sells more it will lower the market price, a monopsonist takes into account the fact that it will raise the market prices if it buys more. Thus, it buys less and pays less than would a market with an equivalent number of competitive buyers.

Now that you've analyzed price-discriminating monopolies, you should understand them better. To see whether you do, try to provide a price discrimination explanation for the following:

Q.6 Why does a price-discriminating monopolist make a higher profit than a normal monopolist?

1. Theaters have special rates on Monday and Tuesday nights.
2. Retail tire companies run special sales about half the time.
3. Restaurants generally make most of their profit on alcoholic drinks and just break even on food.
4. College-town stores often give students discounts.

Now that you've answered those, see if you can extend your understanding by listing the central characteristics of markets that make them highly susceptible to price discrimination.

If you answered, "The market demand is made up of distinguishable individuals who have different demand elasticities," you've got it.

THE WELFARE LOSS FROM MONOPOLY

As we saw above there is no necessary reason to believe that a monopolist is guaranteed a profit. Thus, profits can't be the primary reason that the economic model we're using sees monopoly as bad. If not because of profits, then what standard is the economic model using to conclude that monopoly is undesirable?

One reason can be seen by reconsidering graphically the normal monopolist equilibrium and perfectly competitive equilibrium in reference to producer and consumer surplus. This we do in Figure 12-5. In a competitive equilibrium, the total consumer and producer surplus is the area between the demand curve and the marginal cost curve up to market equilibrium quantity Q_C. The monopolist reduces output to Q_M and raises price to P_M. The benefit lost to society from reducing output from Q_C to Q_M is measured by the area under the demand curve between output levels Q_C and Q_M. That area is represented by the shaded areas labeled A, B, and D. Some of that loss is regained. Society gains the opportunity cost of the resources that are freed up from reducing production—the value of the resources in their next-best use indicated by the shaded area A. So the net cost to society of decreasing output from Q_C to Q_M is represented by areas B and D. (Area C is the monopolist's profit. It is neither a gain nor a loss to society. It represents a transfer of income from the consumer to the monopolist that would occur with a rise in price. Since both monopolist and consumer are members of society, the gain and loss net out.) The triangular areas B and D are the net cost to society from the existence of monopoly.

Q.7 Why is area C in Figure 12-5 not considered a loss from monopoly?

As discussed in Chapter 7, this area designated by B and D is often called the *deadweight loss* or *welfare loss triangle*. That welfare cost of monopoly is one of the reasons economists oppose monopoly. That cost can be summarized as follows: Because monopolies

Figure 12-5   The Welfare Loss from Monopoly

The welfare loss from a monopoly is represented by the triangles B and D. The rectangle C is a transfer from consumer surplus to the monopolist. The area A represents the opportunity cost of diverted resources. This is not a loss to society since the resources will be used in producing other goods.

charge a price higher than marginal cost, people's decisions don't reflect the true cost to society. Price exceeds marginal cost. Because price exceeds marginal cost, people's choices are distorted; they choose to consume less of the monopolist's output and more of some other output than they would if markets were competitive. That distinction means that the marginal cost of increasing output is lower than the marginal benefit of increasing output, so there's a welfare loss.

BARRIERS TO ENTRY AND MONOPOLY

The standard model of monopoly just presented is simple, but, like many things simple, it hides some issues. One issue the standard model of monopoly hides is in this question: What prevents other firms from entering the monopolist's market? You should be able to answer that question relatively quickly. If a monopolist exists, it must exist due to some type of barrier to entry (a social, political, or economic impediment that prevents firms from entering the market). Three important barriers to entry are natural ability, economies of scale, and government restrictions. In the absence of barriers to entry, the monopoly would face competition from other firms, which would erode its monopoly.

This recognition is one of the main reasons why economists generally support free international trade and oppose tariffs. Tariffs are a barrier to entry to foreign firms and thus provide monopoly power to U.S. firms, allowing them to charge the consumer more than they otherwise could.

Studying how these barriers to entry are established enriches the standard model and lets us distinguish different types of monopoly.

Natural Ability

A barrier to entry that might exist is that a firm is better at producing a good than anyone else. It has unique abilities that make it more efficient than all other firms. The barrier to entry in such a case is the firm's natural ability. The defense attorneys in the Microsoft antitrust case argued that it was Microsoft's superior products that led to its capture of 90 percent of the market.

Such monopolies based on ability usually don't provoke the public's ire. Often in the public's mind such monopolies are "just monopolies." The standard economic model doesn't distinguish between a "just" and an "unjust" monopoly. The just/unjust distinction raises the question of whether a firm has acquired a monopoly based on its ability, or

The welfare loss from monopoly is a triangle, as in the graph below. It is not the loss that most people consider. They are often interested in normative losses that the graph does not capture.

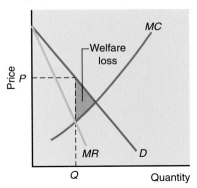

If there were no barriers to entry, profit-maximizing firms would always compete away monopoly profits.

 12.2

In Chapter 7 you learned how effective price ceilings increase market price, reduce output, and reduce the welfare of society. With any type of price control in a competitive market, some trades that individuals would like to have made are prevented. Thus, with competitive markets, price controls of any type are seen as generally bad (though they might have some desirable income distribution effects).

When there is monopoly the argument is not so simple. The monopoly price is higher than the marginal cost and society loses out; monopolies create their own deadweight loss. In the monopoly case price controls can actually lower price, increase output, and reduce deadweight loss. Going through the reasoning why provides a good review of the tools.

The exhibit below shows you the argument.

APPLYING THE TOOLS

Can Price Controls Increase Output and Lower Market Price?

The monopoly sets its price at $MR = MC$. Output is Q_M and price is P_M; the welfare loss is the shaded triangle A. Now say that the government comes in and places a price ceiling on the monopolist at the competitive price, P_C. Since the monopolist is compelled by law to charge price P_C, it no longer has an incentive to restrict output. Put another way, the price ceiling—the dashed line P_C—becomes the monopolist's demand curve and marginal revenue curve. (Remember, when the demand curve is horizontal, the marginal revenue curve is identical to the demand curve.) Given the law, the monopolist's best option still is to produce where $MC = MR$, but that means charging price P_C and increasing output to Q_C. As you can see from the exhibit, the price ceiling causes output to rise and price to fall.

If, when there is monopoly, price controls can increase efficiency, why don't economists advocate price controls more than they do? Let's review four reasons why.

1. For a price control to increase output and lower price, it has to be set within the right price range—below the monopolist's price and above the price where the monopolist's marginal cost and marginal revenue curves intersect. It is unclear politically that such a price will be chosen. Even if regulators could pick the right price initially, markets may change. Demand may increase or decrease, putting the price control outside the desired range.

2. All markets are dynamic. The very existence of monopoly profits will encourage other firms in other industries to try to break into that market, keeping the existing monopolist on its toes. Because of this dynamic element, in some sense no market is ever a pure textbook monopoly.

3. Price controls create their own deadweight loss in the form of rent seeking. Price controls do not eliminate monopoly pressures. The monopolist has a big incentive to regain its ability to set its own price and will lobby hard to remove price controls. Economists see resources spent to regain their monopoly price as socially wasteful.

4. Economists distrust government. Governments have their own political agendas—there is no general belief among economists that governments will try to set the price at the competitive level. Once one opens up the price control gates in cases of monopoly, it will be difficult to stop government from using price controls in competitive markets.

The arguments are, of course, more complicated, and will be discussed in more detail, but this should give you a good preview of some of the policy arguments to come in later chapters.

based on certain unfair tactics such as initially pricing low to force competitive companies out of business but then pricing high. Many public debates over monopoly focus on such normative issues, about which the economists' standard model has nothing to say.

Economies of Scale

An alternative reason why a barrier to entry might exist is that there are significant economies of scale. If sufficiently large economies of scale exist, it would be inefficient

Figure 12-6 (a and b)   A Natural Monopolist

This graph in (a) shows the average cost curve for a natural monopoly. One firm producing Q_1 would have average cost of C_1. If total production remains at Q_1 and another firm enters the market, sharing quantity produced, each firm would produce $Q_{1/2}$ goods at average cost C_2. If three firms each produced $Q_{1/3}$, the average cost for each would be C_3. In a case of a natural monopoly, as the number of firms in the industry increases, the average cost of producing a fixed number of units increases.

The graph in (b) shows that a natural monopolist would produce Q_M and charge a price P_M. It will earn a profit shown by the red shaded box. If the monopolist were required to charge a price equal to marginal cost, P_C, it would incur a loss shown by the blue shaded box.

(a)   (b)

to have two producers since if each produced half of the output, neither could take advantage of the economies of scale. Such industries are called natural monopolies. A **natural monopoly** is *an industry in which a single firm can produce at a lower cost than can two or more firms.* A natural monopoly will occur when the technology is such that indivisible setup costs are so large that average total costs fall within the range of potential outputs. I demonstrate that case in Figure 12-6(a).

If one firm produces Q_1, its cost per unit is C_1. If two firms each produce half that amount, $Q_{1/2}$, so that their total production is Q_1, the cost per unit will be C_2, which is significantly higher than C_1. In cases of natural monopoly, as the number of firms in the industry increases, the average total cost of producing a fixed number of units increases. For example, if there were three firms in the industry and they each had a third of the market, each firm would have an average cost of C_3.

Until the 1990s local telephone service was a real-world example of such a natural monopoly. It makes little sense to have two sets of telephone lines going into people's houses. I say "until recently" because technology changes and now, with wireless communications and cable connections, the technical conditions that made local telephone service a natural monopoly are changing. Such change is typical; natural monopolies are only natural given a technology.

A natural monopoly can also occur when a single industry standard owned by one firm is more efficient than multiple standards. An example is the operating system of computers. It is much more efficient (because the communication among users is easier) for there to be a single standard rather than multiple standards.

From a welfare standpoint natural monopolies are different than other types of monopolies. In the case of a natural monopoly, even if a single firm makes some monopoly

In a natural monopoly a single firm can produce at a lower cost than can two or more firms.

Q.8   Why is the competitive price impossible for an industry that exhibits strong economies of scale?

profit, the price it charges may still be lower than the price two firms making normal profit would charge because its average total costs will be lower. In the case of a natural monopoly not only is there no welfare loss from monopoly, there can actually be a welfare gain since a single firm producing is so much more efficient than many firms producing. Such natural monopolies are often organized as public utilities. For example, most towns have a single water department supplying water to residents.

Figure 12-6(b) shows the profit-maximizing level of output and price that a natural monopolist would choose. To show the profit-maximizing level of output, I've added a marginal cost curve that is below the average total cost curve and also falling. (If you don't know why this must be the case, a review of costs is in order.) A natural monopolist uses the same $MC = MR$ rule that a monopolist uses to determine output. The monopolist will produce Q_M and charge a price P_M. Average total costs are C_M and the natural monopolist earns a profit shown by the red shaded box.

Where natural monopoly exists, the perfectly competitive solution is impossible, since average total costs are not covered where $MC = P$. A monopolist required by government to charge the competitive price P_C, where $P = MC$, will incur a loss shown by the blue shaded box because marginal cost is always below average total cost. Some output restriction is necessary in order for production to be feasible. In such cases monopolies are often preferred by the public as long as they are regulated by government. I will discuss the issues of regulating natural monopolies in a later chapter.

Government-Created Monopolies

A third reason monopolies can exist is that they're created by government. The support of laissez-faire by Classical economists such as Adam Smith and their opposition to monopoly arose in large part in reaction to those government-created monopolies, not in reaction to any formal analysis of welfare loss from monopoly.

NORMATIVE VIEWS OF MONOPOLY

Many laypeople's views of government-created monopoly reflect the same normative judgments that Classical economists made. Classical economists considered, and much of the lay public considers, such monopolies unfair and inconsistent with liberty. Monopolies prevent people from being free to enter whatever business they want and are undesirable on normative grounds. In this view, government-created monopolies are simply wrong.

This normative argument against government-created monopoly doesn't extend to all types of government-created monopolies. The public accepts certain types of government-created monopoly that it believes have overriding social value. An example is patents. A **patent** is *a legal protection of a technical innovation that gives the person holding the patent a monopoly on using that innovation.* To encourage research and development of new products, government gives out patents for a wide variety of innovations, such as genetic engineering, Xerox machines, and cans that can be opened without a can opener.

A second normative argument against monopoly is that the public doesn't like the income distributional effects of monopoly. Although, as we saw in our discussion of monopoly, monopolists do not always earn an economic profit, they often do, which means that the monopoly might transfer income in a way that the public (whose normative views help determine society's policy toward monopoly) doesn't like. This distributional effect of monopoly based on normative views of who deserves income is another reason many laypeople oppose monopoly: They believe it transfers income from "deserving" consumers to "undeserving" monopolists.

Q_9 If a patent is a monopoly, why does the government give out patents?

A third normative reason people oppose government-created monopoly that isn't captured by the standard model of monopoly is that the possibility of government-created monopoly encourages people to spend a lot of their time in political pursuits trying to get the government to favor them with a monopoly, and less time doing "productive" things. It causes *rent-seeking* activities in which people spend resources to gain monopolies for themselves.

Each of these arguments probably plays a role in the public's dislike of monopoly. As you can see, these real-world arguments blend normative judgments with objective analysis, making it difficult to arrive at definite conclusions. Most real-world problems require this blending, making applied economic analysis difficult. The economist must interpret the normative judgments about what people want to achieve and explain how public policy can be designed to achieve those desired ends.

Let's now consider how economic theory might be used to analyze monopoly and to suggest how government might deal with that monopoly.

> Possible economic profits from monopoly lead potential monopolists to spend money to get government to give them a monopoly.

GOVERNMENT POLICY AND MONOPOLY: AIDS DRUGS

Let's consider the problem of acquired immune deficiency syndrome (AIDS) and the combination of medicinal drugs, including azidothymidine (AZT), used to treat it. AZT, used in combination with other drugs in mixtures called cocktails, is believed to arrest AIDS completely. These drugs were developed by a small group of pharmaceutical companies, which have patents on them. Those patents give the drug companies a monopoly. Patents are given on medicine to encourage firms to find cures for various diseases. The monopoly the patent gives them lets them charge a high price so that the firms can expect to make a profit from their research. Whether such patents are in the public interest isn't an issue, since the patent has already been granted.

What is an issue is what to do about these drugs. Currently demand for them is highly inelastic, so the price pharmaceutical companies can charge is high even though their marginal cost of producing them is low. Whether they are making a profit depends on their cost of development. But since that cost is already spent, that's irrelevant to the current marginal cost; development cost affects their *ATC* curve, not their marginal cost curve. Thus, the pharmaceutical companies are charging an enormously high price for drugs that may help save people's lives and that cost them a very small amount to produce.

What, if anything, should the government do? Some people have suggested that the government come in and regulate the price of the drugs, requiring the firms to charge only their marginal cost. This would make society better off. But most economists have a problem with that policy. They point out that doing so will significantly reduce the incentives for drug companies to research new drugs. One reason drug companies spend billions of dollars for drug research is their expectation that they'll be able to make large profits if they're successful. If drug companies expect the government to come in and take away their monopoly when they're successful, they won't search for cures. So forcing these pharmaceuticals to charge a low price for their drugs would help AIDS victims, but it would hurt people suffering from diseases that are currently being researched and that might be researched in the future. So there's a strong argument not to regulate.

But the thought of people dying when a cheap cure—or at least a partially effective treatment—is available is repulsive to me and to many others. African countries, where 70 percent of all people infected with the virus that causes AIDS live, have threatened to license production of these drugs to local manufacturers and make them available at cost. U.S. pharmaceutical companies pressured the United States to cut off foreign aid

> **Q.10** The medicinal drug tetracycline sold for animals costs about ⅟₂₀ the cost of the same drug sold for human beings. What is the likely explanation?

if they did so. Indeed, some companies have felt the pressure and have made drugs for AIDS available to AIDS patients in poor nations at a much lower price than they do to others (an example of price discrimination). In 1998 Glaxo Wellcome and several other pharmaceutical companies agreed to cut their prices 50 to 75 percent in developing countries. Still, the cost of the drug regimen is between $200 and $400 a month—far above monthly income in those countries.

An alternative policy suggested by economic theory is for the government to buy the patents and allow anyone to make the drugs so their price would approach their marginal cost. Admittedly this would be expensive. It would cause negative incentive effects, as the government would have to increase taxes to cover the buyout's costs. But this approach would avoid the problem of the regulatory approach and achieve the same ends. However, it would also introduce new problems, such as determining which patents the government should buy.

Whether such a buyout policy makes sense remains to be seen, but in debating such issues the power of the simple monopoly model becomes apparent.

CONCLUSION

We've come to the end of the presentation of the formal models of perfect competition and monopoly. Working through the models takes a lot of effort, but, it's effort well spent. In Chapter 1, I quoted Einstein: "A theory should be as simple as possible, but not more so." This chapter's analysis isn't simple; it takes repetition, working through models, and doing thought experiments to get it down pat. But it's as simple as possible. Even so, it's extremely easy to make a foolish mistake, as I did in my Ph.D. oral examination when I was outlining an argument on the blackboard. [*What* did you say the output would be for this monopolist, Mr. Colander?*] As I learned then, it takes long hours of working through the models again and again to get them right.

Chapter Summary

- The price a monopolist charges is higher than that of a competitive market due to the restriction of output; a monopolist can make a profit in the long run.

- A monopolist's profit-maximizing output is where marginal revenue equals marginal cost.

- A monopolist can charge the maximum price consumers are willing to pay for the quantity the monopolist produces.

- To determine a monopolist's profit, first determine its output (where $MC = MR$). Then determine its price and average total cost at that output level. The difference between price and average total cost at the profit-maximizing level of output is profit per unit. Multiply this by output to find total profit.

- If a monopolist can (1) identify groups of customers who have different elasticities of demand, (2) separate them in some way, and (3) limit their ability to resell its product between groups, it can price discriminate.

- A price-discriminating monopolist earns more profit than a normal monopolist because it can charge a higher price

to those with less elastic demands and a lower price to those with more elastic demands.

- Because monopolists reduce output and charge a price that is higher than marginal cost, monopolies create a welfare loss to society.

- Three important barriers to entry are natural ability, increasing returns to scale, and government restrictions.

- Natural monopolies exist in industries with strong economies of scale. Because their average total costs are always falling, it is more efficient for one firm to produce all the output.

- The competitive price is impossible in a natural monopoly because marginal cost is always below average total cost. No firm would enter an industry where not even normal (zero economic) profit can be made.

- Normative arguments against monopoly include the following: (1) monopolies are inconsistent with freedom, (2) the distributional effects of monopoly are unfair, and (3) monopolies encourage people to waste time and money trying to get monopolies.

Key Terms

monopoly   *(261)*   natural monopoly   *(273)*   patent   *(274)*   price discriminate   *(269)*

Questions for Thought and Review

1. Demonstrate graphically the profit-maximizing positions for a perfect competitor and a monopolist. How do they differ?

2. Monopolists differ from perfect competitors because monopolists make a profit. True or false? Why?

3. Why is marginal revenue below average revenue for a monopolist?

4. Explain the effects on college education of the development of a teaching machine that you plug into a student's brain and that makes the student understand everything. How would your answer differ if a college could monopolize production of this machine?

5. Say you place a lump sum tax (a tax that is treated as a fixed cost) on a monopolist. How will that affect her output and pricing decisions?

6. A monopolist is selling fish. But if the fish don't sell, they rot. What will be the likely elasticity at the point on the demand curve at which the monopolist sets the price?

7. Provide a price discrimination argument for the existence of the four unexplained examples of price discrimination in the text.

8. Airlines are always running sales. On closer look, however, existing fares can be cheaper than restricted flights. What accounts for the practice of advertising "bargain" fares that may not be the lowest fare available? What conditions in the airline market make this practice possible?

9. Demonstrate the welfare loss created by a monopoly.

10. Will the welfare loss from a monopolist with a perfectly elastic marginal cost curve be greater or less than the welfare loss from a monopolist with an upward-sloping marginal cost curve?

11. In the late 1990s, the Government Accounting Office reported that airlines block new carriers at major airports. What effect does this have on fares and the number of flights at those airports? How much are airlines willing to spend to control the use of gates to block new carriers?

12. Copyrights provide authors with a monopoly. What effect would eliminating copyrights have on the price and output of textbooks? Should copyrights be eliminated?

13. How is efficiency related to the number of firms in an industry characterized by strong economies of scale?

Problems and Exercises

1. A monopolist with a straight-line demand curve finds that it can sell two units at $12 each or 12 units at $2 each. Its fixed cost is $20 and its marginal cost is constant at $3 per unit.
   a. Draw the MC, ATC, MR, and demand curves for this monopolist.
   b. At what output level would the monopolist produce?
   c. At what output level would a perfectly competitive firm produce?

2. State what's wrong with the following graphs:

(a)

(b)

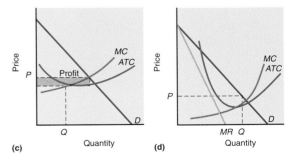

(c)

(d)

3. Wyeth-Ayerst Laboratories developed Norplant, a long-acting contraceptive, in the early 1990s. In the United States, the firm priced the contraceptive at $350, and in other countries, the firm priced it at $23.
   a. Why would the firm price it differently in different countries?
   b. Was the pricing fair?
   c. What do you think will happen to the price over time? Why?

4. Assume your city government has been contracting with a single garbage collection firm that has been granted an exclusive franchise, or sole right to pick up trash within the entire city limits. However, it has been proposed that the companies be allowed to compete for business with residents on an individual basis. The city government has estimated the price residents are willing to pay for various numbers of garbage collections per month and the total costs per resident as shown in the following table.

Pickup (Q)	Price per Pickup (Demand)	Total Revenue (TR)	Marginal Revenue (MR)	Total Cost (TC)	Marginal Cost (MC)	Average Total Cost (ATC)
0	$4.20	0	—	$ 3.20	—	—
1	$3.80	___	___	$ 4.20	___	___
2	$3.40	___	___	$ 5.60	___	___
3	$3.00	___	___	$ 7.80	___	___
4	$2.60	___	___	$10.40	___	___
5	$2.20	___	___	$13.40	___	___
6	$1.90	___	___	$16.80	___	___

a. What are the fixed costs per month of garbage collection per resident?

b. Considering that the current garbage collection firm the city has contracted with has a monopoly in garbage collection services, what is the current number of collections residents receive per month and the price charged residents for each collection? What is the economic profit received from each resident by the monopoly firm?

c. If competitive bidding were allowed and therefore a competitive market for garbage collection services developed, what would be the number of collections per month and the price charged residents per collection? What is the economic profit received from each resident by the competitive firms?

d. Based on the above analysis, should the city government allow competitive bidding? Why? Would you ex-

pect there to be any quality differences between the monopolistic and competitive trash collection firms?

5. Econocompany is under investigation by the U.S. Department of Justice for violating antitrust laws. The government decides that Econocompany has a natural monopoly and that, if it is to keep its business, it must sell at a price equal to marginal cost. Econocompany says that it can't do that and hires you to explain to the government why it can't.

a. You do so in reference to the following graph.

b. What price would it charge if it were unregulated?

c. What price would you advise that it should be allowed to charge?

6. New York City has issued 11,787 taxi licenses, called *medallions*, and has not changed that number since 1937.

a. What does that limitation likely do to the price of taxi medallions?

b. In the early 1990s, the New York City Taxi Commission promulgated a rule that required single-cab medallion owners to drive their cabs full-time. What will that rule do to the price of the medallion?

c. If New York City increased the number of medallions by 1,000, selling the additional 1,000 at the market rate, and gave half the proceeds to owners of exising medallions, what would happen to the price of medallions?

d. What would happen to the wealth of existing medallion owners?

Web Questions

1. In the late 1990s Congress passed a law allowing groups of states to establish dairy compacts. One is the Northeast Dairy Compact Commission. Go to its home page at www.dairycompact.org and use the information you find to answer the following questions:

a. What is the mission of the Northeast Dairy Compact Commission?

b. What do you think happened to the price of milk after this commission was established?

c. What are the welfare effects of the Commission according to the standard model? What might the standard model be missing?

2. Go to the Bionomics Institute's home page at www.bionomics.org and search for an article entitled "Vitamin B: Your Daily Dose of Bionomics" to answer the following questions about natural monopoly:

a. What is a natural monopoly?

b. What criticism does Gary Becker have about the standard model of natural monopoly?

c. What does this alternative view of natural monopoly suggest about government regulation of natural monopoly?

Answers to Margin Questions

1. If you doodle too much, your doodles will become worthless. Besides, if you want to pass the next test you have to study. *(262)*

2. At output 4, the marginal cost of $12 (between $8 and $16) equals the marginal revenue of $12 (between $15 and $9), making it the profit-maximizing output. It has the highest total profit, $34. *(264)*

3. To determine the profit-maximizing price and output, one must determine where the marginal revenue curve equals marginal cost. So one must first draw the marginal revenue curve and see where it intersects marginal cost. That intersection determines the quantity, as in the graph below. Carrying the line up to the demand curve determines the price. *(265)*

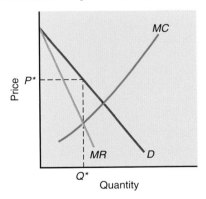

4. A monopolist produces less output than a perfectly competitive firm because it takes into account the fact that increasing output will lower the price of all previous units. *(266)*

5. To determine profit, follow the following four steps: (1) draw the marginal revenue curve, (2) find the level of output where MC = MR indicated in the graph below by Q*, (3) find the price the monopolist would charge indicated by P* and extend a horizontal line from the demand curve at that price to the price axis, (4) determine the average total cost at Q* shown by C* and extend a horizontal line from the ATC curve at that cost to the price axis. The box created is the

monopolist's profit. The profit is the shaded box shown in the graph below. *(267)*

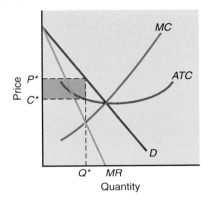

6. A price-discriminating monopolist makes a greater profit than a normal monopolist because a price-discriminating monopolist is able to charge a higher price to those consumers who have less elastic demands. *(270)*

7. Area C represents the profit going to a monopolist. It is not considered a loss since, while consumers lose it, monopolists gain it. It is a redistribution of resources rather than an efficiency loss. *(270)*

8. The marginal cost curve for an industry that exhibits strong economies of scale is always below average total costs. Therefore, the competitive price, where P = MC, will always result in losses for firms. Firms would not enter into such an industry and there would be no supply. *(273)*

9. The government gives out patents to encourage research and development of new products. This suggests that the public and government believe that certain monopolies have overriding social value. *(274)*

10. A likely explanation for medicinal drugs being sold at a much lower cost for animals than for human beings is differing elasticities of demand. The demand for drugs for human beings is highly inelastic, whereas the demand for medicinal drugs for animals is elastic. When there is a price-discriminating monopolist for these drugs, those with more inelastic demands are charged higher prices. *(275)*

The Algebra of Competitive and Monopolistic Firms

In the Appendix to Chapter 5, I presented the algebra relevant to supply and demand. To relate that algebra to competitive firms, all you must remember is that the market supply curve equals the marginal cost curve for the competitive industry. Let's review it briefly.

Say that marginal costs, and thus market supply, for the industry is given by

$$P = 2Q_S + 4$$

Let's also say that the market demand curve is

$$Q_D = 28 - \tfrac{1}{4}P$$

To determine equilibrium price and quantity in a competitive market, you must equate quantity supplied and quantity demanded and solve for price. First, rewrite the marginal cost equation with quantity supplied on the left:

$$Q_S = \tfrac{1}{2}MC - 2$$

Then set quantity demanded equal to quantity supplied and $MC = P$. Then solve for equilibrium price:

$$Q_S = Q_D \Rightarrow 28 - \tfrac{1}{4}P = \tfrac{1}{2}P - 2$$
$$112 - P = 2P - 8$$
$$3P = 120$$
$$P = 40$$

Thus, the equilibrium price is $40. Competitive firms take this price as given and produce up until their marginal cost equals price. The industry as a whole produces 18 units.

Now let's consider the algebra relevant for a monopolistic firm. In the monopolistic case, supply and demand are not enough to determine where the monopolist will produce. The monopolist will produce where marginal revenue equals marginal cost. But, for the monopolist, the industry demand curve is the demand curve, which means that in order to determine where the monopolist will produce, we must determine the marginal revenue curve that goes along with the above demand curve. There are two ways to do that.

First, if you know calculus you can determine the marginal revenue curve in the following manner: Since marginal revenue tells us how much total revenue will change with each additional unit produced, you first specify the demand curve in terms of quantity produced.

$$P = 112 - 4Q$$

Since $TR = PQ$ we can multiply this by Q to get total revenue. Doing so gives us:

$$TR = PQ = 112Q - 4Q^2$$

To find marginal revenue, take the first derivative of total revenue with respect to Q.

$$P = 112 - 8Q$$

Second, if you don't know calculus, all you need to remember is the trick shown in a box in the chapter on how to graph the marginal revenue curve. Remember, the marginal revenue curve starts at the same price as the demand curve and bisects the quantity axis at one-half the value of the quantity axis intercept of the demand curve. The marginal revenue curve, because it bisects the quantity axis at one-half the value of the quantity axis intercept of the accompanying demand curve, must fall twice as fast as the market demand curve. That is, its slope is twice the slope of the market demand curve.

Knowing that its slope is twice the market demand curve slope, you can write the marginal revenue curve with the same price axis intercept as the demand curve and a slope of two times the slope of the demand curve. (Warning: this only works with linear demand curves.) The price-axis intercept of the demand curve is the value of P where Q equals 0: 112. The quantity-axis intercept of the demand curve is the value of Q where P equals 0: 28. So, the marginal revenue curve has a price-axis intercept at 112 and a quantity-axis intercept at 14. Mathematically, such a curve is represented by

$$P = 112 - (112/14)P$$

or

$$P = 112 - 8Q$$

Now that we've determined the monopolist's marginal revenue curve, we can determine its equilibrium quantity by setting $MR = MC$ and solving for Q. Doing so gives us:

$$112 - 8Q = 2Q + 4$$
$$-10Q = -108$$
$$Q = 10.8$$

The monopolist then charges the price consumers are willing to pay for that quantity. Mathematically, substitute 10.8 into the demand equation and solve for price:

$$P = 112 - 4(10.8)$$
$$P = \$68.80$$

Comparing the price and quantity produced by a monopolist and those of a competitive industry shows that the monopolist charges a higher price and produces a lower output.

Questions for Thought and Review

1. The market demand curve is $Q_D = 50 - P$. The marginal cost curve is $MC = 4Q + 6$.
    a. Assuming the marginal cost curve is for a competitive industry as a whole, find the profit-maximizing level of output and price.
    b. Assuming the marginal cost curve is for only one firm which comprises the entire market, find the profit-maximizing level of output and price.
    c. Compare the two results.

2. The market demand curve is $Q_D = 160 - 4P$. A monopolist's total cost curve is $TC = 6Q^2 + 15Q + 50$.
    a. Find the profit-maximizing level of output and price for a monopolist.
    b. Find its average cost at that level of output.
    c. Find its profit at that level of output.

3. Suppose fixed costs for the monopolist in question 2 increases by 52.
    a. Find the profit-maximizing level of output and price for a monopolist.
    b. Find its average cost at that level of output.
    c. Find its profit at that level of output.

4. The market demand curve is $Q_D = 12 - \frac{1}{3}P$. Costs do not vary with output.
    a. Find the profit-maximizing level of output and price for a monopolist.
    b. Find the profit-maximizing level of output and price for a competitive industry.

Monopolistic Competition, Oligopoly, and Strategic Pricing

13

After reading this chapter, you should be able to:

- Describe two methods of determining market structure.

- List the four distinguishing characteristics of monopolistic competition.

- Demonstrate graphically the equilibrium of a monopolistic competitor.

- State the central element of oligopoly.

- Explain why decisions in the cartel model depend on market share and decisions in the contestable market model depend on barriers to entry.

- Illustrate a strategic decision facing a duopolist using the prisoner's dilemma.

Competition, you know, is a lot like chastity.
It is widely praised, but alas, too little practiced.

Carol Tucker

As soon as economists start talking about real-world competition, market structure becomes a focus of the discussion. **Market structure** refers to *the physical characteristics of the market within which firms interact.* It involves the number of firms in the market and the barriers to entry. Monopoly and competition are the two polar cases of market structure. Real-world markets generally fall in between, and it is essential to introduce briefly two market structures between perfect competition and monopoly: monopolistic competition and oligopoly. They not only provide you with a sense of how the models can apply to the real world; but also help cement in your mind the concepts introduced in Chapter 12.

Perfect competition has an almost infinite number of firms; monopoly has one firm. **Monopolistic competition** is *a market structure in which there are many firms selling differentiated products; there are few barriers to entry.* **Oligopoly** is *a market structure in which there are only a few firms; there are often significant barriers to entry.*

In monopolistic competition, firms' decisions are independent; in oligopoly, firms' decisions are interdependent.

THE PROBLEMS OF DETERMINING MARKET STRUCTURE

Any estimate of the distribution of market structures must be treated with care. Defining an industry is a complicated task—inevitably, numerous arbitrary decisions must be made. Similarly, defining the relevant market of a given industry is complicated. For example, there are fewer than 12,000 banks in the United States, and banking is considered reasonably competitive. However a particular small town may have only one or two banks, so there will be a monopoly or oligopoly with respect to banks in that town. Is the United States or the town the relevant market? The same argument exists when we think of international competition. Many firms sell in international markets and, while a group of firms may compose an oligopoly in the United States, the international market might be more accurately characterized by monopolistic competition.

Another dimension of the definitional problem concerns deciding what is to be included in an industry. If you define the industry as "the transportation industry," there are many firms. If you define it as "the urban transit industry," there are fewer firms; if you define it as "the commuter rail industry," there are still fewer firms. Similarly with the geographic dimension of industry. There's more competition in the global market than in the local market. The narrower the definition, the fewer the firms.

Classifying Industries

One of the ways in which economists classify markets is by cross-price elasticities (the responsiveness of the change in the demand for a good to change in the price of a related good). Industrial organization economist F. M. Sherer has suggested the following rule of thumb: When two goods have a cross-price elasticity greater than or equal to 3, they can be regarded as belonging to the same market.

The **North American Industry Classification System (NAICS)** is *an industry classification that categorizes firms by type of economic activity and groups firms with like production processes.* It was adopted by the United States, Mexico, and Canada in 1997 and replaces the Standardized Industrial Classification (SIC) codes developed in the 1930s. All firms are placed into 20 broadly defined two-digit sectors. These two-digit sectors are further subdivided into three-digit subsectors, four-digit industry groupings, five-digit industries, and six-digit national industry groupings. Each subgrouping becomes more and more narrowly defined. Table 13-1 lists the 20 sectors and shows the subgroupings for one sector, Information, to give you an idea of what's included in each.

Q-1 Which would have more output: the two-digit industry 21 or the four-digit industry 2111? Explain your reasoning.

When economists talk about industry structure, they generally talk about industries in the four- to six-digit subsector groupings in the United States. This is a convention. Economists are often called on to give expert testimony in court cases, and if an economist wants to argue that an industry is more competitive than its opponents say it is, he or she challenges this convention of using a four- to six-digit classification of industry, asserting that the classification is arbitrary (which it is) and that the relevant market should be the two- to three-digit classification.

Table 13-1   Industry Groupings in the North American Industry Classification System

Two-Digit Sectors	Three- to Six-Digit Subsectors
11 Agriculture, forestry, fishing, and hunting	
21 Mining	
22 Utilities	
23 Construction	
31–33 Manufacturing	
42 Wholesale trade	
44–45 Retail trade	
48–49 Transportation and warehousing	513 Broadcasting and telecommunications
51 Information	5133 Telecommunications
52 Finance and insurance	51332 Wireless telecommunications carriers, except satellite
53 Real estate and rental and leasing	513321 Paging
54 Professional, scientific, and technical services	
Management of companies and enterprises	
56 Administrative and support, and waste management and remediation services	
Education services	
Health care and social assistance	
71 Arts, entertainment, and recreation	
Accommodation and food services	
81 Other services (except public administration)	
Public administration	

Determining Industry Structure

To measure industry structure, economists use one of two methods: the concentration ratio or a Herfindahl index.

A **concentration ratio** is *the percentage of the total industry sales that the top firms of the industry have*. The most commonly used concentration ratio is the four-firm concentration ratio. For example, a four-firm concentration ratio of 60 tells you that the top four firms in the industry produce 60 percent of the industry's output. The higher the ratio, the closer the industry is to an oligopolistic or monopolistic type of market structure.

The **Herfindahl index** is *an index of market concentration calculated by adding the squared value of the individual market shares of all the firms in the industry*. For example, say that 10 firms in the industry each have 10 percent of the market:

Herfindahl index $= 10^2 + 10^2 + 10^2 + 10^2 + 10^2 + 10^2 + 10^2 + 10^2 + 10^2 + 10^2 = 1,000$

The Herfindahl index gives higher weights to the largest firms in the industry because it squares market shares.

The two measures can differ because of their construction, but generally if the concentration ratio is high, so is the Herfindahl index. Table 13-2 presents the four-firm concentration ratio and the Herfindahl index of selected industries.

The Herfindahl index plays an important role in government policy; it is used as a rule of thumb by the U.S. Department of Justice in determining whether an industry is sufficiently competitive to allow a merger between two large firms in the industry. If the Herfindahl index is less than 1,000, the Department of Justice assumes the industry is sufficiently competitive, and it doesn't look more closely at the merger. We'll discuss this in more detail in Chapter 16.

A Herfindahl index is a method used by economists to classify how competitive an industry is.

Because it squares market shares, the Herfindahl index gives more weight to firms with large market shares than does the concentration ratio measure.

Table 13-2 Concentration Ratios and the Herfindahl Index

Industry	Four-Firm Concentration Ratio	Herfindahl Index
Meat packing	29	325
Canned fruits and vegetables	21	214
Cereal breakfast foods	86	NA
Women's and misses' dresses	6	24
Book publishing	17	190
Greeting card publishing	84	2,840
Soap and detergent	60	1,306
Men's footwear	28	378
Women's footwear	38	492
Bolts, nuts, rivets, and washers	13	102
Computing equipment	43	793
Radio and TV sets	49	751
Burial caskets	52	1,247

Conglomerate Firms and Bigness

Neither the four-firm concentration ratio nor the Herfindahl index gives us a picture of corporations' bigness. That's because many corporations are conglomerates—companies that span a variety of unrelated industries. For example, a conglomerate might produce both shoes and automobiles.

To see that concentration ratios are not an index of bigness, say there were only 11 firms in the entire United States, each with a 9 percent share of each industry. Both indexes would classify the U.S. economy as unconcentrated, but many people would seriously doubt whether that were the case. Little work has been done on classifying conglomerates or in determining whether they have any effect on an industry's performance.

The Importance of Classifying Industry Structure

A basic rule of economics is that less concentrated industries are more likely to resemble perfectly competitive markets. In terms of formal modeling it's important to classify industries because the number of firms in an industry plays an important role in determining whether firms will tend to explicitly take other firms' actions into account. In monopolistic competition, there are so many firms that individual firms tend not to explicitly take into account rival firms' likely responses to their decisions. Collusion is difficult. In oligopoly there are fewer firms, and each firm is more likely to explicitly engage in **strategic decision making**—*taking explicit account of a rival's expected response to a decision you are making*. In oligopolies all decisions, including pricing decisions, are strategic decisions. Collusion is much easier. Thus, one distinguishes between monopolistic competition and oligopoly by whether or not firms explicitly take into account competitors' reactions to their decisions.

Why is the distinction important? Because it determines whether economists can model and predict the price and output of an industry. Nonstrategic decision making can be predicted relatively accurately if individuals behave rationally. Strategic decision making is much more difficult to predict, even if people behave rationally. What one person does depends on what he or she expects other people to do, which in turn depends on what others expect the one person to do. Consistent with this distinction, economists' model of monopolistic competition has a definite prediction. A model of monopolistic

Q-2 If the four-firm concentration ratio of an industry is 60 percent, what is the highest Herfindahl index that industry could have? What is the lowest?

Oligopolies take into account the reactions of other firms; monopolistic competitors do not.

Q-3 Your study partner, Jean, has just said that monopolistic competitors use strategic decision making. How would you respond?

Market structures change over time. Take, for instance, the automobile industry, which has always been used as the classic oligopoly model. Starting in the 1970s, however, foreign automakers have made large inroads into the U.S. market and have added new competition to it. Foreign companies such as Honda, Nissan, and Toyota have entered the U.S. market, as seen in the accompanying pie chart, which lists major automobile companies and their market shares.

The four-firm concentration ratio is over 75 percent, so the industry is still

APPLYING THE TOOLS

Foreign Competitive Oligopolies

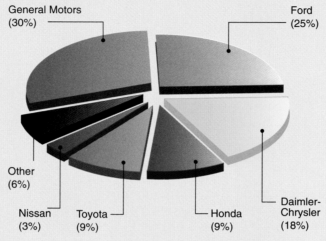

classified as an oligopoly. GM still considers what Ford's and Chrysler's reactions will be, but with the addition of foreign competition, there are getting to be too many firms for one firm to consider the reactions of all the other firms. The auto industry is becoming more monopolistically competitive.

Such change in industry structure is to be expected. Monopoly and oligopoly create the possibility that firms can make above-normal profits. Above-normal profits invite entry, and unless there are entry barriers, the result will likely be a breakdown in that monopoly or oligopoly.

General Motors (30%)   **Ford (25%)**   **Other (6%)**   **Nissan (3%)**   **Toyota (9%)**   **Honda (9%)**   **Daimler-Chrysler (18%)**

Market Shares in the Automotive Industry
Source: *Automotive News, 2000.*

competition will tell us: Here's how much will be produced and here's how much will be charged. Economists' models of oligopoly don't have a definite prediction. There are no unique price and output decisions at which an oligopoly will rationally arrive; there are a variety of rational oligopoly decisions, and a variety of oligopoly models.

CHARACTERISTICS OF MONOPOLISTIC COMPETITION

The four distinguishing characteristics of monopolistic competition are:

1. Many sellers.
2. Differentiated products.
3. Multiple dimensions of competition.
4. Easy entry of new firms in the long run.

Let's consider each in turn.

Many Sellers

When there are only a few sellers, it's reasonable to explicitly take into account your competitors' reaction to the price you set. When there are many sellers, it isn't. In monopolistic competition firms don't take into account rivals' reactions. Here's an example. There are many types of soap: Ivory, Irish Spring, Yardley's Old English, and so on. So when Ivory decides to run a sale, it won't spend a lot of time thinking about Old English's reaction. There are so many firms that one firm can't concern itself with the reaction of any specific firm. The soap industry is characterized by monopolistic competition. In contrast, there are only a few major automobile firms, so when GM sets its price, it will explicitly consider what Ford's reaction may be. If GM raises its price, will Ford go along and also raise price? Or will it hold its price at its current level and try to sell its cars on the basis of lower prices? The automobile industry is an oligopoly.

The fact that there are many sellers in monopolistic competition also makes collusion difficult since, when there are many firms, getting all of them to act as one is difficult. In economists' models monopolistically competitive firms are assumed to act independently.

Product Differentiation

The "many sellers" characteristic gives monopolistic competition its competitive aspect. Product differentiation gives it its monopolistic aspect. In a monopolistically competitive market, the goods that are sold aren't homogeneous, as in perfect competition; they are differentiated slightly. Irish Spring soap is slightly different from Ivory, which in turn is slightly different from Yardley's Old English.

So in one sense each firm has a monopoly in the good it sells. But that monopoly is fleeting; it is based on advertising to let people know, and to convince them, that one firm's good is different from the goods of competitors. The good may or may not really be different. Bleach differs little from one brand to another, yet buying Clorox makes many people feel "safe" that they're getting pure bleach. I generally don't buy it; I generally buy generic bleach. Ketchup, however, while made from the same basic ingredients no matter what brand, differs among types (in my view).

 13.1

Because a monopolistic competitor has some monopoly power, advertising to increase that monopoly power (and hence increase the firm's profits) makes sense as long as the marginal benefit of advertising exceeds the marginal cost. Despite the fact that their goods are similar but differentiated, to fit economists' monopolistically competitive model, firms must make their decisions as if they had no effect on other firms.

Multiple Dimensions of Competition

In perfect competition, price is the only dimension on which firms compete; in monopolistic competition, competition takes many forms. Product differentiation reflects firms' attempt to compete on perceived attributes; advertising is another form competition takes. Other dimensions of competition include service and distribution outlets. These multiple dimensions of competition make it much harder to analyze a specific industry, but the alternative methods of competition follow the same two general decision rules as price competition:

In monopolistic competition, competition takes many forms.

- Compare marginal costs and marginal benefits; and
- Change that dimension of competition until marginal costs equal marginal benefits.

Ease of Entry of New Firms in the Long Run

The last condition a monopolistically competitive market must meet is that entry must be relatively easy; that is, there must be no significant entry barriers. Barriers to entry create the potential for long-run economic profit and prevent competitive pressures from pushing price down to average total cost. In monopolistic competition if there were long-run economic profits, other firms would enter until no economic profit existed.

OUTPUT, PRICE, AND PROFIT OF A MONOPOLISTIC COMPETITOR

Although a full analysis of the multiple dimensions of monopolistic competition cannot be compressed into two dimensions, a good introduction can be gained by considering it within the standard two-dimensional (price, quantity) graph.

To do so we simply consider the four characteristics of monopolistic competition and see what implication they have for the analysis. First, we recognize that the firm has some monopoly power; therefore, a monopolistic competitor faces a downward-sloping demand curve. The downward-sloping demand curve means that in making decisions about output, the monopolistic competitor will, as will a monopolist, use a marginal revenue curve that is below price. At its profit-maximizing output, marginal cost will be less than price (not equal to price as it would be for a perfect competitor). We consider that case in Figure 13-1(a).

The monopolistic competitor faces the demand curve D, marginal revenue curve MR, and marginal cost curve MC. This demand curve is its portion of the total market demand curve. Using the $MC = MR$ rule discussed in Chapter 12, you can see that the firm will choose output level Q_M (because that's the level of output at which marginal revenue intersects marginal cost). Having determined output, we extend a dotted line up to the demand curve and see that the firm will set a price equal to P_M. This price exceeds marginal cost. So far all we've done is to reproduce the monopolist's decision.

Where does the competition come in? Competition implies zero economic profit in the long run. (If there's profit, a new competitor will enter the market, decreasing the existing firms' demand [shifting it to the left].) In long-run equilibrium a perfect competitor makes only a normal profit. Economic profits are determined by ATC, not by MC, so the competition part of monopolistic competition tells us where the average total cost curve must be at the long-run equilibrium output. It must be equal to price, and it will be equal to price only if the ATC curve is tangent to the demand curve at the output the firm chooses. We add that average total cost curve to the MC, MR, and de-

Q-4 How do the equilibrium for a monopoly and for a monopolistic competitor differ?

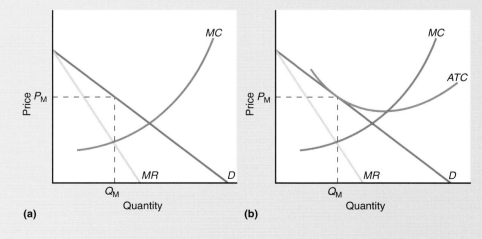

Figure 13-1 (a and b)
Monopolistic Competition

In **(a)** you can see that a monopolistically competitive firm prices in the same manner as a monopolist. It sets quantity where marginal revenue equals marginal cost. In **(b)** you can see that the monopolistic competitor is not only a monopolist but also a competitor. Competition implies zero economic profit in the long run. Economic profits are determined by the average total cost (ATC) curve. In long-run equilibrium, ATC must be equal to price. It will be equal to price only if the ATC curve is tangent to the demand curve at the output the firm chooses.

mand curves in Figure 13-1(b). Profit or loss, I hope you remember, is determined by the difference between price and average total cost at the quantity the firm chooses.

To give this condition a little more intuitive meaning, let's say, for instance, that the monopolistically competitive firm is making a profit. This profit would set two adjustments in motion. First, it would attract new entrants. Some of the firm's customers would then defect, and its portion of the market demand curve would decrease. Second, to try to protect its profits the firm would likely increase expenditures on product differentiation and advertising to offset that entry. (There would be an All New, Really New, Widget campaign.) These expenditures would shift its average total cost curve up. These two adjustments would continue until the profits disappeared and the new demand curve is tangent to the new average total cost curve. A monopolistically competitive firm can make no long-run economic profit.

Comparing Monopolistic Competition with Perfect Competition

If both the monopolistic competitor and the perfect competitor make zero economic profit in the long run, it might seem that, in the long run at least, they're identical. They aren't, however. The perfect competitor perceives its demand curve as perfectly elastic, and the zero economic profit condition means that it produces at the minimum of the average total cost curve where the marginal cost curve equals price. We demonstrate that case in Figure 13-2(a).

The monopolistic competitor faces a downward-sloping demand curve for its differentiated product. It produces where the marginal cost curve equals the marginal revenue curve, and not where MC equals price. In equilibrium, price exceeds marginal

> The difference between a monopolist and a monopolistic competitor is in the position of the average total cost curve in long-run equilibrium.

Figure 13-2 (a and b)   A Comparison of Perfect and Monopolistic Competition

The perfect competitor perceives its demand curve as perfectly elastic, and zero economic profit means that it produces at the minimum of the *ATC* curve, as represented in (**a**). A monopolistic competitor, on the other hand, faces a downward-sloping demand curve and produces where marginal cost equals marginal revenue, as represented in (**b**). In long-run equilibrium the *ATC* curve is tangent to the demand curve at that level, which is *not* at the minimum point of the *ATC* curve. The monopolistic competitor produces Q_M at price P_M. A perfect competitor with the same marginal cost curve would produce Q_C at price P_C.

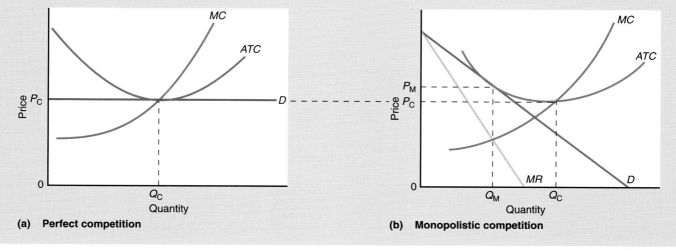

(a) Perfect competition   **(b) Monopolistic competition**

cost. The average total cost curve of a monopolistic competitor is tangent to the demand curve at that output level, which cannot be at the minimum point of the average total cost curve since the demand curve is sloping downward. The minimum point of the average total cost curve (where a perfect competitor produces) is at a higher output (Q_C) than that of the monopolistic competitor (Q_M). I demonstrate the monopolistically competitive equilibrium in Figure 13-2(b) to allow you to compare monopolistic competition with perfect competition.

The perfect competitor in long-run equilibrium produces at a point where $MC = P = ATC$. At that point, ATC is at its minimum. A monopolistic competitor produces at a point where $MC = MR$. Price is higher than marginal cost. For a monopolistic competitor in long-run equilibrium:

> For a monopolistic competitor in long-run equilibrium, $(P = ATC) \geq (MC = MR)$.

$$(P = ATC) \geq (MC = MR)$$

At that point, ATC is *not* at its minimum.

What does this distinction between a monopolistically competitive industry and a perfectly competitive industry mean in practice? It means that for a monopolistic competitor, since increasing output lowers average cost, increasing market share is a relevant concern. If only the monopolistic competitor could expand its market, it could do better. For a perfect competitor, increasing output offers no benefit in the form of lower average cost. A perfect competitor would have no concern about market share (the firm's percentage of total sales in the market).

Comparing Monopolistic Competition with Monopoly

An important difference between a monopolist and a monopolistic competitor is in the position of the average total cost curve in long-run equilibrium. For a monopolist, the average total cost curve can be, but need not be, at a position below price so that the monopolist makes a long-run economic profit. The average total cost curve of a monopolistic competitor must be tangent to the demand curve at the price and output chosen by the monopolistic competitor. No long-run economic profit is possible.

Advertising and Monopolistic Competition

While firms in a perfectly competitive market have no incentive to advertise (since they can sell all they want at the market price), monopolistic competitors have a strong incentive. That's because their products are differentiated from the others; advertising plays an important role in providing that differentiation.

> Goals of advertising include shifting the firm's demand curve to the right and making it more inelastic.

Goals of Advertising Goals of advertising include shifting the firm's demand curve to the right and making it more inelastic. Advertising works by providing consumers with information about the firm's product and by making people want only a specific brand. That allows the firm to sell more, to charge a higher price, or to enjoy a combination of the two. It is advantageous to the firm if the marginal revenue of advertising exceeds the marginal cost of advertising. Advertising has two effects: It shifts the demand curve to the right, and it shifts the average total cost curve up.

When many firms are advertising, the advertising might be done less to shift the demand curve out than to keep the demand curve where it is—to stop consumers from shifting to a competitor's product. In either case, firms advertise to move the demand curve further out and to make it more inelastic than it would be if the firms weren't advertising.

Does Advertising Help or Hurt Society? Our perception of products (the degree of trust we put in them) is significantly influenced by advertising. Think of the following pairs of goods:

13.2

Rolex	Timex
Cheerios	Oat Circles
Clorox bleach	generic bleach
Bayer	generic aspirin

Each of these names conveys a sense of what it is and how much trust we put in the product, and that determines how much we're willing to pay for it. For example, most people would pay more for Cheerios than for Oat Circles. Each year firms in the United States spend more than $150 billion on advertising. A 30-second commercial during the Super Bowl can cost as much as $3 million. That advertising increases firms' costs but also differentiates their products.

Are we as consumers better off or worse off with differentiated products? That's difficult to say. There's a certain waste in much of the differentiation that occurs. It shows up in the graph by the fact that monopolistic competitors don't produce at the minimum point of their average total cost curve. But there's also a sense of trust that we get from buying names we know and in having goods that are slightly different from one another. I'm a sophisticated consumer who knows that there's little difference between generic aspirin and Bayer aspirin. Yet sometimes I buy Bayer aspirin even though it costs more.

Edward Chamberlin, who, together with Joan Robinson, was the originator of the description of monopolistic competition, believed that the difference between the cost of a perfect competitor and the cost of a monopolistic competitor was the cost of what he called "differentness."[1] If consumers are willing to pay that cost, then it's not a waste but, rather, it's a benefit to them.

We must be careful about drawing any implications from this analysis. Average total cost for a monopolistically competitive firm includes advertising and costs of differentiating a product. It's debatable whether we as consumers are better off with as much differentiation as we have, or whether we'd all be better off if all firms produced a generic product at a lower cost.

Q.5 Why do monopolistically competitive firms advertise and perfect competitors do not?

CHARACTERISTICS OF OLIGOPOLY

The central element of oligopoly is that there are a small number of firms in an industry so that, in any decision it makes, each firm must take into account the expected reaction of other firms. Oligopolistic firms are mutually interdependent and can be collusive or noncollusive.

Most industries in the United States have some oligopolistic elements. If you ask almost any businessperson whether he or she directly takes into account rivals' likely response, the answer you'll get is "In certain cases, yes; in others, no."

Most retail stores that you deal with are oligopolistic in your neighborhood or town, although by national standards they may be quite competitive. For example, how many grocery stores do you shop at? Do you think they keep track of what their competitors are doing? You bet. They keep a close eye on their competitors' prices and set their own accordingly.

Oligopolistic firms are mutually interdependent.

---

[1]Joan Robinson, a Cambridge, England, economist, called this the theory of imperfect competition, rather than the theory of monopolistic competition.

MODELS OF OLIGOPOLY BEHAVIOR

No single general model of oligopoly behavior exists. The reason is that an oligopolist can decide on pricing and output strategy in many possible ways, and there are no compelling grounds to characterize any of them as *the* oligopoly strategy. Although there are five or six formal models, I'll focus on two informal models of oligopoly behavior that give you insight into real-world problems rather than exercise your reasoning and modeling abilities as my earlier discussion did. The two models we'll consider are the cartel model and the contestable market model. These should give you a sense of how real-world oligopolistic pricing takes place.

Why, you ask, can't economists develop a simple formal model of oligopoly? The reason lies in the interdependence of oligopolists. Since there are few competitors, what one firm does specifically influences what other firms do, so an oligopolist's plan must always be a contingency or strategic plan. If my competitors act one way, I'll do X, but if they act another way, I'll do Y. Strategic interactions have a variety of potential outcomes rather than a single outcome such as shown in the formal models we discussed. An oligopolist spends enormous amounts of time guessing what its competitors will do, and it develops a strategy of how it will act accordingly.

The Cartel Model

A **cartel** is *a combination of firms that acts as if it were a single firm;* a cartel is a shared monopoly. If oligopolies can limit entry by other firms, they have a strong incentive to cartelize the industry and to act as a monopolist would, restricting output to a level that maximizes profit to the combination of firms. Thus, the **cartel model of oligopoly** is *a model that assumes that oligopolies act as if they were monopolists that have assigned output quotas to individual member firms of the oligopoly so that total output is consistent with joint profit maximization.* All firms follow a uniform pricing policy that serves their collective interest.

Since a monopolist makes the most profit that can be squeezed from a market, cartelization is the best strategy for an oligopoly. It requires each oligopolist to hold its production below what would be in its own interest were it not to collude with the others. Such explicit formal collusion is against the law in the United States, but informal collusion is allowed and oligopolies have developed a variety of methods to collude implicitly. Thus, the cartel model has some relevance.

The model has some problems, however. For example, various firms' interests often differ, so it isn't clear what the collective interest of the firms in the industry is. In many cases a single firm, often the largest or dominant firm, takes the lead in pricing and output decisions, and the other firms (which are often called *fringe firms*) follow suit, even though they might have preferred to adopt a different strategy.

This dominant-firm cartel model works only if the smaller firms face barriers to entry, or the dominant firm has significantly lower cost conditions. If that were not the case, the smaller firms would pick up an increasing share of the market, eliminating the dominant firm's monopoly. An example of such a dominant-firm market was the copier market in the 1960s and 1970s, in which Xerox set the price and other firms followed. That copier market also shows the temporary nature of such a market. As the firms became more competitive on cost and quality, Xerox's market share fell and the company lost its dominant position. The copier market is far more competitive today than it used to be.

In other cases the various firms meet—sometimes only by happenstance, at the golf course or at a trade association gathering—and arrive at a collective decision. In the

If oligopolies can limit the entry of other firms and form a cartel, they increase the profits going to the combination of firms in the cartel.

13.3

Q-6 Why is it difficult for firms in an industry to maintain a cartel?

United States meetings for this purpose are illegal, but they do occur. In yet other cases the firms engage in **implicit collusion**—*multiple firms make the same pricing decisions even though they have not explicitly consulted with one another.* They "just happen" to come to a collective decision.

In some cases firms collude implicitly—they just happen to make the same pricing decisions. This is not illegal.

Implicit Price Collusion Implicit price collusion, in which firms just happen to charge the same price but didn't meet to discuss price strategy, isn't against the law. Oligopolies often operate as close to the fine edge of the law as they can. For example, many oligopolistic industries allow a price leader to set the price, and then the others follow suit. The airline and steel industries take that route. Firms just happen to charge the same price or very close to the same price.

It isn't only in major industries that you see such implicit collusion. In small towns, you'll notice that most independent carpenters charge the same price. There's no explicit collusion, but were a carpenter to offer to work for less than the others, he or she would feel unwelcome at the local breakfast restaurant.

Or let's take another example: the Miami fish market where sport fishermen sell their catch at the dock. When I lived in Miami I often went to the docks to buy fresh fish. There were about 20 stands, all charging the same price. Price fluctuated, but it was by subtle agreement, and close to the end of the day the word would go out that the price could be reduced.

I got to know some of the sellers and asked them why they priced like that when it would be in their individual interest to set their own price. Their answer: "We like our boat and don't want it burned." They may have been talking in hyperbole, but social pressures play an important role in stabilizing prices in an oligopoly.

Cartels and Technological Change Even if all firms in the industry cooperate, other firms, unless they are prevented from doing so, can always enter the market with a technologically superior new product at the same price or with the same good at a lower price. It is important to remember that technological changes are constantly occurring, and that a successful cartel with high profits will provide incentives for significant technological change, which can eliminate demand for its monopolized product.

Why Are Prices Sticky? Informal collusion happens all the time in U.S. businesses. One characteristic of informal collusive behavior is that prices tend to be sticky. They don't change frequently, so the existence of informal collusion is an important reason why prices are sticky. But it's not the only reason.

Another reason is that firms don't explicitly collude, but they have certain expectations of other firms' reactions, which changes their perceived demand curves. Specifically, they perceive a kinked demand curve facing them. This kinked demand curve is used especially to explain why firms often do not use lower-price strategies to increase sales.

Let's go through the reasoning behind the kinked demand curve. If a firm increases its price, and the firm believes that other firms won't go along, its perceived demand curve for increasing price will be very elastic (D_1 in Figure 13-3). It will lose lots of business to the other firms that haven't raised their price. The relevant portions of its demand curve and its marginal revenue curve are shown in blue in Figure 13-3.

If it decreased its price, however, the firm assumes that all other firms would immediately match that decrease, so it would gain very few, if any, additional sales. A large fall in price would result in only a small increase in sales, so its demand is very inelastic (D_2 in Figure 13-3). This less elastic portion of the demand curve and the corresponding marginal revenue curve are shown in red in Figure 13-3.

Q.7 Is the demand curve as perceived by an oligopolist likely to be more or less elastic for a price increase or a price decrease?

Figure 13-3   The Kinked Demand Curve

One explanation of why prices are sticky is that firms face a kinked demand curve. When we draw the relevant marginal revenue curve for the kinked demand we see that the corresponding *MR* curve is discontinuous. It has a gap in it. Shifts in marginal costs between *c* and *d* will not change the price or the output that maximizes profits.

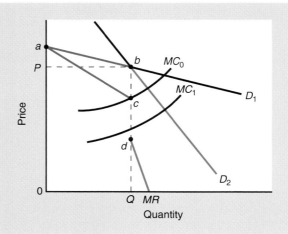

When the demand curve has a kink, the marginal revenue curve must have a gap.

Notice that when you put these two curves together you get a rather strange demand curve (it's kinked) and an even stranger marginal revenue curve (one with a gap). I didn't make a mistake in drawing the curves; that's the way they come out given the assumptions. When the demand curve has a kink, the marginal revenue curve must have a gap.

If firms do indeed perceive their demand curves to be kinked at the market price, we have another explanation of why prices tend to be sticky. Shifts in marginal cost (such as MC_0 to MC_1) will not change the firm's profit maximization position. A large shift in marginal cost is required before firms will change their price. Why should this be the case? The intuitive answer lies in the reason behind the kink. If the firm raises its price, other firms won't go along, so it will lose lots of market share. However, when the firm lowers price, other firms will go along and the firm won't gain market share. Thus, the firm has strong reasons not to change its price in either direction.

I should emphasize that the kinked demand curve is not a theory of oligopoly pricing. It does not say why the original price is what it is; the kinked demand curve is simply a theory of sticky prices.

The Contestable Market Model

In the contestable market model of oligopoly, pricing and entry decisions are based only on barriers to entry and exit, not on market structure. Thus, even if the industry contains only one firm, it could still be a competitive market if entry is open.

A second model of oligopoly is the *contestable market model*. The **contestable market model** is *a model of oligopoly in which barriers to entry and barriers to exit, not the structure of the market, determine a firm's price and output decisions*. Thus, it places the emphasis on entry and exit conditions, and says that the price that an oligopoly will charge will exceed the cost of production only if new firms cannot exit and enter the market. The higher the barriers, the more the price exceeds cost. Without barriers to entry or exit, the price an oligopolist sets will be equivalent to the competitive price. Thus, an industry that structurally looks like an oligopoly could set higher competitive prices and output levels.

Comparison of the Contestable Market Model and the Cartel Model

Because of the importance of social pressures in determining strategies of oligopolies, no one "oligopolistic model" exists. Oligopolies with a stronger ability to collude (i.e., more social pressures to prevent entry) are able to get closer to a monopolist solution. Equilibrium of oligopolies with weaker social pressures and less ability to prevent new entry is closer to the perfectly competitive solution. That's as explicit as we can be.

An oligopoly model can take two extremes: (1) the cartel model, in which an oligopoly sets a monopoly price; and (2) the contestable market model, in which an oligopoly with no barriers to entry sets a competitive price. Thus, we can say that an oligopoly's price will be somewhere between the competitive price and the monopolistic price. Other models of oligopolies give results in between these two.

Much of what happens in oligopoly pricing is highly dependent on the specific legal structure within which firms interact. In Japan, where large firms are specifically allowed to collude, we see Japanese goods selling for a much higher price than those same Japanese goods sell for in the United States. For example, you may well pay twice as much for a Japanese television in Japan as you would in the United States. From the behavior of Japanese firms, we get a sense of what pricing strategy U.S. oligopolists would follow in the absence of the restrictions placed on them by law.

Q.8 What are the two extremes an oligopoly model can take?

Strategic Pricing and Oligopoly

Notice that both the cartel model and the contestable market model use **strategic pricing** decisions—*firms set their price based on the expected reactions of other firms*. Strategic pricing and interdependence are central characteristics of oligopoly.

One can see the results of strategic decision making all the time. For example, consider a firm that announces that it will not be undersold—that it will match any competitor's lower price and will even go under it. Is that a pro-competitive strategy, leading to a low price? Or is it a strategy to increase collusive information and thereby prevent other firms from breaking implicit pricing agreements? Recent work in economics suggests that it is the latter.

Let's now see how a specific consideration of strategic pricing decisions shows that the cartel model and the contestable market model are related.

Strategic pricing and interdependence are central characteristics of an oligopoly.

New Entry as a Limit on the Cartelization Strategy One of the things that limits oligopolies from acting as a cartel is the threat from outside competition. The threat will tend to be more effective if this outside competitor is much larger than the firms in the oligopoly.

For example, small-town banks have a tendency to collude (implicitly, of course), offering lower interest to savers and charging higher interest to borrowers than big banks charge, even though their average costs aren't significantly higher. When I ask small-town banks why this is, they tell me that my perceptions are faulty and that I should mind my own business. But if a big bank, which couldn't care less about increasing the wealth of a small-town banker, enters the town and establishes a branch office, interest rates to savers seem to go up and interest rates to borrowers seem to go down. The big bank can add significant competition—competition that couldn't come from within the town.

On a national scale, the outside competition often comes from international firms. For example, implicit collusion among U.S. automobile firms led to foreign firms' entry into the U.S. automobile market. There are many such examples of this outside competition breaking down cartels with no barriers to entry. Thus, a cartel with no barriers to entry faces a long-run demand curve that's very elastic. This means that its price will be very close to its marginal cost and average cost. This is the same prediction that came from the contestable market theory.

Price Wars Whenever there's strategic decision making there's the possibility of a price war. Price wars are the result of strategic pricing decisions gone wild. Thus, in any oligopoly it's possible that firms can enter into a price war where prices fall below average total cost.

The reasons for such wars are varied. Since oligopolistic firms know their competitors, they can personally dislike them; sometimes a firm's goal can be simply to drive a disliked competitor out of business, even if that process hurts the firm itself. Passion and anger play roles in oligopoly pricing because interpersonal and interfirm relations are important.

Alternatively, a firm might follow a predatory pricing strategy—a strategy of pushing the price down temporarily to drive the other firm out of business to increase long-term profits. If the predatory pricing strategy is successful, the firm can charge an even higher price because potential entrants know that the existing firm will drive them out if they try to enter. It's this continual possibility that strategies can change that makes oligopoly prices so hard to predict.

GAME THEORY, OLIGOPOLY, AND STRATEGIC DECISION MAKING

The inability to come to an explicit conclusion about what price and quantity an oligopoly will choose doesn't mean that economic reasoning and principles don't apply to oligopoly. They do. Most oligopolistic strategic decision making is carried out with the implicit or explicit use of **game theory** (*the application of economic principles to interdependent situations*). Game theory is economic reasoning applied to decision making.

To give you a sense of game theory, I'll present the **prisoner's dilemma,** *a well-known game that demonstrates the difficulty of cooperative behavior in certain circumstances.* The standard prisoner's dilemma can be seen in the following example: Two suspects are caught and are interrogated separately. Each prisoner is offered the following options:

- If neither prisoner confesses, each will be given a 6-month sentence on a minor charge.

- If one prisoner confesses and the other does not, the one who confesses will go free and the other will be given a 10-year sentence.

- If they both confess, they'll each get a 5-year sentence.

What strategy will each choose? If neither can count on the other not to confess, the optimal strategy (the one that maximizes expected benefits) will be for each to confess, because each must assume the other will do the same. Confessing is the rational thing for each prisoner to do. That's why it's called the *prisoner's dilemma.* Trust gets one out of the prisoner's dilemma. If the prisoners can trust each other, the optimal strategy is not to confess, and they both get only a light sentence. But trust is a hard commodity to come by without an explicit enforcement mechanism.

In the prisoner's dilemma, where mutual trust gets each one out of the dilemma, confessing is the rational choice.

Prisoner's Dilemma and a Duopoly Example

13.4

The prisoner's dilemma has its simplest application to oligopoly when the oligopoly consists of only two firms. So let us consider the strategic decisions facing a "foam peanut" (packing material) **duopoly**—*an oligopoly with only two firms.* Let us assume that the average total cost and marginal cost of producing foam peanuts are the same for both firms, and are such that only two firms can exist in the industry. These costs are shown in Figure 13-4(a).

Assume that a production facility with a minimum efficient scale of 4,000 tons is the smallest that can be built. In Figure 13-4(b), the marginal costs are summed and the industry demand curve is drawn in a way that the competitive price is $500 per ton and the competitive output is 8,000 tons. The relevant industry marginal revenue curve is also drawn.

Figure 13-4 (a and b)   Firm and Industry Duopoly Cooperative Equilibrium

In (a) I show the marginal and average total cost curve for either firm in the duopoly. Thus to get the average and marginal cost for the industry, you double each. In (b) the industry marginal cost curve (the horizontal sum of the individual firms' marginal cost curves) is combined with the industry demand and marginal revenue curves. At the competitive solution for the industry, output is 8,000 and price is $500. As you can see in (a), at that price economic profits are zero. At the monopolistic solution, output is 6,000 and price is $600. As you can see in (a), ATC is $575 at an industry output of 6,000 (firm output of 3,000), so each firm's profit is 25 × $3,000 = $75,000 (the shaded area in (a)).

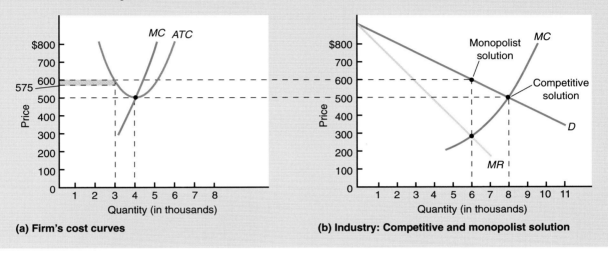

(a) Firm's cost curves

(b) Industry: Competitive and monopolist solution

If the firms collude fully, they will act as a joint monopolist setting total output at 6,000 tons where MR = MC (3,000 tons each). This gives them a price of $600 with a cost of $575 per ton, for a joint economic profit of $150,000, or $75,000 each. The firms prefer this equilibrium to the competitive equilibrium where they earn zero economic profit.

If they can ensure that they will both abide by the agreement, the monopolist output will be the joint profit-maximizing output. But what if one firm cheats? What if one firm produces 4,000 tons (1,000 tons under the counter)? The additional 1,000 tons in output will cause the price to fall to $550 per ton. The cheating firm's average total costs fall to $500 as its output rises to 4,000, so its profit rises to $200,000. The noncheating firm's profit moves in the opposite direction. Its average total costs remain $575, but the price it receives falls to $550, so it loses $75,000 instead of making $75,000. This gives it a large incentive to cheat also. The division of profits and output split is shown in Figure 13-5. If the noncheating firm decides to become a cheating firm, it eliminates its loss and the other firm's profit, and the duopoly moves to a zero profit position.

In Figure 13-5(a), you can see that the firm that abides by the agreement and produces 3,000 units makes a loss of $75,000; its average total costs are $575 and the price it receives is $550. In Figure 13-5(b) you can see that the cheating firm makes a profit of $200,000; its average costs are $500, so it is doing much better than when it did not cheat. The combined profit of the cheating and the noncheating firms is $200,000 − $75,000 = $125,000, which is lower than if they cooperated. By cheating, the firm has essentially transferred $125,000 of the other firm's profit to itself and has reduced their combined profit by $25,000. Figure 13-5(c) shows how output is split between the two

Figure 13-5 (a, b, and c)   Firm and Industry Duopoly Equilibrium When One Firm Cheats

In this Figure I demonstrate the three different outcomes. Figures (a) and (b) show the noncheating and the cheating firms' output and profit, respectively, while (c) shows the industry output and price.

Say they both cheat. The price is $500 and output is 8,000 (4,000 per firm) (point A in (c)). Both firms make zero profit since their average total costs of $500 equal the price they receive.

If neither cheats, the industry output is 6,000, the price is $600, and their ATC is $575. This outcome gives them a profit of $75,000 each and would place them at point C in (c). This outcome was considered in Figure 13-4.

If one firm cheats and the other does not, the output is 7,000 and the industry price is $550 (point B in (c)). The noncheating firm's loss is shown by the shaded area in (a); its costs are $575, its output is 3,000, the price it receives is $550, and its loss is $75,000. The cheating firm's profit is shown by the shaded area in (b). Its average total costs are $500, the price it receives is $550, and its output is 4,000, so its profit is $200,000. So if one firm is cheating, it pays to be that firm; it doesn't pay to be honest when the other firm cheats.

(a) Noncheating firm's loss   **(b) Cheating firm's profit**   **(c) Cheating solution**

firms. If both firms cheat, the equilibrium output moves to the competitive output, 8,000, and both of the firms make zero profit.

It is precisely to provide insight into this type of strategic situation that game theory was developed. It does so by analyzing the strategies of both firms under all circumstances and placing the combination in a payoff matrix—a box that contains the outcomes of a strategic game under various circumstances.

Duopoly and a Payoff Matrix

The duopoly presented above is a variation of the prisoner's dilemma game. The results can be presented in a payoff matrix that captures the essence of the prisoner's dilemma. In Figure 13-6, each square shows the payoff from a pair of decisions listed in the columns and rows. The blue triangles show A's profit; the gold triangles show B's profit. For example, if neither cheats, the result for both is shown in the upper left-hand square, and if they both cheat, the result is shown in the lower right-hand square.

Notice the dilemma they are in if detecting cheating is impossible. If they can't detect whether the other one cheated and each believes the other is maximizing profit, each must expect the other one to cheat. But if firm A expects firm B to cheat, the relevant payoffs are in the second row. Given this expectation, if firm A doesn't cheat, it loses $75,000. So firm A's optimal strategy is to cheat. Similarly for firm B. If it expects firm A to cheat, its relevant payoffs are in the second column. Firm B's optimal strategy is to cheat. But if they both cheat they end up in the lower right-hand square with zero profit.

Figure 13-6   The Payoff Matrix of Strategic Pricing Duopoly

The strategic dilemma facing each firm in a duopoly can be shown in a payoff matrix that captures the four possible outcomes. **A**'s strategies are listed horizontally; **B**'s strategies are listed vertically. The payoffs of the combined strategies for both firms are shown in the four boxes of the matrix, with **B**'s payoff shown in the gold shaded triangles and **A**'s payoff shown in the blue shaded triangles. For example, if **A** cheats but **B** doesn't, **A** makes a profit of $200,000 but **B** loses $75,000.

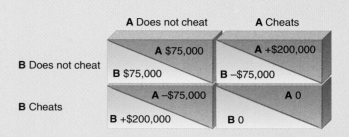

Their combined optimal strategy is to cartelize and achieve the monopoly payoff, with both firms receiving a profit of $75,000. However, each must expect that if it doesn't cheat and the other does cheat, it will lose $75,000. To avoid losing that $75,000, both firms will cheat, which leads them to the payoff in the lower right-hand corner—the competitive solution with zero profit for each firm.

G ame theory has offered significant insight into the structure of economic problems but arrives at the conclusion that a number of alternative solutions are possible. A new branch of economics—*experimental economics*—has developed that offers insight into which outcome will be forthcoming. Let's consider an example.

When game theorists have done experiments, they have found that people believe that the others in the game will work toward a cooperative solution. Thus, when the gains from cheating are not too great, often people do not choose the individual profit-maximizing position, but instead choose a more cooperative strategy,

BEYOND THE TOOLS

Game Theory and Experimental Economics

at least initially. Such cooperative solutions tend to break down, however, as the benefits of cheating become larger. Additionally, as the number of participants gets larger, the less likely it is that the cooperative solution will be chosen and the more likely it is that competitive solutions will be chosen.

Experimental economists have also found that the structure of the game plays an important role in deciding the solution. For example, posted-price markets, in which the prices are explicitly announced, are more likely to reach a collusive result than are nonposted or uncertain-price markets, where actual sale prices are not known.

In reality, of course, cheating is partially detectable, and even though explicit collusion and enforceable contracts are illegal in the United States, implicit collusive contracts are not. Moreover, in markets where similar conditions hold time after time, the cooperative solution is more likely since each firm will acquire a reputation based on its past actions, and firms can retaliate against other firms that cheat. But the basic dilemma remains for firms and tends to push oligopolies toward a zero profit competitive solution.

Oligopoly Models, Structure, and Performance

The fourfold division of markets that I've considered so far has all been based on the structure of the markets. By *structure* I mean the number, size, and interrelationship of firms in an industry. A monopoly (one firm) is the least competitive; perfectly competitive industries (an almost infinite number of firms) are the most competitive. Classification by

KNOWING THE TOOLS

A Comparison of Various Market Structures

Structure / Characteristics	Monopoly	Oligopoly	Monopolistic competition	Perfect competition
Number of firms	1	Few	Many	Almost infinite
Barriers to entry	Significant	Significant	Few	None
Pricing decisions	$MC = MR$	Strategic pricing, between monopoly and perfect competition	$MC = MR$	$MC = MR = P$
Output decisions	Most output restriction	Output somewhat restricted	Output restricted somewhat by product differentiation	No output restriction
Interdependence	Only firm in market, not concerned about competitors	Interdependent strategic pricing and output decision	Each firm acts independently	Each firm acts independently
Profit	Possibility of long-run economic profit	Some long-run economic profit possible	No long-run economic profit possible	No long-run economic profit possible
P and MC	$P > MC$	$P > MC$	$P > MC$	$P = MC$

Q.9 The Herfindahl index is 1,500. Using a contestable market approach, what would you conclude about this industry?

structure is easy for students to learn and accords nicely with intuition. The cartelization model fits best with this classification system because it assumes the structure of the market (the number of firms) is directly related to the price a firm charges. It predicts that oligopolies charge higher prices than do monopolistic competitors.

The contestable market model gives far less weight to market structure. According to it, markets that structurally look highly oligopolistic could actually be highly competitive—much more so than markets that structurally look less competitive. This contestable market model view of judging markets by performance, not structure, has had many reincarnations. Close relatives of it have previously been called the *barriers-to-entry* model, the *stay-out pricing* model, and the *limit-pricing* model. These models provide a view of competition that doesn't depend on market structure.

To see the implications of the contestable market approach, let's consider an oligopoly with a four-firm concentration ratio of 60 percent and a Herfindahl index of 1,500. Using the structural approach we would say that, because of the multiplicity of oligopoly models, we're not quite sure what price firms in this industry would charge, but that it seems reasonable to assume that there would be some implicit collusion and that the price would be closer to a monopolist price than to a competitive price. If that same market had a four-firm concentration ratio of 30 percent and a Herfindahl index of 700, the industry would be more likely to have a competitive price.

A contestable market model advocate would disagree, arguing that barriers to entry and exit are what's important. If no significant barriers to entry exist in the first case but significant barriers to entry exist in the second case, the second case would be more monopolistic than the first. An example is the Miami fish market mentioned earlier, where there were 20 sellers (none with a large percentage of the market) and significant barriers to entry (only fishers from the pier were allowed to sell fish there and the slots at the pier were limited). Because of those entry limitations, the pricing and output decisions would be close to the monopolistic price. If you took that same structure but had free entry, you'd get much closer to competitive decisions.

As I presented the two views, I emphasized the differences in order to make the distinction clear. However, I must also point out that there's a similarity in the two views. Often barriers to entry are the reason there are only a few firms in an industry. And when there are many firms, that suggests that there are few barriers to entry. In such situations, which make up the majority of cases, the two approaches come to the same conclusion.

Q-10 The Herfindahl index is 1,500. Using a structural analysis of markets approach, what would you conclude about this industry?

CONCLUSION

As you can see, the real world gets very complicated very quickly. I'll show you just how complicated in Chapter 14. But don't let the complicated real world get you down on the theories presented here. It's precisely because the real world is so complicated that we need some framework, like the one presented in this chapter. That framework lets us focus on specific issues—and hopefully the most important. Because the framework is so important, as a conclusion to this chapter I have summarized the primary market structures in the box "A Comparison of Various Market Structures."

Chapter Summary

- Industries are classified by economic activity in the North American Industry Classification System (NAICS). Industry structures are measured by concentration ratios and Herfindahl indexes.

- A concentration ratio is the sum of the market shares of individual firms with the largest shares in an industry.

- A Herfindahl index is the sum of the squares of the individual market shares of all firms in an industry.

- Conglomerates operate in a variety of different industries. Industry concentration measures do not assess the bigness of these conglomerates.

- Monopolistic competition is characterized by (1) many sellers, (2) differentiated products, (3) multiple dimensions of competition, and (4) ease of entry for new firms.

- The central characteristic of oligopoly is that there are a small number of interdependent firms.

- In monopolistic competition firms act independently; in an oligopoly they take account of each other's actions.

- Monopolistic competitors differ from perfect competitors in that the former face a downward-sloping demand curve.

- A monopolistic competitor differs from a monopolist in that a monopolistic competitor makes zero economic profit in long-run equilibrium.

- An oligopolist's price will be somewhere between the competitive price and the monopolistic price.

- Game theory and the prisoner's dilemma can shed light on strategic pricing decisions.

- A contestable market theory of oligopoly judges an industry's competitiveness more by performance and barriers to entry than by structure. Cartel models of oligopoly concentrate on market structure.

Key Terms

cartel   (292)

cartel model of oligopoly
(292)

concentration ratio   (284)

contestable market model
(294)

duopoly   (296)

game theory   (296)

Herfindahl index   (284)

implicit collusion   (293)

market structure   (282)

monopolistic competition
(283)

North American Industry
Classification System
(NAICS)   (283)

oligopoly   (283)

prisoner's dilemma   (296)

strategic decision making
(285)

strategic pricing   (295)

Questions for Thought and Review

1. Which industry is more highly concentrated: one with a Herfindahl index of 1,200 or one with a four-firm concentration ratio of 55 percent?

2. What are the ways in which a firm can differentiate its product from that of its competitors? What is the overriding objective of product differentiation?

3. What are the "monopolistic" and the "competitive" elements of monopolistic competition?

4. Does the product differentiation in monopolistic competition make us better or worse off? Why?

5. Both a perfect competitor and a monopolistic competitor choose output where $MC = MR$, and neither makes a profit in the long run. How is it, then, that the monopolistic competitor produces less than a perfect competitor?

6. If a monopolistic competitor is able to restrict output, why doesn't it earn economic profits?

7. What are some of the barriers to entry in the restaurant industry? In the automobile industry?

8. Is an oligopolist more or less likely to engage in strategic pricing compared to a monopolistic competitor?

9. What is the difference between the contestable market model and the cartel model of oligopoly? How are they related?

10. Is a contestable model or cartel model more likely to judge an industry by performance? Explain your answer.

11. What did Adam Smith mean when he wrote, "Seldom do businessmen of the same trade get together but that it results in some detriment to the general public"?

12. Private colleges of the same caliber generally charge roughly the same tuition. Would you characterize these colleges as a cartel type of oligopoly?

13. Describe a situation you have faced in your lifetime that can be characterized as a prisoner's dilemma.

14. In the late 1990s, Kellogg's, which controlled 32 percent of the breakfast cereal market, cut the prices of some of its best-selling brands of cereal to regain market share lost to Post, which controlled 20 percent of the market. General Mills had 24 percent of the market. The price cuts were expected to trigger a price war. Based on this information, what market structure best characterizes the market for breakfast cereal?

Problems and Exercises

1. Suppose a monopolistic competitor has a constant marginal cost of $6 and faces the demand curve given in the following table:

Q	20	18	16	14	12	10	8	6
P	$ 2	4	6	8	10	12	14	16

a. What output will the firm choose?

b. What will be the monopolistic competitor's average fixed cost at the output it chooses?

2. A firm is convinced that if it lowers its price, no other firm in the industry will change price; however, it believes that if it raises its price, some other firms will match its increase, making its demand curve more inelastic. The current price is $8 and its marginal cost is constant at $4.

a. Sketch the general shape of the firm's MR, MC, and demand curves.

b. If the marginal cost falls to $3, what would you predict would happen to price?

c. If the marginal cost rises to $5, what would you predict would happen to price?

d. Do a survey of five or six firms in your area. Ask them how they believe other firms would respond to their increasing or decreasing price. Based on that survey, discuss the relevance of this kinked demand model compared to the one presented in the book.

3. You're the manager of a firm that has constant marginal cost of $6. Fixed cost is zero. The market structure is monopolistically competitive. You're faced with the following demand curve:

a. Determine graphically the profit-maximizing price and output for your firm in the short run. Demonstrate what profit or loss you'll be making.
b. Do the same for the long run.
c. Thanks to a technological innovation, you have zero marginal cost. Demonstrate the new profit-maximizing price and output in the short run. Demonstrate graphically the short-run profit at that new profit-maximizing output.

4. The pizza market is divided as follows:

Pizza Hut	20.7%
Domino's	17.0
Little Caesars	6.7
Pizza Inn/Pantera's	2.2
Round Table	2.0
All others	51.4

a. How would you describe its market structure?
b. What is the approximate Herfindahl index?
c. What is the four-firm concentration ratio?

5. In 1982 Robert Crandell, CEO of American Airlines, phoned the Braniff Airways CEO and said, "Raise your fares 20 percent and I'll raise mine the next morning."
a. Why would he do this?
b. If you were the Braniff Airways CEO, would you have gone along?

c. Why should Crandell not have done this?
6. Two firms, TwiddleDee and TwiddleDum, make up the entire market for wodgets. They have identical costs. They are currently colluding explicitly and are making $2 million each. TwiddleDee has a new CEO, Mr. Notsonice, who is considering cheating. He has been informed by his able assistant that if he cheats he can increase the firm's profit to $3 million, but that cheating will reduce TwiddleDum's profit to $1 million. You have been hired to advise Mr. Notsonice.
a. Construct a payoff matrix for him that captures the essence of the decision.
b. If the game is only played once, what strategy would you advise?
c. How would your answer to b change if the game were to be played many times?
d. What change in the profit made when colluding (currently $2 million) would be needed to change your advice in b?
7. In 1993, the infant/preschool toy market four-firm concentration ratio was 72 percent. With 8 percent of the market, Mattel was the fourth largest firm in that market. Mattel proposed to buy Fisher-Price, the market leader with 27 percent. At this time the new Clinton administration was trying to develop a set of rules dealing with such mergers. Your assignment is to help it decide by answering questions a through d.
a. Why would Mattel want to buy Fisher-Price?
b. What arguments can you think of in favor of allowing this acquisition?
c. What arguments can you think of against allowing this acquisition?
d. How do you think the four-firm concentration ratio for the entire toy industry would compare to this infant/preschool toy market concentration ratio?
e. What did the Clinton administration decide? (Requires library or online research.)

Web Questions

1. Go to the home page of the U.S. Department of Justice (DOJ) at www.usdoj.gov and search to find the document "Horizontal Merger Guidelines." Use the table of contents to find the sections "Product Market Definition" and "Concentration and Market Shares."
a. How does the DOJ determine the relevant product market?
b. Explain how the definition of market depends on cross-price elasticity of demand.
c. What measure of market concentration does the DOJ use?
d. Above what level for the market concentration measure does the DOJ believe the market to be highly concentrated?

2. Go to the U.S. Census Bureau's home page at www.census.gov and search to find the North American Industry Classification System (NAICS) to answer the following questions:
a. What are the industry codes for potato farming, tire manufacturing, and family clothing stores?
b. The NAICS replaced the Standard Industrial Classification (SIC). How did the SIC classify industries? How does the NAICS classify industries?
c. Why did the Census Bureau change its method of classification? Will the new classification be more or less helpful than the SIC when classifying firms to determine market structure? Explain.

3. The Organization of Petroleum Exporting Countries (OPEC) is an international cartel. Go to its home page at www.opec.org to answer the following questions:
   a. What are OPEC's objectives? How does it meet those objectives?

   b. What countries are members of OPEC? What percentage of world oil production comes from these nations? In what way is OPEC a cartel?
   c. What significant oil-exporting countries are not members? What has OPEC done to limit the effect of non-member production on its pricing decisions?

Answers to Margin Questions

1. The smaller the number of digits, the more inclusive the classification. Therefore, the two-digit industry would have significantly more output. *(283)*

2. The highest Herfindahl index for this industry would occur if one firm had the entire 60 percent, and all other firms had an infinitesimal amount, making the Herfindahl index slightly over 3,600. The lowest Herfindahl index this industry could have would occur if each of the top four firms had 15 percent of the market, yielding a Herfindahl index of 900. *(285)*

3. I would respond that monopolistic competitors, by definition, do not take into account the expected reactions of competitors to their decisions; therefore, they cannot use strategic decision making. I would tell Jean she probably meant, "*Oligopolies* use strategic decision making." *(285)*

4. Both a monopoly and a monopolistic competitor produce where marginal cost equals marginal revenue. The difference is in the positioning of the average total cost curve. For a monopolistic competitor, that average total cost curve must be tangent to the demand curve because a monopolistic competitor makes no profits in the long run. A monopoly can make profits in the long run, so its average total cost can be below the price. *(288)*

5. Monopolistically competitive firms advertise because their products are differentiated from others. Advertising can convince people that a firm's product is better than that of other firms and increase the demand curve it faces. Perfect competitors, in contrast, have no incentive to advertise since their products are the same as every other firm's product and they can sell all they want at the market price. *(291)*

6. Maintaining a cartel requires firms to make decisions that are not in their individual best interests. Such decisions are hard to enforce unless there is an explicit enforcement mechanism, which is difficult in a cartel. *(292)*

7. The demand curve perceived by an oligopolist is more elastic above the current price because it believes that others will not follow price increases. If it increased price, it would see quantity demanded fall by a lot. The opposite is true below the current price. The demand curve below current price is less elastic. Price declines would be matched by competitors and the oligopolist would see little change in quantity demanded with a price decline. *(293)*

8. The two extremes an oligopoly model can take are: (1) a cartel model, which is the equivalent of a monopoly; and (2) a contestable market model, which, if there are no barriers to entry, is the equivalent of a competitive industry. *(295)*

9. The contestable markets approach looks at barriers to entry, not structure. Therefore, we can conclude nothing about the industry from the Herfindahl index. *(300)*

10. In a market with a Herfindahl index of 1,500, the largest firm would have, at most, slightly under 40 percent of the market. The least concentrated such an industry could be would be if seven firms each had between 14 and 15 percent of the market. In either of these two cases, the industry would probably be an oligopolistic industry and could border on monopoly. *(301)*

Globalization, Technology, and Real-World Competition

14

After reading this chapter, you should be able to:

- Define the monitoring problem and state its implications for economics.

- Explain how corporate takeovers can limit X-inefficiency.

- Discuss why competition should be seen as a process, not a state.

- List two actions firms take to break down monopoly and three they take to protect monopoly.

- Explain how globalization and technology have changed competition.

- Discuss why oligopoly is the best market structure for technological change.

It is ridiculous to call this an industry. This is rat eat rat; dog eat dog. I'll kill 'em, and I'm going to kill 'em before they kill me. You're talking about the American way of survival of the fittest.

Ray Kroc (founder of McDonald's)

In earlier chapters we've seen some nice, neat models, but as we discussed in Chapter 13, often these models don't fit reality directly. Real-world markets aren't perfectly monopolistic; they aren't perfectly competitive either. They're somewhere between the two. The monopolistic competition and oligopoly models in Chapter 13 come closer to reality and provide some important insights into the "in-between" markets, but, like any abstraction, they, too, fail to capture aspects of the actual nature of competition. In this chapter I remedy that shortcoming and give you a sense of what actual firms, markets, and competition are like. This chapter also discusses two issues that are very much in the news—technology and globalization—and relates these concepts to the models we developed earlier.

When reading this chapter, think about the two uses of competition discussed in Chapter 11: competition as a process, the end state of which is zero profits, and competition as a market structure. In this chapter the focus is on competition as a process—it is a rivalry between firms and between individuals. This competitive process is active in all market forms and is key to understanding real-world competition.

THE GOALS OF REAL-WORLD FIRMS AND THE MONITORING PROBLEM

Maybe the best place to start is with the assumption that firms are profit maximizers. There's a certain reasonableness to this assumption; firms definitely are concerned about profit, but are they trying to maximize profit? The answer is: It depends.

Short-Run versus Long-Run Profit

Q-1 What are two reasons why real-world firms are not pure profit maximizers?

14.1

The first insight is that if firms are profit maximizers, they aren't just concerned with short-run profit; most are concerned with long-run profit. Thus, even if they can, they may not take full advantage of a potential monopolistic situation now, in order to strengthen their long-run position. For example, many stores have liberal return policies: "If you don't like it, you can return it for a full refund." Similarly, many firms spend millions of dollars improving their reputations. Most firms want to be known as good citizens. Such expenditures on reputation and goodwill can increase long-run profit, even if they reduce short-run profit. (New Internet firms focus almost entirely on the long run, and many of the most well known have yet to make a profit.)

The Problem with Profit Maximization

Most real-world production doesn't take place in owner-operated businesses; it takes place in large corporations.

A second insight into how real-world firms differ from the model is that the decision-makers' income is often a cost of the firm. Most real-world production doesn't take place in owner-operated businesses; it takes place in large corporations with eight or nine levels of management, thousands of stockholders whose stock is often held in trust for them, and a board of directors, chosen by management, overseeing the company by meeting two or three times a year. Signing a proxy statement is as close as most stock-owners get to directing "their company" to maximize profit.

Managers' Incentives Why is the structure of the firm important to the analysis? Because economic theory tells us that, unless someone is seeing to it that they do, self-interested decision makers have little incentive to hold down their pay. But their pay is a cost of the firm. And if their pay isn't held down, the firm's profit will be lower than otherwise. Most firms manage to put some pressure on managers to make at least a pre-designated level of profit. (If you ask managers, they'll tell you that they face enormous pressure.) So the profit motive certainly plays a role—but to say that profit plays a role is not to say that firms maximize profit. Having dealt with many companies, I'll go out on a limb and say that there are enormous wastes and inefficiencies in many U.S. businesses.

This structure presents a problem in applying the model to the real world. The general economic model assumes individuals are utility maximizers—that they're motivated by self-interest. Then, in the standard model of the firm, the assumption is made that

Table 14-1   Compensation of CEOs of Selected Companies (base pay plus bonuses and stock options)

Company	Salary in 1998
Abbott Laboratories	$39,601,058
Ameritech	9,637,916
CBS Corp.	13,426,152
Citigroup Inc.	52,135,054
Coca-Cola Co.	20,469,799
Dayton Hudson Group	6,416,477
Gap Inc.	47,142,590
Hewlitt-Packard	10,927,382
Home Depot	3,116,434
Lucent Technologies	30,772,979
U.S. Airways	34,247,666
Wachovia Corp.	9,599,084

Source: AFL-CIO (http://www.paywatch.org).

 14.2

firms, composed of self-interest-seeking individuals, are profit-seeking firms, without explaining how self-interest-seeking individuals who manage real-world corporations will find it in their interest to maximize profit for the firm. Economists recognize this problem, which was introduced in an earlier chapter. It's an example of the **monitoring problem**—*the need to oversee employees to ensure that their actions are in the best interest of the firm.*

Need for Monitoring Monitoring is required because employees' incentives differ from the owner's incentives, and it's costly to see that the employee does the owner's bidding. The monitoring problem is now a central problem focused on by economists who specialize in industrial organization. They study internal structures of firms and look for a contract that managers can be given: an **incentive-compatible contract** in which *the incentives of each of the two parties to the contract are made to correspond as closely as possible.* The specific monitoring problem relevant to firm structure is that often owners find it too costly to monitor the managers to ensure that managers do what's in the owners' interest. And self-interested managers are interested in maximizing the firm's profit only if the structure of the firm requires them to do so.

When appropriate monitoring doesn't take place, high-level managers can pay themselves very well. U.S. managers are very well paid and, as can be seen in Table 14-1, many receive multimillion-dollar salaries. But are these salaries too high? That's a difficult question. Most of the high salaries are not pure salaries, but include stock options and bonuses for performance.

One way to get an idea about an answer is to compare U.S. managers' salaries with those in Japan, where the control of firms is different. Banks in Japan have significant control over the operations of firms, and they closely monitor their performance. The result is that, in Japan, high-level managers on average earn about one-fourth of what their U.S. counterparts make, while wages of low-level workers are comparable to those of low-level workers in the United States. Given Japanese companies' success in competing with U.S. companies, this suggests that high managerial pay in the United States reflects a monitoring problem inherent in the structure of corporations. There are, of course, other perspectives. Considering what some sports, film, and music stars receive places the high salaries of U.S. managers in a different light.

The monitoring problem is that employees' incentives differ from the owner's incentives. Because monitoring these employees is expensive, some economists are studying ways to change the situation.

Self-interested managers are interested in maximizing firm profit only if the structure of the firm requires them to do so.

Q-2 Why would most economists be concerned about third-party payment systems in which the consumer and the payer are different?

What Do Real-World Firms Maximize?

If firms don't maximize profit, what do they maximize? What are their goals? The answer again is: It depends.

Real-world firms often have a set of complicated goals that reflect the organizational structure and incentives built into the system. Clearly, profit is one of their goals. Firms spend a lot of time designing incentives to get managers to focus on profit.

But often intermediate goals become the focus of firms. For example, many real-world firms focus on growth in sales; at other times they institute a cost-reduction program to increase long-run profit. At still other times they may simply take it easy and not push hard at all, enjoying the position they find themselves in—being what British economist Joan Robinson called **lazy monopolists**—*firms that do not push for efficiency, but merely enjoy the position they are already in.* This term describes many, but not all, real-world corporations. When Robinson coined the term, firms faced mostly domestic competition. Today, with firms facing more and more global competition, firms are a bit less lazy than they were—as we'll discuss later in this chapter.

Although profit is one goal of a firm, often firms focus on other intermediate goals such as cost and sales.

THE LAZY MONOPOLIST AND X-INEFFICIENCY

Lazy monopolists are not profit maximizers; they see to it that they make enough profit so that the stockholders aren't squealing, but don't push as hard as they could to hold their costs down. They perform as efficiently as is consistent with keeping their jobs. The result is what economists call **X-inefficiency** (*firms operating far less efficiently than they could technically*). Such firms have monopoly positions, but they don't make large monopoly profits. Instead, their costs rise because of inefficiency; they may simply make a normal level of profit or, if X-inefficiency becomes bad enough, a loss.

The standard model avoids dealing with the monitoring problem by assuming that the owner of the firm makes all the decisions. The owners of firms who receive the profit, and only the profit, would like to see that all the firm's costs are held down. Unfortunately, very few real-world firms operate that way. In reality owners seldom make operating decisions. They hire or appoint managers to make those decisions. The managers they hire don't have that same incentive to hold costs down. Therefore, it isn't surprising to many economists that managers' pay is usually high and that high-level managers see to it that they have "perks" such as chauffeurs, jet planes, ritzy offices, and assistants to do as much of their work as possible.

Q-3 *Why doesn't a manager have the same incentive to hold costs down as an owner does?*

The equilibrium of a lazy monopolist is presented in Figure 14-1. A monopolist would produce at price P_M and quantity Q_M. Average total cost would be C_M, so the monopolist's profit would be the entire shaded rectangle (areas A and B). The lazy monopolist would allow costs to increase until the firm reached its normal level of profit. In Figure 14-1, costs rise to C_{LM}. The profit of the lazy monopolist is area B. The remainder of the potential profit is eaten up in cost inefficiencies.

What places a limit on firms' laziness is the degree of competitive pressures they face. All economic institutions must have sufficient revenue coming in to cover costs, so all economic institutions have a limit on how lazy and inefficient they can get—a limit imposed by their monopoly position. They can translate the monopoly profit into X-inefficiency, thereby benefiting the managers and workers in the firm, but once they've done so, they can't be more inefficient. They would go out of business.

The competitive pressures a firm faces limit its laziness.

How Competition Limits the Lazy Monopolist

If all individuals in the industry are lazy, then laziness becomes the norm and competitive pressures don't reduce their profits. Laziness is relative, not absolute. But if a new

Figure 14-1   True Cost Efficiency and the Lazy Monopolist

A monopolist producing efficiently would have costs C_M and would produce at price P_M and quantity Q_M. A lazy monopolist, in contrast, would let costs rise until the minimum level of profit is reached, at C_{LM}. Profit for the monopolist is represented by the entire shaded area, whereas profit for the lazy monopolist is squeezed down to area B.

firm comes in all gung-ho and hardworking, or if an industry is opened up to international competition, the lazy monopolists can be squeezed and must undertake massive restructuring to make themselves competitive. Many U.S. firms have been undergoing such restructuring in order to make themselves internationally competitive.

A second way in which competitive pressure is placed on a lazy monopolist is by a **corporate takeover,** in which *another firm or a group of individuals issues a tender offer (that is, offers to buy up the stock of a company to gain control and to install its own managers).* Usually such tender offers are financed by large amounts of debt, which means that if the takeover is successful, the firm will need to make large profits just to cover the interest payments on the debt.

Managers don't like takeovers. A takeover may mean losing their jobs and the perks that go along with the jobs, so they'll often restructure the company on their own. Such restructuring frequently means incurring large amounts of debt to finance a large payment to stockholders. These payments put more pressure on management to operate efficiently. Thus, the threat of a corporate takeover places competitive pressure on firms to maximize profits.

Were profit not a motive at all, one would expect the lazy monopolist syndrome to take precedence. Thus, it's not surprising that nonprofit organizations often display these lazy monopolist tendencies. For example, some colleges, schools, libraries, jails, and nonprofit hospitals have a number of rules and ways of doing things that, upon reflection, benefit the employees of the institution rather than the customers. At most colleges, students aren't polled about what time they would prefer classes to meet; instead, the professors and administrators decide when they want to teach. I leave it to you to figure out whether your college exhibits these tendencies and whether you'd prefer that your college, library, or hospital change to a for-profit institution. Studying these incentive-compatible problems is what management courses are all about.

Motivations for Efficiency Other Than the Profit Incentive

I'm not going to discuss management theory here other than to stimulate your thinking about the problem. However, I'd be remiss in presenting you this broad outline of the monitoring problem without mentioning that the drive for profit isn't the only drive that pushes for efficiency. Some individuals derive pleasure from efficiently run organizations. Such individuals don't need to be monitored. Thus, if administrators are well

A corporate takeover, or simply the threat of a takeover, can improve a firm's efficiency.

Q-4   In what way does the threat of a corporate takeover place competitive pressures on a firm?

intentioned, they'll hold down costs even if they aren't profit maximizers. In such cases, monitoring (creating an organization and structure that gives people profit incentives) can actually reduce efficiency! It's amazing to some economists how some nonprofit organizations operate as efficiently as they do—some libraries and colleges fall into that category. Their success is built on their employees' pride in their jobs, not on their profit motive.

Most economists don't deny that such inherently efficient individuals exist, and that most people derive some pleasure from efficiency, but they believe that it's hard to maintain that push for efficiency year in, year out, when some of your colleagues are lazy monopolists enjoying the fruits of your efficiency. Most people derive some pleasure from efficiency, but, based on their observation of people's actions, economists believe that holding down costs without the profit motive takes stronger willpower than most people have.

Individuals have complicated motives; some simply have a taste for efficiency.

THE FIGHT BETWEEN COMPETITIVE AND MONOPOLISTIC FORCES

Even if all the assumptions for perfect competition could hold true, it's unlikely that real-world markets would be perfectly competitive. The reason is that perfect competition assumes that individuals accept a competitive institutional structure, even though changing that structure could result in significant gains for sellers or buyers. The simple fact is that *self-interest-seeking individuals don't like competition for themselves* (although they do like it for others), and when competitive pressures get strong and the invisible hand's push turns to shove, individuals often shove back, using either social or political means. That's why you can understand real-world competition only if you understand how the invisible hand, social forces, and political pressures push against each other to create real-world economic institutions. Real-world competition should be seen as a process—a fight between the forces of monopolization and the forces of competition.

When competitive pressures get strong, individuals often fight back through social and political pressures. Competition is a process—a fight between the forces of monopolization and the forces of competition.

How Monopolistic Forces Affect Perfect Competition

Let's consider some examples. During the Depression of the 1930s, competition was pushing down prices and wages. What was the result? Individuals socially condemned firms for unfair competition, and numerous laws were passed to prevent it. Unions were strengthened politically and given monopoly powers so they could resist the pressure to push down wages. The Robinson-Patman Act was passed, which made it illegal for many firms to lower prices. Individual states passed similar laws, and it was under one of these that Wal-Mart lost a 1993 court case in which it was accused of charging too-low prices in its pharmacies.

As another example, consider agricultural markets, which have many of the conditions for almost perfect competition. To my knowledge, not one country in the world allows a competitive agricultural market to exist. As you'll see in Chapter 18, the United States has myriad laws, regulations, and programs that prevent agricultural markets from working competitively. U.S. agricultural markets are characterized by price supports, acreage limitations, and quota systems. Thus, where perfectly competitive markets could exist, they aren't allowed to. An almost infinite number of other examples can be found. Our laws and social values and customs simply do not allow perfect competition to work because government emphasizes other social goals besides efficiency. When competition negatively affects these other goals (which may or may not be goals that most people in society hold), government prevents competition from operating.

The United States has a myriad of laws, regulations, and programs that prevent agricultural markets from working competitively.

Q-5 Explain, using supply and demand curves, why most agricultural markets are not perfectly competitive.

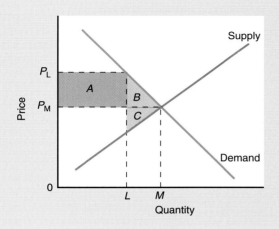

Figure 14-2   Movement Away from Competitive Markets

In the case where suppliers of $0L$ can restrict suppliers of LM from entering the market, they can raise the price of the good from P_M to P_L, giving the suppliers of $0L$ area A in additional income. The suppliers kept out of the market lose area C in income. The consumers, however, lose both areas A and B, giving them strong incentive to fight collusion. Often the costs of organizing for consumers are higher than the costs for the suppliers, so consumers accept the market restrictions.

Economic Insights and Real-World Competition

The extreme rarity of perfectly competitive markets *should not* make you think that economics is irrelevant to the real world. Far from it. In fact, the movement away from perfectly competitive markets could have been predicted by economic theory.

Consider Figure 14-2. Competitive markets will exist only if suppliers or consumers don't collude. If the suppliers producing $0L$ can get together and restrict entry, preventing suppliers who would produce LM from entering the industry, the remaining suppliers can raise their price from P_M to P_L, giving them the shaded area A in additional income. If the cost of their colluding and preventing entry is less than that amount, economic theory predicts that these individuals will collude. The suppliers kept out of the market lose only area C, so they don't have much incentive to fight the restrictions on entry. Consumers lose the areas A plus B, so they have a strong incentive to fight. However, often their cost of organizing a protest is higher than the suppliers' cost of collusion, so consumers accept the restrictions.

Suppliers introducing restrictions on entry seldom claim that the reason for the restrictions is to increase their incomes. Usually they couch the argument for restrictions in terms of the general good but, while their reasons are debatable, the net effect of restricting entry into a market is to increase suppliers' income to the detriment of consumers.

How Competitive Forces Affect Monopoly

Don't think that because perfect competition doesn't exist, competition doesn't exist. In the real world, competition is fierce; the invisible hand is no weakling. It holds its own against other forces in the economy.

Competition is so strong that it makes the other extreme (perfect monopolies) as rare as perfect competition. For a monopoly to last, other firms must be prevented from entering the market. In reality it's almost impossible to prevent entry, and therefore it's almost impossible for perfect monopoly to exist. Monopoly profits send out signals to other firms who want to get some of that profit for themselves.

Q-6 Why is it almost impossible for a perfect monopoly to exist?

Breaking Down Monopoly To get some of the profit, firms will break down a monopoly through political or economic means. If the monopoly is a legal monopoly, high profit will lead potential competitors to lobby to change the law underpinning that monopoly. If the law can't be changed—say, the monopolist has a **patent** (*a legal right to be*

Establishing an initial presence in a market can be more effective than obtaining a patent when trying to extract monopoly profit.

the sole supplier of a good)—potential competitors will generally get around the obstacle by developing a slightly different product or by working on a new technology that avoids the monopoly but satisfies the relevant need.

Say, for example, that you've just discovered the proverbial better mousetrap. You patent it and prepare to enjoy the life of a monopolist. But to patent your mousetrap, you must submit the technical drawings of how your better mousetrap works to the patent office. That gives all potential competitors (some of whom have better financing and already existing distribution systems) a chance to study your idea and see if they can think of a slightly different way (a way sufficiently different to avoid being accused of infringing on your patent) to achieve the same end. They often succeed—so often, in fact, that many firms don't apply for patents on new products because the information in the patent application spells out what's unique about the product. That information can help competitors more than the monopoly provided by the patent would hurt them. Instead many firms try to establish an initial presence in the market and rely on inertia to protect what little monopoly profit they can extract.

Reverse Engineering Going to the patent office isn't the only way competitors gather information about competing products. One of the other ways routinely used by firms is called **reverse engineering**—*the process of a firm buying other firms' products, disassembling them, figuring out what's special about them, and then copying them within the limits of the law.*

Variations on reverse engineering and cloning go on in all industries. Consider the clothing industry. One firm I know of directs its secretaries to go to top department stores on their lunch hour and buy the latest fashions. The secretaries bring the clothes back and, that afternoon, the seamstresses and tailors dismantle each garment into its component parts, make a pattern of each part, and sew the original up again. The next day the secretary who chose that garment returns it to the department store, saying "I don't really like it."

Meanwhile the firm has express-mailed the patterns to its Hong Kong office, and two weeks later its shipment of garments comes in—garments that are almost, but not perfectly, identical to the ones the secretaries bought. The firm sells this shipment to other department stores at half the cost of the original.

If you ask businesspeople, they'll tell you that competition is fierce and that profit opportunities are fleeting—which is a good sign that competition does indeed exist in the U.S. economy.

Competition and Natural Monopoly

The view one takes of the fight between competitive and monopolistic forces influences one's view of what government policy should be in relation to natural monopolies—industries whose average total cost is falling as output increases. We saw in Chapter 12 that natural monopolies can make large profits and that consequently there have been significant calls for government regulation of these monopolies to prevent their "exploitation" of the consumer.

New technologies can compete with and undermine natural monopolies.

Over the past decade economists and policymakers have become less supportive of such regulation. They argue that even in these cases of natural monopoly, competition works in other ways. High monopoly profits fund research on alternative ways of supplying the product, such as sending TV signals through electrical lines or sending phone messages by satellite. New technologies provide competition to existing firms. When this competition doesn't work fast enough, people direct their efforts toward government, and political pressure is brought to bear either to control the monopoly through regulation or to break up the monopoly.

Regulating Natural Monopolies In the past, the pressure to regulate natural monopolies has been stronger than competitive pressure that lowers prices. Regulated natural monopolies have been given the exclusive right to operate in an industry but, in return, they've had to agree to have the price they charge and the services they provide regulated. Regulatory boards control the price that natural monopolies charge so that it will be a "fair price," which they generally define as a price that includes all costs plus a normal return on capital investment (a normal profit, but no economic profit). Most states have a number of regulatory boards.

When firms are allowed to pass on all cost increases to earn a normal profit on those costs, they have little or no incentive to hold down costs. In such cases, X-inefficiency develops with a passion, and such monopolies look for capital-intensive projects that will increase their rate bases. To fight such tendencies, regulatory boards must screen every cost and determine which costs are appropriate and which aren't—an almost impossible job. For example, nuclear power is an extremely capital-intensive method of producing electric power, and regulated electric companies favored nuclear power plants until they were told that some nuclear power plant construction costs could not be passed on.

Once regulation gets so specific that it's scrutinizing every cost, the regulatory process becomes extremely bureaucratic, which itself increases the cost. Moreover, to regulate effectively, the regulators must have independent information and must have a sophisticated understanding of economics, cost accounting, and engineering. Often regulatory boards are made up of volunteer laypeople who start with little expertise; they are exhausted or co-opted by the political infighting they have had to endure by the time they develop some of the expertise they need. As is often the case in economics, there's no easy answer to the problem.

Because of the problems with regulation, more and more economists argue that even in the case of natural monopoly, no regulation is desirable, and that society would be better off relying on direct competitive forces. They argue that regulated monopolies inevitably inflate their costs so much and are so inefficient and lazy that a monopoly right should never be granted.

Deregulating Natural Monopolies In the 1980s and 1990s such views led to the deregulation and competitive supply of both electric power and telephone services.[1] Regulators are making these markets competitive by breaking down the layers of the industry into subindustries and deregulating those subindustries that can be competitive. For example, the phone industry can be divided into the phone line industry, the caller service industry, the pay phone industry, and the directory information industry. By dividing up the industry, regulators can carve out that part that has the characteristics of a natural monopoly and open the remaining parts to competition.

Let's take a closer look at the electrical industry. It used to be that electricity was supplied by independent firms, each providing electricity for its own customers. Today, however, electricity is supplied through a large grid that connects to many regions of the country. (This grid was developed to provide backup power to different sections of the country.) Given this grid, electricity generated in one area can easily be sent all over the country. Now that many suppliers can compete for customers, a reasonable competition in power supply is feasible. Many states have adopted provisions to open their electricity markets to multiple providers.

14.3

When firms are allowed to pass on all cost increases to earn a normal profit on those costs, they have little or no incentive to hold down costs.

Q.7 What is the problem with regulations that set prices relative to costs?

[1]Telephone regulation will be discussed more fully in Chapter 16, on antitrust regulation.

Economies of scale can create natural monopolies.

The power line industry, however, cannot be competitive. It would be extremely costly for each company to run a separate power line into your house. That is, the power line industry exhibits *economies of scale*. Because of the economies of scale, the power line industry is the natural monopoly aspect of electrical power supply. The deregulation of electricity involves splitting off the production of electricity from the maintenance of the line—and choosing an appropriate charge for electric line maintenance. While in the newspapers you will likely read that the electrical power industry is being deregulated, that is not quite correct. Only those portions of the market where competition is likely to exist are being deregulated.

HOW FIRMS PROTECT THEIR MONOPOLIES

The image I've presented of competition being motivated by profits is a useful one. It shows how a market economy adjusts to ever-changing technology and demands in the real world. Competition is a dynamic, not a static, force.

Firms do not sit idly by and accept competition. They fight it.

Firms do not sit idly by and accept competition. They fight it. How do monopolies fight real-world competition? By spending money on maintaining their monopoly. By advertising. By lobbying. By producing products that are difficult to copy. By not taking full advantage of their monopoly position, which means charging a low price that discourages entry. Often firms could make higher short-run profits by charging a higher price, but they forgo the short-run profits in order to strengthen their long-run position in the industry.

Cost-Benefit Analysis of Creating and Maintaining Monopolies

Q-8 What decision rule does a firm use when deciding whether to create or maintain a monopoly?

Preventing real-world competition costs money. Monopolies are expensive to create and maintain. Economic theory predicts that if firms have to spend money on creating and protecting their monopoly, they're going to "buy" less monopoly power than if it were free. How much will they buy? They will buy monopoly power until the marginal cost of such power equals the marginal benefit. Thus, they'll reason:

- Does it makes sense for us to hire a lobbyist to fight against this law that will reduce our monopoly power? Here is the probability that a lobbyist will be effective, here is the marginal cost, and here is the marginal benefit.

- Does it make sense for us to buy this machine? If we do, we'll be the only one to have it and are likely to get this much business. Here is the marginal cost, and here is the marginal benefit.

- Does it make sense for us to advertise to further our market penetration? Here are the likely various marginal benefits; here are the likely marginal costs.

Examples of firms spending money to protect or create monopolies are in the news all the time. The farm lobby fights to keep quotas and farm support programs. Drug companies spend a lot of resources to discover new drugs they can patent. A vivid example of the length to which firms will go to create a monopoly position is Owens-Corning's fight to trademark its hue of pink fiberglass. Owens-Corning has spent more than $200 million to advertise and promote its color "pink" and millions more in the court to protect its right to sole use of that hue. Owens-Corning has weighed the costs and benefits and believes that its pink provides sufficient brand recognition to warrant spending millions to protect it.

Establishing Market Position

Some economists, such as Robert Frank, have argued that today's economy is becoming more and more like a monopoly economy. Modern competition, he argues, is a winner-take-all competition. In such a competition, the winner (established because of brand loyalty, patent protection, or simply consumer laziness) achieves a monopoly and can charge significantly higher prices than its costs without facing competition. The initial competition, focusing on establishing market position, is intense.

In "winner-take-all" markets, the initial competition is on establishing market position.

To see how important establishing a market position is in today's economy, consider the initial public offering (IPO) of the new firms that were so highly valued by Wall Street in the late 1990s. Many of these new firms had no profits and no likelihood of profits for a number of years, but they were selling at extraordinarily high stock prices. Why? The reasoning was that these companies were spending money to establish brand names. As their names became better known, they would establish a monopoly position, and eventually their monopoly positions would be so strong that they couldn't help but make a profit. I didn't buy stock in any of these companies, even though for some firms that argument is probably true. (It was for Microsoft.) The problem is that for other firms, it will not be true—in any competitive process there are winners and losers, and I, like most people, have no way of differentiating between the two.

DRIVING FORCES IN TODAY'S ECONOMY

Many economists consider competition today to be different from competition 10 or 20 years ago. The differences may be simply a matter of degree, but the reasons are closely tied to globalization and technology. Let's now consider both of these issues, and explain their importance for competition.

Modern competition is different because of globalization and technology.

Globalization

Over the past 20 years markets have become more global in a number of ways. Through the General Agreement on Tariffs and Trade and the World Trade Organization, tariffs and other barriers to trade have been lowered significantly. Political tensions among world superpowers have eased, leading firms to be more confident that they can diversify their production and their sources of inputs. Communication costs have fallen dramatically, which has lowered the cost of searching for the lowest-cost source of inputs and location for production. The global economy gives firms a lot more places to search, and the Internet reduces the costs of that search significantly.

U.S. companies' strategic decision makers must take into account more than just domestic competitors. They face competition from foreign firms and see their potential market as the world, not just the United States.

Globalization has two effects on firms. The first is positive; it increases the size of the gain to the winner. Because the world economy is so much larger than the domestic economy, the rewards for winning globally are much larger than the rewards for winning domestically. The second effect is negative; globalization makes it much harder to win, or even to stay in business. A company may be the low-cost producer in a particular country yet may face foreign competitors that can undersell it. The global economy increases the number of competitors for the firm. Consider the automobile industry. Three companies are headquartered in the United States, but more than 20 automobile companies operate worldwide. U.S. automakers face stiff competition from foreign automakers; unless they meet that competition, they will not survive.

The global economy increases the number of competitors for the firm.

These two effects are, of course, related. When you compete in a larger market, you have to be better to survive, but if you do survive the rewards are greater.

Globalization increases competition by allowing greater specialization and division of labor, which, as Adam Smith first observed in *The Wealth of Nations*, increases growth and improves the standard of living for everyone. Thus, in many ways, globalization is simply another name for increased specialization. Globalization allows (indeed, forces) companies to move operations to countries with a comparative advantage. As they do so, they lower costs of production. Globalization leads to companies specializing in smaller portions of the production process because the potential market is not just one country but the world. Such specialization can lead to increased productivity as firms learn from doing.

Surviving in a Global Economy In order to survive in the global economy, companies must be continually looking for ways to organize production that will improve efficiency and lower costs. One important way they are doing this is by breaking down the production process into its component parts and considering new ways of organizing not only production but also the firm.

Specialization in the modern economy involves dividing production (which includes manufacturing, distribution, sales, research, management, and advertising) into component parts, and searching for the cheapest method of producing each component. Firms may keep production within the company but parcel out portions of it to divisions located in different parts of the world. Or they may simply outsource (buy from another firm) the part of production that can be done more cheaply by other domestic or foreign firms. Globalization lets companies take advantage of cost differentials across countries for different aspects of production. An example of a cost differential is the cost of labor. Labor is a significant input to production whose costs differ widely among countries. Table 14-2 lists hourly compensation for workers in various countries.

For example, average hourly wages in manufacturing are $18.56 in the United States but only $5.24 in Taiwan. Labor-intensive parts of production might be relocated to Taiwan. Keep in mind that labor costs are only one part of the decision to relocate production. Firms also take into account differences in the quality of labor, the infrastructure, and regulations within countries. The fact remains, however, that barriers among countries have been lowered, allowing companies to reconsider moving parts of their operations across the world. Firms are using comparative advantage not just in

Globalization leads to specialization which leads to increased productivity.

Q.9 How does globalization reduce the cost of production?

14.4

Table 14-2   Hourly Compensation for Production Workers

Country	Cost in U.S. Dollars
United States	$18.56
Canada	15.69
Mexico	1.83
Japan	18.05
Korea	5.03
Taiwan	5.24
Germany	27.20
Hong Kong	5.47

Source: International Comparisons of Manufacturing Hourly Compensation Costs, 1998. Bureau of Labor Statistics, (http://stats.bls.gov).

producing an entire product but in producing portions of the product. Firms are reevaluating the entire production process, asking where the production process for each component should occur.

Consider automobiles again. GM, Ford, and Daimler-Chrysler all have production facilities throughout the world. When you buy a GM car, its components will likely have come from 50 different companies, and a Toyota car may have more U.S.-made components than a GM car. Components of the U.S. Air Force's F-16 fighter aircraft are produced in 11 countries, and the aircraft is assembled in 4 countries.

Production within companies is often divided among many countries.

This specialization and division of labor due to globalization means that competition takes place not just in the market for finished products but in numerous layers of the production process. Global competition helps hold down prices and wages firms pay to the factors of production. Those layers that do not face significant global competition may still be able to use lower-cost inputs to production, while maintaining their own high product prices. For example, U.S. legal work, as yet, gets very little international competition because (1) services are difficult to transport cheaply, (2) countries regulate the practice of law within their borders, and (3) laws tend to be country-specific. Hence the prices U.S. lawyers get for their services remain high. The manufacturing layer of production, however, is quite susceptible to foreign competition. This competition has placed downward pressure on U.S. manufacturing prices. Faced with increasing foreign competition, manufacturing workers are forced to accept lower pay. If the workers don't accept lower pay, the company will outsource the manufacturing to a foreign country in which costs are lower.

Consider the letters for the game Scrabble. Until recently these wooden tiles were made in a small Vermont town. In 1998, a Hong Kong company offered to produce the tiles at a lower price, and now Vermont lumber is shipped to Hong Kong, where the Scrabble tiles are made and shipped back to the United States. Hasbro, which makes Scrabble, is still a U.S. company; its marketing and distribution is run from the United States, but the production of its tiles is outsourced to a foreign firm. This is only one of many possible examples.

Does Globalization Eliminate Jobs? It is sometimes argued that global competition eliminates jobs in the United States. To some degree this is absolutely true, but it is important to see global trade as something that increases total production and simultaneously creates jobs. Lowering costs of production can lead to lower product prices, which benefits consumers. Lower prices boost sales and, as sales rise, demand for the inputs to production rises, which can raise the prices of inputs and/or profits. This potentially benefits laborers and others who supply the various inputs to production. Consumers, producers, and suppliers of the factors of production all can potentially benefit.

The reality is that over the past decade the U.S. economy has added 19 million jobs even though U.S. markets have faced increased global competition. How has that happened? U.S. firms, even small ones, more and more see themselves as global companies and are structuring themselves to compete on the global market. As they do so, their costs of production fall or the design of their products improves, putting them in a better position to sell their products. This increases the demand for those aspects of production—generally advertising, marketing, financial services, management, and distribution—which are still U.S.-based. This has helped keep the demand high for U.S. goods and, hence, increased the demand for U.S. labor.

Globalization eliminates jobs, but it also creates jobs.

Until recently, European firms have led a far more sheltered life. European governments' movement toward the European Union (EU) and the euro, the common European currency, are both attempts to add broader competition within European markets and to better prepare European firms to compete in the global economy. Trade restrictions between EU members have been eliminated, and when the euro becomes the only currency among member nations in 2002, comparison shopping will be much easier.

Technology

The second major driving force in the economy in recent years has been **technological development**—*the discovery of new or improved products or methods of production*. As we saw in Chapter 10, technological advance lowers the costs of production and makes economies more efficient—producing more output with the same number of inputs.

Technological advance and globalization go together; technological advance requires large investments of time and money in very specialized areas. Globalization allows for that specialization and the possibility for large revenues to fund research. In addition, specialization allows producers to learn more about the particular aspects of production in which they specialize. As they learn more, they not only become more productive but are more likely to produce technological advances because they gain a deeper understanding of their specialty.

For example, instead of producing an entire line of clothing, companies might specialize in the production of certain types of carbon-based fibers and explore ways of making more useful material. The result of such specialization can be a technological advance, such as Gore-Tex—a material that insulates but also "breathes," and thus keeps individuals dry and cool on warm rainy days, and dry and warm on cold rainy or snowy days. Instead of spreading resources to the entire process of making a jacket, a company can concentrate on just one aspect—fibers.

> *Technological advance and globalization go together; Globalization leads to specialization which leads to technological advance.*

TECHNOLOGY, EFFICIENCY, AND MARKET STRUCTURE

Given the significance of technology, an important question is: What causes technology to grow? Market incentives are an important part of the answer. Before markets existed, economies grew slowly. After markets came into existence in the 1700s, technology advanced more rapidly because individuals gained incentives, in the form of profits, to discover new and cheaper ways of doing things. Globalization of our economy provides an even greater incentive to develop new technologies because the revenue that can be captured from a global market with 6 billion people (world population) is much greater than the revenue that can be generated from 275 million people (U.S. population).

Are some market structures more conducive to growth than others? The answer economists have come to is a tentative yes, and it is an answer that makes certain market structures look better than the way they were presented earlier. Let's review what we've learned about market structure. In the basic supply/demand framework, perfect competition is seen as the benchmark—it leads to efficient outcomes. All other market structures lead to some deadweight loss. But the supply/demand framework does not consider technological issues. It implicitly assumes that technology is unchanging or is unaffected by market structure. If market structure does affect technological advance, another type of efficiency must be considered. This efficiency might be called dynamic efficiency. **Dynamic efficiency** refers to *a market's ability to promote cost-reducing or product-enhancing technological change*. Market structures that best promote technological change are dynamically efficient. Oligopoly provides the best market structure for technological advance. To see why, let's look at the four market structures: perfect competition, monopolistic competition, monopoly, and oligopoly.

> *In considering market structures, dynamic efficiency must be considered as well as static efficiency.*

Perfect Competition and Technology

Perfectly competitive firms have no incentive to develop new technologies. Moreover, perfect competitors earn no profits and consequently may not be able to acquire the funds to devote to research and development that leads to technological change. Even if they did, they would gain little from it. A perfectly competitive market would quickly transfer the gains of the innovation to other firms, making it difficult for the innovating firm to recoup the costs of developing the new technology.

Monopolistic Competition and Technology

Monopolistic competition is somewhat more conducive to technological change because firms have some market power. The promise of gaining additional market power provides the incentive to fund research in new technologies. But, as we learned earlier, monopolistic competitors also lack long-run profits. Easy entry limits their ability to recoup their investment in technological innovation. Eventually, their increased market share will deteriorate and they will return to earning normal profits.

Through its support of patents, the United States does provide incentives to innovate. Patents allow the development of new products through the promise of monopoly profits for a specified period of time. Of course, a firm with a patent will change the market structure into a monopoly.

Monopoly and Technology

On the other end of the spectrum is pure monopoly. Monopolies may earn the profits needed for research and development, but they seldom have the incentive to innovate. Since a monopolist's market is protected from entry, the easiest path is the lazy monopolist path. Since almost all monopolies are created by government (the government gives a monopoly to a specific company), pure monopolists don't face the threat of new competitors. Until recently, European telephone companies and European domestic airlines were monopolies. These industries developed far fewer innovations than did the equivalent U.S. firms that faced more competition, and European industry prices were much higher than those in the United States. A European phone call, for instance, could cost five times more than a U.S. phone call.

In response to these observations, European governments have moved toward privatization and more competition. Both telecommunications and domestic airlines have been privatized, and their monopolies are slowly being removed. The result has been a fall in prices of their products. Whether this privatization will lead to more technological progress remains to be seen, but most economists believe that it will.

Oligopoly and Technology

That leaves oligopoly. Oligopoly is the market structure that is most conducive to technological change. Since the typical oligopolist realizes ongoing economic profit, it has the funds to carry out research and development. Moreover, the belief that its competitors are innovating also forces it to do so. Oligopolists are constantly searching for ways to get an edge on competitors, so most technological advance takes place in oligopolistic industries.

The computer industry is an example of an oligopolistic market that has demonstrated tremendous innovation. Technological progress has been rapid, following *Moore's law*—every 18 months the cost of computer speed is cut by half. Another example is the telecommunications industry, which has been oligopolistic since the breakup of AT&T and has had enormous technological change.

Oligopoly tends to be most conducive to technological change.

Q.10 Why is oligopoly the best market structure for technological advance?

Some economists, especially those who favor a model in which the threat of competition is enough to keep a firm behaving competitively (a contestable market approach), argue that market structure does not matter for technological progress. It is the conditions of entry that matter. They argue that it is primarily developments in pure science that lead to technological advance. Businesses sample technological advances and develop those that have market potential. They argue that technological advances lead to the formation of oligopolies; oligopolies don't necessarily lead to technological advances. The cigarette industry and the aluminum industry are highly oligopolistic but have had little technological advance. In the steel industry, companies outside the group of existing producers started minimills that led to technological advance. The process did not originate with the oligopolistic steel companies.

Network Externalities, Standards, and Technological Lock-In

Network externalities lead to market standards and affect market structure.

In support of the view that technology determines market structure, economists have focused on those aspects of production that involve *network* externalities. An externality, as explained in Chapter 5, is an effect of a decision on a third party that is not taken into account by the decision maker. A **network externality** occurs *when greater use of a product increases the benefit of that product to everyone*. Telephones exhibit network externalities. If you were the only person in the world with a telephone, it would be pretty useless. As the number of people with telephones increases, the telephone's value to communication becomes enormous. Another example of a product with network externalities is the Windows 2000 operating system. It is of much more use to you if many other people use it too, because you can then communicate with other Windows users and purchase software based on that platform.

Network externalities are important to market structure because they lead to the development of industry standards. Standards become important because network externalities involve the interaction among individuals and processes. Many examples of the development of industry standards exist. Some are television broadcast standards (they differ in the United States and Europe, which is why U.S. TVs cannot be used in Europe), building standards (there is a standard size of doors), and electrical current standards (220 or 110; AC or DC).

Standards and Winner-Takes-All Industries Network externalities have two implications for the economic process. First, they increase the likelihood that an industry becomes a winner-takes-all industry. Early in the development of new products, there may be two or three competing standards, any one of which could be a significant improvement over what existed before. As network externalities broaden the use of a product, the need for a single standard becomes more important and eventually one standard wins out. The firm that gets its standard accepted as the industry standard gains an enormous advantage over the other firms. This firm will dominate the market. Microsoft and its Windows operating system is an example of how getting your product accepted as the standard can do wonders for the firm. Once a standard develops, even if the other firms try to enter with a better technological standard, they will have a hard time competing because everyone is already committed to the existing industry standard. Deviating from that standard will reduce the benefits of the network externality.

The first-mover advantage helps explain the high stock prices of start-up technology companies.

First-Mover Advantage Firms in an industry developing a standard will have a strong incentive to be the first to market with the product; they will be willing to have large losses initially in their attempt to set the industry standard. The "first-mover advantage" helps explain why the stock of small technology companies sold for extremely high prices even though they were having large losses. The large losses were created because the firms were spending money to gain market share so that their products would become the industry standard. If the firm is successful in getting its product accepted as the standard, the demand for the product will rise and it will have enormous profits in the future.

Technological Lock-In The second implication of network externalities is that the market might not gravitate toward the most efficient standard. Economists debate how standards can be inefficient and yet be maintained by the first-mover advantage. Some economists argue that the inefficiency can be quite large; others argue that it is small. One aspect of the debate has centered around the QWERTY keyboard on computers. Research by Paul David showed that the arrangement of the keys in the QWERTY keyboard was designed to slow people's typing down so that the keys would not stick on the early mechanical typewriters. As the technology of typewriters improved, the need to slow down typing soon ended, but because the QWERTY keyboard was introduced first, it had become the standard. Other, more efficient keyboards have been proposed but not adopted. The QWERTY keyboard has remained, even with its built-in inefficiencies. David suggested that QWERTY is a metaphor for **technological lock-in**—*when prior use of a technology makes the adoption of subsequent technologies difficult.*

> QWERTY is a metaphor for technological lock-in.

David's technological lock-in argument suggests that many of our institutions and technologies may be inefficient. Other economists argue that the QWERTY keyboard was not that inefficient and if it had been, other keyboards would have been adopted. I am not sure who is right in this debate, but it may soon be made obsolete by another technological development: voice recognition software, which will make keyboarding a relic of the past.

The QWERTY debate is a part of a larger debate about the competitive process and government involvement in that process. The issues are somewhat the same as they were in the earlier discussion of government regulation of natural monopolies. Many economists see government involvement as necessary to protect the economy and the consumer. They advocate what economist Brian Arthur calls "a nudging hand" approach, in which the government keeps the initial competition fair.

Other economists see monopoly as part of the competitive process—something that will be eliminated as competitive forces act against it. Standards will develop, but they will be temporary. If the standards are sufficiently inefficient, they will be replaced, or an entirely new product will come along that makes the old standard irrelevant. For such economists, neither natural monopoly nor technological lock-in is a reason for government interference. Government interference, even the nudging hand, would stop the competitive process and make the society worse off.

> Modern debates about policy regarding competition take dynamic issues into account, but still leave open a debate about what the role of government should be.

Who is right? My own view leans toward the competitive process view with a nudge here or there, but one cannot be dogmatic about it; each case must be decided on its own merits. Moreover, even in those cases where explicit regulation is not called for, the government must set up appropriate rules and property rights to see that the competitive playing field is reasonably level.

An example of what I mean by setting appropriate rules can be seen in the ongoing process of ending local telephone service monopolies and allowing consumers choice in both local and long-distance carriers. Whether this process will be a success depends on the charge the local telephone firms are allowed to make for access to their phone lines into individuals' houses. Government must determine the charge and set up the initial rules. Unless it does, the competitive process won't work properly.

CONCLUSION

The stories of competition and monopoly have no end. Both are continuous processes. Monopolies create competition. Out of the competitive struggle, other monopolies emerge, only to be beaten down by competition. Globalization and technology are big parts of that struggle. Individuals and firms, motivated by self-interest, try to use the changes brought by globalization and technology to their benefit. By doing so they change both the global nature of the economy and the direction of technological change itself.

Chapter Summary

- The goals of real-world firms are many. Profit plays a role, but the actual goals depend on the incentive structure embodied in the structure of the firm.

- The monitoring problem arises because the incentives faced by managers are not always to maximize the profit of the firm. Economists have helped design incentive-compatible contracts to help alleviate the monitoring problem.

- Monopolists facing no competition can become lazy and not hold down costs as much as they can. X-inefficiency refers to firms operating less efficiently than they could technically.

- The competitive process involves a continual fight between monopolization and competition. Suppliers are willing to pay an amount equal to the additional profit gained from the restriction. Consumers are willing to pay an amount equal to the additional cost of products to avoid a restriction. Consumers, however, face a higher cost of organizing their efforts.

- Firms compete against patents that create monopolies by making slight modifications to existing patents and engaging in reverse engineering to copy other firms' products within the limits of the law.

- The U.S. government is deregulating natural monopolies by dividing the firms into various subindustries, carving out that part that exhibits the characteristics of a natural monopoly, and opening the remaining parts to competition.

- Firms protect their monopolies by such means as advertising, lobbying, and producing products that are difficult for other firms to copy.

- Firms will spend money on monopolization until the marginal cost equals the marginal benefit.

- X-inefficiency can be limited by the threat of competition or takeovers. Corporate takeovers often mean change in management.

- Globalization increases competition by providing more competitors to domestic firms at all levels of production and by allowing firms to specialize. Globalization also increases the gain to the industry leader by reducing costs of production and by increasing the size of the market.

- Oligopoly provides the best market structure for technological advance because oligopolists have an incentive to innovate in the form of additional profits and because they have the profits to devote to investing in the research and development of new technologies.

Key Terms

corporate takeover   (309)

dynamic efficiency   (318)

incentive-compatible
    contract   (307)

lazy monopolist   (308)

monitoring problem   (307)

network externality   (320)

patent   (311)

reverse engineering   (312)

technological development
    (318)

technological lock-in
    (321)

X-inefficiency   (308)

Questions for Thought and Review

1. Describe the monitoring problem. How does an incentive-compatible contract address the monitoring problem?

2. Are managers and high-level company officials paid high salaries because they're worth it to the firm, or because they're simply extracting profit from the company

to give themselves? How would you tell whether you're correct?

3. Define *X-inefficiency*. Can a perfect competitor be X-inefficient? Explain why or why not.

4. Some analysts have argued that competition will eliminate X-inefficiency from firms. Will it? Why?

5. Nonprofit colleges must be operating relatively efficiently. Otherwise for-profit colleges would develop and force existing colleges out of business. True or false? Why?

6. If it were easier for consumers to collude than for suppliers to collude, there would often be shortages of goods. True or false? Why?

7. If it were easier for consumers to collude than for suppliers to collude, the price of goods would be lower than the competitive price. True or false? Why?

8. Monopolies are bad; patents give firms monopoly; therefore, patents are bad. True or false? Why?

9. Natural monopolies should be broken up to improve competition. True or false? Why?

10. Technically competent firms will succeed. True or false? Why?

11. Monsanto Corporation lost its U.S. patent protection for its highly successful herbicide Roundup in the year 2000. What do you suppose will be Monsanto's strategy for Roundup in the short run? In the long run?

12. Why would a company want to sacrifice short-run profits to establish market position?

13. What effect has globalization had on the ability of firms to specialize? How has this affected the competitive process?

14. Why would globalization lead to greater technological advance?

15. What two characteristics does a market structure need to have for firms in that industry to engage in technological advance?

16. Taking into consideration changing technologies, why might the basic supply/demand framework not lead to the most efficient outcome?

17. How do network externalities increase the winner-take-all nature of a market?

Problems and Exercises

1. The title of an article in *The Wall Street Journal* was "Pricing of Products Is Still an Art, Often Having Little Link to Costs." In the article, the following cases were cited:

   ● Vodka pricing: All vodkas are essentially indistinguishable—colorless, tasteless, and odorless—and the cost of producing vodka is independent of brand name, yet prices differ substantially.

   ● Perfume: A $100 bottle of perfume may contain $4 to $6 worth of ingredients.

   ● Jean and "alligator/animal" shirts: The "plain pocket" jeans and the Lacoste knockoffs often cost 40 percent less than the brand-name items, yet the knockoffs are essentially identical to the brand-name items.

   a. Discuss whether these differences undermine economists' analysis of pricing.

   b. What do each of these examples likely imply about fixed costs and variable costs?

   c. What do they likely imply about costs of production versus costs of selling?

   d. As what type of market would you characterize each of the above examples?

2. Demonstrate graphically the net gain to producers and the net loss to consumers if suppliers are able to restrict their output to Q_r in the following graph. Demonstrate the net deadweight loss to society.

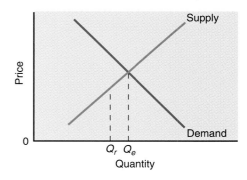

3. Airlines and hotels have many frequent flier and frequent visitor programs in which individuals who fly the airline or stay at the hotel receive bonuses that are the equivalent of discounts.

   a. Give two reasons why these companies have such programs rather than simply offer lower prices.

   b. Can you give other examples of such programs?

   c. What is a likely reason why firms don't monitor these programs?

   d. Should the benefits of these programs be taxable?

4. Up to how much is the monopolist depicted in the accompanying graph willing to spend to protect its market position? Demonstrate your answer graphically.

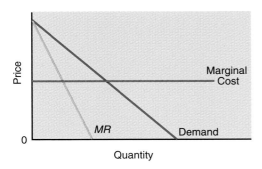

5. In 1998 the hourly cost to employers per German industrial worker was $27.20. The hourly cost to employers per U.S. industrial worker was $18.56, while the average cost per Taiwanese industrial worker was $5.24.
   a. Give three reasons why firms produce in Germany rather than in a lower-wage country.
   b. Germany has just entered into an agreement with other EU countries that allows people in any EU country, including Greece and Italy, which have lower wage rates, to travel and work in any EU country, including high-wage countries. Would you expect a significant movement of workers from Greece and Italy to Germany right away? Why or why not?
   c. Workers in Thailand are paid significantly less than workers in Taiwan. If you were a company CEO, what other information would you want before you decided where to establish a new production facility?

Web Questions

1. Nike coordinates the production and sales of shoes worldwide. Go to Nike's homepage at www.nikebiz.com to read about its World Shoe Project and read "Our Chronology" (nikebiz.com/story/chrono.shtml) to answer the following questions:
   a. What is Nike's World Shoe Project? How does Nike's selling strategy in developing countries differ from its selling strategy in the United States?
   b. What are the reasons Nike cites for selling shoes globally today?
   c. What are the reasons Nike cites for locating production of shoes in foreign countries?
   d. From your reading of "Our Chronology," how have technology and globalization affected Nike since its incorporation as BRS in 1962?
2. Research Dell Corporation's history since its inception in 1984 by going to its home page at www.dell.com and clicking on "About Dell." Answer the following questions:
   a. What product does Dell sell? What was Dell's innovation in this market?

   b. In what countries does Dell sell its products? Which geographic area provides the largest source of revenue?
   c. In what countries does Dell produce its product?
   d. How does Dell plan to continue its growth in the future?
3. The Coalition for Affordable Power–Texas is an advocacy group working toward establishing affordable and reliable electricity in Texas. Go to its home page at www.captx.org to learn more about the group's lobby efforts. Answer the following questions:
   a. What changes to the electricity market does the coalition believe will reduce the cost of electricity to consumers?
   b. What does the coalition believe are the benefits of competition?
   c. What part of the electricity market will remain regulated? What part will be opened to competition?
   d. What specific regulations does the coalition want to remain in place for electricity providers?

Answers to Margin Questions

1. Firms are not interested in just short-run profits. They are also interested in long-run profits. So, a firm might sacrifice short-run profits for higher long-run profits. Also, those making the decisions for the firm are not always those who own the firm. *(306)*
2. Most economists are concerned about third-party payment systems because of the problems of monitoring. It is the consumers who have the strongest incentive to make sure that they are getting value for their money. Any third-party payment system reduces the consumers'

vigilance and therefore puts less pressure on holding costs down. *(307)*
3. A manager does not have the same incentive to hold costs down as an owner does because when an owner holds costs down, the owner's profits are increased, but when a manager holds costs down, the increased profits accrue to the owner, not the manager. Thus the manager has less direct motivation to hold costs down than an owner does. This is especially true if the costs being held down are the manager's perks and pay. *(308)*

4. The threat of a corporate takeover places competitive pressures on firms because it creates the possibility of the managers being replaced and losing all their perks and above-market-equilibrium pay. *(309)*

5. Most agricultural markets are not perfectly competitive because the gains from moving away from competitive markets are fairly large and, for small deviations from competitive markets, the costs are fairly small to those suppliers and consumers who are kept out. This can be seen in the graph below.

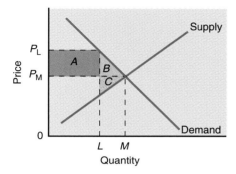

If suppliers producing 0*L* got together and limited supply to *L*, they could push the price up to P_L and could gain the rectangle A for themselves. Consumers and suppliers who are kept out of the market lose triangles *B* and *C* respectively, which, in the diagram, are not only each smaller than *A*, but also *B* and *C* combined are smaller than *A*. Of course, the area A is lost to the consumers, but the costs of organizing those consumers to

fight and protect competition are often prohibitively large. *(310)*

6. It is almost impossible for perfect monopoly to exist because preventing entry is nearly impossible. Monopoly rents are a signal to potential entrants to get the barriers of entry removed. *(311)*

7. The problem with cost-based regulation that sets prices relative to costs is that this removes the incentive for firms to hold down costs and can lead to X-inefficiency. While, in theory, regulators could scrutinize every cost, in practice that is impossible—there would have to be a regulatory board duplicating the work that a firm facing direct market pressure undertakes in its normal activities. *(313)*

8. If the additional benefits of creating or maintaining a monopoly exceed the cost of doing so, do it. If it doesn't, don't. *(314)*

9. Globalization reduces the cost of production in two ways. First, it allows companies to specialize in smaller portions of the production process, which increases competition and lowers cost at all levels of the production process. Second, it allows companies to locate parts of the production process in those countries with comparative advantage in that portion of the production process. *(316)*

10. Oligopoly is the best market structure for technological advance because oligopolists have the profits to devote to research and development and have the incentive to innovate. Innovation may provide the oligopolist with a way to increase market share. *(319)*

Government Policy and Market Failures

15

After reading this chapter, you should be able to:

- Explain what an externality is and show how it affects the market outcome.

- Describe three methods of dealing with externalities.

- Define a public good and explain the problem with determining the value of a public good to society.

- Explain how informational problems can lead to market failure.

- List five reasons why government's solution to a market failure could worsen the market failure.

The business of government is to keep the government out of business—that is unless business needs government aid.

Will Rogers

There is an ongoing (indeed unending) debate: Should the government intervene in markets such as health care or agriculture? The supply/demand framework you learned in the previous chapters was created to provide some insight into answering that question, and in Chapters 5 and 7 we began exploring the issues. Now that we've been through the foundation of supply and demand and various market structures, we're ready to explore economic policy questions more deeply and develop a fuller understanding of some of the roles of government first presented in Chapter 5. This chapter presents the general economic framework, and Chapter 17 discusses how economists use that framework.

Perfect competition serves as a benchmark for judging policies. A foundation for this benchmark is in the work of Stanford economist Kenneth Arrow, who showed that the market translates self-interest into society's interest. (Arrow was given a Nobel Prize in 1972 for this work.) Arrow's ideas are based on many assumptions that can only be touched on in an introductory book. I will, however, discuss one here—the interpretation of the term *society's welfare*. In the economic framework society's welfare is interpreted as coming as close as one can to a *Pareto optimal position*—a position from which no person can be made better off without another being made worse off. (Pareto optimal policies will be discussed more in Chapter 17.)

Let's briefly consider what Arrow proved. He showed that if the market was perfectly competitive, and if there was a complete set of markets (a market for every possible good) now and in the future, the invisible hand would guide the economy to a Pareto optimal position. If these assumptions hold true, the supply curve (which represents the marginal cost to the suppliers) would represent the marginal cost to society. Similarly, the demand curve (which represents the marginal benefit to consumers) would represent the marginal benefit to society. In a supply/demand equilibrium, not only would an individual be as well off as he or she possibly could, given where he or she started from, but so too would society. A perfectly competitive market equilibrium would be in a Pareto optimal position.

A number of criticisms exist to using perfect competition as a benchmark:

1. *The Nirvana criticism:* A perfectly competitive equilibrium is highly unstable. It's usually in some person's interest to restrict entry by others, and, when a market is close to a competitive equilibrium, it is in few people's interest to stop such restrictions. Thus,

KNOWING THE TOOLS

Pareto Optimality and the Perfectly Competitive Benchmark

perfect competition will never exist in the real world. Comparing reality to a situation that cannot occur (i.e., to Nirvana) is unfair and unhelpful because it leads to attempts to achieve the unachievable. A better benchmark would be a comparison with workable competition—a state of competition that one might reasonably hope could exist.

2. *The second-best criticism:* The conditions that allow the conclusion that perfect competition leads to a Pareto optimal position are so restrictive that they are never even approached in reality. If the economy deviates in hundreds of ways from perfect competition, how are we to know whether a movement toward a competitive equilibrium in one of those ways will move the economy closer to perfect competition?

3. *The normative criticism:* Even if the previous two criticisms didn't exist, the perfect competition benchmark still isn't appropriate because there is nothing necessarily wonderful about Pareto optimality. A Pareto optimal position could be a horrendous position, depending on the starting position. For example, say the starting position is the following: One person has all the world's revenues and all the other people are starving. If that rich person would be made worse off by having some money taken from him and given to the starving poor, that starting position would be Pareto optimal. By most people's normative criteria, it would also be a lousy position.

Critics of the use of the perfect competition benchmark argue that society has a variety of goals. Pareto optimality may be one of them, but it's only one. They argue that economists should take into account all of society's goals—not just Pareto optimality— when determining a benchmark for judging policies.

The economic framework can be called the *invisible hand framework*. It says that if markets are perfectly competitive they will lead individuals to make voluntary choices that are in the society's interest. It is as if individuals are guided by an invisible hand to do what society wants them to do.

 15.1

MARKET FAILURES

For the invisible hand to guide private actions toward the social good, a number of conditions must be met. When those conditions are not met, economists say that there is a **market failure**—*a situation in which the invisible hand pushes in such a way that individual decisions do not lead to socially desirable outcomes*. In this chapter we consider three sources of market failures: externalities, public goods, and imperfect information.

Three important sources of market failure are externalities, public goods, and imperfect information.

Any time a market failure exists there is a reason for possible government intervention to improve the outcome. But it is important to remember that even if these market failures exist, it is not clear that government action will improve the result, since the politics of implementing the solution often lead to further problems. These problems of government intervention are often called *government failures*, so after discussing the three sources of market failures, we will discuss government failures. The economic policy debate will then be framed as a matter of choosing which failure is likely to be the lesser of two evils.

Economic policy is often a choice between market failure and government failure.

EXTERNALITIES

An important requirement for the invisible hand to guide markets in society's interest is that market transactions have no side effects on anyone not involved in them. As I discussed in Chapter 5, such side effects are called **externalities**—*the effect of a decision on a third party that is not taken into account by the decision maker.* Externalities can be either positive or negative. Secondhand smoke and carbon monoxide emissions are examples of **negative externalities**, which occur *when the effect of a decision not taken into account by the decision maker is detrimental to others.* **Positive externalities** occur *when the effect of a decision is not taken into account by the decision maker is beneficial to others.* An example is education. When you purchase a college education, it affects not only you but others as well. Innovation is another example. The invention of the personal computer has had significant beneficial effects on society, which were not taken into account by the inventors. When there are externalities, the supply and/or demand curves no longer represent the marginal cost and marginal benefit curves to society.

An externality is an effect of a decision on a third party not taken into account by the decision maker.

A Negative Externality Example

Say that you and I agree that I'll produce steel for you. I'll build my steel plant on land I own, and start producing. We both believe our welfare will improve. But what about my plant's neighbors? The resulting smoke will pollute the air they breathe. The people involved in the market trade (you and I) are made better off, but people external to the trade are made worse off. Thus, there is a negative externality. My production of steel has a cost to society that neither you nor I take into account.

The effect of a negative externality is shown in Figure 15-1. The supply curve S represents the marginal private cost to society of producing steel. The demand curve D rep-

Q-1 Why does the existence of an externality prevent the market from working properly?

Figure 15-1   The Effect of a Negative Externality

When there is a negative externality, the marginal private cost will be below the marginal social cost and the competitive price will be too low to maximize social welfare.

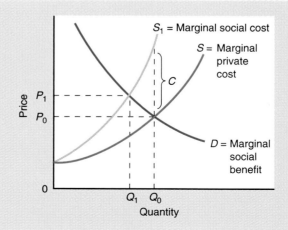

resents the marginal social benefit of consuming the steel. When there are no external-ities, the marginal private costs and benefits represent the marginal social costs and ben-efits, so the supply/demand equilibrium (P_0, Q_0) represents the point where the marginal social benefit equals the marginal social cost. At that point society is as well off as possible.

But now consider what happens when production results in negative externalities. In that case people not involved in production also incur costs. This means that the supply curve no longer represents both the marginal private and marginal social costs of supply-ing the good. Marginal social cost is greater than the marginal private cost. This case can be represented by adding a curve in Figure 15-1 called the *marginal social cost curve*. The **marginal social cost** includes all the marginal costs that society bears—or *the marginal pri-vate costs of production plus the cost of the negative externalities associated with that production*.

Since in this case the externality represents an additional cost to society, the mar-ginal social cost curve lies above the marginal private cost curve. The distance between the two curves represents the additional marginal cost of the externality. For example, at quantity Q_0, the private marginal cost faced by the firm is P_0. The marginal cost from the externality at quantity Q_0 is shown by distance C. The externality cost is not taken into account, and the supply/demand equilibrium is at too high a quantity, Q_0, and at too low a price, P_0.

Notice that the market solution results in a level of steel production that exceeds the level that equates the marginal social costs with the marginal social benefits. If the market is to maximize welfare, some type of government intervention may be needed to reduce production from Q_0 to Q_1 and raise price from P_0 to P_1.

A Positive Externality Example

Private trades can also benefit third parties not involved in the trade. These are positive externalities. Again, an example is education. Consider a person who is working and takes a class at night. He or she will bring the knowledge from class back to co-workers through day-to-day interaction on projects. The co-workers will be learning the mate-rial from the class indirectly. They are outside the initial decision to take the class, but they benefit nonetheless.

In the case of positive externalities, the market will not provide enough of the good. Let's see how. In Figure 15-2, we start again with the standard demand and supply

When there are externalities the marginal social cost differs from the marginal private cost.

Q-2 If a positive externality ex-ists, does that mean that the mar-ket works better than if no externality exists?

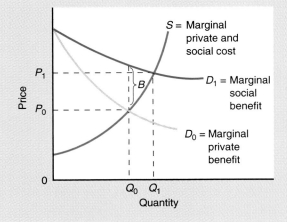

Figure 15-2   A Positive Externality

When there is a positive exter-nality, the marginal social bene-fit will be above the marginal private benefit and the market price will be too low to maxi-mize social welfare.

APPLYING THE TOOLS

Common Resources
and the Tragedy
of the Commons

Individuals tend to overuse commonly owned goods. Let's consider an example—say that grazing land is held in common. Individuals are free to bring their sheep to graze on the land. What is likely to happen? Each grazing sheep will reduce the amount of grass for other sheep. If individuals don't have to pay for grazing, when deciding how much to graze their sheep they will not take into account the cost to others of their sheep's grazing. The result may be overgrazing—killing the grass and destroying the grazing land. This is known as the *tragedy of the commons*. A more contemporary example of the tragedy of the commons is fishing. The sea is a common resource; no one owns it, and whenever people catch fish, they reduce the number of fish that others can catch. The result will likely be overfishing.

The tragedy of the commons is an example of the problems posed by externalities. Catching fish imposes a negative externality. Because of the negative effect on others, the social cost of catching a fish is greater than the private cost. Overfishing has been a problem in the United States and throughout the world. Thus, the tragedy of the commons is caused by individuals not taking into account the negative externalities of their actions.

Why doesn't the market solve the externality problem? Some economists argue that in the tragedy of the commons examples it would, if given a chance. The problem is a lack of property rights (lack of ownership). If rights to all goods were defined, the tragedy of the commons would disappear. In the fishing example, if someone owned the sea, he or she would charge individuals to fish. By charging for fishing rights the owner would internalize the externality and thus avoid the tragedy of the commons.

Positive externalities make the marginal private benefit below the marginal social benefit.

curves. The supply curve S represents the marginal private cost of the course. The demand curve D_0 is the marginal private benefit to those who take the course. Since others not taking the course also benefit, the marginal social benefit, shown by D_1, is above the marginal private benefit. The **marginal social benefit** equals *the marginal private benefit of consuming a good plus the benefits of the positive externalities resulting from consuming that good.* The vertical distance between D_0 and D_1 is the additional benefit that others receive at each quantity. At quantity Q_0, the market equilibrium, the marginal benefit of the externality is shown by distance B. At this quantity, the marginal social benefit exceeds the marginal social cost. The market provides too little of the good. The optimal price and quantity for society are P_1 and Q_1, respectively. Again, some type of intervention to increase quantity and lower price may be warranted.

ALTERNATIVE METHODS OF DEALING WITH EXTERNALITIES

Externalities can be dealt with via:
1. direct regulation,
2. incentive policies, and
3. voluntary solutions.

Ways to deal with externalities include (1) direct regulation, (2) incentive policies (tax incentive policies and market incentive policies), and (3) voluntary solutions.

Direct Regulation

In a program of **direct regulation,** *the amount of a good people are allowed to use is directly limited by the government.* Let's consider an example. Say we have two individuals, Ms. Thrifty, who uses 10 gallons of gasoline a day, and Mr. Big, who uses 20 gallons of gas a day. Say we have decided that we want to reduce total daily gas consumption by 10 percent, or 3 gallons. The regulatory solution might require both individuals to reduce consumption by some specified amount. Likely direct regulatory reduction strategies would be to require an equal quantity reduction (each consumer reducing consumption by 1.5 gallons) or an equal percentage reduction (each consumer reducing consumption by 10 percent).

Both of those strategies would work, but neither would be **efficient** (*achieving a goal at the lowest cost in total resources without consideration as to who pays those costs*). This is because direct regulation does not take into account that the costs of reducing consumption may differ among individuals. Say, for example, that Ms. Thrifty could easily (i.e., almost costlessly) reduce consumption by 3 gallons while Mr. Big would find it very costly to reduce consumption by even 0.5 gallon. In that case, either regulatory solution would be **inefficient** (*achieving a goal in a more costly manner than necessary*). It would be less costly (more efficient) to have Ms. Thrifty undertake most of the reduction. A policy that would automatically make the person who has the lower cost of reduction *choose* (as opposed to being *required*) to undertake the most reduction would achieve the same level of reduction at a lower cost. In this case the efficient policy would get Ms. Thrifty to choose to undertake the majority of the reduction.

Incentive Policies

Two types of incentive policies would each get Ms. Thrifty to undertake the larger share of reduction. One is to create a tax incentive to achieve the desired reduction; the other is to create a type of property right embodied in a permit or certificate, and to allow individuals to trade those property rights freely.

Tax Incentive Policies Let's say that the government imposes a tax on gasoline consumption of 50 cents per gallon. This would be an example of a **tax incentive program** (*a program using a tax to create incentives for individuals to structure their activities in a way that is consistent with the desired ends*). Since Ms. Thrifty can almost costlessly reduce her gasoline consumption, she will likely respond to the tax by reducing gasoline consumption, say, by 2.75 gallons. She pays only $3.63 in tax but undertakes most of the conservation. Since Mr. Big finds it very costly to reduce his consumption of gasoline, he will likely respond by reducing gasoline consumption by very little, say by 0.25 gallon. He pays $9.88 in tax but does little of the conservation.

In this example, the tax has achieved the desired end in a more efficient manner than would the regulatory solution—the person for whom the reduction is least costly cuts consumption the most. Why? Because the incentive to reduce is embodied in the price, and individuals are forced to choose how much to change their consumption. The tax has made them internalize the externality. The solution also has a significant element of fairness about it. The person who conserves the most pays the least tax.

Let's now consider how the tax incentive solution will solve the problem in our earlier example of steel production creating an externality. Figure 15-3 shows the situation. Say the government determines that the additional marginal social cost of producing steel equals C. If the government sets the pollution tax on steel production at C, the firm will reduce its output to Q_1 on its own. Such taxes on externalities are often called **effluent fees**—*charges imposed by government on the level of pollution created*. The efficient tax equals the additional cost imposed on society but not taken into account by the decision maker. With such a tax, the cost the suppliers face is the social cost of supplying the good. With the tax, the invisible hand guides the traders to equate the marginal social cost to the marginal social benefit and the equilibrium is socially optimal.

Market Incentive Policies A second incentive policy that gets individuals to internalize an externality is a **market incentive plan** (*a plan requiring market participants to certify that they have reduced total consumption—not necessarily their own individual consumption—by a specified amount*). Such a program would be close to the regulatory solution but involves a major difference. If individuals choose to reduce consumption by more than the required amount, they will be given a marketable certificate that they

Q-3 It is sometimes said that there is a trade-off between fairness and efficiency. Explain one way in which that is true and one way in which that is false.

Economists tend to like incentive policies to deal with externalities.

Q-4 In what sense is the tax incentive approach fair?

Figure 15-3   Regulation through Taxation

If the government sets a tax sufficient to take into account a negative externality, individuals will respond by reducing the quantity of the pollution-causing activity supplied to a level that individuals would have supplied had they included the negative externality in their decision.

Incentive policies are more efficient than direct regulatory policies.

can sell to someone who has chosen to reduce consumption by less than the required amount. By buying that certificate, the person who has not personally reduced consumption by the requisite amount will have met the program's requirements. Let's see how the program would work with Mr. Big and Ms. Thrifty.

In our example, Mr. Big finds it very costly to reduce consumption while Ms. Thrifty finds it easy. So we can expect that Mr. Big won't reduce consumption much and will instead buy certificates from Ms. Thrifty, who will choose to undertake significant reduction in her consumption to generate the certificates, assuming she can sell them to Mr. Big for a high enough price to make that reduction worth her while. So, as was the case in the tax incentive program, Ms. Thrifty undertakes most of the conservation—but she reaps a financial benefit for it.

Obviously there are enormous questions about the administrative feasibility of these types of proposals, but what's important to understand here is not the specifics of the proposals but the way in which incentive policies are *more efficient* than the regulatory policy. As I stated before, *more efficient* means *less costly* in terms of resources, with no consideration paid to who is bearing those costs. Incorporating the incentive into a price and then letting individuals choose how to respond to that incentive lets those who find it least costly undertake most of the adjustment.

More and more, governments are exploring incentive policies for solving problems. Sin taxes (taxes on goods government believes to be harmful) are an example of the tax incentive approach. (These will be discussed further in Chapter 17.) Marketable permits for pollution, discussed in the accompanying box, are an example of the marketable certificate approach. You can probably see more examples discussed in the news.

Voluntary Reductions

A third possibility to address externalities is to make the reduction voluntary, leaving individuals free to choose whether to follow what is socially optimal or what is privately optimal. Let's consider how a voluntary program might work in our Mr. Big and Ms. Thrifty example. Let's say that Ms. Thrifty has a social conscience and undertakes most of the reduction while Mr. Big has no social conscience and does not reduce consumption significantly. It seems that this is a reasonably efficient solution. But what if the costs were reversed and Mr. Big had the low cost of reduction and Ms. Thrifty had the high cost? Then the voluntary solution would not be so efficient. Of course, it could be argued that when people choose to do something voluntarily it makes them better off.

APPLYING THE TOOLS

Marketable Permits for Pollution

Marketable permits are being used more and more to deal with environmental issues. In many areas, air quality permits are required of firms before they may begin production. The only way a new firm may start production is if it buys permits from existing firms, which are allowed to sell permits only if they decrease air pollution by the amount of the permit.

Another example of the use of marketable permits is a program instituted in California to deal with a drought. The only way a construction firm is allowed to build a new house is if it reduces existing water usage by a specific amount. To do this, the firm goes around to existing home owners, offering to put in water-saving devices for free. In some areas, more than 60 percent of the existing homes have introduced these water-saving devices, which were paid for by the construction firms and hence indirectly by the new home buyers.

On the national level, the United States introduced Project XL, which lets firms reduce air pollutants below existing requirements and, in doing so, free themselves from some specific regulations. This allows the firms to trade some pollution internally for others, achieving some of the flexibility that the marketable permits provide on an inter-firm level.

So one could argue that even in the case where Ms. Thrifty has a high cost of reduction and voluntarily undertakes most of the reduction, she also has a high benefit from reducing her consumption.

15.2

The largest problem with voluntary solutions is that a person's willingness to do things for the good of society generally depends on that person's belief that others will also be helping.

If a socially conscious person comes to believe that a large number of other people won't contribute, he or she will often lose that social conscience: Why should I do what's good for society if others won't? This is an example of the **free rider problem** (*individuals' unwillingness to share in the cost of a public good*), which economists believe will often limit, and eventually undermine, social actions based on voluntary contributions. A small number of free riders will undermine the social consciousness of many in the society and eventually the voluntary policy will fail.

There are exceptions. During times of war and extreme crisis, voluntary programs are often successful. For example, during World War II the war effort was financed in part through successful voluntary programs. But for other long-term social problems that involve individuals accepting significant changes in their actions, generally the results of voluntary programs haven't been positive.

Q.5 What are two reasons to be dubious of solutions based on voluntary action that is not in people's self-interest?

Economists believe that a small number of free riders will undermine the social consciousness of many in the society and that eventually a voluntary policy will fail.

The Optimal Policy

An **optimal policy** is *one in which the marginal cost of undertaking the policy equals the marginal benefit of that policy.* If a policy isn't optimal (that is, the marginal cost exceeds the marginal benefit or the marginal benefit exceeds the marginal cost), resources are being wasted because the savings from a reduction of expenditures on a program will be worth more than the gains that would be lost from reducing the program, or the benefit from spending more on a program will be worth more than the cost of expanding the program.

Let's consider an example of this latter case. Say the marginal benefit of a program significantly exceeds it marginal cost. That would seem good. But that would mean that we could expand the program by decreasing some other program or activity whose marginal benefit doesn't exceed its marginal cost, with a net gain in benefits to society. To spend too little on a beneficial program is as inefficient as spending too much on a non-beneficial program.

If a policy isn't optimal, resources are being wasted because the savings from reduction of expenditures on a program will be worth more than the gains that will be lost from reducing the program.

Some environmentalists want to rid the world of all pollution while most economists want to reduce pollution to the point where the marginal cost of reducing pollution equals the marginal benefit.

This concept of optimality carries over to economists' view of most problems. For example, some environmentalists would like to completely rid the economy of pollution. Most economists believe that doing so is costly and that since it's costly, one would want to take into account those costs. That means that society should reduce pollution only to the point where the marginal cost of reducing pollution equals the marginal benefit. That point is called the *optimal level of pollution—the amount of pollution at which the marginal benefit of reducing pollution equals the marginal cost*. To reduce pollution below that level would make society as a whole worse off.

PUBLIC GOODS

15.3

A **public good** is *a good that is nonexclusive (no one can be excluded from its benefits) and nonrival (consumption by one does not preclude consumption by others)*. As I discussed in Chapter 5, in reality there is no such thing as a pure public good, but many of the goods that government provides—education, defense, roads, and legal systems—have public good aspects to them. Probably the closest example we have of a pure public good is national defense. A single individual cannot protect himself or herself from a foreign invasion without protecting his or her neighbors as well. Protection for one person means that many others are also protected. Governments generally provide goods with significant public aspects to them because private businesses will not supply them, unless they transform the good into a mostly private good.

What is and is not considered a public good depends on technology. Consider roads—at one point roads were often privately supplied, since with horses and buggies, the road owners could charge tolls relatively easily. Then, with the increased speed of the automobile, collecting tolls on most roads became too time-consuming. At that point the nonexclusive public good aspect of roads became dominant—once a road was built, it was most efficiently supplied to others at a zero cost—and government became the provider of most roads. Today, with modern computer technology, sensors that monitor road use can be placed on roads and in cars. Charging for roads has once again become more feasible. In the future we may again see more private provision of roads. Some economists have even called for privatization of existing roads, and private roads are being built in California and in Bangkok, Thailand.

One of the reasons that pure public goods are sufficiently interesting to warrant a separate discussion is that a modification of the supply/demand model can be used to neatly contrast the efficient supply of a private good with the efficient supply of a public good. The key to understanding the difference is to recognize that once a pure public good is supplied to one individual, it is simultaneously supplied to all, whereas a private good is supplied only to the individual who purchased it. For example, if the price of an apple is 50 cents, the efficient purchase rule is for individuals to buy apples until the marginal benefit of the last apple consumed is equal to 50 cents. The analysis focuses on the individual. If the equilibrium price is 50 cents, the marginal benefit of the last apple sold in the market is equal to 50 cents. That benefit is paid for by one individual and is enjoyed by one individual.

Now consider a public good. Say that the marginal benefit of an additional missile for national defense is 50 cents to one individual and 25 cents to another. In this case the value of providing one missile provides 75 cents (25 + 50) of total social benefit. With a public good the focus is on the group. The societal benefit in the case of a public good is the *sum* of the individual benefits (since each individual gets the benefit of the good). With private goods, we count only the benefit to the person buying the good, since only one person gets it.

Figure 15-4   The Market Value of a Public Good

The market demand curve for a public good is constructed differently than for a private good. Since a public good is enjoyed by many people without diminishing its value to others, the market demand curve is constructed by adding the marginal benefit each individual receives from the public good at each quantity. For example, the value of the first unit to the market is $1.10, the sum of individual A's value ($0.50) and individual B's value ($0.60). In other words, vertically sum the individual demand curves to construct the market demand curve for a public good.

The above reasoning can be translated into supply and demand curves. The market demand curve represents the marginal benefit of a good to society. As we saw in Chapter 4 in the case of a private good, the market demand curve is the *horizontal sum* of the individual demand curves. The total amount of a private good supplied is split up among many buyers. While the market demand curve for a private good is constructed by adding all the quantities demanded at every price, the market demand curve in the case of public goods is the *vertical sum* of the individual demand curves at every quantity. The quantity of the good supplied is not split up; the full benefit of the total output is received by everyone.

With private goods you sum demand curves horizontally; with public goods you sum it vertically.

Figure 15-4 gives an example of a public good. In it we assume that society consists of only two households—A and B, with demand curves D_A and D_B. To arrive at the market demand curve for the public good, we vertically add the price that each individual is willing to pay for each unit since both receive a benefit when the good is supplied. Thus, at quantity 1 we add $0.60 to $0.50. We arrive at $1.10, the marginal benefit of providing the first missile. By adding together the willingness to pay by individuals A and B for quantities 2 and 3, we generate the market demand curve for missiles. Extending this example from two individuals to the economy as a whole you can see that, even though the benefit of a public good is small to each person, the total benefit is large. With 275 million people in the United States, the benefit of that missile would be $138 million even if each person valued it on average at 50 cents.

Adding demand curves vertically is easy to do in textbooks, but not in practice. With private-good demand curves individuals reveal their demand when they buy a good. If they don't buy it, it wasn't worth the price. Since individuals do not purchase public goods, their demand is not revealed by their actions. Government must guess at it. If a public good is to be financed by a tax on the citizens who benefit from it, individuals have an incentive to conceal their willingness to pay for it. This is why in the supply of public goods we see the free rider problem. The self-interested citizen wants to benefit from the public good without bearing the cost of providing it. Similarly, if respondents think they will not be taxed, but will benefit from the public good, they have an incentive to exaggerate their willingness to pay.

Q-6 Why is it so difficult for government to decide the efficient quantity of a public good to provide?

INFORMATIONAL PROBLEMS

The final case of market failure I want to address is caused by imperfect information. The perfectly competitive model assumes that individuals have perfect information about what they are buying. So, if they voluntarily buy a good, it is a reasonable presumption that they expect that they are making themselves better off by doing so. But what happens if the buyer doesn't have perfect information? Say someone convinces you that he is selling you an expensive diamond, but it is actually glass. You are convinced, so you buy it. Or alternatively, say someone convinces you her used car is a cherry (in perfect condition). You buy it only to discover later that it is a lemon (faulty) and won't run no matter what you do to it.

Real-world markets often involve deception, cheating, and inaccurate information. For example, car dealers know about defects in the cars they sell but do not always reveal those defects to consumers. Another example is when consumers who want health insurance do not reveal their health problems to the insurance company. In both cases, it is in the interest of the knowledgeable person not to reveal information that the other person or firm would need to know to make an informed decision about the transaction. Hence, imperfect information can be a cause of market failure.

When there is a lack of information, or when buyers and sellers don't have equal information, markets in some goods may not work well. Let's consider the used car example more carefully to make the point. Let's say that owners of used cars know everything about their cars, but buyers know nothing. If sellers are profit maximizers, they will reveal as little as possible about the car's defects; they will reveal as much as they can about its good qualities.

To make the example specific, let's say also that only two types of cars exist—"lemons" that are worth $4,000 and "cherries" that are worth $8,000. The market initially consists of equal quantities of lemons and cherries. Say also that the buyers cannot distinguish between lemons and cherries. What will happen? Individuals, knowing that they have a 50 percent chance of buying a lemon, may well offer around $6,000 (the average of $4,000 and $8,000). Given that price, individuals with cherries will be very hesitant to sell, and individuals with lemons will be anxious to sell. Eventually, buyers will recognize that the sellers of cherries have left the market. In the end only lemons will be offered for sale, and buyers will only offer $4,000 with the expectation that cars offered would be lemons. When the market for cherries—good used cars—has disappeared, the result is a market failure.

Such a market failure is called an **adverse selection problem**—*a problem that occurs when buyers and sellers have different amounts of information about the good for sale*. In the case of adverse selection, only lemons—those with the most problems—remain in the market. Take the example of medical insurance. Insurance providers need to make a profit. To do so, they set rates that reflect their estimate of the costs of providing health care. The problem is that individuals have better information about their health than do the insurance providers. Health insurers want a diverse group to spread out the costs, but face a greater demand among those with the worst health problems. Seeing that their customers have more health problems than average, medical insurance providers raise the rates. Those who are in good health find those charges to be too high and reduce the quantity of health insurance they purchase. The providers, therefore, are left with a group with an even higher incidence of health problems and higher medical costs than the general population. Less than the desired amount of low-cost insurance exists for people in good health.

Workplace safety is another example of imperfect information causing market failure. Although businesses have an incentive to provide a safe working environment to

---

Imperfect information can be a cause of market failure.

Adverse selection problems can occur when buyers and sellers have different amounts of information about the good for sale.

Q-7 How would you expect medical insurance rates to change if medical insurers could use information contained in DNA to predict the likelihood of major medical illnesses?

limit costs, they may not choose a level of safety that would be preferred by employees. If the employer does not disclose unsafe working conditions, and those conditions cannot be easily identified by workers, there is again an informational problem. Employees may not be adequately compensated for the risks they face.

POLICIES TO DEAL WITH INFORMATIONAL PROBLEMS

What should society do about informational problems that lead to market failures? One answer is to regulate the market and see that individuals provide the right information. Another is for the government to license individuals in the market, requiring those with licenses to reveal full information about the good being sold. Government has set up numerous regulatory commissions and passed laws that require full disclosure of information. The Federal Trade Commission, the Consumer Product Safety Commission, the Occupational Safety and Health Administration, the Food and Drug Administration, and state licensing boards are all examples of regulatory solutions designed to partially offset informational market failures.

But these regulatory solutions have problems of their own. The commissions and their regulations introduce restrictions on individuals that can potentially slow down the economic process, and can prevent trades that people want to make. Consider as an example the Food and Drug Administration (FDA). It restricts what drugs may be sold until sufficient information about the drugs' effects can be disclosed. The FDA testing and approval process can take 5 or 10 years, is extraordinarily costly, and raises the price of drugs. The delays have caused some people to break the law by taking the drugs before they are approved.

A Market in Information

Economists who lean away from government regulation suggest that the problem presented by the information examples above are not really a problem of market failure but instead a problem of the lack of a market. Information is valuable, and is an economic product in its own right. Left on their own, markets will develop to provide the information that people need, and are willing to pay for. (For example, a large number of consumer magazines provide such information.) In the car example, the buyer can hire a mechanic who can test the car with sophisticated diagnostic techniques and determine whether it is likely a cherry or a lemon. Firms can offer guarantees that will provide buyers with assurance that they can either return the car or have it fixed if the car is a lemon. There are many variations of such market solutions. If the government regulates information, these markets may not develop; people might rely on government instead of markets. Thus, the informational problem is not a problem of the market; it is a problem of government regulation.

Information problems may be a problem of the lack of a market.

Licensing of Doctors

Let's consider another informational problem that contrasts the market approach with the regulatory approach: medical licensing.[1] Currently all doctors are required to be licensed in order to practice, but this was not always the case.

---

[1]The arguments presented here about licensing doctors also apply to dentists, lawyers, college professors, cosmetologists (in some states, cosmetologists must be licensed), and other professional groups.

In the early 1800s, medical licenses were not required by law in the United States, so anyone who wanted to could set up shop as a physician. The most popular type of medical treatment at the time was heroic therapy, which consisted primarily of blood-letting, blistering, and the administration of massive doses of mineral poisons, such as mercury.[2] The practitioners of two alternative types of medicine—homeopathy (which focused on natural healing) and eclecticism (which combined a variety of approaches)—together laid the foundation of modern medicine. These practitioners challenged the status quo by arguing that heroic therapy was not helping people. They pressured Congress to pass licensure laws requiring that all doctors earn a license to practice medicine by receiving training in homeopathy and eclecticism. Ever since, it has been illegal to practice medicine without a license.

To get that license, one must go through a pre-med program in college, four years of medical school, and a residency in a hospital for anywhere from one to seven years, as well as pass a series of National Medical Board examinations.

Licensing of doctors is justified by information problems. Since individuals often don't have an accurate way of deciding whether a doctor is good, government intervention is necessary. The information problem is solved because licensing requires that all doctors have at least a minimum competency. People have the *information* that a doctor must be competent because they see the license framed and hanging on the doctor's office wall.

Sometimes even when people have the information available, they don't use it *rationally*. Without licensing, businesses would be established to sell a whole set of schemes, such as using laetrile to fight cancer or using vitamin C to fight everything. According to scientific research, laetrile does not cure cancer and vitamin C does not cure everything.

A small number of economists, of whom Milton Friedman is the best known, have proposed that licensure laws be eliminated, leaving the medical field unlicensed. While such a proposal is supported by only a few economists, it's instructive to consider their proposal: Let anyone practice medicine who wishes to.

They argue that licensure was instituted as much, or more, to restrict supply as it was to help the consumer. Specifically, critics of medical licensure raise these questions:

> Why, if licensed medical training is so great, do we even need formal restrictions to keep other types of medicine from being practiced?

> Whom do these restrictions benefit: the general public or the doctors who practice mainstream medicine?

> What have the long-run effects of licensure been?

Even the strongest critics of licensure agree that, in the case of doctors, the informational argument for government intervention is strong. But the question is whether licensure is the right form of government intervention. Why doesn't the government simply provide the public with information about which treatments work and which don't? That would give the freest rein to *consumer sovereignty* (*the right of the individual to make choices about what is consumed and produced*). As for the rationality argument, critics of licensure simply reject it out of hand. They ask: Who is the government to decide for people what is, or isn't, good for them? If people have the necessary information but still choose to treat cancer with laetrile or treat influenza with massive doses of vitamin C, why should the government tell them they can't?

If the informational alternative is preferable to licensure, why didn't the government choose it? Friedman argues that government didn't follow that path because the

Some economists argue that licensure laws were established to restrict supply, not to help the consumer.

---

[2]Bloodletting involved extracting blood from the body, based on the theory that the person's problem stemmed from "too much blood." Blistering involved causing blisters to form on the body, based on the theory that when they burst, they would expel the poisonous matter that was making the person ill.

licensing was done as much for the doctors as for the general public. Licensure has led to a monopoly position for doctors. They can restrict supply and increase price and thereby significantly increase their incomes. Friedman further argues that the group most hurt by the decision to choose the licensure alternative is the poor, who often can't afford the higher fees licensed doctors charge.

Let's now take a closer look at the informational alternative.

The Informational Alternative to Licensure

The informational alternative is to allow anyone to practice medicine, but to have the government certify doctors' backgrounds and qualifications. The government would require that doctors' backgrounds be made public knowledge. Each doctor would have to post the following information prominently in his or her office:

1. Grades in college.
2. Grades in medical school.
3. Success rate for various procedures.
4. References.
5. Medical philosophy.
6. Charges and fees.

According to supporters of the informational alternative, these data would allow individuals to make informed decisions about their medical care. Like all informed decisions, they would be complicated. For instance, doctors who take only patients with minor problems can show high "success rates," while doctors who are actually more skilled but who take on problem patients may have to provide more extensive information so people can see why their success rates shouldn't be compared to those of the doctors who take just easy patients. But despite the problems, supporters of the informational alternative argue that it's better than the current situation.

Current licensure laws don't provide any of this information to the public. All a patient knows is that a doctor has managed to get through medical school and has passed the medical board exams (which are, after all, only sets of multiple-choice questions). The doctor may have done all this 30 years ago, possibly by the skin of his or her teeth, but, once licensed, a doctor is a doctor for life. (A well-known doctor joke is the following: What do you call the person with the lowest passing grade point average in medical school? Answer: Doctor.) Thus, the informational alternative would provide much more useful data to the public than the current licensing procedure.

Let's now consider two examples of how the informational alternative would work.

Two Examples Say you're wondering whether that new mole on your arm is cancerous. What do you do? Under our current system, you ask your private physician, or you go to your local hospital and ask. The physician, most likely, won't know. He or she had two or three lectures on skin cancer in medical school and may have seen some in practice, but probably isn't a specialist in cancer. So all you get is a referral to a specialist (cost: $50).

Why not go to the specialist in the first place? By agreement among doctors, specialists usually will see only those patients who have been referred to them by a general physician.[3] Now let's say that you go to the specialist, who looks at the mole and recognizes

Q-8 Who would benefit and who would lose if an informational alternative to licensing doctors were used?

---

[3]Sometimes the general physician and the specialist are in the same group practice, and they each contribute a percentage of their income to a common pool, which is later divided among the members of the pool. Thus, when the doctors are in a group practice, the referring doctor gets a percentage of the specialist's fee. In such cases it's not even clear that your doctor has an incentive to send you to the most competent specialist!

immediately that it's just a mole (cost: $70). But she orders a biopsy, just to be sure (cost: $140). She's right and you're relieved, but you're also $260 poorer. To find out from the specialist whether the mole was cancerous cost you $260 and about four hours of your time. Many people without insurance won't pay the cost. They'll just hope the mole isn't cancerous.

15.4   Consider this hypothetical informational alternative: You go to a person who hasn't been to medical school, but who's been through a special one-year training program in diagnosing malignant carcinomas (skin cancer). The success rate of detection by such persons is 99.8 percent; the fee is $10 if no biopsy is needed, $30 if one is. The process is quick, easy, and inexpensive.

As a second example, consider surgery. This should be the strongest case for licensure. Would you want an untrained butcher to operate on you? Of course not. But opponents of licensure point out that it's not at all clear how effectively licensure prevents butchery. Ask a doctor, "Would you send your child to any board-certified surgeon picked at random?" The honest answer you'd get is "No way. Some of them are butchers." How do they know that? Being around hospitals, they have access to information about various surgeons' success and failure rates; they've seen them operate and know whether or not they have manual dexterity.

Advocates of the informational alternative suggest that you ask yourself, "What skill would you want in a surgeon?" A likely answer would be "Manual dexterity. Her fingers should be magic fingers." Does the existing system of licensure ensure that everyone who becomes a surgeon has magic fingers? No. To become licensed as a surgeon requires a grueling seven-year residency after four years of medical school, but manual dexterity, as such, is never explicitly tested or checked!

The informational alternative wouldn't necessarily eliminate the seven-year surgical residency. If the public believed that a seven-year residency was necessary to create skilled surgeons, many potential surgeons would choose that route. But there would be other ways to become a surgeon. For example, in high school, tests could be given for manual dexterity. Individuals with superb hand/eye coordination could go to a one-year technical college to train to be "heart technicians," who would work as part of a team doing heart surgery.

Clearly open-heart surgery is the extreme case, and most people will not be convinced that it can be performed by unlicensed medical personnel. But what about minor surgery? According to informational alternative advocates, many operations could be conducted more cheaply and better (since people with better manual dexterity would be doing the work) if restrictive licensing were ended. Or, if you don't accept the argument for human medical treatments, how about for veterinarians? For cosmetologists? For plumbers? Might the informational alternatives work in these professions?

Some Words of Caution If you were convinced that the informational alternative was preferable to medical licensure, beware. The preceding discussion of licensure and the informational alternative presented only the arguments in favor of that alternative. It highlights the benefits of the informational alternative and the problems with the licensure alternative.

I presented the alternatives in a one-sided way to stimulate your thinking, not to convince you that doctors are monopolists concerned only with their own incomes and that eliminating the medical monopoly will solve our country's health care woes. Reality is far more complicated than that. A complete presentation would have discussed problems of the informational alternative and how, if chosen, the alternative could be implemented. In the real world, systems for qualifying professionals have serious problems; arguments can be made against informational and certification alternatives that likely would convince you that neither is the answer.

Ultimately, we need an intimate knowledge of the actual practice and institutions to judge whether reforms would really make things better or worse. Therein lies the problem of reform. Just about the only individuals who have detailed knowledge are those who have a vested interest in the current system. So the information you're likely to get about potential reforms may well be biased toward only those reforms that will help the vested interest.

Ultimately, we need institutional knowledge to judge whether reforms will work.

GOVERNMENT FAILURE AND MARKET FAILURES

The above three types of market failure—externalities, public goods, and informational problems—give you a good sense of how markets can fail. They could be extended almost infinitely; all real-world markets in some way fail. But the point of the above discussions was to provide you not only with a sense of the way in which markets fail but also with a sense that economists know that markets fail and many of them support markets and oppose regulation anyway. Simply to point out a market failure is not necessarily to call for government to step in and try to rectify the situation. Why? The reason can be called **government failure**—when *the government intervention in the market to improve the market failure actually makes the situation worse.*

Why are there government failures? Let's briefly list some important reasons:

1. *Government doesn't have an incentive to correct the problem.* Government reflects politics, which reflects individuals' interests in trying to gain more for themselves. Political pressures to benefit some group or another will often dominate over doing the general good.

2. *Governments don't have enough information to deal with the problem.* Regulating is a difficult business. To intervene effectively, even if it wants to, government must have good information, but just as the market often lacks adequate information, so does the government. Individuals have the information and will be in a better position to decide the best plan of action.

3. *Intervention in markets is almost always more complicated than it initially seems.* Almost all actions have unintended consequences. Government attempts to offset market failures can prevent the market from dealing with the problem more effectively. The difficulty is that generally the market's ways of dealing with problems work only in the long run. As government deals with the short-run problems, it eliminates the incentives that would have brought about a long-run market solution.

4. *The bureaucratic nature of government intervention does not allow fine-tuning.* When the problems change, the government solution often responds far more slowly. An example is the Interstate Commerce Commission, which continued to exist years after its regulatory job had been eliminated.

5. *Government intervention leads to more government intervention.* Given the nature of the political process, opening the door in one area allows government to enter into other areas where intervention is harmful. Even in those cases where government action may seem to be likely to do some good, it might be best not to intervene, if that intervention will lead to additional government action in cases where it will not likely do good.

Q.9 Would an economist necessarily believe that we should simply let the market deal with a pollution problem?

Q.10 If one accepts the three reasons for market failure, how might one still oppose government intervention?

CONCLUSION

As a textbook writer, I wish I could say that some conclusions can be drawn about whether the government should, or should not, enter into the economy. I certainly have views about particular instances (in case you haven't guessed, I'm a highly opinionated individual), but to lay out arguments and information that would convince a reasonable person to agree with me would take an entire book for each area in which government might intervene.

Should the government intervene in the market? It depends.

What I can do in this textbook is to stimulate your interest in discovering for yourself the information and the subtleties of the debates for and against government intervention. Just about every time you read, hear, or are asked the question "Should the government intervene in a market?" the answer is "It depends." If your first impulse is to give any answer other than that one, you may have trouble maintaining the appropriate objectivity when you start considering the costs and benefits of government intervention.

Chapter Summary

- Three sources of market failure are externalities, public goods, and imperfect information.

- An externality is the effect of a decision on a third party that is not taken into account by the decision maker. Positive externalities provide benefits to third parties. Negative externalities impose costs on third parties.

- The markets for goods with negative externalities produce too much of the good for too low of a price. The markets for goods with positive externalities produce too little of the good for too great a price.

- Economists generally prefer incentive-based programs to regulatory programs because incentive-based programs are more efficient. An example of an incentive-based program is to tax the producer of a good that results in a negative externality by the amount of the externality.

- Voluntary solutions are difficult to maintain for long periods of time because other people have an incentive to be free riders—to enjoy the benefits of others' volunteer efforts without putting forth effort themselves.

- An optimal policy is one in which the marginal cost of undertaking the policy equals its marginal benefit.

- Public goods are nonexclusive and nonrival. It is difficult to measure the benefits of public goods because people do not reveal their preferences by purchasing them in the marketplace.

- Theoretically, the value of a public good can be calculated by summing the value that each individual places on every quantity. This is vertically summing individual demand curves.

- Individuals have an incentive to withhold information that will result in a lower price if one is a seller and a higher price if one is a consumer. Because of this incentive to withhold information, the markets for some goods disappear. Such market failures are known as adverse selection problems.

- Licensure and full disclosure are two solutions to the information problem.

- Government intervention may worsen the problem created by the market failure. Government failure occurs because (1) governments don't have an incentive to correct the problem, (2) governments don't have enough information to deal with the problem, (3) intervention is more complicated than it initially seems, (4) the bureaucratic nature of government precludes fine-tuning, and (5) government intervention often leads to more government intervention.

Key Terms

adverse selection problem (336)

direct regulation (330)

efficient (331)

effluent fees (331)

externality (328)

free rider problem (333)

government failure (341)

inefficient (331)

marginal social benefit (330)

marginal social cost (329)

market failure (327)

market incentive plan (331)

negative externality (328)

optimal policy (333)

positive externality (328)

public good (334)

tax incentive program (331)

Questions for Thought and Review

1. State three reasons for a potentially beneficial role of government intervention.

2. Explain why a market incentive program is more efficient than a direct regulatory program.

3. How would an economist likely respond to the statement "There is no such thing as an acceptable level of pollution"?

4. Would a high tax on oil significantly reduce the amount of pollution coming from the use of oil? Why or why not?

5. Would a high tax on oil significantly reduce the total amount of pollution in the environment?

6. More than half of 30 economists polled recently stated that the federal gasoline tax should be $1 or higher. What do you suppose were their reasons?

7. If you are willing to pay $1,000 for a used stereo that is a "cherry" and $200 for a used stereo that is a "lemon," how much will you be willing to offer to purchase a stereo if there is a 50 percent chance that the stereo is a lemon? If owners of cherry stereos want $700 for their cherries, how will your estimate of the chance of getting a cherry change?

8. Define the adverse selection problem. Does your understanding of adverse selection change your view of commercial dating services? If so, how?

9. If neither buyers nor sellers could distinguish between "lemons" and "cherries" in the used-car market, what would you expect to be the mix of lemons and cherries for sale?

10. Automobile insurance companies charge lower rates to married individuals than they do to unmarried individuals. What economic reason is there for such a practice? Is it fair?

11. Should government eliminate the Food and Drug Administration's role in restricting which drugs may be marketed? Why or why not?

12. List five ways you are affected on a daily basis by government intervention in the market. For what reason might government be involved? Is that reason justified?

Problems and Exercises

1. There's a gas shortage in Gasland. You're presented with two proposals that will achieve the same level of reduction in the use of gas. Proposal A would force everybody to reduce their gas consumption by 5 percent. Proposal B would impose a 50-cent tax on the consumption of a gallon of gas, which would also achieve a 5 percent reduction. Demand curves for two groups are shown below.
   a. Show the effect of both proposals on each group.
   b. Which group would support a regulatory policy? Which would support a tax policy?

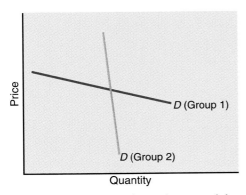

2. The marginal cost, marginal social cost, and demand for fish are represented by the curves in the following graph. Suppose that there are no restrictions on fishing.
   a. Assuming perfect competition, what is the catch going to be, and at what price will it be sold?
   b. What are the socially efficient price and output?
   c. Some sports fishers propose a ban on commercial fishing. As the community's economic adviser, you're asked to comment on it at a public forum. What do you say?

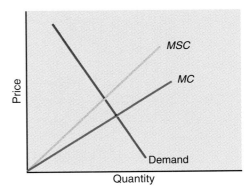

3. You are in Seattle, watching the Seattle Stomp—a dance home owners do in their trash cans.
   a. What can you say about trash fees in Seattle? Be as specific as possible.
   b. What change in fee structure might eliminate the Seattle Stomp?

4. In *At the Hand of Man*, Raymond Bonner argues that Africa should promote hunting, charging large fees for permits to kill animals (for example, $7,500 for a permit to shoot an elephant).

a. What are some arguments in favor of this proposal?

b. What are some arguments against?

5. California passed an air quality law that required 3.75 percent of all the cars sold in the state to emit zero pollution by 1998, and required 10 percent of all cars sold in the state to meet this standard by 2003.

a. What was the likely impact of this law?

b. Can you think of any way in which this law might actually increase pollution rather than decrease it?

c. How might an economist suggest modifying this law to better achieve economic efficiency?

6. Economics professors Thomas Hopkins and Arthur Gosnell of the Rochester Institute of Technology estimated that in the year 2000, regulations cost the United States $662 billion, or about $5,700 per family.

a. Do their findings mean that the United States has too many regulations?

b. How would an economist decide which regulations to keep and which to do away with?

7. In the 1990s a debate about dairy products concerned the labeling of milk produced from cows who have been injected with the hormone BST, which significantly increases their milk production. Since the FDA has determined that this synthetically produced copy of a milk hormone is indistinguishable from the hormone produced naturally by the cow, and has also determined that milk from cows treated with BST is indistinguishable from milk from untreated cows, some people have argued that no labeling requirement is necessary. Others argue that the consumer has a right to know.

a. Where do you think most dairy farmers stand on this labeling issue?

b. If consumers have a right to know, should labels inform them of other drugs, such as antibiotics, normally given to cows?

c. Do you think dairy farmers who support BST labeling also support the broader labeling law that would be needed if other drugs were included? Why?

8. Financial analysts are currently required to be licensed. Should they be licensed? Why or why not?

9. An advanced degree is required in order to teach at most colleges. In what sense is this a form of restricting entry through licensure?

10. Who would benefit and who would lose if an informational alternative to licensing doctors were introduced?

Web Questions

1. The Emissions Trading Educational Initiative (ETEI) is a project of the Environmental Defense Fund and the Emissions Marketing Association to educate the public about emissions trading. Visit their website at www.etei.org. Answer the following questions:

a. What is "cap and trade"?

b. What type of market failure does cap and trade address in Case Study #1? Explain your answer.

c. Is cap and trade efficient?

d. What is the solution to the market failure in Case #1? Has the program been successful?

2. Visit the home page for Occupational Safety and Health Administration (OSHA) at www.osha.gov. Answer the following questions:

a. When was OSHA established and what is its mission?

b. What market failure is OSHA designed to address?

c. Who is covered by OSHA? Who is not covered?

d. How does OSHA enforce its workplace standards?

Answers to Margin Questions

1. An externality is an effect of a decision not taken into account by the decision maker. When there are externalities, the private price no longer necessarily reflects the social price, and therefore the market may not work properly.   (328)

2. No. The existence of a positive externality does not mean that the market works better than if no externality existed. It means that the market is not supplying a sufficient amount of the resource or activity, and insufficient supply can be as inefficient as an oversupply. (329)

3. An example of the trade-off between fairness and efficiency is whether to allow nontaxpayers to enjoy the benefits of a public park maintained through local taxes. It would cost too much to exclude them from enjoying the park, so the exclusion is inefficient, but not to exclude that person is unfair to the taxpayers who pay to maintain the park. An example of a policy that might be seen as both fair and efficient is a gas tax designed to deter pollution. Consumers choose to reduce their gas use based on the new price, so the solution is efficient. The solution has an element of fairness in it since those causing the pollution are those paying more.   (331)

4. The tax incentive approach to pollution is fair in the following sense: individuals whose actions result in more pollution pay more. Individuals whose actions re-

sult in less pollution pay less. In some broader sense this may not be fair if one takes into account the initial positions of those polluting. For example, the poor may have older cars which get fewer miles per gallon and have to pay a higher cost of pollution resulting from gasoline use. *(331)*

5. Voluntary actions that are not in people's self-interest may not work in large groups because individuals will rely on others to volunteer. There is also a potential lack of efficiency in voluntary solutions since the person who voluntarily reduces consumption may not be the person who faces the least cost of doing so. *(333)*

6. It is difficult for government to decide the efficient quantity of a public good because public goods are not purchased by individuals in markets. Individuals do not reveal the value they place on public goods. Individuals also face incentives to overstate the value they place on public goods if they do not have to pay for them, and to understate the value if they do have to share the cost. *(335)*

7. Since adverse selection is a problem in the medical insurance industry, with fuller information, I would expect that average medical rates would decline since the adverse selection problem would disappear. Medical insurers would be able to offer lower-cost insurance to people who are less likely to get sick and who perhaps choose not to be covered at today's high rates. *(336)*

8. If an informational alternative to licensing were introduced, existing doctors would suffer a significant monetary loss, and students who would likely go on to medical school in existing institutions would face lower potential incomes when they entered practice. Gainers would likely be (1) those who did not want to go through an entire medical school schedule but were willing to learn a specialty that required far less education and in which they had a particular proclivity to do good, and (2) consumers, who would get more for less. *(339)*

9. An economist would not necessarily believe that we should simply let the market deal with the pollution problem. Pollution clearly involves externalities. Where economists differ from many laypeople is how they would handle the problem. An economist is likely to look more carefully into the costs, try to build price incentives into whatever program is designed, and make the marginal private cost equal the marginal social cost. *(341)*

10. One can accept all three explanations for market failure and still oppose government intervention if one believes that government intervention will cause worse problems than the market failure. *(341)*

Antitrust Policy and Regulation

16

After reading this chapter, you should be able to:

- Explain the difference between the structure and the performance methods of judging competition.

- Give a brief history of U.S. antitrust policy.

- State the resolution of the IBM, AT&T, and Microsoft antitrust cases.

- Differentiate among horizontal, vertical, and conglomerate mergers.

- List five reasons why unrelated firms would want to merge.

- Compare U.S. antitrust policy with antitrust policy of other countries.

- List three alternatives to antitrust policy that government can use to affect the competitive process.

We have always known that
heedless self-interest was bad morals;
we now know that it is bad economics.

Franklin Delano Roosevelt

In the courtroom everyone waits for the Microsoft star witness, an economist who is arguing that Microsoft does not have a monopoly. On the stand he testifies, "The market is too dynamic, too much in flux for a monopoly to exist."

"But how about the fact that Microsoft intentionally tied its Web browser to its Windows operating system in order to harm Netscape's ability to compete?" the government lawyer asks.

"Those were technical decisions," the economist answers, "necessary to make the Web browser operate efficiently."

"Yeah, right," replies the government lawyer.

The above is a paraphrase of what went on recently in a federal court in an antitrust case the government brought against Microsoft. It captures a very real aspect of all theoretical discussions of market structure and policy. Once theory is translated into policy, market structure and behavior play an important role in how the economy functions. One way in which theory is translated into policy is through antitrust policy and regulation. In this chapter we consider both.

ANTITRUST POLICY: JUDGMENT BY PERFORMANCE OR STRUCTURE?

Antitrust policy is *the government's policy toward the competitive process*. It's the government's rulebook for carrying out its role as referee. In volleyball, for instance, the rulebook would answer such questions as: When should a foul be called? When has a person caught and thrown rather than hit the ball over the net? In business a referee is needed for such questions as: When can two companies merge? What competitive practices are legal? When is a company too big? To what extent is it fair for two companies to coordinate their pricing policies? When is a market sufficiently competitive or too monopolistic?

The United States has seen wide swings in economists' prescriptions concerning such questions, depending on which of the two views of competition has held sway. The two competing views are:

1. **Judgment by performance:** *We should judge the competitiveness of markets by the performance (behavior) of firms in that market.*

2. **Judgment by structure:** *We should judge the competitiveness of markets by the structure of the industry.*

To show how the U.S. government has applied these two views of competition in promoting workable and effective competition, this chapter considers government's application of antitrust laws to regulate business. It then considers how recent structural changes in the economy are altering the government's role in refereeing the market.

Antitrust policy is government's policy toward the competitive process.

Judgment by performance is the view that competitiveness of a market should be judged by the behavior of firms in that market; judgment by structure is the view that competitiveness of a market should be judged by the structure of that market.

HISTORY OF U.S. ANTITRUST LAWS

Although U.S. ideology has always been strongly in favor of laissez-faire and government noninvolvement in business, there has simultaneously been a populist (pro-people) sensibility that fears bigness and monopoly. These fears of bigness and monopoly burst forth in the late 1800s as many firms were merging or organizing together to form trusts or cartels. As stated in Chapter 13, a *cartel*—or, as we'll use the term in this chapter, a *trust*—is a combination of firms in which the firms haven't actually merged but nonetheless act essentially as a single entity. A trust sets common prices and governs the output of individual member firms. A trust can, and often does, act like a monopolist.

In the 1870s and 1880s, trusts were forming in a number of industries, including railroads, steel, tobacco, and oil. Some of these trusts' actions are typified by John D. Rockefeller's Standard Oil. Standard Oil demanded that railroads pay it kickbacks on freight rates. These payments allowed Standard Oil to set lower prices for its products than other companies, which had to pay the railroads full price on freight. Standard Oil thus could sell at lower prices than its competitors.

If prices had remained low, this would have had a positive effect on consumers and a negative effect on Standard Oil's competitors. But prices didn't remain low. By 1882, Standard Oil had driven many of its competitors out of business, and the writing was on the wall for those competitors that remained. At that time, Standard Oil created a trust and "invited" its few surviving competitors to join. Then Standard Oil Trust used the monopoly power it had gained to close down refineries, raise prices, and limit the production of oil. The price of oil rose from a competitive level to a monopolistic level, and the consumer, as well as Standard Oil's competitors, ended up suffering.

The Sherman Antitrust Act

Public outrage at the formation and activities of trusts such as Standard Oil led to the passage of the Sherman Act, the Clayton Act, and the Federal Trade Commission Act.

Public outrage against trusts like Standard Oil's was high. The organizers of the trusts were widely known as *robber barons* because of their exploitation of natural resources and their other unethical behavior. The trusts were seen as making enormous profits, preventing competition, and in general bullying everyone in sight. In response the U.S. Congress passed the **Sherman Antitrust Act** of 1890—*a law designed to regulate the competitive process.*

The Sherman Act contained two main sections:

Section 1: Every contract, combination in the form of trust or otherwise, or conspiracy in restraint of trade or commerce among the several States, or with foreign nations, is hereby declared to be illegal.

Section 2: Every person who shall monopolize, or attempt to monopolize, or combine or conspire with any other person or persons, to monopolize any part of the trade or commerce among the several States, or with foreign nations, shall be deemed guilty of a misdemeanor, and, on conviction thereof, shall be punished by a fine not exceeding five thousand dollars, or by imprisonment not exceeding one year, or by both said punishments, in the discretion of the court.

Q-1 What were the two provisions of the Sherman Antitrust Act?

The Sherman Act was broad and sweeping, but vague.

The Sherman Act was meant to be as sweeping and broad as its language sounds. After all, it was passed in response to a public outcry against trusts. But if you look at it carefully, in some respects it is vague and weak. For example, offenses under Section 2 were initially only misdemeanors, not felonies.[1] It's unclear what constitutes "restraint of trade." Moreover, although the act prohibits monopolization, it does not explicitly prohibit monopolies. In short, with the Sherman Act, Congress passed the buck to the courts, letting them decide U.S. antitrust policy.[2]

The following story summarizes the courts' role in antitrust policy. Three umpires are describing their job. The youngest of the three says, "I call them as I see them." The middle-aged umpire says, "No, that's not what an umpire does. An umpire calls them the way they are." The senior umpire says, "You're both wrong. They're nothing until I call them." And that's how it is with the courts and monopoly. Whether a firm is behaving monopolistically isn't known until the court makes its decision.

As Congress was passing the Sherman Act, economists too were debating the implications of trusts and whether it was in the public interest to restrict them. Part of the debate concerned whether the mergers reflected technological changes in production and expanding transportation systems that made increased economies of scale more important (in which case restricting trusts might not be in the public interest since doing so might prevent firms from taking advantage of economies of scale), or whether trusts

---

[1]Under federal law, a misdemeanor is any misconduct punishable by only a fine or by a jail sentence of a year or less. A felony requires a sentence of more than a year.

[2]Subsequent amendments to the Sherman Act have strengthened it. For example, offenses under Section 2 are now felonies, not misdemeanors.

simply represented attempts at monopolization to restrict output and generate monop-oly profits (in which case restricting trusts would more likely be in the public interest since doing so would reduce monopoly).

A second part of the debate concerned how fast economic forces would operate and how fragile competition was. Some economists argued that competition was strong and that it would limit the profit trusts and monopolies made and force them to charge the competitive price (in which case restricting trusts might not be in the public interest). These economists were reflecting the performance viewpoint—that competition should be relied on to break down the monopolies. They argued that bigness doesn't imply the absence of market competition and that the government's role should merely be to make sure that no significant barriers to entry are created.

Other economists, reflecting the structure viewpoint, argued that competition was fragile and that it wouldn't operate unless there were a large number of small firms. They argued that trusts and monopolies (even if they don't charge monopolistic prices) are bad, that the trusts should be broken up by government, and that laws should not al-low new monopolies or trusts to be formed. However, the debate was for the courts, not economists, to settle.

> Economists reflecting the performance viewpoint argued that competition was strong and would ultimately limit monopolies. Economists reflecting the structure viewpoint argued that trusts should be broken up by government.

The Standard Oil and American Tobacco Cases: Judging Market Competitiveness by Performance

In 1911, the U.S. Supreme Court established its interpretation of the Sherman Act by handing down its opinions in cases involving Standard Oil and the American Tobacco Company. The Court determined that both companies were structural monopolies; each company controlled 90 percent of its market. However, the Court decided that the monopolistic structure of the markets did not violate the Sherman Antitrust Act. A company's violation of the act was determined not by the structure of the industry but by the particular firm's performance—that is, by whether or not the firm engaged in "unfair business practices." This judgment by performance, not judgment by structure, is often called the *abuse theory* because a firm is legally considered a monopoly only if it commits monopolistic abuses.

 16.2

In these two cases the distinction was academic. Both Standard Oil and American Tobacco were judged guilty (very guilty) of unfair business practices and were broken up. But the academic distinction played an important role in determining the industrial struc-ture of the United States. It allowed structural monopolies to continue to exist, but it prohibited them from using certain monopolistic practices, such as demanding kickbacks.

> Standard Oil and the American Tobacco Company were judged guilty, not because of their struc-ture, but because of their per-formance.

In 1920, this structure/performance distinction was important in a case involving U.S. Steel. Here the Supreme Court ruled that, while U.S. Steel was a structural mo-nopoly, it was not a monopoly in performance. That is, the firm had not used unfair business practices to become a monopolist and thus was not in violation of antitrust law. Unlike Standard Oil, U.S. Steel was not required to break up into a group of smaller companies.

> Q-2 What was the resolution of the Standard Oil case?

The Clayton Act and the Federal Trade Commission Act

In an attempt to give more guidance to the courts and to provide for more vigorous en-forcement of the antitrust provisions, in 1914 Congress passed the Clayton Antitrust Act and the Federal Trade Commission Act.

The **Clayton Antitrust Act** is *a law that made four specific monopolistic practices illegal* when their effect was to lessen competition:

1. Price discrimination, that is, selling identical goods to different customers at different prices.

> The Clayton Antitrust Act made four specific monopolistic prac-tices illegal:
> 1. Price discrimination.
> 2. Tie-in contracts.
> 3. Interlocking directorships.
> 4. Purchase of a competitor's stock.

2. Tie-in contracts, in which the buyer must agree to deal exclusively with one seller and not to purchase goods from competing sellers.

3. Interlocking directorships, in which memberships of boards of directors of two or more firms are almost identical.

4. Buying stock in a competitor's company when the purpose of buying that stock is to reduce competition.

In establishing the Federal Trade Commission (FTC) in 1914, Congress gave it the power to regulate competition and police markets. The **Federal Trade Commission Act** is *a law that made it illegal for firms to use "unfair methods of competition" and to engage in "unfair or deceptive acts or practices,"* whether or not those actions had any impact on competition. Other than that broad mandate, Congress gave the FTC little direction as to what rules it was to use to regulate trade and police markets. As a result, for more than 20 years the commission was rather ineffective. In 1938, however, it was given the job of preventing false and deceptive advertising, which remains one of its primary roles.

The ALCOA Case: Judging Market Competitiveness by Structure

Q-3 What was the resolution of the ALCOA case?

16.3

Judgment by performance was the primary criterion governing U.S. antitrust policy until 1945. In 1945 the U.S. courts changed their interpretation of the law with the Aluminum Company of America (ALCOA) case. In the ALCOA case, the company was found guilty of violating the antitrust statutes even though the court did not rule that ALCOA had been guilty of unfair practices. What ALCOA had done was to use its knowledge of the market to expand its capacity before any competitors had a chance to enter the market. In addition, it had kept its prices low to prevent potential entry by competitors, an activity known as *predatory pricing*. It showed no signs of exploiting its monopoly power to charge high prices or to force competing firms out of business. Thus, on performance standards, it was not violating the law. But in the ALCOA case, the structure of the market, not the company's performance, was used to determine whether ALCOA was in violation of antitrust law.

Judging Markets by Structure and Performance: The Reality

Judgment by structure seems unfair on a gut level. After all, in economics the purpose of competition is to motivate firms to produce better goods than their competitors are producing, and to do so at lower cost. If a firm is competing so successfully that all the other firms leave the industry, the successful firm will be a monopolist, and on the basis of judgment by structure will be guilty of antitrust violations. Under the judgment-by-structure criterion, a firm is breaking the law if it does what it's supposed to be doing: producing the best product it can at the lowest possible cost.

An important reason supporting the structure criterion is practicality.

Supporters of the judgment-by-structure criterion recognize this problem but nonetheless favor the structure criterion. An important reason for this is practicality.

Contextual Judgments and the Capabilities of the Courts Judgment by performance requires that each action of a firm be analyzed on a case-by-case basis. Doing that is enormously time-consuming and expensive. In some interpretations, actions of a firm might be considered appropriate competitive behavior; in other interpretations, the same actions might be considered inappropriate. For example, say that an automobile company requires that in order for its warranty to hold, owners of its warranted vehicles

APPLYING THE TOOLS

Wal-Mart, State Laws, and Competition

It isn't only the federal government that has laws on competition. States have a variety of laws that govern competitive practices. One such state law is Arkansas's Unfair Practices Act, which prohibits selling, or advertising for sale, items below cost "for the purpose of injuring competitors and destroying competition." In the early 1990s, three Arkansas pharmacies sued Wal-Mart for violating this law by selling its goods at "too low" a price. The background of the case is the following.

Wal-Mart had been expanding aggressively throughout the United States in the 1980s and early 1990s, reaching a total of about 3,000 stores in 1996. It does not deny that it, like many other stores, sells some goods at below cost. But it argues that when it sells below cost it does not do so to "destroy competition" or "injure competitors," but rather to maintain low prices for consumers. It claims that its pricing policies promote, not destroy, competition.

In principle, most economists agree with Wal-Mart; new competition, by its very nature, hurts existing businesses—that's the way the market competitive process works. Those who don't sell for the lowest price lose, and those who sell for the lowest price gain. But most economists also recognize that Wal-Mart's brand of competition can have externalities affecting the social fabric of small-town economies. A new Wal-Mart store can undermine the town centers and replace them with commercial sprawl on the outskirts of these towns. Whether these externalities are a reason to limit Wal-Mart's aggressive pricing policies is a debatable question.

Wal-Mart initially lost its suit in Arkansas; however, in 1995 the Arkansas Supreme Court overturned the lower court decision and held that Wal-Mart's pricing was not part of a strategy to price below cost over a prolonged period of time. While Wal-Mart won this suit, the threat of other states suits will likely discourage Wal-Mart from following quite as aggressive a pricing policy as it otherwise would have.

must use only the company's parts and service centers. Is this requirement of the automobile company intended to create a monopoly position for its parts and service center divisions or to ensure proper maintenance? The answer depends on the context of the action.

But judging each case contextually is beyond the courts' capabilities. There are so many firms and so many actions that the courts can't judge all industries on their performance. They must devise a way to limit the issues they look at. In order to apply the performance criterion reasonably, the Supreme Court must set out certain guidelines to tell firms in what situations the Court will take a closer look at their performance. Because the available information concerns structure, those guidelines inevitably refer to market structure, even though it is firms' performance that will ultimately be judged. So even though judging by structure may have problems, it is necessary.

It's very much like the procedure college admissions offices use in deciding which applicants to accept. They judge applicants on their "total performance," not just on their quantitative scores on standardized tests. However, they often use a certain quantitative score as a cutoff point in order to reduce applications to a manageable number. Applicants below the cutoff point are automatically rejected; applicants above it are considered one by one.

Another argument in favor of judging competitiveness by structure is that structure can be a predictor of future performance. Advocates of the structure criterion argue that a monopolist may be pricing low now, but it is, after all, a monopolist, and it won't price low in the future. The low price will eliminate competition now, and, once the competition is gone, the firm will not be able to resist the temptation to use its monopoly power.

Determining the Relevant Market and Industry Supporters of the performance criterion admit that this standard has problems, but they point out that the structure

Choosing the relevant market when evaluating competitiveness is difficult to do.

criterion also has problems. As you saw in Chapter 13, it's difficult to determine the relevant market (local, national, or international) and the relevant industry (three-digit or five-digit NAICS code) necessary to identify the structural competitiveness of any industry.

Such questions have been the center of many antitrust court cases. For example, in the ALCOA case, the company argued that metals such as copper and steel were interchangeable with aluminum, and that therefore the relevant industry to consider was the metals industry. If the Court had chosen metals, not aluminum, as the relevant industry, ALCOA wouldn't have been found to have a monopoly. The Court decided, however, that aluminum had sufficiently unique properties to constitute its own market. Since it determined that ALCOA had 90 percent of the aluminum market, ALCOA was declared a monopoly and was broken up.

The arguments in the Du Pont case (1956) again centered around the definition of *industry*. The Supreme Court found that Du Pont was innocent of monopolizing the production of cellophane even though Du Pont was the only producer of cellophane. The Court reasoned that the relevant industry was not the cellophane industry but rather the flexible wrap industry, which also included aluminum foil and wax paper. Du Pont did not have a monopoly of the flexible wrap industry and thus, the Court said, was not in violation of the antitrust laws.

Similar ambiguities exist with the decision about the relevant geographic market. In the Pabst Brewing case (1966), the definition of the market played a key role. Pabst wanted to merge with the Blatz Brewing Company. On a national scale, both companies were relatively small, accounting together for about 4.5 percent of beer sales in the United States as a whole. Pabst argued that the United States was the relevant market. The Court, however, decided that Wisconsin, where Pabst had its headquarters, was the relevant market, and since the two firms held a 24 percent share of that market, the merger was not allowed.

What should one make of this debate? The bottom line is that both structure and performance criteria have ambiguities, and in the real world there are no definitive criteria for judging whether a firm has violated the antitrust statutes. A firm isn't at fault or in the clear until the courts make the call.

Recent Antitrust Enforcement

In recent years antitrust law has worked mainly through its deterrent effect. Many potential mergers are never even proposed because firms know they would not be allowed. Few major antitrust cases have been brought, in part because a century of experience has taught business what the law allows, and in part because the government has been lenient in its interpretation of the antitrust laws. That leniency has three interrelated causes. The first is a change in the American ideology. Whereas in the 1950s and 1960s the prevailing ideology saw big business as "bad," by the 1980s the view changed to one that was more complex—big business was seen as a combination of good and bad. In this new ideological framework, the political pressure to push antitrust enforcement waned.

Second, as the United States became more integrated into the global economy, big business faced significant international competition and hence competition created by U.S. market structure became less important.

Third, as technologies became more complicated, the issues in antitrust enforcement also became more complicated for the courts to handle. By the time the legal system had resolved a case, the technology would have changed so much that the issues in that case were no longer relevant.

Q₄ What was the resolution of the Du Pont case?

Both structure and performance criteria have ambiguities, and in the real world there are no definitive criteria for judging whether a firm has violated the antitrust statutes.

Since the 1980s the United States has been more lenient in antitrust cases because of a change in ideology, the globalization of the U.S. economy, and the increasing complexity of technology.

We have a saying at this company—our competitors are our friends and our customers are our enemies.
—James Randall, former president of ADM

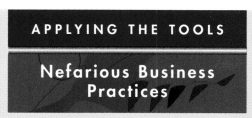

APPLYING THE TOOLS

Nefarious Business Practices

The U.S. antitrust laws concern far more than mergers and market structure; they also place legal restrictions on certain practices of businesses such as price-fixing. By law, firms are not allowed to *explicitly* collude in order to fix prices above the competitive level. A key aspect of the law is the explicit nature of the collusion that is disallowed. Airlines, gas stations, and firms in many other industries have prices that generally move in tandem—when one firm changes its price, others seem to follow. Such practices would suggest that these firms are implicitly colluding, but they are not violating the law unless there is explicit collusion.

To prove explicit collusion is difficult—there must be a smoking gun, and there is seldom sufficient evidence of explicit collusion to prosecute businesses. There are exceptions, however. In 1996, Archer Daniels Midland (ADM), a major supplier of food and grains, was caught red-handed when one of its former officials gave prosecutors tapes of meetings in which price-fixing occurred. Meeting secretly around the world, in countries like Mexico, France, Canada, and Japan, ADM executives tried to set prices of Lysine, a feed additive, and citric acid. One of ADM's officials, working undercover for the FBI, secretly recorded these meetings. Faced with the taped evidence against them, ADM agreed to pay $100 million in fines—the largest criminal antitrust fine in history up to that year. Since 1996 four other companies have been fined even greater sums, with Roche Holding paying a fine of $500 million.

Company	Fine (in millions)
Roche Holding	$500
BASF	225
SGL Carbon	135
Ucar International	110
ADM	100

THREE RECENT ANTITRUST CASES

The modern era of antitrust policy has been marked by important cases in the computer and telecommunication market. One such case was against IBM.

The IBM Case

In 1967 the U.S. Department of Justice sued IBM for violating the antitrust laws. The department argued that the company had a 72 percent share of the general-purpose electronic digital computing industry, and that it had acquired that market share because of unfair business practices such as bundling of hardware, software, and maintenance services at a single price (that is, requiring customers to buy all three together). If you wanted IBM equipment (hardware), you also had to take IBM service and software whether you wanted them or not. When you bought an IBM machine you bought everything, so other companies had little chance to compete. Moreover, the department argued that IBM constantly redesigned its computers, making it impossible for other companies to keep up and compete fairly on the sale of any IBM mainframe-compatible item.

IBM argued that the relevant market was broader, that it included all types of computers such as military computers, programmable calculators, and other information-processing products. It further claimed that its so-called unfair practices were simply a reflection of efficient computer technology. Fast-moving technological developments required it to continually redesign its products merely to provide its customers with the

In technology industries the market is continually changing.

latest, best equipment. And, it said, the only way to provide the best level of service to its customers was to include its maintenance services in the price of its products.

By 1982 the market had changed. Many of the government's objections had become moot, and the government withdrew its case. Mainframe computers were being replaced with personal computers, a market in which Apple and DEC had become serious competitors, and the globalization of the computer industry made IBM's dominance in the United States far less important.

IBM may have triumphed in the antitrust case against it, but in doing so it may have lost the war. Here's why.

About the same time as the case was at its height, IBM was negotiating with a young upstart company about an operating system for a small part of its market—the personal computer (PC) market, which was just developing. Bill Gates, the president of the young company, offered to sell its disk operating system (DOS) to IBM for $75,000. IBM refused to buy it; to have bought DOS would have given IBM greater control over the PC market, and would have made a court-ordered breakup of IBM more likely. Instead, IBM left Bill Gates to license DOS to IBM and everyone else, while IBM concentrated on mainframe computers and the production of PCs.

In the early 1990s, the cost of that decision was clear. The mainframe market was dying, and IBM was hemorrhaging losses. Meanwhile, Bill Gates had become a multi-billionaire, and his company—Microsoft—had become a controlling force in the PC market. Now the tables were turned and in 1994 Microsoft entered into a consent decree with the U.S. government, agreeing to make it easier for other firms, such as IBM, to compete with it.

The losses at IBM ended in the mid-1990s and its competitive position improved. Thus, ultimately it weathered the antitrust case, but its history was forever changed by it.

The AT&T Case

The other major antitrust case of the 1980s, the AT&T case, demonstrates another aspect of U.S. antitrust policy and shows how technological change plays an important role in competition and questions of industrial market structure.

AT&T as a Regulated Monopoly Up until 1982, AT&T was what was called a *regulated monopoly*. It had the exclusive right to provide telephone service in the United States. AT&T controlled most of the telecommunications market: long-distance and local telephone service, and the production of telephones themselves as well as other communications equipment.

Why was it given that right? Because it was felt that economies of scale and network externalities made supplying telephone service a **natural monopoly** (*an industry in which significant economies of scale make the existence of more than one firm inefficient*). Telephone service required lines to be brought into every house; those lines had to be buried underground or strung overhead on poles and connected to all other houses. It made little sense to have more than one company stringing competing lines. Moreover, government decided that universal telephone service was socially desirable, and AT&T was required to provide universal service. Unregulated companies likely would have practiced *cream skimming* (providing service to low-cost areas and avoiding high-cost areas).

In return for its monopoly, AT&T was subjected to regulatory control by the Federal Communications Commission and by state utility commissions. This government regulation was designed to limit the company's profit to a fair level and prevent it from abusing its monopoly.

Under AT&T's monopoly, phone service in the United States was the best and cheapest in the world, although some believed it could and should have been even

---

The IBM case was dropped by the United States, but the prosecution likely led to IBM's problems in the 1990s. It won but it also lost.

Q-5 What was the resolution of the IBM case?

A natural monopoly is an industry in which significant economies of scale make the existence of more than one firm inefficient.

cheaper. Some economists argued that AT&T's guarantee of a "fair" return on its investment gave it a strong incentive to act as a lazy monopolist and to invest heavily, thereby increasing costs. If a company knows it can pass on its costs to customers (and add on a profit margin as well), it has little incentive to hold down costs. But even if service was more expensive than it needed to be, on the whole most agreed that the system worked well.

Technological Change and Competition In the 1970s technological changes fundamentally altered the nature of the long-distance telephone industry. The development of satellite transmission and fiber optics made physical line connections no longer the only option, so long-distance telephone service was no longer a natural monopoly. In fact, significant competition began to develop, and AT&T's new competitors claimed that they weren't being allowed reasonable access to the AT&T-controlled local telephone network. AT&T charged competing firms high fees for access to all their local lines—fees that competitors argued were unfair.

The issue was complicated by the fact that the regulatory commissions, in an attempt to see that everyone had low-cost local service, had set local charges low and long-distance rates high. As long as AT&T controlled both local and long-distance calling, this had no effect on AT&T. But when competitors began to undercharge AT&T on long-distance service, the rate-setting system (which implicitly subsidized local service with AT&T's long-distance profits) concerned AT&T greatly. AT&T's high access charges were an attempt to see that the competitors used some of their own profits to help subsidize local rates.

As a result of these claims and counterclaims, the Department of Justice introduced an antitrust suit against AT&T in 1978, alleging that potential competitors were not being allowed reasonable access to AT&T's local telephone network. The case had merit, but so did AT&T's defense: the problem was in the setting of rates for local and long-distance calls. As is now usual for any contested antitrust case, the case went on and on, and no conclusion was in sight.

Resolution of the AT&T Case Then, in January 1982 AT&T and the Department of Justice announced that they had settled the case and that AT&T had agreed to be broken up. Specifically, AT&T agreed that by January 1, 1984, it would divest itself of 22 local operating companies (known as the *Baby Bells*), which accounted for $87 billion of AT&T's $136 billion in assets. AT&T kept its long-distance telephone service, its manufacturing division, and its research facilities. In return, AT&T was subject to far less regulation than before. After the settlement, AT&T could enter any unregulated business it desired, such as data transmission and computers.

The result of this settlement was an enormous upheaval in the telephone industry. Local rates for phone service went up twofold or even threefold, while long-distance rates fell substantially. Two major competitors, MCI and Sprint, emerged, and competition for long-distance business became fierce. (Now more than 800 firms offer long-distance service.)

Developments Since the AT&T Case AT&T may have lost the antitrust case against it, but it also won the war, at least temporarily. With its newfound freedom from regulation, it quickly entered into the competitive fray in a variety of industries. Its entry into the personal computer market didn't fare well, but it did much better in the broader information flow industry. It developed technology that could be used for two-way information transmittal and, ironically, became a potential competitor of cable TV monopolies, since its fiber-optic networks could be used to transmit TV programs. It bought McCaw Communications, a cellular phone company in 1994, making it a major

Q-6 What was the resolution of the AT&T case?

The AT&T case was settled by AT&T agreeing to be split up into regional companies handling local service, and AT&T itself competing in the long-distance market.

player in the wireless communications market, and expanded into the Internet access market, becoming the largest direct Internet service provider in 1996. As it was expanding in these areas, it was pulling out of others. Specifically, AT&T split into three companies in 1995. One of these companies retained the name AT&T; its focus was communications services. The other two companies were Lucent Technologies, which produces and services communications systems and networking technology, and National Cash Register (NCR), which concentrated on support and services of computer systems.

This split up was, in part, due to the fast-changing technology and regulations governing the telecommunications industry. For example, as compression technology (the ability to reduce signals to digital notation and compress them) of telephone signals advanced, and as regulations were modified to take these advances into account, local and long-distance suppliers became direct competitors. As that happened, it became clear that the Baby Bells were becoming hesitant to buy equipment and services from AT&T: You don't become dependent on your direct competitor. This threatened to cut sales for AT&T. The creation of Lucent Technologies as a separate company eliminated the conflict-of-interest problem.

To take account of the fast-moving technological changes in telecommunications, in 1996 Congress passed a sweeping overhaul of the telecommunications law. This new law allowed for long-distance carriers, local phone companies, and cable television companies to enter one another's market. It eliminated many of the regulations that previously existed. This change recognized the changing market conditions due to changing technology that had essentially merged various markets such as cable, telephone service, and cellular phone service into a combined "information flow" market.

Under this new law the Baby Bells have been merging with one another and are competing with AT&T, cable companies, and wireless communications companies to provide a wide variety of expanding telecommunications services. Internet on the TV; videophones; interactive TV; combined TVs and computers; online movies for rent on demand; combined cellular and wire phones—all are in the telecommunications future.

The telecommunications revolution that led to the breakup of AT&T has continued, leading to an ever-changing competitor landscape. Cable and phone companies are all competing to be suppliers of high-speed Internet access and are merging. (AT&T bought TeleCommunications Inc. (TCI) in 1999, for example.) Digital phone companies are competing with cellular phone companies. Firms are taking an international focus; U.S. companies are entering and buying up non-U.S. companies, and non-U.S. companies are entering the U.S. market. (In 1996, British Telecom merged with MCI.) Long-distance companies are entering local markets, and local companies are entering long-distance markets. (In 1996 Worldcom, a long-distance phone company, bought MFS Communications, a local phone company, and became the first company to offer both local and long-distance phone service since the breakup of AT&T in 1984. Others are quickly following suit.) Given these changes, government antitrust policy regarding telecommunications firms is likely to stay in the news.

Given the merger activity, government antitrust policy regarding telecommunications is likely to stay in the news.

The Microsoft Case

One of the most important antitrust cases brought in the 1990s was the Microsoft case. This is an extremely interesting case to consider both because of its similarities to the IBM case and because of the issues it raises about competition, the competitive process, and government's role in that competitive process.

Microsoft makes computer software. From its small start some 20 years ago, it now has about 50 percent of the world's total software market. It has an even larger share of the world's operating system software market. Between 80 and 90 percent of all computers use its Windows or DOS operating systems.

Since all software must be compatible with an operating system, the widespread use of Microsoft operating systems gives Microsoft enormous power—power that competitors claim it has used to gain competitive advantage for its other divisions. Competitors' calls for action, and reports of monopolistically abusive acts by Microsoft, led the U.S. Department of Justice in 1998 to charge Microsoft with violating antitrust laws.

The government suit against Microsoft charged the company with being a monopoly and using that monopoly power in a predatory way. Specifically, the charges were as follows:

1. Possessing monopoly power in the market for personal computer operating systems.

2. Tying other Microsoft software products to its Windows operating system.

3. Entering into agreements that keep computer manufacturers that install Windows from offering competing software.

Microsoft's 80–90 percent market share in PC operating systems has remained unchanged for about a decade. The U.S. Department of Justice argued that this long-standing monopoly position was the result of unfair business practices. Microsoft argued that Windows sold so well because it is a superior product. Microsoft further argued that, because it faces competition from technological change, it is not a monopolist.

Because of their experience with the AT&T and IBM cases, prosecutors were initially hesitant to bring charges against Microsoft. They knew that the case would be extremely complicated, contentious, and long. And they fully expected that the competitive issues would change significantly in the interim. They eventually decided to bring the case, however, because the judge granted them an expedited process—the case would be resolved much faster than previous cases—and because they felt that Microsoft had violated a 1994 consent that it had entered into following an earlier investigation.

Is Microsoft a Monopolist? The computer software industry is a market with barriers to entry that originate from two sources—network externalities and economies of scale. Network externalities exist because as the number of applications supported by a single platform increase the value of the platform also increases. Economies of scale exist because the cost of developing a new platform and new software is significant, while the cost of producing it is minimal. It is a potential candidate for monopoly.

Is Microsoft a monopoly in the market for operating systems? Looking only at the market within a static framework, Microsoft, given its stable 90 percent share, almost definitely has a monopoly. Looking at the market from a dynamic perspective, the issue is much more complicated. Competing operating systems exist—Macintosh (developed by Apple), OS/2 (developed by IBM), and Linux are all competitors to Windows.

The Linux operating system is a particularly strong potential competitor because it is an "open-source" operating system. All programmers can get the code and modify it, allowing them to tailor it for their software and streamline the structure of their programs. Linux reduces the costs of software development and leads to more efficient programs.

Another potential competitive force is the merging of software and hardware. As the power of computers increases according to Moore's law, it is becoming more and more feasible to design specific chips to do specific jobs, incorporating into a single chip aspects that were previously separated into hardware and software. Within 10 years the entire PC structure—a machine to handle a multitude of tasks—could become obsolete, and instead the market may consist of $10 or $15 machines that will perform specific tasks more efficiently than can a multipurpose machine like the PC. Each of these

Whether one sees Microsoft as a monopolist depends on whether one views it in a static or dynamic framework.

changes could eliminate Microsoft's monopoly advantage. In this dynamic view of the market, Microsoft's monopoly is at best temporary, and will survive only if it out-competes the other technologies.

Is Microsoft a Predatory Monopolist? The U.S. Department of Justice argued that Microsoft used its monopoly in the operating systems market to gain a larger share of the software market and engaged in unfair practices against its competitors to maintain the barriers to entry in the operating system market. Let's first look at its actions to gain market share in the software market.

Competing software companies alleged that companies like Novell (now Corel)—which had the leading word-processing software, WordPerfect—were put at a significant disadvantage because Microsoft combined its software with the Windows operating system. Not surprisingly, Microsoft's word-processing system, Word, has become the dominant one. By directing the development of new software to favor Windows, Microsoft strengthened the barrier to entry created by network externalities. Microsoft also penalized computer manufacturers that installed Windows if they installed competing software. IBM, for example, was denied Windows 95 when it decided to pre-install its PCs with Lotus, a direct competitor to Microsoft's Excel.

Microsoft was also alleged to have engaged in unfair practices in addressing the threat of competition in the operating system market. Direct competitive threats came mainly from two firms—Netscape and Sun Microsystems. Netscape and Sun were developing programs that operated across multiple platforms and were developing potential alternative platforms themselves.

Netscape designed and marketed a very popular Web browser called Netscape Navigator. Navigator posed a threat to Microsoft not only because it could serve as a platform for other software applications and circumvent the need for Windows but also because Navigator could work on many operating systems, increasing the ability of software to work on systems other than Windows. In response to that threat, Microsoft attempted to get Netscape to agree to stop developing Navigator as a competing platform in exchange for a "special relationship" with Microsoft. Netscape wouldn't agree. In response, Microsoft withheld for three months the source code Netscape needed to provide its browser on the Windows platform. This gave Microsoft an advantage to offer its own Web browser, Internet Explorer, with Windows 95. Microsoft then bundled its browser to Windows (essentially offering it at no cost) and made it virtually impossible for consumers to remove the Internet Explorer icon from the PC screen. Installing Windows 95 actually disabled competing Internet browsers. Microsoft also prohibited computer manufacturers such as Compaq from offering Netscape as an alternative browser when they sold PCs with Windows.

The government argued that this competition was unfair and predatory. Microsoft argued that Internet Explorer was an improvement to Windows 95; it was part of Windows. Netscape Navigator, which had been more popular than Internet Explorer and had seen its sales climbing rapidly, was in a matter of a few years nearly replaced by the Microsoft browser.

Another potential competitor was Sun Microsystems, which was developing Java, a programming language designed to create software applications on a variety of platforms, not just Windows. Sun Microsystems had entered into an agreement with Microsoft that allowed Microsoft to distribute the Java code under explicit instructions not to change it. But Microsoft created a version of Java that kept it tied to Windows and changed the platform-neutral characteristics of Java. Microsoft also instructed other companies not to cooperate with Sun. These actions stunted the development of a program that would allow software to run across multiple platforms and thus reduce the network externality barriers to trade that Microsoft enjoyed.

Microsoft used its power in one market to give it advantages in other markets.

Resolution of the Microsoft Case So, is Microsoft a monopoly? And has it been involved in anticompetitive practices? The answer the court gave was yes. The judge concluded that Microsoft violated Section 2 of the Sherman Act by attempting to maintain its monopoly power by anti-competitive means. He also ruled that Microsoft violated Section 1 of the Sherman Act by unlawfully tying its Web browser to its operating system. In a strongly worded decision he stated that "Microsoft mounted a deliberate assault upon entrepreneurial efforts that, left to rise or fall on their own merits, could well have enabled the introduction of competition into the market. . . ." As a remedy the government proposed breaking up Microsoft into two companies, but since Microsoft vowed to appeal the judge's ruling and any court remedy, the case will likely remain unsettled for years.

As all this was going on, the competitive nature of the market changed enormously. America Online (AOL), which was the world's largest Internet service provider, bought out Netscape. AOL then merged with Time Warner, in a move that combined a bricks and mortar content company that was a major force in traditional media with a major Internet company. (This merger will likely be reviewed by the government to determine its competitive effects, and may ultimately not be allowed.) Microsoft argued that, even if it had had a monopoly before (which it claims it did not), these changes reduced that monopoly and eliminated the need for any drastic policy settlement such as breaking up Microsoft. Whatever decision is ultimately arrived at will likely take years to implement, and this case will be much in the news in the early 2000s.

Assessment of Antitrust Policy

Economic scholars' overall assessment of antitrust policy is mixed. In certain cases, such as the IBM case, most agree that antitrust prosecution went too far. But most believe that other decisions (as in the 1911 Standard Oil and American Tobacco cases) set a healthy precedent by encouraging a more competitive U.S. business environment. Almost all agree that antitrust enforcement has not reduced the size of firms below the minimally efficient level, the level at which a firm can take full advantage of economies of scale. But they are mixed in their judgments as to whether the enforcement was needed. Performance advocates generally believe that it was not, while structural advocates generally believe that it was. They are also mixed in their judgment about whether any type of antitrust action is feasible in a technologically dynamic industry such as computers or telecommunications.

Economists' judgment on antitrust is mixed.

MERGERS, ACQUISITIONS, AND TAKEOVERS

Other than the Microsoft case, antitrust activity was minimal in the 1990s. But industrial structure has changed significantly. The nature of those changes was treated in an earlier chapter, where I discussed how firms are increasingly looking for alternative ways of structuring themselves so that they can achieve economies of scope and economies of scale that go along with specialization. To do this, firms are simultaneously merging and breaking up. Firms are allowed to break up as much as they want; when they merge, however, they must see that any merger falls within the antitrust guidelines. Let's consider the various subcategories and types of mergers that are possible, in order to put recent merger activity into perspective.

Acquisitions and Takeovers

Merger is *a general term meaning the act of combining two firms*. The picture it conveys is of two firms combining to form one firm. That picture isn't always appropriate, however. For example, often the firm buying another company is essentially what's called a *shell* *corporation*, which exists primarily to buy up other firms. A combination that is technically a merger but has distinguishing characteristics all its own is the **takeover**—*the purchase of one firm by a shell firm that then takes direct control of all the purchased firm's operations*. The term *takeover* is used to emphasize that little true merging is taking place. Takeovers change the control over the firm, but do not affect market concentration.

Another kind of merger is an **acquisition**—*a merger in which a company buys another company and the purchaser has the right of direct control over the resulting operation (but does not always exercise that right)*. It is a merger, but it is not a merger of equals, and the acquiring firm does not necessarily take over direct control of the acquired firm's operations. In a merger of equals, neither firm takes over the other, and it's not clear who'll be in charge after the merger.

Takeovers and acquisitions are said to be *friendly* or *hostile*. In a friendly takeover, one corporation is willing to be acquired by the other. A **hostile takeover** is *a merger in which the firm being taken over doesn't want to be taken over*. How can that happen?

Remember the discussion of corporations from Chapter 3. Corporations are owned by stockholders, but are managed by a different group of individuals. The two groups' interests do not necessarily coincide. When it is said that a corporation doesn't want to be taken over, that means that the corporation's managers don't want the company to be taken over. In a hostile takeover, the management of each corporation presents its side to the shareholders of both corporations. The shareholders of the corporation that is the takeover target ultimately decide whether or not to sell their shares. If enough shareholders sell, the takeover succeeds.

In a hostile takeover, the shareholders ultimately decide whether to sell their shares.

Mergers

Mergers are also classified by the types of businesses that are merging.

Horizontal mergers are companies in the same industry merging together.

Horizontal Mergers Most U.S. antitrust policy has concerned **horizontal mergers**—*the combining of two companies in the same industry*. The creation of Standard Oil is an example of a horizontal merger. Since the passage of the Cellar-Kefauver Act of 1950, almost all mergers of companies with substantial market shares in the same industry have been prohibited, even though enforcement was loosened in the 1980s. For example, in 1986 the FTC blocked a proposed merger between Coca-Cola and 7UP because the market share after the merger would have been 80 percent.

Exactly what is considered substantial market share has changed over time. The general guideline government used in the 1970s and early 1980s was that, in highly concentrated industries, the government would challenge all mergers involving the following combinations of market share:

Acquiring Firm	Acquired Firm
4%	4% or more
10%	2% or more
15%	1% or more

For less-concentrated industries, the guidelines used slightly different percentages. In 1982, the Department of Justice changed the guidelines and began looking at all mergers in which the Herfindahl index, after the merger, would be above 1,000. Special highly restrictive rules regarding mergers existed for industries with Herfindahl indexes above 1,800. Since then the rules have evolved and have become more flexible; for example, in 1997 the government issued new rules that allow some mergers if the companies can show that the merger will lower price, or will improve a product or service, even if the merger doesn't meet the guidelines.

BEYOND THE TOOLS

White Knights and Golden Parachutes

The specific nature of a merger is of great interest to people working for the corporations involved. It determines whether employees will move up or down in the corporate pecking order, or even whether they'll keep their jobs at all. When a firm is threatened by a hostile takeover, top management is likely to hunt for another firm, a friendly one that will be a "white knight" coming to the rescue. The white knight firm, it is hoped, will keep all the management employees in their jobs. When their jobs are at stake, it is often questionable whether management searches out the firm that will pay shareholders the best price. Management's interest is likely to be in keeping their jobs, not in making money for the shareholders.

Strategies have been developed to protect shareholders from management's interest overriding shareholders' interest. One such strategy is the *golden parachute*. The board of directors of the corporation provides that if the corporation should be acquired by another corporation, people holding top management jobs are guaranteed large payments of money—as high as $100 or $200 million in some cases. This is a golden parachute. It means that management can feel comfortable when the corporation is approached by a potential buyer and will make decisions based on the shareholders' interest, not on whether management jobs will be left undisturbed.

Golden parachutes afford shareholders some assurance that if their firm receives an acquisition or takeover offer, management will consider it. Golden parachutes protect top managers because either they'll keep their jobs or, if they lose their jobs, their pain will be soothed by compensation in big bucks. Golden parachutes do nothing for low-level managers and ordinary workers, who may suffer demotions or layoffs after two firms have merged.

Vertical Mergers A **vertical merger** is *a combination of two companies that are involved in different phases of producing a product*, one company being a buyer of products the other company supplies. For example, if a computer company merges with an electronic chip company, a vertical merger has taken place. Similarly, if a clothes manufacturer buys a retail boutique, that's a vertical merger. If either of the merged firms is able to limit access of other buyers or sellers to the market, such a merger is in violation of the Clayton Act.

A famous vertical merger case is the Du Pont/General Motors case (1961), in which Du Pont was required to sell its 23 percent share of General Motors because Du Pont was a major supplier to the automobile industry. The Supreme Court felt Du Pont's ownership share of GM was restricting competition. Similarly in the Brown Shoe/Kinney Shoe case (1962), Brown Shoe, primarily a wholesaler, was forbidden to buy Kinney Shoe, which was a chain of shoe retailers.

In most of the 1980s, the U.S. government challenged any vertical merger in which the supplying firm had a 10 percent or more market share and the buyer company purchased 6 percent or more of the market. This rule was loosened some as the 1980s progressed, although specific new guidelines have not yet replaced it. The U.S. government challenges few vertical mergers.

Conglomerate Mergers A third type of merger is a conglomerate merger. **Conglomerate mergers** involve *the merging of two relatively unrelated businesses*. Conglomerate mergers are generally approved by the U.S. antitrust laws under the assumption that they do not significantly restrict competition. Thus, when GM bought Electronic Data Systems Corporation in 1984, no antitrust action was taken to prevent the merger because the two firms were unrelated.

Why would two unrelated firms want to merge? Or why would one want to be bought out by another? There are five general reasons:

1. *To achieve economies of scope.* Although the businesses are unrelated, some overlap is almost inevitable, so economies of scope are likely. For example, one

Vertical mergers are combinations of two companies, one of which supplied inputs to the other's production.

Q.7 If Ben and Jerry's, a maker of ice cream, bought a dairy farm, what type of merger would it be?

 16.4

Conglomerate mergers are combinations of unrelated businesses. Five reasons why unrelated firms merge include:
1. To achieve economies of scope;
2. To get a good buy;
3. To diversify;
4. To ward off a takeover bid; and
5. To strengthen their political-economic influence.

firm's technical or marketing expertise may be helpful to the other firm, or the conglomerate's increased size may give it better bargaining power with its suppliers.

2. *To get a good buy.* Firms are always on the lookout for good buys. If a firm believes that another firm's stock is significantly undervalued, it can buy that stock at its low price and then sell it at a profit later when the stock is no longer undervalued.

3. *To diversify.* Many industries have a cyclical nature. In some parts of the business cycle they do poorly; in other parts of the business cycle they do just fine. Buying an unrelated company allows a firm to diversify and thereby to even out the cyclical fluctuation in its profits.

4. *To ward off a takeover bid.* Firms are always susceptible to being bought out by someone else. Sometimes they prevent an unwanted buyout by merging with another firm in order to become so large that they're indigestible. For example, in 1989 Time, Inc., merged with Warner Communications to reduce the likelihood that Time would be taken over by a third firm, Paramount. (Since then Time Warner has merged with America Online for other reasons.)

5. *To strengthen their political-economic influence.* The bigger you are, the more influence you have. Individuals who run companies like to have and use influence. Merging can increase their net influence considerably.

Recent Merger Activity and Deacquisitions

Figure 16-1 presents the number of mergers in the United States each year since 1892. As you can see mergers rose significantly in the late 1990s. The primary reasons for the increase in the number of mergers are globalization, deregulation, and technological change. Globalization leads to mergers because firms can gain instant foreign distribution networks and knowledge of local markets from mergers and can also lower costs by restructuring production to low cost areas. Deregulation of the telecommunications, electricity, and financial industries has encouraged mergers that take advantage of economies of scale and scope. Bank mergers and phone company mergers are examples.

Q₋8 When the long-distance phone company AT&T merged with the cellular phone company McCaw to create AT&T Wireless Services, what type of merger was it?

Figure 16-1   Mergers in the United States since 1892

The number of mergers in the United States has fluctuated substantially in the last 100 years.

Source: Federal Trade Commission, national press, and author extrapolations.

The acceleration of technological change in recent years is another contributor to merger activity. Firms are looking for ways to develop new technologies or take advantage of new technologies, and merging with another company is one way to acquire a new technology. The merger of America Online and Time Warner is an example of an Internet (technology) company combining with a "content" company.

At the same time that these mergers are taking place, firms are also engaging in **deacquisitions**—*one company's sale of parts of either another company it has bought, or parts of itself.* Sometimes regulators require such deacquisitions as a condition of a merger. Deacquisition also occurs as firms focus on those areas where they have comparative advantage and where growth is highest, and sell off aspects of their firms that are not part of their core business. For example, automobile firms are breaking off their component manufacturing operations. Hewlett-Packard voluntarily split into two companies—Hewlett-Packard, which focuses on computers, and Agilent, which focuses on non-computer aspects of their business. The motto of the 2000s is that firms have to continually reinvent themselves.

As I mentioned at the beginning of this section, voluntarily breaking up companies is becoming much more prominent as firms try to find their niche in the global marketplace. Companies are continually spinning off portions of their business where they do not believe they have a comparative advantage, and buying businesses where they think they do have a comparative advantage. This process is likely to continue, making the U.S. market structure a continually changing landscape.

The U.S. market structure is a continually changing landscape.

Assessment of Mergers and Acquisitions

I've introduced a lot of terms in this section and, ideally, started you thinking about the issues involved in deciding on a merger and acquisition policy. This chapter does not arrive at definite conclusions, and in this it reflects the economics profession, which has no one position on what policy the United States should follow toward mergers.

But the economics profession's failure to come to an undivided view on mergers isn't necessarily a failing of economists. Mergers have both costs and benefits, and reasonable people will assess them differently.

INTERNATIONAL COMPETITION AND ANTITRUST POLICY IN OTHER COUNTRIES

As I discussed in Chapter 14, the nature of competition is changing in the United States. Ten or 20 years ago, when people talked about competition, they meant competition among U.S. firms. Now, however, they often mean international competition.

Because of this internationalization of competition, the political climate in the United States is changing. More and more, U.S. antitrust policymakers see the international market as the relevant market. The policy focus of government is shifting from "Is U.S. industry internally competitive so that it does not take advantage of the consumer?" to "Is U.S. industry internationally competitive so that it can compete effectively in the world economy?"

Other countries' approaches toward antitrust are a likely harbinger of future U.S. antitrust policy. The reason is that other countries, because most are smaller than the United States, have consistently seen the international market as the relevant market and have designed their antitrust laws accordingly. Their domestic markets were simply too small to take advantage of economies of scale.

What's interesting about other countries' antitrust laws is how lax they are when compared to U.S. laws. No other country forces companies to break up for antitrust violations,

Q.9   Does Japan have stricter or less strict antitrust laws than the United States has?

Britain: British Monopoly Commission
While it has the power to recommend structural reorganization, the British Monopoly Commission generally has not done so. Instead, it has pushed for price reductions in certain industries. After World War II, a number of major industries were nationalized, putting the government in direct control of prices, but many of these industries have been privatized in the past few years.

Japan: Fair Trade Commission
The Japanese Fair Trade Commission is weak and subordinated to the Ministry of International Trade and Industry and other government agencies. In retailing, small firms continue to dominate with the support of government. But the 1980s saw the beginnings of a retailing system with large stores, like the system in the United States. The Fair Trade Commission may take a role in suppressing that development.

Germany: Federal Cartel Office
The Federal Cartel Office is relatively small. Often it allows and even encourages cartels. It does have the authority to push for price reductions if it determines that the cartel has abused its power.

France: Commission on Competition
The Commission on Competition has been very weak and has often advocated mergers. In the 1960s, France actively promoted large-scale mergers, and during that period the government nationalized large industries without hearing objections from the Commission on Competition.

European Union: The European Commission
In 1990, the EU's rules regarding mergers officially took precedence over member nations' local rules in those cases in which the merger involved significant activities in more than one member state. There were many such mergers; as expected, the expansion of the market that was made possible by the integration of the EU economies in 1992 generated significant merger activity as firms consolidated and tried to take advantage of new trading possibilities.

It wasn't only EU member firms that were merging. The largest percentage of growth in EU merger activity has been between EU firms and non-EU, especially U.S., firms. At times this has resulted in conflict between the EU Commission and other countries' antitrust agencies. For instance, the Commission had serious concerns regarding the 1997 merger between Boeing and McDonnell Douglas, but backed down after the United States pressured them to allow the merger. This case was unusual; for the most part the EU Commission has been very lenient in allowing mergers and, from 1991 to 1998, the Commission disallowed only 10 mergers.

---

although some push for price rollbacks in cases of extreme monopolization. Even when, for example, the United States tried to export its stringent antitrust laws during its military occupation of Germany and Japan after World War II, those laws were repealed by those nations soon after the occupation ended.

One important reason other countries oppose antitrust regulation is that they recognize the importance of economies of scale. In many countries that have only small markets, the minimum efficient production level requires high concentration.

A second reason is their history. Most countries don't have the same populist worldview that exists in the United States. The ideological and cultural underpinning of strong antitrust laws (individualistic competition based on small producers) fits in nicely with the American populist worldview. In the United States, many people believe that bigness is bad. That belief is not as prevalent in other countries.

A third reason that other countries don't have strong antitrust laws is cultural. In the United States, government and business are often seen as enemies of each other. In cultures such as Japan's or Germany's, government and business are seen as allies, working together to increase exports and compete internationally.

Other countries oppose antitrust laws because of economies of scale, lack of strong ideology supporting competition, and strong cultural ties between government and business.

REGULATION, GOVERNMENT OWNERSHIP, AND INDUSTRIAL POLICIES

Antitrust policy is not the only way in which governments affect the competitive process. Other ways include (1) regulating the activities of firms, (2) government ownership—taking charge of the firms and operating them directly, and (3) industrial policy—influencing firms with laws and taxes. While I consider these issues in other parts of the book, here I want to briefly discuss some of the central elements of these three means of affecting the competitive process.

The government can also affect the competitive process by (1) regulation, (2) government ownership, and (3) industrial policy.

Regulation

Regulation involves the setting of the rules that firms must follow if they are to conduct business. There are two types of regulation—price regulation and social regulation. *Price regulation* is regulation directed at industries that have natural monopoly elements. In order to allow them to take advantage of the economies of scale, firms are given an exclusive right to conduct business, but are subject to pricing controls. Examples include the Federal Energy Regulatory Commission, which regulates gas and oil pipelines and other energy-related areas, and the Federal Communications Commission, which regulates cable television, telephones, television, and other communications areas. *Social regulation* is concerned with the conditions under which goods and services are produced, the safety of those goods and the side effects of production on society. Examples of social regulatory bodies include the Food and Drug Administration (FDA), the Environmental Protection Agency (EPA), and the Equal Employment Opportunity Commission (EEOC).

Two types of regulation are price regulation and social regulation.

Price Regulation Price regulation is usually imposed in those industries where there seems to be a natural monopoly, as discussed in an earlier chapter. In such cases, a single producer is most efficient because two firms could not take advantage of the economies of scale. But if the firm is to have the monopoly, then it will be able to charge high prices to consumers and transfer the consumer surplus into its profit. Thus, when such monopolies are granted, government must also regulate the price they charge. Usually this has taken the form of requiring the firm to charge its average total cost plus a profit margin.

That sounds reasonable in theory, but the practice has problems. The first is that the regulated firm does not have an incentive to hold down costs. Cost increases lead directly to price increases. X-inefficiency will exist. Regulatory boards have tried to counteract that tendency of rising costs by permitting firms to pass on only "legitimate" costs, but generally the people on the regulatory boards do not have the accounting expertise to review costs and determine whether costs are legitimate or not, especially when the companies have a strong incentive to make all costs look legitimate.

Price regulated firms often do not have an incentive to hold down costs.

The problem is worsened by the fact that the boards are often made up of individuals from the industry that is being regulated. This gives the commission necessary expertise, but it also creates a potentially unhealthy connection between the regulatory commission and the firms being regulated. Some economists have argued that the connection is so close that the regulatory board simply reflects the regulated firms' interests, and that it protects them from competition arising from technological change.

Another problem critics have seen in regulation is that, once established, regulation may tend to extend far beyond natural monopolies and be introduced into industries where competition could work. Still another problem is that regulation continues even after technological change has created competitive market conditions. For example, the trucking and airline industries were both regulated industries even though they became industries with significant competition. Often the regulatory boards simply function as a way of allowing an industry to operate as a legal cartel, holding prices up rather than keeping them down.

Problems with price regulation have led to deregulation in recent years.

The above criticisms have led to significant deregulation over the last 20 years. Trucking, airlines, and aspects of phone service have all been deregulated, and electric power generation is currently being deregulated, as discussed in an earlier chapter. In general, most economists' assessments of the results of this deregulation have been positive and some economists have estimated deregulation saves consumers approximately $50 billion annually.

Social Regulation[3] Whereas most economists are skeptical of pricing regulation, they are far more divided on social regulation. Social regulation differs from pricing regulation in that:

1. Social regulation applies to most firms, and is not designed specifically for a natural monopoly. For example, when the Occupational Safety and Health Administration (OSHA) issues a requirement that all workers have a periodic break from work, it applies to all firms in the United States that fall under OSHA's control.

2. Social regulation affects large aspects of business: working conditions, the quality of the products, and the production processes firms are allowed to use.

Whereas pricing regulation has declined in the last 20 years, social regulation has increased substantially. Economists debate whether this is good or bad. Critics of social regulation point out that regulation has high administrative and compliance costs and that those costs hurt consumers more than the regulation benefits them. They believe that this occurs because the social regulation laws are too often poorly written and ambiguous, and put into law without information on what is reasonable and feasible. The result is higher prices, far less technical progress than there otherwise would have been, and fewer new entrants into a field as the regulatory burdens become unbearable for small firms.

Advocates of social regulation agree with some of the above but argue that the benefits of social regulation are worth the costs, and that the objections are simply a call for better regulation. They argue that social regulation has made manufacturing much safer in the United States, has improved the quality of life and the environment enormously, introduced far more justice into the economy, and reduced discrimination against minorities.

Judging between these two views is difficult because measurement of both the costs and benefits is difficult or impossible. In such cases, the economic cost/benefit framework cannot provide a definitive answer.

Government Ownership

Instead of regulation, an alternative way of dealing with the problems of natural monopolies is for the government to own the firms itself. European countries have used this approach much more often than has the United States. Instead of regulating the telephone (or other natural monopoly) industry, governments took it over and ran it with state employees. Since the 1980s most countries have been selling off government-owned businesses to private owners. Why? Most governments have found that government-owned firms did not have an incentive to hold costs down or to introduce new technology. Workers in government-owned firms, who were guaranteed jobs, used political threats to hold their wages high. Since the government firms faced little competition,

Government-owned firms tend not to have an incentive to hold costs down.

---

[3]Social regulation is discussed more fully in Chapter 17.

they could raise prices and pass on the higher costs to consumers. The result was that European prices for telephone service, airline travel, and electricity were much higher than in the United States. Economic integration in Europe has been accompanied by privatization of many of the formerly government-owned industries; the hope is that the larger markets will provide the needed competition.

Industrial Policies

In the 1980s and 1990s, a rallying cry for many politicians was that the U.S. economy needed an industrial policy. An **industrial policy** is *a formal policy that government takes toward business*. These politicians wanted the United States to follow a policy like Japan's, where a branch of government—the Ministry of International Trade and Industry (MITI)—played an active role in guiding business decisions. Economists generally opposed such a policy, and when the Japanese economy faltered in the 1990s, the calls went away.

In thinking about government's relation with business, it is important to remember that, in actual fact, the United States has always had, and always will have, a type of industrial policy. That policy is embodied in its tax code, its laws, and its regulatory structure, and in the positions the government takes in international negotiations about tariffs and trade. An example is the U.S. government's strong support of international copyrights and patents, which prevent foreign firms from making "knockoffs" without paying a royalty to the U.S. firm. The policy is, however, an implicit policy of working with business, not an explicit policy of directing business.

Many close connections between government and business have developed. For example, the military works closely with its suppliers, and the relationship between them has been called a *military-industrial complex*. This combination of business and government plays important roles in making decisions about what is produced. For example, in 1989 Congress seemed about to cut production of the B-2 Stealth bomber. Northrup, the plane's manufacturer, took out full-page newspaper ads, pointing out that parts of the B-2 were produced in 48 states and that thousands of jobs would be lost if the government canceled the contract. Congress gave in, as it has done on many other defense items that are widely regarded as nonessential to national security. Many other business-government alliances exist in the United States, and there are similar government-drug complexes, government–higher-education complexes and government–high-tech complexes. In a democracy where politicians are dependent on business for funding their campaigns, such complexes are inevitable.

CONCLUSION

We've come to the end of our discussion of market structure and government policy toward the competitive process. What conclusion should we come to? That's a tough question because the problem has so many dimensions. What we can say is that market structure is important, and generally more competition is preferred to less competition. We can also say that, based on experience, government-created and protected monopolies have not been the optimal solution, especially when industries are experiencing technological change. But how government should deal with monopolies that develop as part of the competitive process is less clear. Competition has both dynamic elements and market structure elements, and often monopolies that develop as part of the competitive process are temporary—and they will be overwhelmed by other monopolies. Thus the debate about government entering into the market to protect competition has no single answer, which makes cases like the Microsoft antitrust case difficult to resolve.

Q-10 Why have European countries recently privatized many government-owned firms in the telecommunications, electricity, and airline industries?

An industrial policy is a formal policy that government takes toward business.

  16.5

Chapter Summary

- Judgment by performance means judging the competitiveness of markets by the behavior of firms in that market. Judgment by structure means judging the competitiveness of markets by how many firms operate in the industry and their market shares.

- There is a debate on whether markets should be judged on the basis of structure or on the basis of performance.

- Antitrust policy is the government's policy toward the competitive process.

- Important antitrust laws include the Sherman Antitrust Act, the Clayton Act, and the Federal Trade Commission Act.

- The antitrust suit against IBM filed in 1967 was withdrawn in 1982 because the computer market had changed, making the charges against IBM moot.

- The antitrust suit against AT&T ended in a settlement that required AT&T to be broken up into one long-distance and equipment company (AT&T) and seven regional local telephone companies (Baby Bells). Since then the Baby Bells have been merging, firms are now allowed to compete in both local and long-distance markets, and AT&T has both divided itself and merged with other companies.

- In 1998 the U.S. government filed an antitrust suit against Microsoft alleging that Microsoft abused its market power to maintain its monopoly position. In 1999 the courts found that Microsoft has a monopoly that is protected by barriers to entry and that Microsoft engaged in practices to maintain that monopoly power.

- Three types of mergers are horizontal, vertical, and conglomerate.

- A horizontal merger is the combination of two companies in the same industry, a vertical merger is the combination of two companies in different industries, and a conglomerate merger is the combination of two companies in relatively unrelated industries.

- Five reasons that two unrelated firms would want to merge are economies of scope, a good buy, diversification, warding off a takeover bid, and strengthening political-economic influence.

- The increasing internationalization of the U.S. market has changed U.S. antitrust policy from looking at just domestic competition to considering international competition.

- Three alternatives to antitrust policy are regulation, government ownership, and industrial policy.

Key Terms

acquisition   (360)

antitrust policy   (347)

Clayton Antitrust Act (349)

conglomerate merger (361)

deacquisition   (363)

Federal Trade Commission Act   (350)

horizontal merger   (360)

hostile takeover   (360)

industrial policy   (367)

judgment by performance (347)

judgment by structure (347)

merger   (359)

natural monopoly   (354)

Sherman Antitrust Act (348)

takeover   (360)

vertical merger   (361)

Questions for Thought and Review

1. What is the difference between judgment by performance and judgment by structure?

2. Distinguish the basis of judgment for the Standard Oil and the ALCOA cases.

3. How would the U.S. economy likely differ today if Standard Oil had not been broken up?

4. How did the Clayton Antitrust Act clarify the Sherman Antitrust Act?

5. Colleges require that students take certain courses at that college in order to get a degree. Is that an example of a tie-in contract that limits consumers' choices? If so, should it be against the law?

6. Colleges give financial aid to certain students. Is this price discrimination? If so, should it be against the law?

7. Should interlocking directorships be against the law? Why or why not?

8. If you were an economist for a firm that wanted to merge, would you argue that the three-digit or five-digit NAICS industry is the relevant market? Why?

9. If you were an economist for Mattel, manufacturer of the doll Barbie, which was making an unsolicited bid to take over Hasbro, manufacturer of G.I. Joe, would you argue that the relevant market is dolls, preschool toys, or all toys including video games? Why? Would your answer change if you were working for Hasbro?

10. Has telephone service improved since AT&T was broken up? What does this imply about antitrust laws?

11. How did the antitrust suit against IBM affect IBM's future business?

12. In what market did Microsoft have a monopoly in the late 1990s? What technological advances threatened that monopoly?

13. Under the 1997 Department of Justice guidelines, would a merger be allowed between the number three firm in an industry and a firm with 2 percent of the market? The number four firm in the industry has 11 percent of the market.

14. Should the United States have a policy against conglomerate mergers? Why or why not?

15. How has the globalization of the U.S. economy changed U.S. antitrust policy?

16. What two methods does government have for dealing with natural monopolies? What problems are associated with each?

17. How would you design an industrial policy to avoid the problems inherent in industrial policies?

Problems and Exercises

1. You're working at the Department of Justice. Ms. Ecofame has just brought in a new index, the Ecofame index, which she argues is preferable to the Herfindahl index. The Ecofame index is calculated by cubing the market share of the top 10 firms in the industry.
   a. Calculate an Ecofame guideline that would correspond to the 1997 Department of Justice guidelines.
   b. State the advantages and disadvantages of the Ecofame index as compared to the Herfindahl index.

2. Using a monopolistic competition model, a cartel model of oligopoly, and a contestable market of oligopoly, discuss and demonstrate graphically, where possible, the effect of antitrust policy.

3. In 1993 Mattel proposed acquiring Fisher-Price for $1.2 billion. In the toy industry, Mattel is a major player with 11 percent of the market. Fisher-Price has 4 percent. The other two large firms are Tyco, with a 5 percent share, and Hasbro, with a 15 percent share. In the infant/preschool toy market, Mattel has an 8 percent share and Fisher-Price has a 27 percent share, the largest. The other two large firms are Hasbro, with a 25 percent share, and Rubbermaid, with a 12 percent share.
   a. What are the approximate Herfindahl and four-firm concentration ratios for these firms in each industry?

   b. If you were Mattel's economist, which industry definition would you suggest using in court if you were challenged by the government?
   c. Give an argument why the merger might decrease competition.
   d. Give an argument why the merger might increase competition.

4. In 1992 American Airlines offered a 50-percent-off sale and cut fares. In 1993 Continental Airlines and Northwest Airlines sued American Airlines over this action.
   a. What was the likely basis of the suit?
   b. How does the knowledge that Continental and Northwest were in serious financial trouble play a role in the suit?

5. Demonstrate graphically how regulating the price of a monopolist can both increase quantity and decrease price.
   a. Why did the regulation have the effect it did?
   b. How relevant to the real world do you believe this result is in the "contestable markets" view of the competitive process?
   c. How relevant to the real world do you believe this result is in the "cartel" view of the competitive process?

Web Questions

1. In 1999, four companies (Showa Denko Carbon, Inc.; UCAR International, Inc.; Tokai Carbon Co., Ltd.; and SGL Carbon AG) pleaded guilty to fixing prices in the worldwide market for graphite electrodes. Go to the U.S. Department of Justice's home page at www.usdoj.gov and search for information on this suit to answer the following questions:
   a. What was the combined market share of the four price-fixing conspirators?

   b. By what percentage did the price of graphite electrodes in the United States increase over the course of the conspiracy?
   c. What antitrust act makes the practice engaged in by the defendants illegal?
   d. What was the combined fine for all four conspirators for the illegal act?

2. The Web site www.antitrust.org is dedicated to issues involving antitrust regulation. Go to the site and select the Mergers button to find out specific information about

how the U.S. Department of Justice handles potential entry in its decisions to allow mergers. Entry conditions are found by clicking on "Economics" on the menu. Answer the following questions about the importance of entry to merger guidelines:

a. What are the three conditions for entry as stated in the merger guidelines?

b. What merger highlights *entry* as important to the decision by the U.S. Department of Justice to disallow the merger? What barriers, according to the Department of Justice, limited entry?

Answers to Margin Questions

1. The Sherman Antitrust Act contained two main sections. The first stated that every contract, combination, or conspiracy in restraint of trade was illegal. The second stated that every person who shall monopolize or attempt to monopolize shall be deemed guilty of a misdemeanor. These provisions, while sounding strong, were so broad that they were almost unenforceable, and the interpretation was left to the courts. *(348)*

2. In the Standard Oil case, the Court determined that Standard Oil controlled 90 percent of the market. It said that this monopolistic structure of the market did not necessarily violate the Sherman Antitrust Act. However, the Court also decided that Standard Oil had engaged in systematic abuse and unfair business practices, and therefore was guilty of antitrust violations and must be broken up. *(349)*

3. In the ALCOA case, the Supreme Court changed the interpretation of the law. Here it found ALCOA was not guilty of any unfair practices. It agreed that ALCOA had simply used its knowledge of the market to expand capacity before any competitors had a chance to enter, and had kept its price low to prevent other entry. Thus, on performance standards, it was not violating the law. But the Court decided the structure of the market, not the company's performance, was the appropriate standard by which to judge cases, and, therefore, ALCOA was in violation of the antitrust law. *(350)*

4. In the 1956 Du Pont case, the Supreme Court found that Du Pont was innocent of monopolization of the production of cellophane, even though it was the only producer. The Court's reasoning was that the relevant market was the entire flexible wrap industry, not just cellophane. Since Du Pont did not dominate the flexible wrap industry, it was not in violation of antitrust law. *(352)*

5. In the late 1960s, the Department of Justice filed suit against IBM for violating the antitrust laws. It alleged that IBM had a monopoly of the general-purpose electronic digital computing industry and that it had acquired its market share because of unfair business practices. The case dragged on for 13 years but never went to court. In 1982, the government withdrew its lawsuit. The antitrust case, however, had significant effects on IBM. It is likely that the experience caused IBM to shy away from the then-small personal computer market. This decision by IBM very likely was the beginning of the serious problems that IBM faced in the 1990s. *(354)*

6. In 1978, the Department of Justice sued AT&T, alleging that its potential competitors were not being allowed reasonable access to AT&T's local telephone network. The case was resolved in January 1982, when AT&T agreed to let itself be broken up. Specifically, AT&T divested itself of 22 operating companies and focused thereafter only on long-distance telephone service, manufacturing, and research and development. This settlement left AT&T free to enter into any unregulated business it desired, and in the 1990s AT&T expanded with fiber-optic networks and merged with McCaw Communication. Ironically, these expansions placed it in direct competition with the still-regulated Baby Bells, which had inherited AT&T's monopoly rights. *(355)*

7. If Ben & Jerry's bought a dairy farm, it would be a vertical merger because Ben & Jerry's would be buying one of its suppliers. *(361)*

8. AT&T's merger with McCaw was a mixture of a horizontal merger and a conglomerate merger. It is a horizontal merger to the degree that one interprets the industry broadly as a "communications industry." It is a conglomerate merger if one interprets the industry narrowly and distinguishes the wireless communications industry from the wire communications industry. *(362)*

9. Japan has antitrust laws that are significantly less strict than those of the United States. *(363)*

10. European countries have been privatizing firms in telecommunications, electricity, and airline industries because the government-owned firms were inefficient, resulting in higher costs for consumers and less innovation. *(367)*

Microeconomic Policy, Economic Reasoning, and Beyond

17

After reading this chapter, you should be able to:

- List three reasons why economists sometimes differ in their views on social policy.

- Explain why liberal and conservative economists often agree in their views on social policy.

- Explain the cost/benefit approach the typical economist takes to analyze regulations.

- Describe three types of failure of market outcomes.

- Explain why economists are doubtful government can correct failure of market outcomes.

- Explain how politics sometimes makes a positive and sometimes a negative contribution to economic policy.

*If an economist becomes certain of the solution
of any problem, he can be equally certain that
his solution is wrong.*

H. A. Innis

One important job of economists is to give advice to politicians and other policy-makers on a variety of questions relating to social policy: How should unemployment be dealt with? How can society distribute income fairly? Should the government redistribute income? Would a program of equal pay for jobs of comparable worth (a pay equity program) make economic sense? Should the minimum wage be increased? These are tough questions.

The supply/demand model is a tool, not a rule.

In Chapter 15 I discussed the supply/demand framework that economists use to think about such issues. In this chapter I consider economic reasoning in a broader context.

The reason for doing so is that economic reasoning, and the supply/demand model are tools, not rules. To draw policy implications from it, the supply/demand model has to be placed in context. Used in the proper context, the supply/demand model is enormously strong, something no one should be without. Used out of context, it can lead to conclusions that don't seem right, and that maybe are not right. Consider the assembly-line chicken-production example in Chapter 10. Some of you may have felt that the assembly-line production of chickens was somehow not right—that the efficiency of the production process somehow did not outweigh the chickens' suffering. Yet the economic model, which focuses on efficiency, directs production toward that assembly line. This chapter considers when you might want to use economic reasoning, and when you might not.

The chapter is divided into two parts. The first part of the chapter extends the supply/demand model to a broader cost/benefit framework, tying together the discussion we had about economic reasoning in the introductory chapters with the chapters that developed the foundations of the supply/demand model. It shows you how economic reasoning is used in practice. The second part of the chapter turns economic reasoning back upon itself, considering not only the benefits (which are considerable) but also the costs of using economic reasoning. In doing so I discuss how markets that are working perfectly may still lead to outcomes that are undesirable.

ECONOMISTS' DIFFERING VIEWS ABOUT SOCIAL POLICY

Economists' views on social policy differ widely because (1) their objective economic analyses are colored by their subjective value judgments; (2) their interpretations of economic evidence and of how political and social institutions work vary widely; and (3) their proposals are often based on various models that focus on different aspects of problems.

Economists have many different views on social policy because:

1. Economists' suggestions for social policy are determined by their subjective value judgments (normative views) as well as by their objective economic analyses.

2. Policy proposals must be based on imprecise empirical evidence, so there's considerable room for differences of interpretation not only about economic issues but also about how political and social institutions work. Economic policy is an art, not a science.

3. Policy proposals are based on various models that focus on different aspects of a problem.

All three reasons directly concern the role of ideology in economics. However, any policy proposal must embody both economic analysis and value judgments because the goals of policy reflect value judgments. When an economist makes a policy proposal, it's of this type: "If A, B, and C are your goals, then you should undertake policies D, E, and F to achieve those goals most efficiently." In making these policy suggestions, the economist's role is much the same as an engineer's: he or she is simply telling someone else how to achieve desired ends most efficiently. Ideally the economist is as objective as possible, telling someone how to achieve his or her goals (which need not be the economist's goals).

How Economists' Value Judgments Creep into Policy Proposals

Even though economists attempt to be as objective as possible, value judgments still creep into their analyses in three ways: interpretation of policymakers' values, interpretation of empirical evidence, and choice of economic models.

Interpretation of the Policymaker's Values In practice, social goals are seldom so neat that they can be specified A, B, and C; they're vaguely understood and vaguely expressed. An economist will be told, for instance, "We want to make the poor better off" or "We want to see that middle-income people get better housing." It isn't clear what *poor, better off,* and *better housing* mean. Nor is it clear how judgments should be made when a policy will benefit some individuals at the expense of others, as real-world policies inevitably do.

Faced with this problem, some academic economists have argued that economists should recommend only **Pareto optimal policies**—*policies that benefit some people and hurt no one*. The policies are named in honor of the famous Italian economist Wilfredo Pareto, who first suggested that kind of criterion for judging social change.[1] It's hard to object to the notion of Pareto optimal policies because, by definition, they improve life for some people while hurting no one.

I'd give you an example of a real-world Pareto optimal policy if I could, but unfortunately I don't know of any. Every policy inevitably has some side effect of hurting, or at least seeming to hurt, somebody. In the real world, Pareto optimal policies don't exist. Any economist who has advised governments on real-world problems knows that all real-world policies make some people better off and some people worse off.

But that doesn't mean that economists have no policy role. In their policy proposals, economists try to spell out the effect of a policy on the distribution of income and wealth, whether a policy will help a majority of people, who those people are, and whether the policy is consistent with the policymaker's value judgments. Doing so isn't easy because the policymaker's value judgments are often vague and must be interpreted by the economist. In that interpretation, the economist's own value judgments often slip in.

Interpretation of Empirical Evidence Value judgments creep into economic policy proposals through economists' interpretations of empirical evidence, which is almost always imprecise. For example, say an economist is assessing the elasticity of a product's demand in the relevant price range. She can't run an experiment to isolate prices and quantities demanded; instead she must look at events in which hundreds of other things changed, and do her best to identify what caused what. In selecting and interpreting empirical evidence, our values will likely show through, try as we might to be objective. People tend to focus on evidence that supports their position. Economists are trained to be as objective as they can be, but pure objectivity is impossible.

Let's consider an example. In the 1980s, some economists proposed that a large tax be imposed on sales of disposable diapers, citing studies that suggested disposable diapers made up between 15 and 30 percent of the garbage in a landfill. Others objected, citing studies that showed disposable diapers made up only 1 or 2 percent of the refuse going into landfills. Such differences in empirical estimates are the norm, not the exception. Inevitably, if precise estimates are wanted, more studies are necessary. (In this case, the further studies showed that the lower estimates were correct.) But policy debates don't wait for further studies. Economists' value judgments influence which incomplete study they choose to believe is more accurate.

Choice of Economic Models Similarly with the choice of models. A model, because it focuses on certain aspects of economic reality and not on others, necessarily reflects certain value judgments, so economists' choice of models must also reflect certain value judgments. Albert Einstein once said that theories should be as simple as possible, but

---

In practice, social goals are seldom neat; they're generally vaguely understood and vaguely expressed.

Pareto optimal policies are policies that benefit some people and hurt no one.

Q.1 If someone suggests that economists should focus only on Pareto optimal policies, how would you respond?

---

[1]Pareto, in his famous book *Mind and Society,* suggested this criterion as an analytic approach for theory, not as a criterion for real-world policy. He recognized the importance of the art of economics and that real-world policy has to be judged by much broader criteria.

not more so. To that we should add a maxim: Scientists should be as objective and as value-free as possible, but not more so.

This book presents the mainstream economic model. That model directs us to certain conclusions. Two other general models that some economists follow are a **Marxian (radical) model** which is *a model that focuses on equitable distribution of power, rights, and income among social classes* and a **public choice (conservative) model** which is *a model that focuses on economic incentives as applied to politicians*. These two models, by emphasizing different aspects of economic interrelationships, sometimes direct us to other conclusions.

Let's consider an example. Mainstream economic analysis directs us to look at how the invisible hand achieves harmony and equilibrium through the market. Thus, when mainstream economists look at labor markets, they generally see supply and demand forces leading to equilibrium. When Marxist economists look at labor markets, their model focuses on the tensions among the social classes, and they generally see exploitation of workers by capitalists. When public choice economists look at labor markets, they see individuals using government to protect their monopolies. Their model focuses on political restrictions that provide rents to various groups. Each model captures different aspects of reality. That's why it's important to be as familiar with as many different models as possible.

Q-2 How does a radical analysis of labor markets differ from a mainstream analysis?

Each model captures different aspects of reality. That's why it's important to be as familiar with as many different models as possible.

The Need for a Worldview

John Maynard Keynes, an economist who gained fame in the 1930s, once said that economists should be seen in the same light as dentists—as competent technicians. He was wrong, and his own experience contradicts that view. In dealing with real-world economic policy, Keynes was no mere technician. He had a definite worldview, which he shared with many of the policymakers he advised. An economist who is to play a role in policy formation must be willing to combine value judgments and technical knowledge. That worldview determines how and when the economic model will be applied.

AGREEMENT AMONG ECONOMISTS ABOUT SOCIAL POLICY

Liberal and conservative economists agree on many policy prescriptions because they use the same models, which focus on incentives and individual choice.

Despite their widely varying values, both liberal and conservative economists agree more often on policy prescriptions than most laypeople think they do. They're economists, after all, and their models focus on certain issues—specifically on incentives and individual choice. They believe economic incentives are important, and most economists tend to give significant weight to individuals' ability to choose reasonably. This leads economists, both liberal and conservative, to look at problems differently than other people do.

Many people think economists of all persuasions look at the world coldheartedly. In my view, that opinion isn't accurate, but it's understandable how people could reach it. Economists are taught to look at things in an "objective" way that takes into account a policy's long-run incentive effects as well as the short-run effects. Many of their policy proposals are based on these long-run incentive effects, which in the short run make the policy look coldhearted. The press and policymakers usually focus on short-run effects. Economists argue that they aren't being coldhearted at all, that they're simply being reasonable, and that following their advice will lead to less suffering than following others' advice will. This is not to say that all advice economists give will lead to significant benefits and less suffering in the long run. Some of it may be simply misguided.

The problem economists face is similar to the one parents face when they tell their children that they can't eat candy or must do their homework before they can play. Explaining how "being mean" is actually "being nice" to a six-year-old isn't easy.

A former colleague of mine, Abba Lerner, was well known for his strong liberal leanings. The government of Israel asked him what to do about unemployment. He went to Israel, studied the problem, and presented his advice: "Cut union wages." The government official responded, "But that's the same advice the conservative economist gave us." Lerner answered, "It's good advice, too." The Israeli Labor government then went and did the opposite; it raised wages, thus holding on to its union support in the short run.

Another example comes from a World Bank economist. She had to advise a hospital in a developing country to turn down the offer of a free dialysis machine because the marginal cost of the filters it would have to buy to use the machine significantly exceeded the costs of life-saving medicines that would save even more lives. Economic reasoning involves making such hard decisions.

The best way to see the consistency and the differences in economists' policy advice is to consider some examples. Let's start with a general consideration of economic views on government regulation.

> Q-3 When can "being mean" actually be "being nice"?

ECONOMISTS' COST/BENEFIT APPROACH TO GOVERNMENT REGULATION

Say that 200 people die in a plane crash. Newspaper headlines trumpet the disaster while news magazines are filled with stories about how the accident might have been caused, citing speculation about poor maintenance and lack of government regulation. The publicity spreads the sense that "something must be done" to prevent such tragedies. Politicians quickly pick up on this, feeling that the public wants action. They introduce a bill outlawing faulty maintenance, denounce poor regulatory procedures, and demand an investigation of sleepy air controllers. In short, they strike out against likely causes of the accident and suggest improved regulations to help prevent any more such crashes.

Economists differ in their views on government regulation of airlines and other businesses, but most find themselves opposing some of the supposedly problem-solving regulations proposed by politicians. They generally adopt a **cost/benefit approach** to problems—*assigning costs and benefits, and making decisions on the basis of the relevant costs and benefits*—which requires them to determine a quantitative cost and benefit for everything, including life. What's the value of a human life? All of us would like to answer, "Infinite. Each human life is beyond price." But if that's true, then in a cost/benefit framework, everything of value should be spent on preventing death. People should take no chances. They should drive at no more than 30 miles per hour with airbags, triple-cushioned bumpers, double roll bars—you get the picture.

It might be possible for manufacturers to make a car in which no one would die as the result of an accident. But people don't want such cars. Many people don't buy the auto safety accessories that are already available, and many drivers ignore the present speed limit. Instead, many people want cars with style and speed.

> Many regulations are formulated for political expediency and do not reflect cost/benefit considerations.

> Cost/benefit analysis is analysis in which one assigns a cost and benefit to alternatives, and draws a conclusion on the basis of those costs and benefits.

The Value of Life

Far from regarding human life as priceless, people make decisions every day that reflect the valuations they place on their own lives. Table 17-1 presents one economist's

Table 17-1   The Value of a Human Life

Such figures are increasingly being used in state and federal courts to support claims for loss of enjoyment of life.

Basis for Calculation	Value of Life (in 2000 dollars)
Automotive air bag purchases	$ 516,000
Smoke detector purchases	542,000
EPA requirements for sulfur scrubbers	724,000
Wage premiums for dangerous police work	1,231,000
Auto safety features	3,620,000
EPA regulations of radium content in water	3,620,000
Wage premiums for dangerous factory jobs	4,633,000
Seat belt usage	4,640,000
OSHA rules for workplace safety	5,212,000
Premium tire usage	5,200,000

Source: Stan V. Smith, Ph.D., adjunct professor, DePaul College of Law, and president, Corporate Financial Group, Chicago. Used by permission. (Adjustments made by author.)

estimates of some of these quantitative decisions. These values are calculated by looking at people's revealed preferences (the choices they make when they must pay the costs). To find them, economists calculate how much people will pay to reduce the possibility of their death by a certain amount. If that's what people will pay to avoid death, the cost to them of death can be calculated by multiplying the inverse of the reduction in the probability of death by the amount they pay. (What is relevant for these calculations is not the actual probabilities but the decision maker's estimate of the probabilities.)

For example, say someone will buy a car whose airbags add up to $500 to the vehicle's cost, but won't buy a car whose airbags add more than $500 to its cost. Also say that the buyer believes that an airbag will reduce the chance of dying in an automobile accident by 1/720. That means that to increase the likelihood of surviving an auto accident by 1/720, the buyer will pay $500. That also means that the buyer is implicitly valuing his or her life at roughly $360,000 (720 × $500 = $360,000).

Alternatively, say that people will pay an extra $52 for a set of premium tires that reduces the risk of death by 1/100,000. As opposed to having a 3/100,000 chance per year of dying in a skid on the highway, people with premium tires all round have a 2/100,000 chance of dying (3/100,000 − 2/100,000 = 1/100,000). Multiplying 100,000 (the inverse of the reduction in probability) by $52, the extra cost of the set of premium tires, you find that people who buy these tires are implicitly valuing their lives at $5,200,000.[2] Another way of determining the value that society places on life is to look at awards juries give for the loss of life. One study looking at such awards found that juries on average value life at about $3.5 million.

No one can say whether people know what they're doing in making these valuations, although the inconsistencies in the valuations people place on their lives suggest that to some degree they don't, or that other considerations are entering into their decisions. But even given the inconsistencies, it's clear that people are placing a finite value on life. Most people are aware that in order to "live" they must take chances on

Q-4 If Table 17-1 correctly describes the valuation individuals place on life with regard to air bag purchases and seat belt usage, how would you advise them to alter their behavior in order to maximize utility?

Economists argue that individuals' revealed choices are the best estimate that society can have of the value of life, and that in making policy society shouldn't pretend that life is beyond value.

---

[2]For simplicity of exposition, I'm not considering risk preferences or other benefits of these decisions such as lowering the chance of injury.

losing their lives. Economists argue that individuals' revealed choices are the best estimate that society can have of the value of life, and that in making policy society shouldn't pretend that life is beyond value.

Placing a value on human life allows economists to evaluate the cost of a crash. Say each life is worth $2 million. If 200 people die in that plane accident and a $200 million plane is destroyed, the cost of the crash is $600 million.

 17.1

Right after the accident, or even long after the accident, tell a mother and father you're valuing the life of their dead daughter at $2 million and the plane at $200 million, and you'll see why economists have problems with getting their views across. Even if people can agree rationally that a value must be placed on life—that they implicitly give their own lives a value—it's not something they want to deal with emotionally, especially after an accident. Using a cost/benefit approach, an economist must be willing to say, if that's the way the analysis turns out, "It's reasonable that my son dies in this accident because the cost of preventing the accident by imposing stricter government regulations would have been greater than the benefit of preventing it."

Economists take the emotional heat for making such valuations. Their cost/benefit approach requires them to do so.

Comparing Costs and Benefits of Different Dimensions

After the marginal cost and marginal benefit data have been gathered and processed, one is ready to make an informed decision. Will the cost of a new regulation outweigh the benefit, or vice versa? Here again, economists find themselves in a difficult position in evaluating a regulation about airplane safety. Many of the costs of regulation are small but occur in large numbers. Every time you lament some "bureaucratic craziness" (such as a required weekly staff meeting or a form to be signed assuring something has been done), you're experiencing a cost. But when those costs are compared to the benefits of avoiding a major accident, the dimensions of comparison are often wrong.

For example, say it is discovered that a loose bolt was the probable cause of the plane crash. A regulation requiring airline mechanics to check whether that bolt is tightened and, to ensure that they do so, requiring them to fill out a form each time the check is made, might cost $1. How can we compare $1 to the $600 million cost of the crash? Such a regulation obviously makes sense from the perspective of gaining a $600 million benefit from $1 of cost.

Cost/benefit analysis sometimes leads one to uncomfortable results.

But wait. Each plane might have 4,000 similar bolts, each of which is equally likely to cause an accident if it isn't tightened. If it makes sense to check that one bolt, it makes sense to check all 4,000. And the bolts must be checked on each of the 4,000 flights per day. All of this increases the cost of tightening bolts to $16 million per day. But the comparison shouldn't be between $16 million and $600 million. The comparison should be between the marginal cost ($16 million) and the marginal benefit, which depends on how much tightening bolts will contribute to preventing an accident.

Let's say that having the bolts checked daily reduces the probability of having an accident by 0.001. This means that the check will prevent one out of a thousand accidents that otherwise would have happened. The marginal benefit of checking a particular bolt isn't $600 million (which it would be if you knew a bolt was going to be loose), but is:

$$0.001 \times \$600 \text{ million} = \$600,000$$

That $600,000 is the marginal benefit that must be compared to the marginal cost of $16 million.

Given these numbers, I leave it to you to decide: Does this hypothetical regulation make sense?

Q-5 Why should you be very careful about any cost/benefit analysis?

17.2

Cost/benefit analysis is often biased toward quantifiable costs.

Q-6 When using marginal cost/marginal benefit analysis, do "other things remain constant"? Explain.

Economics teaches people to be "reasonable."

Putting Cost/Benefit Analysis in Perspective

The numbers in our plane crash example are hypothetical. The numbers used in real-world decision making are not hypothetical, but they are often ambiguous. Measuring costs, benefits, and probabilities is difficult, and economists often disagree on specific costs and benefits.

Cost/benefit analyses are often used to justify what someone already wants to do. For example, from the 1950s to the 1980s the U.S. Army Corps of Engineers always seemed to come up with conclusions that their projects—dams, canals, and the like—made sense from a cost/benefit analysis point of view. In the 1990s many of the corps' projects were reassessed, and in that reassessment many of the projects no longer made so much sense—the earlier analyses had not taken into account larger environmental costs.

Costs have many dimensions, some more quantifiable than others. Cost/benefit analysis is often biased toward quantifiable costs and away from nonquantifiable costs, or it involves enormous ambiguity as nonquantifiable costs are quantified.

The subjectivity and ambiguity of costs are one reason why economists differ in their views of regulation. In considering any particular regulation, some economists will favor it and some will oppose it. But their reasoning process—comparing marginal costs and marginal benefits—is the same; they differ only on the estimates they calculate.

The Problem of Other Things Changing

One problem economists have concerns the "other things equal" assumption discussed in Chapters 4 and 5. Supply and demand analysis assumes that all other things remain equal. But in a large number of issues it is obvious that other things do not remain equal. However, it is complicated to sort out how they change, and the sorting-out process is subject to much debate. The more macro the issue, the more other things change, and hence the more debate.

Let's consider the minimum wage example we discussed in earlier chapters. Suppose you can estimate the supply and demand elasticities for labor. Is that enough to enable you to estimate the number of people who will be made unemployed by a minimum wage? To answer that, ask yourself: Are other things likely to remain constant? The answer is: No; a chain of possible things can change. Say the firm decides to replace these workers with machines. So it will buy some machines. But machines are made by other workers, and so the demand for workers in the machine-making industry will rise. So the decrease in employment in the first industry may be offset by an increase in employment elsewhere.

But there are issues on the other side too. For example, workers who get the higher wage may not receive a net benefit if other things change. Say you had a firm that was paying a wage lower than the minimum wage but was providing lots of training, which was preparing people for much better jobs in the future. Now the minimum wage goes into effect. The firm keeps hiring workers, but it eliminates the training. Its workers are actually worse off.

How important are such issues? That's a matter of empirical research, which is why empirical research is central to economics. Unfortunately, the data aren't very good, which is why there is so much debate about policy issues in economics.

There are many more examples of "other things changing," but the above should be sufficient to give you an idea of the problem.

The Cost/Benefit Approach in Context

Economics teaches people to be reasonable—sickeningly reasonable, some people would say. I hope that you have some sense of what I mean by that. The cost/benefit approach

KNOWING THE TOOLS

Economic Efficiency and the Goals of Society

Economic efficiency means achieving a goal at the lowest possible cost. For the definition to be meaningful, the goal must be specified. Efficiency in the pursuit of efficiency is meaningless. Thus, when we talk about economic efficiency, we must have some goal in mind. In the supply/demand framework, we *assume* the goal is to maximize total output. Each of the three failures of market only goal of society.

outcomes that we discuss in this section represents a situation in which the goals of society cannot be captured by a single measure—where society's goal is more complicated than to maximize total output—and thus the assumed goal of efficiency—maximizing total output—is not the only goal of society.

to problems (which pictures a world of individuals whose self-interested actions are limited only by competition) makes economists look for the self-interest behind individuals' actions, and for how competition can direct that self-interest into the public interest.

In an economist's framework,

- Well-intentioned policies often are prevented by individuals' self-interest-seeking activities.
- Policies that relieve immediate suffering often have long-run consequences that create more suffering.
- Politicians have more of an incentive to act fast—to look as if they're doing something—than to do something that makes sense from a cost/benefit point of view.

The marginal cost/marginal benefit approach is telling a story. That story is embodied in the supply/demand framework. Supply represents the marginal costs of a trade, and demand represents the marginal benefits of a trade. Equilibrium is where quantity supplied equals quantity demanded—where marginal cost equals marginal benefit. That equilibrium maximizes the combination of consumer and producer surplus and leads to an efficient, or Pareto optimal, outcome. The argument for competitive markets within that supply/demand framework is that markets allow the society to achieve **economic efficiency**—*achieving a goal, in this case producing a specified amount of output, at the lowest possible cost.* Alternatively expressed, the story is that, given a set of resources, markets produce the greatest possible output. When the economy is efficient, it is on its production possibility curve, producing total output at its lowest opportunity cost.

The supply/demand framework is logical, satisfying, and (given its definitions and assumptions) extraordinarily useful. That's why we teach it. It gives students who understand it the ability to get to the heart of many policy problems. It tells them that every policy has a cost, every policy has a benefit, and if the assumptions are met, competition sees to it that the benefits to society are achieved at the lowest possible cost. Applied to policy issues, the framework gets you to face trade-offs that you would often rather avoid, and that you likely wouldn't see if you didn't use it. It is what "thinking like an economist" is all about.

> The marginal cost/marginal benefit story is embodied in the supply/demand framework.

> **Q-7** True or false? The goal of society is efficiency.

FAILURE OF MARKET OUTCOMES

A good story emphasizes certain elements and deemphasizes others to make its point. When the moral of the story is applied, however, we have to be careful to consider all the relevant elements—especially those that the story didn't emphasize. That's why in the second part of this chapter I will discuss some implicit assumptions that the supply/demand framework pushes to the back of the analysis and that therefore often don't get addressed in principles courses. I classify these as failures of market outcomes. A **failure of market outcomes** occurs *when, even though the market is functioning properly (there are no market failures), it is not achieving society's goals.*

Three separate types of failures of market outcomes will be considered:

1. *Failures due to distributional issues:* Whose surplus is the market maximizing?

2. *Failures due to rationality problems of individuals:* What if individuals don't know what is best for themselves?

3. *Failures due to violations of inalienable or at least partially inalienable rights of individuals:* Are there certain rights that should not be for sale?

I'll discuss an example of each of the three failures of market outcomes and contrast them with market failures discussed in Chapter 15. Then I will conclude with a brief discussion of why, even though most economists recognize these failures of market outcomes, they still favor the use of markets for the large majority of goods that society produces.

Distribution

Say that the result of market forces is that some people don't earn enough income to be able to survive—the demand for their labor intersects the supply for their labor at a wage of 25 cents an hour. Also assume there are no market failures, as described in Chapter 15. (Information is perfect, trades have no negative externalities, and all goods are private goods.)

The market solution to a wage that is so low the worker can't survive is starvation—people who don't earn enough die. Not all low-wage workers must die, however. After some low-wage workers die, the supply of labor shifts back, raising the wage for the survivors. This process takes time, but eventually all remaining workers will receive a subsistence wage. This is the long-run market solution. Implicit within the supply/demand framework is a Darwinian "survival of the fittest" approach to social policy. Most people would regard the market solution—starvation—as an undesirable outcome. Even though the market is doing precisely what it is supposed to be doing—equating quantity supplied and quantity demanded—most people would not find the outcome acceptable.

Distribution of Total Surplus Let me now relate this distributional issue to the supply/demand framework by considering distribution of consumer and producer surplus. For most discussions of economic policy, an implicit assumption is that the goal of policy is to create as much total surplus as possible. In a world of only one good and one person, that goal would be clear. But with many goods and many people, what is meant by total surplus in terms of social welfare can be unclear. One reason is that society does not value all surplus equally. In the above starvation example, *the reason most people do not like the market outcome is that they care about not only the size of the total surplus but also how total surplus is distributed.* The supply/demand framework does not distinguish among those who get producer and consumer surplus, and thus avoids that distribution issue.

Examples of Distributional Issues Let's consider two real-world examples where distributional issues are likely to play a significant role in value judgments about the market outcome. Our economy produces $200-an-ounce olive oil, but it does not provide a minimum level of health care for all. This happens because income distribution is highly unequal. The high income of the wealthy means there is demand for $200-an-ounce bottles

Failure of market outcomes occurs when, even though it is functioning properly, the market is not achieving society's goals.

17.3

Implicit within the supply/demand framework is a "survival of the fittest" approach to social policy.

BEYOND THE TOOLS

The Ambiguity
of Total Surplus

To talk about consumer and producer surplus we must figure out a way of taking into account people's valuation of surplus. The market does that—it allows each person to vote with their income in the buying of goods. This means that whoever has the income plays a role in determining how we measure total surplus. This presents a circular reasoning problem in moving from total surplus to social welfare, and in talking about efficiency as if it involves maximizing total surplus. If the distribution of income is one of society's goals, then efficiency cannot unambiguously be defined without also specifying distributional goals.

Let's consider an extreme example to show the problems this can present. Say we start with two individuals, Jules and Jim, and two goods, apples and oranges. Jules likes only oranges and Jim likes only apples. If Jim has all the income, only apples count for determining total output because Jim likes only apples. Since no oranges are traded, oranges are given no weight because Jules has no income. Now, say that Jules has all the income. In that case only oranges contribute to total output. More generally, when two individuals have different tastes, the way in which income is distributed can change the contribution of goods to total output.

Economists get around part of the problem theoretically either by assuming individuals have the same tastes or by assuming that income can be costlessly redistributed. This separates the issue of equity from the issue of efficiency. In practice, economists recognize that these conditions do not hold. They know that in the real world it is extraordinarily difficult to redistribute income. You can't go up to Bill Gates and tell him, "Hey, you need to give $10 billion to some poor people." For this reason economists are careful to apply the producer and consumer surplus analysis only to those cases where the conditions are "reasonable" approximations of reality—where distributional and taste issues do not play a big role in a policy recommendation. Of course, economists may disagree on what are "reasonable" approximations of reality. That is why economic policy is an art, not a science.

of olive oil. (It's all the rage in Silicon Valley.) Businesses establish production facilities to produce it (or any one of a million other luxury items), and it is sold on the market. Selling $200-an-ounce bottles of olive oil is efficient if one's goal is to maximize total consumer and producer surplus. However, given the distribution of income, it would be inefficient to produce health care for the poor. The poor just don't have sufficient income to demand it. Since they have little income, the poor are given little weight in the measure of consumer surplus.

A second example of where distribution of income likely makes a big difference in our normative judgments, and where we would likely not apply the consumer and producer surplus reasoning, concerns the demand for the AIDS drug cocktail (see Chapter 12). The cocktail can stop AIDS from killing people; thus, the desire for the AIDS cocktail among individuals with AIDS is high. The desire for the drug among those without AIDS is minimal.

In some African countries, 30 percent of the population has AIDS. Since consumer surplus reflects desire, one might think that in Africa the consumer surplus from the desire for the AIDS drug cocktail would be enormous. But it isn't. Most people in Africa have relatively little income; in fact, most have so little income that they cannot afford the cocktail at all. Since the price of the cocktail is above their total income, they get no consumer surplus from the cocktail at all in the supply/demand framework—it would be "inefficient" to supply it to them. In the supply/demand framework you can only have a demand for a good if you have the desire *and* the income to pay for it.

The point of these examples is not to convince you that the consumer surplus concept is useless. Far from it. For the majority of goods, it is a useful shorthand that demonstrates the power of competitive markets. The point of the examples is to show you the type of case where overriding the supply/demand framework in policy considerations may be socially desirable and efficient if society's goals include a particular distribution of

For many goods maximizing total surplus is a useful shorthand.

consumer surplus. The sole purpose of society is not to maximize consumer and producer surplus. Society has other goals. Once these other goals are taken into account, the competitive result may not be the one that is desired.

Societies integrate other goals into market economics by establishing social safety nets (programs such as welfare, unemployment insurance, and Medicaid). When individuals are below a certain income, what they receive does not depend solely on what they earn in the market. How high to set a given social safety net is a matter of debate, but favoring the market outcome in most cases is not inconsistent with favoring a social safety net in others.

Consumer Sovereignty and Rationality Problems

John Drunk drinks more than is good for him; he just has to have another drink. He buys liquor voluntarily, so that means buying it makes him better off, right? Not necessarily. Even when they have full information, individuals sometimes do not do what is in their own best interest. If they don't do what's best for themselves, then the market solution—let people enter freely into whatever trades they want to—is not necessarily the best solution. Again, the market is working, but the outcome may be a failure.

This problem is sometimes called *rationality failure of individuals*. The supply/demand framework starts with the proposition that individuals are completely **rational**—that *what individuals do is in their own best interest*. Reflecting on this, however, as we did in Chapter 7, we see that that is not always the case. Most of us are irrational at times; we sometimes can "want" something that we really "don't want." Think of smoking, chocolate, or any other of our many vices.

Even if we don't have serious addictions, we may have minor ones; often we don't know what we want and we are influenced by what people tell us we want. Businesses spend lots of money on advertising to convince us that we want certain things. Individuals can be convinced they want something that, if they thought further about it, they would not want. The fact that individuals don't know what they want can be a second reason for government intervention—getting people what is good for them.

Let's look at an example: The U.S. government has taken the position that if people could be induced to stop smoking, they would be better off. **Sin taxes**—*taxes that discourage activities society believes are harmful (sinful)*—are meant to do just this. Based on the consumer surplus argument, a tax on smoking would create deadweight loss; it would reduce the combination of consumer and producer surplus. But in this case consumer surplus does not reflect individuals' welfare.

Notice the difference between the argument for taxes to change behavior (sin taxes) and the argument for taxes to raise revenue discussed in Chapter 7. When government wants to raise revenue it takes into account how much deadweight loss is created by the tax. With sin taxes, government is trying to discourage the use of the good that is being taxed. When society takes the position that individuals' demands in the marketplace do not reflect their true welfare, it is not at all clear that the market result is efficient. (See the accompanying box.)

Inalienable Rights

Nice Guy wants to save his son, who needs an operation that costs $300,000. He doesn't have that kind of money, but he knows that Slave Incorporated, a newly created company, has been offering $300,000 to the first person who agrees to become a slave for life. He enters into the contract, gets his money, and saves his son. Again, the market is working just as it is supposed to. There's no negative externality, and there's no in-

Q-8 A cocaine addict purchases an ounce of cocaine from a drug dealer. Since this was a trade both individuals freely entered, is society better off?

APPLYING THE TOOLS

Elasticity and Taxation to Change Behavior

A good way to see how economists view the difference between the effect of a sin tax and the effect of a tax to raise revenue is to ask: Would a policymaker rather have an elastic or an inelastic demand curve for the good being taxed? If the purpose is to raise revenue while creating only a minimal amount of deadweight loss, an inelastic demand is preferable. If the purpose is to change behavior, as it is in the example of an alcohol-dependent individual, a more elastic demand curve is better because a relatively small tax can cause a relatively large reduction in purchases.

Consider an example of taxation to reduce consumption. If government believes that smoking is bad for people, it can decrease the amount people smoke by placing a tax on cigarettes. If the demand for cigarettes is inelastic, then the tax will not significantly decrease smoking; but if the demand is elastic, then it will. If demand is inelastic, government may choose alternative methods of affecting behavior, such as advertising campaigns. If the purpose of taxation is to raise taxes, an inelastic demand would be better; that's why most states rely on general sales taxes for revenue—such taxes allow them to raise revenue with relatively little effect on the efficiency of the market.

The following table provides a quick review of when a tax will be most effective, given a particular goal of government.

Goal of Government	Most Effective When
Raise revenue, limit efficiency loss	Demand or supply is inelastic
Change behavior	Demand or supply is elastic

formation problem—Nice Guy knows what he's doing and Slave Inc. knows what it's doing. Both participants in the trade believe that it is making them better off.

Many people's view of the trade will likely be different; they would regard such a market outcome—an outcome that allows slavery—as a market outcome failure. That is why governments have developed laws that make such trades illegal.

As Amartya Sen pointed out (and won a Nobel Prize for doing so), most societies regard certain rights as inalienable. By definition, inalienable rights cannot be sold or given away. There can be no weighing of costs and benefits. For example, the right to freedom is an inalienable right, so slavery is wrong, and any trade creating slavery should not be allowed, regardless of any issues of consumer and producer surplus.

The Need to Prioritize Rights To understand why market outcomes might be undesirable, we have to go back and consider markets in a broader perspective. Markets develop over time as individuals trade to make themselves better off. But markets don't just come into existence—they require the development of property rights for both suppliers and consumers. Each side must know what is being traded. So markets can exist only if there are property rights.

Property rights, in turn, are included in a broader set of rights that are part of society's constitution—the right to vote, the right to free speech, the right to the pursuit of happiness, the right to life. Property rights are subrights to the right to pursue happiness. If that right to property rights conflicts with other rights, society must make a judgment about which right has priority. Thus, within the written or unwritten constitution of a society, rights needs to be prioritized.

Examples of Inalienable Rights Let's consider a couple of examples. Say I come up to you with a gun and offer you this deal: Your money or your life. This can be viewed

Q-9 True or false? If someone chooses to sell himself into slavery, the individual, and thus society, is better off.

as a trade. Because I have the gun, I control whether you live or die. You control the money you have. If we make the "trade," you'll be better off because I don't shoot you and I'll be better off because I'll have more money. But it is not an acceptable trade, because the right to your life was inalienable—no one but you owns it; I cannot claim to own it. So, even if the gun gave me the power over your life, it did not give me the right to it. Other moral prohibitions that are related to inalienable rights include those against prostitution, selling body parts, and selling babies.

My point is not that the moral judgment our society has made about these rights is correct; they may or may not be correct. Nor is my point that such trades should not be subjected to the market. My point is that society must make these judgments. Such issues are moral questions, and do not have to stand up to the consumer and producer surplus arguments. If something is wrong, it is wrong; whether it is efficient is irrelevant.

Moral judgments must be made about where markets should exist, and someone might decide that the market should be allowed everywhere (that is the libertarian view), but such moral judgments can override consumer surplus arguments about markets achieving efficiency. Consider again the efficient-chicken-farming example discussed in Chapter 10. If you believe that it is immoral to treat chickens the way "efficient" farming requires them to be treated, then the fact that the farming is efficient may be irrelevant to you.

Moral judgments underlie all policy prescriptions.

GOVERNMENT FAILURE

Distributional issues, issues of rationality, and the existence of inalienable rights are representative of the types of problems that can arise in the market. For most economists these issues play a role in interpreting the policy results that follow from the economic model presented, even when there is no market failure. But it is important to remember that even these failures of market outcomes do not necessarily call for government action. The reason is government failure.

As I discussed in Chapter 15, if the failure is to be corrected someone must formulate and enact the policy, and if we believe that government's attempt to correct it will do more harm than good, then we can still support the market as the lesser of two evils. For the government to correct the problem, it must

For the government to correct a problem it must
1. *recognize the problem*
2. *have the will to deal with it and*
3. *have the ability to deal with it.*

1. Recognize the problem.
2. Have *the will* to do something positive about the problem.
3. Have *the ability* to do something positive about the problem.

Government seldom can do all three of these well. Often the result is that government action is directed at the wrong problem at the wrong time.

Probably the most vocal group of economists on the subject of government failure are *public choice economists*. This group, started by James Buchanan and Gordon Tullock, has pointed out that politicians are subject to the laws of supply and demand, like everyone else. Often the result of politics is that the redistribution that takes place does not go from rich to poor, but from one group of middle class to another group of middle class. Public choice economists argue that when the government enters the market, the incentives are not to achieve its goal in the least-cost manner; the incentives are to provide a policy that its voting constituency likes. The result is larger and larger government, with little benefit for society, and public choice economists advocate as little government intervention as possible regardless of whether there are market failures or failures of market outcomes.

APPLYING THE TOOLS

The Conventional
Policy Wisdom
among Economists

Where do economists come out on whether government can correct a failure of market outcomes? The easy answer is that they conclude that to make a policy decision we must weigh the costs of market failure against the costs of government failure. But those costs are often poorly specified and difficult to estimate. Thus, policy considerations require subjective judgments. Let me give you my interpretation of how economists fit these broader considerations into their analysis.

Most economists downplay the distribution issues for the majority of goods, and use distribution in their policy consideration only for the extreme examples, such as those I presented in the text. They believe that it is far better to be open about the distributional goals and to give money directly to individuals, rather than to hide the redistribution by changing the pricing structure through subsidizing goods. Let's take an example: The European Union's agricultural policy currently provides large amounts of price supports for European agricultural production. To keep farmers in business, the prices of agricultural goods are kept high. If the social decision were to keep farmers in business, most economists, however, would prefer to see the EU provide direct subsidies to farmers. Then the policy of redistribution is clear to everyone, and is far less costly in terms of both efficiency and implementation.

The "rights argument" plays a role in all economists' policy arguments. Almost all economists oppose selling citizenship. All oppose slavery. All see economic policy as being conducted within a constitutional setting, and that means that inalienable rights come before market efficiency.

There are, of course, areas of ambiguity—allowing the regulated sale of body parts from individuals who have died is one such area. Let's consider it. There is currently a shortage of organs for transplants. When someone dies, from a medical perspective his or her organs can usually be "harvested" and used by someone else—but only if the deceased had signed a donor card. If the family of the deceased donor were given $5,000 for burial expenses, some economists argue, the shortage of transplant organs would disappear and everyone would be better off—the family could give the deceased a much nicer funeral and people needing the organs could live. Our society is moving cautiously in that direction; Pennsylvania has recently announced that it is giving $300 in funeral expenses to the survivors of those who donate organs. My feeling is that economists are more open to such market solutions than the general public, but there is nothing in economics that requires such solutions.

The argument about problems arising from rationality issues is also accepted by most economists, but they downplay it for most nonaddictive goods. The reason is that while it is true that individuals may not know what they want, it is far less likely that the government will know better. Based on that view, on average, the acceptance of consumer sovereignty, and the market result, is probably warranted. Exceptions include children and some elderly. How to deal with addictive goods is still very much in debate among economists, and there is no conventional wisdom.

POLITICS AND ECONOMIC POLICY

Economic policy is, and must be, applied within a political context. This means that political elements must be taken into account. Politics enters into the determination of economic policy in two ways, one positive and one negative. Its positive contribution is that politicians take market failures and failures of market outcomes into account when formulating policy. Ultimately the political system decides what externalities should be adjusted for, what is a desirable distribution, what rights are above the market, and when people's demand does not reflect their true demand. To the extent that the government's political decisions reflect the will of society, government is making a positive contribution.

The negative contribution is that political decisions do not always reflect the will of society.[3] The political reality is that, in the short run, people are often governed by

Q.10 In what way does government positively contribute to economic policy? In what way does it negatively contribute to economic policy?

---

[3]By even discussing the "will of society" I am avoiding a very difficult problem in political philosophy of what that will is, and how it is to be determined. I leave it to your political science courses to discuss such issues.

emotion, swayed by mass psychology, irrational, and interested in their own rather than the general good. Politicians and other policymakers know that; the laws and regulations they propose reflect such calculations. Politicians don't get elected and reelected by constantly saying that all choices have costs and benefits. What this means is that while policymakers listen to the academic economists from whom they ask advice, and with whom in private they frequently agree, in practice they often choose to ignore that advice.

Because government both adjusts for failures of market outcomes and is subject to short-run political pressures, the way in which economic reasoning influences policy can be subtle. Sometimes we see elaborate charades acted out: Politicians put forward bills that from a cost/benefit viewpoint don't make sense but that make the politicians look good. They hope the bills won't pass, but they also hope that presenting them will allow enough time to pass so that emotions can cool and a more reasonable bill can be put forward. Other times, compromise bills are proposed that incorporate as much cost/benefit policy as possible, but also appeal to voters' emotional sense. In short, economic policy made in the real world reflects a balancing of cost/benefit analysis and special interest desires.

CONCLUSION

Adam Smith, the creator of modern economics, was a philosopher; his economics was part of his philosophy. Before he wrote the *Wealth of Nations*, in which he set out his argument for markets, he wrote a book called *The Theory of Moral Sentiments*, in which he laid out his broader philosophy. That foundation, in turn, was part of the Scottish Enlightenment, which spelled out what was meant by a good society, and how they believed individuals' and society's rights should be considered. Any economic policy issue must be interpreted within such a broad philosophical framework. Clearly, an introductory course in economics cannot introduce you to these broader philosophical and political issues. But it can point out to you their importance, and that economic policy arguments must fit within that broader context.

Economics provides the tools, not the rules, for policy.

This chapter was written to give you a sense of that broader context—economics provides the tools, not the rules, for policy. Cost/benefit analysis and the supply/demand framework are powerful tools for analyzing issues and coming up with policy conclusions. But to apply them successfully, they must be applied in context.

Applying economics is much more than muttering "supply and demand." Economics involves the thoughtful use of economic insights and empirical evidence.

Thomas Carlyle, who, as we saw in an earlier introductory quotation, argued that all you have to do is teach a parrot the words *supply and demand* to create an economist, was wrong. Economics involves the thoughtful use of economic insights and empirical evidence. If this chapter gave you a sense of the nature of that thoughtful application along with the core of economic reasoning, then it succeeded in its purpose.

Chapter Summary

- Economists differ because of different underlying value judgments, because empirical evidence is subject to different interpretations, and because their underlying models differ.

- Value judgments inevitably work their way into policy advice, but good economists try to be objective.

- Economists tend to agree on certain issues because their training is similar. Economists use models that focus on economic incentives and rationality.

- The economic approach to analyzing issues is a cost/benefit approach.

- Economists generally have reservations about regulations.

- Collecting and using empirical evidence is an important part of economics.

- People make choices every day that reveal the value that they place on their lives. The value of life is calculated by multiplying the inverse of the reduction in the probability of death by the amount individuals pay for that reduction.

- Collecting and interpreting empirical evidence is difficult, which contributes to disagreements among economists.

- Economics involves the thoughtful use of economic insights and empirical evidence.

- The cost/benefit approach and the supply/demand framework deemphasize the possibility that market outcomes may be undesirable to society.

- Three failures of market outcomes are failures due to distributional issues, failures due to rationality problems of individuals, and failures due to violations of inalienable rights.

- Although an implicit assumption in most policy discussions is that the goal of policy is to maximize consumer

and producer surplus, society does care about how that total surplus is distributed.

- The supply/demand framework assumes that individuals are rational. Individuals are not always rational in practice. Their actions are swayed by addictions, advertising, and other pressures.

- Some rights, called inalienable rights, cannot be bought and sold. What rights are inalienable are moral judgments that do not have to stand up to the same cost/benefit framework.

- Economics provides the tools, not the rules, for policy.

Key Terms

cost/benefit approach *(375)*	failure of market outcomes *(380)*	Pareto optimal policies *(373)*	rational *(382)*

cost/benefit approach (375)

economic efficiency (379)

failure of market outcomes (380)

Marxian (radical) model (374)

Pareto optimal policies (373)

public choice (conservative) model (374)

rational (382)

sin taxes (382)

Questions for Thought and Review

1. Could anyone object to a Pareto optimal policy? Why?

2. Would it be wrong for economists to propose only Pareto optimal policies?

3. Would all economists oppose price controls? Why or why not?

4. Should body organs be allowed to be bought or sold? Why or why not?

5. In cost/benefit terms, explain your decision to take an economics course.

6. How much do you value your life in dollar terms? Are your decisions consistent in that valuation?

7. If someone offered you $1 million for one of your kidneys, would you sell it? Why or why not?

8. Why might an economist propose a policy that has little chance of adoption?

9. In the 1970s legislators had difficulty getting laws passed requiring people to wear seat belts. Now not only do

most people wear seat belts, many cars have air bags too. Do people value their lives more now than in the 1970s?

10. Why are economists' views of politicians cynical?

11. Michael Tanner and Stephen Moore of the Cato Institute recently calculated the hourly wage equivalent of welfare for a single mother with two children for each of the 50 United States. Their estimates ranged from $17.50 an hour for Hawaii to $5.33 in Mississippi. What do you suppose were their policy recommendations? What arguments can be made to oppose those prescriptions?

12. Economist Steven D. Levitt estimated that, on average, for each additional criminal locked up in the United States, 15 crimes are eliminated. In addition, although it costs about $30,000 a year to keep a prisoner incarcerated, the average prisoner would have caused $53,900 worth of damage to society per year if free. If this estimation is correct, does it make economic sense to build more prisons?

Problems and Exercises

1. Say that the cost of a car crash is $8,000. Assume further that installing a safety device in a car at a cost of $12 will reduce the probability of an accident by 0.05 percent. The plant makes 1,000 cars each day.

   a. If the preceding are the only relevant costs, would you favor or oppose the installation of the safety device?

   b. What other costs might be relevant?

2. In a study of hospital births, the single most important prediction factor of the percentage of vaginal births as opposed to Caesarean (C-section) births was ownership status of hospitals—whether they were for-profit or nonprofit.

a. Which had more C-sections, and why?

b. What implications about the health care debate can you draw from the above results?

c. How might the results change if the for-profit hospital received a fixed per-patient payment as it would in a managed care system?

3. The technology is now developing so that road use can be priced by computer. A computer in the surface of the road picks up a signal from your car and automatically charges you for the use of the road.

a. How could this technological change contribute to ending bottlenecks and rush-hour congestion? Demonstrate graphically.

b. How will people likely try to get around the system?

c. If people know when the prices will change, what will likely happen immediately before? How might this be avoided?

4. In the early 1990s, the 14- to 17-year-old population fell because of low birth rates in the mid-1970s. Simultaneously, aging baby boomers who decided to have kids combined to increase the number of babies and hence to increase the number of parents needing baby-sitters. What effect will these two events likely have on:

a. The number of times parents go out without their children?

b. The price of baby-sitters?

c. The average age of baby-sitters?

5. As organ transplants become more successful, scientists are working on ways to transplant animal organs to humans. Pigs are the odds-on favorites as "donors" since their organs are about the same size as human organs.

a. What would the development of such organ farms likely do to the price of pigs?

b. If you were an economic adviser to the government, would you say that such a development would be Pareto optimal (for humans)?

c. Currently, there is a black market in human organs. What would this development likely do to that market?

6. If one uses a willingness-to-pay measure in which life is valued at what people are willing to pay to avoid risks that might lead to death, the value of a U.S. citizen's life is $2.6 million, a Swede's life is worth $1.2 million, and a Portuguese's life is worth $20,000 (according to an article in *The Journal of Transport Economics and Policy*).

a. What policy implications does this value schedule have?

b. Say you operate an airline. Should you spend more on safety precautions in the United States than you do in Portugal?

c. Should safety standards be lower in Portugal and Sweden than in the United States?

7. According to U.S. government statistics, the cost of averting a premature death differs among various regulations. Car seat belt standards cost $100,000 per premature death avoided, while hazardous waste landfill disposal bans cost $4.2 trillion per premature death avoided.

a. If you were choosing between these two regulations, which would you choose? Why?

b. If these figures are correct, should neither, one, the other, or both of these regulations be implemented?

8. A 29-year old politician, Anthony Zielinski, who was a member of the Milwaukee Board of Supervisors, proposed that the county government sell the organs of dead welfare recipients to help pay off the welfare recipients' welfare costs and burial expenses.

a. What was the likely effect of that proposal?

b. Why was that the effect?

9. Technology will soon exist such that individuals can choose the sex of their offspring. Assume that technology has now arrived and that 70 percent of the individuals choose male offspring.

a. What effect will that have on social institutions such as families?

b. What effect will it have on dowries—payments made by the bride's family to the groom—which are still used in a number of developing countries?

c. Why might an economist suggest that if 70 percent male is the expectation, families would be wise to have daughters rather than sons?

Web Questions

1. Find out whether you could survive on the minimum wage by going to www.aflcio.org/articles/minimum_wage/paycalc.htm. (If you do not support yourself, answer the questions assuming you are the head of a household with two children.)

a. Are you able to provide for your monthly budgeted expenses? By how much do you overspend?

b. Compare your budget to that of the average head of a household earning the minimum wage. How would your lifestyle change if you had to adjust your budget to a minimum-wage income?

2. Some groups are now lobbying local governments to institute "living wage" policies. Go to the New Party's home page at www.newparty.org/livwag/ to answer the following questions:

a. What is a living wage?

b. How does the living wage compare to the federal minimum wage?

c. What are the New Party's arguments in favor of the living wage?

3. The U.S. Constitution spells out various rights of its citizens. Go to the Cornell Law School home page at www.law.cornell.edu/ and look up the U.S. Constitution.
   a. List six rights granted by the U.S. Constitution.
   b. Are all these rights inalienable?

c. Should any of these rights be allowed to be bought and sold on a market? Why or why not?
d. Go to the Libertarian Party's home page at www.lp.org/ and read its Statement of Purpose. From your reading, do Libertarians believe that individuals should have the right to buy and sell rights granted to them by the constitution? Explain your answer.

Answers to Margin Questions

1. I would respond that in the real world, Pareto optimal policies don't exist, and all real-world policies make someone better off and someone worse off. In making real-world policy judgments, one cannot avoid the difficult distributional and broader questions. It is those more difficult questions, which are value-laden, that make economic policy an art rather than a science. *(373)*

2. A radical analysis of the labor market differs from the mainstream analysis in that it emphasizes the tensions among social classes. Thus, a radical analysis will likely see exploitation built into the institutional structure. Mainstream analysis is much more likely to take the institutional structure as given and not question it. *(374)*

3. Oftentimes being "mean" in the short run can actually involve being "nice" in the long run. The reason is that often policy effects that are beneficial in the long run have short-run costs, and people focusing on those short-run costs see the policy as "mean." *(375)*

4. To maximize life, one would expect that the marginal value per dollar spent should be equal in all activities. Thus, if Table 17-1 is correct, it would suggest that you should be far less concerned about seat belt usage and far more concerned about whether your automobile has air bags or not. *(376)*

5. Costs and benefits are ambiguous; economists often disagree enormously on specific costs and benefits, or the costs and benefits are difficult or impossible to quantify. Thus, you should be extremely careful about using a cost/benefit analysis as anything more than an aid to your analysis of the situation. *(378)*

6. Other things do not always remain constant. The more macro the issue, the more things are likely to change. These changes must be brought back into the analysis, which complicates things enormously. *(378)*

7. False. Efficiency is achieving a goal as cheaply as possible. Stating efficiency as a goal does not make sense. *(379)*

8. No. The cocaine addict may be responding to the cravings created from the addiction, and not from any rational desire for more cocaine. Society may not be better off. *(382)*

9. False. Society may find that personal freedom is an inalienable right. Selling such a right would make society worse off. *(383)*

10. Government makes a positive contribution by adjusting for market failures and failures of market outcomes. Government may make a negative contribution because government is swayed by short-run political pressures. *(385)*

Politics and Economics:
The Case of Agricultural Markets

18

After reading this chapter, you should be able to:

- Describe the competitive nature of agricultural markets.

- Explain the good/bad paradox in farming.

- State the general rule of political economy in a democracy.

- Explain how a price support system works.

- Explain, using supply and demand curves, the distributional consequences of four alternative methods of price support.

- Discuss real-world pressures politicians face when designing agricultural policy.

American farmers have become welfare addicts, protected and assisted at every turn by a network of programs paid for by their fellow citizens. If Americans still believe in the virtue of self-reliance, they should tell Washington to get out of the way and let farmers practice it.

Stephen Chapman

In 1999 the government's 2000 budget was delayed as the Senate, House, and president fought over the Northeast Dairy Compact, a law that established minimum prices for Northeast dairy farmers. Midwestern senators fought against the compact because dairy farmers in their region would be hurt by it. Northeast senators fought in favor of it because farmers in their region would be helped. Eventually, after enormous political infighting, the government reached a settlement that allowed the compact to exist for two more years.

APPLYING THE TOOLS

The Cost of a
Box of Wheaties

When people think of agricultural products, they often think of the products they buy, like Wheaties. Doing so gives them the wrong impression of the cost of agricultural products. To see why, let's consider an 18-ounce box of Wheaties that costs you, say, $3.35.

If you look at the ingredients, you'll see that you're buying wheat, sugar, salt, malt syrup, and corn syrup. So you're buying agricultural products, right? Well, a little bit. Actually, the total cost of those agricultural ingredients is probably somewhere around 25 cents, less than 10 percent of the cost of the box of Wheaties. What are you spending the other 90 percent on? Well, there's packaging, advertising, transporting the boxes, processing the ingredients, stocking the grocery store shelves, and profits. These are important components of Wheaties, but they aren't agricultural components.

The point of this example is simple: Much of our food expenditure isn't for agricultural goods; it's for the services that transform agricultural goods into processed foods, convince us we want to eat those foods, and get those foods to us.

As this incident shows, agricultural markets provide good examples of the interaction between the invisible hand and political forces. Considering the economics of agricultural markets shows us how powerful a tool supply and demand analysis is in helping us understand not only the workings of perfectly competitive markets but also the effects of government intervention in a market.

While the chapter is about agricultural markets, please bear in mind that the lessons of the analysis are applicable to a wide variety of markets in which the invisible hand and politics interact. As you read the chapter, applying the analysis to other markets will be a useful exercise.

THE NATURE OF AGRICULTURAL MARKETS

In many ways, agricultural markets fit the classic picture of perfect competition. First, there are many independent sellers who are generally *price takers*. Second, there are many buyers. Third, the products are interchangeable: Farm A's wheat can readily be substituted for farm B's wheat. And fourth, prices can, and do, vary considerably. On the basis of these inherent characteristics, it is reasonable to talk about agricultural markets as competitive markets.

In other ways, however, agricultural markets are far from perfectly competitive. The competitiveness of many agricultural markets is influenced by government programs. In fact, neither the United States nor any other country allows the market, unhindered, to control agricultural prices and output. For example, the U.S. government sets a minimum price for milk; buys up large quantities of wheat and stockpiles it; and licenses tobacco growers, allowing only those with licenses to grow tobacco.

I could have made the list of government programs much longer, because the government has a program for just about every major agricultural market. The point is clear, however: The competitive market in agriculture is not a story of the invisible hand alone. It's the story of a constant struggle between political and economic forces. Whenever the invisible hand pushes prices down, various coalitions of political forces generally work to push them back up. Farm states know this and are strongly encouraging their farmers to engage in *value-added farming* in which farmers take over some of the other activities that give agricultural goods their value to the consumer.

Agricultural markets involve a constant struggle between political and economic forces.

THE GOOD/BAD PARADOX IN AGRICULTURE

Agriculture is characterized by what might be called a **good/bad paradox** (*the phenomenon of doing poorly because you're doing well*). This good/bad paradox shows up in a variety of ways. Looking at the long run, we see that the enormous increase in agricultural productivity over the past few centuries has reduced agriculture's importance in U.S. society and has forced many farmers off the farm. Looking at the short run, we see that when harvests are good, farmers often fare badly financially; when harvests are poor, some farmers do very well financially. Let's consider these two cases in some detail.

The Long-Run Decline of Farming

Most countries, the United States included, began as predominantly agricultural societies. When the United States was founded a little more than 200 years ago, 97 percent of the labor force was engaged in farming. Today less than 3 percent of the U.S. labor force works in agriculture.

The decline in the number of farmers isn't the result of the failure of U.S. agriculture. Rather, it's the result of its tremendous success—the enormous increase in its productivity. It used to take the majority of the population to provide food for the United States. Today it takes only a small proportion to produce more food than the U.S. population can consume.

Figure 18-1 shows how success can lead to problems. In the long run the demand for wheat is inelastic (i.e., the percentage change in quantity demanded is small relative to the percentage change in price), as it is for most agricultural products, so the figure shows the equilibrium in the inelastic portion of the demand curve.

In this example, initially farmers are selling quantity Q_0 for price P_0. Their total income is P_0Q_0, shown by rectangles A and B. Now say that increases in productivity shift the supply curve out from S_0 to S_1. Output increases from Q_0 to Q_1, and price falls to P_1. Income falls to P_1Q_1, shown by the B and C rectangles. Farmers have gained the C rectangle but lost the A rectangle. The net effect is the difference in size between the two rectangles. So in this example, the net effect is negative.

In short, productivity has increased but total revenue has fallen, and many farmers have stopped farming altogether. They've done good by producing a lot, but the result

The good/bad paradox is the phenomenon of doing poorly because you're doing well.

Figure 18-1   The Good/Bad Paradox

The good/bad paradox is demonstrated in this graph. At price P_0 the quantity of wheat produced is Q_0. Total income is P_0Q_0. But if the supply of wheat increases from S_0 to S_1 due to increased productivity, the price of wheat will fall from P_0 to P_1 and quantity demanded will increase from Q_0 to Q_1. The increase in farmers' income (area C) is small. The decrease in farmers' income (area A) is large. Overall, the increased productivity has led to a decrease in farmers' incomes.

for themselves is bad. This good/bad paradox will occur whenever the supply curve shifts outward in the inelastic range of the demand curve.

Due to competition among farmers, most benefits of productivity increases in agriculture have gone to consumers in the form of lower prices. As an example, consider chicken. In the early 1930s, when Herbert Hoover was president of the United States and running for reelection, he promised prosperity to the country by saying there would be "two chickens in every pot." That promise meant a lot because, in today's money, chicken then cost $8 a pound. In the early 2000s, the price of chicken has fallen to under $2 a pound, only about one-quarter of its price in 1930.

The Short-Run Cyclical Problem Facing Farmers

The long-run good/bad paradox for farmers is mirrored by a short-run good/bad paradox: Good harvests often mean bad times and a fall in income; poor harvests often mean a rise in income.

A fact of life that farmers must deal with is that agricultural production tends to be highly unstable because it depends on weather and luck. Crops can be affected by too little rain, too much rain, insects, frost, heat, wind, hail—none of which can be easily controlled. Say you're an apple grower and you're having a beautiful spring—until the week that your trees are blossoming, when it rains continually. Bees don't fly when it rains, so they don't pollinate your trees. No pollination, no apple crop. There goes your apple crop for this year, and there goes your income.

The short-run demand for most agricultural goods is even more inelastic than the long-run demand. Because short-run demand is so inelastic, short-run changes in supply can have a significant effect on price. The result is that good harvests for farmers in general can lower prices significantly, while poor harvests can raise prices significantly. When the short-run price effect overwhelms the short-run quantity effect (as it does when demand is inelastic), farmers face the short-run good/bad paradox.

The Difficulty of Coordinating Farm Production

This good/bad paradox caused by inelastic demand isn't lost on farmers. They, quite naturally, aren't wild about passing on the gains to consumers instead of keeping the gains themselves. However, because agriculture is competitive, it is not in any one farmer's interest to decrease his or her supply in order to avoid encountering the paradox. Competitive farmers take the market price as given. That's the definition of a competitive industry. While it is in the industry's interest to have a "bad year" (to reduce total supply), it is in each individual farmer's interest to have a good year (to increase output) even if the combination of *all* farmers having a good year would cause all farmers to have a bad year.

It is, however, in farmers' joint interest to figure out ways to have continually "bad" years—which are, of course, actually "good" years for them. In other words, it's in their interest to figure out ways to limit the production of all farmers.

In a competitive industry, limiting production is easier said than done. It is difficult for farmers to limit production privately, among themselves, because although they make up only a small percentage of the total U.S. population, there are still a lot of them—3.5 million. That's too many to coordinate easily.

Ways around the Good/Bad Paradox

The difficulty of organizing privately to limit supply can be avoided by organizing through government. The U.S. political structure provides an alternative way for farmers (and other suppliers) to coordinate their actions and limit supply. Suppliers can

Q.1 What is the good/bad paradox?

Due to competition among farmers, most benefits of productivity increases in agriculture have gone to consumers in the form of lower prices.

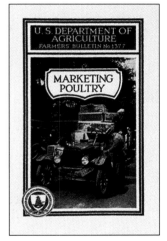

Marketing Poultry, *a 1936 Department of Agriculture publication, is representative of the major role government has played in agriculture.*

Q.2 How can it be in the interest of the agricultural industry to have a "bad year"?

Q.3 What are two ways around the good/bad paradox?

organize and get government to establish programs to limit production or hold price high, thereby avoiding the good/bad paradox. And that's what farmers did, which is why so many government agricultural programs exist today. (For a history of the U.S. government farm programs, go to the Colander Web site: www.mhhe.com/economics/colander.) These programs have been a combination of **price stabilization programs**—*programs designed to eliminate short-run fluctuations in prices, while allowing prices to follow their long-run trend line* and **price support programs**—*programs designed to maintain prices at levels higher than the market prices.*

The General Rule of Political Economy

If farmers are helped by farm programs, who is hurt? The answer is taxpayers and consumers. One would expect that these broad groups would strongly oppose farm programs because farm programs cost them in two ways: (1) higher taxes that government requires in order to buy up surplus farm output, and (2) higher prices for food. It's not easy for a politician to tell nonfarm constituents, "I'm supporting a bill that means higher prices and higher taxes for you." Nevertheless, the farm lobby has been quite successful in seeing that these programs are retained.

Economists who specialize in the relationship between economics and politics (known as *public choice economists*) have suggested that the reasons for farm groups' success involve the nature of the benefits and costs. The groups that are hurt by agricultural subsidies are large, but the negative effect on each individual in that group is relatively small. Large groups that experience small costs per individual don't provide a strong political opposition to a small group that experiences large gains. This seems to reflect a **general rule of political economy** in a democracy: *When small groups are helped by a government action and large groups are hurt by that same action, the small group tends to lobby far more effectively than the large group; thus, policies tend to reflect the small group's interest, not the interest of the large group.*

This bias in favor of farm programs is strengthened by the historical representation of farmers in Congress. Right from its beginnings in 1787, the U.S. political system has reflected the importance of agriculture. The Constitution gives representation in the Senate equally to all states. Only representation in the House of Representatives is based on a state's population. Since farm states have smaller populations than urban states, this arrangement gives farmers relatively more political power per capita than nonfarmers.

Farmers' strong political representation in Congress establishes a core of lawmakers who favor price supports. That core is supplemented with individuals who like the countryside filled with farms rather than with suburban sprawl. Consumers and taxpayers in general, who would be hurt by price supports, generally lack the political organization necessary to make their will known and counter the pressure for price controls.

The general rule of political economy states that small groups that are significantly affected by a government policy will lobby more effectively than large groups that are equally affected by that same policy.

Farmers' strong political representation in Congress establishes a core of lawmakers who favor price supports.

FOUR PRICE SUPPORT OPTIONS

Let's now consider the theory underlying some alternative farm price support options. In doing so, we'll try to understand which options, given the political realities, would have the best chance of being implemented, and why.

In a price support system, the government maintains a higher-than-equilibrium price, as diagrammed in Figure 18-2. At support price P_1, the quantity people want to supply is Q_S, but the quantity demanded at that price is Q_D.

At price P_1, there's excess supply, which exerts a downward pressure on price (arrow A). To maintain price at P_1, some other force (arrow B) must be exerted; otherwise the invisible hand will force the price down.

In a price support system, the government maintains a higher-than-equilibrium price.

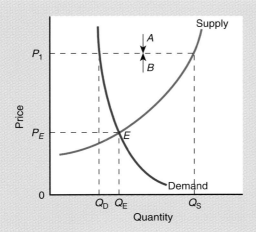

Figure 18-2   A Price Support System

In a price support system, the government maintains a higher-than-equilibrium price. At support price P_1, the quantity of product demanded is only Q_D, while the quantity supplied is Q_S. This causes downward pressures on the price, P_1, which must be offset by various government measures.

The government has various options to offset the downward pressure on price:

1. Using legal and regulatory force to prevent anyone from selling or buying at a lower price.

2. Providing economic incentives to reduce the supply enough to eliminate the downward pressure on price.

3. Subsidizing the sale of the good to consumers so that while suppliers get a high price, consumers have to pay only a low price.

4. Buying up and storing, giving away, or destroying enough of the good so that the total demand (including government's demand) increases enough to eliminate downward pressure on price.

Four price support options are:
1. Regulatory force.
2. Economic incentives to reduce supply.
3. Subsidizing the sale of goods to consumers.
4. Buying up and storing, giving away, or destroying the good.

These methods distribute the costs and benefits in slightly different ways. Let's consider each in detail.

Supporting the Price by Regulatory Measures

Suppose the government simply passes a law saying that, from now on, the price of wheat will be at least $5 per bushel. No one may sell wheat at a lower price. If the competitive equilibrium price is higher than $5, the law has no effect. When the competitive equilibrium is below the price floor (say the competitive equilibrium is $3.50 per bushel), the law limits suppliers from selling their wheat at that lower price.

The price floor helps some suppliers and hurts others. Those suppliers who are lucky enough to sell their wheat benefit. Those suppliers who aren't lucky and can't find buyers for their wheat are hurt. How many suppliers will be helped and how many will be hurt depends on the elasticities of supply and demand. When supply and demand are inelastic, a large change in price brings about a small change in quantity supplied, so the hurt group is relatively small. When the supply and demand are elastic, the hurt group is larger.

In Figure 18-3(a), at $5 suppliers would like to sell quantity Q_2 but they can sell only Q_1. They end up with a surplus of wheat, $Q_2 - Q_1$. Consumers, who must pay the higher price, $5, and receive only Q_1 rather than Q_e, are also hurt.

The Need for Rationing The law may or may not specify who will, and who will not, be allowed to sell, but it must establish some noneconomic method of rationing the

Figure 18-3 (a, b, c, and d) Alternative Methods of Government Price Supports

Alternative methods have different distributional consequences. The consequences of regulatory measures are shown in (a); the consequences of providing economic incentives to reduce supply in (b); the consequences of subsidizing the sale in (c); and the consequences of buying up and storing the good in (d).

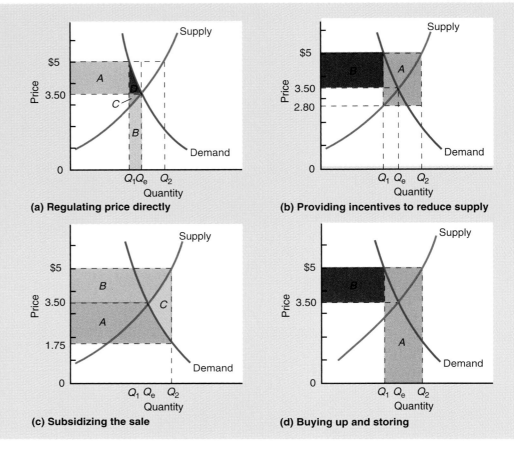

(a) Regulating price directly

(b) Providing incentives to reduce supply

(c) Subsidizing the sale

(d) Buying up and storing

limited demand among the suppliers. If it doesn't, buyers are likely, for example, to buy from farmers who are their friends. If individual farmers have a surplus, they'll probably try to dispose of that surplus by selling it on the black market at a price below the legal price. To maintain the support price, the government will have to arrest farmers who sell below the legal price. If the number of producers is large, such a regulatory approach is likely to break down quickly, since individual incentives to sell illegally are great and the costs of enforcing the law are accordingly high.

In understanding who benefits and who's hurt by price floors, it's important to distinguish between two groups of farmers: the farmers who were producing before the law went into effect, and the farmers who entered the market afterward. In Figure 18-3(a), the first group supplies Q_e; the second group, which would want to enter the market when the price went up, would supply $Q_2 - Q_e$. Why must the second group be clearly identified? Because one relatively easily enforceable way to limit the quantity supplied is to forbid any new farmers to enter the market. Only people who were producing at the beginning of the support program will be allowed to produce, and they will be allowed to produce only as much as they did before the program went into effect. Restricting production to the existing suppliers will reduce the quantity supplied to Q_e, leaving only $Q_e - Q_1$ to be rationed among suppliers.

To use this method of restriction is to **grandfather**—*to pass a law affecting a specific group but providing that those in the group before the law was passed are not subject to the law.*

With a price floor, some method of nonprice rationing must determine how the limited demand will be distributed among suppliers.

To grandfather in existing suppliers is one of the easiest provisions to enact into law and one of the easiest to enforce; thus, it is one of the most widely used. For example, when supply limitations were placed on tobacco, existing growers were all allowed to grow tobacco on land they were currently using for tobacco production. They could not, however, devote any new land to growing tobacco. (Later, tobacco farmers were allowed to sell their acreage allocations, so that if old land was taken out of tobacco production, new land could be added.)

Grandfathering is one of the politically easiest ways of restricting supply.

When it comes to grandfathering groups out of production, foreign producers are perhaps the politically easiest targets. To keep the domestic price of a good up, foreign imports must be limited as well as domestic production. U.S. taxpayers might put up with subsidizing U.S. farmers, but they're likely to balk at subsidizing foreign farmers. So most farm subsidy programs are supplemented with tariffs and quotas on foreign imports of the same commodity. (See Chapter 19 for definitions and further discussion of tariffs and quotas.)

Distributional Consequences Notice that with the equilibrium in the inelastic portion of the demand curve, even though the average farmer is constrained as to how much can be sold, he or she is made better off by that constraint because the total revenue going to all farmers is higher than it would be if supply weren't constrained. The farmer's total revenue from this market increases by rectangle A in Figure 18-3(a) and decreases by the rectangle composed of the combined areas B and C. Of course, making the farmer better off is not cost-free. Consumers are made worse off because they must pay more for a smaller supply of wheat. There's no direct cost to taxpayers other than the cost of enforcing and administering the regulations.

Notice in the diagram the little triangle made up of areas C and D, which shows an amount of income that society loses but farmers don't get. It's simply wasted. As discussed in Chapter 7, that little triangle is the welfare loss of producer and consumer surplus to society from the restriction.

Providing Economic Incentives to Reduce Supply

A second way in which government can keep a price high is to provide farmers with economic incentives to reduce supply.

Looking at Figure 18-3(b), you see that at the support price, $5 per bushel, the quantity of wheat supplied is Q_2 and quantity demanded is Q_1. To avoid a surplus, the government must somehow find a way to shift the quantity supplied back from Q_2 to Q_1. For example, it could pay farmers not to grow wheat, as it did in the acreage control programs established under President John F. Kennedy in the early 1960s. How much would such an economic incentive cost? Given the way the curves are drawn, to reduce the quantity supplied to Q_1, the government would have to pay farmers $2.20 ($5.00 − $2.80) for each bushel of wheat they didn't grow. This payment of $2.20 would induce suppliers producing $Q_2 − Q_1$ not to produce, reducing the quantity supplied to Q_1. The payment is shown by the A rectangle.

The Need for Rationing There is, however, a problem in identifying those individuals who would truly supply wheat at $5 a bushel. Knowing that the government is paying people not to grow wheat, people who otherwise had no interest in growing wheat will pretend that at $5 they would supply the wheat, simply to get the subsidy. To avoid this problem, often this incentive approach is combined with our first option, regulatory restrictions. Farmers who are already producing wheat at Q_e are grandfathered in; only they are given economic incentives not to produce. All others are forbidden to produce.

Q.4 Which of the four methods of price support would farmers favor least? Why?

Distributional Consequences When economic incentives are supplied, the existing farmers do very well for themselves. Their income goes up for two reasons. They get the A rectangle from the government in the form of payments not to grow wheat, and they get the B rectangle from consumers in the form of higher prices for the wheat they do grow. Farmers are also free to use their land for other purposes, so their income rises by the amount they can earn from using the land taken out of wheat production for something other than growing wheat. Consumers are still being hurt as before: They are paying a higher price and getting less. In addition, they're being hurt in their role as taxpayers because the lightly shaded area (rectangle A) represents the taxes they must pay to finance the government's economic incentive program. Thus, this option is much more costly to taxpayers than the regulatory option.

Subsidizing the Sale of the Good

Q.5 Which of the four methods of price support would taxpayers favor least? Why?

A third option is for the government to subsidize the sale of the good in order to hold down the price consumers pay but keep the amount suppliers receive high. Figure 18-3(c) shows how this works. Suppliers supply quantity Q_2 and are paid $5 per bushel. The government then turns around and sells that quantity at whatever price it can get—in this case, $1.75. No direct transfer takes place from the consumer to the supplier. Both are made better off. Consumers get more goods at a lower price. They are benefited by area A. Suppliers get a higher price and can supply all they want. They are benefited by area B. What's the catch? The catch, of course, is that taxpayers foot the entire bill, paying the difference between the $5 and the $1.75 ($3.25) for each bushel sold. The cost to taxpayers is represented by areas A, B, and C. This option costs taxpayers the most of any of the four options.

Buying Up and Storing, Giving Away, or Destroying the Good

Q.6 Which of the four methods of price support would consumers favor least? Why?

The final option is for the government to buy up all the quantity supplied that consumers don't buy at the support price. This option is shown in Figure 18-3(d). Consumers buy Q_1 at price $5; the government buys $Q_2 - Q_1$ at price $5, paying the A rectangle.

Distributional Consequences In this case consumers transfer the B rectangle to suppliers when they pay $5 rather than $3.50, the competitive equilibrium price. The government (i.e., the taxpayers) pays farmers rectangle A. The situation is very similar to our second option, in which the government provides suppliers with economic incentives not to produce. However, it's more expensive since the government must pay $5 per bushel rather than paying farmers $2.20 per bushel. In return for this higher payment, the government is getting something in return: $Q_2 - Q_1$ of wheat.

18.1

The Need to Dispose of Surplus Of course, if the government buys the surplus wheat, it takes on the problem of what to do with this surplus. Say the government decides to give it to the poor. Since the poor were already buying food, in response to a free food program they will replace some of their purchases with the free food. This replacement brings about a drop in demand—which means that the government must buy even more surplus. Instead of giving it away, though, the government can burn the surplus or store it indefinitely in warehouses and grain elevators. Burning up the surplus or storing it, at least, doesn't increase the amount government must buy.

Why, you ask, doesn't the government give the surplus to foreign countries as a type of humanitarian aid? The reason is that just as giving the surplus to our own poor creates problems in the United States, giving the surplus to the foreign poor creates problems in the countries involved. To the degree that the foreign poor have any income, they're likely to spend most of it on food. Free food would supplant some of their demand, thus lowering the price for those who previously sold food to them. Giving anything away destroys somebody's market, and when markets are destroyed someone gets upset. So when the United States has tried to give away its surplus food, other foreign countries have put enormous pressure on the United States not to "spoil the world market."

Which Group Prefers Which Option?

The four price support options I've just described can, of course, be used in various combinations. It's a useful exercise at this point to think through which of the options farmers, taxpayers, and consumers would likely favor and to relate the history of the farm programs to these options.

The first option, regulation, costs the government the least, but it benefits farmers the least. Since existing farmers are likely to be the group directly pushing for price supports, government is least likely to choose this approach. If it is chosen, most of the required reduction in quantity supplied will probably come from people who might enter farming at some time in the future, not from existing farmers.

The second option, economic incentives, costs the government more than the first option but less than the third and fourth options. Farmers are benefited by economic incentive programs in two ways. They get paid not to grow a certain crop, and they can sometimes get additional income from using the land for other purposes. When farmers aren't allowed to use their land for other purposes, they usually oppose this option, preferring the third or fourth option.

The third option, subsidies on the sales to keep prices down, benefits both consumers (who get low prices) and farmers (who get high prices). Taxpayers are harmed the most by this option. They must finance the subsidy payments for all subsidized farm products.

The last option, buying up and storing or destroying the goods, costs taxpayers more than the first two options but less than the third, since consumers pay part of the cost. However, it leaves the government with a surplus to deal with. If there's a group who can take that surplus without significantly reducing their current demand, then that group is likely to support this option.

ECONOMICS, POLITICS, AND REAL-WORLD POLICIES

The two farm programs most prevalent in the United States have been the **land bank program** (in which *government supports prices by giving farmers economic incentives to reduce supply*) and the **nonrecourse loan program** (in which *government "buys" goods in the form of collateral on defaulting loans*). Programs that support prices through regulation, our first option, generally haven't been applied to existing farmers. They have, however, often been used to prevent new farmers from entering the market—which isn't surprising since the political impetus for farm programs comes from existing farmers. The third option, to subsidize the sale of the good so the farmer gets a high price and the consumer pays a low price, hasn't been used because, as discussed previously, it would be the most costly to taxpayers.

Q-7 What two farm programs have been the most prevalent in the United States?

Interest Groups

The actual political debate is, of course, much more complicated than presented here. For example, other pressure groups are involved. Recently, farm groups and environmental groups have combined forces and have become more effective in shaping and supporting farm policy. Thus, recent new restrictions on supply in farming often operate

APPLYING THE TOOLS

Changes in U.S.
Agricultural Policy

In 1996 the U.S. government voted for sweeping reforms designed to eliminate major aspects of the farm support programs by 2002. What made that politically possible was a combination of three forces: (1) the government deficit, which put pressure on government to eliminate costly programs; (2) the ability of U.S. farmers to sell abroad, which reduced the benefits of the existing farm support program to them; and (3) the general pro-market ideology that gained favor in the late 1990s and early 2000s.

When we look at the reforms more carefully, they look less sweeping than they initially appeared. There are three reasons why. First, three of the programs that most sharply limit production—peanut, sugar, and dairy programs—were left untouched because of strong lobbying efforts directed at members of Congress. Second, while in a number of areas direct price supports will be eliminated, other indirect price support systems will not. The most important of these is the program that allows farmers to borrow money cheaply from the government, using the expected crop as collateral. This program allows the farmer to default on the loan, instead of paying it back, should the price of their crop be less than the prices set as collateral. This means that if agricultural prices fall significantly, the "buy-up-and-store" option discussed in the text will still exist and will hold prices up. This method of price support is extraordinarily costly to taxpayers.

Third, to "compensate" farmers for their elimination of direct price supports, the government gave direct grants to farmers. These grants started at $5.8 billion in 1998 and will fall to $4 billion in 2002, when the law ends. With agricultural prices high, as they were at the time the law was passed, the net result of this "compensation" was that the total payments to farmers were initially higher than they were under the old price support system. As prices fell in 1999 large emergency grants were given to farmers, and most observers expect government agricultural supports to continue.

Q.8 Are taxpayers, farmers, and consumers separate groups that are independent of each other?

in ways that environmentalists would favor, such as regulating the types of fertilizer and chemicals farmers can use.

Moreover, the three interest groups discussed here—farmers, taxpayers, and consumers—aren't entirely distinct one from another. Their memberships overlap. All taxpayers are also consumers, farmers are both taxpayers and consumers, and so on. Thus, much of the political debate is simply about from whose pocket the government is going to get money to help farmers. Shall it be the consumer's pocket (through higher prices)? Or the taxpayer's (through higher taxes)? That said, the political reality is that consumer and taxpayer interests and the lobbying groups that represent them generally examine only part of the picture—the part that directly affects them. Accordingly, politicians often act as if these groups had separate memberships. Politicians weigh the options by attempting to balance their view of the general good with the power and preferences of the special interest groups that they represent or that contribute to their election campaigns.

International Issues

18.2

If you think government is significantly involved in U.S. agriculture, you should see its role in other countries, such as the members of the European Union and Japan.

The final real-world complication that must be taken into account is the international dimension. If you think government is significantly involved in U.S. agriculture, you should see its role in other countries such as the members of the European Union (EU) and Japan. For example, more than half the EU's budget is devoted to farm subsidies, and most of its farms stay in business only because of protection. Our agricultural policy is, in part, determined by trade negotiations with these other countries. For example, a reduction in EU subsidies could bring about a reduction in our subsidies.

The early 2000s also saw major debates about genetically modified seeds. The EU was threatening to prevent import of any crop that was genetically modified. Since much U.S. seed is genetically modified, such an import ban would be a significant barrier to trade and this debate should be much in the news.

CONCLUSION

This chapter has focused on agricultural markets, but it should be clear that the discussion is about much more than just agriculture; it's about the interrelationship between economics and politics. If individuals are self-interested maximizers, it's reasonable to assume that they're maximizers in all aspects of their lives. What they can't achieve in the economic sphere, they might be able to achieve in the political sphere.

To understand the economic policies that exist, we must consider how people act in both spheres. Consideration of the economics underlying government policies often leads to useful insights. For example, as discussed in Chapter 7, a military draft can be seen as a mechanism for focusing the costs of defense away from the taxpayer and onto a specific group of individuals—young people. The government's support for the arts can be seen as a transfer from general taxpayers to a specific group of individuals who like the arts. Government support for education can be seen as a transfer from general taxpayers to a specific group of individuals: students and instructors. These groups maintain strong lobbies to achieve their political ends, and the interaction of the various lobbying groups typically strongly influences what policies government will follow.

Economics doesn't tell you whether government intervention or any particular policy is good or bad. That, you must decide for yourself. But what economics can do is pose the policy question in terms of gains and losses for particular groups. Posing the question in that framework often cuts through to the real reasons behind various groups' support for this or that policy. Often people support programs that transfer money from other taxpayers and consumers to themselves. They are, however, unlikely to say that is their motive. For example, I've seldom heard teachers say that the reason they favor government support for education is that those policies transfer money to them.

The economic framework directs you to look beyond the reasons people say they support policies; it directs you to look for the self-interest. The supply/demand framework provides a neat graphical way to picture the relative gains and losses resulting from various policies.

But as usual there's an *on the other hand*. Just because some groups may support policies for self-serving reasons, it is not necessarily the case that the policies are bad or shouldn't be adopted. Reality is complicated, with many more gray answers than black-and-white ones.

Q.9 Is the military draft a cheaper way of maintaining defense than a volunteer army?

Q.10 Economic theory tells us that a volunteer army is preferable to an army maintained by a draft. True or false? Why?

Chapter Summary

- Agricultural markets have many qualities of perfectly competitive markets: sellers are price takers, there are many buyers, products are interchangeable, and prices vary considerably. The competitiveness of agricultural markets is affected by significant government intervention.

- The good/bad paradox is the result of the inelastic demand in most agricultural markets. Increases in productivity increase supply; but, because demand is inelastic, the percentage decline in price is greater than the percentage increase in equilibrium quantity. Total revenue declines.

- A general rule of political economy in a democracy is that policies tend to reflect small groups' interests, not the interests of large groups.

- Because farmers are a small, easily identifiable group, and because farm states get larger representation relative to population in the Senate, the farm lobby is very strong.

- A price support program works by government maintaining higher-than-equilibrium prices through regulations, economic incentives, subsidies, and buying up and storing or destroying.

- Regulatory price supports cost government the least, but benefit the farmers the least.

- Economic incentive price supports cost the government and taxpayers more than regulatory price supports, but less than subsidy price supports or buying up and storing the good.

- Subsidy price supports benefit consumers, who pay lower prices, and farmers, who receive higher prices. Subsidy price supports cost taxpayers the most.
- Buying up and storing the good gives government a surplus to deal with.
- Two prevalent farm programs in the United States are the land bank program, in which government gives farmers economic incentives to reduce supply, and the nonrecourse loan program, in which government "buys" goods in the form of collateral on defaulting loans.
- Agricultural policy is affected by interest groups (consumers, taxpayers, and farmers) and international issues (farm policies of our trading partners).

Key Terms

general rule of political economy   *(394)*
good/bad paradox   *(392)*
grandfather   *(396)*

land bank program   *(399)*
nonrecourse loan program   *(399)*
price stabilization programs   *(394)*

price support programs   *(394)*

Questions for Thought and Review

1. If the demand for farm products were elastic rather than inelastic, would the good/bad paradox still exist? Why or why not?

2. Demonstrate, using supply and demand curves, the distributional consequences of a price support system achieved through acreage restriction.

3. Which would a taxpayers' group prefer: price support achieved through buying up the surplus or through providing economic incentives for not producing? Why?

4. What is the most costly method of price support to the taxpayer? Demonstrate graphically.

5. What is the least costly method of price support to the taxpayer? Demonstrate graphically.

6. Why do tariffs and quotas generally accompany price support systems?

7. How does the elasticity of supply affect the cost of price supports in each of the four options?

8. Why is grandfathering an attractive option for governments when they institute price supports?

9. All government intervention in markets makes society worse off. True or false? Evaluate.

10. What type of price support program is the nonrecourse loan? the land bank program?

Problems and Exercises

1. Show graphically how the effects of an increase in supply will differ according to the elasticities of supply and demand.
   a. Specifically, demonstrate the following combinations:
      (1) An inelastic supply and an inelastic demand.
      (2) An elastic supply and an inelastic demand.
      (3) An elastic supply and an elastic demand.
      (4) An inelastic supply and an inelastic demand.
   b. Demonstrate the effect of a government guarantee of the price in each of the four cases.
   c. If you were a farmer, which of the four combinations would you prefer?

2. Congratulations. You've been appointed finance minister of Farmingland. The president wants to protect her political popularity by increasing farmers' incomes. She's considering two alternatives: (a) bolstering agricultural prices by adding governmental demand to private demand; and (b) giving farmers financial incentives to restrict supply and thereby increase price. She wants to use the measure that's least costly to the government. The conditions of supply and demand are illustrated in the accompanying diagram. (S_1 is what the restricted supply curve would look like. P_s is the price that the president wants to establish.) Which measure would you advise?

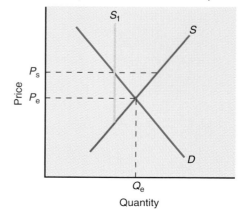

3. The Pure Food and Drug Act of 1906 is known as "Dr. Wiley's Law." It is generally regarded by noneconomic historians as representing the triumph of consumer interests over producer interests.
    a. Why might an economist likely be somewhat wary of this interpretation?
    b. What evidence would a skeptical economist likely look for to determine the motives behind the passage of this law?
    c. What would be the significance of the fact that the Pure Food and Drug Act was passed in 1906, right when urbanization and technological change were fostering new products that competed significantly with existing producers' interests?

4. The U.S. government makes it against the law to grow peanuts unless the grower has been granted a government quota. It also essentially forbids peanut imports and sets a minimum U.S. price of peanuts at about 50 percent higher than the price of peanuts on the world market. This program costs the government $4 million a year in administrative costs.
    a. Are there likely any other costs associated with the program?
    b. Demonstrate graphically how to come up with about $250 million of additional costs.
    c. When "peanut land"—land with peanut quotas—is sold, what is the likely price of that land compared to equivalent land without a peanut quota?

    d. Say that, under the World Trade Organization, the United States agrees to allow open imports of peanuts into the United States and guarantees that all sellers receive the existing price. What will happen to the governmental costs of the program?
    e. Say the government limits the guaranteed high price to U.S. producers. What will it have to do to make that guarantee succeed?

5. Say that a law, if passed, will reduce Mr. A's wealth by $100,000 and increase Mr. B's wealth by $100,000.
    a. How much would Mr. A be willing to spend to stop passage of the law?
    b. How much would Mr. B be willing to spend to ensure passage of the law?
    c. What implications for social policy do your answers to *a* and *b* have?

6. In 1992 the U.S. Bureau of Land Management set a fee for ranchers who graze their animals on public land equal to $1.86 per animal unit per month—the amount of forage needed to feed one cow and its calf, or five sheep, for a month. The market rate for grazing on private land is $9 per animal unit per month.
    a. Why do you think there is a difference?
    b. What are the advantages of setting the lower fee?
    c. Would you expect excess demand for government grazing land? Why? Demonstrate graphically.

Web Questions

1. The U.S. Department of Agriculture provides a Foreign Agriculture Service that reports prices for agricultural goods. Go to its home page at www.fas.usda.gov, look up the commodity pages, and search for recent world and domestic sugar prices. Answer the following questions:
    a. What is the cost of raw sugar on world markets? What is the cost of domestic raw sugar?
    b. What accounts for the difference between domestic and world price for raw sugar?
    c. At the Foreign Agriculture Service home page, search for and read the report "Import Requirements for Sugar." How does U.S. trade policy help maintain high U.S. domestic sugar prices?

2. Capital Hill Blue is an online news source. Go to its home page at www.capitolhillblue.com/ and search in its archives for the article "Sacred Cow Farm Subsidies Under Attack." Read the article and answer the following questions:
    a. What three crops were hardly affected by the farm bill in 1997?
    b. How would curtailing sugar and peanut programs benefit consumers?
    c. How does the sugar program harm our environment?
    d. Go to the American Sugar Alliance home page at www.sugaralliance.org. What benefits does the alliance say U.S. sugar policy provides?

Answers to Margin Questions

1. The good/bad paradox is the phenomenon of doing poorly because you're doing well. It exists when demand for your product is inelastic. Specifically, as it applies to agriculture, it means that when most farmers produce a lot, prices are low and their net income drops. (393)

2. Because demand is inelastic, it is in the interest of the agricultural industry for the supply of agricultural goods to decline from bad weather or other supply disruptions. The percentage rise in price will be greater than the percentage decline in quantity demanded, and total revenue for the industry will rise. (393)

3. There are two ways around the good/bad paradox. One is for suppliers to coordinate their activity and limit supply. The second way is for suppliers to lobby and get government to establish programs to limit production, stabilizing the price and holding it high. Because of the difficulty of coordinating the large number of farmers, it is this second track that U.S. farmers have followed. (393)

4. Farmers are least likely to support the regulatory method of price support, in which regulatory force is used to prevent anyone from selling or buying at a lower price. Although such a policy benefits farmers, it benefits them far less than other price support policies. (398)

5. Taxpayers will likely least favor the price support method of subsidizing the sale of goods to consumers, because this method costs taxpayers the most. The low price paid by consumers and the high price received by farmers necessitate large subsidies. (398)

6. Consumers would least favor the price support method of providing economic incentives to reduce supply and the price support method of regulatory force. Both these methods reduce the supply and push up the price. Some consumers would benefit from the buying up, giving away, or destroying method, which suggests that consumers on average would prefer this to the regulatory or the economic incentive method. (398)

7. The land bank program, which gives farmers incentives to reduce supply, and the nonrecourse loan program,

which buys up goods, have been the two most prevalent U.S. farm programs. (399)

8. While this chapter discusses taxpayers, farmers, and consumers as separate groups independent of each other, in reality they are not. Each individual is, generally, both a taxpayer and a consumer, while farmers are generally members of all three groups. It is nonetheless useful to treat them as separate groups because specific interests predominate: for example, farmers' interests as farmers significantly outweigh their interests as taxpayers or as consumers. (400)

9. In terms of actual money payment by the government, having a military draft likely is a cheaper way of maintaining defense than is a volunteer army. However, a military draft can be seen as a type of hidden tax on a specific group of individuals—young people who are subject to the draft—to the degree that they are paid less than the going wage. If that hidden tax is also included in the cost, the military draft is not a cheaper way of maintaining defense. Because it involves inefficiencies in who can participate, it can, indeed, be seen as more expensive than an all-volunteer army. (401)

10. False. Economic theory tells us nothing about what is preferable. Choices about what is preferable can only be made by specifying one's value judgments. Such choices belong in normative economics and in the art of economics, where distributional effects, broader sociological issues, and value judgments are included in the analysis. (401)

International Trade Policy

After reading this chapter, you should be able to:

- Explain the principle of comparative advantage.

- List three determinants of the terms of trade.

- Discuss why countries impose trade restrictions.

- Summarize why economists generally oppose trade restrictions.

- Explain three policies countries use to restrict trade.

- Explain how free trade associations both help and hinder international trade.

One of the purest fallacies is that trade follows the flag. Trade follows the lowest price current. If a dealer in any colony wished to buy Union Jacks, he would order them from Britain's worst foe if he could save a sixpence.

Andrew Carnegie

If economists had a mantra, it would be "Trade is good." Trade allows specialization and division of labor and thereby promotes technological growth. Consistent with that mantra, most economists oppose trade restrictions. Not everyone agrees with economists; almost every day we hear calls from some sector of the economy to restrict foreign imports in order to save U.S. jobs and protect U.S. workers from unfair competition. In this chapter we consider why economists generally favor free trade, and why, despite what economists tell them, countries impose trade restrictions.

APPLYING THE TOOLS

The Gains to International Traders

Trade does not take place on its own—markets and trade require entrepreneurs to bring it about. The market is not about abstract forces; it is about real people operating to improve their position. Many of the gains from trade do not go to the countries involved but rather to the trader. And the gains that traders get can be enormous.

Consider, for example, the beautifully knit Peruvian sweaters often sold at art fairs and college campuses for $75 apiece. The Peruvian women knitting those sweaters are paid only a small fraction of that $75—say $6 apiece—and the trader makes the difference. So much of the benefits of trade do not go to the producer or the con-sumer; they go to the trader. Another example is the high-priced sneakers ($105) that many "with-it" students wear. Those sneakers are likely made in China, and the cost of mak-ing a pair of sneakers is about $8. The trader has other costs, of course; there are, for example, costs of transportation and advertising—someone has to convince you that you need those "with-it" sneakers. (Just do it, right?) But that advertising is not done in China, and a portion of the benefits of the trade are accruing to adver-tising firms, which can pay more to creative people who think up those crazy ads.

THE PRINCIPLE OF COMPARATIVE ADVANTAGE

The reason two countries trade is that trade can make both countries better off. The reasoning showing that this is true underlies the principle of comparative advantage presented in Chapter 2. There, I also went through the geometry of trade. The basic idea of the **principle of comparative advantage** is that *as long as the relative opportunity costs of producing goods (what must be given up in one good in order to get another good) differ among countries, then there are potential gains from trade.* (If the idea is not clear to you, Appendix A to this chapter goes through the reasoning and the geometry in more de-tail.) Let's review this principle by considering the story of I.T., an imaginary interna-tional trader, who convinces two countries to enter into trades by giving both countries some of the advantages of trade; he keeps the rest for himself.

> The principle of comparative ad-vantage states that as long as the relative opportunity costs of pro-ducing goods differ among coun-tries, then there are potential gains from trade.

The Gains from Trade

19.1

Here's the situation. On his trips to the United States and Saudi Arabia, I.T. noticed that no trade between them was taking place. He also noticed that the opportunity cost of producing a ton of food in Saudi Arabia was 10 barrels of oil and that the opportunity cost for the United States of producing a ton of food was 1/10 of a barrel of oil. At the time, the United States' production was 60 barrels of oil and 400 tons of food, while Saudi Arabia's production was 400 barrels of oil and 60 tons of food.

I.T. made the United States and Saudi Arabia the following offer: If the United States would specialize in food, devoting the resources then being used to produce 60 barrels of oil to producing food, it could increase its food production from 400 tons to 1,000 tons. I.T. would then give the United States 120 barrels of oil in exchange for 500 of those tons. That would leave 500 tons of food to the United States (100 tons more than it had before the deal) and give it double the amount of oil—120 barrels (com-pared to its pre-deal 60 barrels). By accepting this deal, the United States wound up with more of both commodities without increasing the resources it expended.

He told Saudi Arabia that if it would specialize in oil, devoting the resources used to produce 60 tons of food to producing oil and thus increasing its oil production from 400 barrels to 1,000 barrels, he would give it 120 tons of food—double the amount of food it had before the deal—in exchange for 500 barrels of that oil. Like the United States,

Q.1   In terms of oil and food, exactly how much richer is I.T. after the trade?

Over the past 50 years, international issues have become increasingly important for the U.S. economy. That statement would be correct even if the reference period went back as far as the late 1800s. The late 1800s and the first 40 years of the 1900s together formed an isolationist period for the United States in which the country turned inward in both economic and foreign policies.

In the 1600s, 1700s, and most of the 1800s, international trade was vital to the American economy. The American nation grew out of colonial possessions of England, France, and Spain. These "new world" colonial possessions were valued for their gold, agricultural produce, and natural resources. From a European standpoint, international trade was the colonies' reason for being.*

A large portion of the U.S. government's income during much of the 1800s came from tariffs. Our technology was imported from abroad, and international issues played a central role in wars fought here. (An important cause of the U.S. Civil War was differences of views about tariffs on manufactured goods. The South opposed them because it wanted cheap manufactured goods, while the North favored them because it wanted to protect its manufacturing industries.) Up until the 1900s, no one would have studied the U.S. economy independently of international issues. Not only was there significant international trade; there was also significant immigration.

Only in the late 1800s did the United States adopt an isolationist philosophy in both politics and trade. So, relative to that isolationist period, the U.S. economy has become more integrated with the world economy. However, in a broader historical perspective, that isolationist period

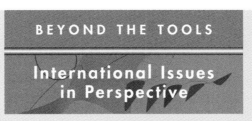

BEYOND THE TOOLS

International Issues in Perspective

was an anomaly, and the 1990s simply returned international issues to the key role they've usually played.

A second important insight is that international trade has social and cultural dimensions. While much of the chapter deals specifically with economic issues, we must also remember the cultural and social implications of trade.

Let's consider an example from history. In the Middle Ages, Greek ideas and philosophy were lost to Europe when hordes of barbarians swept over the continent. Europeans only rediscovered the ancient ideas and philosophy in the Renaissance as a by-product of trade between the Italian merchant cities and the Middle East. (The Greek ideas that had spread to the Middle East were protected there from European upheavals.) *Renaissance* means rebirth: a rebirth in Europe of Greek learning. Many of our traditions and sensibilities today are based on those of the Renaissance, and that Renaissance was caused, or at least significantly influenced, by international trade. Had there been no trade, our entire philosophy of life might be different than it is.

Another example is the major change in socialist countries in the 1990s. Through the 1960s China, the Soviet Union, and the Eastern European countries were relatively closed societies—behind the Iron Curtain. That changed in the 1970s and 1980s as these socialist countries opened up trade with the West as a way to speed their own economic development. That trade, and the resulting increased contact with the West, gave the people of those countries a better sense of the material goods available in the West. That trade also spread Western ideas of the proper organization of government and the economy to these societies. A strong argument can be made that along with trade came the seeds of discontent that changed those societies and their economies forever.

---

*The American Indian standpoint was, I suspect, somewhat different.

Saudi Arabia wound up with more of both commodities without increasing the resources it expended. Thus, both countries ended up with more than they initially had of both goods.

Dividing Up the Gains from Trade

As the above story suggests, when countries avail themselves of comparative advantage there are high gains of trade to be made. Who gets these gains is unclear. The principle of comparative advantage doesn't determine how those gains of trade will be divided up among the countries involved and among traders who make the trade possible. While there are no definitive laws determining how real-world gains from trade will be apportioned, economists have developed some insights into how those gains are likely to be divided up. The first insight concerns how much the trader gets. The general rule is:

Three determinants of the terms of trade are:

1. The more competition, the less the trader gets.
2. Smaller countries get a larger proportion of the gain than larger countries.
3. Countries producing goods with economies of scale get a larger gain from trade.

Q.2 In what circumstances would a small country not get the larger percentage of the gains from trade?

The more competition that exists among traders, the less likely it is that the trader gets big gains of trade; more of the gains from trade will go to the citizens in the two countries, and less will go to the traders.

What this insight means is that where entry into trade is unimpaired, most of the gains of trade will pass from the trader to the countries. Thus, the trader's big gains from trade occur in markets that are newly opened.

This insight isn't lost on trading companies. Numerous import/export companies exist whose business is discovering possibilities for international trade in newly opened markets. Individuals representing trading companies go around hawking projects or goods to countries. For example in 1999 at the end of the NATO bombing campaign in Kosovo, what the business world calls the *import/export contingent* flew to Kosovo with offers of goods and services to sell. Many of these same individuals had been in Iraq and Iran in the early 1990s, in Saudi Arabia when oil prices rose in the 1970s, and in the Far East when China opened its doors to international trade in the 1980s.

A second insight is:

Once competition prevails, smaller countries tend to get a larger percentage of the gains of trade than do larger countries.

The reason, briefly, is that more opportunities are opened up for smaller countries by trade than for larger countries. The more opportunities, the larger the relative gains. Say, for instance, that the United States begins trade with Mali, a small country in Africa. Enormous new consumption possibilities are opened up for Mali—prices of all types of goods will fall. Assuming Mali has a comparative advantage in fish, before international trade began cars were probably extraordinarily expensive in Mali, while fish was cheap. With international trade, the price of cars in Mali falls substantially, so Mali gets the gains. Because the U.S. economy is so large compared to Mali's, the U.S. price of fish doesn't change noticeably. Mali's fish are just a drop in the bucket. The price ratio of cars to fish doesn't change much for the United States, so it doesn't get much of the gains of trade. Mali gets almost all the gains from trade.

There's an important catch to this gains-from-trade argument. The argument holds only once competition among traders prevails. That means that Mali residents are sold cars at the same price (plus shipping costs) as U.S. residents. International traders in small countries often have little competition from other traders and keep large shares of the gains from trade for themselves. In the preceding example, the United States and Saudi Arabia didn't get a large share of the benefits. It was I.T. who got most of the benefits. Since the traders often come from the larger country, the smaller country doesn't get the benefits of the gains from trade; the larger country's international traders do.

A third insight is:

Gains from trade go to the countries producing goods that exhibit economies of scale.

Trade allows an increase in production. If there are economies of scale, that increase can lower the average cost of production of a good. Hence, an increase in production can lower the price of the good in the producing country. The country producing the good with the larger economies of scale has its costs reduced by more, and hence gains more from trade than does its trading partner.

REASONS FOR TRADE RESTRICTIONS

Let's now turn to a different question: If trade is beneficial, as it is in our example of I.T., why do countries restrict trade? Here are some reasons why:

1. Unequal internal distribution of the gains from trade.
2. Haggling by companies over the gains from trade.
3. Haggling by countries over trade restrictions.
4. Specialized production: learning by doing and economies of scale.
5. Macroeconomic aspects of trade.
6. National security.
7. International politics.
8. Increased revenue brought in by tariffs.

Reasons for restricting trade include:
1. Unequal internal distribution of the gains from trade.
2. Haggling by companies over the gains from trade.
3. Haggling by countries over trade restrictions.
4. Specialized production: learning by doing and economies of scale.
5. Macroeconomic aspects of trade.
6. National security.
7. International politics.
8. Increased revenue brought in by tariffs.

Unequal Internal Distribution of the Gains from Trade

In the example of the argument for trade discussed at the beginning of the chapter, I.T. persuaded Saudi Arabia to specialize in the production of oil rather than food, and persuaded the United States to produce more food than oil. That means, of course, that some U.S. oil workers will have to become farmers, and in Saudi Arabia some farmers will have to become oil producers.

Often people don't want to make radical changes in the kind of work they do—they want to keep on producing what they're already producing. So when these people see the same kinds of goods that they produce coming into their country from abroad, they lobby to prevent the foreign competition. Sometimes they're successful. A good example is the "voluntary" quotas—numerical limits—placed on Japanese cars exported to the United States in the 1980s. These quotas saved U.S. jobs, but, by reducing competition, forced consumers to pay higher prices for cars. Economists have estimated that it costs consumers, in higher car prices, about $100,000 for each job saved. Table 19-1 lists economists' estimates of the cost to consumers of saving a job in some other industries.

Had I.T. been open about the difficulties of trading, he would have warned the countries that change is hard. It has very real costs that I.T. didn't point out when he made his offers. But these costs of change are relatively small compared to the gains from trade. Moreover, they're short-run, temporary costs, whereas gains from trade are permanent, long-run gains. Once the adjustment has been made, the costs will be gone but the benefits will still be there.

For most goods, the benefits for the large majority of the population so outweigh the small costs to some individuals that, decided on a strict cost/benefit basis, international trade is still a deal you can't refuse. With benefits so outweighing costs, it would seem that transition costs could be forgotten. But they can't.

Table 19-1   Cost of Saving Jobs in Selected Industries

Industry	Cost of Production (per job saved)
Specialty steel	$1,000,000
Color TVs	420,000
Ceramic tiles	135,000
Clothing	36,000–82,000
Agriculture	20,000 (per farmer)
Dairy	1,800 (per cow)

Source: GATT, 1993 (http://www.wto.org).

Benefits of trade are generally widely scattered among the entire population. In contrast, costs of free trade often fall on specific small groups.

Q₃ Why does the EU place high barriers against agricultural products?

Because eliminating trade restrictions often imposes high costs on a small subgroup in society, government has instituted trade adjustment assistance programs to compensate for the losses.

Telling people who claim to be hurt that they aren't really being hurt isn't good politics.

Benefits of trade are generally widely scattered among the entire population. In contrast, costs of free trade often fall on small groups of people who loudly oppose the particular free trade that hurts them. Though the benefits of free trade to the country at large exceed the costs of free trade to the small group of individuals, the political push from the few (who are hurt) for trade restrictions often exceeds the political push from the many (who are helped) for free trade. The result is trade restrictions on a variety of products. You'll likely see TV ads supporting such restrictions under the heading SAVING U.S. JOBS. But you'll see few ads in favor of free trade to keep prices low for consumers.

It isn't only in the United States that the push for trade restrictions focuses on the small costs and not on the large benefits. For example, the European Union (EU) places large restrictions on food imports from nonmember nations. If the EU would remove those barriers, food prices in EU countries would decline significantly. For example, it is estimated that meat prices would fall by about 65 percent. Consumers would benefit, but farmers would be hurt. The farmers, however, have the political clout to see that the costs are considered and the benefits aren't. The result: The EU places high duties on foreign agricultural products.

The cost to society of relaxing trade restrictions has led to a number of programs to assist those who are hurt. Such programs are called **trade adjustment assistance programs**—*programs designed to compensate losers for reductions in trade restrictions.*
The argument for these programs is the following:

Trade will make most members of society better off, but will make a particular subgroup in society worse off. Because of the country's political dynamics, this subgroup can prevent free trade. If I structure programs so that they transfer some of society's gains to individuals who are made worse off by trade, I can eliminate their opposition and thereby make society better off.

Since a trade adjustment program compensates those who are hurt by trade, one might think that such programs will eliminate the opposition to free trade. Unfortunately, they generally do not.

Governments have tried to use trade adjustment assistance to facilitate free trade, but they've found that it's enormously difficult to limit the adjustment assistance to those who are actually hurt by international trade. As soon as people find that there's assistance for people injured by trade, they're likely to try to show that they too have been hurt and deserve assistance. Losses from free trade become exaggerated and magnified. Instead of only a small portion of the gains from trade being needed for trade adjustment assistance, much more is demanded—often even more than the gains.

Telling people who claim to be hurt that they aren't really being hurt isn't good politics. That's why offering trade adjustment assistance as a way to relieve the pressure to restrict trade is a deal many governments can refuse.

Haggling by Companies over the Gains from Trade

Many naturally advantageous bargains aren't consummated because each side is pushing for a larger share of the gains from trade than the other side thinks should be allotted. This is another example of the prisoner's dilemma.

To see how companies haggling over the gains of trade can restrict trade, let's reconsider the original deal that I.T. proposed. I.T. got 380 tons of food and 380 barrels of oil. The United States got an additional 100 tons of food and 60 barrels of oil. Saudi Arabia got an additional 100 barrels of oil and 60 tons of food.

Suppose the Saudis had said, "Why should we be getting only 100 barrels of oil and 60 tons of food when I.T. is getting 380 barrels of oil and 380 tons of food? We want an additional 300 tons of food and another 300 barrels of oil, and we won't deal unless we get them." Similarly the United States might have said, "We want an additional 300 tons of food and an additional 300 barrels of oil, and we won't go through with the deal unless we get them." If either the U.S. or the Saudi Arabian company that was involved in the trade for its country (or both) takes this position, I.T. might just walk—no deal. Tough bargaining positions can make it almost impossible to achieve gains from trade.

The side that drives the hardest bargain gets the most gains from the bargain, but it also risks making the deal fall through. Such strategic bargaining goes on all the time. **Strategic bargaining** means *demanding a larger share of the gains from trade than you can reasonably expect*. If you're successful, you get the lion's share; if you're not successful, the deal falls apart and everyone is worse off.

Haggling by Countries over Trade Restrictions

Another type of trade bargaining that often limits trade is bargaining between countries. Trade restrictions and the threat of trade restrictions play an important role in that kind of haggling. Sometimes countries must go through with trade restrictions that they really don't want to impose, just to make their threats credible.

Once one country has imposed trade restrictions, other countries attempt to get those restrictions reduced by threatening to increase their own restrictions. Again, to make the threat credible, sometimes countries must impose or increase trade restrictions simply to show they're willing to do so.

Ultimately, strategic bargaining power depends on negotiators' skills and the underlying gains from trade that a country would receive. A country that would receive only a small portion of the gains from trade is in a much stronger bargaining position than a country that would receive significant gains. It's easier for the former to walk away from trade.

The United States is currently using such strategic bargaining in its attempt to get the European Union to lower its restrictions on imports of U.S. agricultural goods. The U.S. Congress often threatens to restrict imports from the EU significantly if the EU doesn't ease its trade restrictions against U.S. goods. For example, in the late 1990s the United States imposed punitive tariffs totaling $100 million aimed to hurt a variety of European imports to the United States.

The problem with strategic trade policies is that they can backfire. One rule of strategic bargaining is that the other side must believe that you'll go through with your threat. Thus, strategic trade policy can lead a country that actually supports free trade to impose trade restrictions, just to show how strongly it believes in free trade.

Even though most economists support free trade, they admit that in bargaining it may be necessary to adopt a strategic position. A country may threaten to impose trade restrictions if the other country does so. When such strategic trade policies are successful, they end up eliminating or reducing trade restrictions.

When should trade restrictions be used, and when should they not be used for strategic purposes? Economic theory does not tell us. That question is part of the practice of the art of economics.

Specialized Production

My discussion of comparative advantage took it as a given that one country was inherently more productive than another country in producing certain goods. But when one looks at trading patterns, it's often not at all clear why particular countries have a productive advantage in certain goods. There's no inherent reason for Switzerland to specialize in the production of watches or for South Korea to specialize in the production of cars. Much in trade cannot be explained by inherent resource endowments.

Strategic bargaining can lead to higher gains from trade for the side that drives the hardest bargain, but it can also make the deal fall through.

Q.4 In strategic trade bargaining, it is reasonable to be unreasonable. True or false? Explain.

If they don't have inherent advantages, why are countries and places often so good at producing what they specialize in? Two important explanations are that they *learn by doing* and that *economies of scale* exist.

Learning by Doing **Learning by doing** means *becoming better at a task the more often you perform it*. Take watches in Switzerland. Initially production of watches in Switzerland may have been a coincidence; the person who started the watch business happened to live there. But then people in the area became skilled in producing watches. Their skill made it attractive for other watch companies to start up. As additional companies moved in, more and more members of the labor force became skilled at watchmaking, and word went out that Swiss watches were the best in the world. That reputation attracted even more producers, so Switzerland became the watchmaking capital of the world. Had the initial watch production occurred in Austria, not Switzerland, Austria might be the watch capital of the world.

When there's learning by doing, it's much harder to attribute inherent comparative advantage to a country. One must always ask: Does country A have an inherent comparative advantage, or does it simply have more experience? Once country B gets the experience, will country A's comparative advantage disappear? If it will, then country B has a strong reason to limit trade with country A in order to give its own workers time to catch up as they learn by doing.

Economies of Scale In determining whether an inherent comparative advantage exists, a second complication is **economies of scale**—*the situation in which costs per unit of output fall as output increases*. Many manufacturing industries (such as steel and autos) exhibit economies of scale. The existence of significant economies of scale means that it makes sense (that is, it lowers costs) for one country to specialize in one good and another country to specialize in another good. But who should specialize in what is unclear. Producers in a country can, and generally do, argue that if only the government will establish barriers, they'll be able to lower their costs per unit and eventually sell at lower costs than foreign producers.

A number of countries follow trade strategies to allow them to take advantage of economies of scale. For example, in the 1970s and 1980s Japan's government consciously directed investment into automobiles and high-tech consumer products, and significantly promoted exports in these goods to take advantage of economies of scale.

Most countries recognize the importance of learning by doing and economies of scale. A variety of trade restrictions are based on these two phenomena. The most common expression of the learning-by-doing and economies-of-scale insights is the **infant industry argument,** which is that *with initial protection, an industry will be able to become competitive*. Countries use this argument to justify many trade restrictions. They argue, "You may now have a comparative advantage, but that's simply because you've been at it longer, or are experiencing significant economies of scale. We need trade restrictions on our _____ industry to give it a chance to catch up. Once an infant industry grows up, then we can talk about eliminating the restrictions."

Macroeconomic Aspects of Trade

The comparative advantage argument for free trade assumes that a country's resources are fully utilized. When countries don't have full employment, imports can decrease domestic aggregate demand and increase unemployment. Exports can stimulate domestic aggregate demand and decrease unemployment. Thus, when an economy is in a recession, there is a strong macroeconomic reason to limit imports and encourage exports. These macroeconomic effects of free trade play an important role in the public's view of

---

Learning by doing means becoming better at a task the more you perform it.

19.2

In economies of scale, costs per unit of output go down as output increases.

Q.5 Is it efficient for a country to maintain a trade barrier in an industry that exhibits economies of scale?

The infant industry argument says that with initial protection, an industry will be able to become competitive.

imports and exports. When a country is in a recession, pressure to impose trade restrictions increases substantially.

National Security

Countries often justify trade restrictions on grounds of national security. These restrictions take two forms:

1. Export restrictions on strategic materials and defense-related goods.
2. Import restrictions on defense-related goods. For example, in a war we don't want to be dependent on oil from abroad.

For a number of goods, national security considerations make sense. For example, the United States restricts the sale of certain military items to countries that are likely to be fighting the United States someday. The problem is where to draw the line about goods having a national security consideration. Should countries protect domestic agriculture? All high-technology items, since they might be useful in weapons? All chemicals? Steel? The national security argument has been extended to a wide variety of goods whose importance to national security is indirect rather than direct. When a country makes a national security argument for trade, we must be careful to consider whether a domestic political reason may be lurking behind that argument.

International Politics

International politics frequently provides another reason for trade restrictions. The United States forbids trade with Cuba to punish that country for trying to extend its Marxist political and economic policies to other Latin American countries. Until 1991, the United States restricted exports to and imports from the Union of South Africa because it disapproved of South Africa's racist apartheid policies. U.S. grain exports to the Soviet Union were stopped in 1979 to protest the Soviet invasion of Afghanistan. The list can be extended, but you get the argument: Trade helps you, so we'll hurt you by stopping trade until you do what we want. So what if it hurts us too? It'll hurt you more than us.

Increased Revenue Brought In by Tariffs

A final argument made for one particular type of trade restriction—a tariff—is that tariffs bring in revenues. In the 19th century, tariffs were the U.S. government's primary source of revenue. They are less important as a source of revenue today for some developed countries because those countries have instituted other forms of taxes. However, tariffs remain a primary source of revenue for many developing countries. They're relatively easy to collect and are paid by people rich enough to afford imports. These countries justify many of their tariffs with the argument that they need the revenues.

WHY ECONOMISTS GENERALLY OPPOSE TRADE RESTRICTIONS

Each of the preceding arguments for trade restrictions has some validity, but most economists discount them and support free trade. The reason is that, in their considered judgment, the harm done by trade restrictions outweighs the benefits.

Economists' first argument for free trade is that, viewed from a global perspective, free trade increases total output. From a national perspective, economists agree that particular instances of trade restriction may actually help one nation, even as most other

Economists generally oppose trade restrictions because:

1. From a global perspective, free trade increases total output.
2. Trade restrictions lead to retaliation.
3. International trade provides competition for domestic companies.

Q.6 What was the long-run effect on the steel industry of the trade restrictions on the import of steel during the 1950s and 1960s?

Very few of the infant industries protected by trade restrictions have ever grown up.

19.3

Q.7 How can free trade improve national security?

Yes, some restrictions might benefit a country, but almost no country can limit its restrictions to the beneficial ones.

nations are hurt. But they argue that the country imposing trade restrictions can benefit *only if the other country doesn't retaliate* with trade restrictions of its own. Retaliation is the rule, not the exception, however, and when there is retaliation, trade restrictions cause both countries to lose.

A second reason most economists support free trade is that trade restrictions reduce international competition. International competition is desirable because it forces domestic companies to stay on their toes. If trade restrictions on imports are imposed, domestic companies don't work as hard, and they become less efficient. For example, in the 1950s and 1960s the United States imposed restrictions on imported steel. U.S. steel industries responded to this protection by raising their prices and channeling profits from their steel production into other activities. By the 1970s the U.S. steel industry was a mess, internationally uncompetitive, and using outdated equipment to produce overpriced steel. Instead of making the steel industry stronger, restrictions made it a flabby, uncompetitive industry.

Economists dispose of the infant industry argument by reference to the historical record. In theory the argument makes sense. But very few of the infant industries protected by trade restrictions have ever grown up. What tends to happen instead is that infant industries become dependent on the trade restrictions and use political pressure to keep that protection. As a result, they often remain immature and internationally uncompetitive. Most economists would support the infant industry argument only if the trade restrictions included definite conditions under which the restrictions would end.

Most economists agree with the national security argument for export restrictions on goods that are directly war related. Selling bombs to Iraq, with whom the United States was at war in early 1991, doesn't make much sense (although it should be noted that the United States did exactly that throughout the 1980s when the United States supported Iraq in its war with Iran).

Economists point out that the argument is often carried far beyond goods directly related to national security. For example, in the 1980s the United States restricted exports of sugar-coated cereals to the Soviet Union purportedly for reasons of national security. Sugar-frosted flakes may be great, but they were unlikely to help the Soviet Union start a war.

Another argument that economists give against the national security rationale is that trade restrictions on military sales can often be evaded. Countries simply have another country buy the goods for them. Such third-party sales—called *transshipments*—are common in international trade and limit the effectiveness of any absolute trade restrictions for national security purposes.

Economists also argue that by fostering international cooperation, international trade makes war less likely—a significant contribution to national security.

Economists' final argument against trade restrictions is: Yes, some restrictions might benefit a country, but almost no country can limit its restrictions to the beneficial ones. Trade restrictions are addictive—the more you have, the more you want. Thus, a majority of economists take the position that the best response to such addictive policies is "Just say no."

VARIETIES OF TRADE RESTRICTIONS

Let's now turn to the policies countries can use to restrict trade. These include tariffs, quotas, voluntary restraint agreements, embargoes, regulatory trade restrictions, and nationalistic appeals. I'll consider each in turn and also review the geometric analysis of each.

Table 19-2   Trade-Weighted Tariff Averages by Country after the Uruguay Round

These rates will be continually changing as the changes negotiated by the WTO come into effect.

Country	%	Country	%
Argentina	30.9	Mexico	33.7
Australia	12.2	New Zealand	11.3
Austria	7.1	Norway	2.0
Brazil	27.0	Peru	29.4
Canada	4.8	Phillipines	22.2
Chile	24.9	Poland	9.9
Colombia	35.1	Romania	33.9
Costa Rica	44.1	Senegal	13.8
Czech Rep.	3.8	Singapore	5.1
El Salvador	30.6	Slovak Rep.	3.8
European Union	3.6	South Africa	17.2
Finland	3.8	Sri Lanka	28.1
Hong Kong	0.0	Sweden	3.1
Hungary	6.9	Switzerland	1.5
Iceland	11.5	Thailand	28.0
India	32.4	Tunisia	34.1
Indonesia	36.9	Turkey	22.3
Jamaica	50.0	United States	3.5
Japan	1.7	Uruguay	30.9
Korea Rep.	8.3	Venezuala	30.9
Macau	0.0	Zimbabwe	4.6
Malaysia	9.1		

Source: General Agreement on Tariffs and Trade (GATT), The Results of the Uruguay Round of Multilateral Trade Negotiations, November, 1994. (http://www.wto.org)

Tariffs

Tariffs are *taxes governments place on internationally traded goods*—generally imports. (Tariffs are also called *customs duties*.) Tariffs are the most-used and most-familiar type of trade restriction. Tariffs operate in the same way a tax does: They make imported goods relatively more expensive than they otherwise would have been, and thereby encourage the consumption of domestically produced goods. On average, U.S. tariffs raise the price of imported goods by about 3 percent. Table 19-2 presents average tariff rates for industrial goods for a number of countries and the European Union.

Probably the most infamous tariff in U.S. history is the Smoot-Hawley Tariff of 1930, which raised tariffs on imported goods an average of 60 percent. It was passed at the height of the Great Depression in the United States in the hope of protecting American jobs. It didn't work. Other countries responded with similar tariffs. As a result of these trade wars, international trade plummeted from $60 billion in 1928 to $25 billion in 1938, unemployment worsened, and the international depression deepened. These effects of the tariff convinced many, if not most, economists that free trade is preferable to trade restrictions.

The dismal failure of the Smoot-Hawley Tariff was the main reason the **General Agreement on Tariffs and Trade (GATT),** *a regular international conference to reduce trade barriers,* was established in 1947 immediately following World War II. In 1995 GATT was replaced by the **World Trade Organization (WTO),** *an organization whose functions are generally the same as GATT's—to promote free and fair trade among countries.* Unlike GATT,

Three policies used to restrict trade are:

1. Tariffs (taxes on internationally traded goods).
2. Quotas (quantity limits placed on imports).
3. Regulatory trade restrictions (government-imposed procedural rules that limit imports).

the WTO is a permanent organization with an enforcement system (albeit weak). Since then, rounds of negotiations have resulted in a decline in worldwide tariffs.

Quotas

A quota limiting foreign quantity supplied to Q_1 is the equivalent of a tariff of T.

Q.8 What is the difference between a tariff and a quota?

Quotas are *quantity limits placed on imports*. Their effect in limiting trade is similar to the effect of a tariff. Chapter 5 showed the geometry of quotas and tariffs. The results of tariffs and quotas in terms of price and quantity are the same, as you can see in the graph in the margin. (If the graph doesn't look familiar, I suggest a review of Chapter 5.)

The issues involved with tariffs and quotas can be seen in a slightly different way than in Chapter 5 by assuming our country is small relative to the world economy, and that imports compete with domestic producers. The small-country assumption means that the supply from the world to this country is perfectly elastic at the world price, $2, as in Figure 19-1(a).

The world price of the good is unaffected by this country's demand. This assumption allows us to distinguish the world supply from domestic supply. In the absence of any trade restrictions, the world price of $2 would be the domestic price. Domestic low-cost suppliers would supply 100 units of the good at $2. The remaining 100 units demanded are being imported.

In Figure 19-1(a) I show the effect of a tariff of 50 cents placed on all imports. Since the world supply curve is perfectly elastic, all of this tax, shown by the shaded region, is borne by domestic consumers. Price rises to $2.50 and quantity demanded falls to 175. With a tariff, the rise in price will increase domestic quantity supplied from 100 to 125, and will reduce imports to 50. Now let's compare this situation with a quota of 50,

---

Figure 19-1 (a and b)   Foreign Supply of a Good When the Domestic Country Is Small

This exhibit shows the effects of a tariff in (a) and of a quota in (b) when the domestic country is small. The small-country assumption means that the world supply is perfectly elastic, in this case at $2.00 a unit. With a tariff of 50 cents, world supply shifts up by 50 cents. Domestic quantity demanded falls to 175 and domestic quantity supplied rises to 125. Foreign suppliers are left supplying the difference, 50 units. The domestic government collects revenue shown in the shaded area. The figure in (b) shows how the same result can be achieved with a quota of 50. Equilibrium price rises to $2.50. Domestic firms produce 125 units and consumers demand 175 units. The difference between the tariff and the quota is that, with a tariff, the domestic government collects the revenue from the higher price. With a quota, the benefits of the higher price accrue to the foreign and domestic producers.

(a) With a tariff

(b) With a quota

shown in Figure 19-1(b). Under a quota of 50, the final price would be the same, but higher revenue would accrue not to the government but instead to foreign and domestic producers. One final difference: Any increase in demand under a quota would result in higher prices because it would have to be filled by domestic producers. Under a tariff, any increase in demand would not affect price.

19.4

Voluntary Restraint Agreements

Imposing new tariffs and quotas is specifically ruled out by the WTO, but foreign countries know that WTO rules are voluntary and that, if a domestic industry brought sufficient political pressure on its government, the WTO would be forgotten. To avoid the imposition of new tariffs on their goods, countries often voluntarily restrict their exports. That's why Japan has agreed informally to limit the number of cars it exports to the United States.

The effect of such voluntary restraint agreements is similar to the effect of quotas: They directly limit the quantity of imports, increasing the price of the good and helping domestic producers. For example, when the United States encouraged Japan to impose "voluntary" quotas on exports of its cars to the United States, Toyota benefited from the quotas because it could price its limited supply of cars higher than it could if it sent in a large number of cars, so profit per car would be high. Since they faced less competition, U.S. car companies also benefited. They could increase their prices because Toyota had done so.

Voluntary restraint agreements are often not all that voluntary.

Embargoes

An **embargo** is *a total restriction on import or export of a good*. Embargoes are usually established for international political reasons rather than for primarily economic reasons.

An example is the U.S. embargo of trade with Iraq. The U.S. government hoped that the embargo would so severely affect Iraq's economy that Saddam Hussein would lose political power. It did make life difficult for Iraqis, but it didn't bring about the downfall of the Hussein government.

An embargo is a total restriction on import or export of a good.

Regulatory Trade Restrictions

Tariffs, quotas, and embargoes are the primary *direct* methods to restrict international trade. There are also indirect methods that restrict trade in not-so-obvious ways; these are called **regulatory trade restrictions** (*government-imposed procedural rules that limit imports*). One type of regulatory trade restriction has to do with protecting the health and safety of a country's residents. For example, a country might restrict imports of all vegetables grown where certain pesticides are used, knowing full well that all other countries use those pesticides. The effect of such a regulation would be to halt the import of vegetables.

A second type of regulatory restriction involves making import and customs procedures so intricate and time-consuming that importers simply give up. For example, France requires all imported VCRs to be individually inspected in Toulouse. Since Toulouse is a provincial city, far from any port and outside the normal route for imports after they enter France, the inspection process can take months.

Some regulatory restrictions are imposed for legitimate reasons; others are designed simply to make importing more difficult and hence protect domestic producers from international competition. It's often hard to tell the difference. A good example of this difficulty occurred in 1988, when the EU disallowed all imports of meat from animals that had been fed growth-inducing hormones, as the accompanying box details.

Q.9 How might a country benefit from having an inefficient customs agency?

Some regulatory restrictions are imposed for legitimate reasons; others are designed simply to make importing more difficult.

Trade restrictions, in practice, are often much more complicated than they seem in textbooks. Seldom does a country say, "We're limiting imports to protect our home producers." Instead the country explains the restrictions in a more politically acceptable way. Consider the fight between the European Union (EU) and the United States over U.S. meat exports. In 1988 the EU, in line with Union-wide internal requirements, banned all imports of any meat from animals treated with growth-inducing hormones, which U.S. meat producers use extensively. The result: the EU banned the meat exported from the United States.

The EU claimed that it had imposed the ban only because of public health concerns. The United States claimed that the ban was actually a trade restriction, pointing out that its own residents ate this kind of meat with confidence because a U.S. government agency had certified that the levels of hormones in the meat were far below any danger level.

The United States retaliated against the EU by imposing 100 percent tariffs on Danish and West German hams, Italian tomatoes, and certain other foods produced by EU member nations. The EU threatened to respond by placing 100 percent tariffs on $100 million worth of U.S. walnuts and dried fruits, but instead entered into bilateral meetings with the United States. Those meetings allowed untreated meats into the EU for human consumption and treated meats that would be used as dog food. In response, the United States removed its retaliatory tariff on hams and tomato sauce, but retained its tariffs on many other goods. In the 1990s, Europe's dog population seemed to be growing exponentially as Europe's imports of "dog food" increased by leaps and bounds. In 1996 the United States asked the WTO to review the EU ban. It did so in 1997, finding in favor of the United States. In 1999 the WTO stood by its earlier ruling and the United States reimposed the 100 percent tariffs.

Which side is right in this dispute? The answer is far from obvious. Both the United States and the EU have potentially justifiable positions. As I said, trade restrictions are more complicated in reality than in textbooks.

Nationalistic Appeals

Finally, nationalistic appeals can help to restrict international trade. "Buy American" campaigns and Japanese xenophobia[1] are examples. Many Americans, given two products of equal appeal except that one is made in the United States and one is made in a foreign country, would buy the U.S. product. To get around this tendency, foreign and U.S. companies often go to great lengths to get a MADE IN THE U.S.A. classification on goods they sell in the United States. For example, components for many autos are made in Japan but shipped to the United States and assembled in Ohio or Tennessee so that the finished car can be called an American product.

FREE TRADE ASSOCIATIONS

Most politicians feel a strong push from constituents to impose trade barriers. Even politicians who accept free trade in principle support restrictions in practice. They have, however, found it possible to support a limited type of free trade in which a few countries agree to have free trade with each other. A **free trade association** (or *customs union*) is a *group of countries that allows free trade among its members and, as a group, puts up common barriers against all other countries' goods.*

A free trade association is a group of countries that allows free trade among its members and puts up common barriers against all other countries' goods.

The European Union (EU) is the most famous free trade association. All barriers to trade among the EU's member countries were removed in 1992. In the coming decade more European countries can be expected to join the EU. In 1993, the United States and Canada agreed to enter into a similar free trade union, and they, together with Mexico, created the North American Free Trade Association (NAFTA). Under

---

[1]*Xenophobia* is a Greek word meaning "fear of foreigners." Pronounce the *x* like *z*.

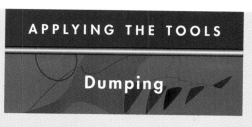

APPLYING THE TOOLS

Dumping

The WTO allows countries to impose trade restrictions on imports if they can show that the goods are being dumped. *Dumping* is selling a good in a foreign country at a lower price than in the country where it's produced. On the face of it, who could complain about someone who wants to sell you a good cheaply? Why not just take advantage of the bargain price? The first objection is the learning-by-doing argument. To stay competitive, a country must keep on producing. Dumping by another country can force domestic producers out of business. Having eliminated the competition, the foreign producer has the field to itself and can raise the price. Thus, dumping can be a form of predatory pricing.

The second argument against dumping involves the short-term macroeconomic and political effects it can have on the importing country. Even if one believes that dumping is not a preliminary to predatory pricing, it can displace workers in the importing country, causing political pressure on that government to institute trade restrictions. If that country's economy is in a recession, the resulting unemployment will have substantial macroeconomic repercussions, so pressure for trade restrictions will be amplified.

NAFTA, tariffs and other trade barriers among these countries are being gradually reduced. Some other trading associations include Mercosur (among South American countries) and Asean (among Southeast Asian countries).

Economists have mixed reactions to free trade associations. They see free trade as beneficial, but are concerned about the possibility that these regional free trade associations will impose significant trade restrictions on nonmember countries. They also believe that bilateral negotiations between member nations will replace multilateral efforts among members and nonmembers. Whether the net effect of these bilateral negotiations is positive or negative remains to be seen.

One way countries strengthen trading relationships among groups of countries is through a most-favored-nation status. The term **most-favored nation** refers to *a country that will be charged as low a tariff on its exports as any other country.* Thus, if the United States lowers tariffs on goods imported from Japan, which has most-favored-nation status with the United States, it must lower tariffs on those same types of goods imported from any other country with most-favored-nation status.

This status is often used as a bargaining tool to gain political or economic concessions from the country desiring the most-favored-nation status. In the 1990s the United States reviewed China's most-favored-nation status almost annually in an effort to correct China's human rights violations and intellectual property rights encroachments.

Q-10 What is economists' view of limited free trade associations such as the EU or NAFTA?

A most-favored nation is a country that will pay as low a tariff on its exports as will any other country.

CONCLUSION

International trade will become more and more important for the United States. With international transportation and communication becoming easier and faster, and with other countries' economies growing, the U.S. economy will inevitably become more interdependent with the other economies of the world. As international trade becomes more important, the push for trade restrictions will likely increase. Various countries' strategic trade policies will likely conflict, and the world will find itself on the verge of an international trade war that would benefit no one.

Concern about that possibility leads most economists to favor free trade. As often happens, economists advise politicians to follow a politically unpopular policy—to take the hard course of action. Whether politicians follow economists' advice or whether they follow the politically popular policy will play a key role in determining the course of the U.S. economy in the 2000s.

Chapter Summary

- According to the principle of comparative advantage, as long as the relative opportunity costs of producing goods (what must be given up in one good in order to get another good) differ among countries, there are potential gains from trade, even if one country has an absolute advantage in everything.

- Three insights into the terms of trade include:
  1. The more competition exists in international trade, the less the trader gets and the more the involved countries get.
  2. Once competition prevails, smaller countries tend to get a larger percentage of the gains from trade than do larger countries.
  3. Gains from trade go to countries that produce goods that exhibit economies of scale.

- Reasons that countries impose trade restrictions include unequal internal distribution of the gains from trade, hag-

gling by companies over the gains from trade, haggling by countries over trade restrictions, learning by doing and economies of scale, macroeconomic aspects of trade, national security, international political reasons, and increased revenue brought in by tariffs.

- Economists generally oppose trade restrictions because of the history of trade restrictions and their understanding of the advantages of free trade.

- Trade restrictions include: tariffs, quotas, embargoes, voluntary restraint agreements, regulatory trade restrictions, and nationalistic appeals.

- Free trade associations help trade by reducing barriers to trade among member nations. Free trade associations could hinder trade by building up barriers to trade with nations outside the association; negotiations among members could replace multilateral efforts to reduce trade restrictions among members and nonmembers.

Key Terms

economies of scale (412)
embargo (417)
free trade association (418)
General Agreement on Tariffs and Trade (GATT) (415)
infant industry argument (412)
learning by doing (412)
most-favored nation (419)
principle of comparative advantage (406)
quotas (416)
regulatory trade restrictions (417)
strategic bargaining (411)
tariffs (415)
trade adjustment assistance programs (410)
World Trade Organization (WTO) (415)

Questions for Thought and Review

1. Widgetland has 60 workers. Each worker can produce 4 widgets or 4 wadgets. Each resident in Widgetland currently consumes 2 widgets and 2 wadgets. Wadgetland also has 60 workers. Each can produce 3 widgets or 12 wadgets. Wadgetland's residents consume 1 widget and 9 wadgets. Is there a basis for trade? If so, offer the countries a deal they can't refuse.

2. Why does competition among traders affect how much of the gains to trade are given to the countries involved in the trade?

3. Why do smaller countries usually get most of the gains from trade? What are some reasons why a small country might not get the gains of trade?

4. Which country will get the larger gain from trade—a country with economies of scale or diseconomies of scale? Explain your answer.

5. Suggest an equitable method of funding trade adjustment assistance programs. Why is it equitable? What problems might a politician have in implementing such a method?

6. If you were economic adviser to a country that was following your advice about trade restrictions and that country fell into a recession, would you change your advice? Why, or why not?

7. The U.S. trade balance improved significantly in 1991 when the U.S. economy went into recession. Is this consistent with economic predictions? Why or why not?

8. What are two reasons economists support free trade?

9. Demonstrate graphically how the effects of a tariff differ from the effects of a quota.

10. How do the effects of voluntary restraint agreements differ from the effects of a tariff? How are they the same?

11 Mexico exports many vegetables to the United States. These vegetables are grown using chemicals that are not allowed in U.S. vegetable agriculture. Should the United States restrict imports of Mexican vegetables? Why or why not?

12. When the United States placed a temporary price floor on tomatoes imported from Mexico, U.S. trade representative Mickey Kantor said, "The agreement will pro-vide strong relief to the tomato growers in Florida and other states, and help preserve jobs in the industry." What costs did Americans bear from the price floor?

13. A study by the World Bank on the effects of Mercosur, a regional trade pact among four Latin American countries, concluded that free trade agreements "might confer significant benefits, but there are also significant dangers." What are those benefits and dangers?

Problems and Exercises

1. Suppose there are two states that do not trade—Iowa and Nebraska. Each state produces the same two goods—corn and wheat. For Iowa the opportunity cost of producing 1 bushel of wheat is 3 bushels of corn. For Nebraska the opportunity cost of producing 1 bushel of corn is 3 bushels of wheat. At present, Iowa produces 20 million bushels of wheat and 120 million bushels of corn, while Nebraska produces 20 million bushels of corn and 120 million bushels of wheat.
   a. Explain how, with trade, Nebraska can end up with 40 million bushels of wheat and 120 million bushels of corn while Iowa can end up with 40 million bushels of corn and 120 million bushels of wheat.
   b. If the states ended up with the numbers given in a, how much would the trader get?

2. Country A can produce, at most, 40 olives or 20 pickles, or some combination of olives and pickles such as the 20 olives and 10 pickles it is currently producing. Country B can produce, at most, 120 olives or 60 pickles, or some combination of olives and pickles such as the 100 olives and 50 pickles it is currently producing.
   a. Is there a basis for trade? If so, offer the two countries a deal they can't refuse.
   b. How would your answer to a change if you knew that there were economies of scale in the production of pickles and olives rather than the production possibilities described in the question? Why? If your answer is yes, which country would you have produce which good?

3. The world price of textiles is P_w, as in the accompanying figure of the domestic supply and demand for textiles.

The government imposes a tariff t, to protect the domestic producers. For this tariff:
   a. Shade in the gains to domestic producers.
   b. Shade in the revenue to government.
   c. Shade in the costs to domestic producers.
   d. Are the gains greater than the costs? Why?

4. In 1998 the hourly cost to employers per German industrial worker was $27.20. The hourly cost to employers per U.S. industrial worker was $18.56, while the average cost per Taiwanese industrial worker was $5.24.
   a. Give three reasons why firms produce in Germany rather than in a lower-wage country.
   b. Germany has just entered into an agreement with other EU countries that allows people in any EU country, including Greece and Italy, which have lower wage rates, to travel and work in any EU country, including high-wage countries. Would you expect a significant movement of workers from Greece and Italy to Germany right away? Why or why not?
   c. Workers in Thailand are paid significantly less than workers in Taiwan. If you were a company CEO, what other information would you want before you decided where to establish a new production facility?

5. Peter Sutherland, the director-general of GATT, published a pamphlet on the costs of trade protection. He subtitled the pamphlet "The Sting: How Governments Buy Votes on Trade with the Consumer's Money."
   a. What does he likely mean by this subtitle?
   b. If a government is out to increase votes with its trade policy, would it more likely institute tariffs or quotas? Why?

6. One of the basic economic laws is "the law of one price." It says that given certain assumptions one would expect that if free trade is allowed, the price of goods in countries should converge.
   a. Can you list what three of those assumptions likely are?
   b. Should the law of one price hold for labor also? Why or why not?
   c. Should it hold for capital more so or less so than for labor? Why or why not?

Web Questions

1. Go to the WTO's home page at www.wto.org to find out how trade disputes are settled.
   a. What is the procedure for settling disputes?
   b. What is the timetable for the settlement procedure?
   c. What happens if one of the countries does not abide by the settlement?

2. Two of the free trade associations mentioned in the chapter were Asean (www.aseansec.org) and Mercosur (www.americasnet.com/mauritz/mercosur/english/). Go to their home pages and answer the following questions for each:
   a. What countries belong to the trade association?
   b. When was the association established?
   c. What is the association's stated objective?
   d. What is the combined gross domestic product of all members?

Answers to Margin Questions

1. I.T. ended up with 380 tons of food and 380 barrels of oil after the trade.   *(406)*

2. The percentage of gains of trade that goes to a country depends upon change in the price of the goods being traded. If trade led to no change in prices in a small country, then that small country would get no gains from trade. Another case in which a small country gets a small percentage of the gains from trade would occur when its larger trading partner was producing a good with economies of scale and the small country was not. A third case is when the traders who extracted most of the surplus or gains from trade come from the larger country; then the small country would end up with few of the gains from trade.   *(408)*

3. The EU places high barriers against agricultural products to protect its farmers. As in the case with many of the international trade barriers, this is primarily for political, not economic, purposes.   *(410)*

4. True. In strategic trade bargaining it is reasonable to be unreasonable. The belief of the other bargainer that you will be unreasonable leads you to be able to extract larger gains from trade. Of course, this leads to the logical paradox that if "unreasonable" is "reasonable," unreasonable really is reasonable, so it is only reasonable to be reasonable. Sorting out that last statement can be left for a philosophy or logic class.   *(411)*

5. Whether or not it is efficient for a country to maintain barriers to trade in an industry that exhibits economies of scale depends upon the marginal costs and marginal benefits of maintaining those barriers. Having significant economies of scale does mean that average costs of production will be lower; however, trade restrictions might mean that the industry might be able to inflate its costs.   *(412)*

6. The U.S. steel industry became internationally uncompetitive and produced overpriced steel. The restrictions produced an uncompetitive industry.   *(414)*

7. Free trade fosters international cooperation, making war less likely.   *(414)*

8. A tariff is a type of tax that the government places on internationally traded goods. A quota is a quantity restriction that a country places on internationally traded goods.   *(416)*

9. An inefficient customs agency can operate with the same effect as a trade restriction, and if trade restrictions would help the country then it is possible that an inefficient customs agency could also help the country.   *(417)*

10. Most economists have a mixed view of limited free trade associations such as NAFTA or the EU. While they see free trade as beneficial, they are concerned about the possibility that these limited trade associations will impose trade restrictions on nonmember countries. Whether the net effect of these will be positive or negative is a complicated issue.   *(419)*

APPENDIX A

The Geometry of Absolute Advantage and Comparative Advantage

The chapter briefly went through an example of the gains of trade. This appendix presents that same example geometrically, together with another example. In doing so it contrasts the concept of absolute advantage with the concept of comparative advantage.

WHY DO NATIONS TRADE?

International trade exists for the same reason that all trade exists: Party A has something that party B wants and party B has something that party A wants. Both parties can be made better off by trade.

The Principle of Absolute Advantage

Trade between countries in different types of goods is relatively easy to explain. For example, trade in raw materials and agricultural goods for manufactured goods can be easily explained by the **principle of absolute advantage:**

> A country that can produce a good at a lower cost than another country is said to have an absolute advantage in the production of that good. When two countries have absolute advantages in different goods, there are gains of trade to be had.

The principle of absolute advantage explains trade of, say, oil from Saudi Arabia for food from the United States. Saudi Arabia has millions of barrels of easily available oil, but growing food in its desert climate and sandy soil is expensive. The United States can grow food cheaply in its temperate climate and fertile soil, but its oil isn't as easily available or as cheap to extract. Because it can produce a certain amount of oil with fewer resources, Saudi Arabia has an absolute advantage over the United States in producing oil. Because it can produce a certain amount of food with fewer resources, the United States has an absolute advantage over Saudi Arabia in producing food. When each country specializes in the good it has an absolute advantage in, both countries can gain from trade.

In Figure A19-1, I consider a hypothetical numerical example that demonstrates how the principle of absolute advantage can lead to gains from trade. For simplicity, I assume constant opportunity costs.

Figures A19-1(b) and (d) show the choices for the United States; Figures A19-1(a) and (c) show the choices for Saudi Arabia. In Figures A19-1(a) and (b) you see that the United States and Saudi Arabia can produce various combinations of food and oil by devoting differing percentages of their resources to producing each. Comparing the two tables and assuming the resources in the two countries are comparable, we see that Saudi Arabia has an absolute advantage in the production of oil and the United States has an absolute advantage in the production of food.

For example, when the United States and Saudi Arabia devote equal amounts of resources to oil production, Saudi Arabia can produce 10 times as much as the United States. Alternatively, when the United States devotes 60 percent of a given amount of resources to oil production,

it gets 60 barrels of oil. But when Saudi Arabia devotes 60 percent of that same amount of resources to oil production, it gets 600 barrels of oil. The information in the tables is presented graphically in Figures A19-1(c) and (d). These graphs represent the two countries' production possibility curves without trade. Each combination of numbers in the table corresponds to a point on the curve. For example, point B in each graph corresponds to the entries in row B, columns 2 and 3, in the relevant table.

Let's assume that, without any international trade, the United States has chosen point C (production of 60 barrels of oil and 400 tons of food) and Saudi Arabia has chosen point D (production of 400 barrels of oil and 60 tons of food).

Now I.T. (International Trader), who understands the principle of absolute advantage, comes along and offers the following deal to Saudi Arabia:

> If you produce 1,000 barrels of oil and no food (point A) and give me 500 barrels of oil while keeping 500 barrels for yourself, I guarantee you 120 tons of food, double the amount of food you're now getting. I'll put you on point G, which is totally above your current production possibility curve. You'll get more oil and more food. It's an offer you can't refuse.

I.T. then flies off to the United States, to whom he makes the following offer:

> If you produce 1,000 tons of food and no oil (point F) and give me 500 tons of food while keeping 500 tons for yourself, I'll guarantee you 120 barrels of oil, double the amount you're now getting. I'll put you on point H, which is totally above your current production possibility curve. You'll get more oil and have more food. It's an offer you can't refuse.

Both countries accept; they'd be foolish not to. So the two countries' final consumption positions are as follows:

	Oil (barrels)	Food (tons)
Total production	1,000	1,000
U.S. consumption	120	500
Saudi consumption	500	120
I.T.'s profit	380	380

For arranging the trade, I.T. makes a handsome profit of 380 tons of food and 380 barrels of oil.

I.T. has become rich because he understands the principle of absolute advantage. Unfortunately for I.T., the principle of absolute advantage is easy to understand, which means that he will quickly face competition. Other international traders come in and offer the countries even better deals than I.T. offered, squeezing his share. With

Figure A19-1 (a, b, c, and d)   Absolute Advantage: The United States and Saudi Arabia

Looking at tables (**a**) and (**b**), you can see that if Saudi Arabia devotes all its resources to oil, it can produce 1,000 barrels of oil, but if it devotes all of its resources to food, it can produce only 100 tons of food. For the United States, the story is the opposite: devoting all of its resources to oil, the United States can only produce 100 barrels of oil—10 times less than Saudi Arabia—but if it devotes all of its resources to food, it can produce 1,000 tons of food—10 times more than Saudi Arabia. Assuming resources are comparable, Saudi Arabia has an absolute advantage in the production of oil, and the United States has an absolute advantage in the production of food. The information in the tables is presented graphically in (**c**) and (**d**). These are the countries' production possibility curves without trade. Each point on each country's curve corresponds to a row on that country's table.

Percentage of resources devoted to oil	Oil produced (barrels)	Food produced (tons)	Row
100%	1,000	0	A
80	800	20	B
60	600	40	C
40	400	60	D
20	200	80	E
0	0	100	F

(a) Saudi Arabia's production possibility table

Percentage of resources devoted to oil	Oil produced (barrels)	Food produced (tons)	Row
100%	100	0	A
80	80	200	B
60	60	400	C
40	40	600	D
20	20	800	E
0	0	1,000	F

(b) United States' production possibility table

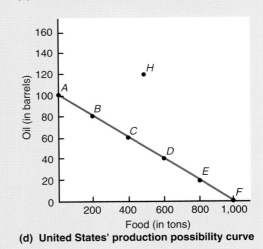

(c) Saudi Arabia's production possibility curve

(d) United States' production possibility curve

free entry and competition in international trade, eventually I.T.'s share is squeezed down to his costs plus a normal return for his efforts.

Now obviously this hypothetical example significantly overemphasizes the gains a trader makes. Generally the person arranging the trade must compete with other traders and offer both countries a better deal than the one presented here. But the person who first recognizes a trading opportunity often makes a sizable fortune. The second and third persons who recognize the opportunity make smaller fortunes. Once the insight is generally recognized, the possibility of making a fortune is gone. Traders still make their normal returns, but the instantaneous fortunes are not to be made without new insight. In the long run, benefits of trade go to the producers and consumers in the trading countries, not the traders.

I.T. realizes this and spends part of his fortune on buying a Greek island, where he retires to contemplate more deeply the nature of international trade so he can triple his remaining fortune. He marries, has a daughter whom

Table A19-1   Germany's Comparative Advantage over Algeria in the Production of Autos and Food

(a) Germany				(b) Algeria			
% of Resources Devoted to Autos	Autos Produced	Food Produced	Row	% of Resources Devoted to Autos	Autos Produced	Food Produced	Row
100%	100	0	A	100%	20	0	A
80	80	40	B	80	16	1	B
60	60	80	C	60	12	2	C
40	40	120	D	40	8	3	D
20	20	160	E	20	4	4	E
0	0	200	F	0	0	5	F

he names I.T. Too, and dies. But before he dies he teaches his daughter about international trade and how new insights can lead to fortunes. His dying words to his daughter are "Keep searching for that new insight."

The Principle of Comparative Advantage

Many years pass. I.T. Too grows up, and one day, while walking along the beach, she contemplates the possibilities of trade between Germany and Algeria in automobiles and food. No other traders have considered trade between these two countries because Germany is so much more productive than Algeria in all goods. No trade is currently taking place because Germany has an absolute advantage in production of both autos and food. Assuming the resources in the two countries are comparable, this case can be seen in Table A19-1.

But I.T. Too is bright. She remembers what her father taught her about opportunity costs back in her first economics lesson. She reasons as follows: Germany's opportunity cost of producing an auto is 2/1. That means Germany must give up 2 tons of food to get 1 additional auto. For example, if Germany is initially producing 60 autos and 80 tons of food, if it cuts production of autos by 20, it will increase its food output by 40. For each car lost, Germany gains 2 tons of food. When Algeria cuts its production of autos by 4, it gains 1 ton of food. Algeria's opportunity cost of producing another auto is 1/4. It must give up 1 ton of food to get an additional 4 autos.

I.T. Too further reasons that if Algeria needs to give up only 1/4 unit of food to get an auto while Germany needs to give up 2 tons of food to produce 1 auto, there are potential gains to be made, which can be split up among the countries and herself. Then, like her father before her, she can make the countries offers they can't refuse. She walks

the beach mulling the following: "*Absolute advantage* is not necessary for trade; *comparative advantage* is." A smile comes over her face; she understands.

Flying happily over the Mediterranean Sea, she formulates her insight precisely. She calls it the **principle of comparative advantage**: *As long as the relative opportunity costs of producing goods (what must be given up in one good in order to get another good) differ among countries, there are potential gains from trade, even if one country has an absolute advantage in everything.*

It is comparative advantage, not absolute advantage, that forms a basis of trade. If one country has a comparative advantage in one good, the other country must, by definition, have a comparative advantage in the other good.

Having formulated her idea, she applies it to the Germans and Algerians. She sees that, unexpectedly, Germany has a comparative advantage in producing food and Algeria has a comparative advantage in producing cars. With this insight firmly in mind, she leaves her island, flies to Germany, and makes the Germans the following offer:

> You're currently producing and consuming 60 autos and 80 tons of food (row C of Table A19-1(a)). If you'll produce only 48 autos but 104 tons of food and give me 22 tons of food, I'll guarantee you 13 autos for those 22 tons of food. You'll have more autos (61) and more food (82). It's an offer you can't refuse.

She then goes to Algeria and presents the Algerians with the following offer:

> You're currently producing 4 tons of food and 4 automobiles (row E of Table A19-1(b)). If you'll produce only automobiles (row A) and turn out 20 autos, keeping 5 for yourself and giving 15 of them to me,

I'll guarantee you 5 tons of food for the 15 autos. You'll have more autos (5) and more food (5). It's an offer you can't refuse.

Neither Germany nor Algeria can refuse. They both agree to I.T. Too's offer. The final position appears as follows:

	Autos	Food
Total production	68	104
Germany consumption	61	82
Algerian consumption	5	5
I.T. Too's profit	2	17

I.T. Too then proceeds to visit various other countries, making similar offers. They accept the offers because it's in their interest to accept them. Countries (and people) trade because trade benefits them.

As was the case with her father, her initial returns are the greatest. Then, as other people recognize the principle of comparative advantage and offer the countries better deals than hers, her share shrinks until her return just covers her opportunity cost and the costs of transporting the goods. But because the principle of comparative advantage is more difficult to understand than the principle of absolute advantage, the competing traders enter in much more slowly. Her above-normal returns last longer than did her father's, but eventually they're competed away. When her profits declines to only normal levels, she sells out and retires.

Competitiveness, Exchange Rates, and Comparative Advantage

In microeconomics, most of our analysis is conducted in real terms without reference to a numeraire (price level) or exchange rate. These financial issues are traditionally covered in macroeconomics, where the study of money and financial issues is a central focus. Money and financial markets are necessary to make trade and payment imbalances possible. However, it would be inappropriate to not at least mention those issues here, since exchange rates play a central role in determining a country's absolute advantage. In fact, without implicit exchange rates, absolute advantage cannot be determined.

In turn, absolute advantage plays a big role in whether a country can have a temporary trade surplus or trade deficit—phenomena that we ruled out by assumption in this micro analysis of trade so that we keep the presentation challenging, but learnable. In micro, trade surpluses or deficits are not considered.

Generally a low exchange rate encourages exports from a country and discourages imports; a high exchange rate discourages exports and encourages imports. An example of the importance of exchange rates can be seen by considering the United States and Japan: in the mid-1980s a dollar bought 200 yen, but in the mid-1990s the dollar bought only 100 yen. That change halved the absolute advantage of Japan and significantly discouraged our consumption of Japanese products. The resurgence of the U.S. auto industry was in large part due to that change in the exchange rate.

Key Terms

principle of absolute advantage   *(423)*

principle of comparative advantage   *(425)*

Questions for Thought and Review

1. Suppose that two countries, Machineland and Farmland, have the following production possibility curves.

Machineland

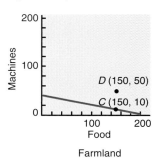

Farmland

a. Explain how these two countries can move from points *A* and *C*, where they currently are, to points *B* and *D*.
b. If possible, state by how much total production for the two countries has risen.
c. If you were a trader, how much of the gains from trade would you deserve for discovering this trade?
d. If there were economies of scale in the production of both goods, how would your analysis change?

2. Suppose Greece and France each produced only Kalamata olives and Roquefort cheese. Their production possibility curves are given in the following tables:

Greece

% of Resources Devoted to Olives	Olives Produced (millions of olives)	Roquefort Produced (thousands of pounds)
100%	500	0
80	400	100
60	300	200
40	200	300
20	100	400
0	0	500

France

% of Resources Devoted to Olives	Olives Produced (millions of olives)	Roquefort Produced (thousands of pounds)
100%	200	0
80	160	10
60	120	20
40	80	30
20	40	40
0	0	50

Currently, contrary to expectations, Greece produces 300 million olives and 200,000 pounds of Roquefort, while France produces 40 million olives and 40,000 pounds of Roquefort.

a. What is the opportunity cost of producing olives in each country? What is the opportunity cost of producing Roquefort in each country?

b. The European Commission rules that traditional foods have trademark protection. Only Roquefort made in France can be Roquefort and only olives produced in Greece can be Kalamata olives. Now Greece and France, following the new ruling, must each produce their respective trademarked goods and trade. Are they made better off? Why?

c. Show your answer graphically by selecting points now attainable that were previously not attainable.

3. Suppose there are two countries, Busytown and Lazyasiwannabe, with the following production possibility tables:

Busytown

% of Resources Devoted to Cars	Cars Produced (thousands)	Gourmet Meals Produced (thousands)
100%	60	0
80	48	10
60	36	20
40	24	30
20	12	40
0	0	50

Lazyasiwannabe

% of Resources Devoted to Cars	Cars Produced (thousands)	Gourmet Meals Produced (thousands)
100%	50	0
80	40	10
60	30	20
40	20	30
20	10	40
0	0	50

a. Draw the production possibility curves for each country.

b. Which country has the absolute advantage in producing cars? In producing gourmet meals?

c. Which country has the comparative advantage in producing cars? In producing gourmet meals?

d. Suppose each country specializes in the production of one good. Explain how Busytown can end up with 36,000 cars and 22,000 meals and Lazyasiwannabe can end up with 28,000 meals and 24,000 cars.

Who Gets What?
The Distribution of Income

20

After reading this chapter, you should be able to:

- State what a Lorenz curve is.

- Explain how the poverty definition is both an absolute and a relative measure.

- Discuss U.S. income inequality in a global context.

- Summarize the statistical findings on income and wealth distribution.

- State two alternative ways to describe income distribution.

- Explain three problems in determining whether an equal income distribution is fair.

- List three side effects of redistributing income.

- Summarize the U.S. tax and expenditure programs to redistribute income.

> *"God must love the poor," said Lincoln, "or he wouldn't have made so many of them." He must love the rich, or he wouldn't divide so much mazuma among so few of them.*
>
> H. L. Mencken

In 1998, Sanford I. Weill, the CEO of Citigroup, Inc., earned $52 million (base pay plus stock options); that's $1 million per week. Assuming he worked 70 hours per week (you have to work hard to earn that kind of money), that's $14,286 per hour.

Today, the average doctor earns $160,000 per year; that's $3,077 per week. Assuming she works 70 hours per week (she's conscientious, makes house calls, and spends time with her hospitalized patients), that's $44 per hour.

Joe Smith, a cashier in a fast-food restaurant, earns $6.00 per hour. But to earn enough for his family to be able to eat, he works a lot of overtime, for which he is paid time-and-a-half, or $9.00 per hour. So he makes $26,520 per year, or $510 per week, by working 70 hours per week.

Nguyen, a peasant in Vietnam, earns $250 a year; that's $4.80 per week. Assuming he works 70 hours per week (you have to work hard at that rate of pay just to keep from starving), that's 7 cents per hour.

Are such major differences typical of how income is distributed among people in general? Are such differences fair? And if they're unfair, what can be done about them? This chapter addresses such issues. (I should warn you, however: If you're looking for answers, this chapter won't provide them; it will simply make the assumptions on both sides clear.)

The issues addressed in these questions play a fundamentally important role in policy debates today. The reason why is that in the last 20 years the income distribution in the United States has changed considerably. Many formerly middle-income people have moved into the upper-income levels; their wealth and their control of real assets have grown considerably. But simultaneously, lower-income people's income has stagnated or fallen. This change is bringing income distribution issues to center stage in modern policy debates.

WAYS OF CONSIDERING THE DISTRIBUTION OF INCOME

There are several different ways to look at income distribution. In the 1800s, economists were concerned with how income was divided among the owners of businesses (for whom profits were the source of income), the owners of land (who received rent), and workers (who earned wages). That concern reflected the relatively sharp distinctions among social classes that existed in capitalist societies at that time. Landowners, workers, and owners of businesses were separate groups, and few individuals moved from one group to another.

Time has changed that. Today workers, through their pension plans and investments in financial institutions, are owners of over 50 percent of all the shares issued on the New York Stock Exchange. Landowners as a group receive only a small portion of total income. Companies are run not by capitalists, but by managers who are, in a sense, workers. In short, the social lines have blurred.

This blurring of the lines between social classes doesn't mean that we can forget the question "Who gets what?" It simply means that our interest in who gets what has a different focus. We no longer focus on classification of income by source. Instead we look at the relative distribution of total income. How much income do the top 5 percent get? How much do the top 15 percent get? How much do the bottom 10 percent get? **Share distribution of income** is the name given to *the relative division of total income among income groups*.

A second distributional issue economists are concerned with is the **socioeconomic distribution of income** (*the allocation of income among relevant socioeconomic groupings*). How much do blacks get relative to whites? How much do the old get compared to the young? How much do women get compared to men?

The share distribution of income is the relative division or allocation of total income among income groups.

The socioeconomic distribution of income is the relative division or allocation of total income among relevant socioeconomic groups.

THE SHARE DISTRIBUTION OF INCOME

The U.S. share distribution of income measures aggregate family income, from the poorest segment of society to the richest. It ranks people by their income and tells how much the richest 20 percent (a quintile) and the poorest 20 percent receive. For example, the poorest 20 percent might get 5 percent of the income and the richest 20 percent might get 40 percent.

The Lorenz Curve

A Lorenz curve is a geometric representation of the share distribution of income among families in a given country at a given time.

Q₋₁ When drawing a Lorenz curve, what do you put on the two axes?

Figure 20-1(a) presents the share distribution of income for the United States in 1998. In it you can see that the 20 percent of Americans receiving the lowest level of income got 3.6 percent of the total income. The top 20 percent of Americans received 49.2 percent of the total income. The ratio of the income of the top 20 percent compared to the income of the bottom 20 percent was about 14:1.

A **Lorenz curve** is *a geometric representation of the share distribution of income among families in a given country at a given time*. It measures the cumulative percentage of *families* on the horizontal axis, arranged from poorest to richest, and the cumulative percentage of *family income* on the vertical axis. Since the figure presents cumulative percentages (all of the families with income below a certain level), both axes start at zero and end at 100 percent.

A perfectly equal distribution of income would be represented by a diagonal line like the one in Figure 20-1(b). That is, the poorest 20 percent of the families would have 20 percent of the total income (point A); the poorest 40 percent of the families would have 40 percent of the income (point B); and 100 percent of the families would have 100

Figure 20-1 (a and b)   A Lorenz Curve of U.S. Income, 1998

If income were perfectly equally distributed, the Lorenz curve would be a diagonal line. In (**b**) we see the U.S. Lorenz curve based on the numbers in (**a**) compared to a Lorenz curve reflecting a perfectly equal distribution of income.

Income quintile	Percentage of total family income	Cumulative percentage of total family income
Lowest fifth	3.6 %	3.6%
Second fifth	9.0	12.6
Third fifth	15.0	27.6
Fourth fifth	23.2	50.8
Highest fifth	49.2	100.0

(a)

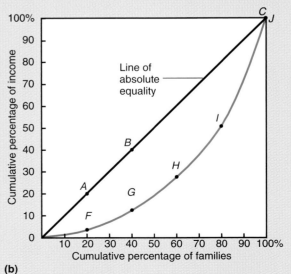

(b)

Source: *Current Population Reports*, U.S. Bureau of the Census, 1999 (http://www.census.gov).

percent of the income (point C). An unequal distribution of income is represented by a Lorenz curve that's below the diagonal line. All real-world Lorenz curves are below the diagonal because income is always distributed unequally in the real world.

The colored line in Figure 20-1(b) represents a Lorenz curve of the U.S. income distribution presented in Figure 20-1(a)'s table. From Figure 20-1(a) you know that, in 1998, the bottom 20 percent of the families in the United States received 3.6 percent of the income. Point F in Figure 20-1(b) represents that combination of percentages (20 percent and 3.6 percent). To find what the bottom 40 percent received, we must add the income percentage of the bottom 20 percent and the income percentage of the next 20 percent. Doing so gives us 12.6 percent (3.6 plus 9.0 percent from column 2 of Figure 20-1(a)). Point G in Figure 20-1(b) represents the combination of percentages (40 percent and 12.6 percent). Continuing this process for points H, I, and C, you get a Lorenz curve that shows the share distribution of income in the United States in 1998.

U.S. Income Distribution over Time

Lorenz curves are most useful in visual comparisons of income distribution over time and between countries. Figure 20-2 presents Lorenz curves for the United States in 1929, 1970, and 1998. They show that from 1929 to 1970 the share distribution of income became more equal. (The curve for 1970 is closer to being a diagonal than the curve for 1929.) Income of the bottom fifth of families rose by a much higher proportion than did income of the top fifth. That was a continuation of a trend that had begun in the 1920s. In the 1970s that trend stopped and began to reverse. As you can see, from 1970 to 1998 income distribution became less equal. (The curve for 1998 is further from being diagonal than is the curve for 1970.) The income of the bottom fifth of families fell by over 10 percent, while the income of the top fifth rose significantly.

Important reasons for the initial increase in equality are the redistribution measures instituted by the U.S. government between the 1930s and the 1970s, including welfare

From 1929 to 1970, income inequality in the United States decreased. From 1970 to 1998, it increased.

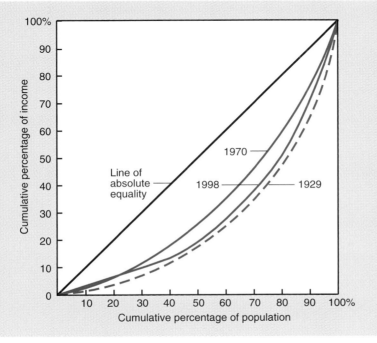

Figure 20-2   Lorenz Curves for the United States: 1929, 1970, and 1998

The amount of inequality of income distribution has fluctuated in the United States. Until about 1970, it decreased; since then it has increased.

programs, unemployment insurance, Social Security, progressive taxation (taxation of higher income at higher rates, lower income at lower rates), and improved macroeconomic performance of the economy.

The trend back toward greater inequality starting in the 1970s was caused by a fall in the real income of the poor. This was due to wage increases that didn't keep up with price increases during that period, a movement away from progressive taxation, and a reduction in government funding for some social programs; this trend toward inequality will likely become a hot political topic if U.S. economic growth slows.

The distribution of income over time is also affected by demographic factors. Many families have relatively low income in their early years, relatively higher income in their middle years, and then relatively low income again in their retirement years. The Lorenz curve reflects these differences, so even if lifetime income were equally distributed, income in any one year would not be. Moreover, when the percentages of these groups change, the Lorenz curve will change. For example, when the baby-boom generation's members retire and are no longer working, their collective income will fall. That decline in income relative to the income of the smaller number of working families will affect the Lorenz curve.

DEFINING POVERTY

Much of the government's concern with income distribution has centered on the poorest group—those in poverty. Defining poverty is not easy. Do we want to define it as an *absolute* amount of real income that does not change over time? If poverty were defined as an *absolute* amount of real income, few in the United States would be in poverty today; most of today's poor have higher real incomes than did the middle class 50 or 60 years ago. Or do we want to define it as a *relative* concept that rises as the average income in the society rises? For example, anyone with an income of less than one-fifth of the average income could be defined as being in poverty. If that relative concept of poverty were chosen, then the proportion of people classified as poor would always be the same.

The Official Definition of Poverty

The United States uses a definition of poverty that is a combination of a relative and an absolute measure. Thus, it satisfies neither those who favor an absolute measure nor those who favor a relative measure, and there are both calls to increase and calls to decrease the **poverty threshold**—*the income below which a family is considered to live in poverty*. The official definition of poverty is the following:

> A family is in poverty if it has an income equal to or less than three times an average family's minimum food expenditures as calculated by the U.S. Department of Agriculture.

That minimum food budget includes 4 eggs, 1½ pounds of meat, 3 pounds of potatoes, about 4 pounds of vegetables, and other foods; the cost is about $26.28 per person per week. Tripling that amount to about $78.85 (since food is said to require one-third of a family's income) and multiplying it by 52 (the number of weeks in a year), we arrive at a poverty level of about $4,100 per person per year, or about $16,400 for a family of four.

As Table 20-1 shows, using the official poverty measure, the number of people in poverty decreased in the 1960s and then began increasing in the 1970s. The number of poor rose to over 30 million in the 1980s. Then, due to a recession in the early 1990s, it rose even more, but it declined throughout the remainder of the 1990s as the U.S.

Q.2 Is the U.S. definition of poverty an absolute or a relative definition?

Poverty is defined by the U.S. government as having an income being equal to or less than three times an average family's minimum food expenditures as calculated by the U.S. Department of Agriculture.

Table 20-1   Number and Percentage of Persons in Poverty, 1960–1998

	Number of People (in millions)	Percentage of Population	Poverty Income of Family of 4 (in current dollars)
1960	39.9	22.2%	$ 3,022
1970	24.4	12.6	3,986
1980	29.3	13.0	8,414
1990	33.6	13.5	13,359
1991	35.7	14.2	13,924
1992	36.9	14.5	14,335
1993	39.3	15.1	14,764
1994	38.1	14.5	15,142
1995	36.4	13.8	15,569
1996	36.5	13.8	16,036
1997	35.6	13.3	16,400
1998	34.5	12.7	16,660

Source: *Current Population Reports*, U.S. Bureau of the Census, 1999 (http://www.census.gov).

economy continued to grow. In 1998, 34.5 million Americans lived below the poverty threshold.

Debates about the Definition of Poverty

The minimum food budget used to determine the poverty line was determined in the 1960s and has not been recalculated to account for rising standards of living. This, it is in principle an absolute measure. However, it is adjusted by the rate of inflation rather than by the rise in the price of the originally selected foods. Since food prices have risen by less than the rise in the general price level, the index of poverty has gone up by more than it would have had the fixed ratio of food to income remained constant. That means the definition includes significant aspects of relativity.

Those who favor a relative measure of poverty argue that our current poverty measure is too low. They point out that since food is now closer to a fourth of a family's total budget, it would make sense to increase the poverty threshold by multiplying food expenditures by a number a bit less than four rather than by three. Doing so would raise the poverty threshold to $19,500, and would add 12 million people to the poverty roll.

Those who favor an absolute measure of poverty argue that the current measure is too high. They point out that U.S. poverty figures do not include in-kind (noncash) transfers, such as food stamps and housing assistance. Nor does the current poverty measure take into account underreporting of income, or the savings people have. (Many elderly people may have low incomes but significant wealth, which they could choose to spend.) If we make adjustments for in-kind transfers and underreporting of income, the official number of people in poverty decreases to about 60 percent of the official number (i.e., to about 20.7 million people). University of Texas economist Daniel Slesnick takes it further and points out that, since the price of food has increased at less than the rate of inflation, a much lower level of expenditures than the amount used to calculate the poverty threshold will provide a "nutritionally adequate diet." Slesnick calculated that when one takes the decrease in the relative price of food into account, the number of people in poverty falls to less than 5 million (one-seventh the official count).

The moral of this debate: Like most economic statistics, poverty statistics should be used with care.

There are arguments both that the poverty line is too high and too low.

The Costs of Poverty

People who favor policies aimed at achieving equality of income argue that poverty brings significant costs to society. One is that society suffers when some of its people are in poverty, just as the entire family suffers when one member doesn't have enough to eat. Most people derive pleasure from knowing that others are not in poverty.

Another cost of poverty is that it increases incentives for crime. In contrast, as people's incomes increase, they have more to lose by committing crimes, and therefore fewer crimes are committed. As the economy has boomed in the 1990s the crime rate has decreased.

Those who favor equality of income argue that the increased poverty in the late 1970s and 1980s represents a failure of the economic policies of that period. Others respond that the widening gap between rich and poor is not the result of government tax and spending policies. It has more to do with demographic changes. For example, the number of single-parent families increased dramatically during this period, while rapid growth of the labor force depressed wages for young unskilled workers.

Advocates of reducing poverty respond that this argument is unconvincing. They argue that the tax cuts of the 1980s favored the rich while decreased funding for government programs hurt the poor. To compensate, they argue, free day care should be provided for children so that single parents can work full-time, and government should supplement the low wages of the working poor. They argue that demographic changes are not a valid excuse for ducking a question of morality.

INTERNATIONAL DIMENSIONS OF INCOME INEQUALITY

When considering income distribution, we usually are looking at conditions within a single country. For example, the richest 5 percent of the U.S. population gets approximately 30 times what the poorest 5 percent of the American people get.

There are other ways to look at income. We might judge income inequality in the United States relative to income inequality in other countries. Is the U.S. distribution of income more or less equal than another country's? We could also look at how income is distributed among countries. Even if income is relatively equally distributed within countries, it may be unequally distributed among countries.

Comparing U.S. Income Distribution with That in Other Countries

The United States has less income inequality than most developing countries but more income inequality than many developed countries.

Q.3 How does the income distribution in the U.S. compare with that in other countries?

Figure 20-3 gives us a sense of how the distribution of income in the United States compares to that in other countries. We see that the United States has significantly more income inequality than Sweden, but significantly less than Brazil (or most other developing and newly industrialized countries).

An important reason why the United States has more income inequality than Sweden is that Sweden's tax system is more progressive. Until recently (when Sweden's socialist party lost power), the top marginal tax rate on the highest incomes in Sweden was 80 percent, compared to about 40 percent in the United States. Given this difference, it isn't surprising that Sweden has less income inequality. In a newly industrialized country like Brazil, where a few individuals earn most of the income and, to a large degree, control the government, the government is not likely to begin redistributing income to achieve equality.

A second measure economists use to talk about the degree of income inequality is the Gini coefficient of inequality. The Gini coefficient is derived from the Lorenz curve by comparing the area between the (1) Lorenz curve and the diagonal (area A) and (2) the total area of the triangle below the diagonal (areas A and B). That is:

Gini coefficient = Area A/ (Areas A + B)

A Gini coefficient of zero would be perfect equality, since area A is zero if income is perfectly equally distributed. The highest the Gini coefficient can go is 1. So all Gini coefficients must be between zero and one. The lower the Gini coefficient, the closer income distribution is to being equal. The Gini coefficient for the United States was 0.46 in 1998.

The following table gives Gini coefficients for a number of other countries. The Gini coefficients for transitional economies such as the Slovak Republic are most likely higher today

KNOWING THE TOOLS

The Gini Coefficient

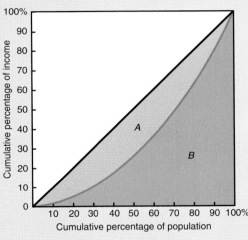

because they are now market economies and their incomes are less equally distributed.

Gini Coefficients for Selected Countries	
Algeria	.353
Bangladesh	.283
Brazil	.601
Canada	.315
Czech Republic	.266
Denmark	.247
Germany	.281
Guatemala	.596
Hungary	.279
Indonesia	.342
Japan	.350
Latvia	.270
Netherlands	.315
Panama	.568
Philippines	.429
Romania	.255
Slovak Rep.	.195
South Africa	.584
Thailand	.462
United Kingdom	.326
United States	.460

Source: *World Development Report*, 1998/99, The World Bank (http://www. worldbank.org).

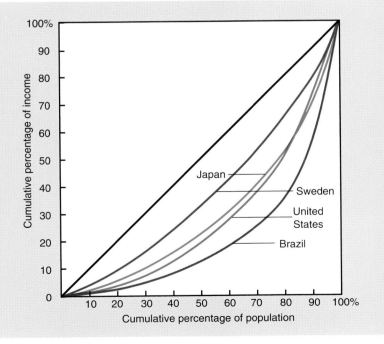

Figure 20-3   U.S. Income Distribution Compared to that of Other Countries

Among countries of the world, the United States has neither the most equal nor the most unequal distribution of income.

Source: *World Development Report*, The World Bank, 1998/1999 (http://www.worldbank.org).

Income Distribution among Countries

When we consider the distribution of world income, the picture becomes even more unequal than the picture we see within countries. The reason is clear: Income is highly unequally distributed among countries. The average per capita income of the richest 5 percent of the countries in the world is more than 100 times the average income of the poorest 5 percent of the countries of the world. Thus, a Lorenz curve of world income would show much more inequality than the Lorenz curve for a particular country. Worldwide, income inequality is enormous. A minimum level of income in the United States would be a wealthy person's income in a poor country like Bangladesh.

The Total Amount of Income in Various Countries

To gain a better picture of income distribution problems, you need to consider not only the division of income but also the total amounts of income in various countries. Figure 20-4 presents per capita income (gross domestic product) for various countries. Looking at the enormous differences of income among countries, we must ask which is more important: the distribution of income or the absolute level of income. Which would you rather be: one of four members in a family that has an income of $3,000 a year, which places you in the top 10 percent of Bangladesh's income distribution, or one of four members of a family with an income of $12,000 (four times as much), which places you in the bottom 10 percent of the income earners in the United States?

THE DISTRIBUTION OF WEALTH

Wealth is the value of assets individuals own less the value of what they owe.

In considering equality, two measures are often used: *equality of wealth* and *equality of income*. Because of space limitations, my focus will be on income, but I want to mention wealth. **Wealth** is *the value of the things individuals own less the value of what they owe*. It is a *stock* concept representing the value of assets such as houses, buildings, and machines.

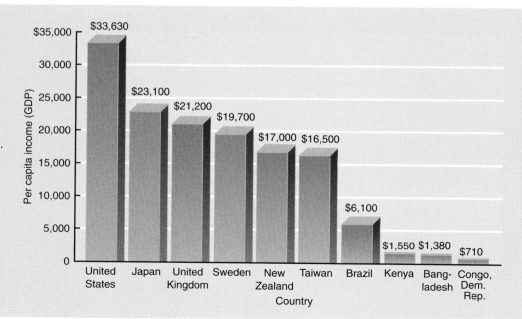

Figure 20-4   Per Capita Income (Gross Domestic Product) in Various Countries, 1999

Income is unequally distributed among the countries of the world. These relative comparisons change considerably over time as exchange rates fluctuate.

Source: *CIA World Factbook*, Central Intelligence Agency, 1999 (http://www.ocdi.gov) and various country home pages.

For example, a farmer who owns a farm with a net worth of $1 million is wealthy compared to an investment banker with a net worth of $225,000.

Income is *payments received plus or minus changes in value in a person's assets in a specified time period.* In contrast to wealth, income is a *flow* concept. It's a stream through time. That farmer might have an income of $20,000 a year while the investment banker might have an income of $80,000 a year. The farmer, with $1 million worth of assets, is wealthier than the investment banker, but the investment banker has a higher income than the farmer.

Income is payments received plus or minus changes in value of a person's assets in a specified time period.

A Lorenz Curve of the Distribution of Wealth

Figure 20-5 compares the Lorenz curve for wealth in the United States with the Lorenz curve for income in the United States. You can see that wealth in the United States is more unequally distributed than income and that the bottom 40 percent of the U.S. population has essentially zero wealth.

Wealth is significantly more unequally distributed in the United States than is income.

How Much Wealth Do the Wealthy Have?

Relative comparisons such as those depicted by Lorenz curves don't give you a sense of how much wealth it takes to be "wealthy." The following numbers provide you with a better sense. Bill Gates (who founded Microsoft), the richest person in the United States, had a net worth of about $85 billion in 1999. Five of the wealthiest people in the United States were from the Walton family (whose father founded Wal-Mart) and they each had $17 billion. Most of us have little chance of joining that group; in fact, most of us have little possibility of becoming one of the top 5 percent of the wealthholders in the United States, which would require total wealth of at least $4 million. Once there was a time when people's ultimate financial goal was to be a millionaire. In the 2000s,

Billionaires often lose a billion here, gain a billion there; sometimes they even become multibillionaires. Seldom do they become poor.

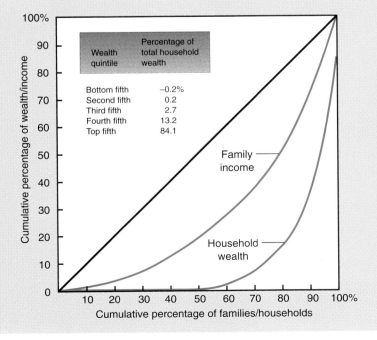

Wealth quintile	Percentage of total household wealth
Bottom fifth	−0.2%
Second fifth	0.2
Third fifth	2.7
Fourth fifth	13.2
Top fifth	84.1

Figure 20-5   Wealth Distribution in the United States and Wealth Compared to Income

Wealth is much more unequally distributed than income in the United States. In fact, the lowest 40 percent of the population has 0 percent of the wealth; these people have borrowed as much as they own.

Source: U.S. Bureau of the Census and Edward N. Wolf, New York University (with permission).

the ultimate financial goal for the wealthiest people is to be a billionaire. The millionaire's club is no longer highly exclusive.

Of course, people in the club don't always stay there; the club is constantly changing. For example, a number of families who were in the club earlier are no longer in it. Many of the Japanese billionaires lost billions in the fall of the Japanese stock market, and fell off the top 10 in the world list of wealthiest people. Today, some of these people and families might only be multimillionaires. (It's tough to stay a billionaire.)

SOCIOECONOMIC DIMENSIONS OF INCOME INEQUALITY

The size distribution of inequality is only one of the dimensions that inequality of income and wealth can take. As I mentioned before, the distribution of income according to source of income (wages, rents, and profits) was once considered important. Today's focus is on the distribution of income based on race, ethnic background, geographic region, and other socioeconomic factors such as gender and type of job.

Income Distribution According to Socioeconomic Characteristics

Table 20-2 gives an idea of the distribution of income according to socioeconomic characteristics.

You can see that income differs substantially by type of job, leading some economists to argue that a new professional/nonprofessional class distinction is arising in the

Table 20-2   Various Socioeconomic Income Distribution Designations

Median Income, 1998		
By Occupational Category	Female	Male
Executive, administrators, and managerial	$34,755	$51,351
Professional specialists	36,261	51,654
Technical and related support	27,849	40,546
Sales	23,197	37,248
Administrative support, including clerical	23,835	31,153
Precision production, craft, and repair	23,907	31,631
Machine operators, assemblers, and inspectors	19,015	27,890
Transportation and material moving	21,449	30,422
Handlers, equipment cleaners, helpers, and lab	16,550	21,871
Service workers	15,647	22,515
Farming, forestry, and fishing	15,865	18,855

By Age, 1998	Median Household Income
Less than 25	$23,564
25–45	44,260
45–65	48,658
Over 65	21,589

Median Income				
By Sex	1970	1980	1990	1998
Male	$7,537	$15,340	$27,866	$35,345
Female	3,138	6,772	19,816	25,862

By Race, 1998	Median Household Income
White	$40,912
Black	25,351
Hispanic	28,330

Source: *Current Population Reports, Consumer Income,* U.S. Bureau of the Census, 1999 (http://www.census.gov).

United States. Substantial differences also exist between the incomes of women and men, and between whites and blacks.

Income Distribution According to Class

As I stated above, early economists focused on the distribution of income by wages, profits, and rent because that division corresponded to their class analysis of society. Landowners received rent, capitalists received profit, and workers received wages. Tensions among these classes played an important part in economists' analyses of the economy and policy.

Even though class divisions by income source have become blurred, other types of socioeconomic classes have taken their place. The United States has a kind of upper class. In fact, a company in the United States publishes the *Social Register*, containing the names and pedigrees of about 35,000 socially prominent people who might be categorized "upper-class." Similarly, it is possible to further divide the U.S. population into a middle class and a lower class.

Class divisions are no longer determined by income source. For example, upper-class people do not necessarily receive their income from rent and profits. Today we have "upper-class" people who derive their income from wages and "lower-class" people who derive their income from profits (usually in the form of pensions, which depend on profits from the investment of pension funds in stocks and bonds).

The Importance of the Middle Class What has made the most difference in today's class structure in the United States compared to its class structure in earlier periods and to the structure in today's developing countries is the tremendous growth in the relative size of the middle class. Economists used to see the class structure as a pyramid. From a base composed of a large lower class, the pyramid tapered upward through a medium-sized middle class to a peak occupied by the upper class (Figure 20-6(a)). The class structure is still pyramidal in developing countries. In the United States and other developed countries, the pyramid has bulged out into a diamond, as shown in Figure 20-6(b). The middle class has become the largest class, while the upper and lower classes are smaller in relative terms.

This enormous increase in the relative size of the middle class in developed countries has significantly blurred the distinction between capitalists and workers. In early capitalist society, the distributional fight (the fight over relative income shares) was largely between workers and capitalists. In modern capitalist society, the distributional

The United States has socioeconomic classes with some mobility among classes. This is not to say such classes should exist; it is only to say that they do exist.

In the United States the middle class is the largest class.

Q-4 How have distributional fights about income changed over time?

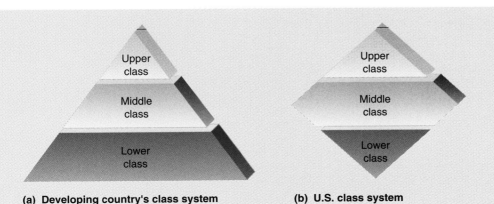

(a) Developing country's class system

(b) U.S. class system

Figure 20-6 (a and b)   The Class System as a Pyramid and as a Diamond

The class system in developing countries is a pyramid; in the United States the class system is more diamond-shaped.

fight is among various types of individuals. Union workers are pitted against nonunion workers; salaried workers are pitted against workers paid by the hour. The old are pitted against the young; women are pitted against men; blacks are pitted against Hispanics and Asians, and all three groups are pitted against whites.

Distributional Questions and Tensions in Society While mainstream economists tend to focus on the size distribution of income, nonmainstream economists tend to emphasize class and group structures in their analysis. Radical economists emphasize the control that the upper class has over the decision process and the political process. Conservative economists emphasize the role of special interests of all types in shaping government policy. Both radical and conservative analyses bring out the tensions among classes in society much better than does the mainstream, classless analysis.

When people feel they belong to a particular class or group, they will often work to further the interests of that class or group. They also generally have stronger feelings about inequalities among classes or groups than when they lack that sense of class or group identity. Using a classless analysis means overlooking the implications of class and group solidarity in affecting the tensions in society.

Those tensions show up every day in political disputes over the tax system, in the quiet fuming of individuals as they see someone else earning more for doing the same job, and in strikes and even riots. Such tensions exist in all countries. In some transitional and developing countries they break out into the open as armed insurrections or riots over food shortages.

Those tensions have been kept to a minimum in American society. A majority of Americans believe that income distribution is sufficiently fair for them to accept their share more or less contentedly. To remedy the unfairness that does exist, they don't demand that the entire system be replaced. Instead they work for change within the present system. They look to affirmative action laws, comparable worth laws, minimum wage laws, and social welfare programs for any improvement they perceive to be necessary or desirable. There's much debate about whether these government actions have achieved the desired ends, but the process itself reduces tensions and has worked toward the maintenance of the entire system.

People's acceptance of the U.S. economic system is based not only on what the distribution of income is but also on what people think it should be, what they consider fair. It is to that question that we now turn.

INCOME DISTRIBUTION AND FAIRNESS

Judgments about whether the distribution of income is fair or should be changed are normative ones, based on the values the analyst applies to the situation. Value judgments necessarily underlie all policy prescriptions.

Philosophical Debates about Equality and Fairness

Depending on one's values, any income distribution can be justified. For example, Friedrich Nietzsche, the 19th-century Germany philosopher, argued that society's goal should be to support its supermen—its best and brightest. Lesser individuals' duty should be to work for the well-being of these supermen. Bertram de Juvenal, a 20th-century philosopher, has argued that a high level of income inequality is necessary to sustain the arts, beauty, education, and civilization. He and others say that a world of equally distributed income would be a world without beauty. Even if we don't personally own beautiful,

Both radical and conservative analyses bring out the tensions among classes in society much better than does mainstream classless analysis.

expensive homes or aren't devoted opera fans, these philosophers argue, our lives are improved because some people do own such homes and because opera performances exist. Inequality creates diversity in our lives, and that diversity enriches the lives of everyone.

Other philosophers disagree strongly. They argue that equality itself is the overriding goal. That view is embodied in the Declaration of Independence: "We hold these truths to be self-evident, that all men are created equal." And for many people the inherent value of equality is not open to question—it is simply self-evident.

Believing that equality is an overriding goal does not necessarily imply that income should be equally distributed. For example, John Rawls (a Harvard University professor who believes that equality is highly desirable and that society's goal should be to maximize the welfare of the least well-off) agrees that to meet that goal some inequality is necessary. Rawls argues that if, in pursuing equality, you actually make the least well-off worse off than they otherwise would have been, then you should not pursue equality any further. For example, say under one policy there would be perfect equality and everyone would receive $10,000 per year. Under another policy, the least well-off person receives $12,000 per year and all others receive $40,000. Rawls argues that the second policy is preferable to the first even though it involves more inequality.

Economists, unlike philosophers, are not concerned about justifying any particular distribution of income. In their objective role, economists limit themselves to explaining the effects that various policies will have on the distribution of income; they let the policymakers judge whether those effects are desirable.

However, in order to judge economic policies, you, in your role as a citizen who elects policymakers, must make certain judgments about income distribution because all real-world economic policies have distribution effects. Accordingly, a brief discussion of income distribution and fairness is in order.

Fairness and Equality

The U.S. population has a strong general tendency to favor equality—equality is generally seen as fair. Most people, including me, share that view. However, in some instances equality of income is not directly related to people's view of fairness. For example, consider this distribution of income between John and Fred:

John gets $50,000 a year.

Fred gets $12,000 a year.

Think a minute. Is that fair?

The answer I'm hoping for is that you don't yet have enough information to make the decision.

Here's some more information. Say that John gets that $50,000 for holding down three jobs at a time, while Fred gets his $12,000 for sitting around doing nothing. At this point, many of us would argue that it's possible John should be getting even more than $50,000 and Fred should be getting less than $12,000.

But wait! What if we discover that Fred is an invalid and unless his income increases to $15,000 a year he will die? Most of us would change our minds again and argue that Fred deserves more, regardless of how much John works.

But wait! How about if, after further digging, we discover that Fred is an invalid because he squandered his health on alcohol, drugs, and fried foods? In that case some people would likely change their minds again as to whether Fred deserves more.

By now you should have gotten my point. Looking only at a person's income masks many dimensions that most people consider important in making value judgments about fairness.

Q.5 Is it self-evident that greater equality of income would make the society a better place to live? Why?

While economists in their objective role limit themselves to explaining the effects of various policies on the distribution of income, individuals, in order to judge economic policies, must make value judgments and concern themselves about the distributional effects of economic policy.

Q.6 You are dividing a pie among five individuals. What would be a fair distribution of that pie?

Fairness has many dimensions and it is often difficult to say what is fair and what isn't.

Three problems in determining whether an equal income distribution is fair are:

1. People don't start from equivalent positions.
2. People's needs differ.
3. People's efforts differ.

Fairness as Equality of Opportunity

The concept of fairness is crucial and complicated, and it deserves deeper consideration than just a gut reaction.

When most people talk about believing in equality in income, they mean they believe in equality of opportunity for comparably endowed individuals to earn income. If equal opportunity of equals leads to inequality of income, that inequality in income is fair. Unfortunately, there's enormous latitude for debate on what constitutes equal opportunity of equals.

In the real world, needs differ, desires differ, and abilities differ. Should these differences be considered relevant differences in equality? You must answer that question before you can judge any economic policy, because to make a judgment on whether an economic policy should or should not be adopted, you must make a judgment about whether a policy's effect on income is fair. In making those judgments, most people rely on their immediate gut reaction. I hope what you have gotten out of the discussion about John and Fred and equality of opportunity is the resolve to be cautious about trusting your gut reactions. The concept of fairness is crucial and complicated, and it deserves deeper consideration than just a gut reaction.

THE PROBLEMS OF REDISTRIBUTING INCOME

Let's now say that we have considered all the issues discussed so far in this chapter and have concluded that some redistribution of income from the rich to the poor is necessary if society is to meet our ideal of fairness. How do we go about redistributing income?

First, we must consider what programs exist and what their negative side effects might be. The side effects can be substantial and can subvert the intention of the program so that far less money is available overall for redistribution and inequality is reduced less than we might think.

Three Important Side Effects of Redistributive Programs

Three side effects of redistribution of income include:

1. The labor/leisure incentive effect.
2. The avoidance and evasion incentive effect.
3. The incentive effect to look more needy than you are.

Q-7 When determining the effects of programs that redistribute income, can one reasonably assume that other things will remain equal?

Three important side effects that economists have found in programs to redistribute income are:

1. A tax may result in a switch from labor to leisure.
2. People may attempt to avoid or evade taxes, leading to a decrease in measured income.
3. Redistributing money may cause people to make themselves look as if they're more needy than they really are.

All economists believe that people will change their behavior in response to changes in taxation and income redistribution programs. These responses, called *incentive effects of taxation*, are important and must be taken into account in policymaking. But they differ significantly in the importance they assign to incentive effects, and empirical evidence doesn't resolve the question. Some economists believe that incentive effects are so important that little taxation for redistribution should take place. They argue that when the rich do well, the total pie is increased so much that the spillover benefits to the poor are greater than the proceeds they would get from redistribution. For example, supporters of this view argue that the growth in capitalist economies was made possible by entrepreneurs. Because those entrepreneurs invested in new technology, income in society grew more. Moreover, those entrepreneurs paid taxes. The benefits resulting from entrepreneurial action spilled over to the poor, making the poor far better off than any redistribution would. The fact that some of those entrepreneurs became rich is irrelevant because all society was better off due to their actions.

Other economists believe that there should be significant taxation for redistribution. While they agree that sometimes the incentive effects are substantial, they see the goal of equality overriding these effects. (Incentive effects are discussed in more detail in Chapter 21.)

Politics, Income Redistribution, and Fairness

We began this discussion of income distribution and fairness by making the assumption that our value judgments determine the taxes we pay—that if our values led us to the conclusion that the poor deserved more income, we could institute policies that would get more to the poor. Reality doesn't necessarily work that way. Often politics, not value judgments, plays a central role in determining what taxes individuals will pay. The group that can deliver the most votes will elect lawmakers who will enact tax policies that benefit that group at the expense of groups with fewer votes.

Often politics, not value judgments, plays a central role in determining what taxes an individual will pay.

On the surface, the democratic system of one person/one vote would seem to suggest that the politics of redistribution would favor the poor, but it doesn't. One would expect that the poor would use their votes to make sure income was redistributed to them from the rich. Why don't they? The answer is complicated.

One reason is that many of the poor don't vote because they assume that one vote won't make much difference. As a result, poor people's total voting strength is reduced. A second reason is that the poor aren't seen by most politicians as a solid voting bloc. There's no organization of the poor that can deliver votes to politicians. A third reason is that those poor people who do vote often cast their votes with other issues in mind. An anti-income-redistribution candidate might have a strong view on abortion as well, and for many the abortion view is the one that decides their vote.

A fourth reason is that elections require financing. Much of that financing comes from the rich. The money is used for advertising and publicity aimed at convincing the poor that it's actually in their best interests to vote for a person who supports the rich. People are often misled by that kind of biased publicity.

Reasonable-sounding arguments can be made to support just about any position, and the rich have the means to see that the arguments supporting their positions get the publicity. Of course, some of their arguments are also correct. The issues are usually sufficiently complicated that a trained economist must study them for a long time to determine which arguments make sense.

INCOME REDISTRIBUTION POLICIES

The preceding discussion should have provided you with a general sense of the difficulty of redistributing income. Let's now consider briefly how income redistribution policies and programs have worked in the real world. In considering this, it is helpful to keep in mind that there are two direct methods and one indirect method through which government redistributes income. The direct methods are (1) *taxation* (policies that tax the rich more than the poor) and (2) *expenditures* (programs that help the poor more than the rich). The indirect method involves the establishment and protection of property rights. Let's first consider direct methods.

Direct methods of redistribution are taxation and expenditures programs.

Taxation to Redistribute Income

The U.S. federal government gets its revenue from a variety of taxes. The three largest sources of revenue are the personal income tax, the corporate income tax, and the Social Security tax.

Taxes can be progressive, proportional, or regressive.

Q.8 A progressive tax is preferable to a proportional tax. True or false? Why?

State and local governments get their revenue from income taxes, sales taxes, and property taxes. The rates vary among states.

As I stated in Chapter 7, tax systems can be progressive, proportional (sometimes called *flat rate*), or regressive. A **progressive tax** is one in which *the average tax rate increases with income*. It redistributes income from the rich to the poor. A **proportional tax** is one in which *the average rate of tax is constant regardless of income level*. It is neutral in regard to income distribution. A **regressive tax** is one in which *the average tax rate decreases as income increases*. It redistributes income from poor to rich.

Federal Income Taxes In the early 1940s, the federal personal income tax was made highly progressive, with a top tax rate of 90 percent on the highest incomes. The degree of progressivity went down significantly through various pieces of legislation after World War II until 1986, when the income tax system was amended to provide for an initial rate of 15 percent and a top rate of 28 percent. The changes did not reduce the actual progressivity of the personal income tax as much as they seemed to, because the 1986 reforms eliminated many of the loopholes in the U.S. Tax Code. Some loopholes had allowed rich people to legally reduce their reported incomes and to pay taxes on those lower incomes at lower rates. In the 1990s, as part of a deficit reduction package, the degree of progressivity was increased again and the top personal income tax rate on high-income individuals was increased to almost 40 percent.

Whereas the personal income tax is progressive, the Society Security tax is initially proportional. All individuals pay the same tax rate on wage income (7.65 percent for employer and 7.65 percent for employee; 15.3 percent for self-employed) up to a cap of about $76,200. Above that income cap, no Social Security tax is due (except for 1.45 percent for medical insurance, which has no cap on the amount to which it is applied). At this income cap the Social Security tax becomes regressive: Higher-income individuals pay a lower percentage of their total income in Social Security taxes than do lower-income individuals. (They also receive relatively less in Social Security benefits, compared to what they put in. So, while the Social Security tax is regressive, taken as a whole the Social Security system is progressive.)

State and Local Taxes State and local governments get most of their income from the following sources:

1. Income taxes, which are generally somewhat progressive.

2. Sales taxes, which tend to be proportional (all people pay the same tax rate on what they spend) or slightly regressive. (Since poor people often spend a higher percentage of their incomes than rich people, poor people pay a higher average tax rate as a percentage of their incomes than rich people.)

3. Property taxes, which are taxes paid on the value of people's property (usually real estate, but sometimes also personal property like cars). Since the value of people's property is related (although imperfectly related) to income, the property tax is considered to be roughly proportional.

When all the taxes paid by individuals to all levels of governments are combined, the conclusion that most researchers come to is that little income redistribution takes place on the tax side. The progressive taxes are offset by the regressive taxes, so the overall tax system is roughly proportional. That is, on average the tax rates individuals pay are roughly equal. Recent changes in the tax laws have increased the rate that high-income people pay and lowered the rate that lower-income people pay. These changes may make the effective tax structure slightly more progressive, but meaningful statistics won't be available for a few years.

Expenditure Programs to Redistribute Income

Taxation has not proved to be an effective means of redistributing income. However, the government expenditure system has been quite effective. Some of the federal government's expenditures that contribute to redistribution include the following:

Expenditure programs have been more successful than taxation for redistributing income.

Social Security The program that redistributes the most money is the **Social Security** system, *a social insurance program that provides financial benefits to the elderly and disabled and to their eligible dependents and/or survivors.* Social Security also has a component called **Medicare,** which is a *multibillion-dollar medical insurance system.*

The amount of an individual's Social Security retirement, disability, or survivors' monthly cash benefits depends on a very complex formula, which is skewed in favor of lower-income workers. The program is not a pension program that pegs benefits to the amount paid in. Many people will get much more than they paid in; some who never paid anything in will get a great deal; and a few who paid in for years will get nothing. (No benefits are payable if you die before you retire and leave no survivors eligible for benefits due to your work.) On the whole, the program has been successful in keeping the elderly out of poverty. In addition, Social Security benefits have helped workers' survivors and the disabled.

Q.9 The U.S. Social Security system is only a retirement system. True or false?

In the early 2000s, there were about 45 million recipients of cash Social Security benefits, many of whom also received Medicare health insurance payments. Total benefits paid in the early 2000s, including Medicare, came to $600 billion each year.

Public Assistance **Public assistance** programs are *means-tested social programs targeted to the poor and providing financial, nutritional, medical, and housing assistance.* (These programs are more familiarly known as *welfare payments*.) Public assistance programs exist in every state of the union, although the amount paid varies greatly from state to state. The main kinds of public assistance are:

Temporary Assistance for Needy Families (TANF). Provides temporary financial assistance to needy families with children under age 19.

Food stamps. Provide nutritional assistance in the form of coupons redeemable at most food stores.

Medicaid. Medical assistance for the poor, paid for by the individual states. It's different from, and usually more generous than, Medicare.

General assistance. State assistance to poor people when emergencies arise that aren't taken care of by any of the other programs.

By far the largest proportion of payments goes to needy families with dependent children, especially since these families are usually so poor that, in addition to qualifying for TANF, they meet the eligibility requirements for food stamps and Medicaid.

TANF is a new program. It was instituted to replace Aid to Families with Dependent Children (AFDC). It has a number of provisions that distinguish it from earlier programs. One important provision is that it establishes a lifetime limit of 60 months (not necessarily consecutive) of benefits. The purpose of the law is to direct welfare recipients to work, and another provision in the law requires welfare recipients to take a job within two years. The law also gives states significant latitude in determining benefits and eligibility criteria. These changes are major ones; they raise many questions about job training and child care. The effects of the new laws will be much in the news over the next few years.

Supplemental Security Income Hundreds of thousands more people would be receiving public assistance if it weren't for **Supplemental Security Income (SSI),** *a federal* *program that pays benefits, based on need, to the elderly, blind, and disabled.* Although SSI is administered through the Social Security offices, it is unlike Social Security benefits because eligibility for SSI payments is based solely on the basis of need. Again unlike Social Security, the recipients pay nothing toward the cost of the program. To be eligible, though, people must have very low incomes and almost no resources except a home, if they are fortunate enough to own one, a wedding ring and engagement ring, and an automobile. In the early 2000s, about $30 billion was paid in SSI benefits each year.

Unemployment Compensation **Unemployment compensation** is *short-term financial assistance, regardless of need, to eligible individuals who are temporarily out of work.* It is limited financial assistance to people who are out of work through no fault of their own and have worked in a covered occupation for a substantial number of weeks in the period just before they became unemployed.

Normally a person can receive unemployment benefits for only about six months in any given year, and the amount of the benefit is always considerably less than the amount the person earned when working.

A person can't just quit a job and live on unemployment benefits. While receiving unemployment benefits, people are expected to actively search for work. Lower-income workers receive unemployment payments that are more nearly equal to their working wage than do higher-income workers, but there is no income eligibility test. In the early 2000s about $22 billion was paid in unemployment benefits each year.

Housing Programs Federal and state governments have many different programs to improve housing or to provide affordable housing. While many of these programs are designed to benefit low-income persons, there are also programs for moderate-income persons and lower-income persons (people whose incomes are lower than moderate but higher than low).

The federal agency overseeing most of these programs, the Department of Housing and Urban Development (HUD), has been criticized for abuse and mismanagement. Hundreds of millions of dollars that could have benefited the poor went instead to developers of housing and other projects, to consultants, and to others who skimmed off money before—or instead of—building or rehabilitating housing. In part because of these problems, federal funding for housing was steadily reduced during the 1980s. In the early 2000s, about $30 billion was allocated to housing programs each year.

How Successful Have Income Redistribution Programs Been?

Most government redistribution works through its expenditure programs, not through taxes.

Figure 20-7 shows approximate Lorenz curves before and after analyzing the effect of both taxes and government programs on the redistribution of income. As you can see, the after-transfer income is significantly closer to being equally distributed. But because of the incentive effects of collecting and distributing the money, that redistribution has come at the cost of a reduction in the total amount of income earned by the society. The debate about whether the gain in equality of income is worth the cost in reduction of total income is likely to continue indefinitely.

While the direct methods of redistributing income get the most press and discussion, perhaps the most important redistribution decisions that the government makes involve an indirect method, the establishment and protection of property rights. Let's take an example: intellectual property rights. Intellectual property consists of things like a book

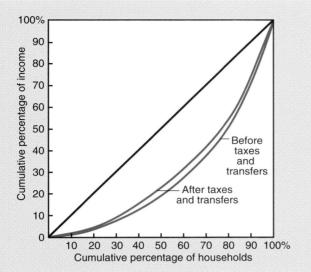

Figure 20-7   Distribution of Income before and after Taxes and Transfers, 1998

Although little redistribution takes place through the tax system, significant redistribution occurs through the transfer system, making the after-tax and transfer distribution of income more equal than the before-tax distribution of income.

Source: *Current Population Reports*, U.S. Bureau of the Census, 1999 (http://www.census.gov).

you've written, a song you've composed, or a picture you've drawn. How these property rights are structured plays a fundamental role in determining the distribution of income.

For example, if strict private property rights are given for, say, a design for a computer screen (e.g., a neat little trash can in the corners and windows of various files) any user other than the designer herself will have to pay for the right to use it. The designer (or the person who gets the legal right to the design) becomes very rich. If no property rights are given for the design, then no payment is made and income is much more equally distributed. Of course, without a promise of high returns to designing a computer screen device, fewer resources will be invested in finding the ideal design. While most people agree that some incentive is appropriate, there is no consensus on whether the incentives embodied in our current property rights structure are too large. I suspect that the trash can (recycling bin) design, while ingenious, would have been arrived at with a much smaller incentive.

The point of the above example is not that property rights in such ideas should not be given out. The point is that decisions on property rights issues have enormous distributional consequences that are often little discussed, even by economists. Ultimately, we can answer the question of whether income redistribution is fair only after we have answered the question of whether the initial property rights distribution is fair.

Q-10 Why are property rights important in the determination of whether any particular income distribution is fair?

CONCLUSION

Much more could be said about the issues involved in income redistribution. But limitations of time and space pressure us to move on. I hope this chapter has convinced you that income redistribution is an important but difficult question. Specifically, I hope I have given you the sense that income distribution questions are integrally related to questions about the entire economic system. Supply and demand play a central role in the determination of the distribution of income, but they do so in an institutional and historical context. Thus, the analysis of income distribution must include that context as well as the analyst's ethical judgments about what is fair.

Chapter Summary

- The Lorenz curve is a measure of the distribution of income among families in a country. The further the Lorenz curve is from the diagonal, the more unequally income is distributed.

- The official poverty measure is an absolute measure because it is based on the minimum food budget for a family. It is a relative measure because it is adjusted for average inflation.

- Income is less equally distributed in the United States than in some countries such as Sweden, but more equally distributed than in other countries such as Brazil. There is more income inequality among countries than income inequality within a country.

- Wealth is distributed less equally than income.

- Income differs substantially by class and by other socioeconomic characteristics such as age, race, and gender.

- Fairness is a philosophical question. People must judge a program's fairness for themselves.

- Income is difficult to redistribute because of incentive effects of taxes, avoidance and evasion effects of taxes, and incentive effects of redistribution programs.

- On the whole, the U.S. tax system is roughly proportional, so it is not very effective as a means of redistributing income.

- Government spending programs are more effective than tax policy in reducing income inequality in the United States.

Key Terms

income *(437)*

Lorenz curve *(430)*

Medicare *(445)*

poverty threshold *(432)*

progressive tax *(444)*

proportional tax *(444)*

public assistance *(445)*

regressive tax *(444)*

share distribution of income *(429)*

Social Security *(445)*

socioeconomic distribution of income *(429)*

Supplemental Security Income (SSI) *(445)*

unemployment compensation *(446)*

wealth *(436)*

Questions for Thought and Review

1. Why are we concerned with the distribution of income between whites and blacks, but not between redheads and blonds?

2. The Lorenz curve for Bangladesh looks like this:

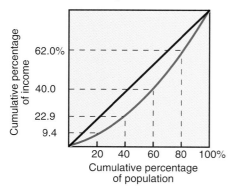

   How much income do the top 20 percent of individuals in Bangladesh receive?

3. If we were to draw a Lorenz curve for lawyers, what would it represent?

4. Should poverty be defined absolutely or relatively? Why?

5. Some economists argue that a class distinction should be made between managerial decision makers and other workers. Do you agree? Why or why not?

6. If a garbage collector earns more than an English teacher, does that mean something is wrong with the economy? Why or why not?

7. Is it ever appropriate for society to:
   Let someone starve?
   Let someone be homeless?
   Forbid someone to eat chocolate?

8. If you receive a paycheck, what percentage of it is withheld for taxes? What incentive effect does that have on your decision to work?

9. Which have been more successful in redistributing income—tax or expenditure programs?

10. There are many more poor people in the United States than there are rich people. If the poor wanted to, they could exercise their power to redistribute as much money as they please to themselves. They don't do that, so they must see the income distribution system as fair. Discuss.

Problems and Exercises

1. The accompanying table shows income distribution data for three countries.

	Percentage of Total Income		
Income quintile	India	Czech Republic	Mexico
Lowest 20%	8.5%	10.5%	4.1%
Second quintile	12.1	13.9	7.8
Third quintile	15.8	16.9	12.5
Fourth quintile	21.1	21.3	20.2
Highest 20%	42.5	37.4	55.4

   a. Using this information, draw a Lorenz curve for each country.
   b. Which country has the most equal distribution of income?
   c. Which country has the least equal?
   d. By looking at the three Lorenz curves, can you tell which country has the most progressive tax system? Why or why not?

2. "There are lies, damned lies, and statistics. Then, there are annual poverty figures." Both liberal and conservative economists believe U.S. poverty statistics are suspect. Here are some reasons:
   (1) They do not take into account in-kind benefits such as food stamps and tax credits.
   (2) They do not consider regional cost-of-living differences.
   (3) They do not take into account unreported income.
   (4) Food accounts for one-fourth of a family's budget, not one-third.
   (5) Ownership of assets such as homes, cars, and appliances is not taken into account.
   a. What would the effect of correcting each of these be on measured poverty?
   b. Would making these changes be fair?

3. The dissident Russian writer A. Amalrik has written:

   . . . The Russian people . . . have . . . one idea that appears positive: the idea of *justice* . . . In practice, "justice" involves the desire that "nobody should live better than I do" . . . The idea of justice is motivated by hatred of everything that is outstanding, which we make no effort to imitate but, on the contrary, try to bring down to our level, by hatred of any sense of initiative, of any higher or more dynamic way of life than the life we live ourselves.

   What implications would such a worldview have for the economy?

4. List four conditions you believe should hold before you would argue that two individuals should get the same amount of income.
   a. How would you apply the conditions to your views on welfare?
   b. How would you apply the conditions to your views on how progressive the income tax should be?
   c. If the income tax were made progressive in wage rates (tax rates increase as wage rates increase) rather than progressive in income, would your conditions be better met? Why?

5. In Taxland, a tax exemption is granted for the first $10,000 earned per year. Between $10,000.01 and $30,000, the tax rate is 25 percent. Between $30,000.01 and $50,000, it's 30 percent. Above $50,000, it's 35 percent. You're earning $75,000 a year.
   a. How much in taxes will you have to pay?
   b. What is your average tax rate? Your marginal tax rate?
   c. Taxland has just changed to a tax credit system in which, in lieu of any exemption, eligible individuals are given a check for $4,000. The two systems are designed to bring in the same amount of revenue. Would you favor or oppose the change? Why?

6. Some economists have proposed making the tax rate progressivity depend on the wage rate rather than the income level. Thus, an individual who works twice as long as another but who receives a lower wage would face a lower marginal tax rate.
   a. What effect would this change have on incentives to work?
   b. Would this system be fairer than our current system? Why or why not?
   c. If, simultaneously, the tax system were made regressive in hours worked so that individuals who work longer hours faced lower marginal tax rates, what effect would this change have on hours worked?
   d. What would be some of the administrative difficulties of instituting the above changes to our income tax code?

Web Questions

1. About.com has information about a variety of economic topics. Go to its website: taxes.about.com/finance/taxes/msubgain.htm.

   a. At what rate are capital gains income taxed?
   b. What is the alternative minimum tax?
   c. What are education credits?

2. The federal government is a great source for information on the web. Go to: www.ssa.gov/pubs/10072.html. Answer the following questions:
   a. What is a social security credit, and how much earnings does it take to get a credit?
   b. How many credits do you need to collect benefits?
   c. What is the charge for a social security number?
   d. What are the eligibility requirements for Medicare?
   e. What is the difference between Part A and Part B Medicare?

Answers to Margin Questions

1. When drawing a Lorenz curve, you put the cumulative percentage of income on the vertical axis and the cumulative percentage of families (or population) on the horizontal axis. *(430)*

2. The U.S. definition of poverty is an absolute measure, but the way poverty is calculated means that some relativity is included in the definition. *(432)*

3. The United States has significantly more income inequality than Sweden and Japan, but significantly less than Brazil. *(434)*

4. In early capitalist society, the distributional fight was between workers and capitalists. In modern capitalist society, the distributional fight is more varied. For example, in the United States minorities are pitted against whites and males against females. *(439)*

5. No, it is not self-evident that greater equality of income would make society a better place to live. Unequal income distribution has its benefits. Still, most people would prefer a somewhat more equal distribution of income than currently exists. *(441)*

6. What is fair is a very difficult concept. It depends on people's needs, people's wants, to what degree people are deserving, and other factors. Still, in the absence of any more information than is given in the question, I would divide the pie equally. *(441)*

7. No, one cannot reasonably assume other things remain constant. Redistributive programs have important side effects that can change the behavior of individuals and subvert the intent of the program. Three important side effects include substituting leisure for labor, a decrease in measured income, and attempts to appear more needy. *(442)*

8. As a general statement, "A progressive tax is preferable to a proportional tax" is false. A progressive tax may well be preferable, but that is a normative judgment (just as its opposite would be). Moreover, taxes have incentive effects that must be considered. *(444)*

9. False. The U.S. Social Security system includes many other aspects, such as disability benefits and survivors' benefits. *(445)*

10. The distribution of initial property rights underlies the initial distribution of income. Those with the property rights will reap the returns from those rights. Ultimately, we can answer the question whether income distribution is fair only after we have answered whether the initial property rights distribution is fair. *(447)*

Work and the Labor Market

21

After reading this chapter, you should be able to:

- Use the theory of rational choice to explain why an increase in the marginal tax rate is likely to reduce the quantity of labor supplied.

- List four factors that influence the elasticity of market labor supply.

- Explain how the demand for labor is a derived demand.

- List four factors that influence the elasticity of market labor demand.

- Define *monopsonist* and *bilateral monopoly*.

- Discuss real-world characteristics of labor markets in terms of market, political, and social forces.

- List three types of discrimination.

Work banishes those three great evils:
boredom, vice, and poverty.

Voltaire

Most of us earn our living by working. We supply labor (get a job) and get paid for doing things that other people tell us they want done. Even before we get a job, work is very much a part of our lives. We spend a large portion of our school years preparing for work. Probably many of you are taking this economics course because you've been told that it will help prepare you for a job—or that it will get you more pay than you're getting in your present job. For you, this course is investment in human capital (skills embodied in workers through experience, education, and on-the-job training). If work in the marketplace isn't already familiar to you, once you get out of school it will become so (unless you're sitting on a hefty trust fund or marry somebody who is).

People tend to define themselves by their work.

Your job will occupy at least a third of your waking hours. To a great extent, it will define you. When someone asks, "What do you do?" you won't answer, "I clip coupons, go out on dates, visit my children . . ." Instead you'll answer, "I work for the Blank Company" or "I'm an economist" or "I'm a teacher." Defining ourselves by our work means that work is more than the way we get income. It's a part of our social and cultural makeup. If we lose our jobs, we lose part of our identity.

There's no way I can discuss all the social, political, cultural, and economic dimensions of work and labor in one chapter, but it's important to begin by at least pointing them out in order to put my discussion of labor markets in perspective. A **labor market** is *a factor market in which individuals supply labor services for wages to other individuals and to firms that need (demand) labor services*. Because social and political pressures are particularly strong in labor markets, we can understand the nature of such markets only by considering how social and political forces interact with economic forces to determine our economic situation.

If the invisible hand were the only force operating, wages would be determined entirely by supply and demand. There's more to it than that, as you'll see, but it shouldn't be surprising to you that my discussion of the invisible hand and the labor market is organized around the concepts of supply and demand.

THE SUPPLY OF LABOR

The labor supply choice facing an individual (that is, the decisions of whether, how, and how much to work) can be seen as a choice between nonmarket activities and legal market activities. Nonmarket activities include sleeping, dating, studying, playing, cooking, cleaning, gardening, and black market trading. Legal market activities include taking some type of paid job or working for oneself, directly supplying products or services to consumers.

Economists focus on the incentive effect when considering an individual's choice of whether and how much to work.

Many considerations are involved in individuals' choices of whether and how much to work and what kind of job to work at. Social background and conditioning are especially important, but the factor economists focus on is the **incentive effect** (*how much a person will change his or her hours worked in response to a change in the wage rate*). The incentive effect is determined by the value of supplying one's time to legal market activities relative to the value of supplying one's time to nonmarket activities. The normal relationship is:

Applying rational choice theory to the supply of labor tells us that the higher the wage, the higher the quantity of labor supplied.

The higher the wage, the higher the quantity of labor supplied.

This relationship between the wage rate and the quantity of labor supplied is shown in Figure 21-1. The wage rate is measured on the vertical axis; the quantity of labor supplied is measured on the horizontal axis. As you can see, the supply curve's upward slope indicates that as the wage rate increases, the quantity of labor supplied increases. Why is that the normal relationship? Because work involves opportunity cost. By working one hour more, you have one hour less to devote to nonmarket activities. Alternatively, if you devote the hour to nonmarket activities, you lose one hour's worth of income from working.

Q-1 Under the usual conditions of supply, what would you expect would happen to the amount of time you study if the wage of your part-time job rises?

Say, for example, that by working you would have made $10 per hour. If you decide to work two hours less, you'll have $20 less to spend, but two hours more available for other activities (including spending the smaller amount of money). When the wage rises, say to $12 per hour, an hour of leisure has a higher opportunity cost. As the cost of leisure goes up, you buy less of it, meaning that you work more.

As I noted in my general discussions of supply and demand, the incentive effects represented by the market supply curve come from individuals' either/or decisions to enter,

Figure 21-1   The Supply of Labor

The supply of labor is generally considered to be upward sloping because the opportunity cost of not working increases as wages get higher.

or leave, the labor market; and from individuals' decisions to work more, or fewer, hours. Given the institutional constraints in the labor market, which require many people to work a fixed set of hours if they work at all, much of the incentive effect of higher wages influences the either/or decisions of individuals. This affects the labor force participation rate (the number of people employed or looking for work as a percentage of people able to work) rather than adjusting the number of hours worked. For example, when wages rise, retired workers may find it worthwhile to go back to work, and many teenagers may choose to find part-time jobs.

Real Wages and the Opportunity Cost of Work

The upward-sloping supply curve of labor tells you that, other things equal, as wages go up, the quantity of labor supplied goes up. But if you look at the historical record, you will see that over the last century real wages in the United States increased substantially but the average number of hours worked per person fell. This difference is partly explained by the income effect. (See the accompanying box.) Higher incomes make people richer, and richer people choose more leisure.

Given that people are far richer today than they were 50 or 100 years ago, it isn't surprising that they work less. What's surprising is that they work as much as they do— eight hours a day rather than the four or so hours a day that would be enough to give people the same income they had a century ago.

The explanation of why people haven't reduced their hours of work more substantially can be found in how leisure has changed. A century ago, conversation was an art. People could use their time for long, leisurely conversations. Letter writing was a skill all educated people had, and cooking dinner was a three-hour event. If today people were satisfied with leisure consisting of long conversations, whittling, and spending quality time with their families rather than skiing, golfing, or traveling, they could get by with working perhaps only four or five hours per day instead of eight hours. But that isn't the case.

Today leisurely dinners, conversations about good books, and witty letters have been replaced by "efficient" leisure: a fast-food supper, a home video, and the instant analysis of current events. Microwave ovens, frozen dinners, Pop-Tarts, cellular telephones, the Internet—the list of gadgets and products designed to save time is endless. All these gadgets that increase the "efficiency" of leisure (increase the marginal utility per hour of leisure spent) cost money, which means people today must work more to enjoy their leisure! In the United States, one reason people work hard is so that they can play hard (and expensively).

Modern gadgets increase the efficiency of leisure but cost money, which means people must work more to enjoy their leisure.

Because labor income is such an important component of most people's total income, when wages change other things often do not stay equal, and at times the effect can seem strange. For example, say that you earn $10 an hour and you decide to work eight hours per day. Suddenly demand for your services goes up and you find that you can receive $40 an hour. Will you decide to work more hours? According to the rational choice rule, you will, but you might also decide that at $40 an hour you'll work only six hours a day—$240 a day is enough; the rest of the day you want leisure time to spend your money. In such a case a higher wage means working less.

Does this violate the rational choice rule? The answer is no, because other things—specifically your income—do not remain equal. The higher wage makes you decide to work more—as the rational choice rule says; but the effect of the higher wage is overwhelmed by the effect of the higher income that allows you to decide to work less.

KNOWING THE TOOLS

Income and Substitution Effects

To distinguish between these two effects, economists have given them names. The decision, based on the rational choice rule, to work more hours when your pay goes up is called the *substitution effect.* You substitute work for leisure because the price of leisure has risen. The decision to work fewer hours when your pay goes up, based on the fact that you're richer and therefore can live a better life, is called the *income effect.*

It's possible that the income effect can exceed the substitution effect, and a wage increase can cause a person to work less, but that possibility does not violate the rational choice rule, which refers to the substitution effect only. For those of you who didn't make a deal with me in the chapter on individual choice, a good exercise is to show the income and substitution effects with indifference curves and to demonstrate how it might be possible for an increase in the wage to lead to a decline in hours of work.

Economists do not try to answer the normative question of whether people are better off today, working hard to play hard, or simply are more harried.

The fast pace of modern society has led a number of people to question whether we, as a society, are better off working hard to play hard. Are we better off or simply more harried? Most economists don't try to answer this normative question; but they do point out that people are choosing their harried lifestyle, so to argue that people are worse off, one must argue that people are choosing something they don't really want. That may be true, but it's a tough argument to prove.

The Supply of Labor and Nonmarket Activities

In addition to leisure, labor supply issues and market incentives play an important role in other nonmarket activities. For example, there's a whole set of illegal activities, such as selling illegal drugs, that are alternatives to taking a legal job.

Let's say that an 18-year-old street kid figures he has only two options: Either he can work at a minimum wage job or he can deal drugs illegally. Dealing drugs involves enormous risks of getting arrested or shot, but it also means earning $50 or $75 an hour. Given that choice, many risk takers opt to sell drugs. When an emergency room doctor asked a shooting victim in New York City why he got involved in selling drugs, he responded, "I'm not going to work for chump change. I make $3,000 a week, tax-free. What do they pay you, sucker?" The doctor had to admit that even he wasn't making that kind of money.

For middle-class individuals who have prospects for good jobs, the cost of being arrested can be high—an arrest can destroy their future prospects. For poor street kids with little chance of getting a good job, an arrest makes little difference to their future. For them the choice is heavily weighted toward selling drugs. This is especially true for the entrepreneurial types—the risk takers—the movers and shakers who might have become the business leaders of the future. I've asked myself what decision I would have made had I been in their position. And I suspect I know the answer.

Prohibiting certain drugs leads to potentially high income from selling those drugs and has significant labor market effects. The incentive effects that prohibition has on the choices of jobs facing poor teenagers is a central reason why some economists support the legalization of currently illegal drugs.

Income Taxation, Work, and Leisure

It is after-tax income, not before-tax income, that determines how much you work. Why? Because after-tax income is what you give up by not working. The government, not you, forgoes what you would have paid in taxes if you had worked. This means that when the government raises your marginal rate (the tax you pay on an additional dollar), it reduces your incentive to work. When the marginal tax rate gets really high—say 60 or 70 percent—it can significantly reduce individuals' incentive to work and earn income.

One main reason why the U.S. government reduced marginal income tax rates in the 1980s was to reduce the negative incentive effects of high taxes. Whereas in the 1950s and 1960s the highest U.S. marginal income tax rate was 70 percent, today (as we noted in Chapter 20) the highest marginal income tax rate is about 40 percent. European countries, which have significantly higher marginal tax rates than the United States, are currently struggling with the problem of providing incentives for people to work.

Reducing the marginal tax rate in the United States hasn't completely eliminated the problem of negative incentive effects on individuals' work effort. The reason is that the amounts people receive from many other government programs are tied to earned income. When your earned income goes up, your benefits from these other programs go down.

Say, for example, that you're getting welfare and you're deciding whether to take a $6-an-hour job. Income taxes and Social Security taxes reduce the amount you take home from the job by 20 percent, to $4.80 an hour. But you also know that the Welfare Department will reduce your welfare benefits by 50 cents for every dollar you take home. This means that you lose another $2.40 per hour, so the marginal tax rate on your $6-an-hour job isn't 20 percent; it's 60 percent. By working an hour, you've increased your net income by only $2.40. When you consider the transportation cost of getting to and from work, the expense of getting new clothes to wear to work, the cost of child care, and other job-associated expenses, the net gain in income is often minimal. Your implicit marginal tax rate is almost 100 percent! At such rates, there's an enormous incentive either not to work or to work off the books (get paid in cash so you have no recorded income that the tax agent can trace).

The negative incentive effect can sometimes be even more indirect. For example, college scholarships are generally given on the basis of need. A family that earns more gets less in scholarship aid; the amount by which the scholarship is reduced as a family's income increases acts as a marginal tax on individuals' income. Why work hard to provide for yourself if a program will take care of you if you don't work hard? Hence, the irony in any need-based assistance program is that it reduces the people's incentive to prevent themselves from being needy. These negative incentive effects on labor supply that accompany any need-based program present a public policy dilemma for which there is no easy answer.

The Elasticity of the Supply of Labor

Exactly how these various incentives affect the amount of labor an individual supplies is determined by the elasticity of the individual's supply curve of labor.

The elasticity of the market supply curve is determined by the elasticity of individuals' supply curves and by individuals entering and leaving the labor force. Both of these, in turn, are determined by individuals' opportunity cost of working. If a large

---

An increase in the marginal tax rate is likely to reduce the quantity of labor supplied because it reduces the net wage of individuals and hence, via individuals' incentive effect, causes them to work less.

Q-2 Why do income taxes reduce your incentive to work?

European countries, which have relatively high marginal tax rates, are struggling with the problem of providing incentives for people to work.

Q-3 What is the irony of any need-based program?

Elasticity of market supply depends on:

1. Individuals' opportunity cost of working.
2. The type of market being discussed.
3. The elasticity of individuals' supply curves.
4. Individuals entering and leaving the labor market.

number of people are willing to enter the labor market when wages rise, then the market labor supply will be highly elastic even if individuals' supply curves are inelastic.

The elasticity of supply also depends on the type of market being discussed. For example, the elasticity of the labor supply facing one firm in a small town will likely be far greater than the elasticity of the labor supply of all firms in that town. If only one firm raises its wage, it will attract workers away from other firms; if all the firms in town raise their wages, any increase in labor must come from increases in labor force participation, increases in hours worked per person, or in-migration (the movement of new workers into the town's labor market).

Existing workers prefer inelastic labor supplies because that means an increase in demand for labor will raise their wage by more. Employers prefer elastic supplies because that means an increase in demand for labor doesn't require large wage increases. These preferences can be seen in news reports about U.S. immigration laws, their effects, and their enforcement. Businesses such as hotels and restaurants often oppose strict immigration laws. Their reason is that jobs such as janitor, chambermaid, and busperson are frequently filled by new immigrants or illegal aliens who have comparatively low expectations.

Because of the importance of the elasticity of labor supply, economists have spent a great deal of time and effort estimating it. Their best estimates of labor supply elasticities to market activities are about 0.1 for heads of households and 1.1 for secondary workers in households. These elasticity figures mean that a wage increase of 10 percent will increase the quantity of labor supplied by 1 percent for heads of households (an inelastic supply) and 11 percent for secondary workers in households (an elastic supply). Why the difference? Institutional factors. Hours of work are only slightly flexible. Since most heads of households are employed, they cannot significantly change their hours worked. Many secondary workers in households are not employed, and the higher elasticity reflects new secondary workers entering the labor market.

Immigration and the International Supply of Labor

International limitations on the flow of people, and hence on the flow of labor, play an important role in elasticities of labor supply. In many industries, wages in developing countries are 1/10 or 1/20 the rate of wages in the United States. This large wage differential means that many people from those low-wage countries would like to move to the United States to earn the higher wages. Because they cannot always meet the legal immigration restrictions that limit the flow, many people come into the United States illegally. In addition to about 700,000 legal immigrants per year, more than 275,000 people per year come illegally. Illegal immigrants take a variety of jobs at lower wages and worse conditions than U.S. citizens and legal immigrants are willing to take. The result is that the actual supply of labor is more elastic than the measured supply, especially in those jobs that cannot be easily policed.

In the early 1990s, the European Union introduced open borders among member countries. That institutional change has brought about a more open flow of individuals into higher-wage EU countries from lower-wage EU countries, although other institutionalized restrictions on flows of people, such as language and culture barriers, prevented the EU from being a unified labor market through the early 2000s.

THE DERIVED DEMAND FOR LABOR

The demand for labor follows the basic law of demand:

The higher the wage, the lower the quantity of labor demanded.

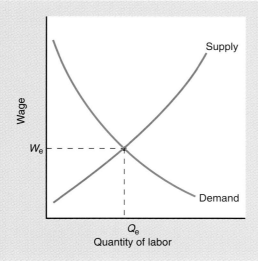

Figure 21-2　Equilibrium in the Labor Market

When the supply and demand curves for labor are placed on the same graph, the equilibrium wage, W_e, is where the quantity supplied equals quantity demanded. At this wage, Q_e laborers are supplied.

This relationship between the wage rate and the quantity of labor demanded is shown by the blue line in Figure 21-2. Its downward slope states that as the wage rate falls the quantity of labor demanded rises. The reason for this relationship differs between the demand for labor by self-employed individuals and by firms.

When individuals are self-employed (work for themselves), the demand for their labor is the demand for the product or service they supply—be it cutting hair, shampooing rugs, or filling teeth. You have an ability to do something, you offer to do it at a certain price, and you see who calls. You determine how many hours you work, what price you charge, and what jobs you take. The income you receive depends on the demand for the good or service you supply and your decision about how much labor you want to supply. In analyzing self-employed individuals, we can move directly from demand for the product to demand for labor.

When a person is not self-employed, determining the demand for labor isn't as direct. It's a two-step process: Consumers demand products from firms; firms, in turn, demand labor and other factors of production. The demand for labor by firms is a **derived demand**—*the demand for factors of production by firms, which depends on consumers' demands*. In other words, it's derived from consumers' demand for the goods that the firm sells. Thus, you can't think of demand for a factor of production such as labor separately from demand for goods. Firms translate consumers' demands into a demand for factors of production.

Derived demand is the demand for factors of production by firms, which depends on consumers' demands.

Factors Influencing the Elasticity of Demand for Labor

The elasticity of the derived demand for labor, or for any other input, depends on a number of factors. One of the most important is (1) *the elasticity of demand for the firm's good*. The more elastic the final demand, the more elastic the derived demand. Other factors influencing the elasticity of derived demand include (2) *the relative importance of the factor in the production process* (the more important the factor, the less elastic is the derived demand); (3) *the possibility of, and cost of, substitution in production* (the easier substitution is, the more elastic is the derived demand); and (4) *the degree to which the marginal productivity falls with an increase in the factor* (the faster productivity falls, the less elastic is the derived demand).

Q-4　Name at least two factors that influence the elasticity of a firm's derived demand for labor.

Four factors that influence
the elasticity of demand for
labor are:
1. The elasticity of demand for
   the firm's good.
2. The relative importance of
   the factor in the production
   process.
3. The possibility of, and cost of,
   substitution in production.
4. The degree to which marginal
   productivity falls with an increase in the factor.

Entrepreneurship is labor services
that involve high degrees of organizational skills, concern, oversight responsibility, and creativity.

Q.5 What would happen to the
demand for labor if a firm's product became more popular?

Each of these relationships follows from the definition of *elasticity* (the percentage change in quantity divided by the percentage change in price) and a knowledge of production. To be sure you understand, ask yourself the following question: If all I knew about two firms was that one was a perfect competitor and the other was a monopolist, which firm would I say is likely to have the more elastic derived demand for labor? If your answer wasn't automatically "the competitive firm" (because its demand curve is perfectly elastic and hence more elastic than a monopolist's), I would suggest that at this point you review the discussion of factors influencing demand elasticity in Chapter 6 and relate that to this discussion. The two discussions are similar and serve as good reviews for each other.

Labor as a Factor of Production

The traditional factors of production are land, labor, capital, and entrepreneurship. When economists talk of the labor market, they're talking about two of these factors: labor and entrepreneurship. **Entrepreneurship** is *labor services that involve high degrees of organizational skills, concern, oversight responsibility, and creativity.* It is a type of creative labor.

The reason for distinguishing between labor and entrepreneurship is that an hour of work is not simply an hour of work. If high degrees of organizational skill, concern, oversight responsibility, and creativity are exerted (which is what economists mean by *entrepreneurship*), one hour of such work can be the equivalent of days, weeks, or even years of simple labor. That's one reason that pay often differs between workers doing what seems to be the same job. It's also why one of the important decisions a firm makes is what type of labor to hire. Should the firm try to hire high-wage entrepreneurial labor or low-wage nonentrepreneurial labor?

In Appendix A, I formally develop the firm's derived demand. Here in the chapter itself I will simply point out that the demand for labor follows the basic law of demand—the lower the price, the higher the quantity demanded. Figure 21-2 shows a demand-for-labor curve combined with a supply-of-labor curve. As you would expect, equilibrium is at wage W_e and quantity supplied Q_e.

Shift Factors of Demand

Factors that shift the demand curve for labor will put pressure on the equilibrium price to change. Let's consider some examples. Say the cost of a competing factor of supply, such as a machine that also could do the job, rises. That would shift the demand for this factor (labor) out, and in doing so put pressure on the wage to rise.

Alternatively, say a new technology develops that requires skills different from those currently being used—for instance, requiring knowing how to use a computer rather than knowing how to use a slide rule. The demand for individuals knowing how to use slide rules will decrease, and their wage will tend to fall.

Another example: Say an industry becomes more monopolistic. What will that do to the demand for labor in that industry? Since monopolies produce less output, the answer is that it would decrease the demand for workers, since the industry would hire fewer of them. The demand for workers would shift in and wages would tend to fall.

Finally, say the demand for the firm's good increases. Then it's clear that the firm's demand for labor will also increase. The way in which these shift factors work is developed in more detail in the appendix to this chapter.

Technology and the Demand for Labor What effect will a change in technology have on the demand for labor? This question has often been debated, and it has no unambiguous answer. What economists do know is that the simple reasoning often used by laypeople when they argue that the development of new technology will decrease the demand for labor is wrong. That simple reasoning is as follows: "Technology makes it possible to replace workers with machines, so it will decrease the demand for labor." This is sometimes called *Luddite reasoning* because it's what drove the Luddites to go around smashing machines in early-19th-century England.

What's wrong with Luddite reasoning? First, look at history. Technology has increased enormously, yet the demand for labor has not decreased; instead it has increased as output has increased. In other words, Luddite reasoning doesn't take into account the fact that total output can change. A second problem with Luddite reasoning is that labor is necessary for building and maintaining the machines, so increased demand for machines increases the demand for labor.

Luddite reasoning isn't *all* wrong. Technology can sometimes decrease the demand for certain types of skills. The computer has decreased demand for calligraphers; the automobile reduced demand for carriage makers. New technology changes the types of labor demanded. If you have the type of labor that will be made technologically obsolete, you can be hurt by technological change. However, technological change hasn't reduced the overall demand for labor; it has instead led to an increase in total output and a need for even more laborers to produce that output.

In the 21st century we're likely to see a continued increase in the use of robots to do many repetitive tasks that blue-collar workers formerly did. Thus, demand for manufacturing labor will likely continue to decline, but it will be accompanied by an increase in demand for service industry labor—designing and repairing robots and designing activities that will fill up people's free time.

International Competitiveness and a Country's Demand for Labor Many of the issues in the demand for labor concern one firm's or industry's demand for labor relative to another firm's or industry's demand. When we're talking about the demand for labor by the country as a whole—an issue fundamentally important to many of the policy issues being discussed today—we have to consider the country's overall international competitiveness. A central determinant of a country's competitiveness is the relative wage of labor in that country compared to the relative wage of labor in other countries.

Wages vary considerably among countries. For example, in 1998 workers in the manufacturing industry earned an average $18.56 an hour in the United States, $27.20 an hour in Germany, and $1.83 an hour in Mexico. Multinational corporations are continually making decisions about where to place production facilities, and labor costs—wage rates—play an important role in these decisions. That means the country's exchange rate plays an important role in determining the demand for labor in a country. For example, in the early 1990s many Japanese automobile companies switched their production of cars to be sold in the United States from production facilities in Japan to facilities in the United States. Why? Because the rise in value of the yen, and fall in value of the dollar, meant that the hourly rate of labor in the United States was about $16 and the hourly rate in Japan was about $20.

But why produce in the United States when the hourly rate in Taiwan, for example, was only 1/4 that in the United States? Or in Mexico, where the hourly rate was only 1/10 that in the United States? The reasons are complicated, but include (1) differences in workers—U.S. workers may be more productive; (2) transportation costs—producing in the country to which you're selling keeps transportation costs down; (3) potential trade restrictions—Japan was under enormous pressure from the U.S. government to reduce its trade surplus with the United States, and producing in the United States helped it avoid future trade restrictions; (4) compatibility of production techniques with social institutions—production techniques must fit with a society's social institutions. If

Luddites oppose technological advances.

Q.6 Name two factors besides relative wages that determine the demand for labor in one country compared to another.

Wages aren't the only consideration when a firm decides where to locate production. Other factors include worker productivity, transportation costs, trade restrictions, and social institutions.

they don't, production will fall significantly. Number (5) is the *focal point phenomenon*— a situation where a company chooses to move, or expand, production to another country because other companies have already moved or expanded there. A company can't consider all places, and it costs a lot of money to explore a country's potential as a possible host country. Japanese businesses know what to expect when they open a plant in the United States; they don't know in many other countries. So the United States, and other countries that Japanese businesses have knowledge about, become focal points. They are considered as potential sites for business, while other, possibly equally good, countries are not. Combined, these reasons lead to a "follow-the-leader" system in which countries fall in and out of global companies' production plans. The focal-point countries expand and develop; the others don't.

THE ROLE OF OTHER FORCES IN WAGE DETERMINATION

Supply and demand forces strongly influence wages, but they do not fully determine wages.

Supply and demand forces strongly influence wages, but they do not fully determine wages. Real-world labor markets are filled with examples of suppliers or demanders who resist these supply and demand pressures through organizations such as labor unions, professional associations, and agreements among demanders. But, as I've emphasized throughout the book, supply and demand analysis is a useful framework for considering such resistance.

For example, say that you're advising a firm's workers on how to raise their wages. You point out that if workers want to increase their wages, they must figure out some way either to increase the demand for their services or to limit the labor supplied to the firm. One way to limit the number of workers the firm will hire (and thus keep existing workers' wages high) is to force the firm to pay an above-equilibrium wage, as in Figure 21-3(a). Say that in their contract negotiations the workers get the firm to agree to pay a wage of W_1. At wage W_1, the quantity of labor supplied is Q_S and the quantity of labor demanded is Q_D. The difference, $Q_S - Q_D$, represents the number of people who want jobs at wage W_1 compared to the number who have them. In such a case, jobs

Figure 21-3   The Labor Market in Action

In (a) you can see the effect of an above-equilibrium wage: If workers force the firm to pay them a wage of W_1, more workers will be supplied (Q_S) than demanded (Q_D). With an excess supply of labor, jobs must be rationed. In (b) you can see the effect of an increase in the supply of labor—for example, because of liberalization in the immigration laws. The supply of labor curve shifts outward from S_0 to S_1. Assuming the demand for labor remains the same, the increase in the supply of labor will cause the wage level to drop from W_0 to W_1.

(a) Maintaining excess supply

(b) An increase in supply

must be rationed. Whom you know, where you come from, or the color of your skin may play a role in whether you get a job with that firm.

As a second example, consider what would happen if U.S. immigration laws were liberalized. If you say the supply curve of labor would shift outward and the wage level would drop, you're right, as shown in Figure 21-3(b). In it the supply of labor increases from S_0 to S_1. In response, the wage falls from W_0 to W_1 and the quantity of labor demanded increases from Q_0 to Q_1.

In analyzing the effect of such a major change in the labor supply, however, remember that the supply and demand framework is relevant only if the change in the supply of labor doesn't also affect the demand for labor. In reality, a change in U.S. immigration laws might increase the demand for products, thereby increasing the demand for labor and raising wages. When you look at the overall effect of a change, you will often find that the final result is less clear-cut. That's why it's important always to remember the assumptions behind the model you're using. Those assumptions often add qualifications to the simple "right" answer.

Q.7 How could an increase in the supply of labor lead to an increase in the demand for labor?

Looking at the overall effects of a change, rather than just the partial equilibrium effects, often makes the final result less clear-cut.

IMPERFECT COMPETITION AND THE LABOR MARKET

Just as product markets can be imperfectly competitive, so too can labor markets. For example, there might be a **monopsony** (*a market in which a single firm is the only buyer*). Alternatively, laborers might have organized together in a union that allows workers to operate as if there were only a single seller. In effect, the union could operate as a monopoly. Alternatively again, there might be a **bilateral monopoly** (*a market with only a single seller and a single buyer*). Let's briefly consider these three types of market imperfections.

A monopsony is a market in which a single firm is the only buyer. A bilateral monopoly is a market in which a single seller faces a single buyer.

Monopsony

When there's only one buyer of labor services, it makes sense for that buyer to take into account the fact that if it hires another worker, the equilibrium wage will rise and it will have to pay more for all workers. The choice facing a monopsonist can be seen in Figure 21-4, in which the supply curve of labor is upward sloping so that the **marginal**

Figure 21-4   Monopsony, Union Power, and the Labor Market

A monopsonist hires fewer workers and pays them less than would a set of competitive firms. The monopsonist determines the quantity of labor, Q_m, to hire at the point where the marginal factor cost curve intersects the demand curve. The monopsonist pays a wage of W_m. A union has a tendency to push for a higher wage, W_u, and a lower quantity of workers, Q_u.

A monopsonist takes into account the fact that hiring another worker will increase the wage rate it must pay all workers.

factor cost (*the additional cost to a firm of hiring another worker*) is above the supply curve since the monopsonist takes into account the fact that hiring another worker will increase the wage rate it must pay to all workers.

Instead of hiring Q_c workers at a wage of W_c, as would happen in a competitive labor market, the monopsonist hires Q_m workers and pays them a wage of W_m. (A good exercise to see that you understand the argument is to show that where there's a monopsonist, a minimum wage simultaneously can increase employment and raise the wage.)

Union Monopoly Power

When a union exists, it will have an incentive to act as a monopolist, restricting supply in order to increase its members' wages. To do so it must have the power to restrict both supply and union membership. There would be a strong tendency for the union to act like a monopolist and to move to an equilibrium somewhat similar to the monopsonist case, except for one important difference. The wage the union would set wouldn't be set below the competitive wage; instead, the wage would be above the competitive wage at W_u, as in Figure 21-4. Faced with a wage of W_u, competitive firms will hire Q_u workers. Thus, with union monopoly power, the benefits of restricting supply accrue to the union members, not to the firm as in the monopsonist case.

Bilateral Monopoly

As our final case, let's consider a bilateral monopoly in which a monopsonist faces a union with monopoly power. In this case, we can say that the equilibrium wage will be somewhere between the monopsonist wage W_m and the union monopoly power wage W_u. The equilibrium quantity will be somewhere between Q_u and Q_m in Figure 21-4. Where in that range the wage and equilibrium quantity will be depends on the two sides' negotiating skills and other noneconomic forces.

Downsizing, Upsizing, and X-Inefficiency

From 1992 to 2000, employment rose in the United States by over 20 million jobs. At the same time there was much concern in the nation about **downsizing**—*a reduction in the workforce*—of major corporations, especially at the level of middle management. Considering these two issues—increased total employment and the downsizing at particular firms—gives us a good sense of how supply and demand analysis carries over into the real world.

Q.8 How is it that total U.S. employment in the late 1990s grew and companies downsized at the same time?

First let's consider the increase in employment during this time period. What were the reasons total employment grew? First, the U.S. economy grew—that growth increased demand for goods, and hence for labor. Second, the value of the dollar remained low relative to the value of the currencies of other major industrial countries. Demand for U.S. exports increased, and hence the demand for U.S. labor increased. Third, union power in the United States declined during this time period, lowering overall wages (adjusted for inflation) in unionized industries, thereby increasing the quantity of labor demanded. Combined, these three forces accounted for the rise in employment.

Some reasons employment grew in the 1990s include:

1. Economic growth.
2. Low value of the dollar.
3. Declining union power.

The downsizing was, in part, a way by which union power was reduced. Firms producing with a high-wage workforce had an incentive to shift their production to firms that had low-wage workforces—that is, to low-wage firms abroad and to low-wage U.S. firms. The term developed for this is wage **outsourcing**—*a firm shifting production from its own plant to other firms, either in the United States or abroad, where wages are lower*. Firms' outsourcing increased the demand for low-wage labor; they *upsized* as firms with high-wage labor downsized.

Why didn't high-wage firms simply cut wages? To some degree, they did, but cutting wages often leads to bitter fights within a firm. Downsizing keeps the angry workers out of the production process and makes the workers who are not laid off feel lucky that they have kept their jobs.

Such outsourcing was only part of the cause of downsizing. A second part was a reduction in X-inefficiency. As discussed in Chapter 14, for a variety of reasons, such as the monitoring problem, managers have a tendency to become lazy and produce inefficiently. When faced with significant international and domestic competition, as firms have been in recent years, they must reduce that inefficiency or go out of business. Thus, downsizing is a normal part of the way the competitive process works. It results from a reduction in demand for labor from inefficient firms and a transfer of demand to more efficient firms, who, it might be said, are upsizing. In this period, upsizing significantly exceeded downsizing, but it was primarily the downsizing that was reported in the press.

Downsizing is a normal part of the way the competitive process works.

POLITICAL AND SOCIAL FORCES AND THE LABOR MARKET

Let's now consider some real-world characteristics of labor markets. For example:

1. English teachers are paid close to what economics teachers are paid even though the quantity of English teachers supplied significantly exceeds the quantity of English teachers demanded, while the quantity of economics teachers supplied is approximately equal to the quantity demanded.

2. On average, women earn about 75 cents for every $1 earned by men.

3. Certain types of jobs are undertaken primarily by members of a single ethnic group. For example, Mohawk Indians make up a large percentage of construction workers on high-rise buildings. They have an uncanny knack for keeping their balance on high, open building frames.

4. Firms often pay higher than "market" wages.

5. Firms often don't lay off workers even when there is a decrease in the demand for their product.

6. It often seems that there are two categories of jobs: dead-end jobs and jobs with potential for career advancement. Once in a dead-end job, a person finds it almost impossible to switch to a job with potential.

7. The rate of unemployment among blacks is more than twice as high as the rate among whites.

Supply and demand analysis alone doesn't explain these phenomena. Each of them can, however, be explained as the result of market, political, and social forces. Thus, to understand real-world labor markets, it is necessary to broaden the analysis of labor markets to include other forces that limit the use of the market. These include legal and social limitations on the self-interest-seeking activities of firms and individuals. Let's consider a couple of the central issues of interaction among these forces and see how they affect the labor market.

To understand real-world labor markets, one must broaden the analysis.

Fairness and the Labor Market

People generally have an underlying view of what's fair. That view isn't always consistent among individuals, but it's often strongly held. The first lesson taught in a personnel or human resources course is that people aren't machines. They're human beings with feelings and emotions. If they feel good about a job, if they feel they're part of a team, then they will work hard; if they feel they're being taken advantage of, they can be highly disruptive.

On some assembly-line jobs, effort is relatively easy to monitor, so individuals can be—and in the past often were—treated like machines. Their feelings and emotions were ignored. Productivity was determined by the speed of the assembly line; if workers couldn't or wouldn't keep up the pace, they were fired.

Efficiency Wages Most modern jobs, however, require workers to make decisions and to determine how best to do a task. Today's managers are aware that workers' emotional state is important to whether they make sound decisions and do a good job. So most firms, even if they don't really care about anything but profit, will try to keep their workers happy. It's in their own interest to do so. That might mean paying workers more than the going market wage, not laying them off even if layoffs would make sense economically, providing day care so the workers aren't worried about their children, or keeping wage differentials among workers small to limit internal rivalry. Such actions can often make long-run economic sense, even though they might cost the firm in the short run. They are common enough that they have acquired a name—**efficiency wages**—*wages paid above the going market wage in order to keep workers happy and productive*.

Views of fairness also enter into wage determination through political channels. Social views of fairness influence government, which passes laws to implement those views. Minimum wage laws, comparable worth laws, and antidiscrimination laws are examples.

Comparable Worth Laws Let's consider one of those, **comparable worth laws**, which are *laws mandating comparable pay for comparable work*—that is, mandatory "fairness." The problem is in defining what is comparable. Do you define comparable work by the education it requires, by the effort the worker puts out, or by other characteristics? Similarly with pay: Compensation has many dimensions and it is not at all clear which are the relevant ones, or whether the political system will focus on the relevant ones.

Economists who favor comparable worth laws point out that social and intrafirm political issues are often the determining factors in setting pay. In fact, firms often have their own implicit or explicit comparable worth systems built into their structure. For example, seniority, not productivity, often determines pay. Bias against women and minorities and in favor of high-level management is sometimes built into firms' pay-setting institutions. In short, within firms, pay structure is influenced by, but is not determined by, supply and demand forces. Comparable worth laws are designed to affect those institutional biases, and thus are not necessarily any more incompatible with supply and demand forces than are current pay-setting institutions.

Job Discrimination and the Labor Market

Discrimination exists in all walks of life: Women are paid less than men, and blacks are often directed into lower-paying jobs. Economists have done a lot of research in order to understand the facts about discrimination and what can be done about it. The first problem is to measure the amount of discrimination and get an idea of how much discrimination is caused by what. Let's consider discrimination against women.

On average, women receive somewhere around 75 percent of the pay that men receive. That has increased from about 60 percent in the 1970s. This pay gap suggests that discrimination is occurring. The economist's job is to figure out how much of this is statistically significant and, of the portion that is caused by discrimination, what the nature of that discrimination is.

Analyzing the data, economists have found that somewhat more than half of the pay difference can be explained by causes other than discrimination, such as length of time

Firms sometimes pay what's called efficiency wages to keep workers happy and productive.

Q.9   Economic theory argues that discrimination should be eliminated. True or false? Why?

BEYOND THE TOOLS

Democracy in the Workplace

In the United States, slavery is illegal. You cannot sell yourself to someone else, even if you want to. It's an unenforceable contract. But work, which might be considered a form of partial slavery, is legal. You can sell your labor services for a specific, limited period of time.

Is there any inherent reason that such partial slavery should be seen as acceptable? The answer to that question is complicated. It deals with the rights of workers, and is based on value judgments. You must answer it for yourself. I raise it because it's a good introduction to Karl Marx's analysis of the labor market (which deals with alienation) and to some recent arguments about democracy in the workplace.

Marx saw selling labor as immoral, just as slavery was immoral. He believed that capitalists exploited workers by alienating them from their labor. The best equivalent I can think of is the way most people today view the selling of sex. Most people see selling sex as wrong because it alienates a person from his or her own body. Marx saw all selling of labor that same way. A labor market makes workers see themselves as objects, not as human beings.

The underlying philosophical issues of Marx's concern are outside of economics. Most people in the United States don't agree with Marx's philosophical underpinnings. But it's nonetheless a useful exercise to think about this issue and ask yourself whether it helps explain why we somehow treat the labor market as different from other markets and limit by law the right of employers to discriminate in the labor market.

Some of Marx's philosophical tenets are shared by the modern democracy-in-the-workplace movement. In this view, a business isn't owned by a certain group, but is an association of individuals who have come together to produce a certain product. For one group—the owners of stock—to have all the say as to how the business is run, and for another group—the regular workers—to have no say, is immoral in the same way that not having a democratic government is immoral. According to this view, work is as large a part of people's lives as is national or local politics, and a country can call itself a democracy only if it has democracy in the workplace.

As with most grandiose ideas, this one is complicated, but it's worth considering because it's reflected in certain laws. Consider, for example, the 1989 federal law that limits firms' freedom to close plants without giving notice to their workers. The view that workers have certain inalienable rights played a role in passing that law.

For those of you who say "Right on!" to the idea of increasing workers' rights, let me add a word of caution. Increasing workers' rights has a cost. It makes it less likely that firms and individuals who can think up things that need doing will do so, and thus will decrease the number of jobs available. It will also increase firms' desire to discriminate. If you know you must let a person play a role in decisions once you hire that person, you're going to be much more careful about whom you hire.

None of these considerations mean that democracy in the workplace can't work. There are examples of somewhat democratic "firms." Universities are run as partial democracies, with the faculty deciding what policies should be set. (There is, however, serious debate about how well universities are run.) But as soon as you add worker democracy to production, more questions come up: What about consumers? Shouldn't they, too, have a voice in decisions? What about the community within which the firm is located?

Economics can't answer such questions. Economics can, however, be used to predict and analyze some of the difficulties such changes might bring about.

---

on the job. But that still leaves a relatively large difference that can be attributed to discrimination.

Three Types of Direct Demand-Side Discrimination In analyzing discrimination, it's important to distinguish various types. The first is discrimination based on relevant individual characteristics. Firms commonly make decisions about employees based on individual characteristics that will affect job performance. For example, restaurants might discriminate against (avoid hiring) applicants with sourpuss personalities. Another example might be a firm hiring more young salespeople because its clients like to buy from younger rather than older employees. If that characteristic can be an identifying factor for a group of individuals, that discrimination becomes more visible.

Three types of discrimination are:

1. Discrimination based on individual characteristics that will affect job performance.
2. Discrimination based on correctly perceived statistical characteristics of the group.
3. Discrimination based on individual characteristics that don't affect job performance or are incorrectly perceived.

A second type of discrimination is discrimination based on group characteristics. This occurs when firms make employment decisions about individuals because they are members of a group with statistical job characteristics that affect job performance. A firm may correctly perceive that young people in general have a lower probability of staying on a job than do older people and therefore may discriminate against younger people.

A third type of discrimination is discrimination based on irrelevant individual characteristics. This discrimination is based on individual characteristics that do not affect job performance or is based on incorrectly perceived statistical characteristics of groups. A firm might not hire people over 50 because the supervisor doesn't like working with older people, even though older people may be just as productive as, or even more productive than, younger people.

Of the three types, the third will be easiest to eliminate; it doesn't have an economic motivation. In fact, discrimination based on individual characteristics that don't affect job performance is costly to a firm, and market forces will work toward eliminating it.

An example of the success of a firm's policy to reduce discrimination is the decision by McDonald's to create a special program to hire workers with learning disabilities. Individuals who are learning disabled often make good employees. They tend to have lower turnover rates and follow procedures better than do many of the more transient employees McDonald's hires. Moreover, through their advertising, McDonald's helped change some negative stereotypes about people with disabilities. So in this case market forces and political forces are working together.

If the discrimination is of either of the first two types and is based on characteristics that do affect job performance, either directly or statistically, the discrimination will be harder to eliminate. Not discriminating can be costly to the firm, so political forces to eliminate discrimination will be working against market forces to keep discrimination.

Whenever discrimination saves the firm money, the firm will have an economic incentive to use subterfuges to get around an antidiscrimination law. These subterfuges will make the firm appear to be complying with the law, even when it isn't. For example, a firm will find some other reason besides age to explain why it isn't hiring an older person.

Institutional Discrimination Institutional discrimination is discrimination in which the structure of the job makes it difficult or impossible for certain groups of individuals to succeed. Consider the policies of colleges and universities. To succeed as a professor, administrator, or other professional in the academic market, one must devote an enormous amount of effort during one's 20s and 30s. But these years are precisely the years when, given genetics and culture, many women have major family responsibilities. This makes it difficult for women to succeed in the academic market. Were academic institutions different—say, a number of positions at universities were designed for high-level, part-time work during this period—it would be easier for women to advance.

Requiring peak time commitment when women are also facing peak family responsibilities is the norm for many companies, too. Thus, women face significant institutional discrimination.

Whether this discrimination is embodied in the firm's structure or in the family is an open question. For example, sociologists have found that in personal relationships women tend to move to be with their partners more than men move to be with their partners. In addition, women in two-parent relationships do much more work around the house and take a greater responsibility for child rearing than men do even when both the man and the woman are employed.

How important are these sociological observations? In discussing discrimination I ask the members of my class if they expect their personal relationships with their partners to be fully equal. The usual result is the following: 80 percent of the women expect

Discrimination based on characteristics that affect job performance is hard to eliminate.

Institutions can have built-in discrimination.

a fully equal relationship; 20 percent expect their partner's career to come first. Eighty percent of the men expect their own careers to come first; 20 percent expect an equal relationship. I then point out that somebody's expectations aren't going to be fulfilled. Put simply, most observers believe that institutional discrimination that occurs in interpersonal relationships is significant.

Economists have made adjustments for these sociological factors, and have found that institutional factors explain a portion of the lower pay that women receive but that other forms of workplace discrimination also explain a portion.

Whether prejudice should be allowed to affect the hiring decision is a normative question for society to settle. In answering these normative questions, our society has passed laws making it illegal for employers to discriminate on the basis of race, religion, sex, age, disability, or national origin. The reason society has made it illegal is its ethical belief in equal opportunity for all, or at least most, individuals. (Homosexuals still aren't protected by federal legislation assuring them equal opportunities.)

The Evolution of Labor Markets

Now that we've briefly considered how noneconomic forces can influence labor markets, let's turn our attention to how labor markets developed.

Labor markets as we now know them developed in the 1700s and 1800s. Given the political and social rules that operated at that time, the invisible hand was free to push wage rates down to subsistence level. Workweeks were long and working conditions were poor. Laborers began to turn to other ways—besides the market—of influencing their wage. One way was to use political power to place legal restrictions on employers in their relationship with workers. A second way was to organize together—to unionize. Let's consider each in turn.

Evolving Labor Laws Over the years, government has responded to workers' political pressure with a large number of laws that limit what can and what cannot be done in the various labor markets. For example, in many areas of production, laws limit the number of normal hours a person can work in a day to eight. The laws also prescribe the amount of extra pay an employee must receive when working more than the normal number of hours. (Generally it's time-and-a-half.) Similarly, the number and length of workers' coffee breaks are defined by law (one coffee break every four hours).

Child labor laws mandate that a person must be at least 16 years old in order to be hired. The safety and health conditions under which a person can work are regulated by laws. (For example, on a construction site all workers are required to wear hard hats.) Workers can be fired only for cause, and employers must show that they had cause to fire a worker. (For example, a 55-year-old employee cannot be fired simply because he or she is getting old.) Employers must not allow sexual harassment in the workplace. (Bosses can't make sexual advances to employees and firms must make a good-faith attempt to see that employees don't sexually harass their co-workers.)

Combined, these laws play an enormously important role in the functioning of the labor market.

Unions and Collective Bargaining Some of the most important labor laws concern workers' right to organize together in order to bargain collectively with employers. These laws also specify the tactics workers can use to achieve their ends. In the latter part of the 1800s, workers had few rights to organize themselves. The Knights of Labor was formed in 1869, and by 1886 it had approximately 800,000 members. But a labor riot in 1886 turned public opinion against these workers and led to the organization's

Figure 21-5   Change in Union Membership, 1895–1998

The graph shows union membership from 1895–1998. As can be seen, after the Depression in the 1930s, unions grew in importance. In the 1980s the importance of unions declined, even though the labor force was growing significantly.

Source: Bureau of Labor Statistics. http://stats.bls.gov.

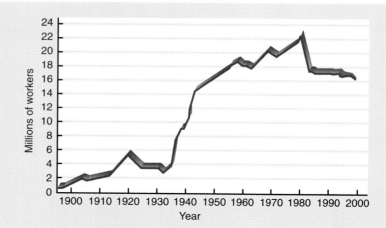

breakup. In its place, the American Federation of Labor developed and began to organize strikes to achieve higher wages.

Business opposed unions' right to strike, and initially the government supported business. Police and sometimes the army were sent in to break up strikes. Under the then-existing legal structure of the economy, unions were seen as monopolistic restraints on trade and an intrusion into management rights.

In the 1930s, society's view of unions changed (in part as a backlash to the strong-arm tactics used by firms to break up unions), and laws such as the National Labor Relations Act (also called the Wagner Act) were passed guaranteeing workers the right to form unions, to strike, and to engage in collective bargaining. As Figure 21-5 shows, from 1935 to 1980 unions grew significantly in size and importance.

Businesses weren't happy with unions' increasing strength, and in 1947 they managed to get the Taft-Hartley Act passed. That act placed limitations on union activities. It allowed states to pass "right-to-work" laws forbidding union membership to be made a requirement for continued employment. Moreover, it made **closed shops,** *firms where the union controls hiring,* illegal. Before anyone can be hired in a closed shop, he or she must be a member of the particular union. Federal law does permit **union shops**—*firms in which all workers must join the union.* Individuals are required to join a union after working for the firm for a period of time. The Taft-Hartley Act also outlawed *secondary boycotts.* In a secondary boycott, in order to strengthen its bargaining position, a union gets unions at other firms to force their firms to refuse to buy a firm's products, under threat of a strike.

Union power weakened further in 1981, when, in response to a strike by air traffic controllers, President Reagan fired all the controllers and refused to hire them back. Private firms similarly won the right to hire permanent replacements for striking workers.

As Figure 21-5 shows, since the 1980s the number of workers in unions has been declining. Moreover, when the growth of the labor force is taken into account, the relative decline in labor union membership is even more significant. Unions don't have the political or economic clout they once had.

Part of the reason, ironically, is their success. By pressuring the government to pass laws that protected workers, unions made themselves less necessary. Another part of the reason is the changing nature of production in the United States. Labor unions were

A closed shop is a firm in which the union controls hiring.

A union shop is a firm in which all workers must join the union.

Part of the reason labor union membership has declined in recent years is the unions' successes.

Table 21-1 (a and b)   Some Useful Labor Information

Occupation	Private or State	U.S. Government
Budget analyst	$29,000	$20,600
Management analyst	32,000	19,000
Secretary	18,000	19,500
Physician assistant	23,000	—
Flight attendant	18,000	17,000
Secondary school teacher	26,000	—
Economist	33,000	24,000
Janitor	16,000	15,000
Retail sales (salary and commission)	17,000	—
Insurance sales	23,000	—

Sources: Author's estimates based on *Occupational Outlook Handbook 00/01* and U.S. Dept. of Labor Statistics (pay varies significantly by region) (http://stats.bls.gov).

(a) Some typical starting salaries of BAs: 2000

Degree	Annual Salary*
Law (3 years)	
High-ranked school	$ 95,000
Intermediate-ranked school	45,000
Low-ranked school	28,000
Engineering	
Bachelor's degree	39,000
Master's degree	53,000
Business	
Bachelor's degree	29,000
Master's (MBA) degree (2 years)	51,000
M.D. (4 years and 3-year internship)	110,000
Ph.D. (5 years)	
In economics	50,000
In humanities	45,000

*These figures are rough estimates based on data from the Department of Labor and informal surveys of author.

(b) Starting salaries for selected professional degrees, 2000

especially strong in manufacturing industries. As the relative number of manufacturing jobs has declined in the United States and the number of service jobs has increased, the base of union membership has been reduced. Unions have somewhat compensated for this change by pushing unionization drives among public sector workers (that is, government employees), and this sector has seen the largest increase in union membership. Today, more than 40 percent of union members work in the public sector. These unions are becoming stronger and will likely be exerting their influence.

CONCLUSION: THE LABOR MARKET AND YOU

This chapter is meant to give you a sense of how the labor market works. But what does it all mean for those of you who'll soon be getting a job or are in the process of changing jobs? I'll try to answer that question in this last section.

Table 21-1 shows a variety of potentially useful statistics about the labor market. Let's consider how some of them might affect you. For example, consider relative pay of

Ph.D.s earn less than MBAs, so therefore one should get an MBA rather than a Ph.D. True or false? Why?

jobs requiring a college degree compared to jobs requiring only a high school diploma. Jobs requiring a college degree pay significantly more, on average, than do jobs requiring only a high school diploma. In recent years the income gap between the two groups has noticeably increased. So the answer to the question of whether it's worthwhile to stick college out for another couple of years and get a degree is probably yes.

Next, consider the salaries of Ph.D.s compared to the salaries of MBAs. A Ph.D. is a person who has gone to graduate school after college, usually for a number of years, and earned an advanced degree called a **D**octorate of **Ph**ilosophy—even though there are many subjects besides philosophy (such as economics) in which one can earn a Ph.D. As you can see, Ph.D.s' starting salaries are lower than salaries of MBAs (masters of business administration) and professionals with other kinds of advanced degrees. Does this mean that Ph.D.s are discriminated against? Not necessarily. It's possible that Ph.D.s' lower pay suggests that Ph.D.s derive a "psychic income" from their work in addition to the amount of money they earn.

Since Ph.D.s are often quite smart, their willingness to accept psychic income as a substitute for higher pay suggests that there's much more to consider in a job than the salary. What's most important about a job isn't the wage, but whether you like what you're doing and the life that job is consistent with. (Of course, their lower salaries also could imply that Ph.D.s really aren't so smart.)

So my suggestion to you is definitely to finish college, especially if you enjoy it. (And with books like this, how could you help but enjoy it?) But go to graduate school only if you really enjoy learning. In picking your job, first and foremost pick a job that you enjoy (as long as it pays you enough to live on). Among jobs you like, choose a job in a field in which the supply of labor is limited, or the demand for labor is significantly

In the late 1800s, many workers worked in sweatshops; they often had quotas that required them to work 60 or more hours a week. Fines were imposed for such indiscretions as talking or smiling. The Bettman Archive.

increasing. Either of those trends is likely to lead to higher wages. After all, if you're doing something you like, you might as well get paid as much as possible for it.

Jobs in which the supply will likely be limited are those in which social or political forces have placed restrictions on entry or those requiring special abilities. If you have some special ability, try to find a job you enjoy in which you can use that ability. You might also look for a job in which entry is restricted, but beware: Jobs that are restricted in supply must be rationed, so while such jobs pay higher wages, you may need personal connections to obtain one of them.

I'm sure most of you are aware that your choice of jobs is one of the most important choices you'll be making in your life. So I'm sure you feel the pressure. But you should also know that a job, unlike marriage, isn't necessarily supposed to be for life. There's enormous flexibility in the U.S. labor market. Many people change jobs six or seven times in their lifetimes. So while the choice is important, a poor choice can be remedied; don't despair if the first job you take isn't perfect. Good luck.

Chapter Summary

- Incentive effects are important in labor supply decisions. The higher the wage, the higher the quantity supplied.

- Elasticity of market supply of labor depends on (1) individuals' opportunity cost of working, (2) the type of market being discussed, (3) the elasticity of individuals' supply curves, and (4) individuals entering and leaving the labor market.

- The demand for labor by firms is derived from the demand by consumers for goods and services. It follows the basic law of demand—the higher the wage, the lower the quantity demanded.

- Elasticity of market demand for labor depends on (1) the elasticity of demand for the firm's good, (2) the relative importance of labor in production, (3) the possibility and cost of substitution in production, and (4) the degree to which marginal productivity falls with an increase in labor.

- Technological advances and changes in international competitiveness shift the demand for labor. Both have reduced demand for some types of labor and increased demand for other types. The net effect has been an increase in the demand for labor.

- A monopsony is a market in which a single firm is the only buyer. A monopsonist hires fewer workers at a lower wage compared to a competitive firm.

- A bilateral monopoly is a market in which there is a single seller and a single buyer. The wage and number of workers hired in a bilateral monopoly depends on the relative strength of the union and the monopsonist.

- Firms are aware of workers' well-being and will sometimes pay efficiency wages to keep workers happy and productive.

- Views of fairness in the labor market have led to laws that mandate comparable pay for comparable work.

- Discrimination may be based on (1) relevant individual characteristics, (2) group characteristics, and (3) irrelevant individual characteristics. The easiest to eliminate is discrimination based on irrelevant individual characteristics. The other two are motivated by market incentives.

- Labor laws have evolved and will continue to evolve. Since the 1980s, labor unions have been declining in importance.

Key Terms

bilateral monopoly (461)

closed shops (468)

comparable worth laws (464)

derived demand (457)

downsizing (462)

efficiency wages (464)

entrepreneurship (458)

incentive effect (452)

labor market (452)

marginal factor cost (462)

monopsony (461)

outsourcing (462)

union shops (468)

Questions for Thought and Review

1. Why are social and political forces more active in the labor market than in most other markets?

2. Welfare laws are bad, not for society, but for the people they are meant to help. Discuss.

3. Which would you choose: selling illegal drugs at $75 an hour (20 percent chance per year of being arrested) or a $6-an-hour factory job? Why?

4. If the wage goes up 20 percent and the quantity of labor supplied increases by 5 percent, what's the elasticity of labor supply?

5. My brother was choosing between being a carpenter and being a plumber. I advised him to take up plumbing. Why?

6. Why might it be inappropriate to discuss the effect of immigration policy using supply and demand analysis?

7. Demonstrate graphically the effect of a minimum wage law. Does economic theory tell us such a law would be a bad idea?

8. Show graphically how a minimum wage can simultaneously increase employment and raise the wage rate.

9. Comparable worth laws require employers to pay the same wage scale to workers who do comparable work or have comparable training. What likely effect would these laws have on the labor market?

10. Why is unemployment nearly twice as high among blacks as among whites? What should be done about the situation?

11. Give four reasons why women earn less than men. Which reasons do you believe are most responsible for the wage gap?

Problems and Exercises

1. A study done by economists Daniel Hamermesh and Jeff Biddle found that people who are perceived as good-looking earn an average of 10 percent more than those who are perceived as homely and 5 percent more than people who are perceived as average-looking. The pay differential was found to be greater for men than for women.
   a. What conclusions can you draw from these findings?
   b. Do the findings necessarily mean that there is a "looks" discrimination?
   c. What might explain the larger pay penalty for males for looks?

2. In the early 1990s a teen subminimum training wage law was passed by which employers were allowed to pay teenagers less than the minimum wage.
   a. What effect would you predict this law would have, based on standard economic theory?
   b. In analyzing the effects of the law, Professors Card and Kreuger of Princeton University found that few businesses used it and that it had little effect. Why might that have been the case?

3. Economists Mark Blaug and Ruth Towse did a study of the market for economists in Britain. They found that the quantity demanded was about 150–200 a year, and that the quantity supplied was about 300 a year.
   a. What did they predict would happen to economists' salaries?
   b. What likely happens to the excess economists?
   c. Why doesn't the price change immediately to bring the quantity supplied and the quantity demanded into equilibrium?

4. Some economists have argued against need-based scholarships because they work as an implicit tax on parents' salaries and hence discourage saving for college.
   a. If the marginal tax rate parents face is 20 percent, and 5 percent of parents' assets will be deducted from a student's financial aid each year for four years a child is in school, what is the implicit marginal tax on that portion of income that is saved? (For simplicity assume the interest rate is zero and that the parents' contribution is paid at the time the child enters college.)
   b. How would your answer differ if parents had two children with the second entering college right after the first one graduated? (How about three?) (Remember that the assets will likely decrease with each child graduating.)
   c. When parents are divorced, how should the contribution of each parent be determined? If your school has need-based scholarships, how does it determine the expected contributions of divorced parents?
   d. Given the above, would you suggest moving to an ability-based scholarship program? Why or why not?

5. Explain each of the following phenomena using the invisible hand or social or political forces:
   a. Firms often pay higher than market wages.
   b. Wages don't fluctuate much as unemployment rises.
   c. Pay among faculty in various disciplines at colleges does not vary much although market conditions among disciplines vary significantly.

6. A recent study by the International Labor Organization estimates that 250 million children in developing countries between the ages of 5 and 14 are working either full- or part-time. The estimates of the percentage of children working within countries is as high as 42 percent in Kenya. Among the reasons cited for the rise in child labor are population increases and poverty.
   a. Why do firms hire children as workers?
   b. Why do children work?
   c. What considerations should be taken into account by countries when deciding whether to implement an international ban on trade for products made with child labor?

7. Interview three married female and three married male professors at your college, asking them what percentage of work in the professor's household each adult household member does.
   a. Assuming your results can be extended to the population at large, what can you say about the existence of institutional discrimination?

   b. If gender-related salary data for individuals at your college are available, determine whether women or men of equal rank and experience receive higher average pay.
   c. Relate your findings in a and b.
   d. Does the existence of institutional discrimination suggest that no discrimination by employers exists? Why or why not?

Web Questions

1. The National Committee on Pay Equity (NCPE) is a central clearinghouse for information on pay equity. Go to its home page at www.feminist.com/fairpay.htm to answer the following questions.
   a. What is pay equity?
   b. What two laws protect workers against wage discrimination?
   c. Does the NCPE believe that most of the pay gap is from women earning less in the same jobs or women working in lower-paying occupations? How does this affect the enforcement of antidiscrimination laws?

2. The Cato Institute is a public policy institute that favors a laissez-faire approach to the market. One of its commentaries, "Immigration Reform Means More High-Tech Jobs," argues that immigration creates jobs in the United States. Search for the commentary on Cato's home page at www.cato.org and read it to answer the following questions:
   a. For what type of workers is the author arguing immigration should be increased?
   b. How do highly skilled immigrants create jobs for Americans?
   c. What was the state of the economy when the article was written? How does this affect the results of the study?
   d. Do you believe the author would argue that the number of visas for unskilled laborers should be increased as well? Why or why not?

Answers to Margin Questions

1. Under usual conditions of supply, one would expect that if the wage of my part-time job rises, the quantity of labor I supply in that part-time job also rises. Institutional constraints such as tax considerations or company rules might mean that the quantity of labor I supply doesn't change. However, under the usual conditions of supply, I will study less if the wage of my part-time job rises. (452)

2. Taxes reduce the opportunity cost, or relative price, of nonwork activities. So you will substitute leisure for labor as marginal tax rates increase. (455)

3. The irony of any need-based program is that such a program reduces people's incentive to prevent themselves from becoming needy. (455)

4. Some factors that influence the elasticity of a firm's derived demand curve include (1) the elasticity of demand for the firm's good; (2) the relative importance of the factor in the production process; (3) the possibility, and cost, of substitution in production; and (4) the degree to which the marginal productivity falls with an increase in the factor. (457)

5. The demand for laborers at that firm would shift out. (458)

6. Differences among countries in productivity, transportation costs, trade restrictions, and social institutions all determine the relative demand for labor in one country compared to another country. (459)

7. If the increase in labor supply leads to an increase in the demand for products in general, the increase in labor supply will also lead to an increase in labor demand. (461)

8. General growth in the economy, the fall in the value of the dollar, and the decline in the power of unions all led to more employment in the late 1990s. Nonetheless, increasing competitive pressures caused many inefficient firms to downsize. The net effect, however, was a rise in total employment. (462)

9. Economic theory does not argue that discrimination should be eliminated. Economic theory tries to stay positive. Discrimination is a normative issue. If one's normative views say that discrimination should be eliminated, economic theory might be useful to help do that most efficiently. (464)

10. There is more to life than income, so it does not necessarily follow that one should take the job that pays the highest wage. (In the author's view, a Ph.D.'s life is far more fulfilling than an MBA's life, although some MBAs may disagree with that.) Each person must decide for him- or herself how to weigh the various dimensions of a job. (470)

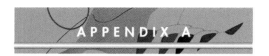

Derived Demand

This appendix considers the issues of derived demand in more detail. Although it focuses on the derived demand for labor, you should note that the formal analysis of the firm's derived demand for labor presented in the chapter is quite general and carries over to the derived demand for capital and for land. Firms translate consumers' demands for goods into derived demands for any and all of the factors of production. Let's start our consideration by looking at the firm's decision to hire.

THE FIRM'S DECISION TO HIRE

What determines a firm's decision to hire someone? The answer is simple. A profit-maximizing firm hires someone if it thinks there's money to be made by doing so. Unless there is, the firm won't hire the person. So for a firm to decide whether to hire someone, it must compare the worker's **marginal revenue product (MRP)** (*the marginal revenue it expects to earn from selling the additional worker's output*) with the wage that it expects to pay the additional worker. For a competitive firm (for which $P = MR$), that marginal revenue product equals the worker's **value of marginal product (VMP)**—the worker's **marginal physical product (MPP)** (*the additional units of output that hiring an additional worker will bring about*) times the price (P) at which the firm can sell the additional product.

Marginal revenue product = $MPP \times P$

Say, for example, that by hiring another worker a firm can produce an additional 6 widgets an hour, which it can sell at $2 each. That means the firm can pay up to $12 per hour and still expect to make a profit. Notice that a key question for the firm is: How much additional product will we get from hiring another worker? A competitive firm can increase its profit by hiring another worker as long as the value of the worker's marginal product (which also equals her marginal revenue product) ($MPP \times P$) is higher than her wage.

To see whether you understand the principle, consider the example in Figure A21-1(a). Column 1 shows the number of workers, all of whom are assumed to be identical. Column 2 shows the total output of those workers. Column 3 shows the marginal physical product of an additional worker. This number is determined by looking at

the change in the total product due to this person's work. For example, if the firm is currently employing 30 workers and it hires one more, the firm's total product or output will rise from 294 to 300, so the marginal product of moving from 30 to 31 workers is 6.

Notice that workers' marginal product decreases as more workers are hired. Why is this? Remember the assumption of fixed capital: More and more workers are working with the same amount of capital and there is diminishing marginal productivity.

Column 4 shows **labor productivity**—*the average output per worker*, which is a statistic commonly referred to in economic reports. It's determined by dividing the total output by the number of workers. Column 5 shows the additional worker's marginal revenue product, which, since the firm is assumed to be competitive, is determined by multiplying the price the firm receives for the product it sells ($2) by the worker's marginal physical product.

Column 5, the marginal revenue product, is of central importance to the firm. It tells the firm how much additional money it will make from hiring an additional worker. That marginal revenue product represents a competitive firm's demand for labor.

Figure A21-1(b) graphs the firm's derived demand for labor, based on the data in column 5 of Figure A21-1(a). The resulting curve is the firm's **derived demand curve for labor,** which *shows the maximum amount of labor, measured in labor hours, that a firm will hire*. To see this, let's assume that the wage is $9 and that the firm is hiring 30 workers. If it hires another worker so it has 31 workers, workers' marginal revenue product of $12 exceeds their wage of $9, so the firm can increase profits by doing so. It increases output and profits since the additional revenue the firm gets from increasing workers from 30 to 31 is $12 and the additional cost the firm incurs is the wage of $9.

Now say the firm has hired 4 additional workers so it has 34 workers. As the firm hires more workers, the marginal product of workers declines. As you can see from the graph in Figure A21-1(b), the marginal revenue product of decreasing from 34 to 33 workers is $6. Since the workers' marginal revenue product of $6 is less than their wage of $9, now the firm can increase profits by laying off some workers. Doing so decreases output but increases profit, because it significantly increases the average product of the remaining workers.

Figure A21-1 (a and b)   Determining How Many Workers to Hire and the Firm's Derived Demand for Labor

The marginal revenue product is any firm's demand curve for labor. Since for a competitive firm $P = MR$, a competitive firm's derived demand curve is its value of the marginal product curve ($P \times MPP$). This curve tells us the additional revenue the firm gets from having an additional worker. From the chart in (a) we can see that when the firm increases from 27 to 28 workers, the marginal product per hour for each worker is 9. If the product sells for $2, then marginal revenue product is $18, which is one point on the demand curve for labor (point A in (b)). When the firm increases from 34 to 35 workers, the value of the marginal product decreases to $4. This is another point on the firm's derived demand curve (point B in (b)). By connecting the two points, as I have done in (b), you can see that the firm's derived demand curve for labor is downward sloping.

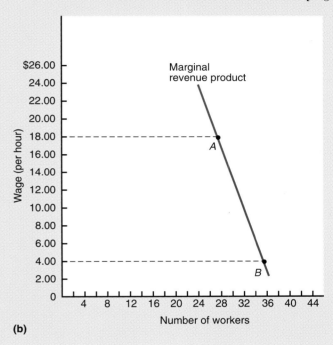

1	2	3	4	5
Number of workers	Total product per hour	Marginal physical product per hour	Average product per hour	Marginal revenue product (MRP)
27	270		10.00	
		9.00		$18
28	279		9.96	
		8.00		16
29	287		9.90	
		7.00		14
30	294		9.80	
		6.00		12
31	300		9.68	
		5.00		10
32	305		9.53	
		4.00		8
33	309		9.36	
		3.00		6
34	312		9.18	
		2.00		4
35	314		8.97	

(a)

(b)

Only when a worker's wage of $9 equals the marginal revenue product does the firm have no incentive to change the number of employees. In this example, the wage ($9) equals workers' marginal revenue product at 32 workers. When the firm is hiring 32 workers, either hiring another worker or laying off one worker will decrease profits. Decreasing from 32 to 31 workers loses $10 in revenue, but increasing from 32 to 33 workers gains $8 in revenue, but costs $9 in wages. Since the marginal revenue product curve tells the firm, given a wage, how many workers it should hire, *the marginal revenue product curve is the firm's demand curve for labor.*

The fact that the demand curve for labor is downward sloping means that as more workers are hired, workers' marginal product falls. This might tempt you to think that the last worker hired is inherently less productive than the first worker hired. But that simply can't be because, by as-

sumption, the workers are identical. Thus, the marginal product of any worker must be identical to the marginal product of any other worker, given that a specified number of workers are working. What the falling marginal product means is that *when 30 rather than 25 workers are working,* the marginal product of any one of those 30 workers is less than the marginal product of any one of 25 of those workers when only 25 are working. When the other inputs are constant, hiring an additional worker lowers the marginal product not only of the last worker but also of any of the other workers.

To understand what's going on here you must remember that when marginal product is calculated, all other inputs are held constant—so if a firm hires another worker, that worker will have to share machines or tools with other workers. When you share tools, you start running into significant bottlenecks, which cause production to

APPLYING THE TOOLS

Difficulties in Determining Marginal Productivities

The economic model of labor markets assumes that marginal productivities can be determined relatively easily. In reality they can't. They require guesses and estimates that are often influenced by a worker's interaction with the person doing the guessing and estimating. Thus, social interaction plays a role in determining wages. If you get along with the manager, his estimate of your marginal productivity is likely to be higher than if you don't. And for some reason, managers' estimates of their own marginal productivity tend to be high. In part because of difficulties in estimating marginal productivities, actual pay can often differ substantially from marginal productivities.

---

fall. That's why the marginal product of workers goes down when a new worker is hired. This assumption that all other factors of production are held constant is an important one. If all other factors of production are increased, it is not at all clear that workers' productivity will fall as output increases.

Why does a firm hire another worker if doing so will lead to a fall in other workers' productivity and, possibly, a fall in the average productivity of all workers? Because the firm is interested in total profit, not productivity. As long as hiring an extra worker increases revenue by more than the worker costs, the firm's total profit increases. A profit-maximizing firm would be crazy not to hire another worker, even if by doing so it lowers the marginal product of the workers.

FACTORS AFFECTING THE DEMAND FOR LABOR

There are many technical issues that determine how the demand for products is translated through firms into a demand for labor (and other factors of production), but we need not go into them in detail. I will, however, state three general principles:

1. Changes in the demand for a firm's product will be reflected in changes in its demand for labor.
2. The structure of a firm plays an important role in determining its demand for labor.
3. A change in the other factors of production that a firm uses will change its demand for labor.

Let's consider each of these principles in turn.

Changes in the Firm's Demand

The first principle is almost self-evident. An increase in the demand for a product leads to an increase in demand for the laborers who produce that product. The increase in demand pushes the price up, raising the marginal revenue product of labor (which, you'll remember, for a competitive firm is the price of the firm's product times the marginal physical product of labor).

The implications of this first principle, however, are not so self-evident. Often people think of firms' interests and workers' interests as being counter to one another, but this principle tells us that in many ways they are not. What benefits the firm also benefits its workers. Their interests are in conflict only when it comes to deciding how to divide up the total revenues among the owners of the firm, the workers, and the other inputs. Thus, it's not uncommon to see a firm and its workers fighting each other at the bargaining table, but also working together to prevent imports that might compete with the firm's product or to support laws that may benefit the firm.

An example of such cooperation occurred when union workers at a solar energy firm helped fight for an extension of government subsidies for solar energy. Why? Because their contract included a clause that if the solar energy subsidy bill passed, the union workers' wages would be significantly higher than if it didn't. This cooperation between workers and firms has led some economists to treat firms and workers as a single entity, out to get as much as they can as a group. These economists argue that it isn't helpful to separate out factor markets and goods markets. They argue that bargaining power models, which combine factor and goods markets, are the best way to analyze at what level wages will be set. In other words, the cost of labor to a firm should be modeled as if it is determined at the same time that its price and profitability are determined, not separately.

The Structure of the Firm and Its Demand for Labor

The way in which the demand for products is translated into a demand for labor is determined by the structure of the firm. For example, let's consider the difference

Table A21-1   The Effect of Monopoly and Firm Structure on the Demand for Labor

1	2	3	4	5	6	7
					Marginal Revenue Product	
Number of Workers	Wage	Price P	Marginal Revenue (Monopolist) MR	Marginal Physical Product MPP	Competitive (MPP × P)	Monopolist (MPP × MR)
5	$2.85	$1.00	$.75	5	$5.00	$3.75
6	2.85	.95	.65	3	2.85	1.95
7	2.85	.90	.55	1	.90	.55

between a monopolistic industry and a competitive industry. For both, the decision about whether to hire is based on whether the wage is below or above the marginal revenue product. But the firms that make up the two industries calculate their marginal revenue products differently.

The price of a competitive firm's output remains constant regardless of how many units it sells. Thus, its marginal revenue product equals the value of the marginal product. To calculate its marginal revenue product we simply multiply the price of the firm's product by the worker's marginal physical product. For a competitive firm:

Marginal revenue product of a worker =

Value of the worker's marginal product =

MPP × Price of product

The price of a monopolist's product decreases as more units are sold since the monopolist faces a downward-sloping demand curve. The monopolist takes that into account. That's why it focuses on marginal revenue rather than price. As it hires more labor and produces more output, the price it charges for its product will fall. Thus, for a monopolist:

Marginal revenue product of a worker =

MPP × Marginal revenue

Since a monopolist's marginal revenue is always less than price, a monopolist industry will always hire fewer workers than a comparable competitive industry, which is consistent with the result we discussed in Chapter 12: that a monopolistic industry will always produce less than a competitive industry, other things equal.

To ensure that you understand the principle, let's consider the example in Table A21-1, a table of prices, wages, marginal revenues, marginal physical products, and marginal revenue products for a firm in a competitive industry and a monopolistic industry.

A firm in a competitive industry will hire up to the point where the wage equals MPP × P (columns 5 × 3).

This occurs at 6 workers. Hiring either fewer or more workers would mean a loss in profits for a firm in a competitive industry.

Now let's compare the competitive industry with an equivalent monopolistic industry. Whereas the firm in the competitive industry did not take into account the effect an increase in output would have on prices, the monopolist will do so. It takes into account the fact that in order to sell the additional output of an additional worker, it must lower the price of the good. The relevant marginal revenue product for the monopolist appears in column 7. At 6 workers, the worker's wage rate of $2.85 exceeds the worker's marginal revenue product of $1.95, which means that the monopolist would hire fewer than 6 workers—5 full-time workers and 1 part-time worker.

As a second example of how the nature of firms affects the translation of demand for products into demand for labor, consider what would happen if workers rather than independent profit-maximizing owners controlled the firms. You saw before that whenever another worker is hired, other inputs constant, the marginal physical product of all similar workers falls. That can contribute to a reduction in existing workers' wages. The profit-maximizing firm doesn't take into account that effect on existing workers' wages. It wants to hold its costs down. If existing workers are making the decisions about hiring, they'll take that wage decline into account. If they believe that hiring more workers will lower their own wage, they have an incentive to see that new workers aren't hired. Thus, like the monopolist, a worker-controlled firm will hire fewer workers than a competitive profit-maximizing firm.

There aren't many worker-controlled firms in the United States, but a number of firms include existing workers' welfare in their decision processes. Moreover, with the growth of the team concept discussed in Chapter 9, existing workers' input into managerial decision making is increasing. In many U.S. firms workers have some say in whether additional workers will be hired and at what wage they will be hired. Other firms have an implicit understanding or a written contract with existing workers that restricts hiring and firing decisions. Some firms, such as IBM, had never laid off a worker; if they had to reduce their workforce, they created early retirement incentives. Ultimately, however, if their business gets bad enough, the invisible hand wins out over the social forces, and they lay off workers. That happened for IBM, and many other large U.S. businesses, in the early 1990s.

Why do firms consider worker's welfare? They do so to be seen as a "good employer," which makes it easier for them to hire in the future. Given the strong social and legal limitations on firms' hiring and firing decisions, one cannot simply apply marginal productivity theory to the real world. One must first understand the institutional and legal structures of the labor market. However, the existence of these other forces doesn't mean that the economic forces represented by marginal productivity don't exist. Rather, it means that firms struggle to find a wage policy that accommodates both economic and social forces in their wage-setting process. For example, in the 1980s and 1990s, a number of firms (such as airline and automobile firms) negotiated two-tier wage contracts. They continued to pay their existing workers a higher wage, but paid new workers a lower wage, even though old and new workers were doing identical jobs. These two-tier wage contracts were the result of the interactions of the social and market forces.

Changes in Other Factors of Production

A third principle determining the derived demand for labor is the amount of other factors of production that the firm has. Given a technology, an increase in other factors of production will increase the marginal physical product of existing workers. For example, let's say that a firm buys more machines so that each worker has more machines with which to work. The workers' marginal physical product increases, and the cost per unit of output for the firm decreases. The net effect on the demand for labor is unclear; it depends on how much the firm increases output, how much the firm's price is affected, and how easily one type of input can be substituted for another—or whether it must be used in conjunction with others.

While we can't say what the final effect on demand will be, we can determine the firm's **cost minimization condition**—where *the ratio of marginal product to the price of*

an input is equal for all inputs.[1] When a firm is using resources as efficiently as possible, and hence is minimizing costs, the marginal product of each factor of production divided by the price of that factor must equal that of all the other factors. Specifically, the *cost minimization condition* is:

$$\frac{MP_l}{w} = \frac{MP_m}{P_m} = \frac{MP_x}{P_x}$$

where

w = Wage rate

l = Labor

m = Machines

x = Any other input

If this cost minimization condition is not met, the firm could hire more of the input with the higher marginal product relative to price, and less of other inputs, and produce the same amount of output at a lower cost.

Let's consider a numerical example. Say the marginal product of labor is 20 and the wage is $4, while the marginal product of machines is 30 and the rental price of machines is $4. You're called in to advise the firm. You say, "Fire one worker, which will decrease output by 20 and save $4; spend that $4 on machines, which will increase output by 30." Output has increased by 10 while costs have remained constant. As long as the marginal products divided by the prices of the various inputs are unequal, you can make such recommendations to lower cost.

CONCLUSION

Changes in these factors make demand for labor shift around a lot. This shifting introduces uncertainty into people's lives and into the economic system. Often people attempt to build up institutional barriers to reduce uncertainty—either through social or political forces. Thus, labor markets function under an enormous volume of regulations and rules. We need to remember that while economic factors often lurk behind the scenes to determine pay and hiring decisions, these are often only part of the picture.

---

[1]This cost minimization condition was explicitly discussed in the appendix to Chapter 9.

Key Terms

cost minimization condition   *(478)*
derived demand curve for labor   *(474)*
labor productivity   *(474)*

marginal physical product *(MPP)*
   (474)
marginal revenue product *(MRP)*
   (474)

value of marginal product *(VMP)*
   (474)

Questions for Thought and Review

1. Using the information in Figure A21-1, answer the following questions:
   a. If the market wage were $7 an hour, how many work-
      ers would the firm hire?
   b. If the price of the firm's product fell to $1, how would
      your answer to *a* change?

2. If firms were controlled by workers, would they likely hire
   more or fewer workers? Why?

3. In the 1980s and the 1990s farmers switched from small
   square bales, which they hired students on summer break
   to stack for them, to large round bales, which can be
   handled almost entirely by machines. What is the likely
   reason for the switch?

4. Should teachers be worried about the introduction of
   computer- and video-based teaching systems? Why or
   why not?

5. A competitive firm gets $3 per widget. A worker's aver-
   age product is 4 and marginal product is 3. What is the
   maximum the firm should pay the worker?

6. How would your answer to question 5 change if the firm
   were a monopolist?

7. Fill in the following table for a competitive firm that has
   a $2 price for its goods.

Number of Workers	TP	MPP	AP	MRP
1	10		___	
2	19	___		___
3	___	8	___	___
4	___		8.5	___
5	___	___	___	$12

8. Your manager comes in with three sets of proposals for a
   new production process. Each process uses three inputs:
   land, labor, and capital. Under proposal A, the firm
   would be producing an output where the *MPP* of land is
   30, labor is 42, and capital is 36. Under proposal B, at the
   output produced the *MPP* would be 20 for land, 35 for labor, and 96 for capital. Under proposal C, the *MPP*
   would be 40 for land, 56 for labor, and 36 for capital. Inputs' cost per hour is $5 for land, $7 for labor, and $6 for
   capital.
   a. Which proposal would you adopt?
   b. If the price of labor rises to $14, how will your answer
      change?

APPENDIX B

Nonwage Income and Property Rights

The four traditional categories of income are wages, rent,
profits, and interest. Wages, discussed in the chapter, are
determined by economic factors (the forces of supply and

demand), with strong influences by political and social
forces, which often restrict entry or hold wages at non-
market-clearing levels. Supply and demand determine

price and income, given an institutional structure that includes property rights and a contractual legal system.

The same holds true for nonwage income: rent, profits, and interest. The forces of supply and demand also determine these forms of income. But, as we have emphasized throughout the book, supply and demand are not necessarily the end of the story. Supply and demand determine price and income, given an institutional structure that includes property rights—the rights given to people to use specified property as they see fit—and the contractual legal system—the set of laws that govern economic behavior of the society. If you change property rights, you change the distribution of income. Thus, in a larger sense, supply and demand don't determine the distribution of income; the distribution of property rights does.

The system of property rights and the contractual legal system that underlie the U.S. economy evolved over many years. Many people believe that property rights were unfairly distributed to begin with; if you believe that, you'll also believe that the distribution of income and the returns to those property rights are unfair. In other words, you can favor markets but object to the underlying property rights. Many political fights about income distribution concern fights over property rights, not fights over the use of markets.

Such distributional fights have been going on for a long time. In feudal times much of the land was held communally; it belonged to everyone, or at least everyone used it. It was common land—a communally held resource. As the economy evolved into a market economy, that land was appropriated by individuals, and these individuals became landholders who could determine the use of the land and could receive rent for allowing other individuals to use that land. Supply and demand can explain how much rent will accrue to a landholder; it cannot explain the initial set of property rights.

The type of issues raised by looking at the underlying property rights are in large part academic for western societies. The property rights that exist, and the contractual legal system under which markets operate, are given. You're not going to see somebody going out and introducing a new alternative set of property rights in which the ownership of property is transferred to someone else. The government may impose shifts at the margin; for example, new zoning laws—laws that set limits on the use of one's property—will modify property rights and create fights about whether society has the right to impose such laws. But there will be no wholesale change in property rights. That's why most economic thinking simply takes property rights as given.

But taking property rights as given isn't a reasonable assumption for the developing countries or the formerly socialist countries now in the process of establishing markets. They must decide what structure of property rights they want. Who should be given what was previously government land and property? Who should own the factories? Do those societies want land to be given to individuals in perpetuity, or do they want it given to individuals for, say, 100 years? As these questions have been raised, economists have redirected their analysis to look more closely at the underlying legal and philosophical basis of supply and demand. As they do so they are extending and modifying the economic theory of income distribution.

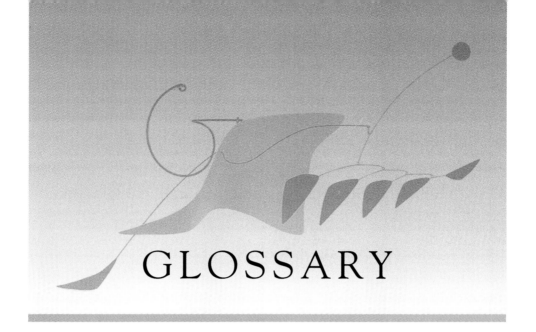

GLOSSARY

A

Ability-to-pay principle. Individuals who are most able to bear the burden of the tax should pay the tax.

Acquisition. A merger in which a company buys another company and the purchaser has the right of direct control over the resulting operation.

Adverse selection problem. Problem that occurs when buyers and sellers have different amounts of information about the good for sale.

Annuity rule. The present value of any annuity is the annual income it yields divided by the interest rate.

Antitrust policy. The government policy toward the competitive process.

Art of economics. The application of the knowledge learned in the achievement of the goals one has determined in normative economics.

Average fixed cost. Fixed cost divided by quantity produced.

Average product. Output per worker.

Average total cost. Total cost divided by the quantity produced.

Average variable cost. Variable cost divided by quantity produced.

B

Balance of trade. The difference between the value of the goods and services a country imports and the value of the goods and services it exports.

Bar graph. Graph where the area under each point is filled in to look like a bar.

Barrier to entry. A social, political, or economic impediment that prevents firms from entering the market.

Benefit principle. Individuals who receive the benefit of a good or service should pay the tax necessary to supply that good.

Bilateral monopoly. Market with only a single seller and a single buyer.

Business cycle. The upward or downward movement of economic activity, or real GDP, that occurs around the growth trend.

Business. Private producing unit in our society.

C

Capitalism. An economic system based on private property and the market in which, in principle, individuals decide how, what, and for whom to produce.

Capitalists. Businesspeople who have acquired large amounts of money and use it to invest in business.

Cartel. A combination of firms that acts as if it were a single firm.

Cartel model of oligopoly. A model that assumes that oligopolies act as if they were monopolists that have assigned output quotas to individual member firms of the oligopoly so that total output is consistent with joint profit maximization.

Clayton Antitrust Act. A U.S. law that outlawed four specific monopolistic practices: price discrimination, tie-in contracts, interlocking directorships, and buying stock in a competitor's company in order to reduce competition.

Closed shop. Firm where unions control the hiring.

Comparable worth laws. Laws mandating comparable pay for comparable work.

Comparative advantage. The ability to be better suited to the production of one good than to the production of another good.

Complements. Goods that are used in conjunction with other goods.

Concentration ratio. The percentage of the total industry that the top firms of the industry have.

Conglomerate merger. The merging of two relatively unrelated businesses.

Constant returns to scale. Situation when long-run average total costs do not change with an increase in output. Also: Output will rise by the same proportionate increase as all inputs.

Consumer sovereignty. Principle that the consumer's wishes rule what's produced.

Consumer surplus. The value the consumer gets from buying a product less its price. Also: The difference between what consumers would have been willing to pay and what they actually pay.

Contestable market model. A model of oligopoly in which barriers to entry and barriers to exit, not the structure of the market, determine a firm's price and output decisions.

Coordinate system. Two-dimensional space in which one point represents two numbers.

Corporate takeover. A firm or a group of individuals issues a tender offer for another company (that is, offers to buy up the stock of a company) to gain control and to install its own managers.

Corporation. Business that is treated as a person, legally owned by its stockholders. Its stockholders are not liable for the actions of the corporate "person."

Cost minimization condition. Situation where the ratio of marginal product to the price of an input is equal for all inputs.

Cost/benefit approach. Assigning costs and benefits, and making decisions on the basis of the relevant costs and benefits.

Cross-price elasticity of demand. The percentage change in demand divided by the percentage change in the price of another good.

D

Deadweight loss. The loss of consumer and producer surplus from a tax.

Deacquisition. One company's sale of parts of either another company it has bought, or parts of itself.

Decision tree. A visual description of sequential choices.

Decreasing returns to scale. Output rises by a smaller proportionate increase than all inputs.

Demand. Schedule of quantities of a good that will be bought per unit of time at various prices, other things constant.

Demand curve. Graphic representation of the relationship between price and quantity demanded.

Demerit goods or activities. Goods or activities the government deems bad for people even though they choose to use the goods or engage in the activities.

Derived demand. The demand for factors of production by firms, which depends on consumers' demands.

Derived demand curve for labor. Curve that shows the maximum amount of labor, measured in labor hours, that a firm will hire.

Diminishing marginal productivity. Increasing one input, keeping all others constant, will lead to smaller and smaller gains in output.

Direct regulation. The amount of a good people are allowed to use is directly limited by the government.

Direct relationship. Relationship in which when one variable goes up, the other goes up too.

Diseconomies of scale. Situation when the long-run average total cost increases as output increases.

Division of labor. The splitting up of a task to allow for specialization of production.

Downsizing. A reduction in the workforce.

Duopoly. An oligopoly with only two firms.

Dynamic efficiency. A market's ability to promote cost-reducing or product-enhancing technological change.

E

Economic decision rule. If the marginal benefits of doing something exceed the marginal costs, do it. If the marginal costs of doing something exceed the marginal benefits, don't do it.

Economic efficiency. Achieving a goal at the lowest possible cost.

Economic forces. The necessary reactions to scarcity.

Economic model. Framework that places the generalized insights of the theory in a more specific contextual setting.

Economic policy. An action (or inaction) taken by government, to influence economic events.

Economic principle. Commonly held economic insight stated as a law or general assumption.

Economic profit. Explicit and implicit revenue minus explicit and implicit cost.

Economically efficient. Method that produces a given level of output at the lowest possible cost.

Economics. The study of how human beings coordinate their wants and desires, given the decision-making mechanisms, social customs, and political realities of the society.

Economies of scale. Situation when long-run average total costs decrease as output increases. Also: Situation in which costs per unit of output fall as output increases.

Economies of scope. Situation when the costs of producing products are interdependent so that it's less costly for a firm to produce one good when it's already producing another.

Efficiency. Achieving a goal as cheaply as possible (using as few inputs as possible).

Efficiency wages. Wages paid above-the-going-market wage in order to keep workers happy and productive.

Efficient. Achieving a goal at the lowest cost in total resources without consideration as to who pays those costs.

Effluent fees. Charges imposed by government on the level of pollution created.

Elastic. The percentage change in quantity is greater than the percentage change in price (E > 1).

Embargo. A total restriction on the import or export of a good.

Employment rate. Number of people who are working as a percentage of the labor force.

Entrepreneur. An individual who sees an opportunity to sell an item at a price higher than the average cost of producing it.

Entrepreneurship. The ability to organize and get something done. Also: Labor services that involve high degrees of organizational skills, concern, oversight responsibility, and creativity.

Equilibrium. A concept in which opposing dynamic forces cancel each other out.

Equilibrium price. The price toward which the invisible hand drives the market.

Equilibrium quantity. The amount bought and sold at the equilibrium price.

European Union (EU). An economic and political union of European countries that is both an economic free trade area and a loose political organization.

Excess demand. Quantity demanded is greater than quantity supplied.

Excess supply. Quantity supplied is greater than quantity demanded.

Exchange rate. The rate at which one country's currency can be traded for another country's currency.

Excise tax. A tax that is levied on a specific good.

Exports. The value of goods sold abroad.

Externality. An effect of a decision on a third party not taken into account by the decision maker.

F

Fallacy of composition. The false assumption that what is true for a part will also be true for the whole.

Federal Trade Commission Act. U.S. law that made it illegal for firms to use "unfair methods of competition" and to engage in "unfair or deceptive acts or practices."

Feudalism. Economic system in which traditions rule.

Firm. An economic institution that transforms factors of production into consumer goods.

Fixed costs. Costs that are spent and cannot be changed in the period of time under consideration.

Foreign exchange market. Market in which one currency can be exchanged for another.

Free rider problem. Individuals' unwillingness to share in the cost of a public good.

Free rider. Person who participates in something for free because others have paid for it.

Free trade association. Group of countries that have reduced or eliminated trade barriers among themselves, and, as a group, puts up common barriers against all other countries' goods.

G

Game theory. The application of economic principles to interdependent situations.

General Agreement on Tariffs and Trade (GATT). Until recently, a regular international conference to reduce trade barriers. It has been replaced by the World Trade Organization (WTO).

General rule of political economy. When small groups are helped by a government action and large groups are hurt by that same action, the small group tends to lobby far more effectively than the large group. Thus, policies tend to reflect the small group's interest, not the interest of the large group.

Global corporations. Corporations with substantial operations on both the production and sales sides in more than one country.

Good/bad paradox. Phenomenon of doing poorly because you're doing well.

Government failures. Situations where the government intervenes and makes things worse.

Grandfather in. To pass a law affecting a specific group but providing that those in the group before the law was passed are not subject to the law.

Graph. Picture of points in a coordinate system in which points denote relationships between numbers.

Gross domestic product (GDP). The total market value of all final goods and services produced in an economy in a one-year period.

Group of Five. Group that meets to promote negotiations and coordinate economic relations among countries. The Five are Japan, Germany, Britain, France, and the United States.

Group of Seven. Group that meets to promote negotiations and coordinate economic relations among countries. The Seven are Japan, Germany, Britain, France, Canada, Italy, and the United States.

H

Herfindahl index. An index of market concentration calculated by adding the squared value of the individual market shares of all firms in the industry.

Horizontal merger. The combining of two companies in the same industry.

Hostile takeover. A merger in which the firm being taken over doesn't want to be taken over.

Households. Groups of individuals living together and making joint decisions.

Human capital. The skills that are embodied in workers through experience, education, and on-the-job training, or, more simply, people's knowledge.

I

Implicit collusion. Multiple firms make the same pricing decisions even though they have not explicitly consulted with one another.

Imports. The value of goods purchased abroad.

Incentive effect. How much a person will change his or her hours worked in response to a change in the wage rate.

Incentive-compatible contract. The incentives of each of the two parties to the contract are made to correspond as closely as possible.

Income. Payments received plus or minus changes in value in one's assets in a specified time period.

Income constraint. A curve that shows us the various combinations of goods an individual can buy with a given income.

Income elasticity of demand. The percentage change in demand divided by the percentage change in income.

Increasing returns to scale. Output rises by a greater proportionate increase than all inputs.

Indifference curve. A curve that shows combinations of goods among which an individual is indifferent.

Indivisible setup cost. The cost of an indivisible input for which a certain minimum amount of production must be undertaken before the input becomes economically feasible to use.

Industrial policy. Formal policy that government takes toward business.

Industrial Revolution. A time when technology and machines rapidly modernized industrial produc-

tion and mass-produced goods replaced handmade goods.

Inefficiency. Getting less output from inputs which, if devoted to some other activity, would produce more output.

Inefficient. Achieving a goal in a more costly manner than necessary.

Inelastic. The percentage change in quantity is less than the percentage change in price ($E < 1$).

Infant industry argument. With initial protection, an industry will be able to become competitive.

Inferior goods. Goods whose consumption decreases when income increases.

Input. What you put into a production process to achieve an output.

International Monetary Fund (IMF). A multinational, international financial institution concerned primarily with monetary issues.

Interpolation assumption. Assumption that the relationship between variables is the same between points as it is at the points.

Inverse relationship. A relationship between two variables in which when one goes up the other goes down.

Invisible hand. The price mechanism, the rise and fall of prices that guides our actions in a market.

Invisible hand theory. A market economy, through the price mechanism, will allocate resources efficiently.

Isocost line. A line that represents alternative combinations of factors of production that have the same costs.

Isoquant curve. A curve that represents combinations of factors of production that result in equal amounts of output.

Isoquant map. A set of isoquant curves that show technically efficient combinations of inputs that can produce different levels of output.

J-K

Judgment by performance. To judge the competitiveness of markets by the behavior (performance) of firms in that market.

Judgment by structure. To judge the competitiveness of markets by the structure of the industry.

L

L. The broadest measure of money.

Labor market. Factor market in which individuals supply labor services for wages to other individuals and to firms that need (demand) labor services.

Labor productivity. The average output per worker.

Laissez-faire. Economic policy of leaving individuals' wants to be controlled by the market.

Land bank program. Program in which government supports prices by giving farmers economic incentives to reduce supply.

Law of demand. Quantity demanded rises as price falls, other things constant. Also can be stated as: Quantity demanded falls and price rises, other things constant.

Law of diminishing marginal productivity. As more and more of a variable input is added to an existing fixed input, eventually the additional output one gets from that additional input is going to fall.

Law of diminishing marginal rate of substitution. As you get more and more of a good, if some of that good is taken away, then the marginal addition of another good you need to keep you on your indifference curve gets less and less.

Law of supply. Quantity supplied rises as price rises. Also can be stated as: Quantity supplied falls as price falls.

Lazy monopolist. Firm that does not push for efficiency, but merely enjoys the position it is already in.

Learning by doing. As we do something, we learn what works and what doesn't, and over time we become more proficient at it. Also: To improve the methods of production through experience.

Limited liability. The liability of a stockholder (owner) in a corporation; it is limited to the amount the stockholder has invested in the company.

Line graph. Graph where the data are connected by a continuous line.

Linear curve. A curve that is drawn as a straight line.

Long-run decision. Decision in which a firm chooses among all possible production techniques.

Lorenz curve. A geometric representation of the share distribution of income among families in a given country at a given time.

Luxuries. Goods that have an income elasticity greater than 1.

M

Macroeconomic externality. Externality that affects the levels of unemployment, inflation, or growth in the economy as a whole.

Macroeconomics. The study of the economy as a whole, which includes inflation, unemployment, business cycles, and growth.

Marginal benefit. Additional benefit above what you've already derived.

Marginal cost. Additional cost to you over and above the costs you have already incurred. Also: Increase (decrease) in total cost from increasing (or decreasing) the level of output by one unit. Also: The change in total cost associated with a change in quantity.

Marginal factor cost. The additional cost to a firm of hiring another worker.

Marginal physical product (MPP). The additional units of output that hiring an additional worker will bring about.

Marginal product. The additional output that will be forthcoming from an additional worker, other inputs constant.

Marginal rate of substitution. The rate at which one good must be added when the other is taken away in order to keep the individual indifferent between the two combinations.

Marginal revenue. The change in total revenue associated with a change in quantity.

Marginal revenue product (MRP). The marginal revenue a firm expects to earn from selling an additional worker's output.

Marginal social benefit. The marginal private benefit of consuming a good plus the benefits of the positive externalities resulting from consuming that good.

Marginal social cost. The marginal private costs of production plus the cost of the negative externalities associated with that production.

Marginal utility. The satisfaction one gets from consuming one additional unit of a product above and beyond what one has consumed up to that point.

Market demand curve. The horizontal sum of all individual demand curves.

Market failures. Situations where the market does not lead to a desired result. Also: Situation in which the invisible hand pushes in such a way that individual decisions do not lead to socially desirable outcomes.

Market force. Economic force that is given relatively free rein by society to work through the market.

Market incentive plan. A plan requiring market participants to certify that they have reduced total consumption—not necessarily their own individual consumption—by a specified amount.

Market structure. The physical characteristics of the market within which firms interact.

Market supply curve. Horizontal sum of all individual supply curves. Also: Horizontal sum of all the firms' marginal cost curves, taking account of any changes in input prices that might occur.

Marxian (radical) model. A model that focuses on equitable distribution of power, rights, and income among social classes.

Medicare. A multibillion-dollar medical insurance system.

Mercantilism. Economic system in which government determines the what, how, and for whom decisions by doling out the rights to undertake certain economic activities.

Merger. The act of combining two firms.

Merit goods or activities. Goods and activities that government believes are good for you, even though you may not choose to consume the goods or engage in the activities.

Microeconomics. The study of individual choice, and how that choice is influenced by economic forces.

Minimum efficient level of production. The amount of production that spreads setup costs out sufficiently for a firm to undertake production profitably.

Minimum wage law. Law specifying the lowest wage a firm can legally pay an employee.

Monitoring costs. Costs incurred by the organizer of production in seeing to it that the employees do what they're supposed to do.

Monitoring problem. The need to oversee employees to ensure that their actions are in the best interest of the firm.

Monopolistic competition. A market structure in which there are many firms selling differentiated products; there are few barriers to entry.

Monopoly. A market structure in which one firm makes up the entire market.

Monopoly power. Ability of individuals or firms currently in business to prevent other individuals or firms from entering the same kind of business.

Monopsony. Market in which a single firm is the only buyer.

Most-favored nation. A country that will be charged as low a tariff on its exports as any other country.

Movement along a demand curve. The graphic representation of the effect of a change in price on the quantity demanded.

Movement along a supply curve. The graphic representation of the effect of a change in price on the quantity supplied.

N

Natural monopoly. An industry in which a single firm can produce at a lower cost than can two or more firms.

Necessity. A good that has an income elasticity less than 1.

Negative externality. The effect of a decision on a third party that is not taken into account by the decision maker is detrimental to others.

Network externality. Phenomenon that greater use of a product increases the benefit of that product to everyone.

NIMBY. Not In My Back Yard. A mindset of approving a project but not wanting it to be nearby.

Nonlinear curve. A curve that is drawn as a curved line.

Nonrecourse loan program. Program in which government "buys" goods in the form of collateral on defaulting loans.

Nontariff barriers. Indirect regulatory restrictions on exports and imports.

Normal goods. Goods whose consumption increases with an increase in income.

Normal profit. The amount the owners of business would have received in the next-best alternative.

Normative economics. The study of what the goals of the economy should be.

North American Free Trade Agreement (NAFTA). A U.S.-Canada-Mexico free trade zone that is phasing in reductions in tariffs.

North American Industry Classification System (NAICS). An industry classification that categorizes firms by type of economic activity and groups firms with like production processes.

O

Oligopoly. A market structure in which there are only a few firms; there are often significant barriers to entry.

Opportunity cost. The benefit forgone by undertaking a particular activity.

Optimal policy. Policy in which the marginal cost of undertaking the policy equals the marginal benefit of that policy.

Output. A result of a productive activity.

Outsourcing. A firm shifting production from its own plant to other firms, either in the United States or abroad, where wages are lower.

P

Pareto optimal policy. Policy that benefits some people and hurts no one.

Partnership. Business with two or more owners.

Patent. A legal right to be the sole supplier of a good. (Note: A patent is good for only a limited time.)

Perfectly competitive. Describes a market in which economic forces operate unimpeded.

Perfectly elastic. Quantity responds enormously to changes in price (E = infinity).

Perfectly inelastic. Quantity does not respond at all to changes in price (E = 0).

Pie chart. A circle divided into "pie pieces," where the individual pie represents the total amount and the pie pieces reflect the percentage of the whole pie that the various components make up.

Positive economics. The study of what is, and how the economy works.

Positive externality. The effect of a decision not taken into account by the decision maker is beneficial to others.

Poverty threshold. The income below which a family is considered to live in poverty.

Present value. A method of translating a flow of future income or saving into its current worth.

Price ceiling. A government-imposed limit on how high a price can be charged.

Price discriminate. To charge different prices to different individuals or groups of individuals.

Price elasticity of demand. The percentage change in quantity demanded divided by the percentage change in price.

Price elasticity of supply. The percentage change in quantity divided by the percentage change in price.

Price floor. A government-imposed limit on how low a price can be charged.

Price stabilization program. Program designed to eliminate short-run fluctuations in prices, while allowing prices to follow their long-run trend line.

Price support program. Program designed to maintain prices at higher levels than the market prices.

Price taker. Firm or individual who takes the market price determined by market supply and demand as given.

Principle of absolute advantage. A country that can produce a good at a lower cost than another country is said to have an absolute advantage in the production of that good. When two countries have absolute advantages in different goods, there are gains of trade to be had.

Principle of comparative advantage. As long as the relative opportunity costs of producing goods (what must be given up in one good in order to get another good) differ among countries, then there are potential gains from trade, even if one country has an absolute advantage in everything.

Principle of diminishing marginal utility. As you consume more of a good, after some point the marginal utility received from each additional unit of a good decreases with each additional unit consumed.

Principle of increasing marginal opportunity cost. In order to get more of something, one must give up ever-increasing quantities of something else.

Principle of rational choice. Spend your money on those goods that give you the most marginal utility (MU) for your money.

Prisoner's dilemma. Well-known game that demonstrates the difficulty of cooperative behavior in certain circumstances.

Private good. A good that, when consumed by one individual, cannot be consumed by other individuals.

Private property rights. Control a private individual or a firm has over an asset or a right.

Producer surplus. Price the producer sells a product for less the cost of producing it.

Production. The transformation of the factors of production—land, labor, and capital—into goods.

Production function. The relationship between the inputs (factors of production) and outputs.

Production possibility curve. A curve measuring the maximum combination of outputs that can be obtained from a given number of inputs.

Production possibility table. Table that lists a choice's opportunity costs by summarizing what alternative outputs you can achieve with your inputs.

Production table. A table showing the output resulting from various combinations of factors of production or inputs.

Productive efficiency. Achieving as much output as possible from a given amount of inputs or resources.

Productivity. Output per unit of input.

Profit. A return on entrepreneurial activity and risk taking. Alternatively, what's left over from total revenues after all the appropriate costs have been subtracted. Also: Total revenue minus total cost.

Profit-maximizing condition. $MR = MC = P$.

Progressive tax. Tax whose rates increase as a person's income increases.

Proletariat. The working class.

Proportional tax. Tax whose rates are constant at all income levels, no matter what a taxpayer's total annual income is.

Public assistance. Means-tested social programs targeted to the poor and providing financial, nutritional, medical, and housing assistance.

Public choice (conservative) model. A model that focuses on economic incentives as applied to politicians.

Public choice economists. Economists who integrate an economic analysis of politics with their analysis of the economy.

Public good. A good that if supplied to one person must be supplied to all and whose consumption by one individual does not prevent its consumption by another individual.

Q

Quantity demanded. A specific amount that will be demanded per unit of time at a specific price, other things constant.

Quantity supplied. A specific amount that will be supplied at a specific price.

Quota. Limitation on how much of a good can be shipped into a country.

R

Rational. What individuals do is in their own best interest.

Regressive tax. Tax whose rates decrease as income rises.

Regulatory trade restrictions. Government-imposed procedural rules that limit imports.

Rent control. A price ceiling on rents, set by government.

Rent-seeking activities. Activities designed to transfer surplus from one group to another.

Reverse engineering. The process of a firm buying other firms' products, disassembling them, figuring out what's special about them, and then copying them within the limits of the law.

Rule of 72. The number of years it takes for a certain amount to double

in value is equal to 72 divided by its annual rate of increase.

S

Scarcity. The goods available are too few to satisfy individuals' desires.

Share distribution of income. The relative division of total income among income groups.

Sherman Antitrust Act. A U.S. law designed to regulate the competitive process.

Shift in demand. The effect of anything other than price on demand.

Shift in supply. The graphic representation of the effect of a change in other than price on supply.

Short-run decision. Decision in which the firm is constrained in regard to what production decisions it can make.

Shutdown point. Point at which the firm will be better off if it temporarily shuts down than it will if it stays in business.

Sin tax. A tax that discourages activities society believes are harmful (sinful).

Slope. The change in the value on the vertical axis divided by the change in the value on the horizontal axis.

Social capital. The habitual way of doing things that guides people in how they approach production.

Social Security. A social insurance program that provides financial benefits to the elderly and disabled and to their eligible dependents and/or survivors.

Socialism. Economic system based on individuals' goodwill toward others, not on their own self-interest, and in which, in principle, society decides what, how, and for whom to produce.

Socioeconomic distribution of income. The allocation of income among relevant socioeconomic groupings.

Sole proprietorship. Business that has only one owner.

Soviet-style socialism. Economic system that uses administrative control or central planning to solve the coordination problems: what, how, and for whom.

Specialization. The concentration of individuals in certain aspects of production.

State socialism. Economic system in which government sees to it that people work for the common good until they can be relied upon to do that on their own.

Stock. Certificates of ownership in a company.

Strategic bargaining. Demanding a larger share of the gains from trade than you can reasonably expect.

Strategic decision making. Taking explicit account of a rival's expected response to a decision you are making.

Strategic pricing. Firms set their price based on the expected reactions of other firms.

Substitute. A good that can be used in place of another.

Sunk costs. Costs that have already been incurred and cannot be recovered.

Supplemental Security Income. A federal program that pays benefits based on need to the elderly, blind, and disabled.

Supply. A schedule of quantities a seller is willing to sell per unit of time at various prices, other things constant. Put another way, a schedule of quantities of goods that will be offered to the market at various prices, other things constant.

Supply curve. Graphical representation of the relationship between price and quantity supplied.

T

Takeover. The purchase of one firm by a shell firm that then takes direct control of all the purchased firm's operations.

Tariff. Tax on imports.

Tax incentive program. A program of using a tax to create incentives for individuals to structure their activities in a way that is consistent with the desired ends.

Team spirit. The feelings of friendship and being part of a team that bring out people's best efforts.

Technical efficiency. As few inputs as possible are used to produce a given output.

Technological change. An increase in the range of production techniques that provides new ways of producing goods.

Technological development. The discovery of new or improved products or methods of production.

Technological lock-in. The use of a technology makes the adoption of subsequent technology difficult.

Technology. The way we make goods.

Total cost. Explicit payments to the factors of production plus the opportunity cost of the factors provided by the owners of the firm.

Total revenue. The amount a firm receives for selling its product or service plus any increase in the value of the assets owned by the firm.

Total utility. The total satisfaction one gets from consuming a product.

Trade adjustment assistance programs. Programs designed to compensate losers for reductions in trade restrictions.

Trade deficit. An excess of imports over exports.

Trade surplus. An excess of exports over imports.

U

Unemployment compensation. Short-term financial assistance, regardless of need, to eligible individuals who are temporarily out of work.

Union shop. Firm in which all workers must join the union.

Unit elastic. The percentage change in quantity is equal to the percentage change in price ($E = 1$).

Utility. The pleasure or satisfaction that one expects to get from consuming a good or service.

Utility-maximizing rule. Utility is maximized when the ratios of the marginal utility to price of two goods are equal.

V

Value of marginal product (VMP). An additional worker's marginal physical product multiplied by the price at which the firm could sell that additional product.

Variable costs. Costs that change as output changes.

Vertical merger. A combination of two companies that are involved in different phases of producing a product.

W

Wage outsourcing. A firm shifting production from its own plant to other firms, either in the United States or abroad, where wages are lower.

Wealth. The value of the things individuals own less the value of what they owe.

Welfare capitalism. An economic system in which the market is allowed to operate but in which government plays dual roles in determining distribution and making the what, how, and for whom decisions.

Welfare loss triangle. A geometric representation of the welfare cost in terms of misallocated resources that are caused by a deviation from a supply/demand equilibrium.

World Bank. A multinational, international financial institution that works with developing countries to secure low-interest loans.

World Trade Organization (WTO). An organization whose functions are generally the same as GATT's were—to promote free and fair trade among countries. Also: Organization committed to getting countries to agree not to impose new tariffs or other trade restrictions except under certain limited conditions.

X-Z

X-inefficiency. Firms operating far less efficiently than they could technically.

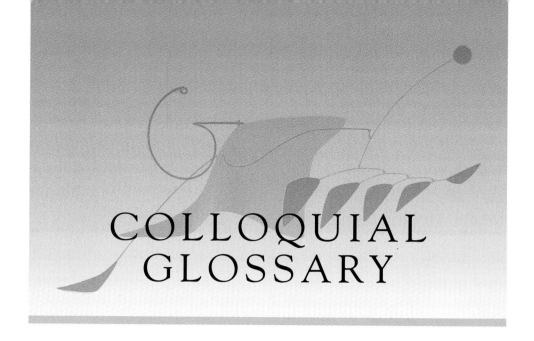

COLLOQUIAL GLOSSARY

A

Ads (noun). Short for "advertisements."

Ain't (verb). An ungrammatical form of "isn't," sometimes used to emphasize a point although the speaker knows that "isn't" is the correct form.

All the rage (descriptive phrase). Extremely popular, but the popularity is likely to be transitory.

Andy Warhol (proper name). American artist who flourished in the period 1960-1980. He was immensely popular and successful with art critics and the intelligentsia but, above all, he gained worldwide recognition in the same way and of the same quality as movie stars and sports athletes do. His renown has continued even after his death.

Armada (proper noun). Historic term for the Spanish navy. Now obsolete.

Automatic pilot (noun). To be on automatic pilot is to be acting without thinking.

B

Baby boom (noun). Any period when more than the statistically predicted number of babies is born. Originally referred to a specific group: those born in the years 1945-1964.

Baby boomers (descriptive phrase). Americans born in the years 1945 through 1964. An enormous and influential group of people whose large number is attributed to the "boom" in babies that occurred when military personnel, many of

whom had been away from home for four or five years, were discharged from military service after the end of World War II.

Backfire (verb). To injure a person or entity who intended to inflict injury.

Balloon (verb). To expand enormously and suddenly.

Beluga caviar (noun). Best, most expensive, caviar.

Benchmark (noun). A point of reference from which measurement of any sort may be made.

Better mousetrap (noun). Comes from the proverb, "Invent a better mousetrap and the world will beat a path to your door."

Bidding (or bid) (verb sometimes used as a noun). Has two different meanings. (1) Making an offer, or a series of offers, to compete with others who are making offers. Also the offer itself. (2) Ordering or asking a person to take a specified action.

Big bucks (noun). Really, really large sum of money.

Big Mac (proper noun). Brand name of a kind of hamburger sold at McDonald's restaurants.

Blow it (verb; past tense: blew it). To do a poor job, to miss an opportunity, to perform unsatisfactorily.

Boost (verb and noun). To give a sudden impetus, or boost, to something or someone.

Botched up (adjective). Operated badly; spoiled.

Bring home (verb). To emphasize or convince.

Buffalo (adjective, as used in this book). "Buffalo chicken wings" are a variety of tempting food developed in, and hence associated with, the city of Buffalo. (Not all chicken wings are Buffalo chicken wings.)

Bus person (noun). Has no relation to transportation. It's a term for the person who clears the tables in a restaurant.

C

CEO (noun). Abbreviation of "chief executive officer."

Call (verb). In sports refereeing, one meaning of "to call" is for the referee to announce his or her decision on a specific point.

Calvin Coolidge (proper name). President of the United States 1923-1928.

Carriage maker (noun). Person or firm that makes carriages, a type of horse-drawn conveyance almost never seen any more except in films. Members of the British royal family ride in carriages on important ceremonial occasions, such as weddings.

Cellophane (noun). A transparent wrapping material. It differs from plastic wrap in that it is made of cellulose, not plastic.

Central Park West (proper noun). A fashionable and expensive street in New York City.

Charade (noun). A pretense, usually designed to convince someone that you are doing something that you are definitely not doing.

Chit (noun). Type of IOU (which see) or coupon with a designated value that can be turned in toward the purchase or acquisition of some item.

Chump change (noun). Insignificant amount of money earned by or paid to a person who is not alert enough to realize that more money could rather easily be earned.

Clear-cut (adjective). Precisely defined.

Clip coupons (verb). To cut coupons out of newspapers and magazines. The coupons give you a discount on the price of the item when you present the item and the coupon at the cashier's counter in a store. Sometimes you are directed to buy the item and then send the coupon and an identifying code from the item's package to the manufacturer, who will mail you the discount.

Clout (noun). Influence or power.

Coined (verb). 'Invented' or 'originated.'

Coldhearted (adjective). Without any sympathy; aloof; inhuman.

Co-opted (adjective). Overwhelmed.

Cornrows (noun). Hair style in which hair is braided in shallow, narrow rows over the entire head.

Corvette (noun). A type of expensive sports car.

Couch (verb). To construct and present an argument.

Crack (noun). A strong form of cocaine.

Cry over spilt milk (verb). To indulge in useless complaint or regret. Note that there is a departure from standard English spelling in this phrase, which uses the spelling "spilt" instead of "spilled." Either is correct, but "spilt" is seldom used. (Another such variation is the rare "spelt" for usual "spelled.")

D

Deadbeat (noun). Lazy person who has no ambition, no money, and no prospects.

Deadweight (noun). Literally, the unrelieved weight of any inert mass (think of carrying a sack of bricks); hence, any oppressive burden.

Decent (adjective). One of its specialized meanings is "of high quality."

Doodle (noun and verb). Idle scribbles, usually nonrepresentational and usually made while actively thinking about something else, such as during a phone conversation or sitting in a class.

Drop in the bucket (noun). Insignificant quantity compared to the total amount available.

Dyed-in-the-wool (adjective). Irretrievably convinced of the value of a particular course of action or of the truth of an opinion. Literally, wool that is dyed after it is shorn from the sheep but before it is spun into thread.

E

'em (pronoun). Careless way of pronouncing "them." Written out, it reproduces the sound the speaker is making.

Establishment (noun and adjective). As a noun, the prevailing theory or practice. As an adjective, something that is used by people whose views prevail over other people's views.

F

Fake (verb). To fake is to pretend or deceive; to try to make people believe that you know what you're doing or talking about when you don't know or aren't sure.

Fire (verb). To discharge an employee permanently. It's different from "laying off" an employee, an action taken when a temporary situation makes the employee superfluous but the employer expects to take the employee back when the temporary situation is over.

Fix (verb). To prepare, as in "fixing a meal." This is only one of the multiplicity of meanings of this verb.

Fleeting (adverb). This word's usage is elegant and correct, but rare. It means transitory or short-lived.

Flop (noun). A dismal failure.

Follow suit (verb). To do the same thing you see others do. Comes from card games where if a card of a certain suit is played, the other players must play a card of that suit, if they have one.

Follow the flag (verb). To be committed to doing business only with firms that produce in your own country or in your "colonies"—that is, territories that belong to your country.

Follow the leader (noun). Name of a children's game. Metaphorically, it means to do what others are doing, usually without giving it much thought.

Funky (adjective). Eccentric in style or manner.

G

G.I. Joe (noun). A toy in the form of a boy (as "Barbie" is a girl). Original meaning was "government issue"—i.e., an item, such as a uniform, issued by the U.S. government to a member of the U.S. armed forces, and, by extension, the person to whom the item was issued.

GM (noun). The General Motors automobile company.

Gadget (noun). Generic term for any small, often novel, mechanical or electronic device or contrivance, usually designed for a specific purpose. For instance, the small wheel with serrated rim and an attached handle used to divide a pizza pie into slices is a gadget.

Gee (expletive). Emphatic expression signaling surprise or enthusiasm.

Get across (verb). To convince.

Get you down (descriptive phrase). Make you depressed about something or make you dismiss something altogether. (Do not confuse with "get it down," which means to understand fully).

Go-cart (noun). A small engine-powered vehicle that is used for racing and recreation.

Gold mine (noun). Metaphorically, any activity that results in making you a lot of money.

Good offices (descriptive phrase). An expression common in 18th century England, meaning "services."

Got it made (descriptive phrase). To succeed.

Grind (noun). Slang for necessary intense effort that may be painful but will likely benefit your understanding.

Groucho Marx (proper name). A famous U.S. comedian (1885-1977).

Gung-ho (adjective). Full of energy and eager to take action.

Guns and butter. (descriptive phrase). Metaphor describing the dilemma whether to devote resources to war or to peace.

H

Haggling (noun). Bargaining, usually in a petty and confrontational manner.

Handy (adjective). Convenient.

Hard liquor (noun). Alcoholic beverages with a high content of pure alcohol. Beer and wine are not "hard liquor" but most other alcoholic drinks are.

Hassle (noun). Unreasonable obstacle. As a verb, "to hassle" means to place unreasonable obstacles or arguments in the way of someone.

Hawking (adjective). Selling aggressively and widely.

Hefty (adjective). Large; substantial.

Hero sandwich (noun). A type of very large sandwich.

Highfalutin (adjective). American slang term, meaning pretentious, self-important, supercilious.

Hog bellies (noun). Commercial term for the part of a pig that becomes bacon and pork chops. (Also called "pork bellies.")

Holds its own (descriptive phrase). Refuses to give up, even in the face of adversity or opposition.

Home free (descriptive phrase). Safe and successful.

Hot dog (noun). A type of sausage.

Hot potatoes (noun). Slang term for anything that everyone wants to avoid confronting.

How come (expression). Why? That is, "How has it come about that . . . ?"

I

"In" (preposition sometimes used as an adjective). Placed within quotation marks to show it is used with a special meaning. Here it is used as an adjective, to indicate: "fashionable or popular, usually just for a short period." Compare, in this glossary, "all the rage."

Incidentals (noun). Blanket term covering the world of small items a person uses on a daily basis as the need happens to arise—that is, needed per incident occurring. Examples are aspirin, combs, and picture postcards.

Iron Curtain (noun). Imaginary but daunting line between Western

Europe and adjacent communist countries. After the political abandonment of Communism in these countries, the Curtain no longer exists.

It'll (contraction). "It will."

J

Jolt (noun). A sudden blow.

Junk food (noun). Food that tastes good but has little nutritional value and lots of calories. It is sometimes cheap, sometimes expensive, and it's quick and easy to buy and eat.

Just say no (admonition). Flatly refuse. This phrase became common in the 1970s after Nancy Reagan, the wife of the then-president of the United States, popularized it in a campaign against the use of addictive drugs.

K

Ketchup (noun). Spicy, thick tomato sauce used on, among other foods, hot dogs.

Kick in (verb). To activate; to start or begin. (Can also mean "to contribute to.")

Kickback (noun). A firm's giving part of the price it has received for its product or service back to the firm or individual who authorized the purchase of that product or service. In effect it is a type of bribe or blackmail demanded or expected by a purchaser's agent.

Klutz (noun). Awkward, incompetent person.

Knockoff (noun). A cheap imitation.

L

Laetrile (noun). Substance derived from peach pits, thought by some people to be a cure for cancer.

Late Victorian (adjective or noun). Embodying some concept typical of the late period of Queen Victoria. Also, a person from that period or who acts like someone from that period. (Queen Victoria was queen of England from 1837 to 1901.)

Lay off (verb). To discharge a worker temporarily.

Levi's (noun). Popular brand of jeans.

Lion's share (noun). By far the best part of a bargain.

Lobby (verb and noun). To lobby is to attempt by organized effort to influence legislation. As a noun, a lobby is an organized group formed to influence legislation. A lobbyist is a member of a lobby.

Lousy (adjective). Incompetent or distasteful.

M

MBA (noun). An academic degree: Master of Business Administration.

Mazuma (noun). U.S. slang term for money. It was used in the first half of the 20th century but is now rare, to say the least.

Medicaid (proper noun). Health insurance program for low-income people. It is administered jointly by the U.S. government and the individual states.

Medicare (proper noun). U.S. government health insurance program for people who are disabled or age 65 and over. There is no means test.

Messed up (adjective). Damaged or badly managed.

Mind your own business (admonition). Don't meddle in other people's affairs; don't ask intrusive questions.

Mind your Ps and Qs (expression). Pay close attention to distinctions. It comes from the similarity of the small printed letters "p" and "q" where the only visual distinction is the location of the downstroke. Also, the letters are right next to each other in our alphabet.

Moot (adjective). Irrelevant because the issue in question has already been decided.

Mousetrap (noun). Producing a better mousetrap is part of the saying, "Make a better mousetrap and the world will beat a path to your door." Metaphorically, producing a better mousetrap stands for doing anything better than it has previously been done.

N

NA (abbreviation). "Not available."

NASDAQ (also sometimes spelled "Nasdaq") (noun). Stock market operated by the National Association of Securities Dealers. The "AQ" stands for "Automated Quotations."

NATO (noun). North American Treaty Organization. Western alliance for joint economic and military cooperation. It includes the United States, Canada, and several European nations.

Nature of the beast (descriptive phrase). Character of whatever you are describing (need not have anything to do with a "beast").

Nirvana (noun). This word is adopted from Buddhism. Its religious meaning is complicated, but it is used colloquially to mean salvation, paradise, harmony, perfection.

No way (exclamation). Emphatic expression denoting refusal, denial, or extreme disapproval.

Nudge (noun and verb). A little push (noun); to give a little push (verb).

O

Off-the-cuff (adjective). A quick, unthinking answer for which the speaker has no valid authority (comes from the alleged practice of writing an abbreviated answer on the cuff of your shirt, to be glanced at during an examination).

Oliver Wendell Holmes (proper name). A justice of the U.S. Supreme Court, famous for his wit, his wisdom, his literary ability, his advocacy of civil rights, and his long life (1841-1935).

On their toes (descriptive phrase). Alert; ready for any eventuality.

P-Q

Ps and Qs. See under "Mind."

Park Avenue (noun). Expensive and fashionable street in New York City.

Pass the buck (descriptive phrase). Evade responsibility by forcing someone else to make the relevant decision.

Peanuts (noun). Slang for a small amount, usually money but sometimes anything with a small value.

Pecking order. Hierarchy.

Peer pressure (descriptive phrase). Push to do what everyone else in your particular group is doing.

Penny-pincher (noun). Person who is unusually careful with money, sometimes to the point of being stingy.

Perks (noun). Short for "perquisites."

Philharmonic (adjective). A philharmonic orchestra is an orchestra that specializes in classical music. Sometimes used as a noun, as in "I heard the Philharmonic."

Pie (noun). Metaphor for the total amount of a specific item that exists.

Pop-Tart (noun). Brand name of a type of junk food. It's a sweet filling enclosed in pastry that you pop into the toaster and when the pastry is hot, it pops out of the toaster.

Populist (noun and adjective). As a noun, this means a member of a political party that purports to represent the rank and file of the people. As an adjective, it means a political party, a group, or an individual that purports to represent rank and file opinion.

Pound (noun). Unit of British currency.

Practice makes perfect (expression). The grammar of this phrase is illogical but the meaning is clear.

Premium tires all round (descriptive phrase). Premium tires are tires of superior quality. When all the tires on your vehicle are premium tires, you have them "all round."

Proxy (noun). A stockholder can give a "proxy" to the firm. It is an authorization that permits the firm's officials to vote for the proposition that the stockholder directs them to vote for. By extension, proxy means a substitute.

Pub (noun). Short for "public house," a commercial establishment where alcoholic drinks are served, usually with refreshments and occasionally with light meals.

R

Raise your eyebrows (verb). To express surprise, usually by a facial expression rather than vocally.

Red flag (noun). A red flag warns you to be very alert to a danger or perceived danger. (Ships in port that are loading fuel or ammunition raise a red flag to signal danger.)

Red-handed (adjective). Indisputably guilty. Comes from being found at a murder or injury scene with the blood of the victim on one's hands.

Right on! (exclamation). Expression of vigorous, often revolutionary, approval and encouragement.

Ritzy (adjective). Very expensive, fashionable, and ostentatious. Comes from the entrepreneur Caesar Ritz, a Swiss developer of expensive hotels, active in the first quarter of the 20th century.

Rule of thumb (descriptive phrase). An estimate that is quick and easy to make and is reliable enough for rough calculations. Comes from using the space from the tip of your thumb to the thumb's first joint to represent an inch.

S

Sacred cow (noun). An institution or practice that social and/or political forces dictate is absolutely protected from change of any kind.

Saks (proper name). A mid-size department store that sells expensive, fashionable items. There are very few stores in the Saks chain, and Saks stores are considered exclusive.

Savvy (adjective). Slang term meaning very knowledgeable. Adaptation of the French verb, "savoir," meaning "to know."

Scab (noun). Person who takes a job, or continues in a job, even though workers at that firm are on strike.

Scraps (noun). Little pieces of leftover food. Also little pieces of anything that is left over: for example, steel that is salvaged from a wrecked car.

Sears Catalog (proper noun). Sears, Roebuck, and Co. is a large chain of stores that sells a wide variety of goods. Before shopping malls, interstate highways, and the Internet, Sears used to have a huge mailing list to which it sent enormous catalogs. A person receiving such a catalog would have information about, and access to, thousands of items, many of which the person might not have known existed before the catalog provided the prospect.

Set up shop (verb). To go into business.

Shivering in their sandals (descriptive phrase). Adaptation of standard English idiom, "shivering in their shoes," which means being afraid.

Shorthand (noun). Any of several systems of abbreviated writing or writing that substitutes symbols for words and phrases. Shorthand was widely used in business until the introduction of mechanical and electronic devices for transmitting the human voice gradually made shorthand obsolete. Today it means to summarize very briefly or to substitute a short word or phrase for a long description.

Shy away (verb). To decisively refrain from something. (Comes from the world of horses, who are said to "shy at" things that startle them.)

Sixpence (noun). A British coin that is no longer in use. It represented six British pennies and its U.S. equivalent in the 2000s would be about a nickel.

Skin of one's teeth (descriptive phrase). To succeed, but just barely. A micromeasure less and one would not have succeeded.

Smoke screen (noun). Metaphorically, anything used intentionally to hide one's true intentions.

Smoking gun (noun). This term has come to stand for any indisputable evidence of guilt or misdeeds.

Soft drink (noun). Nonalcoholic beverage.

Sourpuss (noun). Dour; sulky; humorless. Derives from "sour," which is self-explanatory, and "puss," a slang word for "face."

Squash (verb). To crush or ruin.

Steady (noun). A person to whom you are romantically committed and with whom you spend a lot of time, especially in social activities.

Sticky (adjective). Resistant to change, as if glued on.

Strongarm (adjective). Repressive and violent.

Super Bowl (noun). Important football game played annually that attracts million of viewers (most of them see the game on TV).

Sucker (noun). A gullible person.

T

Tables were turned (descriptive phrase). The advantage of one side over the other reverses so that now the winner is the loser and the loser is the winner.

Tacky (adjective). In very poor taste.

Take the heat (verb). To accept all criticism of one's action or inaction, whether or not one is actually the person that should be blamed.

Time-and-a-half (noun). In labor law, 150 percent of the normal hourly wage.

Tombstone ad (noun). Newspaper advertisement announcing the completion of a stock or bond offering.

Ton (noun). A ton weighs 2,000 pounds and an English ton (often spelled "tonne") weighs 2,240 pounds. In this book the term is used most frequently to mean simply "a large quantity."

Tough (adjective). Very difficult.

Trendy (adjective). A phenomenon that is slightly ahead of traditional ways and indicates a trend. Something trendy may turn into something traditional, or it may fade away without ever becoming mainstream.

Truck (verb). To exchange one thing for another. This was Adam Smith's definition in 1776 and it is still one of the meanings of the verb.

Turf (noun). Territory, especially the figurative territory of a firm.

Turn of the century (expression). The few years at the end of an expiring century and the beginning of a new century. For example: 1998-2002.

Turn up one's nose (verb). To reject.

Twinkies (noun). Brand name of an inexpensive small cake.

U

Union Jack (noun). Nickname for the British flag.

Up in arms (adjective). Furious and loudly protesting. Comes from the use of "arms" to stand for "firearms."

V

Vanity license plate (descriptive phrase). One-of-a-kind motor vehicle license plate issued to your individual specification. It might have your name, your profession, or any individual set of letters and numbers you choose that will fit on the plate.

W-X

Wadget (noun). Term used by economists to stand for any manufactured good except goods designated as widgets, which see.

Wal-Mart (proper name). A very large store that sells thousands of inexpensive items. There are hundreds of Wal-Marts in the United States and the company is beginning to expand into foreign markets.

Wheaties (proper noun). Name of a brand of dry breakfast cereal.

White knight (noun). A company that comes to the rescue of another company. The term comes from the game of chess—some chess sets have white pieces and black pieces—and from the children's book, *Alice Through the Looking Glass*, where the story is structured as a game of chess and a chess piece, the white knight, tries to rescue Alice.

Whiz (noun). An expert.

Whopper (proper noun). Brand name of a kind of hamburger sold at Burger King restaurants.

Widget (noun). The opposite of a wadget, which see.

Wild about (descriptive phrase). Extremely enthusiastic about undertaking a particular action or admiring a particular object or person.

Wind up (descriptive phrase). To discover that you have reached a particular conclusion or destination.

With-it (adjective). Current in one's knowledge.

Wodget (noun). A made-up term for a produced good. Variation of "widget," which see.

Wound up (past tense of verb "wind up"). To have found oneself in a particular situation after having taken particular actions.

Writing on the wall (descriptive phrase). To see the writing on the wall is to realize that a situation is inevitably going to end badly. It comes from the Biblical story that Nebuchadnezzar, king of Babylon, saw a fatal prediction written on a wall.

Y-Z

You bet! (exclamation). Expression meaning "It certainly is." or "Absolutely!"

PHOTO CREDITS

Page 9, Bleichroder Print Collection, Baker Library, Harvard Business School

Page 213, From HORTON HATCHES THE EGG by Dr. Suess TM & copyright © by Dr. Seuss Enterprises, L.P. 1940 renewed 1968. Reprinted by permission of Random House Children's Books, a division of Random House, Inc.

Page 226, © Bettmann/CORBIS

Page 227, © Keystone/The Image Works

Page 393, Courtesy of the United States Department of Agriculture

Page 470, © Bettmann/CORBIS

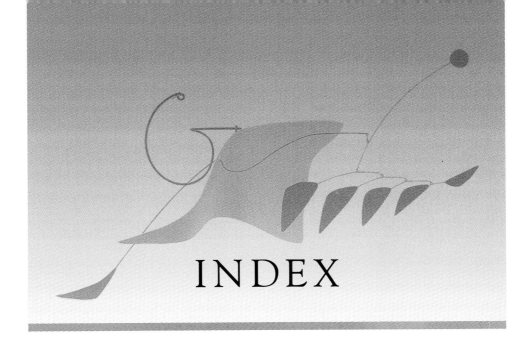

INDEX